MAO'S CHINA

AND AFTER

A History of the People's Republic

THIRD EDITION

MAURICE MEISNER

THE FREE PRESS

THE FREE PRESS
A Division of Simon & Schuster Inc.
1230 Avenue of the Americas
New York, NY 10020

Designed by Carla Bolte

Manufactured in the United States of America

10   9   8   7   6

Library of Congress Cataloging-in-Publication Data

Meisner, Maurice J., 1931–
    Mao's China and after : a history of the People's Republic / Maurice Meisner.—3rd ed.
        p.   cm.
    Includes bibliographical references and index.
    1. China—History—1949–   I. Title.   II. History of the People's Republic.
DS777.55.M455   1999
951.05—dc21   98-31734
                                                                              CIP

ISBN 0-684-85635-2 (alk. paper)

To the memory of Harvey Goldberg

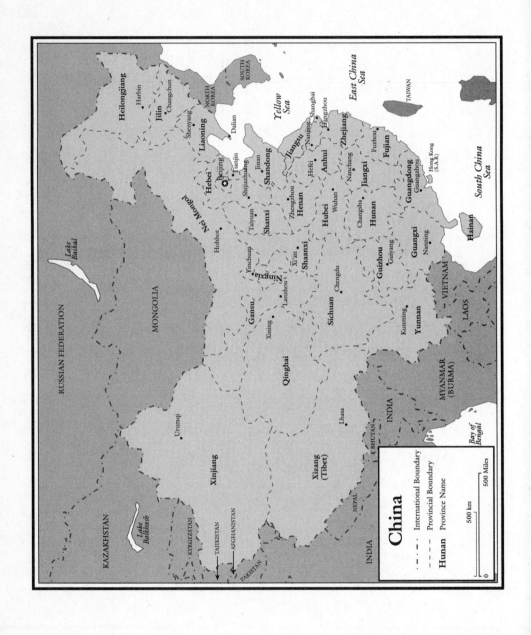

Contents

Preface to the Third Edition

THE MANUSCRIPT for the first edition of *Mao's China* was completed late in the summer of 1976, a few weeks before the death of Mao Zedong. The fact of the passing of Mao (and, as it turned out, the passing of Maoism and the era of peasant revolution) was hastily added to the manuscript as I was preparing to send it to The Free Press for publication.

In *Mao's China* I attempted to evaluate the historical record of the Chinese Communists in power by the standards of their own proclaimed socialist values and Marxist goals and found that record wanting. The first quarter of a century of the People's Republic was a time of immense social and material accomplishments, as well as a time of great inhumanities and crimes. It inaugurated the modern industrial transformation of the world's most populous country, which, over the previous century, had become one of the world's most backward and wretched lands. During the Mao era the Chinese Communists made a notable, if flawed and ultimately failed, attempt to reconcile the imperatives of modernization with the ends of socialism. Conspicuous among the failures of what so many once so hopefully celebrated as "the transition to socialism" in China was the absence of any serious attempt to create the essential democratic political preconditions for the envisioned new society. Maoism was not a doctrine that appreciated the elemental truth that "the self-government of the producers," to recall Karl Marx's famous term, is an essential feature of any society that can claim to be socialist. Thus, at the close of the Mao period, China remained a bureaucratically dominated order that was neither recognizably capitalist nor genuinely socialist.[1] Such, in brief, was the conclusion of the first edition of *Mao's China.*

The writing of the second edition, which was published in 1986 under the title *Mao's China and After,* was undertaken, in part, to correct errors of fact and interpretation on the basis of new information on the Mao period that became available in the early post-Mao years, especially about the ill-fated Great Leap Forward campaign (1958–60) and the Cultural Revolution of the late 1960s. In larger part, the second edition was written to take into account the unanticipated and far-reaching changes that took place in China as a result of Deng Xiaoping's reforms. Writing in the early 1980s, I interpreted the unleashing of market forces as an expedient to serve the nationalist and modernizing aims of the Chinese Communist state, a bureaucratic monolith that seemed to stand as an impregnable barrier to both socialism and capitalism.[2]

My conclusion proved erroneous. For the fact of the matter is that the Communist state, far from being an obstacle to Chinese capitalism, has been its essential agent and promoter. Over the past two decades, China has undergone the most massive and the most intensive era of capitalist development in world history, whatever Deng Xiaoping and other Communist leaders may have intended in 1979. Thus, the writing of the third edition of this history has been undertaken primarily to explore the origins, the peculiar nature, and the social consequences of Chinese capitalism.

The new edition perforce adds fifteen years to the political history of post-Mao China, bringing the story of Chinese Communism to the last year of the millennium, the year that also marks the fiftieth anniversary of the People's Republic. The addition of a decade and a half to the historical account, and an attempt to present an intelligible analysis of the development of Chinese capitalism, has made the text longer than it was in the previous edition. I have attempted to partially compensate for this by purging superfluous words and phrases throughout the text and eliminating sections in my account of the Mao era dealing with events that seem far less significant and interesting today than they did in the 1970s.

I should also note that the traditional Wade-Giles system of romanizing Chinese names and terms has been replaced throughout the book by the now more widely used pinyin system, with the exception of books and articles originally published with titles and names of authors rendered in the older fashion.

. . .

Most of what is written on the following pages is based on the labors of many scholars and journalists who have produced thousands of books, articles, and reports on modern and contemporary China. My debts to them are only partially and very inadequately acknowledged by brief references to their writings in the endnotes and bibliography. I fear I have used their work to arrive at interpretations many of them do not share.

I am grateful to many friends and colleagues who have read parts or all of various editions of the manuscript over the years and offered insightful criticisms and suggestions. Among those who were especially generous with their time and wisdom are Donald Klein, James Sheridan, Arif Dirlik, Robert Pollin, Lin Chun, Robert Marks, and Cui Zhiyuan. I am indebted to Carl Riskin for allowing me to borrow so heavily from *China's Political Economy,* his superb book on China's post-1949 economic history, and his most perceptive other writings. And I owe special thanks to Frederick Vanderbilt Field, a very special friend.

I appreciate enormously the encouragement and commentaries of many of my colleagues in the Department of History at the University of Wisconsin-Madison, especially Theodore Hamerow and Stanley Kutler. Bill Brown and Tom McCormick will never know how many of their insightful comments—mostly made informally over lunch at the Caspian Cafe—eventually found their way into this new edition.

I owe much to the graduate students who participated in my seminar in modern Chinese history for more than two decades and contributed greatly to the making of this book. They did so by raising and discussing so perceptively many of the problems that the book attempts to deal with, by commenting on various bits and pieces of the manuscript that I sometimes inflicted on them, and by generously permitting me to borrow ideas from their papers and dissertations. I learned a great deal from them. I cannot name them all here, but I must gratefully acknowledge the specific contributions of Bob Marks, Paul Pickowicz, Catherine Lynch, Lee Feigon, Brenda Sansom, Wang Yaan-iee, C. K. Kung, Dan Meissner, Tom Lutze, Lisa Brennan, and the late Lin Weinan, who died at a tragically young age.

I also enormously appreciate the reports of Marilyn Young and William Joseph, The Free Press's outside readers of the new chapters that make up Part VI. Their comments cheered me considerably at a dreary point in the preparation of the final version, and their suggestions saved me from more errors of fact and omission than the book now contains.

Belatedly, I wish to express my warm appreciation to Joyce Seltzer, former senior editor at The Free Press, whose "creative interventions" were in good measure responsible for the second edition and who made the initial arrangements for the publication of this edition. I am most grateful to Bruce Nichols, present senior editor at The Free Press, for his encouragement, his professionalism, and his superb management of unruly authors. And I was very fortunate at The Free Press to have the editorial assistance of Caryn-Amy King, who supplied skill, encouragement, and patience—all in abundant measure.

My greatest debt is to Lynn Lubkeman, who, on both matters of substance and style, was as generous with her knowledge and time as she is with her love.

Harvey Goldberg, to whom the second edition of this book was dedicated, died shortly after that volume was published. This new edition is dedicated in memory of Harvey—the greatest of teachers, the firmest of friends, and the most loyal of comrades, in the best sense of that good but much-abused term.

M.M.
Madison, Wisconsin
August 1998

NOTES

1. Maurice Meisner, *Mao's China* (New York: The Free Press, 1977), pp. 386–89.
2. Maurice Meisner, *Mao's China and After* (New York: The Free Press, 1986), pp. 482–85.

PART ONE

THE
REVOLUTIONARY
HERITAGE

1

Western Imperialism and the Weakness
of Chinese Social Classes

T HE HISTORY of revolution in modern China begins in the mid-nineteenth century with a Christian peasant rebellion that failed, and climaxes, although it is by no means the revolutionary conclusion, with a Marxist-led peasant revolution that succeeded in mid-twentieth century. Significantly, the ideologies of both the Taiping Rebellion of 1850–1865 and the Communist revolution, nearly a century later, were drawn not from the millennial Chinese tradition, but from modern Western intellectual sources. Hong Xiuquan, leader of the massive Taiping Rebellion that very nearly overthrew the reigning Manchu dynasty, was a self-proclaimed disciple of the Christian god (and, he believed, the younger brother of Jesus Christ) while Mao Zedong, in his particular fashion, was a modern disciple of Karl Marx. However much their respective ideologies were "Sinified" and adapted to Chinese historical conditions (and there was much adaptation in both cases), neither Hong nor Mao presented himself as a Chinese sage in a Chinese tradition of sages. Instead, both appeared on the Chinese historical scene as iconoclasts, bearers of new social visions and prophets of new social orders based on universal truths derived from Western intellectual and political traditions.

Reflected in the borrowing of Western ideologies to serve Chinese revolutionary ends is the central role of Western imperialism in molding the history of modern China. And one role that imperialism played was profoundly revolutionary, albeit unintentionally so. Imperialism was revolutionary not only in a social and economic sense but also culturally and intellectually. Imperialism not only undermined the old Confucian order—thus making a revolution possible and indeed necessary—it provided, as a by-product, new ideas and ideologies which turned the modern Chinese revolutionary movement against the traditions and institutions of the past. Chinese revolutionaries used Western tools and ideas not only to rid China of the foreign imperialist yoke but also to throw off the yoke of the Chinese tradition. New visions of the future precluded a Confucian-based social order as well as a Western-dominated China. The rejection of the Chinese cultural–historical past proclaimed in the Taiping version of radical Christian egalitarianism struck an iconoclastic chord that reverberated for more than a century.

In view of the general historical picture of China as the land of petrified tradition, portraying Chinese in their "response to the West" as virtually immobilized because of their conservative attachment to traditional Confucian social and cultural values, it is well to keep in mind that modern Chinese revolutionary history began in iconoclastic fashion. The rejection of the Chinese cultural–historical heritage in the Taiping version of radical Christian egalitarianism ushered in a strongly antitraditional impulse that was to be taken up in different fashions by later revolutionary movements, especially by the iconoclastic intelligentsia of the May Fourth era, from whose ranks emerged the founders and early leaders of the Chinese Communist Party.

However much a conservative defense of traditional cultural values may have inhibited conservative Chinese attempts at modernization (and more than culture was involved in the failure of Chinese conservatives to change China), there is little evidence to support the widespread assumption that modern Chinese revolutionary change can be understood in terms of the survival of traditional patterns of thought and behavior. Chinese revolutionaries tended to adopt what were perceived to be the most radical ideas and ideologies the West had to offer, and to derive from those ideas and ideologies radical visions of a future that demanded a fundamental break with the ways of the past. The revolutionary concern was always with the plight and future of China; yet the aim was not to revitalize old Chinese traditions but to find ways to bury them.

Yet ideas and ideologies alone do not create revolutionary situations, much less revolutions. It was the modern Chinese social situation that was potentially revolutionary, making revolutionary ideas (and iconoclastic impulses) historically dynamic forces. Again, in the crucial social realm, foreign imperialism played a decisive role. But it was a contradictory role, both revolutionary and counterrevolutionary, one which created a modern revolutionary situation and yet, at the same time, inhibited the consummation of a modern revolution. Imperialism, as Karl Marx predicted, served as "the unconscious tool of history" in creating conditions for a social revolution in China and, indeed, in all of the pre-capitalist societies of the non-Western world upon which it impinged. However vile the motives which actuated it and however brutal the methods which characterized it, imperialism was a necessary historical force in breaking apart stagnant and tradition-bound societies seemingly incapable of moving into modern history on their own. For Marx imperialism was a force that "batters down all Chinese walls," one that "compels all nations, on pain of extinction, to adopt the bourgeois mode of production; it compels them to introduce what it calls civilization into their midst, i.e., to become bourgeois themselves. In one word, it creates a world after its own image."[1]

But Marx was too sanguine about the ultimate socioeconomic effects of imperialism in China. To be sure, the nineteenth-century Western onslaught did indeed batter down the walls of the old Chinese empire, humiliating China through repeated wars and the unequal treaties imposed in their wake, and contributing to the disintegration of the traditional political structure. And the introduction of modern Western capitalist forces of production undermined and transformed much of the traditional economic order, particularly in and around the treaty ports where foreign political and military power held sway. Yet the new Chinese world was not refashioned in the image of the Western bourgeois world, as Marx had anticipated. Modern capitalism in China, introduced under foreign imperialist auspices, retained an alien character and developed only in limited and distorted form. A modern Chinese bourgeoisie emerged, but it was a numerically small and economically weak class, and one which remained largely dependent upon the forces of foreign imperialism which had given birth to it. Moreover, it was primarily a commercial and financial bourgeoisie, and not an industrial one, largely serving as an intermediary between the Chinese market and the capitalist world market. In a semicolonial country where the modern sector of the economy was dominated by the imperialist presence, it is hardly to be expected that the fledgling Chinese bourgeoisie could have been anything more than an extension of foreign capitalism, however much individual members of that class may have nurtured nationalist resentments against foreign domination. Quite naturally and inevitably, a small and weak bourgeoisie—especially one engaged more in commerce and finance than in industry—was accompanied by a diminutive and ill-formed urban proletariat. When the imperial regime fell in 1911, there were no more than 1,000,000 industrial workers in a land of 400,000,000 people—and most of these worked in small shops lacking mechanical power. Drawn mostly from the peasantry, rather than from the traditional urban artisans, the workers retained strong ties to their native villages and to peasant traditions. These factors, coupled with the numerical paucity of the working class, militated against the development of a modern sense of proletarian class consciousness.

The modern Chinese social structure was thus marked by the feebleness of the modern social classes: a weak bourgeoisie and an even weaker proletariat. But it was not only the modern classes who were puny; the modern Chinese historical situation was marked by the weakness of *all* social classes. For the emergence of the bourgeoisie and proletariat, both of which remained embryonic, was accompanied by a decline in the power and prestige of the traditional ruling gentry-landlord class. While imperialism undermined the foundations of the imperial bureaucratic state with which the gentry was so closely intertwined, gentry-landlord proprietors found it more profitable to continue to exploit peasants in the traditional parasitic fashion—and the fashion became increasingly parasitic as traditional opportunities for bureaucratically obtained wealth (and traditional bureaucratic and Confucian moral checks on exploitation) declined along with the disintegration of the old political order. Because of lack of vision, opportunity, and capital, relatively few members of the old ruling class turned to modern commerce and industry or modern forms of commercial agriculture. The traditional Chinese gentry thus remained mostly traditional in a post-traditional Chinese social and intellectual world; from its ranks there did not emerge any "modernizing elite" capable of promoting economic development or exercising political power. Although the gentry remained economically and politically dominant on the local rural level until the Communist revolution, it was an increasingly weak and parasitic class, morally and intellectually bankrupt, and incapable of national political expression.

The decay of the gentry was a major factor in preventing the reformation of the old imperial order from within, thus hastening the coming of a revolutionary situation. That factor, coupled with the absence of a viable bourgeoisie and a strong centralized state, precluded China from following what Barrington Moore has termed "the conservative route to modernization," similar to that pursued by Meiji Japan. The attempt was made, of course. Following the suppression of the Taiping Rebellion and the humiliations of the Opium Wars, conservative "self-strengtheners" sought to "modernize" China in order to defend the empire from the foreign imperialist threat from without and to preserve the old Confucian sociopolitical order within. But it was a feeble effort. Its futility was revealed in the crushing defeat China suffered in 1895 at Japan's hands and in the last years of the century when China was almost partitioned into a half-dozen foreign colonies. The moribund dynasty lingered on for another decade, and departed quietly from the historical scene in the quasi-revolution of 1911.

The disintegration and collapse of the imperial order, for which the gentry had provided the social base for so long, hastened, in turn, the decline of the gentry in modern times. The end of the empire removed the political symbols of Confucian ideology that traditionally had sanctified the dominant position of the gentry in Chinese society and deprived the members of that class of the bureaucratic network upon which they had been so long dependent for wealth and political protection. The gentry limped into the twentieth century as a dying landlord class, capable of little more than pursuing the most ruthless traditional forms of socioeconomic exploitation, unchecked by traditional political or moral sanctions. The peasants who were the victims of that exploitation eventually were to have the opportunity to repay gentry-landlord ruthlessness in kind, although in a different way—in the ruthlessness of an agrarian social revolution that, in the end, was to eliminate the gentry as a social class in the mid-twentieth century.

For the moment, it is important to take note of a different historical result of the gentry's decay: the tendency, in modern China, for political and military power to become divorced from social and economic power. It is generally the historical case, at least in Western historical experience, that the decline of the power and prestige of a once dominant social class is accompanied by the ascendency of a new social class. Much of our thinking about the rise and decline of social classes, about the relationship between economic and political power in general, and about revolution, is dominated by categories derived from modern Western historical experience. A most prominent part of our historical consciousness is the transition from feudalism to capitalism, an epoch that saw the emergence of new capitalist forces of production and exchange, the undermining of the power of the aristocracy, and the eventual rise of the modern bourgeoisie to social and political dominance.

Yet in modern China this was not precisely the historical case. While the decline of the gentry can be attributed in large measure to the impact of Western imperialism, no social class associated with new capitalist forces of production arose to assume the dominant position in Chinese society that the gentry was forced to abandon. As noted, the modern Chinese bourgeoisie and industrial proletariat were both extraordinarily weak classes. Products of Western capitalism, they were but pale reflections of their Western counterparts.

There remained, of course, the peasant masses who constituted the great majority of the Chinese population. But peasant life remained traditional in an era when the traditional Chinese order was disintegrating; new economic forces increased the already staggering burdens the peasants bore, adding new forms of exploitation to increasingly oppressive traditional forms, but without changing the old agrarian socioeconomic structure or traditional modes of life and thought. By virtue of the very nature of its localized and self-sufficient economic existence, the peasantry was a weak social class, provincial in outlook and without the means to politically articulate its grievances and interests on the national political scene. As in traditional times, modern Chinese society rested on the foundation of peasant labor, but for most of modern Chinese history peasants had little to do or say about the social and political direction that China followed. The Chinese peasantry had the potential for effective political action—and, indeed, for revolution—but it was not a potential that could be realized on its own accord; it required the leadership, organization, and ideology provided by members of other classes to make Chinese peasants modern historical actors and not simply the victims of modern history. As a class by itself, the peasantry was politically impotent as well as without social or economic power.

What was crucial, however, was the decline and decay of the landlord-gentry, the class that had been dominant in Chinese society for more than two millennia, coupled with a modern bourgeoisie that was too embryonic to establish itself as a truly independent social class. An increasingly parasitic gentry survived the fall of the old imperial order in 1911 only because the Chinese bourgeoisie was unable (and, indeed, unwilling) to remove it.

Here we find the social basis for a modern Chinese historical phenomenon of crucial importance: the relative independence of political power from social and economic power. In a situation in which no social class was dominant, in which all were weak, political power tended to be increasingly independent of social class and to dominate society in general. This tendency is apparent in the growth of regionalist political-military power bases during the latter half of the nineteenth century; in the virtually immediate collapse (except in name) of the bourgeois-type republic established by the Revolution of 1911 and the consequent dictatorship of the militarist Yuan Shikai (c. 1912–1916), and the subsequent full-blown emergence of warlordism over the following decade. Independent political power based on military force was characteristic not only of these traditional-type vestiges lingering on to condition the political life of the twentieth century, but also was characteristic of China's modern political parties, the Guomindang and the Chinese Communist Party (CCP). Neither the history of the Guomindang nor the history of the CCP can be understood simply in terms of political parties representing the interests of particular social classes. To be sure, both parties became involved in various ways with various social groups and their interests. But while landlords and the commercial and financial classes of the coastal cities became attached to the Guomindang, it was not simply a party of landlords and bankers; the "bankers of Shanghai" were always more dependent on the military and political power of Chiang Kai-shek than he and his party were on the economic support of the urban monied classes. And while the CCP came to power on the basis of massive peasant support, it did not become a peasant party in the process of the rural-based revolution it led; it was a Party that was to prove to be a good deal more revolutionary than the peasants whose support was decisive for its victory. Both modern political parties operated in a historical situation in which politics and policies were determined not so much by social-class interests but one in which the holders of political and military power determined the fate of social classes.

It was a modern Chinese phenomenon that held special revolutionary potential as well as one with conservative historical implications. The conservative manifestations are apparent in the emergence of semi-independent provincial power bases toward the end of the Qing dynasty; in the warlord satrapies of the twentieth century; and in the Guomindang regime after 1927. In all these cases, political power served not to change Chinese society but to preserve existing socioeconomic relationships, especially in the countryside. The revolutionary potential was to manifest itself in the emergence of an intellectual-political elite that was to give the revolutionary movement a more radical thrust than its social class support might otherwise have warranted.

NOTE

1. Karl Marx and Frederick Engels, "Manifesto of the Communist Party" (1848), in *Selected Works* (Moscow: Foreign Languages Publishing House, 1950), pp. 36–37.

2

The Defection of the Intellectuals

ALTHOUGH TAIPING peasant rebels in the mid-nineteenth century had been the first to mount a revolutionary challenge to the gentry and the Confucian sociopolitical order, the modern history of the Chinese revolution did not truly begin until near the turn of the century when members of the gentry began to turn against the Confucian values and ways of their own class. In the 1890s a small but highly significant number of the sons of the traditional landlord–bureaucratic elite began to lose confidence in the utility (and eventually in the moral validity) of Confucian values and traditional institutions. Influenced by Western ideas and at the same time acutely aware of the inability of the old regime to respond effectively to the increasingly grave threat foreign imperialism posed to the very existence of China, they became intellectually alienated from traditional values and beliefs. And intellectual alienation soon led to social and political alienation. Unwilling to uncritically accept traditionally sanctified values, some proved unwilling to succeed their fathers as rulers in the old system. A portion of young gentry-scholars, the sons of the traditional ruling elite, set themselves adrift from their social class moorings and formed the nucleus of a new strata in Chinese society—a modern intelligentsia from whose ranks were to emerge the leaders of modern revolutionary movements. It was the sons of the gentry—in effect, defectors from their class—who were to provide the ideology and leadership for a revolution that eventually was to destroy the gentry as a social class.

It was not, as often suggested, the traditional prestige of the scholar in China that made intellectuals so politically important in twentieth-century history, but rather the conditions of the modern Chinese historical environment. In a situation characterized by massive social and cultural disintegration, by incredible political chaos, a situation in which all social classes were weak and none dominant, an intelligentsia could operate as a virtually autonomous force and decisively influence the course of historical development.

But intellectuals could not make history on their own. Having cut their ties to their own social class, they became socially independent but remained politically and historically impotent. Only when the intelligentsia felt the need and perceived the opportunity to tie themselves to other social classes, to become the political voice expressing the social and economic discontents of the impoverished masses and to direct their activities into new forms of political action—it was only then that the intelligentsia was able to appreciate and seize upon the potentialities for revolutionary change that the modern Chinese historical situation offered; it was only then that they were able to take advantage of the opportunity to fashion social reality in accordance with their ideas, ideals, and visions. The seeds of the modern Chinese revolution were sown in the 1890s, when the sons of the gentry lost their belief in their moral right to succeed their fathers as rulers and emerged as an independent social stratum. But the modern Chinese revolution, properly speaking, did not begin until three decades later when the history of the intelligentsia became intertwined with the history of the common people.

This crucial historical relationship only began to be forged in the 1920s, with the emergence of a specifically Marxist-oriented segment of the intelligentsia. That intelligentsia, however, did not suddenly appear as a result of any simple act of instant enlightenment produced by the Russian Bolshevik Revolution and the concurrent arrival of the theories of Marx and Lenin. Those who became the leaders of the Chinese Communist Party (CCP) found the Marxist revolutionary message enlightening because they perceived in that message a solution to the crisis of Chinese society. But the manner in which they understood the Chinese situation and the manner in which they applied Marxism to attempt to resolve that plight were influenced profoundly by pre-existing intellectual predispositions.

Nationalism and Iconoclasm

A curious combination of nationalism and cultural iconoclasm is one of the more striking characteristics of the history of the modern Chinese intelligentsia. It is hardly surprising that Chinese intellectuals should be highly nationalistic, for nationalism and anti-imperialism were inherent in the very historical conditions from which the intelligentsia emerged. It was not by chance that the first significant political actions of modern intellectuals came at a time when a more aggressive foreign imperialism threatened China with territorial dismemberment and colonization. In 1895 imperial China was humbled by the military might of a modernizing Japan. And that was the year Sun Yat-sen launched the first of his abortive anti-Manchu revolutionary adventures. And, more significantly, it was the year Kang Youwei organized some 1,300 younger members of the scholar-gentry elite to protest the Beijing government's capitulation to Japan and to advocate far-reaching institutional changes seen as necessary for China's national survival. The event signaled the beginning of the defection of the intellectuals from the old order; it reflected not only widespread dissatisfaction with the traditional system among substantial numbers of the most prominent sons of the ruling class but also their reluctance to take their assigned bureaucratic places in a system in which they had lost confidence. By the mid-1890s, China was no longer a land of complacent Confucian scholars cherishing a comfortable belief in the moral superiority of Chinese civilization in the face of impending national disaster.

In the following years, during the frenzied drive to divide China into spheres of influence for foreign colonization, the political activities of the intellectuals assumed new forms and a greater urgency. Their efforts culminated in the heroic but ill-fated "Hundred Days' Reform" of 1898, the famous coup that attempted to change China from the top but was aborted by a counter-coup that placed China back where it was—in the hands of corrupt bureaucrats and a decaying gentry ruling class.

What was reflected in the political activities and influential writings of the disaffected intellectuals of the 1890s was a new nationalist commitment to China as a nation-state in a world dominated by predatory imperialist nation-states. The overriding concern was not to preserve a particular Chinese culture or a particular Chinese social order (although some tried to salvage as much of the tradition that seemed salvageable) but rather to build a strong Chinese state and society that could survive and prosper in a hostile international arena. It was a concern that conditioned the intellectual understanding and political uses of all new ideas and ideologies, not excluding the internationalist creed of Marxism.

While the emergence of an ardently nationalistic intelligentsia was in a sense dictated by modern Chinese historical circumstances, it is not so easy to understand why the nationalist quest was accompanied by strongly iconoclastic impulses. Nationalism, after all, generally demands a valued national past and it is the general proclivity of nationalists to celebrate and glorify the particular historical and cultural heritage. Yet this was not so for modern Chinese nationalism. The tendency was to discard traditional values and culture as unsuitable for China's survival, and later to condemn them as the source of China's problems.

Yan Fu and Liang Qichao, the major spokesmen for the first generation of the modern Chinese intelligentsia that emerged around the turn of the century, arrived at the conclusion that the basis of modern nation-state power was not simply the material accomplishments of the West but dynamic Western ideas and values that had given rise to those accomplishments—the ideas of struggle and progress, the values conducive to the release of individual human energies for dynamic economic growth and the conquest of nature. And these ideas and values, presented as Western, were offered for Chinese adoption because it was to the absence of such values in the Confucian tradition that the intelligentsia attributed China's modern economic and political weakness.

From declaring the tradition unsuitable to modern national ends, it was but a short step to condemning it as morally deficient as well. As the plight of China deepened, and as the need to explain and find solutions for that plight grew, it was an easy and logical step to take, foreshadowed by the brand of nationalism expounded in the writings of Liang Qichao and Yan Fu. While an iconoclastic rejection of tradition was hardly the nationalist result that Liang or Yan wanted or anticipated, their search for the source of power in the modern world had led them to a fundamental intellectual break with the past, a break they were unable or unwilling to fully recognize. By establishing the preservation and power of the state as the nationalist criterion for judging the value of all ideas and institutions, they imparted two essential messages with essentially iconoclastic implications: one was the conviction that the values necessary for national strength in the modern world were to be sought in the wisdom of Western theories and ideologies, which had provided foreign powers with their economic and political predominance; and the second, logically flowing from the first, was the necessity to discard traditional Chinese beliefs and values that could not serve the overriding interests of national power.

An iconoclastic rejection of the cultural past was thus latent in the very origins of nationalism in China, even though many early nationalists retained a deep emotional tie to traditional Confucian moral values. That iconoclastic potential would be expressed in more forceful fashion by a new generation of young intellectuals in the second decade of the century. Exposed to a wider range of modern Western ideas, their ties to traditional culture became increasingly tenuous. But what gave their anti-traditionalism its special intensity were the political events of the first two decades of the new century. The fall of the monarchy (the symbol of the Confucian moral order) in the Revolution of 1911 deprived traditional values of their final claim to legitimacy, yet political opportunists cynically manipulated elements of the Confucian tradition for purely reactionary purposes, using them as props for a decadent society and the corrupt bureaucrats and militarists who parasitically hovered over it. This continued association of Confucianism with social and political conservatism opened the way to a fiercely iconoclastic assault against the entire traditional cultural heritage.

This nationalistic cultural iconoclasm received its fullest and most politically significant expression in the years 1915–1919, in the New Culture Movement, which called for the total destruction of the traditions and values of the past. The call for China's first cultural revolution was sounded by an ardent young Francophile, Chen Duxiu, who returned to China in 1915 from a self-imposed exile in Japan to found the periodical *Xin qingnian* (*New Youth*)—and to make certain his iconoclastic intentions were sufficiently clear he later gave it a French title as well, *La Jeunesse.* In 1921 this passionate devotee of modern French democracy and culture became the first leader of the Chinese Communist Party.

It is difficult to overestimate the importance of the intellectuals who coalesced around *New Youth,* for their writings molded the beliefs of a whole generation of young students who were to achieve political prominence after the May Fourth incident of 1919 and who were to become the leaders of the modern Chinese revolution. Among their avid readers and followers was the youthful Mao Zedong, who was influenced profoundly by *New Youth*—and whose first published writing (an essay stressing the importance of "physical culture") appeared in that periodical in 1917. One of the enduring influences that *New Youth* conveyed to the young Mao and his contemporaries was the notion that a complete cultural and moral transformation was the primary prerequisite for meaningful social reform and political action. It was not a renovation of traditional culture they wanted, for most saw little or nothing in the Chinese past worth preserving. What they demanded was the total annihilation of all the values, traditions, and customs of the past and their replacement by a wholly new culture based on the Western democratic and scientific values they so admired. The bitter and sarcastic attacks leveled against Confucianism and the merciless condemnation of tradition that filled the pages of *New Youth* reflected not simply the view that the tradition was outmoded and useless but a feeling that it was morally corrupt as well and perhaps always had been so.

This virulently iconoclastic rejection of the Chinese past was accompanied by an ardent faith in the Chinese youth of the present. The youth were to be the bearers of a new culture, and thus the agents for the emergence of a new and young Chinese society, for young people were perceived to be relatively uncorrupted by old traditions and hopefully not yet infected by a diseased culture and a sick society. More amenable to new ideas and values than their elders, the youth were seen as the agents of the cultural transformation upon which the salvation of the nation depended.

Another striking feature of the *New Youth* intellectuals—and, indeed, generally characteristic of the modern Chinese intelligentsia—was an extraordinary faith in the power of ideas to change social reality, an enduring assumption that changes in values and consciousness must necessarily precede social, economic, and political changes. No doubt it is a general proclivity of intellectuals to emphasize (and overemphasize) the importance of ideas, particularly their own, but the intensity and consistency of this tendency in twentieth-century Chinese history seems quite unparalleled and suggests some general predisposition to stress the role of consciousness in determining the direction of historical development.

New Youth was not a Marxist periodical—not at least before Chen Duxiu became a convert to Marxism in late 1919. But it eventually produced Marxists, once political events compelled many of its contributors and readers to abandon their Western liberal beliefs. From the editorial board of *New Youth* came two professors from Peking University, Chen Duxiu and Li Dazhao, who were the cofounders of the CCP. And the early Party membership was largely composed of their young student followers, nurtured on the ideas conveyed in the pages of that extraordinary periodical. The leaders of the Chinese Communist movement—and later the leaders of the People's Republic—sprang from this early group of young revolutionary activists, most notably, of course, Mao Zedong, Li Dazhao's onetime library assistant at Beijing University. To their newly found Marxist faith they brought many of their earlier intellectual predispositions—nationalism, cultural iconoclasm, and a voluntaristic faith in the power of ideas to shape social reality.

These various beliefs were not easy to reconcile. The crucial role attributed to ideas and consciousness went far beyond the bounds of Marxist theory. An ardent nationalism was hardly in tune with the profoundly internationalist content and aims of Marxism, or wholly compatible with the Marxist demand for class struggle and social revolution. And nationalism further clashed with an iconoclastic rejection of China's cultural and his-

torical heritage. Throughout the history of the Chinese Communist movement these conflicting beliefs gave rise to tensions that were to have profoundly important political implications. In new forms and under vastly
different historical circumstances, the problems and tensions that were
generated by the pre-Marxist cultural revolution of 1915–1919 were again
to appear in the Maoist-inspired Cultural Revolution of the 1960s. Centrally involved in both was an iconoclastic assault against the traditions of
the past, the problem of reconciling iconoclastic impulses with nationalist
feelings, an enduring belief in the power of human consciousness to fashion social reality, and an abiding faith in youth as the agents of moral regeneration. A young Mao Zedong was the intellectual product of the first
cultural revolution, and an aging Mao was the political promoter of the
second.

The desertion of the intellectuals received its most extreme expression
in the New Youth era of 1915–1919. The totalistic iconoclasm of the new
intellectuals was a reflection of social rootlessness as well as an intellectual
rejection of the traditions and institutions of the past. Iconoclasm was also
an affirmation of their social independence, for the emergent intelligentsia
formed a new strata in Chinese society not tied to, nor the spokesman for,
any social class. Thus from the dying gentry class emerged an autonomous
intelligentsia committed to building a new social order which would pre-
clude the continued existence of the class from which they had come.

Yet the intelligentsia lacked the means to change Chinese society in accordance with their Western models. For the counterpart to their autonomous status was their social isolation and political powerlessness. The
modern Western bourgeois ideas and institutions they advocated struck
few responsive chords in warlord-dominated China. The modern Chinese
bourgeoisie was too weak and disfigured a class to carry liberal ideas and
promote democracy.

Thus the intellectuals found themselves as much isolated in the modern
cities as they were intellectually and physically separated from the backward countryside. Social isolation and political impotence gave rise to restlessness, frustration, and a growing need to find roots in Chinese society.
The strident calls for cultural transformation were not only their intellectual
prescription for the ills of China but also a reflection of social and political
loneliness, the inability to effect the changes they desired. Not until the
dramatic events of 1919 transformed the Chinese political situation did the
intelligentsia's circumstances change. For many, that transformation led to
disillusionment with Western liberalism, and provided for some a new
Marxist faith which offered the opportunity for effective political action
and the promise of an end to social isolation.

The May Fourth Movement and the Origins of the Chinese Communist Party

The events leading to a fusion of China's "rootless" intellectuals and the common people began on May 4, 1919. On that day, which marks the true beginning of the modern Chinese revolution, more than 3,000 university students in Beijing demonstrated against the decision of the Western democracies at the Versailles peace conference to transfer the former German imperialist concessions in Shandong province to Japan as war booty. The protest culminated in attacks on the homes and offices of ministers of the Beijing government who were in the pay of Japan. The violent clashes with the police and the subsequent arrests served to inflame nationalist resentments against both a weak and corrupt Chinese government and against the foreign governments which for so long had exploited and humiliated China. Demonstrations grew larger and more militant and rapidly spread to virtually all major urban centers.

The political significance of the movement was that it did not remain a student movement. The student activists were soon joined by many of their professors at Beijing University and by industrial workers and merchant associations. The cities of China were swept by massive popular demonstrations, strikes, antiforeign boycotts, and sometimes violent confrontations with the authorities. The May Fourth incident catalyzed the political awakening of a society which long had seemed inert and dormant. A massive wave of popular anti-imperialism engulfed the cities, and the country (if not yet the countryside) was seething with political as well as intellectual ferment.

The dramatically new political situation radically politicized a significant number of intellectuals. Many who had regarded themselves as liberal cosmopolitans emerged as militant nationalists, defending the country against the menace of foreign imperialism. Many who had rejected political participation because they attributed the plight of China to fundamental deficiencies in culture, for which political measures offered only superficial solutions, now began to favor immediate political action to save the nation from the external threat and to resolve the grave social and economic crises that threatened from within. The new spirit of political activism permeating the cities raised hopes that the masses could be organized for effective action and that the intellectuals could be effective in leading them. Concurrently, the intellectuals' views of the West underwent a dramatic transformation. The bitter nationalist resentments aroused by the fateful decision at Versailles, coupled with growing nationalist political activism at home, led to a rapid erosion of the faith that the "advanced" Western nations would instruct China in the principles of democracy and science. The foreign teachers were now perceived as oppressors, and the old image of a Western world providing progressive models for the regeneration of China was replaced by a new image of a West made up of cynical and aggressive imperialist states. Having rejected traditional Chinese intellectual and political values, the intellectuals still looked to the West for guidance; but they now began to look more to Western socialist theories, which were themselves critical of the West as it was, in place of the conventional Western liberal ideologies, which sanctioned the existing capitalist-imperialist order.

It was in this new political and intellectual environment created in the wake of the May Fourth incident that a portion of the Chinese intelligentsia began to turn to the Russian Revolution and the Marxist promise of worldwide revolution. Hitherto, the Bolshevik victory of 1917 had elicited much interest in Chinese intellectual circles but had found few Chinese converts. As faith in Western democracy eroded and with the internal political awakening stimulating new hope for effective and immediate action, the Bolshevik message offered both a new intellectual faith and a new political model. Marxism was seen as the most advanced intellectual product of the modern West, but one that rejected the Western world in its capitalist form and its imperialist relationship with China. The latter was most forcefully demonstrated through the nationalist appeals of the Leninist theory of imperialism (which gave the colonial and semicolonial lands a crucial international revolutionary role) and the new Soviet government's renunciation of old czarist imperialist privileges in China. To become a Marxist was one way for a Chinese intellectual to reject both the traditions of the Chinese past and Western domination of the Chinese present. And to embrace the Russian Revolution and become a Communist was a way to find a program for concrete political action to transform Chinese society—and a way to find a place for the Chinese nation in what was believed to be an international process of revolutionary change.

Although the early Chinese converts to Marxism were inspired by the vision of international revolution that the Bolshevik Revolution seemed to herald, they had come to that new socialist vision through a profoundly nationalist route. Just as two decades earlier the modern Chinese intelligentsia had emerged out of a long process of nationalist alienation from traditional Chinese values, so now the new Marxist intelligentsia grew out of nationalist disillusionment with the Western bourgeois democratic ideologies. The immediate threat of foreign imperialism and a consequent nationalist concern with the fate and future of China were central in both cases. In the Marxist case, nationalism was to be turned to social revolutionary ends, but the nationalist origins of Marxism in China were to remain to condition the manner in which the new doctrine was to be interpreted and employed. It was a necessary condition, for China was a land that required national independence as well as social revolution—and the two tasks were to prove inseparable.

It was on the basis of the nationalist and politically activist impulses generated by the May Fourth Movement, combined with the chiliastic expectations of an imminent international revolutionary upheaval inspired by the writings of Lenin and Trotsky, that the new Chinese converts to Marxism undertook the task of organizing a communist party. The foundations for what was to be the Chinese Communist Party were laid in 1920, when young Marxist activists established a variety of small Communist groups (under a variety of names) in the major cities of China. Similar groups were organized by radical Chinese students studying abroad in Paris, Tokyo, and Berlin. The national Party itself did not formally come into existence until July 1921, when twelve delegates from the different groups met at a secret congress that opened in Shanghai and, after a police raid, concluded its deliberations on a houseboat near Hangzhou. Assisted by a representative from the newly formed (and Moscow-controlled) Third International (Comintern), the congress adopted standard Leninist methods of organization and proclaimed orthodox Marxist-Leninist aims.

The new Party was small in number, youthful in composition, and its members inexperienced in revolutionary practice and Marxist theory. The founding congress could claim to represent a total of only fifty-seven members. In a land which lacked a socialist political tradition, there was little on which to build the new organization; the Party was led by Chen Duxiu and Li Dazhao, who recruited most of their followers from their own students. In a country lacking a Marxist social-democratic intellectual tradition, it was inevitable that both leaders and followers would have only a superficial knowledge of the theory that presumably guided their revolutionary activities. It did not seem a promising beginning.

3

The Abortiveness of
Bourgeois and Proletarian Revolution

THE PERIOD FROM 1921, when the Chinese Communist Party was founded, to 1927, when Chiang Kai-shek launched the bloody counterrevolution that very nearly destroyed the Chinese Communists, was marked by two revolutionary failures. One was the failure of a bourgeois-democratic revolution, or what was sometimes called "the national revolution." The other was the failure of China's nascent urban working class to bring about a socialist reordering of society, although they made a valiant attempt to do so in the great revolutionary upsurge of 1925–1927. The two abortive revolutions were to have momentous consequences. For the failures of the 1920s largely removed both the bourgeoisie and the proletariat from the political scene; and, after 1927, moved the revolution from the cities to the countryside, where Maoism was to grow and the revolutionary victory of 1949 was to be forged.

. . .

When the young intellectuals who founded the CCP began their revolutionary activities in 1921, they believed that their main task was to organize the Chinese proletariat for a socialist revolution that would be part of the international process of socialist transformation that Marx had prophesied and which the Russian Revolution seemed to herald. The results of those early efforts to build a working-class movement were not insignificant. The organization of industrial workers in the large cities, as well as miners and railroad workers in more remote areas, proceeded rapidly. Workers' strikes proliferated—and were often motivated by political aims and nationalist resentments as well as demands for tolerable living and working conditions. Within a few years young Communist activists could claim a national labor federation representing half-a-million workers, and marshal hundreds of thousands for militant May Day demonstrations.

Yet the Communists soon learned that, in a country ruled and plundered by marauding warlord armies, it was naked military power that was crucial in determining the direction of political events, and labor unions and other mass organizations could be repressed and crushed more easily than they could be built. Visions of a socialist revolution in China, if not abandoned, had to be postponed. And the Communists also soon learned that the promised world revolution similarly had been postponed. When the anticipated socialist revolutions failed to materialize in the industrialized countries of Western Europe, and as the Soviet Union remained the lone socialist state in a hostile capitalist world, both Russian national interests and the logic of Leninist revolutionary strategy dictated that the Chinese revolutionary process was in its bourgeois-democratic stage and that the prospects for a socialist revolution lay well in the future—for the possibility of the latter always had been predicated on an international revolutionary explosion, which the Russian Bolshevik Revolution had failed to ignite. The new and pessimistic Soviet assessment of the revolutionary situation in China—and in the world—was communicated to the leaders of the CCP in 1922 by representatives of the Moscow-based Third International (Comintern). The new Chinese converts to Marxism received the disheartening message reluctantly. But both the political authority of Moscow and political conditions in China demanded that the Chinese Communists reconcile themselves to a revolution confined to bourgeois limits. The CCP was to ally itself with the Guomindang. The old revolutionary party, still headed by Sun Yatsen and revitalized by the political activism of the May Fourth Movement, had achieved a tenuous political-military base in and around the city of Guangzhou (Canton). The alliance was designed to achieve the twin goals of national unification and national independence, that is, the elimination of warlord separatism and foreign imperialism. It was an alliance in which the CCP was to be very much the junior partner. The Communists were to recognize the Guomindang as the leader of the bourgeois or "national" revolution and they were to join that party as individual members in a united front. The alliance was formally consummated in January 1924. To the Guomindang at Guangzhou there flowed Soviet arms, money, and military and political advisers—for the purpose of building a modern army that eventually would move northward to unify the country. To the Communists, Moscow offered moral encouragement and political advice.

In retrospect, one is struck by how narrow a definition Comintern ideologists gave the Marxist concept of a "bourgeois-democratic" revolution—at least insofar as China was concerned. A bourgeois revolution is a political transformation that sweeps away obsolete institutions left over from the old feudal (or "precapitalist") order and replaces them with new political institutions favorable to the interests of the bourgeoisie and to the growth of capitalist production and property relationships. Essential in this process is genuine national unification—the establishment of a centralized government with a uniform code of laws, a single national currency, and a uniform system of taxation; in short, the abolition of all the vestiges of feudal separatism and the creation of modern politico-legal conditions conducive to the growth of a national market and to the development of capitalist production. The process also includes, at least ideally, the establishment of a parliamentary democracy, the form of state most appropriate for the class dominance of the bourgeoisie. Furthermore, it assumed that a bourgeois revolution permits some degree of freedom for the political activities of other social classes, especially the growing proletariat, and that it abolishes the remaining feudal relationships that shackle the peasantry, thus hastening the growth of capitalism in the countryside.

In its specifically Leninist form, a bourgeois-democratic revolution in Asia and the Middle East came to include a nationalist revolution to throw off the foreign imperialist yoke. It also included a much greater emphasis on the antifeudal social revolution in the countryside—and, partly to compensate for the weakness of the indigenous bourgeoisie, a far greater political role for the proletariat and especially for the peasantry in the bourgeois phase of the revolutionary process.

Yet the bourgeois revolution that the Guomindang–CCP alliance was designed to carry out was conceived as a much more limited affair. Beneath the facade of the revolutionary rhetoric of the time, the concept was redefined to include no more than the leaders of the Guomindang were willing to accept. And this boiled down to two aims: national unification and national independence. Only lip service was paid to the ideal of a democratic republic; indeed, it was implicitly assumed from the beginning that China's new political order would be essentially a military one. And quite explicitly excluded, or at least postponed, was a social revolution in the countryside. China's "bourgeois-democratic" revolution, in short, was to achieve no more than purely nationalist goals.

A successful nationalist revolution was, of course, desperately needed.

The 1911 Revolution had done little more than remove the anachronistic monarchy. Its political result was neither a strong state nor a democratic one, but rather increased political chaos and fragmentation in the dark age of warlordism that came in its wake. It left undisturbed the web of imperialist political and economic impingements that had made China so dependent on the foreign powers, just as it left untouched the existing internal social structure and especially traditional rural socioeconomic relationships and gentry-landlord dominance in the countryside. By the 1920s, national unification and national independence had become almost universal demands among politically conscious Chinese, uniting much of the traditional ruling class with the modern social classes and political parties. And for the leaders of an isolated and beleaguered Soviet Union, being driven inexorably to Stalin's doctrine of "socialism in one country" and now deeply involved in internal Chinese politics, a nationalist revolution that would yield a friendly Chinese regime was the overriding aim.

But China needed more than a purely nationalist revolution and more was being demanded. New social classes and groups had arrived in the political arena to give the "national revolution" a radical thrust that went far beyond the limited aims upon which the Guomindang–Communist alliance was based. In the cities the new Chinese working class began to revolt against the injustices of early industrialism. In the countryside peasants organized (and were being organized) to overthrow the dominance of the traditional landlord class. And a radical intelligentsia, now politicized and politically organized in modern parties, stood eager to lead a popular revolutionary movement. These forces could not be confined within the narrow limits of a "national" revolution or even a more broadly defined "bourgeois-democratic" one, as the great revolutionary upsurge of 1925–1927 was to demonstrate.

The Revolution of 1925–1927

The alliance with the Guomindang provided Communist revolutionaries wider access to Chinese society and the powerful forces of revolution latent within it. Communists, working under the banner of the Guomindang, renewed their efforts to organize increasingly rebellious workers and peasants. Over the years 1924–1927, the mass revolutionary movement in both town and countryside, partly organized and partly spontaneous, grew with unprecedented rapidity and moved in ever more radical social directions. It was the mass movement that gave China's two modern political parties the enormous strength they so quickly acquired during those years and provided the alliance between them with its extraordinary dynamism. But the increasingly radical character of the popular movement created political tensions and intensified social conflicts that undermined the political united front and resulted in the near destruction of the CCP.

The radical and militant phase of the revolution was signaled by the May Thirtieth Movement of 1925. During the early months of 1925, the city of Shanghai—the center and symbol of the foreign imperialist intrusion—was swept by a wave of workers' strikes. In one instance, a Chinese worker was shot to death by a Japanese foreman. On May 30 workers and students staged a demonstration of protest that culminated in the foreign-governed International Settlement, where British-commanded police dispersed the demonstrators, killing 12 of their number. The incident had an explosive effect, setting off a succession of strikes, demonstrations, antiforeign boycotts in all the major cities and a new massive wave of anti-imperialism throughout the country. The most notorious clash between Chinese and foreigners occurred in the foreign settlement in Guangzhou (Canton) on June 23 when British and French troops killed 50 Chinese demonstrators and wounded many more. The Guangzhou massacre provoked a general strike by Chinese workers in Hong Kong, crippling the colony and British trade for 16 months, and also set off a nationwide boycott against British goods. In a dramatic expression of political militancy, 100,000 Chinese laborers migrated from the British colony to Guangzhou to form the Hong Kong–Canton Strike Committee, which became one of the main centers of the growing revolutionary movement.

The militant mass movement that emerged in the summer of 1925— which was to grow with extraordinary rapidity and force over the next two years—was never a purely nationalist movement and could not be confined to strictly anti-imperialist aims. Powerful nationalist resentments fueled the revolutionary movement, to be sure, and the resentments were exacerbated by the spectacle of foreigners killing Chinese on Chinese soil. But the workers were also driven to revolt by the horrendous conditions of work and life brought by early capitalist industrialism. Workers living in foreign-dominated cities and laboring in foreign-owned factories naturally identified economic exploitation with the foreign presence. It was this combination of socioeconomic oppression and foreign oppression that gave the workers' movement its special militancy.

The urban working-class movement of 1925–1927 was accompanied by the rise of a no less militant peasant movement in the countryside. In addition to a resurgence of peasant protest and revolt through traditional forms, primarily secret societies and banditry, there appeared new and modern rural organizations, the peasant associations. Composed mostly of poorer peasants, and in large measure the product of the ideas and organizing activities of young revolutionary intellectuals, the new organizations posed an increasingly radical threat to the dominance of the gentry. By mid-1925, half-a-million peasants had joined the new associations in Guangdong, the province where the main military–political base of the allied Guomindang–Communist forces was located. Over the next two years, membership in the Guangdong peasant organizations quadrupled and the peasant associations spread rapidly to other provinces. Nationalist and antiforeign sentiments were involved, but the motive force was an elemental demand for social justice and economic survival.

The mass movement sparked by the May Thirtieth incident had an immediate and dramatic effect on both the Guomindang and the CCP. The dynamism of the popular movement in both town and countryside enabled the Guomindang to consolidate its power in Guangzhou and expand it from there. Following the death of Sun Yatsen in March 1925, Chiang Kaishek established himself as the political leader of the Guomindang by virtue of his control of the Russian-trained Nationalist Army and by the end of the year he had extended Guomindang control to all of Guangdong and portions of neighboring provinces. The long-awaited Northern Expedition to unify the country began in the summer of 1926, and warlord armies crumbled before its advance. The popular revolutionary movement aided the new army in its striking victories, while the continuing military successes of Chiang's forces gave further impetus to the workers and peasants.

Just as the May Thirtieth Movement led to a spectacular growth in the power of the Guomindang, so it led to a no less dramatic increase in the power and influence of its Communist allies. The CCP began with less than 100 members in 1921, and had grown to no more than 500 by 1924. At the end of 1925, and on the basis of the mass radicalization of the preceding 6 months, the Party could claim 20,000 members—and by early 1927 its membership had almost tripled to a total of 58,000. Its auxiliary organizations were even larger, particularly the Socialist Youth Corps which attracted ever increasing numbers of militant students and young workers. Moreover, Communist activists, primarily responsible for the organization of industrial unions and peasant associations, exercised enormous influence over the new mass organizations, albeit under the banner of the Guomindang. And Communists held important positions within the Guomindang itself, in the National government based in Guangzhou, and in Chiang Kai-shek's new army.

The successes of the mass movement that gave the Guomindang–CCP alliance its extraordinary political dynamism eventually undermined the political basis of the alliance and soon tore it asunder, leading to the suppression and virtual destruction of the CCP. Once the forces of popular revolution were set in motion they acquired a life of their own that could not be confined within the narrow limits of a "national revolution." Urban workers struck not only at the factories and enterprises owned by foreigners, but those owned by the Chinese bourgeoisie as well; the working-class movement threatened not only foreign property and privileges but property in general. In the countryside, the peasant movement attacked not foreign landlords, but the power of Chinese landlords and rural elites. From the mass nationalist movement there thus arose the threat of social revolution—and it threatened classes and groups that formed the social basis of the Guomindang: the urban bourgeoisie whose ties to, and dependence upon, the Guomindang were solidified in direct proportion to the rising threat of social revolution; and the officer corps of Chiang Kai-shek's army, many of whose members were the sons of the landed gentry, a class that now feared agrarian revolution. With the interests of the propertied classes threatened, the Guomindang emerged more and more as the party of property and order.

As the Nationalist Army moved northward during the latter half of 1926, the workers' and peasant organizations grew to massive proportions, ever more radical in aims and methods, and increasingly revolutionary in character, especially in the countryside. Even the most radical Communists were astonished by the sudden surge and power of the largely spontaneous movement from below. The sense of astonishment (and the feeling of exhilaration) runs throughout Mao Zedong's famous report on the peasant movement in Hunan, a document written during the early months of 1927 in which Mao described the spontaneous revolutionary activities of the peasantry as a force as natural and elemental as "a tornado or tempest, a force so extraordinarily swift and violent that no power, however great, will be able to suppress it."[1]

But social revolution was incompatible with the terms of the Guomindang–Communist alliance. And the Stalinist message from Moscow, duly conveyed to Chinese Communist leaders through the agency of the Comintern, was to restrict the radicalism of the masses, and to preserve the political alliance at all costs. Thus the leaders of the Chinese Party found themselves in the embarrassing and agonizing position of attempting to limit popular radicalism rather than to promote it, to dampen the flames of revolution rather than to place themselves at the head of the insurgent masses. Not all Communists heeded Moscow's "advice," nor could they have enforced Comintern directives even had they wished to do so, for the popular revolution (particularly in the countryside) had acquired a momentum of its own that was beyond the power of any party to control. Although many individual Communists attempted to lead the movement, the Party as a whole remained confused and immobilized. The result was that the rebellious masses were left defenseless and largely leaderless in face of the organized forces of counterrevolution preparing to suppress them.

During the early months of 1927 the popular revolutionary movement reached its apogee, while the Nationalist Army was demonstrating its military supremacy in its victorious march through the provinces of South and Central China. The tension between the purely nationalist aims of the Guomindang and the social-revolutionary aspirations of the masses was nearing its breaking point. The break came when Chiang Kai-shek had acquired the military power (and the financial backing of the higher bourgeoisie of Shanghai) to destroy the mass movement—and to cast off his Russian patrons and Communist allies. The counterrevolution began in Shanghai in April. On March 21–22 a Communist-led working-class uprising had succeeded in seizing control of portions of Shanghai, and the victorious insurgents awaited the arrival of the Nationalist Army. Chiang and his forces entered the city without opposition on March 26, and they were welcomed as liberators. The liberators soon turned executioners. Before dawn on April 12, armed units of the infamous Green Gang and other underworld secret societies, together with selected units of the regular Nationalist Army, attacked the headquarters of Communist and radical trade-union organizations, inaugurating a bloodbath that virtually destroyed both the CCP and the workers' movement in China's largest city and the main center of the organized radical movement. From Shanghai, the repression was carried to all of the areas south of the Yangtze within reach of the Nationalist Army, extending north to warlord areas not yet under the control of the Nationalist government. In an orgy of counterrevolutionary violence, Chiang turned his Soviet-built army to the task of destroying all radical mass organizations as well as the Chinese Communist Party. Trade unions and student organizations were annihilated in the cities, but nowhere was the slaughter greater than in the suppression of the peasant associations in the countryside. Organizations that had mobilized tens of millions of peasants were brutally smashed, and within a few months had vanished from the political scene, leaving few traces of the great agrarian revolution that had risen so swiftly, promising to transform the Chinese countryside. Those killed in the Revolution of 1925–1927 numbered in the hundreds, but the White Terror of 1927–1930 took a toll of human lives that must be counted in the hundreds of thousands.

The Chinese Communist Party was virtually extinguished. Its organizational structure was quickly shattered in a series of lightning blows struck by the Nationalist Army, and its ranks further decimated by a series of belated and desperate attempts to reverse the counterrevolutionary tide, the last of which was the Canton Commune and its bloody suppression in December 1927. At the beginning of 1927 the Chinese Communist Party was a powerful organization with a membership of 58,000. By the end of the year no more than 10,000 remained, and they were scattered, disorganized, demoralized, and leaderless. Some Communists defected, but most had been killed in battle or summarily executed. Those who survived the carnage fled to the more remote areas of the countryside, there to attempt to begin the revolution anew.

The Communists learned bitter lessons from their crushing defeat, and the lessons were to guide their revolutionary strategy in the years that followed. First and foremost was the recognition that in the modern Chinese historical situation military power was decisive in determining the outcome of political and social class struggles. It was the military superiority of the Guomindang that had defeated the revolution in 1927, and that elemental fact of Chinese political life was not lost on the leaders of the CCP. From it grew the Maoist maxim that "political power grows out of the barrel of a gun." The maxim had been practiced by Chiang Kai-shek before Mao expounded it, but Mao was to learn to be a better practitioner of the lesson that Chiang had imparted to him. The Communists now knew that they had to build their own army and that the revolution would of necessity take the form of a military struggle. Many also had learned that Moscow was not the sole repository of revolutionary wisdom, at least not in so far as the Chinese revolution was concerned, for it was that peculiar "united front" strategy formulated in Moscow that had led them to defeat and disaster. United-front strategies were by no means rejected, but the Chinese Communists were now determined to maintain their own political and military independence. And there arose a new appreciation of the revolutionary potentialities of the peasantry. In part, this was a matter of necessity, for the Party was no longer able to operate effectively in the Guomindang-ruled cities; in part, it was to be a new revolutionary preference. In any case, the Communists were no longer bound to orthodox Marxist–Leninist dogmas on the revolutionary limitations of peasants.

The events of 1927 marked the failure not of one revolution but of two: the workers' movement in the cities and the peasant movement in the countryside. The urban proletarian movement had been socialist in nature, or at least potentially so, for it was a revolt against both indigenous and foreign capitalism, and was aimed at the abolition of private property. The socialist potential went unrealized, but it was not historically inevitable that this should have been so. The proletariat constituted only a small minority of the Chinese population, but not an insignificant one. By the mid-1920s the number of industrial workers employed in large-scale enterprises had grown to approximately 2,000,000 and they were highly concentrated and strategically placed in the modern sector of the Chinese economy. To this must be added a far greater number of urban semiproletarians, the perhaps 10,000,000 Mao Zedong once termed "the city coolies," who swelled the ranks of the urban revolutionary movement.[2] The Chinese industrial proletariat proper was not far smaller than its Russian counterpart in 1917.[3] Nor was it any less politically militant. Indeed, few working-class movements anywhere in the twentieth century matched the revolutionary energies, the organizational initiative, the extraordinary heroism, and the spirit of self-sacrifice and dedication to the revolutionary cause which the Chinese proletariat displayed. Moreover, the urban working-class movement developed in a situation that in many respects was highly favorable for revolution. With all social classes weak, political power fragmented, and a militant proletarian movement accompanied by a powerful agrarian revolution, the possibility of a successful revolution based upon a worker-peasant alliance was not beyond the realm of possibility. What was lacking were not the objective preconditions for revolution but rather the subjective prerequisites. A politically immature Communist Party allowed itself to become shackled to the policies of the Comintern and dependent on the actions of the Guomindang. From its ranks emerged no leader with the boldness and vision of a Lenin or a Trotsky to seize upon the possibilities that the revolutionary situation offered. The Chinese Communist leaders did not lead the masses but, however reluctantly and unwittingly, accepted and pursued foreign-made policies that led the mass movement to its tragic end. The disasters that befell both the workers' movement and the Chinese Communist Party in 1927 were in no sense historically inevitable. It was not preordained that the Russians should have created a modern Chinese army and placed that army in the hands of a man who was to use it to crush the revolution. That fatal historical irony came about not because of the weakness of the mass movement but because of the weaknesses and limitations of its leaders—and ultimately because the critical decisions were made in Moscow. It was not to be the last time that the national interests of the Soviet state were to collide with the real interests of the Chinese revolution.

Yet what did happen in 1927, even though it did not necessarily have to happen, was crucial in determining the future and nature of the revolution. The liquidation of the workers' movement and Communist power in the cities proved irreversible. When the Communist revolution revived in the years after the debacle of 1927 it did so in the form of a peasant-based revolution in the more remote rural areas. The urban proletariat, so bloodily suppressed in 1927, remained politically quiescent for most of the next two decades, and the Communists were not to regain power in the urban areas until their victorious peasant armies marched into the cities in 1949.

If the socialist revolutionary potential of 1927 went unrealized, the bourgeois revolution proved abortive as well. To be sure, the victorious northward march of the Guomindang armies in 1927–1928 did manage to achieve a semblance of national unification, albeit upon the ruins of the mass movement. But the new Nationalist government at Nanjing provided no impetus and little opportunity for modern capitalist development in the cities, where its power was based. And it sought to maintain the social status quo in the countryside, where it was content to rely on the local power of the gentry-landlord elite. Even as a purely nationalist revolution, the triumph of the Guomindang was superficial and incomplete, for "national unification" was based less on the elimination of warlordism than on various and tenuous alliances with the more powerful warlord armies of North China. And "national independence" meant arriving at an accommodation with the imperialist powers and a continued dependence on foreign economic influences. The bourgeois revolution thus remained unfinished, and the task of completing it fell to the Communists.

NOTES

1. Mao Tse-tung [Mao Zedong], "Report of an Investigation into the Peasant Movement in Hunan," in *Selected Works of Mao Tse-tung* (London: Lawrence & Wishart, 1954), 1:21–22.
2. Mao Tse-tung, "Analysis of the Classes in Chinese Society" (1926), in *Selected Works* (1954), 1:19.
3. On the eve of the Bolshevik Revolution, the Russian industrial proletariat numbered about 3,000,000.

4

The Maoist Revolution and the Yan'an Legacy

ARADICALLY NEW phase of the Chinese Communist Revolution began inconspicuously in October of 1927 when Mao Zedong led the remnants of a defeated military force to Jinggangshan, a remote mountain region and old bandit hideout bordering the provinces of Hunan and Jiangxi. There Mao built a tiny military base by recruiting peasant vagabonds and uniting his troops with those of several local bandit leaders. In the spring of 1928 the forces at Jinggangshan were augmented by the arrival of 1,000 rebel soldiers led by Zhu De, who was to become the commander of what was to become the Red Army and Mao's comrade in arms during the twenty-one years of revolutionary warfare that were to follow.

It was in the Jinggangshan border area that the Maoist strategy of a rural-based revolution had its origins. From 1928 to 1931, the Maoist forces learned to employ the tactics of guerrilla warfare upon which their survival was dependent. The "Mao-Zhu Army" grew through the recruitment of local peasants and the appeals of a radical program of land redistribution, and eventually secured military predominance in southern Jiangxi, where, in 1931, the Chinese Soviet Republic was established.

While Mao embarked on an independent course of agrarian revolution, this was not the case for the Chinese Communist movement as a whole.

31

During the years when Mao was consolidating a rural base in Jiangxi, other Communists following directives from Moscow were leading small peasant-rebel armies in attacks on the cities. But a demoralized working class failed to respond to revolutionary appeals. The end of 1930 marked the end of Communist hopes to regain their old proletarian bases. What remained of the defeated Communist forces gravitated to Jiangxi or retreated to a dozen smaller rural Soviet bases mostly located along the upper reaches of the Yangtze River. For the next ten years a bitter internal conflict would rage between Comintern-supported Chinese Communist leaders and Maoists for control of the Party and the Red Army. The battles were to be fought in the isolated rural areas where the revolution and the revolutionaries were now confined—and the terrain was to prove favorable to Mao.

The Chinese Soviet Republic, formally proclaimed in November 1931, with its capital at the town of Ruijin in Jiangxi Province, was to survive three years. The Communists established a functioning governmental apparatus, administering a territory of about 15,000 square miles inhabited by approximately 3,000,000 people. The central Soviet area was augmented by a dozen or so smaller rural Soviets, with a total population of about 6,000,000. And the Red Army grew into a formidable fighting force of 300,000.

The history of the Chinese Soviet Republic was brief, and the experiment ended in failure, but the historical experience was by no means insignificant. The Communists established a sizable and functioning civilian governmental apparatus in Jiangxi, and, although the government fell, those who survived its fall emerged as experienced political administrators as well as seasoned revolutionaries. The principles of guerrilla warfare that Mao Zedong and Zhu De originated at Jinggangshan were developed and tested on a far greater scale during the early 1930s. Perhaps most important, the Communists learned essential lessons about the preconditions for the political and social mobilization of the peasantry. They learned that the prerequisite for agrarian revolution was the military predominance of the Red Army and the security it guaranteed, for peasants were willing to sacrifice to change the conditions under which they lived but not in situations they perceived to be hopeless and feared retribution from the forces of counterrevolution. They also learned that radical policies of wholesale social leveling which threatened the productive middle peasants were politically and economically counterproductive in a situation that demanded a broad base of popular support in a rural society existing on a subsistence level. And they learned that meaningful land reform could not be imposed from above by bureaucratic decree but had to be accomplished through the organization and participation of peasants within each village.

Just as Lenin once described the 1905 Russian Revolution as a "dress rehearsal" for the 1917 October Revolution, so the short-lived Jiangxi Soviet was a "rehearsal" for what proved to be the decisive Yan'an period of the Chinese revolution. But it was a rehearsal that was performed at a terrible cost for both the Communists and their peasant supporters. In 1934 the Chinese Soviet Republic began to crumble under the onslaught of Guomindang armies, and in the autumn of that year the Communists abandoned their base in Jiangxi and embarked upon that extraordinary year-long journey to the North that was to become known and celebrated as the Long March.

The Political and Psychological Significance of the Long March

In October 1935 Mao Zedong led what remained of the First Front Army through the last lines of enemy soldiers guarding Mount Liupan in Gansu Province and entered northern Shaanxi Province. In that remote and primitive area of China's vast and sparsely populated Northwest, Communist revolutionaries from many provinces were to find refuge. It was a precarious haven, but one that would provide sufficient time and opportunity to establish a new base area from where the revolution could begin once again.

Of the approximately 80,000 men and 35 women who embarked from Jiangxi on the night of October 15, 1934, fewer than 10,000 survived the torturous trek to arrive with Mao in Shaanxi, just south of the Great Wall. Among the many dead, left along that circuitous route through the treacherous mountains, rivers, and marshes of western China, were many of Mao's closest friends and comrades, killed in the bloody battles fought with pursuing Nationalist troops and warlord armies along the way. Among the missing—and never to be found—were two of Mao's children, who remained behind with sympathetic peasant families in Jiangxi, along with many other children too young to undertake the 6,000-mile march. Also left behind in Jiangxi, to fight a rearguard action against Guomindang troops, was Mao Zedong's brother, Mao Zetan, killed in battle early in 1935.

Measured by any standard of human accomplishment, and quite apart from one's political persuasions, few would disagree with Edgar Snow's assessment that the Long March was "an Odyssey unequaled in modern times."[1] But the heroism and great human drama of the epic should not be

allowed to obscure the fact that it was born out of political and military failure and ended in near disaster. Having successfully withstood Chiang Kai-
shek's first four "encirclement and annihilation" campaigns (1930–33), the
Communists had neither the economic nor military resources to resist the
new "blockhouse" strategy that Chiang's imported German military advisers had devised for the fifth campaign.

Abandoning the Chinese Soviet Republic and leaving the peasants who
had supported them to the terrible reprisals that the returning Guomindang armies inevitably were to inflict was a political defeat of very considerable magnitude. And the fact that the largest part of the Red Army was
destroyed during the ordeals of the next year can hardly be seen as a victory. The exhausted survivors of the Long March who reached Shaanxi celebrated little more than the sheer fact that they had managed to survive.

Yet the Long March was the prelude to what proved to be the victorious
period of the Chinese Communist Revolution, and in that sense it was an
event filled with momentous political and psychological implications. Politically, it was the time when Mao Zedong achieved effective control of the
Chinese Communist Party, a dominance that had eluded him during the
Jiangxi period as his power was eroded by the Comintern-supported
"Twenty-eight Bolsheviks," a group of young Chinese Communists trained
at Sun Yat-sen University in Moscow to do Stalin's bidding in China. It was
not until January 1935, during the course of the Long March, that the
power of the Twenty-eight Bolsheviks was broken and Mao emerged as
chairman of the Party's Politburo. His leadership was not to go unchallenged in later years, but he now was sufficiently in control of the Party
(and enough of the army) to pursue his own revolutionary strategy. The in-
cubus of the Comintern finally had been thrown off, and Mao had achieved
political supremacy in defiance of Stalin. It was an event unprecedented in
the history of Communist parties during the Stalinist era. Thus the Long
March brought Mao to a position of supreme leadership in the Chinese
Communist Party and brought the revolutionaries he led to a relatively secure geographical position—one where they could make good their vow to
fight the Japanese and mobilize Chinese nationalist sentiments for both patriotic and revolutionary ends.

The psychological effects of the Long March are much more intangible.
For Mao, at least, the experience served to reinforce his voluntaristic faith
that people with the proper will, spirit, and revolutionary consciousness
could conquer all material obstacles and mold historical reality in accordance with their ideas and ideals. For those who survived the ordeal—and
for those who were inspired by the story of their survival—the experience,
however bitter it was at the time, gave rise to a renewed sense of hope and

a deepened sense of mission. People must be able to hope before they can act; they must possess not only ideals and a sense of mission, but hope and confidence that they will be able to realize their ideals through their own actions. More than any other event in the history of Chinese Communism, it was the Long March—and the legendary tales to which it gave rise—that provided this essential feeling of hope, the confidence that determined people could prevail under even the most desperate conditions. And more than any other individual, it was Mao Zedong who radiated and inspired this faith in the future. It was a faith not only in those deemed capable of molding the future in accordance with Communist hopes but also in the values regarded as essential to the eventual realization of those hopes. The familiar Maoist virtues of unending struggle, heroic sacrifice, self-denial, diligence, courage, and unselfishness were values espoused not by Mao alone but carried and conveyed by all of the veterans of the Long March, for these were the values they had come to regard as essential to their own survival and to the survival of the revolution to which they had devoted their lives. These ascetic values lay at the core of what later came to be celebrated as "the Yan'an spirit."

Many more died during the Long March than survived it, and this fact alone made its peculiar contribution to "the Yan'an spirit." The survivors' consciousness that they had lived while so many more had perished lent a sacred character to their revolutionary mission and gave rise to an almost religious sense of dedication. Later, Mao found it "odd" that he had survived and commented that "death just did not seem to want him."[2] The Long March, both in reality and later symbolically, was the supreme and ultimate test of survival amidst death. For Mao, the experience undoubtedly contributed enormously to the perception of himself as a man of destiny who would lead his followers to the completion of their revolutionary mission. And if others did not necessarily share Mao's special sense of destiny, they had shared similar experiences, suffered equally heavy personal losses, and had acquired a similar sense of being survivors. This psychological legacy went into the making of Yan'an Communism and manifested itself in a very special commitment to carry on the revolutionary struggle, for only in that way could one justify the incredible sacrifices that had been made and prepare for those yet to be made.

The mere fact of survival thus became a matter of enormous psychological significance. It also was a matter of great political consequence, for it was testimony not only to the validity of the mission, but also to the policies and wisdom of the leader. Indeed, the cult of Mao Zedong, it seems not improbable to suggest, was born out of the Long March, for Mao was the prophet who had led the survivors through the wilderness. And if Shaanxi was not the promised land, later revolutionary successes were to fulfill his prophecies and vindicate his policies. Although one does not find in the Yan'an period anything resembling the more extreme forms of the worship of Mao and his "thought" witnessed after 1949, a certain mystique and sense of awe had already begun to surround his name and person. As early as 1937 Edgar Snow reported that Mao had acquired the reputation of "a charmed life."[3]

In celebrating the heroism of the Long March, later Chinese accounts were to hail it as a great victory which guaranteed the inevitable success of the revolution. Victory did not seem so inevitable at the time, however. While what remained of the First Front Army celebrated their survival, they had little else to celebrate. In assessing the situation in 1936, Mao was a good deal more candid than later writers:

> Except for the Shaanxi–Gansu border area, all revolutionary bases were lost, the Red Army reduced from 300,000 to a few tens of thousands, the membership of the Chinese Communist Party was reduced from 300,000 to a few tens of thousands, and the Party organizations in Guomindang areas were almost entirely wiped out. In short, we received an extremely great historical punishment.[4]

To be sure, Mao attributed the disaster to the ideological and political errors of his recently vanquished Party opponents and duly expressed confidence in ultimate victory and in the new strategy he proposed to achieve that victory. But his appraisal of Communist fortunes at the conclusion of the Long March was bleak and accurate.

The military forces under Mao's control in Shaanxi were augmented in late 1935 by several thousand Communist partisans who had been engaged in guerrilla warfare in the Northwest since 1931 under the leadership of Liu Zhidan, a Whampoa graduate and former Guomindang officer whose heroic exploits had earned him something of a Robin Hood reputation among the peasants of his native Shaanxi. In addition, several thousand other Communist troops who had abandoned a small base area in Hunan Province reached Shaanxi in September 1935, several weeks prior to Mao's arrival. In 1936 these forces were joined by the remnants of two other armies; the army under the command of He Long, who had been operating in Hunan, and the troops led by Zhang Guotao and Zhu De who had broken off from the main line of the Long March and finally arrived by way of Xinjiang. Yet by late 1936 the Red Army in Shaanxi numbered no more than 30,000, a pitifully small force compared to the pursuing forces of Chiang Kai-shek.

The Yan'an Era and Peasant Revolution

The Communist military position in 1936 was precarious and the economic environment in which they now found themselves was unpromising. Northern Shaanxi was one of China's most poor and backward areas. Centuries of erosion had made its lands unfertile, capable of supporting only a relatively small and an extremely impoverished population; "a very poor, backward, underdeveloped, and mountainous part of the country," Mao Zedong later remarked to a foreign visitor.[5] And to Zhou Enlai in 1936, it seemed a most inauspicious place to revive the revolution. "Peasants in Shaanxi are extremely poor," he then complained, "their land very unproductive. . . . The population of the Jiangxi Soviet numbered 3,000,000 whereas here it is at most 600,000. . . . In Jiangxi and Fujian people brought bundles with them when they joined the Red Army; here they do not even bring chopsticks; they are utterly destitute."[6]

And what of Yan'an itself, the town to which pilgrimages are now made to view the sacred revolutionary places, especially the austere wooden houses and the cave dwellings where Mao and others lived and worked during that legendary decade? Although an ancient city, founded some 3,000 years ago, Yan'an could not claim a particularly distinguished history. As Chinese civilization moved southward over the centuries, it became a remote frontier town, used mostly as an advanced military outpost to defend the borders against nomadic invaders from central Asia. It was an impoverished market town of perhaps 10,000 people when it was occupied by Communist troops at the end of 1936 and established as the administrative capital of what was to be called the Shaanxi-Gansu-Ningxia Border Region. The wretched poverty and backwardness of the entire area was reflected in the bleakness of Yan'an. The town's now famous museums and shrines exhibit no ancient glories but are the products of a modern revolutionary history—and, in a sense, are the result of an accident of history. "We didn't pick it" was Mao's terse reply to a sympathetic American writer who once politely praised Yan'an's harsh climate.[7]

But it is Yan'an the time, not Yan'an the place, that Chinese celebrate. Yet how did the time become one to celebrate when the place was so unfavorable? How did a ragged force of revolutionaries, isolated in an area so remote and so lacking in material resources, grow within a decade into a powerful army of more than a million soldiers and acquire the massive peasant support upon which to base its momentous victory?

For those inclined to ponder the role of accidents in history, the Japanese invasion of China is undoubtedly a most intriguing case. Were it not for the Japanese attempt to conquer China in 1937, it can plausibly be argued, the conditions essential to the Communist victory would not have been created. Yan'an would have remained an obscure market town in a remote Chinese province, unknown to Chinese and foreigners alike. No one in Beijing today would be celebrating the "Yan'an spirit" and no foreign "China watchers" would have pondered the "Yan'an syndrome."

The Japanese invasion undermined the foundations of the Guomindang regime, for the Nationalists were driven from the major cities from which they derived their major sources of financial and political support. For the Guomindang, the ravages of war brought incredible economic chaos and bureaucratic corruption—and, eventually, almost total demoralization. More importantly, such administrative authority as the Guomindang exercised in the countryside was largely destroyed. The gentry, upon whom that fragile authority had rested, either fled the rural areas or were left militarily and politically defenseless. At the same time, the Communists, already experienced in working in the villages and adept at guerrilla warfare, were given access to vast areas of the countryside. For while the Japanese invaders were able to occupy the cities, they did not have the manpower to effectively control the rural areas, where Communist guerrilla bases multiplied rapidly during the war years. The retreat of Guomindang forces to the west, and the collapse of Nationalist governmental authority in much of China, allowed the Communists to break out of their remote sanctuary in Shaanxi and expand their military and political influence through vast areas of the countryside in northern and central China. Although the increasingly powerful Yan'an base area remained the political and ideological center of the revolution, Communist cadres operated in many parts of rural China, gaining the political support of tens of millions of peasants and organizing many for guerrilla warfare behind Japanese lines. The gradual growth of Communist political and military nuclei in many parts of rural China during the war years was to prove decisive when the civil war with the Guomindang resumed with full fury in 1946.

Much of the enormous popular support the Communists gained during the war years was based on patriotic appeals for national resistance to the foreign invaders. The new mantle of modern Chinese nationalism had replaced the old "mandate of Heaven" as the symbol of political legitimacy in twentieth-century China. The nationalist credentials which Guomindang leaders lost—at first by their seeming unwillingness to defend the nation against the Japanese threat and then by their obvious inability to do so—were inherited by the Communists. During the war years, Yan'an was not only the revolutionary center but also (for increasing numbers of Chinese) the symbol of Chinese nationalist resistance to the Japanese invaders. From the cities many thousands of students and intellectuals migrated to Yan'an to join the Communist (and now also the nationalist) cause—and there, first at the Northwest Anti-Japanese Red Army University, many were trained, and ideologically "remolded," to become political, administrative, and military cadres for the rapidly expanding Communist base areas.

The Japanese occupation not only intensified the economic crisis in the countryside but gave rise to bitter antiforeign sentiments among the peasants which the Communists were able to transform into a modern mass nationalist movement and utilize for revolutionary political ends. This new political opportunity was greatly facilitated by ruthless Japanese policies—the brutal and indiscriminate military forays into the villages of north and central China, where Japanese soldiers could plunder and punish but could not hold and occupy. The Communist mobilization of peasants on the basis of an anti-Japanese nationalist program contributed enormously to the military and political successes of the Yan'an era.

In view of the strong tendency to interpret Chinese Communism as a species of Chinese nationalism, or to see the revolution as a case of a new elite riding to power on a fortuitous wave of mass nationalism, it is important to keep the whole phenomenon of "peasant nationalism" in historical perspective. The Chinese peasant's identification with China as a political entity and peasant resistance to foreign intruders did not originate in 1937. Both are age-old features of Chinese history. Even armed peasant resistance to modern imperialist incursions has a long history, dating back to the Opium War of 1839–1842. It would be highly misleading to either overestimate the spontaneous origins of the peasantry's modern sense of national consciousness or to underestimate the role of Communist cadres in instilling that sense of modern nationalism. The Communists were ardent Chinese nationalists long before 1937 and they played a crucial role in transforming the elemental antiforeign response of the peasantry to the Japanese invaders into a modern nationalist response. By forging bonds of solidarity between peasants from various localities and regions, the Communists created a nationwide resistance movement and imbued it with a sense of national mission that otherwise would have been absent. In large measure, the Communists brought nationalism to the countryside; they did not simply reflect it.

Furthermore, neither the nationalistic appeals of the Communist Party nor the emergence of a mass nationalist movement made the social-economic grievances of the peasantry any less pressing or Communist promises of agrarian reform any less appealing. Precisely the opposite seems to have been the case in most areas where the Communists achieved their greatest successes in organizing and mobilizing peasant support. The war intensified the already horrendous economic burdens on the peasantry and thus increased the attractiveness of the Communist program for land reform. To be sure, the official land policy of the Yan'an period was a relatively moderate one by Jiangxi standards. Instead of the outright expropriation and division of landlord holdings, a program for reductions in rents and interest rates was adopted, partly to conform to the terms of a tenuous wartime alliance with the Guomindang but more importantly as an attempt to enlist the support of landlords and rich peasants as well as the masses of poor and middle peasants in the struggle against the Japanese invaders. But the reduction of rent to no more than one-third the crop and the elimination of the many extralegal means through which landlords and bureaucrats traditionally exploited peasants were hardly unappealing measures to those who had been subjected to the most merciless forms of social and political, as well as economic, oppression.

Moreover, the officially "moderate" agrarian policies were by no means universally followed. In many cases large landholdings were distributed among land-hungry peasants, especially in areas where landlords fled with retreating Guomindang armies. Where the gentry-landlord elite remained, collaboration between Chinese landlords and Japanese occupiers was not uncommon; in exchange for political services performed—the traditional gentry function of "social control"—the Japanese allowed the gentry their traditional economic privilege of exploiting the peasantry. In such cases, the landlord appeared to the peasant not only in his old role as economic oppressor but also as national traitor. Traditional hatred of the landlord on socioeconomic grounds was intensified by new nationalist resentments, and the Communists appealed to both simultaneously, promoting class as well as national struggle.

Expropriation of gentry landholdings was a highly popular policy in much of the countryside—and where it occurred, and where the Communists had sufficient military strength to guarantee the security of the peasants and their newly acquired land, the Party won the loyalty of masses of peasants. Conditions and policies varied greatly. In some areas, social revolution was sacrificed to obtain the support of all rural classes in the interests of national unity; in others, radical land policies proved more popular; and in some areas, neither nationalist nor socioeconomic appeals were effective. But even where the officially moderate land policies were pursued, traditional agrarian relationships were profoundly transformed: the local political power of the gentry elite was broken, its social authority and prestige undermined, and such reduced economic power as it still held was dependent on the grace of the new holders of political-military power in the local areas—the military and political cadres of the Chinese Communist

Party. In the areas under Communist control in the Yan'an era, the erosion and sometimes the destruction of the power of the gentry-landlord class, the ruling elite of Chinese society for 2,000 years, marked the beginning of the first genuine social revolution in Chinese history since the establishment of the imperial order in 221 B.C.

The Japanese invaders made their unintended contribution to the revolution by removing the Nationalist army and bureaucracy from much of China, thereby permitting the Communists to organize the peasantry for both nationalist and social revolutionary ends. The invasion did not by itself create a revolutionary situation—for that already existed—but it did much to intensify that situation and to provide new opportunities for revolutionary action. But "revolutionary situations," however mature, do not by themselves create revolutions. Only revolutionaries make revolutions, and only when they are able to appreciate the potentialities in the historical situation and to act upon them. To understand the reasons for the Communist successes of the Yan'an years, it is necessary to take into account the subjective as well as the objective forces of the time—and especially the particular intellectual and ideological orientations of Mao Zedong.

The Origins of Maoism

Maoism did not become an official ideological orthodoxy until the early 1940s, but its history as a distinct (and distinctively Chinese) interpretation of Marxism began two decades earlier. To view Maoism as simply the ideological reflection of the "objective" conditions of the Yan'an period is to ignore the truism that people are the producers as well as the products of history and that they make their history, at least in part, on the basis of what they think. Neither Yan'an Communism nor Mao Zedong are exceptions to this proposition; much of what went into the making of the former was molded by the now famous "thoughts" of the latter. And Mao did not arrive in Shaanxi in 1935 with an empty head.

When Mao became a convert to Communism in 1920, many of the intellectual predispositions that were to mold his understanding of Marxism and his concept of revolution were already present, and they were reinforced by his revolutionary experiences in the 1920s and early 1930s. By no means the least important of Mao's early intellectual orientations was a profoundly voluntarist belief that the decisive factor in history (and the making of revolution) is human consciousness—the ideas, the will, and the actions of people. This faith in the ability of dedicated revolutionaries to mold social reality in accordance with their ideas and ideals survived the influence of the more deterministic tenets of Marxist theory, as Mao began to assimilate that theory in the course of his practical revolutionary activities.

To be sure, Mao derived from the objective laws of social development proclaimed in Marxist theory some degree of assurance of the historic inevitability of a socialist future. But, in the final analysis, Mao's faith in socialism was not based upon any real Marxist confidence in the objective forces of historical development. For Mao, the essential factor in determining the course of history was conscious human activity and the most important ingredients for revolution were how people thought and their willingness to engage in revolutionary action. This implied that revolution in China was not dependent on any predetermined levels of social and economic development and that revolutionary action need not be restrained by inherited Marxist-Leninist orthodoxies. It also implied a special concern for developing a "correct ideological consciousness," the ultimately decisive factor in achieving success. Correct thought, in the Maoist view, was the essential prerequisite for effective revolutionary action, and it is this assumption that gave rise to the enormous Maoist stress on "thought reform" and "ideological remolding" developed and refined in the Yan'an era.

The emphasis on ideological solidarity was of central importance for the successful conduct of guerrilla warfare in the Yan'an decade. In conditions of guerrilla war, where centralized organizational control is largely precluded, the forging of strong commitments to a common ideology and a common manner of thinking (and thus of acting) becomes a matter of supreme importance. That Mao and Maoists were already disposed to stress the role of "subjective factors" had a great deal to do with why the Communists adopted the strategy of "people's war" and the tactics of guerrilla warfare—and why they were able to employ those strategic and tactical principles so successfully.

If Mao's voluntarism mitigated the more deterministic implications of Marxist theory, his powerful nationalistic proclivities were equally important in adapting Marxism to the needs of revolution in China. From the beginning of his Marxist intellectual life, Mao's deeply rooted nationalistic impulses gave rise to the belief that the Chinese revolution was central to the world revolutionary process. As early as 1930 Mao predicted that "the revolution will certainly move towards an upsurge more quickly in China than in Western Europe."[8] Implicit in this confidence was a faith that assigned the Chinese nation a very special role in the building of a future international revolutionary order. Internationalist aspirations and goals were no doubt inextricably intertwined with Chinese nationalist impulses. But it was in this treacherous area of what Trotsky once called "messianic revolutionary nationalism" that Mao departed from other Chinese Marxists whose nationalist feelings were restrained by more orthodox Marxist considerations.

The nationalist component in Mao's Marxist world view was reflected not only in his long-standing hostility to the Comintern, but also, and more important, in his conception of the Chinese revolutionary process. Central to this conception was the conviction that the real enemies were not so much within Chinese society as without. The real enemy was foreign imperialism, and in the face of that continuing threat China stood as a potentially proletarian nation in a hostile capitalist-imperialist world order. In confronting the external foe, Chinese of all social classes could gather under the nationalist umbrella hoisted by the CCP. And those who could not, or would not, were excluded from membership in the nation, or at least from "the people," excommunicated as representatives of foreign imperialism. Political circumstances permitting, class struggle thus could be subordinated to national struggle and, indeed, the two could be regarded as more or less synonymous. The notion that all Chinese were potentially revolutionary gave Mao a particularly keen appreciation of the revolutionary potentialities of Chinese nationalism and enabled him to harness nationalist sentiments for Communist ends.

A populist-inspired notion of a "great union of the popular masses"[9] that Mao advocated at the beginning of his revolutionary career in 1919 also survived to influence the Maoist adaptation of Marxism–Leninism. Populist impulses grew to reinforce Mao's nationalist-inspired faith in the basic unity of the Chinese people in the face of external enemies and also led him to attribute to "the people" an almost inherent revolutionary socialist consciousness. "In the masses is embodied great socialist activism" was a Maoist slogan that derived from an early populist faith, expressed in 1919 in the affirmation that "our Chinese people possesses great intrinsic energy."[10]

Mao's populist impulse, with its essentially rural orientation and its romantic celebration of the rural ideal of "the unity of living and working," defined "the people" as the peasant masses (for the peasantry, after all, constituted the overwhelming majority of the Chinese population) and led him to prize the spontaneous revolutionary energies he believed they possessed. Thus, Mao's populism drew him to the countryside when the Communist revolution was still centered in the cities. In his famous (and heretical) "Hunan Report" of February 1927 he had found in the Chinese peasantry an elemental revolutionary force so great that it would sweep away everything before it, including, he predicted, those revolutionary intellectuals who proved unwilling to become one with the peasant masses. Then, as later, he expressed distrust for the "knowledge" brought by urban intellectuals and admiration for the innate "wisdom" of the peasantry.

Many other features of the Maoist mentality were typically populist: a hostility to occupational specialization; an acute distrust of intellectuals and specialists; a profound antipathy to bureaucracy; an antiurban bias; and a romantic mood of heroic revolutionary self-sacrifice. Mao was not simply a populist in Marxist guise (any more than he was simply a Chinese nationalist in Communist dress), but populist ideas and impulses profoundly influenced the manner in which he adapted and employed Marxism.

Mao's populist faith in the peasantry dictated the much celebrated Maoist notion of the "mass line," the various principles and rules by which Communist cadres became intimately involved with the peasant masses. The Maoist maxim that intellectuals and Party cadres must become the pupils of the masses before they can become their teachers was in fact widely practiced in the Yan'an days. Had it been otherwise, the Communists could never have acquired the popular support that was so essential to the strategy of "people's war."

In attributing a latent socialist consciousness to the peasantry, Mao departed not only from Marx but also from Lenin. For Marx the bearer of socialist consciousness was the urban proletariat. And for Lenin, socialist consciousness was to be imposed on the "spontaneous" proletarian mass movement by an elite of revolutionary intellectuals organized into a disciplined Communist Party, with the peasantry playing an ambiguous auxiliary role in the revolutionary process. Mao departed from Leninism not only in his virtually total disinterest in the urban working class but also in his concept of the nature and role of the Party. For Lenin the Party was sacrosanct because it was the incarnation of "proletarian consciousness," and there was no question about who were to be the teachers and who the pupils. For Mao, on the other hand, this was precisely the question, and it remained unresolved; he proved unwilling to define fully the relationship between the organized consciousness of the Party and the spontaneous consciousness of the masses in a purely Leninist fashion. His faith in the Party as the bearer of revolutionary consciousness was never complete, for it was accompanied by a populist faith in the peasant masses, a belief that true revolutionary knowledge and creativity ultimately emanates from the people themselves. Although Mao proved a master in matters of organization and strategy, neither the methods of organization he devised nor the revolutionary strategy he pursued were derived from strictly Leninist principles. While Mao may have acquired absolute faith in his own revolutionary wisdom, his faith in the revolutionary wisdom of the Party was less than absolutely Leninist.

It is most unlikely that orthodox Marxist-Leninists could have appreciated fully the revolutionary opportunities offered by the wartime situation, much less acted upon them to build a Communist movement on a purely peasant base. It was precisely Mao's ideological unorthodoxies that allowed the Communists to seize upon these opportunities during the Yan'an period. It was his voluntarist faith in the power of the human will and consciousness to shape historical reality that permitted him to ignore (or redefine) Marxian socioeconomic prerequisites and social class considerations that might otherwise have restricted the possibilities for revolutionary action. It was his nationalist-populist impulses which made him look to the broadest possible sources of popular support and which directed him from the cities to the countryside. And it was his populist trust in the spontaneous revolutionary energies of the peasant masses that allowed him to develop and pursue the unorthodox strategy of "people's war."

Yan'an Marxism

The Yan'an era was Mao's most productive period as a Marxist theoretician as well as a revolutionary strategist. The bulk of the writings, later canonized as the "thought of Mao Zedong," were composed during the Yan'an period. While Mao's Yan'an writings do more to obscure than to clarify the nature of the Maoist variant of Marxism-Leninism, they nonetheless are important. First, they established Mao's place as an independent Marxist theoretician. Having achieved de facto political independence from Moscow, the Chinese Communists could now claim to have established their ideological independence as well—in the form of a body of Chinese Marxist doctrine that was celebrated for applying the "universal truths" of Marxism-Leninism to specific Chinese historical conditions. Second, Mao's treatises on dialectics provided a rudimentary philosophical basis for some of the distinctive features of Chinese Communist theory and practice. Finally, the Marxist theoretical writings of the Yan'an era (by Mao and others) reaffirmed the Marxist-Leninist orthodoxy of the CCP, conveyed some elemental knowledge of the doctrine to the many newly recruited members of the Party, and rationalized Chinese Communist political practice in terms of Marxist-Leninist theory.

Yet if this latter task was accomplished to the satisfaction of Mao and other Party leaders, it was done without dealing with the most crucial theoretical problem raised by the Chinese Communist Revolution. For

Maoist writings say virtually nothing about the question of how a Communist party, almost totally separated from the cities and the urban proletariat and based entirely on peasant support, could carry out a revolution that aimed to bring about a socialist society, albeit preceded by a "bourgeois" phase of unspecified duration. The question posed not only a Marxist theoretical dilemma but also an enormous practical problem bearing directly on the goals and future of the revolution. For while the peasants were very much interested in socioeconomic reform and the redistribution of land, not even Mao, with all his faith in the inherent "socialist activism" of the peasant masses, really believed that the peasants, as a class, were inclined (spontaneously or otherwise) to socialism. At their radical best, the peasants were interested in the equal distribution of land on the basis of individual peasant proprietorship—an agrarian revolution to be sure, but one which precluded the socialist reorganization of society, by either Marxist or non-Marxist definitions. There is nothing in Maoism or in Chinese social reality to suggest that the peasantry, as such, is the bearer of the socialist future.

Who then were to be the agents of socialist revolution? In Maoist theoretical literature we find little more than repetitions of the Marxist orthodoxy that the socialist revolution is to be led by the proletariat and the Leninist orthodoxy that the Communist Party is the vanguard of the proletariat and the incarnation of "proletarian consciousness." Mao adds only the concept of "the people's democratic dictatorship," a notion born in the united-front strategy of the Yan'an era and formally proclaimed in 1949, on the eve of the establishment of the People's Republic. The formula for the bourgeois stage of the revolution provides for a government representing a coalition of four classes (proletariat, peasantry, petty bourgeoisie, and national bourgeoisie) but a coalition under "proletarian hegemony," which is to say, ultimate political power resides in the Communist Party.

Little is gained by dissecting these ideological formulae. The fact of the matter is that during the crucial Yan'an years the CCP lacked the active support of the urban proletariat and made very little effort to acquire it. Indeed, such an effort was largely precluded by a strategy which dictated that the crucial forces of revolution resided in the peasantry, and that their mobilization would lead to a situation in which the revolutionary rural areas would encircle and eventually occupy the nonrevolutionary cities.

What turned out to be crucial in determining that the revolution would move beyond the bourgeois-democratic phase were the "subjective factors" in history, upon which Maoism itself placed such great emphasis, and most particularly the conscious determination of Communist leaders to pursue socialist goals. However unorthodox their strategy of revolution, Maoists remained firmly committed to orthodox Marxist goals. If they did not identify themselves with the actual proletariat, they did pursue the political and social goals and the historic mission which Marx attributed to that class. And this "subjective factor" was to prove of enormous historical significance in determining the character and direction of the Chinese revolution.

What is thus implicit in Maoist theory, and demonstrated in Maoist practice, is the notion that the bearers of socialism are those who possess "proletarian consciousness" and that the latter exists independently of a specific social class, neither dependent on the actual presence of the proletariat nor attributed to the peasantry. A revolutionary elite (the party and its leaders) holds the socialist goal firmly in mind and directs the mass movement towards its realization. In a broader sense, "proletarian consciousness" is seen as a potential inherent in "the people" as a whole, for all are potentially capable of achieving (through revolutionary action) the spiritual and ideological transformation necessary to acquire a true proletarian spirit and a socialist world view.

This emphasis on the role of consciousness in the making of history and revolution reflects, of course, long-standing Maoist voluntarist and populist predispositions, and the uniquely Maoist treatment of the Marxist theory of class struggle. Mao, to be sure, was always intensely concerned with objective class conditions in Chinese society and was an ardent promoter of class struggle, both in theory and in practice. But he also tended to define "class position" less on the basis of objective social class criteria than by moral and ideological criteria. While for Marx the existence of a potentially revolutionary proletarian class was the prerequisite for the rise of revolutionary proletarian ideas, for Mao the existence of those deemed to possess "proletarian" ideas was sufficient to confirm the existence of a revolutionary class.

The Legacy of Yan'an

The Yan'an period not only proved decisive for the Communist victory of 1949 but bequeathed to the victors a heroic tradition of revolutionary struggle that was to be canonized as the "Yan'an spirit." Since those who fashioned the revolutionary victory were those who became the leaders of the new society born of that victory, it is hardly surprising that the policies they pursued in the post-1949 years were to be significantly influenced by their experiences in those earlier and more heroic days. All Communists were to celebrate the "Yan'an spirit" as the symbol of a heroic revolutionary past. But for many—and it is natural enough for revolutionaries who become rulers—it was a revolutionary past that could be buried safely in the past, an era to be commemorated on appropriate occasions, but not one deemed truly relevant to contemporary needs. For others, especially for Mao and those most inspired by him, the Yan'an experience was not to become simply an object for commemoration but a living revolutionary tradition that provided a model for the future.

The Yan'an heritage that Maoists prized was in part an institutional legacy, and in part a legacy of sacred revolutionary values—and the two parts cannot easily be separated. Much of what was to be distinctively Maoist in the political, economic, and educational life of the People's Republic was foreshadowed by the institutions and practices of the Yan'an years. In the political realm, bureaucratic control from above was mitigated by the much celebrated principles of the mass line; campaigns for "simple administration"; the insistence on decentralized political structures responsive to local needs and conditions; and various *xiafang* ("sending down") and *xiaxiang* ("to the village") campaigns which demanded that Party cadres, government officials, and intellectuals periodically participate in productive labor together with the masses. Such measures tended to reduce (even if they by no means eliminated) the gap between leaders and led. They were harbingers of the anti-bureaucratic campaigns that were to mark the history of the People's Republic during the Mao era.

Moreover, the harsh conditions imposed by war and blockade created the need for economic self-sufficiency in the border regions and guerrilla areas—and gave rise to a variety of experiments and innovations in economic policy. To maintain agricultural production during the war years, the Communists promoted cooperative forms of work organization in the villages, drawing, in part, on traditional methods of mutual aid. New industries were established in the Communist-ruled rural areas, partly to meet military needs and partly to provide the peasantry with essential nonagricultural products previously supplied by trade with the cities. In a wholly rural environment almost entirely lacking in capital resources, the new cooperative industrial undertakings were dependent upon labor-intensive methods, the employment of simple and indigenous technologies, and the use of local resources and raw materials. Self-sufficiency, self-reliance, and local initiative became the slogans and principles of Yan'an economic policy—and from the experiences in employing those principles emerged the ideal of combining industrial with agricultural production in a rural setting. Further, combining education with production molded the educational policies adopted during the Yan'an period. The emphasis was on popular education in part-time schools, night schools, and various work-study programs. Designed not only to promote basic literacy and political consciousness, these policies also provided the practical technological knowledge particularly relevant to the needs of local communities.

While the political, economic, and educational institutions and practices that emerged during the Yan'an era were to prove enormously important in molding the Maoist approach to problems of postrevolutionary development, the system of values that lay behind those institutions and practices was equally significant. The "Yan'an spirit" was in fact largely concerned with spiritual and moral matters and, more specifically, with the kinds of social and ethical values and life orientations once seen as essential to a continuing process of revolutionary transformation. The values which Maoists derived from the Yan'an era, and which are attributed to that heroic revolutionary past, are essentially ascetic and egalitarian. They are the values of selfless struggle and self-sacrifice on behalf of the people, the values of hard work, diligence, self-denial, frugality, altruism, and self-discipline. In the Yan'an decade these values were, in fact, practiced by Chinese Communists, for they were imposed by the harsh imperatives of revolutionary struggle and the spartan and egalitarian way of life such struggle demanded. In the Maoist view, such values were not only responsible for the revolutionary successes of the past but remained essential to bring about the socialist society of the future.

It is paradoxical that, from a Chinese revolutionary process which was so incongruous with the Marxist conception of revolution, institutions and values emerged that (in many respects) were uniquely conducive to the pursuit of ultimate Marxist goals. Certainly neither Marx nor Lenin could have conceived of a socialist-oriented revolution in which the revolutionary forces of the countryside would surround and overwhelm the nonrevolutionary cities, with the urban working class passively awaiting their liberation by revolutionary armies composed of peasants. Yet in the employment of that most unorthodox strategy of revolution in the Yan'an years, there emerged social visions and practices that curiously harmonized with the utopian social goals prophesied in original Marxist theory. The Yan'an practice of combining industrial with agricultural production, and combining education with productive labor, were eminently Marxist measures to achieve a socialist reordering of society.[11] From a Marxist perspective, they were the first and essential steps towards achieving the broader communist goals of abolishing the distinctions between town and countryside, between workers and peasants, and between mental and manual labor—and they were to be hailed as such in later Maoist celebrations of the Yan'an legacy. The requirement of the Yan'an years that officials and intellectuals participate regularly in productive activities struck an at least symbolic blow at the particularly sharp traditional Chinese separation between mental and manual labor. And the Maoist ideal of the Yan'an guerrilla leader, the ideologically pure generalist capable of performing a variety of economic, political, and military tasks, bore strong affinities with the Marxist "all-round" person of the future communist society. In the Chinese Communist Revolution, more than in the case of any other twentieth century socialist revolution, the socialist forms and values of the new society were fashioned (in at least embryonic form) in the very course of the revolutionary struggle itself.

Yet the legacy of Yan'an was not solely one of values that pointed to liberation. The Yan'an era was also the time when Mao and Maoists laid down rigid dogmas and orthodoxies in political and cultural life, conducted witch hunts against those who failed to conform to their orthodoxies, and relentlessly suppressed political and intellectual dissent in general. The incongruity between socioeconomic liberation, on the one hand, and political-intellectual repression on the other, is one that characterized Maoism both before and after 1949.

. . .

The experiences of the Yan'an decade reinforced the Maoist belief in the primacy of moral over material forces, of people over machines, the conviction that the truly creative revolutionary forces reside more in the countryside than in the cities, and the view that ideological-moral solidarity is more important than the artificial unity imposed by any formal bureaucratic organization. More importantly, victory came on the basis of a massive popular social revolution that involved the active support of tens of millions of peasants.

At the end of World War II, when the uneasy Guomindang–CCP truce inevitably collapsed into open civil war, Guomindang armies enjoyed a four-to-one superiority in soldiers over regular Communist military forces and an even greater advantage in modern military technology, largely supplied by the United States. Yet the Communist victory in the massive battles that marked the civil war of 1946–1949, however bloody and difficult, was surprisingly swift. It was, as Stuart Schram so well characterized it, "one of the most striking examples in history of the victory of a smaller but dedicated and well-organized force enjoying popular support over a larger but unpopular force with poor morale and incompetent leadership."[12] On October 1, 1949, Mao Zedong was in Beijing to proclaim the birth of the People's Republic of China, while Chiang Kai-shek and those who remained in his defeated army and bureaucracy had already fled to the island of Taiwan, there to impose their rule on a hostile population and to find a refuge granted by the United States Seventh Fleet.

The Communists rightly attribute their victory to the principles and practices of the Yan'an era. Those principles were not to be entirely forgotten, and in the postrevolutionary era they sometimes were to be recalled to announce the opening of new revolutionary dramas.

NOTES

1. Edgar Snow, *Red Star over China* (New York: Random House, 1938), p. 177.
2. Edgar Snow, "Interview with Mao," *New Republic,* February 27, 1965, pp. 17–23.
3. Snow, *Red Star over China,* p. 67.
4. Mao Tse-tung [Mao Zedong], "Strategic Problems of China's Revolutionary War," in *Selected Works of Mao Tse-tung* (London: Lawrence & Wishart, 1954), 1:193.
5. Cited in Jan Myrdal, *Report from a Chinese Village* (New York: Pantheon, 1965), p. xxvii.
6. Cited in Edgar Snow, *Random Notes on Red China, 1936–1945* (Cambridge, Mass.: Harvard University Press, 1957), pp. 60–61.
7. Anna Louise Strong, *Tomorrow's China* (New York: Committee for a Democratic Far Eastern Policy, 1948), p. 18.
8. Mao Tse-tung, "A Single Spark Can Start a Prairie Fire," in *Selected Works* (1954) 1:118.
9. This was the title of an article by Mao published in the summer of 1919. For a translation of extracts from the article, see Stuart R. Schram, *The Political Thought of Mao Tse-tung* (New York: Praeger, 1963), pp. 105–106.
10. *Ibid.,* p. 106.
11. Among the "postrevolutionary" measures Marx suggests in the *Manifesto* for achieving a socialist society are the "combination of agriculture with manufacturing industries" and the "combination of education with industrial production." Karl Marx and Frederick Engels, *Selected Works* (Moscow: Foreign Languages Publishing House, 1950), 1:51.
12. Stuart R. Schram, *Mao Tse-tung* (New York: Simon & Schuster, 1967), p. 225.

PART TWO

THE
NEW ORDER

1949–1955

5

The New State

THE CHINESE COMMUNISTS did not come to power in 1949 with the messianic revolutionary expectations which the Russian Bolshevik leaders had held so fervently in 1917. For Lenin the Bolshevik Revolution was the prelude to the realization of the Marxist prophecy of world revolution and international socialism. However, utopian revolutionary hopes were soon dashed by the harsh realities of civil war, foreign intervention, and the isolation of the revolution to backward Russia. Instead of a workers' communal "semistate" which would soon "wither away," as Lenin had envisioned in *State and Revolution,* sheer political survival demanded an increasingly centralized and repressive state apparatus. Instead of the promised producers' control of the workplace based on the "free and conscious discipline of the workers themselves," economic survival dictated a bureaucratically imposed discipline from above and the use of capitalist methods and incentives. Instead of the dream of world revolution, all considerations soon were subordinated to the interests of the survival of Soviet power in a single country. As the seeds of Stalinist despotism were being planted, it was not the state but utopian visions that began to wither away. On his deathbed, Lenin somberly questioned the moral and historical validity of the revolution he had led and the crushing of the revolutionary dream over which he had been forced to preside. Near the end, he was moved to confess that he stood "guilty before the workers of Russia."[1]

The Chinese victors of 1949, by contrast, appear as somber realists; not seized by the same chiliastic revolutionary visions as their Russian predecessors, they were not to suffer similar disillusionments. In the early postrevolutionary years, the minds of the Chinese Communist leaders were turned to the immediate political and economic problems of their nation, not to visionary thoughts of world revolution. For more than two decades the Chinese revolution had grown in an insular national mold; it had developed independently of international revolutionary currents and was both physically and spiritually isolated from them. The profoundly nationalistic character of the Chinese revolutionary experience and a vastly different world than that of 1917 had made "proletarian internationalism" a ritualized ideological phrase, no longer a genuine Marxist revolutionary belief. Unlike Lenin or Trotsky, Mao Zedong was an eminently national revolutionary leader, not an international revolutionary spokesman. Moreover, by 1949 the notion of socialism in one country—and even in a single backward country—was no longer an ideological heresy.

China in 1949 differed from Russia in 1917 in many other ways. In 1949 Mao did not need to write a Chinese equivalent of Lenin's utopian treatise on *State and Revolution.* It was sufficient to write "On People's Democratic Dictatorship." In that essay, Mao reaffirmed the commitment to socialist and communist goals but relegated their realization to an unspecified future era, while stressing that the creation of a strong state power and economic construction were the immediate tasks. In China, unlike Russia, the establishment of an authoritarian state (whatever its formal ideological description), which unified the nation and provided political order, was more the fulfillment of a popular hope than the betrayal of a revolutionary promise. Nor did the early socioeconomic policies of the new regime encounter significant popular opposition; what was done was largely in accord with what had been promised and what was expected. In the urban industrial sector, the large degree of managerial authority permitted in both new state-run enterprises and old capitalist ones did not arouse workers' demands for direct control by the producers, as it had in Russia three decades earlier; a long politically dormant Chinese proletariat made few demands and could not serve as the social basis for a "Workers' Opposition." And in the countryside, the new state was to prove capable of satisfying the immediate demands of a long oppressed peasantry.

For the vast majority of the Chinese people and for their new Communist leaders 1949 was a time of great optimism and hope. But their hopes were tempered by a remarkably pragmatic recognition of what was possible. And what was possible at the time was essentially the completion of the long-delayed "bourgeois" phase of the Chinese revolution—national political unification, agrarian reform, and what promised to be a long and arduous process of modern economic development. In the early years these tasks were pursued on the basis of comparatively moderate policies and within a context of political and social stability unusual in postrevolutionary situations. In China, unlike Russia, political victory did not produce chiliastic expectations of the imminent emergence of a perfect order of justice and equality. As Mao put it at the time of the Communist triumph, "our past work is only the first step in a long march of ten thousand *li.*"[2] And the new long march was to be undertaken in China to solve particularly Chinese problems of political and economic construction; there was no expectation that the *deus ex machina* of "world revolution" would make a timely arrival to hasten the process. "Three years of recovery and ten years of development" was the slogan of the time and it reflected the relatively sober temper of the times.

Political stability and economic development were the orders of the day. No one would have characterized Mao as a utopian visionary at the time, for he then accepted, as did most Communist leaders, the fundamental Marxist view that the development of the material forces of production was the essential precondition for the socialist transformation of society. Revolutionary utopianism was not to appear on the historical scene until well after the new order was consolidated and seemingly institutionalized.

. . .

In many respects, the Chinese enjoyed more favorable conditions than had the Russians for consolidating the revolutionary victory in the short term and for establishing preconditions for an eventual socialist transformation. Whereas the Bolsheviks were forced to wage a materially and spiritually debilitating civil war after the October Revolution, in China the civil war had been fought and won during the revolutionary years; when the Communists established state power in 1949, they faced only scattered counterrevolutionary resistance. Moreover, decades of revolutionary struggle had permitted the Communists to develop their own organizational forms and administrative structures and had provided them with considerable governmental experience and many experienced administrators; they were thus much less dependent on the bureaucratic apparatus left over from the old regime than the Bolsheviks had been. And perhaps most significantly, the Chinese Communists came to power with far greater popular support than had their Russian predecessors, especially, of course, in the countryside where 80 percent of the Chinese people lived; unlike Lenin, Mao was not confronted with the problem of a hostile peasantry in a largely agrarian country. While the Communists had few organizational roots in the cities, they had at least the sympathetic cooperation of much of the democratic intelligentsia and the urban population in general, both on nationalist grounds and on the promise to bring order to a weary and long misgoverned people. Nationalism, which was not a significant factor in the Russian Revolution, was an important force that worked in favor of the new leaders of China. The CCP had emerged from the anti-Japanese war as the leader of nationalist resistance to foreign intrusions and the Party's ability to continue to appeal to patriotic sentiments in the early postwar years served to expand the Communist base of popular support.

Moreover, unlike the early Soviet state, the People's Republic was neither completely isolated nor threatened to the same degree by foreign counterrevolutionary intervention. However ambiguous the relationship between Beijing and Moscow, the mere existence of a powerful Communist country on its borders provided the new Chinese state with some measure of security in an otherwise hostile international arena. In addition, there was the prospect of Soviet economic and technical aid, which, while it was to prove far less than anticipated, was nevertheless significant.

But these relative advantages were overshadowed, and perhaps outweighed, by China's terrible backwardness, a backwardness both social and economic—the historical legacy of a century of the failure of both reform and revolution. In 1949 the Chinese Communists inherited a war-ravaged economy far less developed than the Russian economy at the time of the October Revolution. It was this condition of massive backwardness and impoverishment that was the critical factor in the Chinese historical situation and the question of how to deal with it was crucial in determining Chinese social development after 1949.

· · ·

Three months before the formal proclamation of the Chinese People's Republic, Mao Zedong again set forth the principles of "New Democracy" in accordance with which the new government was to be established—and established an ideological rationale for Communist political supremacy. Beginning with the premise that "bourgeois democracy" was bankrupt in a China so long oppressed by the bourgeois democracies of the West, Mao announced that the new state was to be not a bourgeois republic but a "people's republic." And more precisely, the new people's republic was to be "a state of the people's democratic dictatorship, a state under the leadership of the working class and based on the alliance of workers and peasants." Moreover, the new political order was to rest on an even broader social base, for the workers and peasants were to be part of a "national united front" which included the petty bourgeoisie and the national bourgeoisie. In accordance with this formula, indigenous Chinese capitalism (capitalist forces and classes not tied to the external imperialist order) was to be allowed to develop in order to hasten modern economic development. Mao declared that China "must utilize all elements of urban and rural capitalism that are beneficial and not harmful to the national economy. . . . Our present policy is to control, not to eliminate, capitalism." Nevertheless, Mao repeatedly emphasized that the people's democratic dictatorship was to be firmly "under the leadership of the working class and the Communist Party," for its ultimate goal was to transform China from a "new democracy" into a socialist and communist society. Precisely when and how socialism and communism would come about was left ambiguous, although the implication was that it presupposed a lengthy process of economic development that would transform China from an agricultural to a predominantly industrial country.[3]

What is the relationship between these various Maoist propositions and Chinese sociopolitical reality in the early postrevolutionary years? One is first struck by the apparent contradiction in the term "democratic dictatorship" which Mao chose to characterize the new state. Was the People's Republic to be a democracy or a dictatorship? Insofar as Mao was willing to address the question, his ambiguous answer was that it was to be both; whereas democracy was to be extended to "the people," dictatorial methods were to be applied to those excluded from the ranks of "the people." The dictatorial function of the new state was made abundantly clear: the government was to exercise a "dictatorship over the running dogs of imperialism—the landlord class and bureaucratic bourgeoisie, as well as the representatives of those classes, the Guomindang reactionaries and their accomplices." Such groups and classes were to be deprived of democratic rights—and all the forces of state violence were to ensure that their suppression was complete.[4]

In attempting to understand what "democracy" meant in Maoist theory and practice, one enters a much more murky realm. Democracy, Mao wrote, is something to be enjoyed by "the people" as distinct from the reactionaries. One area of ambiguity, of course, is precisely the question that Mao rhetorically posed: "Who are the people?" And, one might add, who is to determine who the people are, and on the basis of what criteria? Implicitly and sometimes explicitly, these questions were to be raised time and again throughout the history of the People's Republic and different answers were to be provided at different times.

In 1949 Mao's answer was deceptively simple; "the people" were the members of the four social classes which presumably had entered into a political united front: the working class, the peasantry, the petty bourgeoisie, and the national bourgeoisie. And "democracy," as the term was used in Maoist theory at the time, meant three things. First, it meant bourgeois democracy in the conventional sense. The people were, according to Mao, to "enjoy the freedoms of speech, assembly, association"; they were to have the right to vote and they were to "elect their own government," a government, in turn, which was to exercise a dictatorship over the reactionaries who fell outside the ranks of the people.[5] Whether the promise of these elementary democratic rights was to be honored is a question to be taken up later—in light of the actual political practice of the new state.

Secondly, democracy referred to a distinctive stage in China's socioeconomic development. More precisely, in Marxist terms, it referred to fulfilling the tasks of the "bourgeois-democratic" phase of historical development. The encouragement of capitalist economic enterprises in the cities and the redistribution of land to the peasants in the countryside were not socialist but democratic measures. And democracy, in this sense, was descriptive of an historical era during which the four popular classes would cooperate in a lengthy process of modern economic development to lay the material foundations for a future socialist society. In the meantime, Chinese society was post-feudal and yet also "pre-socialist," and thus, ipso facto, "democratic."

Thirdly, democracy was to mean the political representation of the four classes defined as "the people." Here one encounters the most murky area of Maoist theory and practice, the question of the relationship between political power and social classes. That the role of the dozen or so non-Communist "democratic" parties, formally represented in the creation of the People's Republic, would be no more than ceremonial—this, needless to say, was predetermined from the outset. Even the best-known of these quasi-parties—such as the Democratic League and the Revolutionary Committee of the Guomindang, presumably the political representatives of portions of the petty bourgeoisie and national bourgeoisie—were political parties more in name than in reality. None had any significant popular following or even much in the way of a formal organizational structure. Having triumphed in the civil war, there was no question (and no one questioned) that real political power in the new state (whatever its formal structure and official ideological description) would be monopolized by the CCP and the Red Army which stood behind it. Nor was much effort made to obscure this elemental political fact in Chinese Communist ideology.

What was ambiguous was the relationship between the political power of the Communist Party and the two major social classes of the postrevolutionary era, the proletariat and the peasantry. On the one hand, official doctrine claimed that the CCP was the party of the proletariat; yet the Party's ties to the urban working class had been severed in 1927 and the latter remained politically passive while the Communist revolution triumphed in the countryside. Indeed, even as late as 1957, when the size of the proletariat had grown enormously and the Communists were well established in the cities, the Party could claim that only 14 percent of its members were workers. On the other hand, no explicit claim was made that the CCP was the party of the peasantry, even though it was the peasants who gave the Maoist party its political victory. And it was from the peasantry that the overwhelming majority of the Party's membership continued to be drawn.[6] Here was the paradox of a revolutionary party claiming to be the party of a politically inactive class but not claiming, at least not explicitly, to be the political representative of the revolutionary class that formed its actual social base.

The paradox was not unraveled when the body that officially established the People's Republic, the Chinese People's Political Consultative Conference, convened in Beijing from September 21–30, 1949. The term, if not the institution, derived from the Communists' futile postwar proposals for a coalition government with the Guomindang. With the Guomindang crushed, there was no longer any need, or any political basis, for a coalition government in any meaningful sense. Nevertheless, the appearance of a genuinely national and other than purely Communist regime was politically useful. A wide variety of non-Communist political and social groups and individuals (or "democratic personalities" as they were called at the time) participated in the Political Consultative Conference,[7] which, having duly consulted, gave its formal approval to a new government organized in accordance with the proposals Mao Zedong had set down three months earlier and appointed Mao head of state.

Many non-Communists were given high positions, or at least provided with high titles, in the administrative organs of the new state. Eleven of the original twenty-four ministries, for example, were headed by non-Party people, three of the six Vice-Chairmen of the Republic were non-Communists, the most illustrious of whom was Song Qingling, the widow of Sun Yatsen. While this aspect of the new state was largely decorative and ceremonial, it was not wholly meaningless. The political cooperation of many non-Communist luminaries reflected the widespread nationalist appeals of the revolution and the broad popular support the new regime enjoyed. And several concrete purposes were served as well: it assisted in enlisting the support of non-Communist Chinese for a national cause, reassured private entrepreneurs and the technical intelligentsia that capitalist enterprises would be allowed to exist for the time being, and gave some credence to the Maoist ideological claim that the new state rested on an alliance of the four classes who constituted "the people"—and the promise implicit in this claim that the new government would pursue relatively moderate policies.

There is no need to linger over the administrative structure of the new government, about which there was nothing exceptional. The major executive organ was under the premiership of Zhou Enlai from the beginning; originally called the Government Administrative Council, its name was changed to the State Council when a formal constitution was promulgated in 1954. Under this organ there emerged a centralized bureaucratic apparatus which extended downwards to the provincial, county *(xian)* and administrative village *(xiang)* levels. As chairman of the republic, it was Mao who originally appointed Zhou as premier and, in different capacities, reappointed him. And it was Zhou who provided much of the continuity and stability that the civilian state structure was to enjoy during its first, often turbulent, twenty-five years.

During the first half-decade, the civilian administration was overshadowed by a military one. The revolution had been won and the new regime had come to power by virtue of a powerful and highly disciplined Red Army, and that army was utilized initially to establish order and a new administrative apparatus within the country as well as to protect it from without. In 1949 China was divided into six military regions and the country remained under what was essentially military control until 1954.

What cemented the civilian and military administrations into a powerful centralized state was the Chinese Communist Party. The political task that confronted the victorious Communists in 1949 was not to put the old pieces back together again—for there were few survivals from the past that could serve the needs of modern national unity—but rather to forge an entirely new political structure. And this had to be undertaken in conditions of extreme economic backwardness, in a country which possessed only the most primitive system of communications and transportation, in a land where the persistence of strong traditional localistic and regional loyalties had retarded the development of a modern national consciousness and where the dominance of largely precapitalist forms of economic life provided only the most fragile material basis for national integration. To achieve modern political unification under such conditions—and in the world's most populous country and territorially one of the largest—was a task of staggering proportions. That it was accomplished so effectively in the years between 1949 and 1952 can be attributed, in large measure, to the fact that the new rulers of China had in their hands a uniquely effective organizational instrument in the Chinese Communist Party.

The Party emerged from the revolutionary years as a highly disciplined and tightly knit organization with a membership of nearly 5,000,000. Two decades of armed struggle had imparted a military-like discipline to its organization and to the habits of its members. Its cadres were not only experienced revolutionary organizers but also experienced governmental administrators—and they possessed a strong sense of national consciousness and purpose. Functioning as a quasi-government long before the formal establishment of the People's Republic, the Party provided the main organizational base, leadership, and methods of mass organization for the new state. The personal popularity of Mao Zedong and the administrative abilities of Zhou Enlai, however great, were no substitute for the Party's organizational apparatus and its dedicated and disciplined cadres.

There is, of course, a distinction between the Party organization and the administrative organs of the state, but the distinction is a thin one. For the most part, the leaders of the Party also held the key positions in the formal state administration, initially symbolized at the top by Mao Zedong, who was both the Party Chairman and the Chairman of the People's Republic. The pattern was repeated down to the lowest levels of the state structure; Party cadres either formally held official posts in the bureaucracy or were placed in positions to supervise the work of non-Party functionaries. A similar situation had, of course, long prevailed in the Red Army, by virtue of the early adoption of the Soviet system of "political commissars" and in accordance with Mao's well-known dictum that "the Party commands the gun." In 1949 the generals of the People's Liberation Army and most of its officers stood high in the Party hierarchy and an elaborate system of political controls was installed throughout the military ranks. In addition, the network of Party organization permeated all mass organizations and quasi-governmental institutions which were established (or reorganized) in 1949 or soon thereafter. In trade unions, peasant associations, the educational system, the "people's courts," and the popular militia, either leadership positions were held by Party members or control was exercised through parallel organizational structures. Between 1949 and 1952 the organizational web of the CCP was woven throughout the fabric of Chinese society.

Although the new political order was officially represented as based on an alliance of four social classes and appropriately decorated with a variety of "democratic personalities," the locus of state power resided in the CCP which officially represented itself as the party of the proletariat. Or more accurately, political power rested with the Party's Central Committee (which had forty-four members in 1949) and more particularly with its 14-member Political Bureau (Politburo); or more precisely still, the levers of state power were in the hands of the five men who made up the latter's

Standing Committee in 1949: Mao Zedong, Liu Shaoqi, Zhou Enlai, Zhu De, and Chen Yun. The political history of the People's Republic is in large measure the internal political history of the CCP and its leading organs.

. . .

In a Marxian sense, the chaotic political situation that the victorious Chinese Communists inherited offered a unique revolutionary advantage. It is a Marxist belief that lasting revolutionary success demands the thorough destruction of the political institutions of the old regime. The working class, Marx wrote in his famous commentary on the Paris Commune of 1871, "cannot simply lay hold of the ready-made state machinery, and wield it for its own purposes"; rather what Marx called the "ubiquitous organs" of centralized state power—the bureaucracy, army, and police—had to be completely eliminated before genuinely revolutionary institutions could take their place.[8] This was a notion Lenin emphasized time and again, and most forcefully in *State and Revolution;* the existing state bureaucracy could not be "taken over" but had to be "smashed." And shortly before his death, Lenin partly attributed the failure of the October Revolution (or at least its failure to realize its promises) to the persistence of old czarist bureaucratic methods.

In this respect, the Chinese political situation of 1949 augured well for the future of the revolution. The Chinese Communists had little need to smash the old state bureaucracy, for little of it remained. Not encumbered by bureaucratic survivals of the old order, the Communists had an unparalleled opportunity to create afresh their own political institutions. But this was not to resolve the perhaps unresolvable problem of bureaucracy. The persistence of traditional bureaucratic patterns of thought and behavior (if not the bureaucratic structures as such), and more importantly, the particular social conditions of the postrevolutionary situation, and indeed the very Leninist organizational structure of the CCP itself were some of the forces which were to foster the rapid growth of bureaucracy. If the Chinese Communists were not burdened by old bureaucratic structures, they soon were to be weighed down by new ones of their own making.

Territorial Unification: The Unfinished Task

When the People's Republic was formally proclaimed in October of 1949, vast areas of China had yet to come under the control of the new government. The military power of the Guomindang had been broken many months before and Chiang Kai-shek had fled to Taiwan. But much of

South China, as well as many of the provinces and outlying dependencies in the West and Northwest, were still occupied by remnants of the Nationalist army or by various warlord armies which had been allied with the Guomindang during the civil war. Therefore the first task of the new state was to extend its military control over these territories.

The Red Army moved to the south with extraordinary rapidity, encountering only scattered resistance. "The battle of the feet," as it was called, was not a serious military struggle but a question of whether Guomindang troops could retreat more rapidly than the Communists advanced. The city of Guangzhou, the last official capital of the Nationalist regime on the mainland, was occupied on October 13, having been abandoned by Guomindang troops the day before. The southwestern provinces were occupied over the next two months. The province of Guizhou was under Communist control by mid-November and Guangxi fell to the Fourth Field Army (commanded by Lin Biao) in early December; Hainan Island, where some of the Guangxi Nationalist troops then retreated, was occupied by the Red Army in April of 1950. The governor of Yunnan surrendered in December of 1949 and Communist control of this most remote area of the Southwest produced a bizarre international by-product; remnant Nationalist forces fled to the Shan region of Burma where they supported themselves by illicit opium trading and with American supplies air-dropped from Taiwan for almost 20 years.

Military operations in the West and Northwest were somewhat more difficult and prolonged. While Sichuan Province was under Red Army control by end of December of 1949, Guomindang resistance in Xinjiang continued until March of the next year. That date marked the termination of organized Guomindang military opposition on the mainland. The reestablishment of Chinese control in Tibet posed not a military problem (for the tiny Tibetan army was crushed in October, 1950) but rather a cultural and political one. The relationship between China and Tibet was marked by more than a thousand years of political ambiguities and cultural hostility. Tibet, incorporated within the Chinese empire by the Qing Dynasty in the eighteenth century, began to slip from Chinese control as the Qing empire began to disintegrate under the foreign onslaught in the late nineteenth century and through British encroachments from colonial India. When the Qing Dynasty collapsed in 1911, Tibet became formally independent. Nevertheless, all twentieth-century Chinese nationalists, Communists and non-Communists alike, consider Tibet to be part of the modern Chinese nation-state, although the political problem was complicated by the passing of the vague British suzerainty over Tibet to an even more vague interest on the part of newly independent India. While the leaders of the People's Republic were determined to reassert Chinese control over Tibet for both nationalist and strategic reasons, they were sensitive to the cultural and political problems involved. Negotiations with India and Tibetan leaders led to a 1951 agreement which recognized Chinese control while providing for a large measure of Tibetan cultural and sociopolitical autonomy. Chinese troops occupied Lhasa in the autumn of that year. This did not resolve the matter, as the Tibetan revolt of 1959 was to demonstrate.

A matter of far greater concern was the occupation of Taiwan by the defeated Guomindang regime, for this not only left unfinished the task of territorial unification but also the civil war. Communist preparations to invade Taiwan, apparently planned for the summer of 1950, were frustrated by President Truman's order of June 27 sending the United States Seventh Fleet to "neutralize" the Taiwan strait. The pretext for intervention was the outbreak of the Korean War. The latter was no more than a pretext, for the Chinese were neither involved in the Korean conflict until General MacArthur's ill-fated "march to the Yalu" directly threatened Chinese borders, nor was there ever any satisfactory explanation of what the Taiwan situation had to do with the war in Korea. Indeed, when the truce ending the Korean hostilities was signed in July of 1953, the "neutralization" of the straits of Taiwan remained in effect. The de facto United States military protectorate over Taiwan allowed the Nationalist regime to linger on and represent itself in international councils as the government of China. And the United States established another base in the military cordon it was establishing around China, in a ring from Korea to Southeast Asia.

Further obstacles to territorial unification existed on China's long northern border with the Soviet Union. In addition to the vast territories which the old czarist empire had annexed from the Qing Dynasty in the late nineteenth century (principally the Maritime provinces in the East and parts of Xinjiang in the West), the Russians had reassumed their old predominance in Manchuria as a result of the Japanese defeat in World War II. They occupied Port Arthur, Dairen, and the Chinese Eastern Railway, and dismantled as much of the industry of Manchuria as they were able to carry away.

The birth of the People's Republic marked China's emergence as a unified, modern nation-state, but fulfillment of the nationalist demand for territorial unification remained incomplete. Foreign intervention prevented the reunification of Taiwan with the mainland and long-standing Russian expansionism precluded recovery of the lost territories in the North. And both situations were fraught with danger.

Repression and Terror

The power of the new Chinese government rested ultimately on the forces of violence which all states wield over society: the army and the police. It would hardly be necessary to repeat this banal truism were it not for the myth that the Maoist state was uniquely characterized by rule through ideological education and "moral suasion." This notion was propagated less by Chinese Communists than by various foreign observers, especially those inclined to find historical parallels between the Confucian past and the Communist present. From the Sinological disposition to accept the Confucian ideological rationalization for the traditional Chinese state—the myth that emperors and mandarins ruled the realm through "moral example"—it was but a short intellectual leap in the dark to cast Mao Zedong in the old imperial role, presiding over a revived "Middle Kingdom" in accordance with a perennial "mandate" to govern on the basis of virtuous example.

Mao Zedong, for one, was never guilty of disseminating such nonsense. "Our present task is to strengthen the people's state apparatus," he wrote in 1949, and he went on to define the nature of the new government in Marxist terms, not according to Confucian ideological precepts: "The state apparatus, including the army, the police and the courts, is the instrument by which one class oppresses another. It is an instrument for the oppression of antagonistic classes; it is violence and not 'benevolence.'"[9] Certainly the new state owed its existence and survival to the means of violence Mao enumerated, most notably the military and police forces; and the leaders of that state have made abundant use of these conventional means of state power to achieve their ends.

To be sure, Mao advocated a "benevolent policy" in governing "the people," employing "democratic" methods of "persuasion and not of compulsion," as distinguished from "the dictatorship over the reactionaries as a class." Even individual members of the reactionary classes were potentially amenable to educational "remolding," although, as classes, landlords and the bureaucratic bourgeoisie were, as Mao stated, to be "eliminated for good."[10] But behind Maoist processes of "persuasion"—educational methods, psychological techniques, and "thought reform" campaigns—there always stood the conventional institutions of "compulsion," the organized forces of violence upon which all states are ultimately dependent. And these forces were not to remain idle.

In addition to the Red Army, the new rulers had at their disposal powerful secret police organizations established during the revolutionary years. All units of the Red Army contained "public security headquarters" and since China was essentially under military rule until 1954, these organs performed police functions in civil society and their personnel supervised the functioning of local police agencies in both the cities and rural districts. Moreover, a secret police apparatus existed within the Party headed by Kang Sheng (in addition to the Control Commission which dealt with internal Party discipline); in view of the Party organization that permeated all levels of the formal state administration as well as mass organizations and large economic enterprises, it is evident that the Party's own police units also exercised considerable control over the civilian population. Furthermore, the establishment of a formal state administration in 1949 was accompanied by the establishment of a formal state secret police organization, the "Public Security Forces," under the jurisdiction of the central government's Ministry of Public Security, headed by Luo Ruiqing from 1949 to 1958, and it rapidly developed into a vast internal security apparatus which penetrated down to the very lowest levels of state administration. In addition to their independent police activities, the Public Security Forces were responsible for the supervision and control of all local civilian police agencies. In the cities, each urban residence committee (consisting of about one hundred households on the average) had a public security section as did each *xiang* administrative unit in the countryside.

It is impossible to specify the political role of these various agencies; the activities of secret police (in China as elsewhere) are, after all, "secret"—and in contemporary China the situation is further obscured by the overlapping functions of the Party, the army, and the formal state administration, each of which has its own police organization; their activities ambiguously merge at various levels of control in civil society. Although never to acquire the gigantic political power of their Soviet counterparts, China's secret police were always a formidable weapon of political control. They are very much part of the state machine, which, as Mao had written, "is an instrument for oppression."

The oppressive functions of the new state were particularly apparent from 1949 to 1953. These were years of great social and economic accomplishments, but also years marked by severe political repression and often political terror. Radical social and political transformations are almost always followed by reigns of terror, for classes and groups economically and politically dominant under the old regime are as reluctant to surrender their privileges as victorious revolutionaries are determined to guarantee the fruits of their victory. Successful revolutions always produce counterrevolutionary reactions and the latter, in turn, impel new rulers to employ all the means of violence they possess to preserve their newly won power.

The counterrevolutionary impulse was comparatively weak in China, for so much of the old order had disintegrated or had been destroyed in the years before 1949. The comprador bourgeoisie and the landlords were rel-atively weak and politically uncohesive social classes, and many of their members with either the money or opportunity to do so had fled to Hong Kong, Taiwan, or, more safely, to the United States. Many who remained opposed or feared the Communists (and often for good reasons), but there were no political banners for them to rally behind. The democratic "Third Force," despised by the Communists and suppressed by the Guomindang, long had proven to be a figment of the political imagination of a small num-ber of dissident intellectuals, its leaders now mostly in exile. And the Guo-mindang, militarily defeated and so long politically bankrupt, inspired neither enthusiasm nor hope even among those who had actively sup-ported it and perhaps still wished to do so. Even the once powerful Song (Soong) and Gong (Kung) families, long the financial pillars of the Nation-alist government, had not only fled China but abandoned the Guomindang in Taiwan as well, retiring to New York and New Jersey with a substantial portion of the old regime's treasury. Other political parties and movements had long since passed from the historical scene. At the end of 1949 and during the early months of 1950, the Communists had little reason to fear any counterrevolution.

Of much greater concern were the internal problems of governing the mainland. To establish administrative control over the country and revive a collapsed economy were formidable tasks which demanded repressive po-litical measures. But internal political resistance of any organized fashion was relatively insignificant and the rulers of the new state harbored no counterrevolutionary fears during these early months.

What raised the spectre of counterrevolution and posed a threat to the survival of the new republic—and consequently precipitated an era of in-ternal political terror—was an external event and, for China, an entirely fortuitous one: the outbreak of war in Korea in late June of 1950. We shall not pause here to inquire into the still murky question of the origins of that conflict except to note that the Chinese were in no way initially involved.[11] The Chinese leaders certainly could not have welcomed a war of potentially grave international consequences in a bordering land at a time when they were preoccupied with the internal consolidation of the new state, when they were beginning to demobilize much of the Red Army, at precisely the time their best military units were being deployed on the southern coast for the anticipated invasion of Taiwan, and when the opening of the land re-form campaign just had been announced. It was not until advancing

United States troops threatened the Manchurian border in November that Chinese troops crossed the Yalu and inflicted on the forces of General MacArthur the greatest defeat in American military history.

In what became a de facto Sino–American war China claimed that its troops were merely "volunteers" assisting a fraternal socialist country, and the United States claimed that its army was acting under the "command" of the United Nations. Both claims were fictitious. For two and a half years Chinese and American armies fought, most of the time in a bloody war of attrition roughly along the boundary line where the war first began and where it was to end. Although China received substantial quantities of Soviet military equipment (but less and more belatedly than anticipated), the war placed a severe burden on a fragile Chinese economy just beginning to recover from the ravages of invasion and civil war. And Chinese losses in manpower were staggering; among the victims was a son of Mao Zedong, Mao Anying, killed in battle in 1951.

While the material and human losses were enormous, the war yielded unanticipated political benefits. The threat of yet another invasion by a foreign power solidified popular nationalist support for the government. The campaign to "Resist America and Aid Korea" appealed successfully to patriotic sentiments, but what was more important were the early Chinese military victories. For over a century China had been humiliated repeatedly by Western military forces, but now, for the first time, a Chinese army had defeated a Western army—and then fought the strongest military power in the world to a stalemate in a major conventional war. This event, perhaps more than any other in China's modern history, served to stimulate intense feelings of national pride and confidence among the Chinese people, feelings shared by many anti-Communist Chinese as well. The Chinese soldier, so long the object of scorn and ridicule, had proven himself in battle—and the lesson was not lost on the world. Just as the unexpected Japanese victory over Russia in 1905 had marked the emergence of Japan as a major power on the world scene (and stimulated nationalist sentiments throughout Asia), so the Chinese military accomplishment shocked Western military minds and dramatically announced that this new China was a nation to be reckoned with in the international arena. It confirmed what Mao had proudly proclaimed in 1949: "Our nation will never again be an insulted nation. We have stood up . . . no imperialist will be allowed to invade our territory again. . . ."[12]

But this is the view in retrospect. At the time—in late 1950 and in 1951—the military clash with the United States had a different effect: the Chinese leaders then were more filled with fears over the survival of the new republic than they were with pride in a new China that finally had "stood up" in the world. The fears were by no means groundless. Not only did the encounter with the United States pose the threat of direct attack on China and a full-scale war (a course advocated by many American military and political leaders), it also raised the spectre of counterrevolution. At the outbreak of the Korean War, the United States had established a military protectorate over Taiwan, thus prolonging the life of the remnant National-ist regime and tying an internal Chinese political conflict to a potentially ex-plosive international one. The very real threat that confronted the Chinese Communists was that deadly combination which had crushed so many rev-olutions—the combination of civil war and foreign invasion. These twin forces of "restoration" had distorted the French Revolution, crushed the Paris Commune, and very nearly destroyed the Russian Bolshevik regime, and the long history of external and internal counterrevolution was very deeply etched in the Marxist historical memory. The Chinese leaders at the time certainly must have been as acutely conscious of the precedents of the past as they obviously were aware of the present danger. If the internal forces of counterrevolution were relatively weak, the threat of foreign inva-sion was very strong. And hardly a year after the founding of the People's Republic there loomed the possibility of a renewed civil war backed by the world's most powerful country.

On Taiwan the revived Nationalist regime did all it could to turn that possibility into a counterrevolutionary reality, assisted and encouraged by the influential "China Lobby" in the United States. Guomindang political agents infiltrated the mainland through Hong Kong and Nationalist army units crossed the presumably "neutralized" Taiwan Strait to conduct com-mando attacks on the China coast. And in the United States, loud political cries were heard urging the Truman administration to carry the Korean War directly to China and to "unleash" Chiang Kai-shek.

The essentially external threat to the survival of the revolution turned the initially moderate policies and practices of the new state into increas-ingly repressive ones—and eventually to a reign of terror throughout most of the country in 1951. The employment of openly terroristic methods was officially sanctioned by Mao's decree of February 21, 1951 on "Regulations Regarding the Punishment of Counterrevolutionaries." Needless to say, there was nothing novel about punishing counterrevolutionaries; Guomin-dang agents, supporters, and sympathizers always had been systematically suppressed in areas under Communist control both before and after 1949, and efforts to quell actual or potential political opposition intensified dur-ing the Korean War. But the purpose of the February decree was somewhat different; it not only extended the scope of political repression by defining more broadly what were deemed to be counterrevolutionary activities, but was also designed to instill an atmosphere of terror in society through public campaigns against all forms of political dissent. In addition to an intensification of secret-police repression in general, the following months saw an endless series of mass meetings in the major urban centers where the more prominent of accused counterrevolutionaries were publicly denounced and sentenced to death while the less prominent were arrested and tried through the regular police and judicial state agencies. Newspapers daily published long lists of the names of those executed and prominently featured grisly accounts of alleged political crimes and punishments. If the purpose of the campaign was to create a public climate of fear and terror as well as to eliminate potential opposition to the state, it was successful on both counts.

The People's Republic has never revealed comprehensive statistics on the number of the victims of the terror (if indeed there are accurate records) and the estimates of outside observers vary greatly, depending on the political proclivities of the observer. However, such fragmentary official reports as are available do suggest that the number was substantial. In the province of Guangdong alone, for example, local authorities reported some 28,000 executions in the 10-month period from October 1950 to August 1951.[13] In a speech delivered in 1957, Zhou Enlai stated that among an unspecified number of counterrevolutionary cases officially handled by the government through 1952, 16.8 percent were sentenced to death, 42.3 percent to "reform through labor," 32 percent placed under "surveillance," and 8.9 percent subject only to "reeducation."[14] Using the government's figure of 800,000 counterrevolutionary trials during the first half of 1951, there were some 135,000 official executions during that 6-month period alone. The real figure is no doubt greater, and taking into account the much longer period involved and the considerable number of executions that took place outside of formal judicial procedures, the estimate of many relatively impartial observers that there were 2,000,000 people executed during the first three years of the People's Republic is probably as accurate a guess as one can make on the basis of scanty information. That figure includes the semi-spontaneous "executions" in the countryside when the long-repressed hatreds of an oppressed peasantry were released during the land reform campaigns of 1950–1952. And many more than 2,000,000 were imprisoned or sent to forced labor camps during these years.

The human toll, whatever the actual number, is not lessened by noting that probably larger percentages of the population were killed in the various reigns of terror which followed in the wake of the French and Russian revolutions. Nor can the figure be reduced by remembering that uncounted millions died annually from famine and malnutrition in pre-1949

China, or by recalling the long lists of official executions and the greater number taken in the wanton slaughters that marked Chiang Kai-shek's White Terror of the late 1920s and early 1930s. On these matters no one kept statistics and few bothered to make estimates.

These macabre comparisons are offered not as revolutionary apologetics but only to maintain some degree of historical perspective on a matter that does not easily lend itself to either moral complacency or moral outrage. In most revolutionary situations, the choice is not between terror or its absence but rather between revolutionary terror or counterrevolutionary terror; and since China had suffered so greatly from the latter over the decades, one should not be too quick to levy moral condemnations on the former. As Barrington Moore has observed, it has been the historical case that "revolutionary violence has been part of the break with a repressive past and of the effort to construct a less repressive future."[15] But it is also the historical case that the gap between the promises of revolution and the actual performances of revolutionaries has been far too great to a priori justify revolutionary violence on future promises alone. In the Chinese case, much more needs to be examined before beginning to attempt to weigh the social accomplishments of the revolution against its human costs.

If there is any cause for surprise in the political history of these early postrevolutionary years, it lies in the relative brevity of the period of overt political terror and the rapidity of the consolidation of the new state order. With the suppression of actual or potential sources of internal opposition, and as the war in Korea ground to a stalemate in 1951 and the fear of a direct United States military attack began to recede, the use of terror as a method of political control began to recede as well. By the end of 1951 the country began to return to more "normal" methods of administrative control and bureaucratic rule, although terror still reigned in parts of the countryside where the completion of the land reform program was to take another year. But if the return to "normalcy" signaled the end of an era of overt political terror, it did not mark the end of a continuing era of political repression. Three years after the establishment of the People's Republic the goal of a strong state had been realized. No doubt the experience of the terror of 1951, and the experience of the Korean War, lent a harsher and more authoritarian cast to the new order than might otherwise have been the case. But if there is any clear lesson to be derived from these political events it is Mao's simple truism that the state is an instrument of oppression and compulsion. And the history of China in those as well as subsequent years has more than amply demonstrated the truth of the Marxist proposition that, as Engels put it and Lenin once repeated, "while the state exists there is no freedom."

NOTES

1. Cited in Isaac Deutscher, *Ironies of History* (London: Oxford University Press, 1966), p. 173.

2. Mao Tse-tung [Mao Zedong], "On the People's Democratic Dictatorship," in *Selected Works of Mao Tse-tung* (Peking: Foreign Languages Press, 1967), 4:422.

3. *Ibid.*, pp. 417–421.

4. *Ibid.*, pp. 417–418.

5. *Ibid.*

6. Of the 12,720,000 Party members in 1957, according to official figures, 1,740,000 were classified as workers, 8,500,000 as peasants, 1,880,000 as intellectuals, and 600,000 as "others." See Franz Schurmann, *Ideology and Organization in Communist China* (Berkeley: University of California Press, 1966), p. 132.

7. Of the 662 delegates to the conference, only 16 were formally CCP members.

8. Karl Marx, "The Civil War in France," in Karl Marx and Frederick Engels, *Selected Works* (Moscow: Foreign Languages Publishing House, 1950), 1:468.

9. Mao, "On the People's Democratic Dictatorship," p. 418.

10. *Ibid.*, p. 419.

11. Interpretations of the origins of the Korean War range from the view that it was an independent North Korean decision; that North Korea was encouraged and manipulated by Moscow; that it was provoked by the Rhee government in South Korea; to the view that it was subtly instigated by the United States. Few diplomatic historians any longer give credence to the once popular theory that it was part of a Chinese design. Indeed, recent evidence indicates that while the Russians were aware that a war was in the making, they failed to communicate the information to Beijing. For a study of the Chinese role, see Allen Whiting, *China Crosses the Yalu: The Decision to Enter the Korean War* (New York: Macmillan, 1960). On the complex causes of the Korean War, see Bruce Cumings' magnificent work, *The Origins of the Korean War* (2 vols., Princeton: Princeton University Press, 1981, 1990).

12. Mao Tse-tung, "Speech to the First Plenary Session of the Chinese People's Political Consultative Conference" (September 21, 1949), in *Selected Works of Mao Tse-tung* (London: Lawrence & Wishart, 1954), 4:411–424.

13. Cited in Ezra Vogel, *Canton under Communism* (Cambridge, Mass.: Harvard University Press, 1969), p. 64.

14. Chou En-lai [Zhou Enlai], "Report on the Work of the Government," delivered to the Fourth Session of the First National People's Congress (June 26, 1957), in Robert R. Bowie and John K. Fairbank, *Communist China 1955–1959: Policy Documents with Analysis* (Cambridge, Mass.: Harvard University Press, 1962), p. 303.

15. Barrington Moore, *Social Origins of Dictatorship and Democracy* (Boston: Beacon Press, 1966), p. 506.

6

The Cities

The Rise and Fall of National Capitalism

I T IS VERY DIFFICULT to govern a country in the aftermath of a revolution and political talent is a scarce commodity."[1] This truism proved less apt in post-1949 China than in most postrevolutionary situations. Three years after the Communist victory China was better governed than at any time in its modern history and there was a relative abundance of political and administrative talent. It was the unique nature of the Chinese revolution, not any special Chinese genius for governing, that was responsible for this unusual postrevolutionary situation. The Chinese Communists had not triumphed in the classic insurrectionary fashion where revolutionaries suddenly are catapulted into the unfamiliar position of rulers. The Chinese Communist victory had come only after more than two decades of armed struggle during which they had been rulers as well as revolutionaries, governing significant territories and populations in accordance with their own organizational methods.

But that experience had been confined to the countryside. In the cities, which fell to the Communists more rapidly than expected, administrative talent was a very scarce commodity indeed. The problem was not wholly unanticipated. As early as 1939 Mao Zedong noted, "The capture of the cities now serving as the enemy's main bases is the final objective of the revolution, an objective which cannot be achieved without adequate work in the cities."[2] And when Communist armies were in fact capturing the cities, Mao announced that "the center of gravity of the Party's work has shifted from the village to the city" and that "we must do our utmost to learn how to administer and build the cities."[3] The task was to prove a formidable one. Although the leaders of the Chinese Communist Party originally had emerged from an urban intelligentsia, most who survived the long revolutionary ordeal had lived and fought in the rural hinterlands for more than 20 years. And for the Red Army's peasant cadres the cities were wholly unfamiliar and strange places. An American scholar living in Beijing at the time observed: "Some of these Communists had never seen a large city before; they did not even know how to turn off the electric lights. . . ."[4] Moreover, unfamiliarity was accompanied by distrust. A revolutionary strategy based on gathering the forces of rural revolution to surround and overwhelm the nonrevolutionary cities bred powerful antiurban feelings. In the pre-1949 years, the revolutionaries viewed the cities as bastions of conservatism, the strongholds of the Guomindang, the centers of foreign imperialism, and the breeding grounds for social inequalities, ideological impurities, and moral corruptions. They entered the cities in 1949 as occupiers as much as liberators, and for the urban inhabitants who had contributed so little to the revolutionary victory feelings of sympathy were intermingled with strong feelings of suspicion. The dichotomy between the revolutionary countryside and the conservative cities, which the whole revolutionary experience produced, had become a notion deeply ingrained in the Maoist mentality, and this ideological residue of the revolution was to play a role in the way in which the new rulers approached one of the crucial problems in the history of the People's Republic—the problem of the relationship between town and countryside.

While China was a largely agrarian country in 1949, more than 60,000,000 Chinese lived in cities with populations of over 100,000 and the urban population was to grow rapidly. Shanghai had some 6,000,000 inhabitants in 1949; over 2,000,000 people lived in Beijing and Tianjin; and more than 1,000,000 in Guangzhou (Canton). The task of governing this unfamiliar terrain was compounded by the chaotic conditions which so tragically marked urban life during the last days of Guomindang rule. In addition to chronic (and now exacerbated) problems of massive unemployment and underemployment, of corrupt and inefficient local administrations, of a population preyed upon by a vast underworld of gangster organizations and secret societies, widespread opium addiction, prostitution, and the lack of elemental standards of sanitation and municipal services, conditions of war and the misrule of a dying regime imposed even more severe problems which destroyed the economic life of the cities and inflicted cruel burdens on their inhabitants. Severe shortages of food led to chronic malnutrition and often famine, to riots, looting, and to new waves of crime in cities long notorious for crime. Factories and workshops closed due to lack of supplies and because workers often were too weakened by malnutrition to work. The wartime and postwar inflation reached staggering proportions. During the final 6 months of Guomindang administration in the cities, the average increase in the cost of living was 25 percent per week. In Beijing, for example, the price of flour rose 4,500 times the year prior to the Communist occupation of the city.[5] Money became virtually useless as various "currency reforms" decreed by the government in Nanjing merely brought new floods of worthless paper to a country which had reverted largely to primitive barter for such goods and services as there were to be exchanged.

Not untypical was the situation in the Manchurian city of Mukden, the most industrialized city in China:

Half a million people have left, either for Communist areas or as refugees to North China. Industrial production is down to almost nothing. A primary factor is lack of food, caused by the seige. Rationed food lasts a worker only ten days out of every month. Many people are forced to live on the large Manchurian soybean cakes, ordinarily used only for cattle and fertilizer. These, probably because of vitamin deficiency, eventually produce night blindness among adults and permanent blindness among children—in some cases even actual disintegration of the eyeballs. Lack of food results in lowered coal output, which cuts electric power, which in turn leads to flooding of coal mines. Production appears to be coming to a complete standstill. This coming winter there will surely be starvation.[6]

In Shanghai, rickshaw drivers were too weakened by malnutrition to haul passengers. And from many Chinese cities came reports of starving people lying untended and dying in the streets.

Such was the final legacy of the Guomindang era—the utter destitution of the cities. Not only were the new Communist rulers ill-prepared to govern cities, the cities they now had to govern were in ruins. The Communists lacked both organized political support among the urban population and the material support of a viable economy. To the burdens of a primitive agricultural economy, there was added a new and unanticipated burden: the ruin of the whole modern sector of the economy. In this condition of total impoverishment the history of the People's Republic began.

The Communists possessed one political asset in the cities: an almost universal antipathy to the Guomindang. The political discontent engendered by the economic miseries of the time was intensified by the increasingly corrupt practices of the dying regime and its resort to wholly terroristic methods of political control, arbitrary arrests and executions, the suppression of the liberal intelligentsia, and the crushing of an anti-Communist, but independent, trade-union movement which had emerged in the early post-World War II years. The vast majority of the urban people, as unfamiliar with the Communists as the rural revolutionaries were with them, could not but welcome the triumph of the countryside over the cities, if for no other reason than that the Communist victory held the promise of peace and order.

While their general disgust with the old regime is well documented, it was rarely expressed in any open or organized political action, and there is little reliable evidence to gauge feelings about the new order. Sentiments varied according to place and social class. From Beijing it was reported that "the Communists come here with the bulk of the people on their side. As one walks the streets, the new feeling of relief and relaxation can definitely be sensed, even though it is hard to describe it in tangible terms."[7] The people of Guangzhou, according to one account, awaited the arrival of the Red Army in a "cautious rather than exuberant" mood and "their main feeling was relief that the city had fallen peacefully."[8]

It was among middle-school and university students that the Communists found their most enthusiastic and active supporters in the urban areas, although genuine idealism often was mixed with opportunism and hypocrisy. Members of the politically uncommitted intelligentsia seemed, for the most part, willing to work within the new order. One liberal professor commented in September, 1948, four months before Beijing fell to the Red Army:

> Most Chinese intellectuals would prefer not to bother about politics. But while they have heard the government repeatedly proclaim its intention of bringing democracy and honest administration to China, they have seen these protestations repeatedly flouted in actual fact. Indeed, far from improving, the government becomes steadily worse, so that today few thinking people hold much hope for its reform. . . . At first, most of us supported the [Nationalist] government, recognizing its many faults, but hoping it would reform. . . . We have become so completely convinced of the hopelessness of the existing government that we feel the sooner it is removed the better. Since the Chinese Communists are obviously the only force capable of making this change, we are now willing to support them as the lesser of two evils. We ourselves would prefer a middle course, but this is no longer possible.[9]

Many of the wealthier members of the bourgeoisie fled along with the Guomindang, but many of those classified by the Communists as belonging to the "national bourgeoisie" remained—a varied assortment of commercial entrepreneurs, petty shopkeepers, owners of small factories and workshops, and managers of industrial and commercial establishments. Nearly ruined by the extralegal exactions of a corrupt bureaucracy and the chaos of civil war, they had little left to lose. They hardly could have been enthusiastic about a government which proclaimed socialism and communism to be its aims, but they could hope that the new rulers would honor the promise to control but not immediately eliminate capitalism. Their attitudes towards the new regime were no doubt highly ambiguous, just as the Communists viewed them in an ambiguous and suspicious fashion.

About the political attitudes and sentiments of the working class and the masses of the urban poor—the downtrodden *lumpenproletariat* of rickshaw drivers, casual "coolie" laborers, beggars, and petty thieves—even less can be said with any degree of accuracy. They made up the great majority of the population of the cities, but they were the least articulate segment of that population. Among the people of the cities, they were the ones who benefited most from the new regime, yet they are the ones about whom the least is known. From their ranks came the bulk of the participants in the victory celebrations of 1949 and the mass demonstrations and meetings in the cities over the following years, but they must have had the most ambiguous feelings about celebrating a revolutionary victory to which they had contributed so little. One can only surmise, on the basis of scanty information, that in 1949 the urban workers greeted the Communist victory with hope and enthusiasm. The members of a class so long victimized by extreme socioeconomic oppression, largely unemployed and half-starved in the last years of the old regime, could only have welcomed the triumph of the new regime, even if they may have found it strange that the leading party in that regime proclaimed itself to be *their* party.

Although the spectacle of an army composed mostly of peasants occupying the cities must have made for deeply ambiguous feelings among the urban populace, the vast majority of the people of the cities probably welcomed the new order, if only because of their deep revulsion with the old one. Hope intermingled with apprehension, for the urban population was as unfamiliar with the Communists as the Communists were with the cities. But the dominant mood was a willingness to cooperate with the new rulers of China to end the chaos in the cities that the discredited Guomindang regime had left behind. Mutual suspicions and distrusts remained, but at the beginning they were subordinated to a mutual desire for peace, social order, an adequate supply of food, the restoration of a shattered economy, and for elemental social reforms. What the Communists lacked in organized political support was compensated for, at least in part, by a general and genuine public eagerness to participate in the work of reviving the social and economic life of the cities.

The first task was to establish public order and restore ordinary municipal services. In striking contrast to the situation in the countryside, where the Communists began with their own organizational forms and cadres, in the cities they had to rely on the bureaucratic apparatus left over from the old regime. Although most high Guomindang officials had fled with the Nationalist Army, many lower level bureaucratic functionaries remained in municipal administrations. To a lesser degree, the same was true for local police forces; old civil police organs and many of their personnel were retained in the interests of restoring order. Over the years, most of the old functionaries were replaced by Party cadres, many of whom were newly recruited from urban youth.

The formal administrative and police structures of the cities were not far different from those which had existed under the Nationalists, but they now were under the control of the public security agencies of both the army and the central government in Beijing. While the formal organization of the old municipal administrations remained, as did many old officials and functionaries, Party members occupied key positions to ensure that local city bureaucracies were responsive to the policies of the new national government. Centralized control was augmented by a variety of formally autonomous urban mass organizations which were in fact intimately tied to the state apparatus. Such nationwide organizations as the All-China Federation of Trade Unions, the All-China Federation of Women, the Students' Association, and various professional associations organized the key classes and groups in urban society. Established on the basis of preexisting organizational structures, these organizations were in essence arms of the centralized state apparatus, dominated by the same Party that controlled the national government. The associations organized and controlled much of the urban population and served as centralized counterweights to the localistic tendencies of urban administrations and economic enterprises.

Beginning in 1952 "urban resident committees" (generally made up of about 100 to 500 households) added another layer of organizational control over the urban population. They were assigned a bewildering variety of functions. In addition to communicating (and popularizing) government policies and programs to their members, they were to communicate to the government the views and opinions of citizens; they had the quasi-judicial function of arbitrating family and neighborhood disputes and the police

function of controlling (and reporting) criminal activities and political dissi-
dence; they were to carry out municipal services, such as public sanitation
and fire prevention, as well as social welfare functions, such as providing relief to needy families and the organization of neighborhood cultural and
recreational programs. Although the welfare and other positive services
provided by the resident committees were both needed and appreciated,
they were basically coercive instruments of control. As Franz Schurmann
has observed: "One of the basic tasks of the residents committees was to
keep an eye on the population under their jurisdiction and to report regularly to the local police station, more or less in the fashion known from
paochia days."[10] The quasi-police and judicial functions of the committees
intruded into private lives and aroused deep popular resentments, just as
had been the case with their pre-1949 counterparts. Yet, despite the reliance on many old bureaucratic forms and many old bureaucrats, Communist political power was quickly and firmly established in the cities. The
revolutionaries in power were not overwhelmed by the remnants of the old
bureaucracy; they simply used them.

If Communist political power was firm, there was little distinctively
"communist" or "socialist" about the ends to which this power was put in
the early years; the urban policies and programs were ones which any
strong national government would have undertaken under the circumstances, and indeed, in large measure, ones which the old Guomindang
regime had attempted to pursue. The establishment of social order; regis-
tration of the population; collection of concealed weapons; control of inflation and introduction of a viable currency system; revival of industrial
production and commerce; restoration of municipal services; improvement
of sanitation facilities; and centralized control over viable local urban administrations were immediate tasks that any new Chinese government
would have confronted. Nor should it have taken a Communist government to deal with the chronic social problems of the cities such as widespread opium addiction, prostitution, and the crime and corruption
wrought by a vast underworld of secret societies and labor gangs.

The problem of opium addiction is a particularly striking example of the
failures of the old regime and the successes of the new one. The drug problem had plagued Chinese society since the late eighteenth century, and
reached epidemic proportions after the Opium War of 1839. By the time
the Nationalist regime inherited the massive problem, most of the trade
was in the hands of Chinese criminal organizations. Guomindang anti-
opium laws and campaigns proved abortive not only because of the inefficiency of the regime but also for reasons of political and economic
expediency; the Guomindang had found politically useful the secret soci-

eties and gangster organizations which profited from the drug trade, while a corrupt bureaucracy and police force found it financially rewarding to protect it. Yet a problem that had persisted and grown under various Chinese governments for almost two centuries was resolved by the new government in two years. The Communists employed a combination of drastic criminal penalties (including execution) for major suppliers and dealers, amnesty for petty traffickers, rehabilitation programs for addicts, and a massive nationwide campaign of education and public "ban opium" rallies, appealing to patriotic sentiments by stressing the nineteenth century imperialist origins of the affliction. By 1952 opium addiction was no longer a major social problem, and few drug addicts were to be found in China.

Other common urban vices were handled with the same efficiency and through similar measures of repression, reformation, mass mobilization, and education. In Guangzhou, one of the most vice-ridden of old Chinese cities, Ezra Vogel summarizes one of the results of the first three years of Communist rule: "Prostitution, opium addiction, gambling, and alcoholism were virtually wiped out. For the first time in a century a public morality was restored so that people did not have to worry about robbery or about walking on the streets alone in the evening. A combination of assistance and tight supervision did not alter human nature but it did bring organized crime under control."[11]

Just as the internal social reforms in the cities fulfilled long-frustrated desires for the regeneration of China, so the departure of foreigners satisfied deep nationalist resentments against a century-long external impingement. The expulsion of foreigners from the cities was not an act of "Communist tyranny," as it was described and condemned in the Western press at the time, but a highly popular Chinese nationalist act, symbolizing the end of the era of imperialist domination. Although the expulsion was marked by occasional incidents of popular antiforeign violence, the process was carried out in a relatively orderly fashion. At first, foreign residents were required to register with the new authorities and their activities and travel were limited and supervised. Foreign businesses were regulated and eventually confiscated and nationalized. In late 1950, under tensions generated by the Korean War, government policy demanded the removal of virtually all Western nationals from Chinese soil. By then most Westerners had already left the country, but the few foreign businessmen, missionaries, and educators who had remained were forced to depart over the next year, hastened on their way by mass anti-imperialist rallies. The majority left peacefully despite the political terror that prevailed at the time and the nationalist passions aroused by the war in Korea. All foreign assets were frozen, foreign-owned property expropriated, and Chinese Christians were forced to terminate ties with foreign churches.

Among the expelled foreigners were a good many who were favorable to the new order and who wished to remain and work in China. And the whole antiforeign campaign created problems in diplomatic relations and trade with Western nations. But these considerations were far outweighed at the time by internal political and psychological needs. As a non-Communist liberal Chinese intellectual explained the situation to an American friend, "Communist antiforeignism is the result of humiliation and oppression suffered by China for the past century. The Communists are out to show their people that they are masters of their own house and that no foreigner can lord it here any more."[12] No concrete political or economic gains or issues were involved; rather it was emotional compensation for a century of humiliation. The expulsion of the foreigners was the necessary psychological prerequisite for China to meet the Western nations on equal terms. Since 1842 Chinese politicians and governments, traditional and modern nationalist, had vowed to throw off the foreign yoke, but the People's Republic was the first government in modern Chinese history to demonstrate that it had the power to do so.

The Urban Economy in the Early Years

The economic policies of the People's Republic were never purely "nationalistic," but in the early years they did largely conform with the Maoist conception of a revolution still in its "national" or "bourgeois-democratic" phase. In the rural areas, the land reform campaign of 1949–1952 produced not a socialist economy but a massive class of petty bourgeois individual peasant cultivators. In the cities socialist and capitalist forms intermingled for a time in a "mixed economy," but of a rather unique kind. The industries, commercial organizations, and banks owned by the "bureaucratic bourgeoisie" (those who had been politically allied with the Guomindang or economically tied to foreign interests) were immediately confiscated and were nationalized without compensation. By 1949 most of the big bourgeoisie had fled the country in any event. Through nationalization, the new state owned most of the modern sector of the economy from the outset. If one defines socialism simply (and perhaps simplistically) as state ownership of property, then most of the urban economy was "socialist" from the beginning. However, significant portions of the economy remained capitalist. In addition to more than a million petty shopkeepers and handicrafts workers who were largely untouched by the new order in the early years, the "national bourgeoisie," defined principally by the criterion of political loyalty, were permitted to continue to privately own their industrial and trading enterprises and operate them in a formally capitalist fashion. Indeed they were encouraged to expand their operations and establish new firms. By 1953 the number of privately owned industrial establishments increased from 123,000 to 150,000 and the number of workers in private firms grew from 1,644,000 to 2,231,000, accounting for 37 percent of China's industrial output.[13]

The operation of the private sector, however, was tightly restricted. Prices, wages, and working conditions were determined by the state. In privately owned factories, trade unions and worker councils, both under Party direction, enforced state policies and regulations, and also played a supervisory role in the management of the enterprises. Most importantly, private factories were dependent on the state for the allocation of raw materials to produce their goods and for outlets to sell them, and private commercial firms depended on the state trading organizations for both wholesale purchases and retail sales. This, in short, was a form of state capitalism, not a laissez-faire economy. The "national bourgeoisie" in the People's Republic was now more dependent on the state bureaucracy than the old and condemned "bureaucratic bourgeoisie" ever had been. The difference was essentially political; it was a new state pursuing new social ends. Yet it was capitalism nonetheless. Owners of capital made profits on the commodities they produced and sold, and although profits were controlled, they were more than adequate to allow the "national" capitalists to enjoy a comfortable bourgeois life style.

More than purely ideological considerations were involved in the revival of "national capitalism." The Communists were not simply attempting to give substance to the promise of "new democracy," nor were they attempting to historically document the Marxist proposition that a "bourgeois-democratic" phase of development must precede a socialist one. The main consideration was more mundane. To reconstruct a wrecked economy and establish a foundation for future economic development, it was expedient to rebuild what had existed and then build upon that. Any program for total expropriation and nationalization would have resulted in organizational chaos. More importantly, the revival of capitalism was necessary to utilize the managerial skills and technical expertise which the bourgeoisie alone possessed. Through a combination of economic and patriotic appeals, the new government enlisted the support of the members of the bourgeoisie and technical specialists who had remained, and encouraged many who had left the country to return, to participate in the task of national economic reconstruction.

The era of "national capitalism" reached its peak in 1952–1953 and declined rapidly thereafter, as private industrial and commercial firms were
nationalized outright, or more typically, reorganized as "joint private-state
enterprises." In the latter case, the state assumed a controlling, and eventually complete, interest in the firms by government capital investments, with
the former private owners usually staying on in managerial roles and receiving dividends of 5 percent on what the government calculated to be their
remaining share of capital. In fact, if not in name, the firms became state-
owned as well as state-managed. By 1956 the private sector of the urban
economy had ceased to exist, and all industrial and commercial enterprises
of any significant size had been effectively nationalized. What little remained of private enterprise was confined to self-employed handicraft
workers, artisans, petty shopkeepers, and peddlers. "National capitalism"
survived only as a vestige—in the form of a tiny bourgeoisie receiving quarterly dividends on what the government determined to be their "capital investments" in the factories and commercial establishments they once
owned, or receiving interest on nonredeemable government bonds they
had received in compensation. Although they continued to enjoy a relatively high standard of living in the cities, the national bourgeoisie was a
dying class since their bonds could not be passed on to their heirs. But if
national capitalism had enjoyed only a brief life in the history of the People's Republic, it had fulfilled the economic role assigned to it; by 1952
urban industry and commerce were flourishing.

The new government sought the cooperation of urban elites who possessed specialized skills needed for national reconstruction: liberal intellectuals and the technological intelligentsia; bureaucrats and urban
administrators left over from the old regime; and the national bourgeoisie.
Once political and economic stability had been achieved, the Communists
moved quickly to end their reliance on what they regarded as the least politically reliable members of the urban population. Beginning in late 1951,
this took the form of three politically repressive campaigns: the thought reform movement directed primarily against intellectuals; the *Sanfan* ("three
anti") campaign against bureaucratic corruption and inefficiency; and the
Wufan ("five anti") campaign which was essentially an attack on the bourgeoisie. Unlike the preceding campaign against "counterrevolutionaries,"
which attempted to eliminate political dissent in society in general, the new
movements had specific goals aimed against particular elite groups in the
cities. And unlike the concurrent land reform campaign which served to
destroy the rural gentry, a class which had nothing to offer to the new society, the urban campaigns aimed not to destroy social groups but rather to
establish firmer political control over them. The thrust was to politicize

people with expertise while preserving them and their talents to serve society. Unlike the gentry and the counterrevolutionaries, the people to be politicized were still regarded as members of "the people."

The first of the major postrevolutionary thought reform campaigns began in the autumn of 1951 when Mao Zedong declared that the reformation of intellectuals was essential for "the thoroughgoing democratic transformation and progressive industrialization of our country."[14] The campaign was thus tied to the completion of the bourgeois-democratic phase of the revolution and the building of the economic preconditions for the future transition to socialism. Beginning with a movement for the intensive study of the writings of Mao, with particular emphasis on the Yan'an talks on art and literature which defined the social and political responsibilities of intellectuals, the campaign spread to all major urban areas employing familiar Maoist techniques of mass meetings, small group "struggle sessions" of criticism and self-criticism, public humiliations, and written and oral "confessions" from those deemed guilty of ideological deviations. Individualistic tendencies and "liberal" bourgeois thought were to be discarded in favor of ascetic Maoist values and a collectivistic mentality of "serving the people." The campaign generally began with intellectuals in universities and spread to middle and elementary school teachers as well as to students and individual writers and artists. There was little overt political coercion (although some intellectuals were sent to the countryside for "reeducation through labor"), but the social and psychological pressures were intense. The vague criterion for success was a subjective judgment, made by the "thought reformers," as to whether confessions and self-criticisms acknowledging past errors and accepting the new social morality were "sincere" or not. While it may be doubted that many intellectuals achieved the desired Maoist inner spiritual transformation, the outer results were patently clear; the campaign ended in 1952 with tighter Party control over the educational system and the closing of the narrow realm of freedom of expression that intellectuals had cautiously enjoyed during the first two years of the People's Republic. Four years later, the "Hundred Flowers" period was to reveal how repression fostered deep resentments.

The *Sanfan* movement against "corruption, waste, and the bureaucratic spirit" was launched early in 1952 and ran simultaneously with the thought reform campaign. The "three anti" movement was designed to remove politically unreliable government officials and Party cadres as well as to correct specific problems in the functioning of the administrative organs of the new state. The mass meetings of citizens to criticize corrupt or oppressive officials, a distinctively Maoist political technique, characterized this campaign as it did virtually all others. While this was something far less than popular control over the bureaucracy, it was a practice entirely foreign to Stalinism both in spirit and method.

Sanfan fell hardest on the bureaucracy, especially old Guomindang officials who had been retained in the urban administrations and who now were dispensable, new Party members hastily recruited during the final years of the civil war who proved unsuited to the new tasks of postrevolutionary administrative work, and older Party cadres who were seen as corrupted by urban bourgeois influences. The latter was a distinctively Maoist theme, the view that city life fostered bureaucratic mentalities and the erosion of revolutionary values. In the end, however, the movement proved to be something less than a massive attack on bureaucracy. Less than 5 percent of administrative functionaries were subjected to formal punishment; some were imprisoned, but most were simply dismissed or demoted.[15]

The *Wufan* campaign (against bribery, tax evasion, fraud, theft of government property, and stealing of state economic secrets) was a movement of greater scope and significance. Directed against corrupt practices in the urban economy in general, its main weight fell on the bourgeoisie and more than 450,000 enterprises were officially investigated by state authorities in 1952 and early 1953. Although some owners were imprisoned for illegal economic activities, the penalties were mostly financial. Through the collection of back taxes, heavy fines and other economic exactions, the remaining assets of the bourgeoisie were further depleted and most firms and factories were forced to become joint state-private enterprises, in effect, well on the way to becoming nationalized.

The campaigns of 1951 and 1952 served to consolidate Communist power in the cities and marked the beginning of the end of the era of "new democracy." By early 1953 the civil administrations, the economy, and the educational institutions of urban China were firmly under the control of the Party and the centralized state apparatus it directed. The new regime was authoritarian and repressive, but the cities were governed honestly and efficiently for the first time in modern Chinese history.

· · ·

In 1949 the Communists had announced their goal to be: "Three years of recovery, then ten years of development." By the end of 1952, with the restoration of the cities and the conclusion of the land reform campaign in the countryside, to be discussed in the next chapter, the new rulers had fulfilled the first half of that promise. The government was now to turn its attention to "ten years of development," the task of industrializing a still backward and impoverished land. But industrialization was to bring unforeseen and, for Mao, undesirable social, political, and ideological consequences. And the industrial development of the cities was to bring more sharply into focus the critical problem of the relationship between town and countryside in the new society, a question that was to dominate the entire history of the People's Republic, just as it had dominated the history of the revolution that produced that republic. A growing antagonism between town and countryside is perhaps inherent in the very process of modern industrialization. But in China the antagonism was to be accentuated by the rural origins and heritage of the revolution and by a curious imbalance between economic and political power in rural and urban areas. In the cities, the Communists had succeeded in reviving the economy and the strong state they had created exercised effective centralized control over the urban areas, but their sociopolitical ties to the growing urban working class remained weak and tenuous. Although strong efforts were made to acquire an urban proletarian base in the early postrevolutionary years, workers or people of working-class origin made up less than 10 percent of the 6,000,000 members of the Chinese Communist Party in 1953, and the percentage was not to increase significantly in the years that followed. In the countryside, on the other hand, the Communists had deep political roots among the peasantry, roots that the land reform campaign of 1950–1952 reinforced. And the Communist Party remained a "peasant party" in the sense that peasants constituted the overwhelming majority of its membership. But those political roots were in an agrarian economy low in productivity and still based on a system of individual peasant proprietorship. The industrialization of the People's Republic thus was to begin on the basis of a fragile petty bourgeois agricultural economy and in cities where the Communists had an ambiguous relationship with the working class.

Yet if the social base of the Chinese Communist Party remained the peasantry, the higher organs of the Party were now based in the cities and the majority of its leaders rapidly became urbanized. They hardly became the "organic" intellectuals of the working class in the sense in which Antonio Gramsci had formulated that conception,[16] but they did identify their fortunes and the future of China with the growth of urban industry, and thus by implication, at least, with China's growing urban proletariat. Other Communist leaders, who might well be characterized as the organic intellectuals of the peasantry, did not so easily accept city life and the prospect of the domination of town over countryside. Foremost among the latter was Mao Zedong, who, when he announced in 1949 the inauguration of the period of "the city leading the village," also warned of the danger that urbanization could corrupt the spirit and ideology of the victorious revolutionaries—that the rural style of "plain living and hard struggle" might give way to the "love of pleasure and distaste for continued hard living" that city life fostered.[17] The warning was to prove prophetic. The existing gap between town and countryside quickly was to widen under the impact of rapid urban industrialization, and the gap was to find expression within the Chinese Communist Party itself—in the form of a division between urban and rural-oriented Communist leaders, between those who placed their hopes for a socialist future in the development of modern urban industry and those who continued to identify themselves with the peasant masses and looked more to the socialist transformation of the countryside.

NOTES

1. John Dunn, *Modern Revolutions* (London: Cambridge University Press, 1972), p. 17.
2. Mao Tse-tung [Mao Zedong], *The Chinese Revolution and the Chinese Communist Party* (1939) (Peking: Foreign Languages Press, 1954), p. 32.
3. Mao Tse-tung, "Report to the Second Plenary Session of the Seventh Central Committee of the Communist Party of China," *Selected Works of Mao Tse-tung* (Peking: Foreign Languages Press, 1961), 4:363–364.
4. Derk Bodde, *Peking Diary* (New York: Henry Schuman, 1950), p. 72. This book is a most perceptive and the most revealing account of the situation in the cities under the Guomindang at the last and the early months of Communist rule.
5. *Ibid.*, p. 100.
6. Quoted in *ibid.*, p. 33.
7. *Ibid.*, p. 99. On the civilian participants in the Red Army's victory parade through the streets of Beijing, Bodde observed that "the enthusiasm of most was too obvious to have been feigned. . . . The reaction of the spectators, on the other hand, was, like that of most Chinese crowds, less outspoken. Nevertheless, they seemed in general quite favorably disposed and obviously deeply impressed by the display of power." [p. 104]
8. Ezra Vogel, *Canton under Communism* (Cambridge, Mass.: Harvard University Press, 1969), pp. 45–46.
9. As related by Derk Bodde in *Peking Diary*, pp. 23–24.
10. Franz Schurmann, *Ideology and Organization in Communist China* (Berkeley: University of California Press, 1966), p. 376. *Baojia* was a traditional system of sociopolitical control imposed by the state; ideally, it was a grouping of a hundred households with each bearing responsibility for the actions and behavior of all other members.
11. Vogel, *Canton under Communism*, p. 67.
12. Bodde, *Peking Diary*, p. 158.
13. Figures calculated by Barry M. Richman, *Industrial Society in Communist China* (New York: Random House, 1969), p. 899.
14. *Jen-min jih-pao* [*Renmin ribao*] (*People's Daily*), October 24, 1951.
15. Schurmann, *Ideology and Organization*, p. 318.
16. For Gramsci's notion of the "organic" intellectual, and his distinction between urban and rural-type intellectuals, see his provocative essay "The Intellectuals" in Antonio Gramsci, *Selections from the Prison Notebooks* (New York: International Publishers, 1971), pp. 5–23.
17. Mao, "Report to the Second Plenary Session of the Seventh Central Committee of the Communist Party of China," *Selected Works* (1961), 4:363–364, 374.

7

Land Reform

The Bourgeois Revolution in the Countryside

I N 1952, THREE YEARS after the establishment of the People's Republic, the landed gentry ceased to exist as a social class. The destruction of the elite that had dominated Chinese society for more than two millennia marked the consummation of a momentous social revolution, but not a socialist one. Although that process of class destruction was carried out under Communist political auspices, the demise of the gentry was socially and economically an eminently bourgeois revolutionary act. Just as the eighteenth-century French Revolution had destroyed the power of the landed aristocracy and removed feudal institutions hindering the growth of bourgeois property, the Chinese Communist revolution in the countryside, by expropriating the landlords and redistributing land among the peasantry, created a massive class of individual peasant proprietors engaged in petty capitalist production.

That the gentry and precapitalist agrarian socioeconomic relationships had survived to the mid-twentieth century reflected the failure of bourgeois revolutionary movements in modern Chinese history. It fell to a Communist Party that aimed to abolish private property to establish the conditions for the flourishing of capitalist property relations in the countryside. This historical paradox was, of course, not without historical precedent. A similar failure on the part of bourgeois political parties in Russia had forced the

Bolsheviks to preside over an agrarian bourgeois revolution, with the result that the first decade of Soviet history saw the emergence and growth of a capitalistic peasantry. In both China and Russia, however, the existence of a bourgeois economy in the countryside was short-lived, and in both countries the same political power that had allowed a bourgeois agrarian revolution to take place also proved to be the instrument that destroyed bourgeois property.

One of the ironies of the history of Marxism might be noted here. The abortiveness of bourgeois revolutionary movements in Russia and China offered a socialist political advantage. Had bourgeois revolutions occurred earlier, before political conditions permitted Marxist revolutionaries to come to power, the peasantries of both countries likely would have become politically conservative forces intent on preserving their smallholdings and thus opposed to revolution. This was the case in most of Western Europe and especially in France. The radicalism of the French peasantry during the Revolution of 1789 was followed by more than a century of political conservatism; Marx often commented on the phenomenon, summed up in his sarcastic comment that "the Bonapartes are the dynasty of the peasants."[1] Such was not the case where the agrarian revolution was retarded and took place in conjunction with, or as part of, a socialist revolutionary process. In Russia, the new peasant smallholders did not have the time to consolidate themselves as a class sufficiently strong to withstand the terror of Stalinist collectivization. In China the political advantage was much greater. The Chinese Communists, unlike the Russian Bolsheviks, came to power on the basis of massive peasant support and with deep organizational roots in the countryside. Peasant resistance to collectivization was to prove minimal, and peasant support for radical social transformation substantial. The socialization of agriculture in China was to proceed in a way strikingly dissimilar from the way it had in the Soviet Union, and with different social and political results.

Land Reform, 1950–1952

When the People's Republic formally was proclaimed in 1949, land reform had been carried out in no more than one-fifth of the villages of China. The Communists were determined to extend the process from their old revolutionary base areas throughout the vast countryside that only recently had come under their control, and to do so quickly. More than an ideological demand to eliminate feudalistic socioeconomic relations in the rural areas (and thus fulfill one of the major promises of "new democracy") lay behind this determination. Also involved were crucial political and economic considerations. For one thing, land reform was necessary to maintain the new regime's base of popular support; "land to the tiller" had been promised to the poor peasants who made up 70 percent of China's rural population of 500,000,000 and from whom the Communists drew the bulk of their political support. The universalization of land reform was a necessity for two other reasons. First, it would destroy the gentry-landlord class (and thus eliminate a potential counterrevolutionary threat), establish Communist political power within the villages, and thus promote the building of a centralized state with firm administrative control over the countryside. Second, land reform was an economic necessity for the new society. It was anticipated that it would expand agricultural production, at least within the limits imposed by traditional technology; establish the political foundation for a technological revolution in agriculture upon which hopes for modern industrial development rested; and provide the base for the future socialist transformation of the countryside.

While the Communists were intent on completing the agrarian social revolution, they were determined to avoid the violence that had marred many of the land reform campaigns in northern provinces during the last years of the civil war. With military victory assured by the spring of 1949, the emphasis turned from the political mobilization of the peasantry to the establishment of a new state order and to a concern for a stable agrarian economy. Party leaders called for an end to revolutionary terror in the villages and attempted to control the spontaneous forces of peasant radicalism, which now seemed politically and economically disruptive to revolutionaries turned rulers. Many of the younger village cadres, now accused of "leftist deviations" and "indiscriminate killings," were expelled from the Party in early 1950. In the meantime, while new national guidelines were being formulated, land reform was slowed or halted and the actions of peasants and local cadres in the newly liberated areas of the southern and central provinces were restrained.

A strong reaction against the violence and disorder of the earlier land reform campaigns figured prominently in Party debates of late 1949 and early 1950. The debate was dominated by two considerations: a determination to destroy the landed gentry as a social class; and an equally strong determination to complete land reform in a manner consistent with maintaining agricultural production. The two aims were by no means inconsistent. The gentry traditionally had been a basically parasitic class, deriving wealth through rents from their landholdings but contributing little or nothing to production. Quite apart from social and political considerations, the simple economic fact of the matter was well put by the anthropologist Fei Xiaotong: "The landlord cannot find a way to eliminate the tenant and get income directly from the land, but the tenant can cultivate the land without the assistance of the landlord."[2] Unlike the bourgeoisie of the cities, whose economic and technical skills were needed and cultivated by the new regime, the gentry had nothing to offer to society. They were a class dispensable on economic grounds as well as socially and politically undesirable.

The results of the deliberations on land reform were summarized in a speech by Liu Shaoqi to the People's Political Consultative Conference on June 14, 1950, and formally adopted by the government two weeks later in the Agrarian Reform Law. Although Liu's speech—eighteen years later—was to be cited as evidence of his alleged "capitalist roadism," there is no reason to believe that Mao Zedong at the time disagreed with the moderate thrust of his report: that the old agrarian system was to be eliminated "step by step and with discrimination" while agricultural production was to be developed at the same time.[3] The need to maintain the productivity of the rural economy during the course of the social revolutionary transformation was recognized as essential to the political as well as the economic viability of the new state by all Communist leaders, including Mao. Indeed, a week before Liu had delivered his speech, Mao had presented a report to the Party's Central Committee foreshadowing the relatively moderate agrarian program that was to be adopted. It was economically necessary, Mao argued, to pursue a policy of "preserving a rich peasant economy, in order to further the early restoration of production in the rural areas."[4] And what Liu proposed as the "general line" to be followed in the land reform campaign—"to rely on the poor peasants and farm laborers, to unite with the middle peasants, and to neutralize the rich peasants"—was a cardinal principle that Mao advocated and practiced before and after 1949. In practical socioeconomic terms this meant protecting the economically efficient farms of the rich as well as the middle peasants from radical egalitarian demands for complete and immediate social leveling.

This concern for maintaining productivity was reflected in the provisions governing the treatment of the estimated 30 percent of the rural population not classified as poor peasants or agricultural laborers under the Agrarian Reform Law and subsequent government directives over the summer of 1950. The lands and properties of landlords (the 4 percent of the rural population who owned about 30 percent of the cultivated land) were to be confiscated and distributed among landless and poor peasants, as were institutional lands (usually indirectly controlled by gentry families) such as property owned by village shrines and temples, monasteries, churches, and schools. But dispossessed landlords were to be given shares of land equal to those of poor peasants "so that they can make their living by their own labor and thus reform themselves through labor." After five years of demonstrated productive activity and political loyalty, the stigma of "land-lord-class status" could be removed. More significant was the provision prohibiting the confiscation of "the land and other properties used by land-lords directly for the operation of industrial and commercial enterprises," a provision in accord with Mao's 1949 injunction that "China must utilize all elements of urban and rural capitalism that are beneficial and not harmful to the national economy," and one which permitted gentry families engaged in entrepreneurial enterprises in the cities and the towns to be reclassified as members of the "national bourgeoisie." Thus while the traditional eco-nomically parasitic role of the gentry was to be eliminated, their economi-cally beneficial functions were to be preserved, even though the latter often involved the exploitation of labor.

More revealing of the Communist willingness to subordinate social con-siderations to immediate economic concerns was the relatively lenient pol-icy adopted toward rich peasants. Although only 6 percent of the rural population, their farms accounted for almost half the total agricultural pro-duction. The Agrarian Law stipulated that the lands "cultivated by them-selves *or by hired labor,* and their other properties, shall be protected from infringement" [emphasis added]. Moreover, rich peasants were permitted to continue to rent land to tenant farmers; only leased land exceeding in size the amount cultivated by themselves and their hired laborers was sub-ject to confiscation.[5] Thus rich peasants were permitted to engage in two traditional types of rural exploitation: they were able to hire agricultural la-borers and to rent parts of their holdings to tenant farmers.

Special efforts were made to increase the economic productivity and win the political cooperation of middle peasants. Although they constituted 20 percent of the rural population, one-third of the leadership of the peas-ants' associations were to be drawn from the middle peasants. None of their lands or properties were subject to confiscation and the introduction of the new category of "well-to-do middle peasant" made it possible for them to draw as much as 25 percent of their income through exploitation, that is by hiring laborers or renting portions of their land.[6]

Although the Agrarian Law of 1950 was a relatively moderate docu-ment, preserving the economic position of middle and most rich peasants, it did retain the main social revolutionary thrust of land reform—the de-struction of the landlord-gentry class. Nevertheless, it provided for less than what had been promised in the slogans around which the poor peas-ant masses had rallied to the Communist cause during the civil war: "the equal distribution of land" and "the land belongs to the man who plows it."

The promise was left unfulfilled because any attempt to achieve complete egalitarianism in the countryside would have created havoc in the rural economy, as the 1947–1949 land reform campaigns in the North had demonstrated. The dilution of social radicalism in the new agrarian program reflected the lessons of that experience as well as new concerns for political and economic stability, concerns that befitted revolutionaries who now had become rulers. These political and economic considerations are evident in the official documents and pronouncements of the time. The destruction of the gentry as a social class was seen as a good and necessary end, but not an end in itself. As the opening paragraph of the new Agrarian Law made clear, the long-range goal was "to set free the rural productive forces, develop agricultural production, and thus pave the way for New China's industrialization."[7] And as Communist leaders emphasized time and again, land reform itself, however egalitarian, would not solve the problem of the poverty of the peasantry, a problem which could be resolved only by increasing total agricultural production and the development of modern industry and technology. Land reform, in any case, was viewed by the Communists, although perhaps not by their peasant supporters at the time, as only the first stage of a long-term social and economic revolution in the countryside, only a first step on the way to the eventual collectivization of agriculture and to industrialization. In the meantime, the interests of the nation would best be served by maintaining social order and economic productivity in the rural areas. Granting temporary concessions to the rich and middle peasants seemed a small price to pay to facilitate a long-term process of development.

From the perspectives held by most Communist leaders in mid-1950, the specific provisions of the law were less important than the means by which the process would be carried out. Unlike the earlier land revolution in North China, where matters were largely left to young and radical peasant cadres and to the spontaneous radicalism of the poor peasantry, the new campaign was to proceed in a more controlled fashion, with land reform cadres acting in accordance with centralized Party and state instructions. If political and economic needs demanded a more gradual approach, then that also was a price that would be paid. As Liu Shaoqi remarked in his June 1950 report, "If deviations occur in some areas after agrarian reform is started and give rise to certain chaotic conditions which cannot be corrected quickly, agrarian reform then should be held up in these areas until the next year."[8]

The campaign was not to follow the orderly course envisioned in the summer of 1950. Once the forces of class struggle within the villages were released, they were not to be easily controlled by official regulations or bureaucratic restraints. Both the resistance of the relatively privileged rural classes and the demands of poorer peasants for land (and for retribution against their former oppressors) were to prove stronger than the leaders in Beijing anticipated.

The movement began peacefully enough in the summer of 1950 with the training of local Party cadres for land reform work, the organization and expansion of local peasant associations and congresses, surveys of landownership, the social classification of the population in the newly liberated areas of South and Central China, educational campaigns, and the popularization of model "pilot" projects. Since there were great regional variations in social and economic conditions, directives from Beijing placed special emphasis on the need for provincial authorities to adapt the movement to local needs. There were, to be sure, serious problems at the outset. In the South, clan organizations (which cut across class lines) were stronger than in the North, and Party organization was weaker. The social and economic power of landlords also was greater in most of the newly liberated areas than it had been in the northern provinces, and the gentry used kinship ties to protect themselves and as much as they could of their properties from the oncoming social revolution; many fled to the cities to hide among relatives, disguised some of their holdings and properties by "lending" them to poorer members of their clans in the villages. Sometimes they simply bribed peasants to resist the transformation of traditional relationships. Moreover, the dispatch of northern land reform workers to the South and West sometimes created political conflicts with local Party officials and cadres. Northerners were intent on carrying out land reform as fully and as quickly as possible, local cadres were often restrained by kinship ties and personal friendships. On the whole, however, the campaign proceeded smoothly and with relatively little physical violence through the end of 1950.

Land reform usually began with the organization of the peasants' association and a people's militia, the former replacing the traditional system of village elders drawn from the wealthier families while the latter replaced what remained of the old *baojia* system of local military "self-defense"—and what remained were mostly "local bullies," armed criminal gangs, usually at the disposal of the gentry, engaged in terror and extortion against peasants. Many of the local bullies were executed or imprisoned when Communist military forces first entered the villages. With Communist political power established through new village organizations, the campaign turned to social and economic ends. First landlords had to refund rent deposits and then the complex process of defining the class status of the villagers and identifying landownership began. These were controversial matters and the decisions were often arbitrary since social class lines within the villages tended to be fluid and overlapping and ownership rights were sometimes uncertain. In general, however, the results conformed to socioeconomic realities, even though tempered by political judgments. The sociologist C. K. Yang, who conducted a study of a village in Guangdong during the last year of Guomindang rule and the first two years of the People's Republic, reported that "The general proportion of the classes [as determined by the land reform surveys] corresponded roughly to what we had learned about the class composition of the village previous to the Communist rule."[9]

The determination of class status and landownership was the prelude to land confiscation and redistribution and it produced a most unusual phenomenon: an effort by villagers to represent themselves as low as possible in the social hierarchy. It also gave rise to fear among the less impoverished villagers:

> A great anxiety and tenseness pervaded the village, for now every family was assigned a status fraught with social, economic and political consequences. Those families listed as landlords waited for the axe to fall. Those listed as rich peasants were extremely uneasy, for they knew their fate was undecided, in spite of the temporary policy of "preservation of the rich peasants' economy." . . . The middle peasants experienced considerable suspense . . . they were uncertain how long their land property could be preserved. Furthermore, many of the relatively well-to-do were in juxtaposition to the rich peasants, and they did not know whether they would some day be "promoted" to that rank.[10]

The drawing of class lines inaugurated a period of open class struggle within the villages. The purpose of land reform was not only to economically dispossess the gentry but to humiliate them socially and discredit them politically in the eyes of the peasantry. Through the mass mobilization of the villagers at "struggle meetings," poor peasants were encouraged to express their long-suppressed anger, to publicly denounce the oppressions and oppressors of the past. The landlords who were the principal targets of these sessions could hope at best to receive a small plot of land to till in return for "bowing their heads" before the masses and sincerely admitting their guilt; at worst, they faced summary execution at mass public trials. A large potential for violence and terror was no doubt inherent in the internal dynamics of the rural social conflict which the land reform movement released, but it is unlikely that the terror that was soon to be unleashed against the gentry would have been so massive had it not been for the Korean War.

The war in Korea broke out the same month the Agrarian Reform Law was promulgated, although it was not until Chinese troops became directly involved at the end of the year—and the spectre of full-scale war with the United States was raised—that it had serious internal political repercussions. Many landlords, hoping that the Communist regime would prove short-lived and that the old regime would be restored, stiffened their resistance. For the new government, the war raised the fear of counterrevolution, which centered on the gentry. Of the two social classes the Communists had vowed to eliminate, the bureaucratic bourgeoisie had largely eliminated itself by fleeing the country, but most members of the gentry remained, either in the countryside or in hiding in the cities. As the war in Korea intensified and as internal political tensions increased in late 1950, directives from Beijing called for more radical agrarian policies, an intensification of the rural class struggle, and for a general speeding-up of the land reform campaign to break the potential threat posed by the continued existence of the gentry class. Political considerations began to outweigh economic concerns, leading to more frequent struggle meetings in the villages and more mass public trials pronouncing harsher judgments. Land reform began to take on the terroristic features of the earlier agrarian revolution in North China, although it was now less spontaneous in character. The campaign remained under central direction and control and became intertwined with the general secret police terror against suspected counterrevolutionaries which continued through most of 1951. Many landlords were executed or sent to labor camps, but the great majority of the approximately 20,000,000 people classified as members of landlord families were provided with small plots of land and reduced to the unaccustomed role of cultivators of the soil, even though still socially designated as "landlords."

Except for regions populated by national minorities, the land reform campaign was substantially completed by the end of 1952. Its great and historic accomplishment was precisely what had been announced when the movement was launched in 1950, the destruction of the gentry as a social class, although that process of class destruction involved more terror and physical violence than originally had been anticipated. Fears that the movement would undermine agricultural production proved unfounded. Between 1950 and 1952, total agricultural output increased at a rate of 15 percent per annum, the largest increase coming in 1952.[11] Although much of the increase can be attributed to the establishment of political order (and the restoration of trade and transport), after a decade of foreign invasion and civil war, agricultural production was still significantly higher in 1952 than in 1936, the best of the prewar years. The disruptive effects of land reform were more than compensated by the new irrigation and flood-control projects begun in 1949 and by a limited expansion of cultivated acreage, organized anti-pest campaigns, and a significant increase in the use of insecticides and fertilizers. And farmers who now tilled their own land had a greater incentive to work more efficiently and adopt better methods of cultivation.

Land reform completed a momentous social revolution in rural China but it did not bring about an economic revolution in agriculture. Productive patterns in the villages were unaltered by land reform alone and technological improvements were slight. To be sure, the fruits of peasant labor were now more equitably distributed and no longer was it possible for "gentlemen" wearing long gowns and cultivating long fingernails to live off the labor of others. Some of the worst horrors of the old system were removed, but general poverty remained. If total food grains production in 1952 was 9 percent higher than during the peak prewar years, as official figures claimed, it hardly kept pace with population growth, much less provide much of a surplus for capital investments in either agriculture or industry. Traditional agricultural technology and productive patterns imposed stringent limits on increases in productivity—and even that was dependent on the vagaries of the weather.

The economic limitations of land reform had been recognized from the beginning. As Liu Shaoqi had warned on the eve of the campaign, "the basic aim of agrarian reform is not purely to relieve the impoverished peasants. . . . The problem of poverty among the peasants can be finally solved only if agricultural production can be greatly developed, if the industrialization of New China can be realized. . . ."[12] Until that modern economic revolution, the burdens of backwardness would have to be borne, although they now might be shared more equally.

Nonetheless, the poor and landless peasants benefited immediately from the confiscation and redistribution of nearly half of China's cultivated land. Tenants and agricultural laborers now had their own plots to till and the poorest owner-cultivators were given additional land, usually of better quality. Even though they now were socially and politically favored under the new system, poor peasants were still relatively poor in villages still suffering from conditions of general poverty. Land reform was a vast process of social leveling, but it was by no means a complete egalitarian leveling. Significant economic distinctions remained among the rural population. Overall the farms of poor peasants were about 90 percent of the average landholding in their locality, middle peasant holdings were somewhat above the established *xiang* norm, and the holdings of rich peasants were generally about twice the average. In addition, the exploitation of labor was not wholly abolished; rich and some middle peasants still rented land to tenants and hired wage laborers.

Moreover, the economic benefits of land reform were offset to some extent by new economic problems it created. Land redistribution created a larger number of small farming units and greater fragmentation, thus intensifying traditional barriers to productivity. Although usury had been abolished, the old problem of adequate rural credit for small owner-cultivators was aggravated; rich and middle peasants who had money to lend were reluctant to do so at the low rates of interest imposed by the new state. And the state had only the most limited means to establish a new rural credit system. The general tax levy was now higher than it had been under previous regimes; it is generally estimated that state taxes after land reform took approximately 30 percent of the gross agricultural yield, about twice the pre-1949 rate, although it was now the richer peasants who bore the heavier burdens. And while most former tenant farmers benefited from land reform, it was not universally the case that land redistribution increased either their productivity or income. In some areas of South China where tenant farms were relatively large and tenant rights relatively secure, land reform sometimes resulted in smaller and less efficient farms and owner-cultivators who were less well off than they had been before as tenant farmers. On the whole, however, material conditions for the majority of the peasants improved, even though the general problem of rural impoverishment remained.

The significance of the land reform campaign cannot be measured in terms of immediate improvement in living standards in any case. No less important in the long run than the elimination of the worst forms of exploitation was the establishment of the social and political foundations for the future economic development and the social transformation of the countryside. A revolution from below, carried out from village to village by the political activation of the peasant masses, created the basis for a centralized state power to firmly establish itself in the villages. The gentry were replaced by a new rural leadership of young peasant activists drawn from the poor peasantry and intimately tied to a national political structure. Although the formal organs of state administration rested at the level of the *xiang,* CCP organization of the peasantry at lower levels extended the authority of the state down into the "natural" village itself. With the breaking down of traditional regional, local, and kinship loyalties and the establishment of central state control, the local isolation of the villages was broken, peasants became part of a national polity and were increasingly drawn into a national market economy.

Undoubtedly the single most important consequence of the penetration of state authority to the villages, and the simultaneous abolition of parasitic landlordism, was to enable the government to appropriate the larger part of the agrarian economic surplus. This, as we shall see, was the essential precondition for China's industrialization.

Another noteworthy result of land reform was a general transformation of the political consciousness of the peasantry. The land reform campaign was not carried out by administrative decrees but through the stimulation of class conflict within each village, a conflict in which all villagers participated and one whose consequences no one could escape. The latent energies and hatreds of the peasantry were released at mass struggle meetings and public trials, where the formerly passive victims of oppression now denounced, judged, and punished their former oppressors. If the ends of land reform were determined from above, the process itself was carried out below, providing peasants with a sense that they themselves were changing the conditions under which they lived and that they could be the masters of their own destiny. Especially for peasants who had not been involved in the pre-1949 revolutionary struggles, land reform was a profoundly traumatic psychological experience and a profoundly revealing political action which instilled a new sense of their own powers and gave them new hope for the future.

The completion of the campaign resulted in the establishment of a system of individual peasant proprietorship that reflected the bourgeois character of the Chinese revolutionary process. The government issued title deeds to the new landowners and the latter were legally free to buy, sell, and rent their lands. Although political power was in the hands of a Party that proclaimed socialist goals, the rural socioeconomic situation in 1953 was favorable to the development of bourgeois property and conducive to the growth of a rural capitalist class.

The Communists had made no secret that they viewed individual peasant proprietorship as a temporary phase in the socioeconomic development of the countryside, as but a transitional step on the way to collectivization. A year before the land reform campaign was launched, Mao had announced that agricultural collectivization was only a matter of time, but he then suggested that it might take a long time:

> As the peasant economy is decentralized, the socialization of agriculture, according to the Soviet Union's experience, will require a long time and much painstaking work. Without the socialization of agriculture there can be no complete and consolidated socialism. And to socialize agriculture we must develop a powerful industry with the state-owned enterprises as its main component.[13]

When and how agricultural production would be collectivized, and the question of the relationship between the industrialization of the cities and the socialization of the countryside, were questions that were to dominate the history of the next decade.

NOTES

1. Karl Marx, "The Eighteenth Brumaire of Louis Bonaparte," in Karl Marx and Frederick Engels, *Selected Works* (Moscow: Foreign Languages Publishing House, 1950), 1:302.

2. Fei Hsiao-t'ung [Fei Xiaotong], *China's Gentry* (Chicago: University of Chicago Press, 1953), p. 119.

3. Liu Shao-ch'i [Liu Shaoqi], "Report on the Agrarian Reform Problem," June 14, 1950. For translated excerpts, see Chao Kuo-chün [Zhao Guojun], *Agrarian Policies of Mainland China: A Documentary Study (1949–1956)* (Cambridge, Mass.: Harvard University Press, 1957), pp. 38–41.

4. *New China's Economic Achievements* (Beijing: Foreign Languages Press, 1952), p. 6.

5. See article 6 of the Agrarian Reform Law, in Chao, *Agrarian Policies,* p. 48.

6. *Ibid.* The Agrarian Reform Law stipulated a limit of 15 percent. It was raised to 25 percent in a governmental directive of August 4, 1950.

7. *Ibid.,* p. 41.

8. *Ibid.,* p. 35.

9. C. K. Yang, *A Chinese Village in Early Communist Transition* (Cambridge, Mass.: MIT Press, 1959), p. 143.

10. *Ibid.,* pp. 143–144.

11. State Statistical Bureau, communiqué, reproduced in *People's China* (Beijing), July 16, 1956.

12. "Report on Agrarian Reform Problem," p. 38.

13. Mao Tse-tung [Mao Zedong], *On People's Democratic Dictatorship* (Beijing: Foreign Languages Press, 1959), p. 14.

8

The Social and Political
Consequences of Industrialization

T HE EARLY HISTORY of the People's Republic is incomprehensible if we read the conservative present of Chinese Communism into its revolutionary past—and thus fail to appreciate how ardently the victors of 1949 were committed to bringing about the socialist goals proclaimed in Marxist theory. For however far Maoist revolutionary practice departed from the premises of Marxism, the leaders of the Chinese Communist Party emerged from their lengthy rural revolutionary experience without having abandoned their vision of a socialist future for China. This vision played a crucial role in determining the policies that the victorious revolutionaries initially pursued. In the first three years of the People's Republic, the Communists wrought more fundamental changes in China's social structure than had occurred over the previous 2,000 years. And at the end of 1952, having decided (perhaps prematurely, as we shall have occasion to suggest), that they had completed the essential "bourgeois" tasks of the revolution, the Communists prepared to move the revolutionary process to a new stage, to what they called "the transition to socialism." If the Communists shared with the Guomindang the eminently nationalist goal of achieving "wealth and power" in the modern world, they differed from their vanquished predecessors in that they viewed the wealth and power of the nation not as the ultimate end but rather as the means to attain Marxian socialist ends. Such, at least, was the case in 1952.

Economic Backwardness and Socialism

If an intellectual commitment to Marxism inspired the effort to bring about a socialist transformation of Chinese society, that same doctrine taught that socialism was impossible under conditions of economic backwardness. Nothing is more central to Marxism than the proposition that socialism presupposes capitalism, that socialism becomes a real historical possibility only on the basis of the material and social accomplishments of modern capitalist production. For Marx (and for Lenin as well) the large-scale capitalist development and organization of modern industry, a high level of specialization in the division of labor based on modern technology, and the collectivistic patterns of social labor thereby produced, are the essential prerequisites for socialism, for only these processes create the necessary conditions of economic abundance on which the future socialist society must inevitably rest. Moreover, there could be no retreat from the course that history dictated. To those who advocated the socialist reorganization of society before capitalism had done its necessary historical work, to those "utopians" who wished to avoid the social evils that capitalist industrialization entailed, Marx once replied that "the country that is more developed industrially only shows, to the less developed, the image of its own future."[1] Indeed, the Marxist predecessors of Mao often warned that a "premature" socialist revolution—one attempted before the full development of capitalist industrialization made the abolition of private property possible—would be historically futile and possibly regressive. Under conditions of economic scarcity, socialism would be what Marx called a "primitive" and "crude" form of "social leveling" that would open the way for more extreme social inequalities and more oppressive kinds of political despotism.

The leaders of the Chinese Communist Party were not unaware of the Marxian-defined material preconditions for socialism, and they were painfully aware that a preindustrial and impoverished China lacked those preconditions. But they confronted a cruel historical paradox. For it was precisely the failure of modern capitalism to develop in China that had permitted socialist revolutionaries to come to power there in the first place, while it was also precisely that failure that denied to revolutionaries in power the material means to realize their socialist goals. Had the bureaucratic capitalism of the Guomindang been successful in establishing a modern industrial economy, as had been the case in Japan and Germany, then the road to revolution would have been closed in China, just as it was closed in other countries that were "latecomers" on the industrial scene and where conservative modernization had proved successful. As it was, the failure of industrialization under conservative regimes had created socioeconomic conditions favorable for revolution under socialist political auspices but left economic conditions that precluded the socialist reorganization of society. The Communists were thus both the beneficiaries and the victims of the retardation of modern capitalist development in China and the consequent heritage of economic backwardness. Possessing state power, they had no alternative but to use that power to pursue a noncapitalist road to socialism.

The Chinese were not the first to face the dilemma. The nineteenth-century Russian Populists had made a socialist virtue out of Russia's economic backwardness by arguing that it was precisely the relative absence of capitalist development that gave Russia special social and moral advantages to allow her to become the pioneer socialist country. Russia could "bypass" the capitalist phase of development and proceed immediately to a socialist restructuring of society on the basis of the precapitalist village commune *(mir)*. By appropriating the modern technology of the advanced industrial nations of the West within a new socialist framework, Russia could avoid the social evils of capitalist industrialization and the moral decadence of bourgeois society. Marx did not dismiss the Populist argument out of hand. He recognized that some of the possible "advantages of backwardness," such as the role of cultural contact, foreign borrowing, and the utilization of traditional communal forms of social life, might telescope the socioeconomic phases of modern historical development.[2] But his ultimate conclusion was that such advantages could be turned to socialist ends only if a revolution in preindustrial Russia coincided with proletarian revolutions in the industrialized countries of Western Europe.[3] In the final analysis, the potentiality for socialism resided in the material and social products which only capitalism had brought into being: modern industry and the modern proletariat.

Marx's conclusion formed the essential theoretical perspectives held by Lenin on the eve of the Bolshevik Revolution of 1917. However much he departed from original Marxism in the realm of revolutionary strategy, for Lenin, the Russian Revolution was to serve as the "spark" that would ignite the long delayed socialist revolutions in Western Europe. Revolution in Russia was not seen as a noncapitalist road to socialism but rather as a political event whose socialist promise was ultimately dependent on the timely intervention of the proletariat of the advanced industrialized countries. But for Lenin, unlike Marx and unlike the Populists, the possibility of bypassing capitalism soon came to be a concrete political question and not merely a theoretical one. When the anticipated socialist revolutions failed to materialize, the Bolsheviks were confronted with the problem of what to do with a successful anti-capitalist revolution in an economically backward and politically isolated country, a problem anticipated neither in the theories of Marx nor of Lenin. While Lenin harbored grave doubts about the historical viability and moral validity of attempting to build a socialist society in conditions of economic and cultural backwardness, his response to the problem generally foreshadowed the "revolution from above" over which Stalin was to preside. Lenin's conclusion, briefly put, was that the survival of Bolshevik political power was dependent on using that power to complete a bourgeois revolution, to carry out in the most rapid fashion possible the yet unfulfilled tasks of capitalist economic development—but under socialist political auspices. Above all, this meant rapid urban industrialization, which in turn presupposed an authoritarian state which would impose its control over the countryside and extract from agricultural production the capital necessary for the industrial development of the cities. Lenin's preoccupation with rapid economic development (which he stressed increasingly after mid-1918) was reinforced by what is often referred to as his "technocratic bias" (epitomized by his striking shorthand formula that "electrification plus Soviets" equals socialism, his slogan "learn from the capitalists," his fascination with the work efficiency and managerial rationality of "Taylorism," and his emphasis on the primacy of heavy industry), as well as by his unqualified praise of the virtues of the centralization of both political and economic life. While the brutalities and irrationalities of Stalinism were in no sense immanent in Leninism, Lenin provided the ideological and policy points of departure for the Stalinist strategy of rapid urban industrialization based on forced rural collectivization. In view of his bitter anti-Populist polemics, it is ironic that Lenin was forced to assume the historical role of the pioneer of a "non-capitalist road to socialism" or, more precisely, a road assumed to have a socialist end. The guiding theoretical premise of postrevolutionary Leninism (and more explicitly of Stalinism) was deceptively simple: the combination of rapid economic development with the existence of socialist state power and the nationalization of the key means of production would more or less automatically guarantee the arrival of a socialist society. And in 1952 the Chinese Communists uncritically accepted this assumption, the ideological rationale for their wholesale adoption of Soviet methods of development and organization.

The First Five Year Plan: Industrialization and the Transition to Socialism

Unlike the Russian Bolsheviks three decades earlier, the Chinese Communists were not haunted by the Marxist dilemmas posed by economic underdevelopment, for the Soviet historical experience had demonstrated to their satisfaction that it was possible to employ the power of a socialist state to industrialize a backward country. Yet if the Chinese could derive psychological and ideological comfort from the Russian experience, there was nothing comforting in the objective economic problems they faced. Even at its peak pre-1949 levels, the modern industrial sector of the Chinese economy was less than half the size of its backward czarist Russian counterpart; and the population of China was fourfold that of Russia. Even this comparison tends to obscure the extent of China's underdevelopment. China's modern industrial base was not only tiny but one built largely under foreign imperialist auspices, and thus far more dependent on external economic relations than had been the case in Russia. Moreover, agricultural technology was even more primitive than it had been in prerevolutionary Russia. And China suffered from a higher rate of illiteracy and a lower level of education, especially in modern science and technology.

Despite the revival of a war-wrecked economy, at the end of 1952, when the government announced the First Five Year Plan, total industrial and agricultural production was still barely higher than the levels attained in the mid-1930s. At a comparable time in Russian postrevolutionary history, when Stalin launched the Soviet Union's First Five Year Plan in 1927, per capita industrial output in Russia was more than four times greater than China's in 1952. Per capita agricultural output in China in 1952 was only about 20 percent of what it had been in the Soviet Union twenty-five years earlier, thus offering a far smaller potential for extracting capital from the rural sector for urban industrialization. Moreover, modern transportation facilities were much less developed.

China thus began its drive for modern industrial development in economic circumstances far less favorable than those from which Soviet industrialization had proceeded. If Russia lacked the Marxian-defined material prerequisites for socialism, this was infinitely more the case in China. Yet the very absence of the objective conditions for socialism served to stimulate efforts to bring those very conditions into being; if China was even more backward than Russia, it was the very consciousness of that backwardness that gave the Chinese Communists an even greater determination to overcome it. Just as Chinese Marxist revolutionaries did not wait

passively on the historical sidelines for capitalism to lay the material and social basis for revolution, Chinese Marxists in power were not disposed to
rely on a "natural" process of economic development to bring about a socialist society or its material prerequisites. The socialist reordering of society and the building of the economic preconditions for it had to be
accomplished by utilizing the political and human resources on hand—and
both had to be done simultaneously, and in the here and now. The beginning of the First Five Year Plan for industrialization in January, 1953 was
thus accompanied by announcements that the bourgeois-democratic phase
of the revolution was passing and that its socialist phase was beginning. On
October 1, 1953, the fourth anniversary of the founding of the People's Republic, the government proclaimed "the general line for the transition to
socialism."

Despite the prominence of the theory of New Democracy in formal
Maoist theory for more than a decade, and its seeming promise of a lengthy
stage of capitalist (or at least semi-capitalist) development, the bourgeois
phase of China's postrevolutionary history was abruptly terminated after a
scant four years. No doubt in good measure responsible for the hasty
prouncement of the "transition to socialism" was Mao Zedong's long-
standing populist-type hostility to all forms of capitalism and his persistent
refusal to intellectually accept the Marxist thesis that socialism presupposes
capitalism.

The Chinese Communists viewed the problem of building a socialist society in an economically backward land as an enormous practical task, but
not as an agonizing Marxist theoretical question, perhaps partly because
they had never been intellectually burdened by orthodox Marxist perspectives on the relationship between political and economic forces in history.
Nevertheless they did not believe that socialism could be built amidst conditions of poverty. The proposition that socialism demanded (even if it did
not necessarily presuppose) industrialization was constantly emphasized in
Chinese Marxist writings and no one emphasized it more strongly than did
Mao Zedong. The development of "a powerful industry with the state-
owned enterprises as its main component" was the prerequisite to the collectivization of agriculture whereas the latter was the prerequisite for a
"complete and consolidated socialism,"[4] Mao insisted at the time.

In 1953 the order of the day was industrialization and the First Five Year
Plan was essentially a plan for the development of heavy industry. To be
sure, at the same time the Communists launched the Five Year Plan they
also announced the beginning of China's transition to socialism. But the
emphasis was less on the transformation of social relations than it was on
modern economic development. "Socialism" at the time meant the more or

less gradual abolition of private property. In the cities this resulted in the nationalization of most of the remaining private sector of the urban economy between 1953 and 1956. In the countryside, it was limited to the gradual introduction of cooperative forms of farming in a rural economy based on individual peasant proprietorship. It was not until late 1955, with the launching of a campaign for rapid collectivization, that rural social relationships were suddenly and dramatically transformed in a socialist direction. But the essence of the Five Year Plan, at least through 1955, was an intensive drive for rapid urban industrialization that aimed to establish the economic foundations for socialism. It was a drive based on the wholesale adoption of Stalinist methods, techniques, and ideological assumptions.

In retrospect it seems strange that the Chinese should have so uncritically accepted the Soviet model of development. Mao, after all, long had warned against the dangers of applying foreign techniques to Chinese conditions. "China has suffered a great deal from the mechanical absorption of foreign material," he wrote in 1940.[5] The Chinese revolution itself was massive historical proof of the Maoist determination to domesticate Western theories and adapt foreign-derived formulae to the concrete needs of the Chinese historical environment. The Chinese Communists, after all, had come to power on their own and by forging their own revolutionary strategy, by rejecting Russian domination, and Mao Zedong had come to power in the CCP in direct defiance of Stalin. Yet however much the Chinese distrusted Stalin's revolutionary advice, they apparently had few reservations about his strategy for postrevolutionary development. The Soviet Union provided the only historical model for industrializing an economically backward country under socialist political auspices. Nor were there any doubts at the time about whether Stalinist means of economic development had led to the desired social ends. The question of whether the Soviet Union was a socialist society or not was never debated; it was simply assumed to be the case. Although the Chinese knew little about the nature of Soviet society other than what they had read in official Soviet textbooks, it was an article of faith that Russia was "the land of socialism," as Mao had put it in 1940, and "a great and splendid socialist state," as he proclaimed in 1949.[6] And although Mao consistently had been critical of "the mechanical absorption of foreign material," he was remarkably uncritical in accepting the Soviet model of development as appropriate for China. If anyone harbored doubts about these views, they did not, and dared not, express them.

Quite apart from the general faith in the Soviet Union as "the land of socialism," there were other more immediate and practical reasons why the Chinese looked to Russia. For one thing, the Chinese leaders saw Russian economic and technological aid as essential for their industrialization program. China hardly could expect such aid from the capitalist countries, especially not in the cold war years, and assistance provided by a presumably socialist country was seen as more desirable in any event. Russian economic aid and technicians began flowing to China with the signing of the Sino-Soviet Treaty of Friendship, Alliance, and Mutual Aid in February 1950, following the first of Mao's two pilgrimages to Moscow. Among other provisions, the Russians agreed to provide China with fifty model industrial units. Russian factories manned by Russian economic specialists demanded the adoption of Soviet methods of economic and managerial organization. With the launching of the First Five Year Plan, Russian economic aid, and perhaps more importantly, access to Russian technology and experience in central planning, became more essential than before. New Sino-Soviet agreements in 1953, 1954, and 1956 attempted to meet these needs. Although Soviet assistance was to prove much more limited than the Chinese had hoped for, and was to have far greater political implications than anticipated, it nevertheless was a highly significant factor in the early industrial development of the People's Republic.

The adoption of the Soviet model of economic development was also closely related to Chinese national security concerns. Long before the victory of 1949, Mao had proclaimed the inevitability of China "leaning to one side" in international affairs. As he put the matter in 1940, "unless there is the policy of alliance with Russia, with the land of socialism, there will inevitably be a policy of alliance with imperialism. . . ."[7] However much the Maoists had come to politically distrust the Russians during the revolutionary years, there was never any question as to which side a Communist-governed China would lean. The need for a political alliance with the Soviet Union in a hostile international arena was powerfully reinforced by American support of Chiang Kai-shek during the civil war and even more by United States intervention in Korea and Taiwan. And the political tie served to reinforce an already strong predisposition to emulate the Soviet model of economic development.

At the beginning Mao Zedong took the lead in advocating the Russian way. "The Communist Party of the Soviet Union is our best teacher and we must learn from it," he proclaimed on the eve of the establishment of the People's Republic.[8] Just as Lenin had advocated "Learn from the capitalists," the Maoist slogan during the early years of the People's Republic was "Learn from the Soviet Union," although Maoists then believed that they were emulating a model of a socialist society as well as learning the technology necessary for modern economic development. The popular rallying cry of the time was "Let's be modern and Soviet."

In the formative years of his intellectual development, during the New Culture era of 1915–1919, Mao had been a follower of the New Youth intellectuals who believed that the panacea for China was learning the principles of "science" and "democracy" from the advanced capitalist countries of the West. Now the Chinese Communists no less uncritically and no less enthusiastically looked to Russia to teach them modern science and modern socialism. Maoists soon were to become disillusioned with their Soviet model, just as the youthful Mao and his intellectual mentors had become disillusioned with their Western bourgeois models almost four decades earlier.

Economic Results of the First Five Year Plan (1953–1957)

The First Five Year Plan began in January 1953 on the orthodox Marxist assumption that socialism presupposed a high level of industrial development and that industrialization could best be accomplished in an economically backward land under the centralized direction of a strong socialist state. Further assumed, in good Leninist and Stalinist fashion, was that the socialist transformation of social relations, or what Maoists called "proletarianization," would follow more or less naturally in the wake of industrialization. Chinese leaders also accepted the Marxist, and the general Western, assumption that industrialization demanded urbanization. Much of the history of the People's Republic would revolve around disputes over these issues. But in 1953 these were the universally accepted premises with which China began its search for "wealth and power"—and for socialism.

The details of the First Five Year Plan were not publicly revealed until mid-1955—precisely at the time, paradoxically, when Maoists began to question its theoretical premises—but its general outline was determined at a meeting of the Party's Central Committee in the autumn of 1952.[9] The Chinese plan was closely patterned on the Soviet First Five Year Plan of 1928–1932 and it was anticipated that China could achieve similar rates of growth in industrial output and employment.[10] While it was expected that industrialization would proceed rapidly, the Chinese leaders at the time held long-term perspectives on the transition to socialism; Mao predicted it would require three five year plans to lay minimally necessary economic foundations for a socialist society, and the remainder of the century "to build a powerful country with a high degree of socialist industrialization."[11]

The State Planning Commission was established in 1952 to determine production targets and quotas and how they were to be accomplished. Over the following years it was supplemented by a variety of more specialized central-government economic ministries and organs of planning and control. The Chinese plan emphasized to an even greater degree than had been the case in the Soviet Union the development of such heavy industries as steel, machine building, fuel, electric power, metallurgy, and basic chemicals. Only 11.2 percent of state capital investment in industry was to go to light industry (consumer production) while 88.8 percent went to heavy industry.[12] The priority was justified because of the structural imbalance of the imperialist-dominated modern sector of the pre-1949 economy, where industrial backwardness in general was aggravated by the dominance of processing industries dependent on imported raw materials.[13] It was assumed that the establishment of a heavy industrial base was the prerequisite for both the development of consumer industries and the technological modernization of agriculture. State investment in the rural sector was negligible.[14]

While the remaining privately owned urban enterprises were nationalized between 1953 and 1956, the socialization of agriculture was seen as a long-term process dependent on the prior socialist industrialization of the cities. According to Li Fuchun: "For the laboring peasants . . . to give up finally the way of the individual small producer . . . calls for a step-by-step process [and] a fairly long period of hard work. . . ."[15]

While intensive efforts were made to develop the heavy industrial base established by the Japanese in Manchuria, the government emphasized the need "to build up new industrial bases [as opposed to the large treaty-port cities like Shanghai and Guangzhou] in North, Northwest and Central China, and make a start with a part of our industrial construction in Southwest China." Of the 694 major industrial enterprises to be built during the 5-year period, 472 were to be located in the interior. The purpose was to correct the geographical imbalance left by the imperialist heritage, and to build new industries closer to sources of raw materials and to areas of consumption and distribution.[16]

The 156 industrial units that the Russians had agreed to supply were regarded by the Chinese planners as "the core of the industrial construction programme" and the economic models for the whole First Five Year Plan.[17] Mao and other Chinese Communist leaders were as effusive in their praise of Soviet generosity as they later were to be bitter in their condemnations of Russian perfidy. At the time, the "fraternal assistance of the Soviet Union" was typically described as "an expression of the noblest and loftiest spirit of internationalism."[18]

In actuality, Russian financial aid was very limited, accounting for only 3 percent of total Chinese state investment for economic development during the period of the First Five Year Plan. And the Russians paid for less than one-third of the cost of even the original 156 industrial units.[19] More significant than Soviet financial assistance was access to their technology and experience in centralized economic planning. The Russians supplied the equipment necessary for the rapid installation of model factories and the personnel (and training of Chinese personnel) necessary for their operation. In addition, the Soviets provided detailed blueprints and technological information for the establishment of a wide variety of other industrial plants and construction projects. Over 12,000 Russian and East European engineers and technicians were sent to China in the 1950s while over 6,000 Chinese students were trained in modern science and technology in Russian universities and some 7,000 Chinese workers were sent to the Soviet Union to acquire experience in modern factories. Thus the Chinese were not wholly dependent on their own meager technological resources. Nevertheless, during the First Five Year Plan "97 percent of the investment for basic development came from the Chinese people themselves."[20]

Between 1952 and 1957 Chinese industry grew at an even more rapid pace than the ambitious 14.7 percent yearly increase set in the Plan.[21] The actual per annum increase was 18 percent, according to official statistics, and 16 percent according to more conservative Western estimates.[22] Total Chinese industrial output more than doubled, and growth rates in key heavy industries were even greater. Rolled steel production, for example, increased from 1.31 million metric tons in 1952 to 4.48 million in 1957; cement from 2.86 million to 6.86 million; pig iron from 1.9 million to 5.9 million; coal from 66 million to 130 million; and electric power from 7.26 billion kilowatt hours to 19.34 billion.[23] In addition, China was now for the first time producing small but significant numbers of trucks, tractors, jet planes, and merchant ships. In all, the Chinese had proved to be excellent students of the Soviet model, for Chinese industrial production between 1952 and 1957 grew more rapidly than Russian industry during the first Soviet Five Year Plan of 1928–1932.[24]

At the same time, of course, urban industrial employment increased substantially, from approximately 6,000,000 workers (including construction workers) in 1952 to an industrial working class of about 10,000,000 in 1957.[25] And China's urban population rose from 70,000,000 to almost 100,000,000 in the 5-year period, with the most rapid growth taking place in the newly industrializing inland cities of the North and the Northwest. In 1957 there were 13 cities with populations of over 1,000,000 as compared to only 5 in 1949.

The First Five Year Plan provided China with a significant and stable modern industrial base, even though it was still a tiny one compared with the advanced industrial countries. But this success was not achieved without social and economic costs, and the major costs were borne by China's 500,000,000 peasants—for the industrialization of the cities was based largely on the exploitation of the countryside. While the cities were rapidly industrializing, agricultural production was stagnating. According to probably inflated official statistics, the output of food grains between 1952 and 1957 increased at an annual rate of 3.7 percent; according to foreign estimates, the increase was more on the order of 2.7 percent, hardly keeping pace with the 2.2 percent average annual population growth. Nevertheless, the capital for urban industrialization was extracted primarily from the countryside by means of a relatively high state grain tax and high quotas of grain which peasants were forced to sell to government stores at low state-fixed prices. The industrialization of the 1950s was a remarkable economic accomplishment by any standard of judgment, but like all economic advances in history it was based on the exploitation of one part of society by the other. Nor did industrialization resolve the chronic problems of urban unemployment and underemployment, problems that were aggravated by the spontaneous migration of millions of peasants from the depressed rural areas to the developing cities.

As much as anyone, it was Mao Zedong who launched the program for rapid urban industrialization. But there was little distinctively "Maoist" about the way in which the process took place. For "Maoism" as a distinctive strategy of socioeconomic development had yet to present itself—and it was to do so only in response to the social and political consequences of Soviet-style industrialization.

Political Results of the First Five Year Plan

The decision to adopt the Soviet model of industrialization necessitated Soviet-type forms of political organization and state administration. Centralized economic planning demanded the bureaucratization and routinization of state and society. The Maoist preference for administrative simplicity gave way to complex and increasingly specialized structures; the cadres of a revolutionary party were transformed into administrators and bureaucratic functionaries; workers in factories were subjected to increasing control by factory managers; the revolutionary ideal of the "guerrilla" generalist was replaced by a new-found faith in the virtues of specialization and the technological specialist; old egalitarian ideals clashed with a new hierarchy of ranks and new patterns of social inequality; the revolutionary faith in the initiative of the masses faded as industrialization demanded authoritarian discipline, social stability, and economic rationality; socialist goals were postponed and partly ritualized in favor of the immediate and all-embracing goal of economic development. The tendency for revolutionaries to become bureaucratic rulers began in 1949, but it was now vastly accelerated. The whole character of political and social life was increasingly determined by the economic targets of the Plan. It was an eminently Stalinist development, albeit without the irrationalities and brutalities of a Stalin to preside over the process.

Bureaucratization was most apparent in the expansion and centralization of the formal state apparatus, particularly in the proliferation of government agencies responsible for the development and control of the modern sector of the economy. The State Planning Commission, similar in organization and function to Stalin's Gosplan, was established in November 1952 to direct the industrialization process. It was originally headed by Gao Gang, the political and economic czar of Manchuria, where Soviet influence was strongest and Soviet political and economic methods most firmly entrenched. Bureaucratic centralization was formalized in 1954 with the creation of the State Council, the main organ of the central government and the successor to the Government Administrative Council; its power, and thus state power in general, lay in its standing committee, whose membership was almost identical with the Politburo of the Party. The State Council generated and directed an enormous number of specialized organs dealing with economic life, a variety of temporary and permanent committees (such as those dealing with Capital Construction, State Economics, State Planning, and Science and Technology), and a multitude of centralized economic ministries. Among the latter, the largest number and the most powerful were concerned with the development of heavy industry; there were, for example, six separate ministries dealing with machine building alone.

Another political result of the Plan was the centralization and expansion in 1954 of the Ministry of State Control, a vast and pervasive bureaucratic apparatus to check inefficiencies and corruption in the industrial sector of the economy and to counter local deviations from state economic directives and quotas. Modeled on its Soviet counterpart and the Soviet system of external economic control, it worked closely with secret-police agencies, and, as had been the case in the Soviet Union, the power of the secret police grew with the power of the Ministry of State Control. But the secret-police forces in China, now centralized under the Ministry of Public Security headed by Luo Ruiqing, never were to acquire a fraction of the terrible power they had in Stalinist Russia. However, the general political structure that began to emerge in China in the mid-1950s increasingly re-

sembled the Soviet state structure of centralized "vertical" forms of bureaucratic rule, just as the Chinese First Five Year Plan resembled the Russian one.

As the formal state bureaucracy grew in size and power, the political and
ideological authority of the CCP was diluted and its functions underwent
subtle changes. In industrial enterprises this tendency was most apparent in
the Chinese adoption of the Soviet system of "one-man management," although (except in Manchuria) the system was introduced in a less extreme
form with less enthusiasm. The rapid development and efficient operation
of large-scale industry demanded a highly specialized system of the division
of labor and responsibility based on the criterion of technological expertise.
Crucial to meeting this need was the skilled factory manager who had clearly
defined lines of responsibility and authority, a man who was responsible for
carrying out directives of the central government from above and with the
power to implement those directives below in the factory over which he had
sole authority. Reflecting the Soviet temper of the times, the need for what
was termed "the system of sole responsibility of management" was justified
by Lenin's dictum: "Any large-scale industry—which is the material source
and foundation of production in socialism—unconditionally must have a
rigorous unified will to direct the collective work of hundreds, thousands,
and even millions of men. But how can the rigorous unity of wills be assured? Only by the wills of the thousands and millions submitting to the will
of a single individual."[26] The introduction of a Soviet-type managerial system was a logical result of the First Five Year Plan and was well in tune with
the general bureaucratization of state and society, for "one-man management" firmly established a chain of command from the central government
in Beijing down to the lowest levels of the individual enterprise.

The system had important consequences for both the role of the Party
organizations in the factories and for the workers who labored in them. As
Franz Schurmann observed:

> In the early 1950s the Chinese, emulating the Soviet experiences, sought to place
> great power in the hands of the managers. The Party's role was to be limited to
> that of moral leadership. The commands that counted came from high echelons
> in the administrative system. Management commanded and the worker had to
> obey. . . . The factory, under one-man management, was conceived of as a coldly
> rational arrangement of individual workers commanded by an authoritarian
> manager.[27]

The professional industrial managers were drawn largely from the pre-1949
technological intelligentsia, for few Party members possessed the necessary

economic expertise. And those Party members who had or acquired such expertise served as economic managers first and as political leaders second. The factory manager was primarily responsible to the economic demands of central government ministries, and increasingly less to the political demands of the factory Party organization. Nor were local Party officials and cadres able to challenge the authority of the manager, for they themselves were responsible to the directives of higher-level Party organs and ultimately to the same Party leaders who controlled the state and determined its economic policies. Although it constantly was repeated that managers were to be under "the ideological leadership of the Party," the significance of this injunction was problematic; it was the Party, after all, which had given the managers their authority in the first place and the operational ideology of the Party at the time was centered on fulfilling the economic targets of the Five Year Plan.

For the workers, the industrialization drive meant subjection to increasingly strict codes of labor discipline. It also meant increasing wage and status differentials within their ranks. The more skilled workers were put in charge of factory work teams or became foremen exercising authority over former fellow workers. In wage policy there was a growing emphasis on material incentives, with monetary rewards for skill, expertise, and productivity, a policy that culminated in the "wage reform" of 1956, formalizing wide wage differentials based on the criteria of skill and output. Before the First Five Year Plan trade unions had acquired some degree of independence as representatives of the interests of the workers, but by the mid-1950s the unions had become instruments of state policy designed to raise workers' productivity.

The political role of the urban workers was of course ambiguous from the beginning, as was necessarily the case in a society born from a rural revolution in which workers had played little part. As industrialization proceeded and as the proletariat consequently grew in size and in socioeconomic importance in the mid-1950s, the question of the relationship of the proletariat to state and society became even more ambiguous. For while the workers benefited economically and materially from industrialization, the manner in which industrialization was carried out left Chinese workers with little more to say about the operation of the factories in which they worked than workers in capitalist countries. The authoritarian managerial system negated any hope of moving toward the socialist principle of workers' control of industry while the general bureaucratization of political life further removed the working class from the centers of political power—from a state which, in theory, they "led," and from a Communist Party which was theoretically the party of the proletariat.

The social composition of the Party, and its patterns of recruitment, are revealing in this respect, even if such statistics do not reveal much about where the real levers of political power lay and who controlled them. In 1949 Communist leaders emphasized the need to build an urban proletarian base for a party then composed almost entirely of peasants, but the results of the effort to make the "party of the proletariat" a real proletarian party met with mixed success at best. In 1957, at the end of the First Five Year Plan, those officially classified as workers made up less than 13 percent of Party membership. Workers were outnumbered by intellectuals and the latter were being recruited at a much more rapid rate. Since the beginning of 1949 Party membership had increased fourfold, from a little over 3,000,000 to 12,700,000, but most of the new members came from the countryside.[28] Moreover, the emphasis in urban recruitment during the mid-1950s was on strengthening the upper levels of the Party by drawing in those who already occupied positions of socioeconomic importance; intellectuals and technicians were favored over workers, and skilled workers were given preference over the non-skilled.

More important than the social composition of the Chinese Communist Party was its transformation into a bureaucratic organization and the erosion of its revolutionary spirit, tendencies particularly reflected in the changing nature and function of Party cadres in the 1950s. The term "cadre" *(ganbu),* narrowly defined, means someone who occupies a leadership position in an organization; for all practical purposes, it refers to a Communist Party member who is a leader in a Party organ or in a Party-dominated institution or mass organization. During the revolutionary years, the concept of the cadre acquired a far broader meaning as a revolutionary leader. Ideally, the cadre is a selfless person imbued with the proper revolutionary values and committed to the achievement of revolutionary goals, a person of "all-round" ability able to perform a variety of tasks and capable of quickly adapting to changing situations and requirements, one who is both "red and expert" but first and foremost politically and ideologically "red" and potentially "expert," a person who faithfully carries out Party policy yet does so with independence and initiative, a person who submits to the discipline of the Party organization but at the same time is intimately tied to the masses; as Mao formulated it, the cadre is both "the teacher and the pupil of the masses," and indeed must be their pupil before he can become their teacher. The ideal cadre is the very antithesis of the bureaucrat who "dozes at his desk" or the official who commands from behind his desk. The Communist revolution owed its success in large measure to the fact that there were indeed many such Party cadres who more or less measured up to this Maoist ideal of revolutionary leadership. They were people committed to the goals and ideals of revolution, not to a vocation or a career.

It was inevitable that the reality, if not the ideal, of the cadre would change after 1949 when revolutionaries became rulers. Cadres filling posts in the new state apparatus had to undertake more specific functions in political and economic administration and were required to learn specialized skills. Once leaders of the masses in a revolutionary situation, Party cadres were becoming state administrators governing the masses—and often doing so from office desks, which further separated a new governing elite from the governed masses. Before 1949 the Party attracted and recruited revolutionaries; after 1949 it increasingly attracted people who saw Party membership as the avenue for a career in government. Moreover, increasing numbers of non-Party people with experience and expertise in administration and economic affairs became cadres after 1949 to run the expanding bureaucracy—and were later recruited into the Party less because of political commitment than because they now occupied leadership positions in the new postrevolutionary order.

During the First Five Year Plan "old revolutionaries," who clung to the simple values and heroic ideals of the revolutionary era, were increasingly overshadowed by the "new cadres," who were more motivated by vocational ethics and the values associated with industrialization. Conflicts and tensions between the "old" and "new" cadres intensified as industrialization proceeded and as the technician and engineer replaced the revolutionary as the new social model. From the "old revolutionaries" there came complaints that the bureaucratization of political and economic life was a repudiation of the revolutionary heritage and a betrayal of socialist ideals. From official quarters came criticisms of the "village habits" and the "guerrilla mentality" of old cadres unable to adapt to the rational division of labor and responsibilities which the new industrial order demanded. The old cadres had come from a revolutionary milieu and were the carriers of the values of a spartan and egalitarian style of life and work. In the early years of the People's Republic they had been treated in a relatively egalitarian fashion, the government providing housing, food, and a small monetary allowance for the basic necessities of life. By 1955, however, cadres were divided into 26 distinct ranks with corresponding salaries ranging from 30 to 560 *yuan* ($12–$224) per month; and in the cities, at least, rank assignments largely were determined by the importance of the cadre in the industrialization process. The new inequality was defended in official theory by the argument that China was not a communist society but only in transition to socialism, a situation which demanded that people be paid according to their contribution and not according to their needs. Old revolutionary cadres who had not reconciled themselves to the new order of things were accused of the ideological heresies of "absolute egalitarianism" and "equality mongering."

The bureaucratization of the Party and its cadres was a development that fitted well the general temper of the times, a temper molded by the all-embracing drive for modern industrialization, and one characterized by a faith in the powers of modern science and technological specialization. "Rationalize," "systematize," and "regularize" were the slogans of the day and they reflected, as Vogel has observed, "a radical departure from the 'guerrilla mentality,'"[29] in effect, an implicit repudiation of the Maoist revolutionary heritage. In the process, the goals proclaimed in Marxist theory tended to become ritualized. While socialist and communist goals were still ardently proclaimed, and no doubt believed, the really operative goal was rapid industrial development, and the actual governing values were those most conducive to industrialization—the values of economic rationality and administrative efficiency.

The Gao Gang Case

While Chinese leaders saw Soviet economic methods as both necessary and desirable, they were not about to allow the Russians to acquire political dominance over China in the process. They had fought too long to prevent Moscow from gaining control of their Party during the revolutionary years to permit the Soviets to reap the political fruits of their victory. It was that fear which lay behind the first major CCP purge in the history of the People's Republic—and one that was to be a prophetic pointer to the future history of Sino-Soviet relations. The principal victim of the 1953–1954 purge was Gao Gang, the head of the Party and state apparatus in Manchuria, and the main issue involved, although unstated at the time, was Russian political influence in Manchuria.

During the revolutionary years, Gao Gang had acquired seemingly impeccable Maoist political credentials. A leader of peasant guerrilla forces in Northwest China in the early 1930s, Gao was one of the founders of the Communist base area in Shaanxi where Mao brought the survivors of the Long March at the end of 1935. During the war years he worked closely with Mao in consolidating control over the Party and was the head of its Northwest China Bureau in Yan'an. After the defeat of the Japanese in 1945, and the subsequent renewal of civil war with the Guomindang, Gao was dispatched with Lin Biao's army to Manchuria, where he came to head the Party and state apparatus of the Northeast. He was also a member of the Politburo, chief of its secretariat, and in 1952 was appointed Chairman of the new State Planning Commission, and thus the man principally responsible for carrying out the First Five Year Plan.

The political downfall of Gao Gang, and the expulsion of his followers from the Party, was determined at a December 1953 Politburo meeting and formalized by the Party's Central Committee in February of 1954. Gao was charged with having set up an "independent kingdom" in Manchuria (independent, that is, of the government in Beijing) and having organized a conspiracy to seize state power. Allegedly, he conveniently responded to the accusations by committing suicide. It is a reflection of the secretiveness that enshrouds political decisions in the People's Republic that the purge was not revealed to the Chinese people until more than a year later, in March 1955.

What was not publicly mentioned at all was the fear of Soviet political penetration that Gao's "independent kingdom" in Manchuria symbolized. While there is little evidence to substantiate the vague charges of any nationwide conspiracy to seize power, there is much to suggest that Gao had close political ties with the Russians, who continued to exercise strong influence in Manchuria long after their postwar military occupation of the region had ended. Soviet aid had restored the heavy industrial base of Manchuria after Soviet troops had carried away much of Manchurian industry as "war booty" during the occupation period. The Russians controlled the joint Sino-Soviet stock companies, established in 1950, and retained their hold on the Chinese Eastern Railroad (and its economic subsidiaries) as well as Dairen and Port Arthur. These were not returned to Chinese control until 1955, after the death of Stalin and the removal of Gao Gang. While Gao Gang reigned in Manchuria, however, Soviet economic and political influence also was dominant. Gao reportedly went on a mission to Moscow as early as 1945.[30] He did so again in July of 1949, when in his capacity as head of the People's Government of the Northeast (Manchuria), he negotiated an economic agreement with the Soviet Union, several months before the formal establishment of the People's Republic in Beijing and before Mao's negotiations with Stalin in February 1950. Moreover, Gao was the foremost advocate of Soviet methods of industrial organization, and nowhere were these methods introduced and pursued more rigorously than in Manchuria, China's major center of heavy industry.

The Gao Gang affair was partly a case of what it was presented to be— a case of a region acquiring an intolerable degree of autonomy from the central government. But Gao's "independent kingdom" in Manchuria was intimately tied to Soviet predominance in an area which historically had been a key object of Russian expansionism in East Asia. To bring Manchuria under the control of Beijing meant throwing off Russian control. It is not entirely fortuitous that the fall of Gao Gang followed shortly after the death of Stalin; it was the apparent weakness of the post-Stalin Soviet leadership that made Beijing sufficiently confident to remove Gao and move against Soviet influence in Manchuria. The move resulted in a temporary improvement in Sino-Soviet relations, and a more equal relationship between the two countries, symbolized by Khrushchev's late 1954 visit to Beijing and the Russian agreement to relinquish their positions in Manchuria.

While the fall of Gao Gang is one of the more opaque episodes in the political history of the People's Republic, there is no doubt that Mao regarded the former czar of Manchuria as Stalin's foremost representative in China. Several years after the event, in a private talk highly critical of Soviet influences in the Chinese Party over the decades, Mao observed: "Stalin was very fond of Gao Gang and made him a special present of a motor car. Gao Gang sent Stalin a congratulatory telegram every 15 August." (August 15, 1945 was the date of the Japanese surrender to the Soviet Union.) And Mao referred to Manchuria and Xinjiang as two former Soviet "colonies" in the People's Republic.[31]

The purge of Gao Gang was accompanied by the purge of Rao Shushi, who controlled the Party and state apparatus in the Shanghai region (East China Central Bureau). Rao also was the head of the Organization Department (Orgburo) of the Party Central Committee and one of the original members of the State Planning Commission. Like Gao, he was accused of running an "independent kingdom," and was charged with being allied with Gao in a conspiracy to seize state power. There is nothing to indicate that Rao Shushi had any Soviet ties or any special pro-Soviet proclivities. What he and Gao had in common was that they controlled the two major industrial centers of China, Manchuria and Shanghai. Why the two were linked in what later became denounced as the "Gao-Rao anti-Party conspiracy" remains obscure, as does the nature of the alleged conspiracy itself.

The Sufan Campaign

The March 1955 Party conference also launched a more general and extensive bureaucratic purge, the *Sufan* movement, or the "Campaign to Wipe Out Hidden Counterrevolutionaries," which continued through the early months of 1956. In the wake of the Gao Gang incident, "hidden" acquired an ominous significance; if leaders so high and powerful as Gao Gang and Rao Shushi could turn out to be counterrevolutionary conspirators, then no one was above suspicion. Unlike the 1951 campaign against counterrevolutionaries, *Sufan* was primarily an internal Party affair marked by constant references to reactionaries "cloaked as Marxist-Leninists." Any Party cadre under suspicion was detained, interrogated, and in the manner of past "rectification" campaigns, required to make written or oral "confessions" detailing past and present political views and associations. An atmosphere of fear pervaded the bureaucracy during the latter half of 1955 as some 150,000 Party and government cadres were investigated. Many tens of thousands who were deemed to hold "wrong attitudes" and labeled as "counterrevolutionaries," were sent to "labor reeducation" camps, usually by administrative decrees which bypassed regular criminal procedures. Most were released and reinstated by mid-1956, often with official apologies for having been falsely accused.

The *Sufan* campaign was undertaken, in part, to eliminate the suspected followers of Gao Gang and Rao Shushi. More significantly, it was an attempt to reestablish centralized Party control over the economic and political bureaucracies which the First Five Year Plan had spawned. The power of the State Planning Commission, dominated by pro-Soviet professionals, was drastically reduced, as was the power of managers in industrial enterprises. Closer Party supervision was established over the various economic control agencies and especially over the Ministry of State Control. The reassertion of Party power over the latter was perhaps the most important development over the long run. While *Sufan* resembled a Stalinist bureaucratic purge in many respects, it differed significantly in that it served to reduce rather than enhance the hitherto growing power and independence of the secret police. As it later was officially interpreted: "The first task of the [*Sufan*] movement was to strengthen the leadership of the Party over public-security work, to put public-security agencies under Party leadership."[32]

The *Sufan* campaign, however extensive, was a rather feeble response to the endemic problem of bureaucracy in a presumably socialist society, for it contributed nothing to the only socialist remedy for the problem—popular control over bureaucratic organs of rule. The evils of bureaucracy, which Mao had so long denounced, remained and grew—and nowhere more than within the Party that Mao headed.

The growing power of Party bureaucrats was dramatically revealed when the *Sufan* movement came down particularly hard on intellectuals in 1955, a development foreshadowed by an extraordinary political-ideological campaign against the Marxist literary critic Hu Feng. A follower of the celebrated Lu Xun, Hu Feng long had been an outspoken critic of official Party literary policies and Party dictates to writers and artists. One of the most prominent nonconformists within the left-wing literary movement, his debates with orthodox Communist literary figures extended back to the mid-1930s. After the establishment of the People's Republic, Hu Feng, committed to Marxist socialist aims and generally supporting Party policies, nevertheless continued to oppose the political stifling of artistic and intellectual creativity and warned of an approaching "cultural desert." He continued to be assailed, as he had been since the late 1930s, for his "subjectivism" and his "bourgeois" deviations from Maoist principles of art and literature. His main protagonist in the earlier debates, Zhou Yang, was now firmly entrenched as the Party's czar on literary and cultural matters.

Although Hu Feng found it difficult to get his writings published after 1949, and while many of his followers were the victims of the thought reform movement of 1951 and the ensuing "literary remolding" campaign, Hu was still treated as a revolutionary writer whose ideological errors were amenable to proper Maoist therapy. Indeed, in a brief era of relative freedom for intellectuals in 1953, Hu was appointed to the executive board of the Chinese Writers' Union. Optimistically seeing the promise of a new birth of freedom, he wrote a report to the Central Committee of the Party in July 1954 criticizing the restrictions imposed by Party literary bureaucrats and appealing for the freedom of writers and artists to express their creative talents. Open discussion of the report soon gave way by the end of the year to a nationwide campaign of vilification against Hu Feng as an archetypal representative of bourgeois ideology. The attack was first led by Hu's old adversary Zhou Yang, but the full weight of the Party was thrown against him when Zhou Enlai joined in the public denunciations. As the *Sufan* movement got under way in the spring of 1955, Hu Feng was portrayed not only as an ideological heretic but as a political subversive as well—an agent of the Guomindang and of imperialism, it was said. In July he was arrested and imprisoned as a "counterrevolutionary."

The campaign against "Hu Fengism" continued after Hu was removed from the scene, for its real purpose was to establish strict ideological controls over the intelligentsia in general. The campaign served both to silence intellectual dissent and to create deep resentments against the Party among intellectuals.

Social Consequences

Since Chinese industrialization proceeded largely on the basis of Soviet methods, it is hardly surprising that it should have produced similar social tendencies. The most significant social result of the First Five Year Plan was the emergence of new patterns of inequality.

The imperatives of rapid industrial development, or at least the imperatives of the manner in which it was pursued, gave rise to two new bureaucratic elites (albeit still embryonic ones) exercising increasingly formal control on the basis of their respective spheres of expertise. One was a political elite of Communist leaders and cadres rapidly becoming administrators and functionaries in the growing state apparatus that presided over the industrialization process; the second was a technological elite of engineers, scientists, and managers responsible for the operation of the expanding modern economic sector. These newly emerging social groups tended to become increasingly motivated by professional and vocational ethics, rather than by Marxist goals and communist values, and increasingly separated from the masses of workers and peasants by virtue of status, power, and material benefits.[33]

For the workers, the First Five Year Plan brought increasingly repressive conditions of life and work. Whether factories were run by professional managers or by Party officials who functioned as managers, the workers were forced to submit to the ever greater labor discipline that the drive for increased productivity demanded. They were subjected to increasingly repressive forms of control at the places they worked and, through the urban neighborhood resident committees, at the places they lived as well. Moreover, inequalities within the ranks of the working class itself grew as larger wage differentials and monetary rewards based on skill and productivity were introduced.

Inequality was most glaringly apparent in a sharpening distinction between town and countryside. The industrialization of the cities was based in good measure on the exploitation of the countryside. While material conditions in the cities improved, the rural economy was largely stagnant, thus widening the economic and cultural gap between the modernizing cities and the backward countryside.

The new educational system, heavily influenced by borrowed Soviet methods and curricula, tended to reinforce these tendencies toward social inequality and stratification. The growth in formal education was highly impressive. Between 1949 and 1957 the number of primary school students more than doubled (from approximately 26,000,000 to more than 64,000,000) and university enrollments increased fourfold, from 117,000 to 441,000. But the urban population benefited from the new educational opportunities far more than did people living in the rural areas. Although officially proclaimed policies gave preference to the children of workers and peasants, in practice the examination requirements for admission to middle-schools and universities strongly favored the sons and daughters of the already privileged strata: the old bourgeoisie, higher Party and government officials, intellectuals, and technicians. And to meet the needs of industrialization, the educational system in general, and university education in particular, overwhelmingly emphasized science and technology. Much like its Soviet counterpart, Chinese higher education functioned to create and perpetuate a privileged technological intelligentsia.

When the First Five Year Plan was launched at the beginning of 1953, the government also had announced the inauguration of the era of "the transition to socialism." While the pursuit of modern economic and industrial development was clear enough, the meaning of socialism became increasingly ambiguous. Chinese society seemed to be moving further away from, rather than closer to, the socialist future that the revolution had promised. Industrialization served to further increase the division between town and countryside; the separation between mental and manual labor tended to grow sharper; new social elites emerged to take up the more complex tasks demanded by the newly emerging industrial order; and the state became stronger and more oppressive, presided over by an increasingly bureaucratized Party. Modern industrial development was conceived as the means to achieve socialist ends, but as time went on industrialization itself became the primary goal while socialist goals tended to be postponed to an ever more distant future.

Mao and "Maoism" were soon to be forced to confront the dilemma of means and ends that the results of the First Five Year Plan posed. And just as the Maoist revolution itself was born and developed in the rural areas, Maoists again were to turn to the countryside to revive the socialist goals and spirit of a revolution that was dying.

NOTES

1. Karl Marx, Preface to *Capital* (Chicago: Kerr, 1906), 1:13.
2. For a fascinating analysis of Marx's consideration of Russian Populist ideas, and their influence on him, see A. Walicki, *The Controversy over Capitalism* (Oxford: Clarendon Press, 1969), pp. 179–194. That Marx entertained the possibility that the traditional village commune might serve as the basis for Russia's modern socialist regeneration is suggested in his March 8, 1881, letter to Vera Zasulich. See Karl Marx and Frederick Engels, *Selected Correspondence* (Moscow: Foreign Languages Publishing House, n.d.), pp. 411–412.
3. In his preface to the 1882 Russian edition of *Capital,* Marx held out the possibility that the precapitalist village commune might serve as a "starting point" for socialist development—but only if a revolution in Russia served as the "signal" for proletarian revolutions in the Western European countries.
4. Mao Tse-tung [Mao Zedong], *On People's Democratic Dictatorship* (Peking: Foreign Languages Press, 1959), p. 14.
5. Mao Tse-tung, "On New Democracy," *Selected Works of Mao Tse-tung* (Peking: Foreign Languages Press, 1967), 2:380.
6. Mao, *Selected Works* (1967), 2:364 and 4:423.
7. Mao, *Selected Works* (1967), 2:364. With the achievement of state power, Mao put the matter in more forceful terms: "All Chinese without exception must lean either to the side of imperi-

alism or to the side of socialism. Sitting on the fence will not do, nor is there a third road" (4:423). In the context of the time, "the side of socialism" was of course the Soviet Union.

8. Mao, *On People's Democratic Dictatorship*, p. 19.

9. The general principles of the plan were publicly outlined in a *People's Daily* editorial on September 16, 1953. The detailed plan, probably revised downward over the following two years, was presented to the Second Session of the First National People's Congress on July 5–6, 1955 by Li Fuchun, then chairman of the State Planning Commission. See Li Fu-ch'un [Li Fuchun], "Report on the First Five Year Plan for Development of the National Economy of the People's Republic of China in 1953–1957," translated in Robert R. Bowie and John K. Fairbank, *Communist China 1955–1959: Policy Documents with Analysis* (Cambridge, Mass.: Harvard University Press, 1962), pp. 42–91.

10. According to official statistics, industrial output grew approximately 18 percent per annum in Russia during the first Soviet Five Year Plan while the industrial working class increased from 3,000,000 to 8,000,000. For an analysis of why the Chinese believed they could match the Russian performance, see Christopher Howe, *Employment, and Economic Growth in Urban China, 1949–1957* (London: Cambridge University Press, 1971), pp. 102–104.

11. Li Fu-ch'un, "Report on First Five Year Plan," p. 48.

12. *Ibid.*, p. 59. As calculated by Li Choh-ming, the actual ratio for the 1953–57 period was 87 percent for heavy industry and 13 percent for light industry. Li Choh-ming, "Economic Development," *China Quarterly*, January–March 1960, p. 40.

13. Li Fu-ch'un, "Report on First Five Year Plan," pp. 46–47.

14. Of total state investment for development during the First Five Year Plan, only 8 percent went to agriculture, forestry and water conservation. (Li Choh-ming, "Economic Development," p. 40; figures taken from 1959 State Statistical Bureau "Communiqué on the Results of the First Five Year Plan for National Development.")

15. Li Fu-ch'un, "Report on First Five Year Plan," pp. 48–49.

16. *Ibid.*, p. 60.

17. *Ibid.*, p. 51.

18. *Ibid.*, p. 44.

19. Li Choh-ming, "Economic Development," p. 38.

20. *Ibid.*, p. 39.

21. Li Fu-ch'un, "Report on First Five Year Plan," pp. 53, 61. A higher rate of growth was envisioned in the original draft of the plan in 1952, although how much higher cannot be determined since the original draft was never published. It was reported, however, that downward revisions were made in 1953 and 1955.

22. For Chinese government figures, see *Ten Great Years* (Peking: Foreign Languages Press, 1960), p. 87. For the general consensus of Western economists, see Joint Economic Committee of the U.S. Congress, *An Economic Profile of Mainland China* (Washington, D.C.: Government Printing Office, 1967), 1:273.

23. See Table 7–12 in Barry M. Richman, *Industrial Society in Communist China* (New York: Random House, 1969), pp. 636–637.

24. Official Soviet statistics claim a 18.5 percent per annum growth rate, but most Western estimates give a figure of about 12 percent.

25. See Tables 8 and 9 in Howe, *Employment and Economic Growth,* p. 14.

26. Tientsin [Tianjin] *Ta Kung-pao* [*Da Gongbao*], December 31, 1953. Quoted in Franz Schurmann, *Ideology and Organization in Communist China* (Berkeley: University of California Press, 1966), p. 255. For a brilliant and lengthy analysis of this complex matter, see pp. 220–308.

27. *Ibid.,* p. 256.

28. Of the 12,720,000 members in 1957, 1,740,000 were officially classified as workers; 1,880,000 as intellectuals; 8,500,000 as peasants; and 600,000 as "others," presumably mostly soldiers. Total membership was approximately 2.5 percent of the population, the lowest Party/population ratio of any Communist country at the time (*ibid.,* pp. 128–139).

29. Ezra Vogel, *Canton under Communism* (Cambridge, Mass.: Harvard University Press, 1969), pp. 127–128. For an analysis of the transformation of cadres into officials, see *idem,* "From Revolutionary to Semi-Bureaucrat: The 'Regularisation' of Cadres," *The China Quarterly,* No. 29 (January–March, 1967), pp. 36–60.

30. According to a Soviet source, Gao Gang and Liu Shaoqi went to the Soviet Union in 1945 to discuss issues arising out of the Soviet occupation of Manchuria and Gao's Northeast China Bureau maintained contacts with the Soviet Communist Party thereafter. See James Harrison, *The Long March to Power* (New York: Praeger, 1972), p. 376.

31. Mao Tse-tung, "Talks at the Chengtu Conference" (March 10, 1958), *Mao Tse-tung Unrehearsed: Talks and Letters, 1956–71,* ed. by Stuart R. Schram (Middlesex: Penguin, 1974), pp. 100–101.

32. Ho Kan-chih [He Ganzhi], *Chung-kuo Hsien-tai Ko-ming-shih* [*Zhongguo Xiandai Gemingshi*] (1958), quoted in Schurmann, *Ideology and Organization,* p. 344.

33. In the mid-1950s, high-level industrial managers and engineers were paid as much as 280 yuan per month while the average workers' salary was 65 *yuan.* Moreover, the higher members of the technological and managerial elite were provided better housing, paid vacations, and often servants. The "wage reform" act of early 1956 formalized and widened salary differentials.

9

Agricultural Collectivization, 1953–1957

IN 1953, WITH THE completion of the land reform campaign, China was basically a land of individual peasant owner-cultivators. A modern Communist state, ironically, had recreated the traditional Chinese ideal of a system of more or less equal family-owned and operated farms. And for a few years the traditional ideal was probably more fully realized than it ever had been in China's long history.

Although there remained socioeconomic differences between the majority of poor peasants, a substantial body of "middle peasants," and a small minority of "rich peasants," differences in land holdings and income were relatively small. Virtually every peasant now had a title deed to land unencumbered by landlords, mortgages, usurers, extralegal bureaucratic exactions, or marauding warlord armies and bandit gangs. It was as close to a "peasants' utopia" as achieved by any society in modern times, the ideal of a relatively egalitarian society in which most families tilled their own farms in relative security. Socially and economically the People's Republic was for a time a "petty bourgeois" society par excellence.

Most peasants were deeply attached to the individual family farm, an attachment strongly reinforced by traditional habits of work, religious practices, and social values. And the majority who benefited from land reform looked forward to a relatively prosperous life that they anticipated work on their own land would bring.

Yet the post–land reform rural situation was conducive neither to prosperity in the countryside nor to the modern economic development of the nation. The fragmentation of plots inhibited the introduction of more efficient work patterns and the use of modern agricultural technology, severely limiting increased productivity. In 1953 and 1954, the production of food grains barely kept pace with population growth. Moreover, the peasants were burdened by high state grain taxes and compulsory deliveries of grain to government stores at fixed low prices. While the state was taking a great deal out of the rural economy to finance urban industrialization, it was putting very little back; under the First Five Year Plan, less than 10 percent of state investment for development went to the agrarian sector.

Quite apart from the poor harvests of 1953 and 1954, there were many other indications of social and economic problems in the countryside. No sooner was land reform completed than the traditional practice of usury reappeared; better off and more economically efficient peasants lent money to poorer tillers, and in some cases the debtors were forced to sell their lands to their creditors.[1] The rural economy, if left to itself, would perforce generate traditional forms of exploitation and reproduce old patterns of socioeconomic differentiation.

Economic difficulties in the countryside also brought a flood of peasant migrants to the cities. While some went to take jobs in industry, most fled to the cities because of food shortages in the countryside. The result was to intensify already serious problems of urban unemployment and underemployment. During the First Five Year Plan the increase in the population of the cities far exceeded urban employment growth, partly because the planners gravely overestimated the capacity of the new industries to absorb a larger work force. And the problem was further aggravated by the demobilization of much of the army in 1954–1955, following the signing of the Korean War truce.

The Communists never assumed that land reform alone would result in either the necessary economic revolution in agricultural production or the desired social reorganization of the rural areas. From the beginning they saw land reform as a necessary but transient stage in a process that would lead to the collectivization of agriculture. But they viewed the transformation from individual peasant proprietorship to collective farming as a long-term process that would proceed gradually through three distinct phases of development. The first step would be the organization of mutual aid teams whereby the members of about six or more households would assist each other in the working of their still individual family farms, initially on a seasonal basis and later as a year-round organization, serving to enlarge the working unit and to forge patterns of cooperative work. Second, mutual aid teams would combine into "semi-socialist" or "lower" agricultural producer cooperatives where land would be pooled and farmed cooperatively, although each family would retain private ownership of land and families would divide the crop (or its proceeds) partly in accordance with the labor contributed and partly according to the amount of property pooled. Finally, "lower" cooperatives eventually would be amalgamated into "higher" or "advanced" cooperative farms, i.e., collectives, which would abolish private land ownership and remunerate its members in accordance with the socialist principle of "to each according to one's labor."

The formation of mutual aid teams and "lower" cooperatives were to be entirely voluntary—and the peasants who joined were free, at least according to official policy, to withdraw from them.[2] Party cadres in the countryside were told to use only methods of persuasion, encouraged to set up model examples of teams and cooperatives, and were continually warned against "commandism." Since Party leaders were well aware of the deep attachment of peasants to the family farm, a matter noted repeatedly in Party documents of the time, the process of socialist transformation presupposed a long period of popular education. Moreover, the general assumption was that the socialization of agriculture demanded the modern means of mechanization and technology which only industrialization could provide; and, since Mao, among others, had said that the necessary level of industrialization would require at least three five-year plans, collectivization was seen as a rather distant goal. Those who called for a more rapid transition were denounced for the heresy of advocating "utopian agrarian socialism." As the Party's Central Committee summed up the matter in February 1953, "Under the present economic conditions of our country, the peasants' individual economy will exist to a very large extent and for a considerable length of time. . . ."[3]

This gradual and cautious approach to rural social change was fully in accord with Mao Zedong's 1949 thesis that modern industrialization was the prerequisite for the socialization of agriculture, and there is no evidence to suggest that he dissented from the policies the Party adopted in 1953. It was not until two years later that Mao was to emerge as the foremost advocate of "utopian agrarian socialism."

The provisions for agricultural development in the First Five Year Plan incorporated these gradualist perspectives. The modest target announced in the Plan was that only one-third of peasant households would be organized into lower-stage agricultural producer cooperatives by the end of 1957. Nothing was said about the establishment of fully socialist collective farms. Agrarian social change was no more rapid than envisioned; by mid-1955, about 15 percent of the peasants had joined the lower cooperatives. But the persistence of a small producer's economy posed far greater economic problems than had been anticipated. The First Five Year Plan assumed a 23 percent increase in agricultural output and subsidiary rural production;[4] in 1953 and 1954, however, agricultural production was falling far short of that goal. Since industrialization was dependent on a developing agrarian economy or, more precisely, on extracting from the countryside a sizable economic surplus for investment in the cities, stagnation in the rural economy threatened the industrialization program and created economic hardships among the peasantry.[5] The plight of the peasants was aggravated by a mid-1954 decision prohibiting the sale of surplus grain on the private market; henceforth all grain beyond that consumed by the peasants themselves was to be sold (at the low controlled rate) to the government, thus reducing the income of many peasants. Peasant income was further reduced (and the program of industrialization endangered) when peasants responded to the food shortages of early 1955 by planting more grain to the neglect of industrial crops. That the demands of the First Five Year Plan had imposed grave hardships on the peasantry was later gingerly conceded by Zhou Enlai: "In 1954, because we did not completely grasp the situation of grain production in the whole country, and purchased a little more grain from the peasants than we should have, discontent arose among a section of the peasants."[6]

Party leaders, long sensitive to "peasant individualism," recognized that land reform would reinforce the peasants' attachment to their own private plots. Thus, they had always insisted that cooperative forms of agriculture be introduced only gradually and only by gaining the voluntary support of the peasants, primarily by demonstrating that cooperatives would raise both production and income. The Communists were determined not to alienate the class to whose support they owed their revolutionary success. Yet by early 1955 the Communists saw peasant individualism as not only a barrier to social change in the countryside, but as a hindrance to the development of the national economy. A stagnant rural economy threatened industrialization and posed a threat to the internal political viability of the new state, its external security, and to the socialist goals of its Communist leadership.

Concerns over agricultural productivity were accompanied by fears about the social direction of the countryside. As Mao complained in mid-1955: "During the past few years, the influence of forces tending to develop spontaneously toward capitalism has been developing daily in the rural areas; new rich peasants have emerged everywhere, and many prosperous middle peasants are exerting efforts to turn themselves into rich peasants. Many poor peasants, due to their lack of means of production, still remain in poverty, some of them having contracted debts; others are selling their land or renting out their land. . . . If this situation is allowed to develop further, there will become increasingly more serious [class] polarization in the rural areas."[7] Communist leaders expressed anxiety about the rise of an exploiting "kulak" class and the recreation of traditional rural social class differentiations, as a result of the "four freedoms" retained by land reform: the freedom to purchase, sell, and rent land; to hire agricultural laborers; to lend money; and to engage in trade on the private market.

Another manifestation of the persistence of peasant individualism was the inclination of the Party's own rural cadres to succumb to petty bourgeois "peasant ideology." In the period after the land reform campaign, many cadres who had been the leaders in that campaign withdrew from political activities to concern themselves with their own farms and the welfare of their families. Since rural cadres were themselves peasants, the phenomenon reflected their own latent desires and their own peasant vision of a good society. In some cases it reflected resentments that the rural areas, the wellspring of the revolution, were being neglected as the new state turned its energies to the industrialization of the cities; in other cases it reflected resentments over being forced to remain in the rural hinterlands when the political center of gravity had moved to the dynamic urban areas. Many rural cadres had only the most vague understanding of the socialist aims of the Party and saw their political role as representing the general peasant desire to become "rich peasants" in a new era of peace and stability. As Party leaders began to complain, "the attitude of some of our comrades to the peasant question still remains at the old stage. . . . They are satisfied that the peasants have obtained land from the landlords, and want to keep things as they are in the villages. . . . They fail to understand that this means . . . allowing capitalism to develop freely in the rural areas."[8]

The situation was largely of the Party's own making. As the emphasis turned to urban industrialization, the Communists were content to rule the countryside through the formal state bureaucratic apparatus, the *xiang* governments and the public security organs attached to them. This was sufficient to serve immediate state needs for political control of the rural areas and the collection of taxes and compulsory grain purchases from the peasantry. Little attention was paid to the development of Party organization within the villages and cadres who remained in the villages, no longer at the forefront of any social movement, tended to retreat to private endeavors.

The New Agrarian Revolution

Communist leaders originally assumed that the organization of the peasantry into mutual aid teams and the gradual development of "lower" agricultural producer cooperatives would be sufficient to blunt capitalist tendencies in the countryside and also increase productivity. By making more efficient use of land, labor, and farm implements through collective efforts, it was believed agricultural production would grow, peasants would be drawn to the virtues of cooperative organization, and the small-producer mentality gradually would be overcome.

There were traditional and earlier Communist precedents for cooperative work in agriculture. In traditional times it was a common practice among peasants, especially those who could not afford to hire agricultural laborers, to exchange labor during planting and harvest seasons, although such arrangements usually were limited to a few families and generally based on kinship bonds. And in the war-time base areas, the Communists had organized peasants into mutual aid organizations and experimental cooperative-type farms as well.[9]

Quantitatively, the post-1949 development of the cooperative movement was impressive, especially since it was organized on a largely voluntary basis. As soon as land redistribution had been completed in a particular area, individual peasant proprietors were organized into mutual aid teams. Unlike traditional forms of work cooperation, the new teams were larger (consisting of six to twenty or more families), cut across kinship lines, and were quickly transformed from seasonal arrangements to permanent organizations. Moreover, the members of the permanent teams engaged in supplementary handicraft production on a collective basis. By the end of 1952, 40 percent of peasant households had joined mutual aid teams and the figure had grown to approximately 65 percent in early 1955. The percentages were higher in North China where land reform had come earlier, and lower in the central and southern regions. And while only 15 percent of the peasantry had been organized into "semi-socialist" cooperatives by early 1955, this was in keeping with the gradualist policies that were being pursued.

However, the mutual aid teams and the cooperatives were beset with a variety of difficulties. The popular enthusiasm of the revolutionary years and the land reform campaigns waned in an era dominated by a mood to return to normalcy after decades of turmoil and struggle. Press reports complained that the mutual aid teams were often only pro forma organizations. Better-off middle peasants, possessing more land and better techniques, often refused to join poor peasants in cooperative efforts. In other

cases, middle and rich peasants came to control newly organized cooperatives, to the detriment of poor peasants. While the mutual aid teams and
cooperatives facilitated state collections of taxes and grain, they failed to
increase productivity. The harvests of 1953 and 1954 were poor, and there
was little to indicate that the "lower" producer cooperatives would fulfill
the expectation that they would increase productivity by 30 to 50 percent
"within two or three years."[10]

Although the majority of peasants had been organized into various
forms of cooperative labor and economic interdependence by the end of
1954, this did not halt the process of growing class differentiations. The
problems were attributed to the system of individual peasant proprietorship and the petty producer mentality that accompanied it. Newspaper articles and Party reports began to quote Lenin's well-known dictum that
"small-scale production gives birth to capitalism and the bourgeoisie constantly, daily, hourly, with elemental force, and in vast proportions."

It was in response to a stagnating rural economy, a problem which
threatened to undermine the whole Five Year Plan for industrial development, and, to a lesser extent, the phenomenon of what Mao later called
"autonomous capitalistic forces [which] have been developing day after
day in the villages," that Beijing once again turned its attention to the
countryside. A Politburo meeting of October 1954 set up a more rapid
timetable for the organization of cooperative farms. In preparation for the
new campaign, a March 1955 Party conference worked out a program to
revitalize Party organizations in the rural areas. The formal decision to
speed up the pace of cooperativization was made by the Party's Central
Committee in May.

Between the October 1954 and May 1955 Party meetings there was
much that happened both in the countryside and within the secret councils
of the Communist leadership—and there is much that remains obscure.
According to Mao Zedong's later account, the decision of October 1954
was to increase the number of lower-stage cooperatives sixfold, from
100,000 to 600,000. And again according to Mao, that target had been
achieved by June of 1955, when there were some 650,000 cooperative
farms in operation comprising 16,900,000 of China's 110,000,000 peasant
households.[11] However, political opposition to the more rapid pace of cooperativization emerged, and in March 1955 the State Council ordered a
halt to further expansion. The May Central Committee meeting resumed
the campaign, but at a much more gradual pace; 400,000 additional cooperatives were to be organized over the next year and one-half. It was not a
decision that Mao found satisfactory, and two months later he was to override it in dramatic fashion.

The secretiveness that shrouds the internal history of the Chinese Communist Party, and the absence of public debate, makes it impossible to be at all precise in reconstructing the political events and the ideological considerations involved in the new agrarian policies embarked upon in 1955. It would appear that by early 1955 the top Party leadership had arrived at a loose consensus—and one that Mao did not share. The majority of the Central Committee believed that an accelerated program of building agricultural cooperatives was necessary if only to ensure meeting the economic requirements for industrialization, and, indeed, satisfying industrial needs was the primary consideration. But they also believed that the cooperatives should be established in an orderly manner and at a gradual pace so as not to endanger productivity. Moreover, the cooperatives were still to be the "lower" or semi-socialist producer cooperatives; it was generally assumed that a high level of technological development and the means to mechanize agricultural production were the essential prerequisites for fully socialist collective farms, a prospect that lay well in the future.

The Soviet experience in collectivization was very much on the minds of Chinese Communists in their debates over agrarian policies, and from that experience they derived two lessons. The first was that collectivization too long delayed could lead to rural class polarization and the solidification of a dominant rich peasant class opposed to the socialist state. But the lesson most deeply impressed was that rapid collectivization imposed from above could have catastrophic results. The Chinese were not unaware of the bloody cataclysm that Soviet collectivization had become under Stalin in the early 1930s: the murder or deportation to Siberia of 10,000,000 peasants; the total disruption of production as vast lands were left untilled and livestock slaughtered; and the famines that came in the wake of the holocaust. It was more out of ideological timidity than historical ignorance that the Chinese made only the most veiled references to those horrors; they could hardly denounce Stalin's methods of agricultural collectivization at the same time they were pursuing his path to industrialization, quite apart from the general ideological and political considerations that made it impossible to be openly critical of Stalin. Yet, however much they were attracted to the Soviet model of development in general, they were determined to avoid the economic and human costs of Stalinist-style collectivization.

The fear of the emergence of a kulak-type class was a matter of less concern. It was generally assumed that the expansion of Party organizations in the rural areas, coupled with the slow and orderly growth of cooperative farming, would be sufficient to check whatever spontaneous capitalist forces had appeared or would appear.

What had become the Party consensus on agrarian policy was summarized in Li Fuchun's report on the First Five Year Plan. The emphasis was on the need for a stable and productive agrarian economy to serve the needs of industrial development. The establishment of cooperative farms would continue, but in a gradual and systematic fashion and on a voluntary basis. The modest goal announced was to expand the existing 600,000 semi-socialist cooperatives to 1,000,000, encompassing about one-third of peasant households, by the end of 1957. The emphasis of the report was on raising agricultural productivity for the purposes of urban industrialization. The peasants, to be sure, were to be led to socialism, but that would be a gradual transition of unspecified duration, dependent on the mechanization of agriculture. In the meantime, the state was to offer "vigorous assistance" to individual peasant proprietors who would make up the vast majority of peasant producers for the foreseeable future.[12]

Such, in brief, were the perspectives on the agrarian question generally held by the leaders of the Chinese Communist Party in early July. Before the month was out, Mao Zedong single-handedly and dramatically dissolved the consensus with his speech on "The Question of Agricultural Cooperation," thereby launching China on a distinctively Maoist road to "agrarian socialism." As a leading Party official later caustically remarked, Mao's speech "settled the debate of the past three years."[13]

The debate was "settled" in a manner unprecedented in the history of the Chinese Communist Party. Mao delivered his speech not to the Central Committee, in which he was in a minority, but rather to a meeting of provincial and regional Party secretaries who were in Beijing at the time for a session of the National People's Congress. In effect, Mao overrode the Central Committee and appealed to the Party at large. It was not until October that the Central Committee convened to formally ratify the new Maoist policies.

At a time when other Party leaders felt that rural cooperatives were being established too hastily, Mao declared the movement was proceeding too slowly.[14] In place of the goal of 1,000,000 cooperative farms to be established by the end of 1957, Mao demanded an additional 300,000 cooperatives and moved up the timetable to the autumn of 1956. By the spring of 1958 no less than half of China's peasant households were to be organized in semi-socialist cooperatives, he declared, and the remaining half were to be included by 1960. However, the significance of Mao's speech lay not in the accelerated timetable he set forth, but rather in the revival of a voluntarist approach to sociohistorical change and a populist faith in the peasant masses to effect that change, the same voluntarist and populist impulses that had characterized Maoism during the revolutionary years. Mao's speech also was an implicit rejection of many of the crucial theoreti-

cal assumptions that had guided Communist policies since 1949, thus foreshadowing the Chinese abandonment of the Soviet model and announcing
the appearance of "Maoism" on the postrevolutionary historical scene.

"Throughout the Chinese countryside a new upsurge in the socialist
mass movement is in sight," were the words with which Mao began, and it
was this belief that permeates the whole report. The peasants were demonstrating a spontaneous "socialist initiative" and there was "an active desire
among most peasants to take the socialist road." The perceptions and the
imagery were strikingly similiar to those of the famous "Hunan Report"
nearly three decades earlier, when Mao began his career as an agrarian revolutionary. In 1927 Mao had found the peasant movement to be an elemental, tornadolike force that would sweep away everything that stood in
its way. Now he saw a "tide of social reform in the countryside" soon to
"sweep the whole country. . . . This is a huge socialist revolutionary movement which involves a rural population of 500,000,000 strong, one which
has very great world significance," he proclaimed, confidently predicting
that "an upsurge in socialist transformation will soon come about all over
the country's rural areas. That is inevitable." Just as in 1927 Mao had perceived the countryside to be the repository of true revolutionary energies,
now in 1955 he again turned to the countryside to find the impetus for radical social change. Just as the "Hunan Report" announced the appearance
of Maoism as an unorthodox strategy of revolution, the 1955 report
marked the emergence of Mao as the advocate of a new and no less unorthodox strategy for the socialist development of a backward land.

Mao's 1955 speech harkened back to the "Hunan Report" in another
respect: the manner in which he perceived the relationship between the
mass movement and the Leninist party. In 1927 he had found the true
sources of revolutionary creativity to reside not in the Party but in the spontaneous movement of the peasantry acting on its own; it was not the Party
that was to judge the revolutionary capacities of the peasantry, but rather it
was the actions of the peasants themselves that were to serve as the criterion to judge the revolutionary sufficiency of the Party.[15] Now again in 1955
Mao counterposed a revolutionary peasantry to a Party that was insufficiently revolutionary. While most of the peasants were striving to achieve
radical social changes, many Party members were "tottering along like a
woman with bound feet, always complaining that others are going too fast."
It was not the peasants who were backward, but rather it was the Party that
had become too timid and conservative. Mao gave the conventional warning to avoid both "leftist" and "rightist" errors, but it was clearly from the
latter that the Party now suffered. "As things stand today," he declared, "the
mass movement is in advance of the leadership" and Party members who

argued that the cooperative movement had "gone beyond the understand-ing of the masses" merely revealed their own lack of faith in the masses. And he was bitterly critical of Party leaders who "cover up their dilatoriness by quoting the experience of the Soviet Union."[16]

For Mao, the experiences and lessons that really mattered were to be de-rived from the history of the Chinese Communist Revolution itself. And the most important lesson, the one revived in 1955, was the celebrated Yan'an principle of the "mass line," which demanded that distinctively Maoist view of the intimate interrelationship between leaders and masses and which also demanded a process of self-education through revolution-ary action. In the postrevolutionary present, just as in the revolutionary past, it was thus necessary to act boldly and act in the here and now: "Both cadres and peasants will change of themselves as they learn from their own experience in the struggle. Get them into action themselves. They will learn while doing, becoming more capable, and large numbers of excellent peo-ple will come forward." Most leaders would emerge from below in the course of the campaign, for the socialist transformation of the countryside was not to be a revolution imposed from above by bureaucratic means. If it was necessary to "send down" cadres from the cities to the rural areas, their first task was "to learn how to work from the movement itself."[17] The "mainstay" of the leadership in organizing the peasants into cooperatives, Mao stressed, was to be "local cadres in the rural areas," the old veteran peasant cadres of the revolution and land reform years as well as newly recruited peasant members of *xiang* Party and Youth League branches. The cadres sent from above were to be only "an auxiliary force" whose function was to "guide and help," rather than "take everything into their own hands."[18] The ideal leader was to be the Yan'an ideal of the local guerrilla leader, the cadre who sprang from the peasants of a particular locality and remained closely tied to them.

Mao's July 31 speech marked not only a departure from existing Party policies on the pace of cooperativization and the methods to be employed, but also set forth new perspectives on the ends the movement was to serve and on the more general question of the relationship between economic de-velopment and social change. The policies that the Communists had pur-sued through mid-1955 had been governed by two hitherto unquestioned assumptions. One was that the major purpose of cooperative farming was to increase agricultural production in order to provide the capital necessary for the industrialization of the cities. As the building of a modern industrial order tended to become the overriding goal, rather than the means to achieve socialist ends, economic productivity and the ability of the state to extract an increasing surplus from the rural economy tended to become the criteria for determining the utility and value of agricultural cooperativization. Secondly, it was assumed that the socialization of the peasantry presupposed the industrialization of the cities, for only modern industry could provide the technology and the mechanization for large-scale collective farming. In 1949 Mao had accepted (and indeed had promoted) these views; by 1955 he had come to reject both assumptions. His July speech implicitly challenged the first and explicitly repudiated the second.

On the one hand, Mao now placed as much emphasis on the social and economic benefits that collectivization would bring to the peasants themselves as he did on its potential for financing industrial development. The majority of peasants remained impoverished, Mao noted, and the socialization of agriculture was the only means "to throw off poverty, improve their standard of living and withstand natural calamities." It was not simply the means to an urban industrial end. Industrialization and the socialist transformation of the countryside were two interlocking revolutionary tasks, Mao argued, warning against attempts to "over-estimate the one and underrate the other." Behind this warning there lay a deep resentment that the First Five Year Plan had led to the exploitation of the rural areas for the benefit of the cities—and a challenge to the whole strategy of urban industrialization and the Soviet model of socioeconomic development.

Secondly, Mao now rejected the proposition he himself had put forward in 1949: the view that the socialization of agriculture was dependent on the prior development of "a powerful industry."[19] Instead, he now argued that "the economic conditions of our country being what they are, technical reform will take longer than social reform."[20] And he estimated that the modern industrial base necessary to carry out a technological revolution in farming would "take roughly four or five five-year plans, that is, twenty to twenty-five years." In the meantime, the socialist transformation of the countryside was not to be delayed: "In agriculture, under the conditions prevailing in our country, cooperation must precede the use of big machinery."

In the summer of 1955 Mao still viewed the socialist transformation of rural China as a fairly lengthy process, even though a more rapid one than many Party leaders thought practical or possible. The movement, he emphasized, was to proceed in accordance with the "principles of voluntariness and mutual benefit." He was no less insistent than others that coercive methods and disruptions in production be avoided. And he was more opposed than anyone to any sort of "revolution from above." But he was confident that the majority of the peasantry—the 70 percent classified as poor and lower-middle peasants—would move to socialism on their own accord and that the remainder would follow their example when they saw the economic benefits of cooperative farms. The immediate program still centered on the organization of lower-stage or semi-socialist cooperatives, and that would take four and one-half years to complete. The establishment of fully socialist collectives would proceed more slowly and also on a voluntary basis, and that would require another decade. The still relatively gradual process Mao envisioned in the summer of 1955 was to be overtaken by the extraordinary events of the winter of 1955–1956.

Formal Party approval of what was already de facto policy came in October in the form of a document entitled "Decisions on Agricultural Cooperation," apparently authored by Chen Boda, one of Mao's closest ideological associates. The document essentially repeated the views Mao had set forth in July and added detailed guidelines for the operation of cooperative farms.[21]

High-level Party opposition to Mao's views remained, but the critics were silent for fear of being labeled "right opportunists" as the Maoist program was implemented in October, just after the fall harvest. In the months between Mao's July speech and the October Central Committee meeting, regional and local Party leaders made frenzied efforts to revitalize rural Party organizations to preside over "the transition to socialism" in the countryside.

Cooperativization proceeded at an extraordinarily rapid pace in the last months of 1955, and the results surpassed Mao's most optimistic expectations. By the end of the year 1,900,000 lower-stage co-ops had been organized, almost 50 percent more than the goal Mao had proposed for the following October. Sixty-three percent of peasant households had joined cooperatives by December 1955, more than a fourfold increase since midyear. The movement below had acquired a momentum of its own, fueled by the egalitarian desires of poorer peasants and the political zeal of local cadres. And Mao responded from above with words that anticipated the full-blown utopianism of the Great Leap Forward era. He described the movement as "a raging tidal wave" that had "swept away all the demons and ghosts," attributing its success to his conviction that "the people are filled with an immense enthusiasm for socialism."[22] The peasants who were transforming the Chinese countryside and who had made 1955 "the year of decision in the struggle between socialism and capitalism" were motivated not only by economic self-interest but more importantly by an inherent spirit of "socialist activism." It was this long-standing faith in the spontaneous "socialist" strivings of the peasantry that was the most striking feature of Mao's views on what he called "the high tide of socialism" in the countryside. The cooperativization movement served to fortify Mao's faith in the revolutionary creativity of the peasantry and in the power of human will and consciousness to shape social reality. Thus he confidently predicted that "by the end of this year [1955] the victory of socialism will be practically assured."[23] It was a prophetic pointer to the future evolution of Maoism—and an echo of its revolutionary past—that Mao saw the actions of peasants in the countryside as decisive for China's "transition to socialism."

Since the goals Mao had set forth in the summer of 1955 were surpassed within a few months, new targets were announced in December. Semi-socialist cooperativization was to be completed by the end of 1956, and the transition to fully socialist collectives would take place over the next four years.[24] In January 1956 the Politburo again accelerated the timetable, calling for full socialist collectivization by 1958.[25]

The revised targets, as well as rapidly changing social conditions in the countryside, demanded revisions in the Party's social class policies. At the beginning, poor and "lower-middle" peasants[26] were to be the nucleus of the movement. Upper or "well-to-do" middle peasants were to be drawn in only gradually, through force of example and education. It was feared that better-off middle peasants (who provided much of the surplus collected by the state) would reduce production to subsistence levels if their economic interests were jeopardized. Rich peasants and former landlords, on the other hand, were prohibited from joining cooperatives. There was particular concern that rich peasants, by virtue of their superior resources, might gain control of the lower-stage coops and perpetuate old socioeconomic inequalities in disguised forms.[27]

But with full-scale collectivization taking place much sooner than anticipated, it was necessary to include the entire rural population, not excluding rich peasants who still owned substantial amounts of land as well as a good portion of the better agricultural implements and livestock. Since the collectives were large organizations formed from an amalgamation of lower-stage coops and generally encompassing an entire village, individual family farming was no longer organizationally feasible or economically desirable. And as collectivization entailed the abolition of private ownership of land and other means of production—in favor of having all peasants remunerated in accordance with the socialist principle of "to each according to one's labor"—the fear that rich peasants might maintain their traditional economic dominance quickly receded as collectivization rapidly proceeded. Thus, in the early months of 1956 the Party removed social class barriers to admission to the new rural organizations, converting most rich peasants and ex-landlords into ordinary peasants, and virtually all rural inhabitants became members of co-ops or collectives, willingly or not.[28]

Collectivization was essentially completed during the first half of 1956, accomplished largely without violence. As the movement from below gained momentum in the early months of the year, most remaining individual peasant proprietors were organized into lower-stage cooperatives and the latter were quickly transformed into "socialist" collectives. By the end of the summer, some 100,000,000 peasant households (or 90 percent of the rural population) were members of approximately 485,000 collective farms, officially called "higher-stage agricultural producer cooperatives." Virtually all the rest were drawn in before the spring planting of 1957. Except for tiny plots that individual households tilled for their own consumption or for sale on the limited private market, private land ownership was abolished, and all peasants, at least in theory, worked the land collectively in accordance with the principle of "equal pay for equal work." Social class distinctions in the countryside seemingly had been eliminated, surviving only in the form of class labels assigned during the land reform campaign, political designations that no longer conformed to new socioeconomic realities.

The rapidity of the transition from "elementary" or "semi-socialist" cooperative farms to "advanced" or fully "socialist" collectives is one of the more surprising features of a movement whose dynamism surprised even the most radical leaders in Beijing. Total collectivization, after all, required peasant families to surrender all rights of private ownership of land, in many cases lands held in the family for generations, and in many more cases land acquired recently and triumphantly during the land reform campaign. In part, rapid collectivization reflected the radical demands of poor peasants for a general social leveling. In part, it was facilitated by central government loans to the more advanced cooperatives.[29] But more important were the difficulties encountered by the "lower-stage" cooperatives in reconciling two different forms of remuneration, one involving a reasonably equitable compensation for the amount of land and capital individual families contributed, voluntarily or otherwise, the other based on payment according to work. As Vivienne Shue has observed:

> The appeal of fully socialist collectives, in which continuing conflicts over land rent and investment could by and large be left behind, became more and more compelling, especially to cadres and poor members. It was largely in an effort to escape the financial complexities and the conflicting interests inherent in elementary co-op organization that so many quick transitions to advanced co-op status were made.[30]

Although the socialization of agriculture took place far more rapidly than anticipated and did not bring the economic chaos some had feared, collectivization was not accomplished without creating serious organizational and other problems. During the most intensive period of the "high tide," the first half of 1956, peasant resistance was minimal. While rich and upper-middle peasants, who constituted about 20 percent of the rural population, were less than enthusiastic about being reduced to the status of ordinary peasants, they peacefully submitted to overwhelming economic, social, and political pressures. There were scattered reports of the slaughter of oxen and other farm animals and vague references in the press to "sabotage" on the part of former landlords and rich peasants, but there was no violent peasant resistance, and the state refrained from employing force. The compulsion generated by the movement itself, and the "commandism" of local cadres, proved sufficient to sweep wealthier peasants into the collectives, willingly or not. Serious signs of dissatisfaction were not evident until after the collectives had been established, and then they took mostly nonviolent forms—the withholding of labor efforts, withdrawals from the new organizations, some spontaneous disbandments of collective farms (especially in the southern provinces, where they had been organized in particularly hasty fashion), and a renewed exodus of peasants to the cities in late 1956 and early 1957.

Despite those problems, agricultural collectivization in China stands in striking contrast to its brutal Soviet precedent. How Stalin brought "socialism" to Russian peasants is well known. Armed forces were sent from the cities to carry out what became a virtual civil war between town and countryside. Villages were surrounded by troops and forced to surrender, and reluctant peasants herded into collectives under machine guns. Those who openly resisted were shot on the spot. Stalin's policy of "liquidating the kulaks as a class" meant the virtual extermination of 10,000,000 peasants, since kulaks were not allowed to join collectives even when they wished to do so. Millions were killed outright and millions more deported to desolate lands in Siberia. Most of the remaining "collectivized" peasants were thrown into sullen opposition to the regime, a political result that came to haunt Moscow during the Nazi invasion. The immediate economic results were catastrophic. Half of Russia's livestock was destroyed, production ceased in many rural areas, and the ensuing famine came near to wrecking the very industrialization drive that collectivization was designed to serve. By contrast, China's collectivization was an almost peaceful social revolution. Collective farms were established without the use of soldiers, resistance was confined to a minority of the rural population and expressed in nonviolent ways, and the country was not thrown into economic chaos.

References to differing historical traditions shed little light on why the Russian and Chinese experiences were so different. Chinese peasants, traditionally, were no less firmly attached to their land than peasants in Russia or elsewhere. Furthermore old collectivistic village traditions were not as strong in traditional China as they had been in czarist Russia, even discounting Russian Populist idealizations of the allegedly "socialist" traditions of the village *mir.* In no premodern society had private ownership of land developed further, or existed longer, than it had in imperial China—and nowhere was the ideal of individual family proprietorship more firmly imbedded. On the basis of social and cultural traditions, the abolition of private property in land should have encountered far more stubborn resistance in China than in Russia.

One reason it did not can be found in the socioeconomic condition of rural China on the eve of collectivization. In China, the rich peasants who survived land reform were, proportionately, a much smaller class than the Russian kulaks and a far less powerful one. And, unlike the kulaks, Chinese rich peasants were not permitted the time or conditions to consolidate themselves as a dominant class of capitalist farmers. Moreover, in China, unlike Russia, the great majority of peasants were impoverished, not excluding most of those who became "middle peasants" as a result of land reform; they had little to lose and could be convinced that they might have something to gain by collectivization. In Russia in the late 1920s, by contrast, two-thirds of the rural inhabitants were "middle-class" peasants who aspired to kulak status and were firmly opposed to socialization.[31] In China in the mid-1950s, two-thirds of the peasants were, as Mao described them, "still badly off." The Chinese countryside simply held a much greater mass of destitute peasants potentially favorable to radical social change.

Yet it is most unlikely that potential could have been tapped had it not been for the particular character of the Chinese Revolution and the nature of the Chinese Communist Party. The Russian Bolsheviks had no significant following among the peasants and hardly any organizational structure in the rural areas. The Russian countryside, after 1917, insofar as it was not left to itself, was loosely ruled by an urban-based administration. The Chinese Revolution, by contrast, had been led by a Communist Party composed mostly of peasants and carried out through the mobilization of tens of millions of rural inhabitants. However much the Party had urbanized itself in the early 1950s, it retained deep organizational roots in the rural areas, which were revitalized in 1955. The socialization of the Chinese countryside was accomplished by local Party cadres and activists who came from, and remained closely tied to, the poorer peasant families. It is inconceivable that so massive a social transformation could have come about so rapidly and relatively peacefully without the active support of very substantial numbers of ordinary peasants. It is equally inconceivable that peasants could have been organized to effect so radical a transformation of their social lives had it not been for the rural revolutionary heritage of the Chinese Communist Party. Mao Zedong had neither the need nor the inclination to carry out a brutal, Stalinist-style "revolution from above."

In view of the vast differences in both the nature and the results of collectivization in China and Russia, it is strange that Mao Zedong, in inaugurating the Chinese campaign in 1955, felt obliged to applaud the agrarian successes of Stalin during "the six years between 1929 and 1934" and to declare that "the Soviet Union's experience is our model."[32] One cannot attribute this homage to Stalin—indeed, a now dead Stalin—to Mao's ignorance of Soviet history, for he was not unaware of the terrible human and economic toll Stalin had exacted during those "six years," and he had no intention of plunging China into a similar disaster. That he felt a need to claim he was following the Soviet "model" is an incongruity that bears on the larger question of the relationship between Maoism and Stalinism, a relationship filled with the most puzzling ambiguities. In the case of collectivization, in any event, Mao invoked the ideological authority of Stalin to launch a very non-Stalinist mass movement—just as in the pre-1949 years he had often hailed Stalin in public pronouncements while defying him in revolutionary practice.

Agricultural collectivization, beyond being celebrated as a decisive act in China's "transition to socialism," was intended to achieve several more immediate and concrete objectives, which it was believed would yield benefits to both the state and the peasantry. First, the establishment of a nationwide network of collective farms would provide the state with greater control over agricultural production and the disposition of the surplus. Party supervision over the operation of collective farms no doubt did facilitate state collections of taxes and grain and provide a more stable supply of food for the urban population and revenue to finance urban industrialization—although that hardly can be counted as a blessing for the peasantry. Second, large-scale collective farming would permit the more rapid dissemination of technological knowledge and the introduction of new agricultural technologies, especially those unsuitable for use on small family farms and ones which individual proprietors lacked the means or interest to adopt; eventually, it was envisioned, collective farms would lend themselves to the modern mechanization of agriculture. In 1956, to coincide with the establishment of the collectives, the government hastily introduced several technological innovations—most notably the double-wheel and blade plough, double-cropping, and close planting—although the initial results were less than salutary.[33] Third, collectivization was intended to eliminate most of the economic inequalities, at least within villages, left over from land reform. That was accomplished through the abolition of private ownership of virtually all means of production: land, large agricultural tools and implements, and draft animals. The result was a general (although not complete) leveling of peasant income in particular localities. This meant that a substantial portion of the rural population, the roughly 25 percent who were formerly rich or upper-middle peasants, were less well off than they had been prior to collectivization. Presumably the poorer families gained, but the gains were rather meager. Collectivization had the effect of reducing subsidiary production on private plots and undermining rural handicrafts, which adversely affected peasant income in general. Moreover, collectivization left untouched wide regional inequalities in rural China, which remained as great in the years after the "high tide" as they were before.

But the greatest appeal of collective farming, to leaders and masses alike, was the promise that once properly established the new system would yield vast increases in agricultural production and productivity, benefiting both the state and the rural population as a whole. While Mao Zedong preferred to believe that most peasants were inspired by socialist ideals, actual Party policies, both during and before collectivization, appealed mainly to the material self-interest of the poorer sectors of the peasantry.[34] For the poor peasants who supported the collectivization campaign with such great enthusiasm, there was every reason to trust Party promises that their efforts would soon bring a higher standard of living. It was the Party-led land reform movement, after all, which had destroyed the old parasitic landlord class and resulted in a significant redistribution of land. And in the years immediately following land reform, Party marketing and credit policies worked to the advantage of poorer peasants—and to the detriment of the trade and money-lending activities of wealthier producers.[35] Now collectivization not only promised immediate benefits that would come from the pooling of the superior assets of rich and upper-middle peasants but also the potential for great economic gains whose fruits, it was promised, could be shared by all in a cooperative social environment. That potential would go unrealized over the remaining two decades of the Maoist era.

Collectivization brought neither the economic disaster some feared nor the economic growth its advocates anticipated. Some collective farms prospered, others were dismal failures, while for the greater number the transition resulted in little economic change.[36] On the whole, per capita peasant income increased little from 1956 until the late 1970s,[37] in part because of the economic crisis that was to be wrought by the Great Leap; in part because of continuing state demands on the rural economy to finance industrialization; and perhaps in larger part because of the failure of most collectives to provide either material or moral incentives to spur peasant production. With the exception of the Great Leap years, collective farms did manage to feed a rapidly growing population over the last two decades of the Maoist era (although not without increasing the rural labor force), and the peasantry did benefit in ways that are not quantifiable in income statistics—through greater security, welfare programs for the destitute and handicapped, the expansion of education and health care in the rural areas, and the beginnings of rural industrialization. But collectivization in general did not yield significant economic gains.

. . .

The first full year of collective farming (1956–57) was plagued by organizational confusion. The collectives were much larger organizations than the "lower-stage" co-ops they replaced, initially averaging 246 households (or about 1,200 people) as opposed to several dozen households. Their operation posed difficult and unfamiliar tasks of economic management and fiscal accounting. With virtually all land, animals, and farm implements now collective property, peasants were to be remunerated according to their labor, mostly in the form of a share of the crop and partly in small cash payments. Each collective was thus faced with the task of calculating, on the basis of very general state guidelines, an equitable system for evaluating labor contributions and calculating "workpoints," a task that inevitably fomented quarrels and bred resentments. In addition, there was much initial uncertainty about responsibility for the care of collectivized animals and equipment, and at times animals perished for lack of adequate attention. The collectives were further confronted with the task of fairly long-term economic planning, determining how much of the crop was to be distributed to its members and how much was to be set aside for welfare and capital investment after meeting state tax and grain delivery obligations. While the young cadres from mostly poor peasant families had proved effective leaders in mobilizing the rural population for the organization of collective farms, they lacked the managerial, bookkeeping, and accounting skills necessary for the effective operation of the new organizations. The dispatch of urban cadres and middle school graduates to the countryside did little to alleviate matters; such skills as they possessed were more than offset by their ignorance of rural life, and their arrogant "city ways" were generally resented by peasants.

Party leaders at first attributed the early economic and organizational problems of collectivization to counterrevolutionary machinations on the part of former landlords and rich peasants, but it was soon recognized that newly collectivized peasants lacked incentives to increase production. Thus through most of 1957 there was a general loosening of state regulations governing collective farms. Mao, in a temporarily less optimistic mood, predicted another five years would be required to establish collectivized agriculture on a sound foundation. In the meantime, government policies offered greater material incentives to the peasantry. State taxes and compulsory grain purchases were reduced to 25 percent of total output in 1956–57; peasants were granted greater freedom to work private plots and sell on the private market; more consumer goods were to be produced; and unwieldly collectives were reduced in size, to an average of 169 households in 1957.

The relaxation of state pressures on the agrarian economy was intended to raise agricultural production. But liberalized government policies also gave rise to a seemingly unresolvable dilemma. The purpose of higher agricultural output was not only to alleviate the economic difficulties of the peasantry but also to provide the state with a greater marketable surplus of grain and raw materials to finance the expansion of urban industry. Yet the very measures taken to give peasants the material means and incentives to increase production deprived the state of the surplus to fulfill the industrial targets of the First Five Year Plan and the more ambitious goals announced for the Second Five Year Plan, due to begin in 1958. By taking a smaller share from the countryside and investing more in consumer industries, the state assisted the peasantry but undermined, at least in the short run, its own plans for rapid industrialization.

The dilemma was to be resolved—and new dilemmas were to be created—when Mao Zedong led the Party to embark on the adventure of the Great Leap Forward in 1958. Just as he had personally intervened in the summer of 1955 to "settle" the debate on collectivization, he now was to intervene with a far more radical scheme to accelerate both agricultural and industrial development, and an attempt to reconcile conflicting interests between the peasantry and the state.

The policies of the Great Leap were to bring to a head a long-simmering Party debate over the whole course of postrevolutionary development and create divisions among Communist leaders that were to prove irreparable. The differences were to remain hidden within the inner councils of the Party for another decade, not to be publicly revealed until the Party itself was burst asunder in the Cultural Revolution. But the origins of the conflict go back to mid-1955, when Mao delivered his speech on agricultural socialization. As rapid cooperativization was quickly followed by rapid collectivization, many Party leaders came to view Mao and his followers as reckless utopians, forcing radical social change much further than could be sustained by China's weak economic base. And Mao was convinced that a bureaucratized Party apparatus had become a conservative obstacle to the new road to socialism he was mapping. The debate became particularly acute in 1957 as Maoists, inspired and emboldened by the successes of the "high tide," proposed ever more radical policies. The conflicts now were no longer confined to the agrarian question. A variety of other political and ideological issues, both international and domestic, had become intertwined with differences over economic policy to widen the scope of the debate. To understand what was being debated on the eve of the Great Leap, and the political atmosphere in which the issues were decided, it is necessary to return to the year 1956 to consider that brief but crucial episode in the history of the People's Republic known as the "Hundred Flowers."

NOTES

1. Although it is impossible to ascertain the extent of this particular practice, it appears to have been fairly widespread. Vogel, for example, has noted that a survey taken in one area of the Guangdong countryside in 1953 revealed that 10 percent of the households of the area were engaged in money lending. Ezra Vogel, *Canton under Communism* (Cambridge, Mass.: Harvard University Press, 1969), p. 142.

2. Official Party policy on this question stipulated that "members withdrawing from a mutual aid team or from a cooperative are entitled to withdraw their investments in capital and reserve funds. But if a member of an APC who bought his shares with land wants to withdraw, it is better if he does so only after the year's crops have been harvested." Cited in Chao Kuo-chun, *Agrarian Policies of Mainland China: A Documentary Study (1949–1956)* (Cambridge, Mass.: Harvard University Press, 1957), pp. 63–64.

3. *Ibid.*, p. 61.

4. The plan called for a 17.6 percent in food grain production and much greater increases in the production of industrial crops. It was emphasized that, "We cannot industrialize our country without an adequate development of agriculture." Li Fu-ch'un, "Report on First Five-Year Plan" in Robert Bowie and John K. Fairbank, *Communist China 1955–1959: Policy Documents with Analysis* (Cambridge, Mass.: Harvard University Press, 1962), p. 62.

5. The report of a Central Committee meeting of October 1955 on cooperativization put the problem in the following fashion: "China's industry is growing rapidly. Facts show that if the development of agricultural cooperation fails to keep pace with it, if the increase in grain and industrial crops lags behind, China's socialist industrialization will run into great difficulties." Cited in Bowie and Fairbank, *Communist China,* pp. 106–107.

6. Chou En-lai [Zhou Enlai], "Report on the Proposals for the Second Five Year Plan for Development of the National Economy," September 16, 1956, in Bowie and Fairbank, *Communist China,* p. 62.

7. Mao Tse-tung [Mao Zedong], "On the Cooperativization of Agriculture," July 31, 1955, in Chao, *Agrarian Policies,* pp. 85–86.

8. Central Committee of CCP, "Decisions on Agricultural Cooperation," October 11, 1955, Bowie and Fairbank, *Communist China,* p. 107.

9. The impetus for the cooperative movement came from Mao's report on economic problems at a Central Committee meeting in December 1942. For perceptive descriptions and analyses of the Yan'an cooperative movement, see Franz Schurmann, *Ideology and Organization in*

Communist China (Berkeley: University of California Press, 1966), pp. 416–427, and Mark Selden, *The Yenan Way in Revolutionary China* (Cambridge, Mass.: Harvard University Press, 1971), pp. 237–254.

10. Teng Tzu-hui [Deng Zihui], "Report to the Rural Work Conference of the Central Committee, New Democratic Youth League," July 15, 1954, in Chao, *Agrarian Policies,* p. 73.

11. Mao Tse-tung, "The Question of Agricultural Cooperation," July 31, 1955, in Bowie and Fairbank, *Communist China,* p. 95.

12. Li Fu-ch'un, "Report of the First Five-Year Plan," in Bowie and Fairbank, *Communist China,* pp. 65–66.

13. The remark is attributed to Chen Yi, Foreign Minister of the People's Republic and a member of the Politburo, and reportedly made in November 1955. See James P. Harrison, *The Long March to Power* (New York: Praeger, 1972), p. 470.

14. Mao's report on "The Question of Agricultural Cooperation" was not published until October 1955, although the new policies it set forth were communicated to Party organizations during the preceding months. The English edition, from which the following discussion and quotations are drawn, was published in Beijing in 1956 and is reprinted in Bowie and Fairbank, *Communist China,* pp. 94–105.

15. "All revolutionary parties and all revolutionary comrades," Mao had declared in the Hunan Report, "will stand before them [the peasants] to be tested, and to be accepted or rejected as they decide," *Selected Works of Mao Tse-tung* (London: Lawrence & Wishart, 1954), 1:22.

16. Mao Tse-tung, "The Question of Agricultural Cooperation," in Bowie and Fairbank, *Communist China,* pp. 94, 101.

17. *Ibid.,* p. 94.

18. *Ibid.,* p. 98.

19. Mao Tse-tung, *On People's Democratic Dictatorship* (Peking: Foreign Languages Press, 1959), p. 14.

20. Mao, "The Question of Agricultural Cooperation," in Bowie and Fairbank, *Communist China,* p. 104.

21. The document was adopted by the Party Central Committee on October 11, 1955. An English translation was published in Beijing in 1956, along with "explanatory notes" by Chen Boda. The new program received formal governmental approval in November 1955, when the State Council promulgated "Draft Model Regulations for the Agricultural Producers' Cooperatives."

22. Mao's views appear in the comments he made on various local reports on the collectivization campaign, compiled in three volumes in January 1956. For the English translation, from which the references here are taken, see Mao Tse-tung, *Socialist Upsurge in China's Countryside* (Peking: Foreign Languages Press, 1957), pp. 44, 160.

23. *Ibid.,* p. 160.

24. *Ibid.,* "Preface," p. 8.

25. "The Draft Program for Agricultural Development in the People's Republic of China, 1956–1967," January 23, 1956, in Bowie and Fairbank, *Communist China,* p. 120.

26. One of the results of land reform was to convert many poor peasants into those conventionally defined as "middle peasants." The term "lower-middle peasants" was invented to refer to middle peasants who, as Mao put it, were "still badly off."

27. The Central Committee document of October 1955 made note of "landlords, rich peasants and counterrevolutionaries [who] have already wormed their way in various guises in cooperatives" and were attempting to turn them to their own ends. However, former landlords and rich peasants were to be permitted to join co-ops "in those places where the great majority of

peasants have joined" and where the co-ops were "on a sound basis." Bowie and Fairbank, *Communist China,* p. 114.

28. "The Draft Program for Agricultural Development in the People's Republic of China, 1956–1967," p. 121; First National People's Congress, "Model Regulations for Higher Stage Agricultural Producer Cooperatives," June 30, 1956, in Chao, *Agrarian Policies,* p. 106.

29. For a highly perceptive discussion of the reasons for the rapidity of the transformation to full collectivization, see Vivienne Shue, *Peasant China in Transition: The Dynamics of Development toward Socialism, 1949–1956* (Berkeley: University of California Press, 1980), pp. 286–317. Shue's book is the most comprehensive and the most analytically interesting study of social change in rural China in the years from land reform through collectivization. Recent "reassessments" of collectivization offer little to challenge the validity of the conclusions reached in this richly documented and insightful volume. For readers interested in what the author of one such reassessment advertises as "striking new conclusions," based, it would appear, on strikingly familiar evidence, see Mark Selden, "Cooperation and Conflict: Cooperative and Collective Formation in China's Countryside," in Mark Selden and Victor Lippit, eds., *The Transition to Socialism in China* (Armonk, N.Y.: M. E. Sharpe, 1982), pp. 32–97.

30. Shue, *Peasant China in Transition,* p. 300.

31. Of Russia's 25 million peasant households in the late 1920s, it is generally estimated that only about 5 million were "poor peasant families," 18 million "middle peasant," and 2 million *kulak,* or "rich peasant." In China the 70 percent of the peasants classified as "poor" or "lower-middle" were destitute or impoverished, whereas in Russia only about 20 percent could be so described.

32. Mao, "The Question of Agricultural Cooperation," p. 102.

33. On the new technology introduced in 1956 and its deficiencies, see Shue, *Peasant China in Transition,* p. 312, and Selden, "Cooperation and Conflict," p. 79.

34. As Vivienne Shue demonstrates in great detail, and convincingly concludes: "The heart of the matter is found . . . in the numerous, deliberate appeals to peasants, on grounds of their own self-interest, to abandon petty-capitalist enterprise and to enter presocialist and then fully socialist institutions." *Peasant China in Transition,* p. 334.

35. On Party policies on rural trade and credit in the years between land reform and collectivization, see Shue, *Peasant China in Transition,* chapters 5 and 6, pp. 195–274.

36. For a report on an area where collective farming failed, see William H. Hinton, "A Trip to Fengyang County: Investigating China's New Family Contract System," *Monthly Review,* Vol. 35, No. 6 (November 1983), pp. 1–28. For a detailed history of a village where it was relatively successful, see William Hinton, *Shenfan* (New York: Random House, 1983).

37. Nicholas R. Lardy, *Agriculture in China's Modern Economic Development* (Cambridge, England: Cambridge University Press, 1983), Table 4.6, p. 160, and discussion pp. 159–163.

PART THREE

UTOPIANISM

1956–1960

10

The Hundred Flowers

Socialism, Bureaucracy, and Freedom

AT THE BEGINNING of 1956 China, in the view of its Communist leaders, was on the verge of completing "the transition to socialism." The events of the latter half of 1955, Mao proclaimed in January of the new year, had proved decisive in determining the outcome of "the struggle between socialism and capitalism" and he predicted that "by the end of this year [1956] the victory of socialism will be practically assured."[1] In the same month, Zhou Enlai and others were celebrating "the high tide of socialist transformation."[2] A year later, in February 1957, Mao was to turn his attention to the problem of "contradictions in a socialist society"; that Chinese society was now socialist was taken for granted, even though it was acknowledged that the new social system had yet to be "fully consolidated."[3]

Whether Chinese society in 1956–1957 was truly socialist is a matter to which we shall return. For the moment it is sufficient to note that seven years after the founding of the People's Republic the leaders of the Chinese Communist Party believed that they had transformed China into a socialist country. And on the basis of how socialism was defined in what was then known as "the Communist camp," they had good and sufficient reason to believe as they did. If socialism is taken to mean the abolition of private property and the control of the means of production by a state in the hands of a socialist party, then China was no less socialist than the Soviet Union, the land still hailed as the "homeland of socialism." By mid-1956 agricultural collectivization largely had been completed and such industrial and commercial enterprises as still remained in private hands were nationalized by the end of the year. Even individual entrepreneurship in handicraft production had been largely reorganized into socialist cooperatives. Like the Soviet Union, China by the end of 1956 was essentially a country with a dual system of property; in the urban economy state property predominated, while collective property prevailed in the rural areas. In both town and countryside, private ownership of property had been abolished, and by the prevailing Marxist-Leninist standard of the time China was a socialist society.

On the assumption that the transition to socialism was completed, or soon would be, the Communists began in early 1956 to chart the future course of socioeconomic development and turned their attention to the problems that the rapid socialization of society had created and the problems yet to be solved. One problem that the arrival of a presumably socialist society had not solved was China's economic backwardness. If the Communists could hail the successes of the First Five Year Plan, they could not but recognize that China's modern industrial sector was still tiny and fragile. If the collectivization of agriculture was being accomplished without plunging the country into economic chaos and without driving the peasantry into political opposition, it nevertheless was taking place without any accompanying technological revolution in agricultural production. China remained a poor country and its people impoverished. No one, not even Mao, believed that a socialist society could long maintain itself, much less flourish, amidst conditions of general economic scarcity. Modern economic development was clearly in order, but it was by no means clear who would issue the order and how it would be carried out. As if to defy the Second Five Year Plan, which was already on the drawing boards at the beginning of 1956, there emerged a radically different Maoist alternative that demanded the wholesale abandonment of the "Soviet model" of development.

For Mao and Maoists, the question of how to achieve a modern economy was inseparable from the question of how to avoid the bureaucratization of state and society that modern economic development fostered. China's "transition to socialism" had been accompanied by a transition from revolutionary forms of organization to bureaucratic forms of rule. The general institutionalization of the postrevolutionary order, and especially the Soviet-borrowed methods of the First Five Year Plan, had given rise to the emergence of new political and economic elites. These developments were perhaps inherent in the process of industrialization, but they clashed with the socialist goals which industrialization presumably was to serve—and clashed more directly with the emerging Maoist vision of the proper course for Chinese society. What came to be known as the "Hundred Flowers" campaign was partly intended to serve, at least on the part of Maoists, an antibureaucratic purpose.

The problem of bureaucracy was a reflection of a larger and more general phenomenon, the growing cleavage between state and society. Socialism, according to Marxist theory, is a historical process whereby the social powers usurped by the state are restored to society. But in the People's Republic, as in the Soviet Union, "the transition to socialism" had produced precisely the opposite historical result: the growth of a vast bureaucratic state apparatus that was increasingly alienated from society. The problem did not go wholly unrecognized. The new Party constitution adopted at the Eighth Congress in September 1956, called for a "maximum effort . . . to combat any bureaucratic practice which estranges the masses or leads to isolation from the realities of life."[4] And in February 1957, Mao spoke of "certain contradictions" which existed "between the government and the masses."[5]

The relationship between state and society was not treated as an abstract theoretical question. In 1956 and 1957 the Communist rulers began to reassess the role of the people over whom they exercised political domination, and confronted the demands of the people themselves. The most dramatic and politically explosive demands came from the urban classes, the industrial working class and the intelligentsia, and posed the most fundamental questions about the nature of a socialist society in general and about the nature of socialism in China in particular. For China's rapidly growing proletariat, "socialist transformation" brought increasingly repressive social and political controls over their lives and an increasingly harsh labor discipline in the factories. Growing unrest among the workers was expressed in 1956 in strikes, which were motivated by political as well as economic discontents. The strikes were scattered and quickly suppressed, but they raised the question of the role of the proletariat in a presumably socialist society that, according to official ideology, was presided over by a state "led by the working class."

For China's intellectuals, the transition to socialism resulted in less freedom, not more. For a time, it seemed that the Communists were willing to grant the Marxist promise that socialism and democracy went hand in hand. The events of 1956–1957 were to reveal the limitations of the Maoist conception of democracy as well as the limits that an entrenched bureaucracy placed on freedom of thought.

What came to be called the "blooming and contending" of 1956–1957 was a time when the most critical questions about the present and future of socialism in China were raised and debated. Questions about the relationship between state and society, between leaders and led, and questions involving human and intellectual freedom were discussed more openly and candidly than ever before in the People's Republic. In part, the questions were posed by the Communist leaders themselves as they reflected on the achievements of "socialist transformation" and industrialization—and the problems which seven years of rapid socioeconomic change had created. In part, the Communists were forced to confront issues which were raised from below by those whom they ruled.

The manner in which the problems or "contradictions" of the time were perceived, the way in which they were resolved or left unresolved, and the outcome of the public debates and the secret Party debates of 1956–1957 are crucial for understanding the nature of socialism in China and the distinctively Maoist theory of socioeconomic development which crystallized during these years.

. . .

The constitution of the People's Republic, promulgated in 1954, formally guaranteed the citizens of China freedom of speech, freedom of assembly, and freedom of the press. That the actual practice and policies of the government were not constrained by such legalities long had been obvious, particularly to China's intellectuals. From the founding of the regime in 1949, they had been subjected to continuous processes of thought reform and ideological remolding; if their thoughts had not been "reformed," they had become painfully aware that unreformed thoughts were best left unsaid. The constitution did nothing to lighten the burden of intellectual conformity the state demanded. Indeed, the *Sufan* campaign and the imprisonment of Hu Feng in 1955 intensified repression and made a mockery of the legal right of "freedom of speech" that had been proclaimed the year before. In 1949 the Communists had come to power with the support of the vast majority of the intelligentsia; now, much of that support had dissipated and the hopes of 1949 had degenerated into passive compliance with the ideological and political dictates of an increasingly repressive state.

In the latter months of 1955 Party leaders began to formulate new policies to regain the active support of a disaffected intelligentsia. It was not the case that the Communists suddenly had come to appreciate the virtues of intellectual freedom. The purpose was largely economic (although Mao Zedong's own motives were rather more complex, as we shall see). As industrialization proceeded, a more rapid development of scientific and tech-

nological research—and the creation of a larger and better trained technological intelligentsia—were required. Instructions were thus issued to draw
up a twelve-year plan for scientific development. At the same time, Mao
proposed a twelve-year program for agriculture which called for a vast technological revolution in agricultural production. An intelligentsia terrified
into silence and driven into political hostility was not likely to provide the
cooperation or intellectual creativity that was required. Intellectual repression was becoming an economic liability.

In the fall of 1955 non-Party representatives to the National People's
Congress were asked to prepare reports on the working conditions of intellectuals. The advice of non-Communist parties was solicited on how best
intellectuals might be "unified" and how they might be reunified with the
CCP. When Mao presented his new agricultural program to the Politburo
in December 1955, he took special pains to urge that intellectuals be
brought into fuller participation in the economic and political life of the
country. It was the first call in the campaign that soon was to proceed under
the slogan "Let a hundred flowers bloom, let a hundred schools of thought
contend."

In January 1956 the Party's Central Committee convened a special conference to deal with the matter. Non-Party representatives of academic institutions and organizations were invited to participate and to hear
speeches by both Mao Zedong and Zhou Enlai. Zhou's speech reflected
the consensus of the Party leadership at the time "On the Question of Intellectuals." The social classification of intellectuals had always posed ideological difficulties, for unlike workers, peasants, or the bourgeoisie, their
class status could not be defined in the usual Marxist way, by their relationship to the means of production. However important intellectuals were in
the economic, political, and cultural life of the country, they remained only
a social "stratum" or "element" and occupied a most ambiguous place in
the four-class alliance upon which the People's Republic presumably
rested. But if intellectuals did not constitute a social class as such, they were
the carriers of class ideologies, and especially bourgeois class ideology, and
thus were politically and ideologically suspect. Zhou attempted to remove
the suspicion by assigning intellectuals a class status they never had been
accorded before. "The overwhelming majority of intellectuals," he announced, "have become government workers in the cause of Socialism and
are already part of the working class." Thus the "question of intellectuals"
was no longer mainly a question of their political and ideological reliability,
but rather a problem of the scarcity of expertise. "The fundamental question now," Zhou stated, "is that the forces of our intelligentsia are insufficient in number, professional skills and political consciousness to meet the

requirements of our rapid Socialist construction." The problem could be resolved through largely technical means. Zhou suggested that through more rational organization and work assignments intellectuals might be better able to "develop their specialized skills to the benefit of the state." And for that same purpose they should be provided with better equipment and more books, better housing and higher wages, more rewards and rapid promotions, and not be burdened unduly with administrative tasks and political study sessions to the neglect of their professional work. Enrollments in universities were to be increased and long-term programs for the development of scientific and technological knowledge were to be undertaken.

The political problem, Zhou suggested, resided more in the Party than among the intellectuals. He complained of "certain unreasonable features in our present employment and treatment of intellectuals, and, in particular, certain sectarian attitudes among some of our comrades towards intellectuals outside the Party," of "unnecessary suspicion" to which intellectuals had been subjected, and a proclivity to label loyal intellectuals as counterrevolutionaries. This did not mean that the intelligentsia was to be freed from political controls and "ideological reform." But the Party would be tolerant: "If they do not turn against the people in speech and action and, even more, if they are prepared to devote their knowledge and energies to serving the people, we must be able to wait for the gradual awakening of their consciousness and help them patiently, while at the same time criticizing their wrong ideology." In the meantime, intellectuals were to be granted a wide realm of professional autonomy in order to master the scientific knowledge that was essential for China's modern economic development.[6]

While the Party was to retain its political and ideological mastery, the intellectuals were recognized as the masters of science and technology, and indeed, encouraged to master a universal body of modern scientific knowledge. The Party was taking the initiative to end what Zhou called "a certain state of estrangement" that existed between the intellectuals and the state. One manifestation of this new confidence in the intelligentsia was Zhou's call for removing barriers for the recruitment of intellectuals into the Party. The result was a 50 percent increase in the number of intellectuals in the Party over the next year. In 1957 there were more intellectuals in China's "party of the proletariat" than there were members of the working class.[7]

It is hardly likely that Mao Zedong could have found Zhou Enlai's speech to his liking, for the new policy implied the creation of a technological intelligentsia that could effectively separate its professional activities from politics and ideology, at least so long as it was not openly hostile to the state and to Marxism. It was a policy that would have accelerated the stratification of professional elites separated from the masses by virtue of their specialized knowledge and privileged social and economic positions. It was precisely this social result of the Soviet-modeled Five Year Plan that Mao was already attempting to reverse and against which he was soon openly to rebel. Mao, to be sure, shared Zhou's desire for modern economic development and the need to master modern science. And Mao was demanding, more strongly than Zhou, that the weight of Party bureaucrats be lifted from the backs of intellectuals. But he was advocating a very different course of economic development than the Party was pursuing at the time and one that had radically different social implications, particularly for intellectuals.

If Mao found uncongenial the social implications of Zhou's speech, there was one political point with which he must have heartily agreed. Among the reasons Zhou advanced for the Party's new policy toward intellectuals was a need for China to end its dependence on the Soviet Union. "We cannot indefinitely rely on the Soviet experts," he stressed, and he was critical of the "sectarian" tendency of the "undue haste, arbitrary learning, and mechanical application" of Soviet methods. It was a reflection of a lack of national self-confidence, he suggested, and he emphasized the need for China to achieve "self-sufficiency" in modern science and technology. This distinctively Maoist theme was to prove a prophetic pointer to the future, and probably neither Zhou nor Mao fully appreciated its significance at the time.

· · ·

When Zhou Enlai spoke "On the Question of Intellectuals" in January 1956, Mao Zedong was pressing the Party to adopt more radical social and economic policies; economic development was to proceed in a manner that was "greater, faster, better and more economical" than it was under the Five Year Plan, while the socialist reorganization of society was to be accelerated as well.[8] At issue in the emerging internal Party dispute was not only the pace of socioeconomic change but its nature. Whereas most Communists were still wedded to the Soviet model of development and thinking in terms of a Second Five Year Plan that was to be basically an extension of the first, Mao was proposing policies that presupposed the wholesale abandonment of the Soviet model. Instead of proceeding in accordance with the dictates of bureaucratic rationality, urban industrialization, and centralized state control, the new Maoist conception flowed from a generalization of the Yan'an model of the "mass line" and, more immediately, was inspired by the populist-type upsurge in the countryside that Mao had launched with his July 1955 speech on agricultural collectivization. The rapid socialist reorganization of society was to be combined with rapid economic development, and industry was to develop simultaneously with agriculture in decentralized fashion and through a populist reliance on the initiative of the masses. The emerging Maoist conception posed a threat to existing state and Party bureaucracies and was bitterly resisted. The debate on the proper course of socioeconomic development raged throughout 1956–1957 and was only resolved (and then only temporarily) in late 1957, when the Maoist conception began to be implemented in the Great Leap Forward campaign.

While the "question of intellectuals" was openly debated, the Party debate on socioeconomic policy remained secret. But the two were intimately related. Zhou Enlai's January 1956 speech flowed quite logically from the premises of the Five Year Plan, for it implied the creation of a Soviet-type technological intelligentsia essential to modern industrial development under bureaucratic auspices. But while Zhou, and most Party leaders, wanted to use intellectuals for economic ends, Mao wanted to use them for political ends as well, as part of a mass socioeconomic movement that would bypass established bureaucratic channels to effect radical social and economic changes. Mao already had come under considerable Party criticism for forcing a too rapid transition to agricultural collectivization. Although his twelve-year plan for agriculture was formally approved by the Central Committee in January 1956, Mao later was to charge that most Party leaders greeted his proposals with indifference. The plan itself was put on the shelf for 18 months as the Party pursued policies of moderation and retrenchment.

It seems likely that Mao was preparing to begin his antibureaucratic drive by announcing a much more dramatic lifting of political restraints on intellectuals than Zhou Enlai proposed. But the launching of the "Hundred Flowers" campaign was delayed by the traumatic impact of Nikita Khrushchev's "secret" speech denouncing Stalin at the Twentieth Soviet Party Congress in February 1956.

· · ·

Khrushchev's condemnation of Stalin's crimes surprised the Chinese as much as it did the rest of the world, and they later complained of the Russian "failure to consult with fraternal parties in advance." It was a resentment they shared with all other Communist parties. Khrushchev delivered the speech at the closing session of the congress and the decision to do so was apparently made at the last minute for the speech bears the marks of hasty composition, and much of it was of an impromptu nature. But it was the internal Chinese political implications of the indictment of Stalin, not the surprise of the occasion, that made for problems.

The leaders of the Chinese Communist Party were not so ignorant of Soviet history as to have found Khrushchev's "revelations" about Stalin very revealing, even though they may have been shocked by some of the more bizarre aspects of Stalin's personality and methods of rule that Khrushchev detailed. Of the greater and general crimes of Stalin they were already well aware. The immediate problem was how to explain the matter to the rank-and-file members of the Chinese Communist Party and to the Chinese people. How were the Chinese leaders to explain why for decades they had extolled as a great revolutionary leader a man who now stood condemned as a bloodthirsty tyrant? Whatever Mao and other Communist leaders privately thought of Stalin, the public record was one of lavish praise. And it was a long record. In 1939 Mao had celebrated Stalin's sixtieth birthday by hailing "Comrade Stalin [as] the saviour of all the oppressed." "Comrade Stalin is the teacher and friend of mankind and of the Chinese people," Mao wrote on the Soviet dictator's seventieth birthday. And on Stalin's death in 1953, Mao lamented the passing of "the greatest genius of the present age." Similar panegyrics had come from other Communist leaders and had filled the Chinese press over the years.

The embarrassing problem could be alleviated, but hardly resolved, by simply not publishing the text of Khrushchev's speech. Just as Khrushchev had concluded his remarks with an admonition not to "wash our dirty linen" in public and had left the matter of publication to the American State Department, so the Chinese refrained from publication, and what details of the speech became publicly known in China appeared only in 1957, in the form of translated excerpts from the English text, which appeared on wall posters written by anonymous hands. The thrust of the speech, even if not its specifics, did of course filter down through Party circles and among the intelligentsia shortly after it was delivered.

The Soviet condemnation of Stalin posed more serious political and ideological issues for the Chinese Communists than such personal embarrassments they suffered because of the idolatrous public praise they had bestowed on the Russian dictator for over a quarter of a century or any annoyance about not having been forewarned about his deidolization. It raised grave questions about the social and moral validity of the socialist system which the Chinese were then emulating. If socialism was a higher stage of sociohistorical development, and Soviet socialism its most advanced model, then how could it have produced and been presided over for so long by a leader whose crimes and brutalities Khrushchev had so vividly, if selectively, described? And it raised the more specific, and for the Chinese, the more immediate problem of the relationship between leader and Party in a presumably socialist society. The major theme of Khrushchev's speech, after all, and his "explanation" for the evils he recounted, was that Stalin was a usurper who had "placed himself above the Party," and placed himself beyond criticism by fostering a "cult of the personality." Had not Mao also placed himself above the Party with his July 1955 speech and the collectivization campaign? And was not Mao also becoming the object of a similar form of hero worship?

The Chinese pondered these questions for more than a month before commenting on Khrushchev's speech. The commentary came on April 5 in the form of an editorial in the *People's Daily* entitled "On the Historical Experience of the Dictatorship of the Proletariat," a treatise probably written by Mao himself. The editorial referred to Stalin's "mistakes" and "errors" only in the most general terms and disclosed few of the details of Khrushchev's denunciation. The new Russian leaders were praised for their "courageous self-criticism of . . . past errors" while Stalin was still portrayed as a great socialist leader who "creatively applied and developed Marxism-Leninism" and carried out Lenin's policies of industrialization and collectivization. Acknowledging that Stalin "made some serious mistakes" in his later years, the Chinese commentary was implicitly more critical of Khrushchev for his failure to explain how those mistakes came about. For the most part the document was a defense of the socialist system Stalin built in Russia—and, by implication, the socialist system that was being built in China—and an attempt to explain (and to explain away) the problem of "the cult of the individual."[9]

The Chinese commentary was hardly more satisfactory than Khrushchev's speech in explaining how the evils of Stalin could have been perpetrated in a presumably socialist society, but Mao, unlike Khrushchev, was unwilling to separate Stalin from the Stalinist era. Khrushchev disposed of the problem by simply attributing all the socialist achievements of the Soviet Union to the party, the masses, and Leninism, and blaming all the failures and horrors of the era on Stalin alone; the evils, he repeated time and again, were due to "the willfulness of one man." Mao, on the other hand, insisted: "We should view Stalin from an historical standpoint, make a proper and all-round analysis to see where he was right and where he was wrong, and draw useful lessons therefrom. Both the things he did right and the things he did wrong were phenomena of the international communist movement and bore the imprint of the times." Thus Stalin was to be credited with the socialist achievements of the Soviet Union as well as held responsible for its defects. And since the achievements exceeded the defects, the historical picture of Stalin was a generally favorable one. Therefore, it was emphasized that "Stalin's works should, as before, still be seriously studied and that we should accept, as an important historical legacy, all that is of value in them, especially those many works in which he defended Leninism and correctly summarized the experience of building up the Soviet Union." To be sure, they were to be studied more critically than before. But for Maoists, Stalin remained a "great Marxist-Leninist revolutionary," albeit an imperfect one—at least on the public record.[10]

Mao also offered an explanation for the problem of "personality cults," but the intent was more to bury the question historically than to confront it politically. "The cult of the individual," it was explained, "is a foul carry-over from the long history of mankind. The cult of the individual is rooted not only in the exploiting classes but also in the small producers. As is well known, patriarchism is a product of small-producer economy." The appearance of such cults in a socialist society was attributed to the "poison-ous ideological survivals of the old society" which "still remain in people's minds for a very long time." While it was "quite natural for the name of Stalin to be greatly honoured throughout the world" for his contributions to socialism, it was to be deplored that he exaggerated his role and succumbed to backward ideological influences. The problem was not likely to appear in China, it was implied, for the Chinese Party "has incessantly fought against elevation of oneself and against individualist heroism." In any event, the necessary measures to prevent the appearance of the problem were on hand: an appropriate balance between "democracy" and "centralism"; modesty and prudence on the part of leaders; and reliance on "the mass line."[11]

. . .

Having temporarily disposed of the question of Stalin, Mao turned to deal with a Party leadership and apparatus increasingly resistant to the radical social and economic policies he was proposing. One way to revive the revolutionary spirit of a Party that was seen to be degenerating into a conservative and routinized bureaucracy was to challenge it from without. The task was first assigned to the non-Party intelligentsia. It was more to revitalize the Party than because of any desire to liberate intellectuals from ideological and political discipline—although Mao saw some limited virtues to be derived from a limited degree of intellectual ferment and opposition—that Mao revived the slogan "let a hundred flowers blossom, let a hundred schools of thought contend," in a speech delivered to the Supreme State Conference on May 2, 1956. It was left to Lu Dingyi, the head of the Central Committee's Propaganda Department, to announce the new Maoist policy when he addressed a meeting of artists, writers and scientists in Beijing on May 26.[12]

The phrase "let a hundred schools of thought contend" applied to scientists, whereas "let a hundred flowers blossom" was directed to writers and artists. The distinction was significant. The natural sciences were declared to have "no class character" and thus scientists were free to advocate and debate different scientific theories without fear of political intrusion; the goal was scientific progress, a politically neutral matter. For writers, artists, and scholars, on the other hand, the realm of freedom was more ambiguously defined. There was, to be sure, the promise of intellectual freedom for all. "History shows," Lu Dingyi observed, "that unless independent thinking and free discussion are encouraged, academic life stagnates." And he proclaimed that the new policy "means that we stand for freedom of independent thinking, of debate, of creative work; freedom to criticize and freedom to express, maintain and reserve one's opinions on questions of art, literature or scientific research."[13] But the promise of freedom was subject to numerous qualifications. While artists and writers were free to "blossom" in the realm of style and subject matter—"socialist realism" was the preferred but no longer the only method permitted—they were offered no license to freely decide the social and political content of their works. Unlike the natural sciences, works in art, literature, history, and philosophy retained a class character and therefore was still to be under political supervision in a country where "the class struggle is still going on." Moreover, the freedom granted was "freedom among the people" and the artistic and literary works produced under the new dispensation were "to serve the people." Lu left hanging the questions of who constituted "the people" and what served them—and who was to make the determination. Furthermore, the ends of the campaign for "blooming and contending" were largely predetermined. "Only through open debate," Lu noted, "can materialism conquer idealism."[14] There could be a free "battle of ideas," but the possibility that non-Marxist ideas might triumph was precluded from the outset.

But what Mao launched through the vehicle of Lu Dingyi's speech was not intended to be another movement to rectify the thoughts of the intellectuals. Mao now was attempting to turn the tables: it was the Party that was to be rectified, and the non-Party intelligentsia was the instrument to be used for that purpose. Lu Dingyi's speech was filled with bitter and sarcastic comments on the arrogance and ignorance of Party members:

They claim to be always right and fail to see the merits of others. . . . They take offence at the critical opinion of others. They always see themselves as the erudite teachers and others as their puny pupils. . . . These comrades had better stop this self-glorification right away . . . they had better be modest, listen more often to others' criticism . . . make a point of learning what they can from people outside the Party . . .

The point I want to make is that it is time for Party members to take note of their own inadequacies and remedy them. There is only one way to do so: to seek advice and learn honestly and modestly from those who know. The great majority of those intellectuals who are not Communist Party members study very hard. Members of the Communist Party must not be behind-hand in learning from them.[15]

Since the natural sciences now had been declared free of class associations, scientists began to protest the interference and the scientific incompetence of Party cadres. Soviet-adopted ideological orthodoxies were criticized, and a remarkably free debate developed on the still politically sensitive subject of genetics. The intelligentsia as a whole, however, was wary of "blooming" and "contending" in the fashion they were now presumably free to do. One speech was hardly sufficient to remove the fears that resulted from six years of repression. Lu Dingyi's speech itself was by no means wholly reassuring; his repeated references to the "reactionary" and "counterrevolutionary" ideas of Hu Feng must have had a chilling effect, as did his warning that "the work of ferreting out hidden counterrevolutionaries has not been completed."[16] Moreover, Lu had been careful to draw distinctions between "friends" and "enemies," between "the people" and "counterrevolutionaries"—and the distinctions were vague. What guarantee did the intellectuals have that openly discussed views might not be used as evidence to condemn them as "enemies" or "counterrevolutionaries" rather than members of "the people?"

Even more inhibiting was the open hostility of most Party officials. While Mao encouraged intellectuals to voice their criticisms, the Party officials they confronted in their day-to-day work were not nearly so encouraging. As Lou Longqi, the head of the Democratic League and a minister in the Beijing government, later explained the problem:

During the past year, not many flowers bloomed and few schools of thought contended in the academic and ideological fields . . . the basic cause lies in the fact that the higher intellectuals are still suspicious . . . this phenomenon is primarily due to the lack of a correct appreciation and comprehension of these two slogans on the part of some Party member cadres. . . . They feel that since the advancement of these slogans, the society has swarmed with heresies. They are therefore over-eager with the work of defending the faith.[17]

Nevertheless, by the summer of 1956, a significant number of intellectuals, especially writers, encouraged by special forums sponsored by the Writers' Union and by literary journals, began to express their views on matters of more than purely literary significance. Criticism of the evils of bureaucracy and the heavy hands of Party bureaucrats was an especially prominent theme and one very much in the desired Maoist spirit of the time. Socialist realism was attacked as "cheap optimism" and calls were heard for the revival of nineteenth-century Western realism to expose rather than hide real social conditions and the economic hardships of the masses. The Party itself was criticized for having disregarded the humanitarian ideals of Marxism. Many of the ideas for which Hu Feng had been imprisoned the year before were now heard and unpublished works written in the early 1950s appeared in print. At Beijing University, courses on Keynesian economics and the philosophy of Bertrand Russell were offered in the 1956–1957 academic year. Birth control, hitherto considered a Malthusian heresy as far as intellectuals were concerned (although it quietly had been discussed and promoted in official circles since 1954), was now being publicly advocated.

Although the Hundred Flowers campaign received formal endorsement at the Eighth Party Congress in September 1956, approval was little more than formal. The Party apparatus, for the most part, and many of its highest leaders were opposed to the campaign from the beginning—and the antibureaucratic thrust of much of what intellectuals were now writing confirmed suspicions that Mao's policy posed a threat to their positions and power. The anti-Stalinist revolt in Hungary in November served to solidify Party hostility to the movement. Although the situations in the two countries were hardly analogous, the analogy was drawn nevertheless. Freedom for Hungarian intellectuals had led to a workers' uprising against the Communist state. Did not critical intellectual ferment among the Chinese intelligentsia portend the same result, especially since unrest among the Chinese working class had resulted in an unprecedented wave of strikes earlier in the year? Whether Party leaders really feared a "Hungarian situation" is dubious, but the revolution in Hungary served as the pretext to launch a counterattack. By the end of the year, Party organs were warning of "poisonous weeds" that had sprung up among the blooming flowers. Criticism of dogmatism and bureaucratism in the Party suddenly turned to Party criticism of "rightism" among the intelligentsia. In the early months of 1957 the campaign was suppressed and intellectuals awaited the retribution of the Party bureaucrats they had been invited to criticize.

The time of retribution was to be delayed, and the Hundred Flowers campaign was to be revived, and in much more radical form, as a result of

Mao's now famous speech "On the Correct Handling of Contradictions Among the People," delivered at the end of February 1957. Mao's lengthy speech is undoubtedly one of the most significant theoretical expressions of "Maoism" in the postrevolutionary era. To understand its significance it is necessary to return to the debate on socioeconomic policy that was raging in late 1956, inexorably dividing the Party into "Maoist" and "non-Maoist" factions.

. . .

In 1956 China's leaders were celebrating the industrial successes of the First Five Year Plan and preparing the Second Five Year Plan, scheduled to begin in 1958. At the time, China's economic planners were still committed to following the Soviet model of development, albeit in somewhat modified form. While the modifications were not insignificant, the general thrust of the proposed Second Five Year Plan, and the fundamental assumptions on which it rested, basically were in accord with the Soviet model which had guided the first. Priority was still to be given to the development of heavy industry, and accordingly, special emphasis was placed on the rapid training of a modern scientific and technological intelligentsia.[18] It was taken for granted that industrialization meant urban industrialization and urbanization; as Zhou Enlai enthusiastically proclaimed in his report on the proposed plan, "we shall build up many new cities and enlarge many existing ones."[19] Moreover, it was assumed that the building of a modern industrial base was the essential prerequisite for the further socialist transformation of society, and thus Mao was under heavy criticism for having forced agricultural collectivization prematurely, because conditions of industrial backwardness precluded the mechanization and technology that a fully socialist agriculture presumably required.

Mao, in turn, was increasingly critical of the Second Five Year Plan, which he felt would only compound the undesirable social, political and ideological consequences that four years of rapid industrialization already had produced. It implied a further expansion and proliferation of bureaucracy and the solidification of professional and bureaucratic elites, an increasing gap between the modernizing cities and the backward countryside, a postponement of radical social change, and a further decay of ideology. In April 1956 Mao had offered an alternative proposal to the Politburo; his speech on "The Ten Great Relationships" (the text of which was only revealed a decade later), was cryptically worded but clearly called for an abandonment of Soviet-type five-year plans and outlined a radically different strategy. Although heavy industry was to grow no less rapidly than before, investment was to be concentrated on the development of light industry and agriculture; in place of the further growth of the advanced coastal sectors, the backward inland and interior areas were to be developed; instead of large-scale urban industrialization, the emphasis would shift to medium and small-scale industries in the countryside; instead of centralized bureaucratic direction (or decentralized regional bureaucratic controls), relatively autonomous local communities were to become the main socioeconomic units; labor-intensive projects were to be favored over capital-intensive ones, and moral incentives were to replace material incentives. Rapid social change was to proceed simultaneously with rapid economic development, and the decisive factor for both was the initiative and consciousness of the masses. Modern economic development was not to proceed more slowly; indeed, it was to proceed more rapidly, but in a far different fashion, and with vastly different social and political implications.[20]

Mao's unorthodox ideas on economic development were largely ignored in the documents on the Second Five Year Plan approved by the Party's Eighth Congress in September 1956. It was now possible to ignore Mao's ideas because he no longer exercised the supreme authority over the Party that he once did. A vast and routinized bureaucratic apparatus is not easily bent to the will of one man, no matter how much personal prestige he may enjoy. In 1955 Mao had overridden the Party's Central Committee—and had appealed directly to the rural cadres and the peasantry—in order to implement his program for rapid collectivization, an event that was a source of continuing resentment among Party leaders. Conditions in 1956 were less conducive for another such *tour de force*. Khrushchev's denunciation of Stalin and the evils of "one-man" rule in February had weakened Mao's position. The Eighth Party Congress, the first held since 1945, was presided over by Liu Shaoqi and Deng Xiaoping. It was Liu and Deng, not Mao, who presented the main reports to the Congress—and to reinforce the new principle of collective leadership, the phrase "guided by the thought of Mao Zedong" was deleted from the new Party constitution. The Eighth Congress further reduced Mao's power by reestablishing the post of General Secretary, which had been abolished in 1937. Appointed to the revived office was Deng Xiaoping, who came to exercise considerable control over the organizational apparatus of the Party. It was with good reason that Mao later complained that in 1956 his views were met with "indifference" by most Party leaders. While Mao's personal prestige remained enormous, the control of the Party organization had fallen into other hands; he remained master of Marxist-Leninist theory but no longer master of policy.

Mao's February 1957 speech "On the Correct Handling of Contradictions Among the People," must be seen in the light of his relative political powerlessness in the Party and his conviction that conservative state and Party organs were blocking radical social change. The debate over questions of economic policy thus became inseparable from the question of personal power. The breaking down of bureaucratic resistance to the alternative policies of socioeconomic development Mao was proposing became the immediate task, and the February speech was designed to do precisely that. It established an ideological justification and set off a train of political events whereby Mao could set himself above the Party (or, at least, above the established Party leadership) and emerge as a supreme leader speaking directly to "the people."

"On the Correct Handling of Contradictions Among the People" served to revive the Hundred Flowers campaign, which the Party bureaucracy had been busily suppressing during the preceding two months. The speech was presented not at a Party meeting but rather to an enlarged session of the Supreme State Conference, an organ of the state apparatus. Just as Mao had used a non-Party forum to deliver his July 1955 speech on agricultural collectivization, he now again went outside regular Party channels to announce policy initiatives and theoretical innovations; in both instances the Maoist position had failed to receive the support the majority of the Politburo, and in both cases the Party was presented with a *fait accompli.* Although the text of the February speech was not published until June (and then only in revised form), the essence of the original quickly circulated among the intelligentsia.

The political significance of Mao's speech was not only that he extended a new invitation to the intellectuals to speak their minds at the very time the Party apparatus had silenced dissenters and was eliminating the "poisonous weeds" produced by the limited "blossoming" of the latter half of 1956, but that he did so on the basis of an argument that suggested the Communist Party did not necessarily possess a monopoly on correct ideas and therefore was subject to criticism from outside its ranks. The renewal of the Hundred Flowers movement was justified not only because of the desirability of stimulating intellectual creativity for purposes of economic development, but also because of the continued existence of "contradictions" in a socialist society. The latter thesis by itself was neither novel nor radical. That contradictions are the motivating force of social development—and that they are inevitable, desirable, and eternal—long had been a principal tenet of Maoist theory. Nor was there anything novel in Mao's distinctions between "antagonistic" and "nonantagonistic" contradictions, and between "the people" and their "enemies." Had Mao confined himself to restating these familiar views, his speech would hardly have raised any political or ideological eyebrows. What made the speech politically significant—and politically threatening—was the introduction of two new propositions, both of which were to prove to be prophetic pointers to the Cultural Revolution. While Mao enumerated many contradictions, the one that he emphasized was that between the "leadership and the led." Not only were there contradictions between the government and the masses in general, but also among "leaders" and "people" in particular. And "leaders" were not simply low-level bureaucratic functionaries. Nowhere did Mao exclude the possibility that the leaders who stood in contradiction to the people might be the very highest officials of the Party, nor the possibility that on certain questions such leaders might be wrong and "the people" right: "Correct and good things have often at first been looked upon not as fragrant flowers but as poisonous weeds," and this might well be the case even in a socialist society.[21] Only a period of trial through ideological struggle could distinguish correct from incorrect ideas. Since it was possible for the Party and even its leaders to fall into error, the Party should be exposed to criticism from the people. "For a Party as much as for an individual," Mao declared, "there is a great need to hear opinions different from its own." Since the people were broadly defined as all those supporting socialism, the range and scope of critical opinion that the Party could hear was potentially very great. Intellectuals, assumed to be basically united in their support of socialism, were thus theoretically free to criticize the Party. And the "democratic parties" who "enjoy the confidence of the people" were enjoined to "exercise supervision over the Communist Party" under a policy of "mutual supervision."[22]

This questioning of the infallibility of the Leninist party had far greater political implications than offering the largely fictious "democratic parties" entrée into the political arena. If the people in general were now free to criticize the Party, then who was to speak for "the people" if not Mao himself? Mao, after all, was not only the chairman of the Party but also the head of the People's Republic. Moreover, as the leader of the people's revolution, Mao had special bonds to the masses which no one else could claim; if the people were free to speak, then Mao was their preeminent spokesman. What Mao's argument on "contradictions among the people" did was to free Mao himself from the Leninist discipline of the Party and enable him to criticize the Party from without in his unique role as the representative of the people. It was a role he soon was to assume.

If the suggestion that the Party was not infallible (and thus subject to criticism from the people—and from Mao) was an implicit threat to Party authorities, especially those who opposed Mao's policies and programs, that threat was reinforced by another proposition, the view that class struggle continues under socialism and that it takes a primarily ideological form.

Much of Mao's treatise proceeded on the premise that socialism had been established in China and that class exploitation was abolished; therefore such social divisions and contradictions that still existed among a basically united people were nonantagonistic in nature. But Mao then qualified the argument by proclaiming that "class struggle is not yet over." Remnants of the old exploiting classes still remain, he observed, although it was not the remnants of social classes but rather the influence of their ideologies that was the source of the struggle: "the class struggle *in the ideological field* between the proletariat and the bourgeoisie will still be long and devious and at times may even become very acute . . . the question whether socialism or capitalism will win is still not really settled."[23] While the proletariat and the bourgeoisie as such may not have been engaged in combat, the conflict between what was deemed to be their respective ideologies was sufficient to proclaim the continued existence of a grave class struggle. The proposition was a logical culmination of a long-held Maoist tendency to define classes and class struggles in terms of conscious attitudes rather than on the basis of objective social criteria—and it marked the appearance of a rigid ideological determinism that henceforth was to govern Maoism. It also directly contradicted the official view expounded only a few months earlier at the Eighth Party Congress to the effect that the struggle between capitalism and socialism had been decided in favor of the latter and that class differences had been reduced to "only a matter of division of labor within the same class."[24]

That Mao chose to proclaim the continued existence of class struggle at the very time he sought to revive the Hundred Flowers campaign had ominous implications. Since "class struggle" was now a matter of a struggle between class ideologies and not between actual social classes, the way was open to condemn as "class enemies" those who expressed incorrect ideas. Nonantagonistic contradictions among the people quickly could be converted into antagonistic class contradictions between the people and their enemies, thus sanctioning the use of "coercive methods" in place of "painstaking reasoning." It was precisely under this rationale that the second phase of "blooming and contending" was to be brought to an end.

The new doctrine had no less threatening political implications for Mao's opponents in the Party. If the Communist Party and its highest leaders were no longer ideologically infallible, as was now suggested, then presumably they were not immune to bourgeois ideological influences. And if class struggle expressed itself in "the ideological field," then ideological and policy conflicts within the Party could be interpreted as class conflicts, and the Party itself could become the political arena for a "class struggle" between the "proletariat" and the "bourgeoisie." These views were to become fully politically explicit only in the Cultural Revolution, but in 1957 Mao established the theoretical basis to arrive at such conclusions, and he was increasingly drawn to them over the following years.

The first political result of Mao's February speech was the revival of the Hundred Flowers movement. But the revival was not immediate. The Party apparatus was opposed, and the intellectuals were suspicious. Party officials hardly could have been enthusiastic about promoting a campaign to resolve the contradiction between "leaders" and the "led," especially since Mao had identified the bureaucratic practices of the Party as the source of the contradiction and had called on the masses to criticize and supervise their leaders as the method to resolve it. And Party resistance reinforced fears among intellectuals that Mao's call was a trap or could prove to be one. The intellectuals, the historian Qian Bozan explained,

> have to speculate for example whether the call for flowers to bloom forth is sincere or just a gesture. They have to guess to what extent, if the call is sincere, flowers will be allowed to blossom forth and whether the call will be recalled after the flowers are in bloom. . . . They have to guess which are the problems that can be brought up for discussion and which are the problems which cannot be discussed. . . . When the leadership cadres of some establishments limit themselves to the giving of lip service to the call without taking action to make flowers blossom forth . . . the intellectuals also refrain from airing their views.[25]

Mao persisted nevertheless. Although the text of his February speech remained unpublished, the major points were revealed in the *People's Daily*. Forums were held in major cities during March and April where intellectuals and leaders of non-Communist groups and parties were assured that the Party was sincere in inviting criticism. Mao again spoke to a gathering of intellectuals and emphasized that the Communists welcomed and required criticism. He prodded the Central Committee to officially sanction "blooming and contending"; at the end of April a Party rectification campaign was launched to eliminate the evils of "bureaucratism, subjectivism, and sectarianism." The campaign was to proceed in a manner as gentle as "a breeze" and "as mild as rain," but it was made clear that it was the Party that was to be rectified and that it was non-Party intellectuals who were to do the rectifying. And criticism was to focus on the eminently political question of the relationship between "leaders and led."

Once Party officials and cadres were ordered not to interfere with free expression, the trickle of dissatisfactions timidly voiced at officially organized meetings in March and April turned into a torrent of social and political criticism in May and early June. The critics became increasingly bold and their accusations increasingly bitter as the virtual absence of official rebuttals seemed to confirm the solemn promises of Party leaders that criticism was genuinely desired. The movement spread and acquired a more and more spontaneous character. Forums sponsored by the "democratic parties" and the United Front Work Department of the Communist Party were supplemented by less formal meetings called by ad hoc organizations. Established newspapers were filled with reports of the speeches and comments of the critics, but harsher criticisms were expressed on big character posters that appeared on the walls of schools and public buildings. Emotions ran high as long-suppressed feelings were expressed in increasingly strident terms.

The atmosphere, for a time, was not unlike that of the early phase of the May Fourth Movement of 1919 when the country was swept by a similar sense of liberation from the oppressions of the past and a similar feeling of freedom to strike out against established orthodoxies and institutions. Indeed, many of the student participants compared themselves to their hallowed May Fourth predecessors. But, unlike the May Fourth Movement, the Hundred Flowers campaign was not allowed to spread from urban intellectual circles to the urban masses. No forums of criticism were set up for workers and peasants. The movement remained largely confined to intellectuals and students, although some members of the intelligentsia spoke about the condition of the masses and spoke on their behalf.

The criticisms which emerged during the brief time they were permitted ranged from everyday petty grievances to wholesale indictments of the sociopolitical order. Many intellectuals confined themselves to pleas for professional autonomy, but others addressed themselves to fundamental social and political questions, such as the monopoly on political power exercised by the Communist Party, a matter brought up for public discussion for the first time in the history of the People's Republic. The Constitution of 1954 provided a "leading role" for the Party, but both the constitution and Maoist theory provided freedom and a meaningful political role for the democratic parties. Yet in political reality, no such role existed. The democratic parties' only "freedom" was to formally ratify decisions already made in secret by the CCP. They were neither consulted in advance nor allowed to debate matters of significance, and the condition prevailed from the National People's Congress down to the *xian* people's councils. What then, it was asked, was the meaning of the heralded "united front," the "democratic dictatorship" of four classes, and the Constitution of the Republic? While the critics detailed specific abuses of power perpetrated by Party organs and members, they also raised the larger question of the validity of one-party rule and the absence of any meaningful distinction between the

Republic's Government and the Party. Although most of those who raised this politically sensitive issue were careful to point out that they accepted the general leadership of the Party, they nonetheless made clear their objections to a "Party-monopolized country."

Calls for "socialist legality" were heard, just as they were then being heard in the Soviet Union and the Eastern European countries. What, it was asked, had become of such constitutional rights as freedom of speech, press, and residence, and especially the "inviolable" guarantee of the "freedom of the person of citizens"? The violations of these freedoms were set forth in great detail. The case of Hu Feng was raised time and again. Why, it was asked, had the imprisoned Hu Feng not been brought to trial? It was proposed that a commission of inquiry investigate illegal arrests that had taken place during the *Sanfan* and *Sufan* campaigns. Demands were made that those who had accepted the current invitation to "bloom and contend" would not suffer similar fates.

Aspects of social as well as political life were attacked. There were complaints, for example, that neither the letter nor the spirit of the Marriage Law of 1950 were being observed; old feudal attitudes toward women persisted even among many Party members, it was charged, and the All-China Federation of Democratic Women demonstrated little concern for the continued oppression of women.

The most striking critiques were those that judged the Communist order on the basis of its own socialist standards. Although the critics of the Hundred Flowers era were soon to be silenced because, it was alleged, they attacked the socialist system, what was being attacked was not socialism but the failure of the Communists to practice their own socialist principles. For the Communist rulers, nothing that emerged from the Hundred Flowers movement was more threatening than the charge that the Communists had betrayed their socialist promises and their revolutionary ideals. The critiques took different forms but they all pointed to the conclusion that the Communists had abandoned their revolutionary traditions, were becoming a "new class," and were promoting socioeconomic inequalities rather than eliminating them. As a leader of the Peasants' and Workers' Democratic Party put the matter:

In leading the masses to carry through the revolution in the past, the Party stood among the masses; after the liberation, it felt the position had changed and, instead of standing among the masses, it stood on the back of the masses and ruled the masses. . . . [leaders] should differ in duties, not in status. Some are deeply conscious of being officials; they occupy special positions even when taking meals and seeing operas.[26]

Party officials and cadres, it was charged, had come to adopt the attitudes of traditional mandarins and Guomindang bureaucrats and enjoyed similar privileges; they lived in special residences, hired servants, sent their children to "aristocratic schools," and enjoyed special access to vacation resorts, recreational facilities, and medical care—all denied to the masses and all enjoyed at the expense of the masses. "Who are the people who enjoy a higher standard of living?" one critic asked. "They are the Party members and cadres who wore worn-out shoes in the past, but travel in saloon cars and put on woolen uniforms now."[27] The conclusion was drawn by a veteran Communist revolutionary in a lengthy letter to Mao and the Central Committee: "There is a privileged class in existence. Even if a national united class has not yet been formed, the embryo of this class is forming and developing."[28] The estrangement of the Party from the masses, particularly from the peasantry, and its power to appropriate an increasingly disproportionate share of the products of the laboring masses, threatened to create a new division between exploiters and exploited.

For the Marxist critics of the regime, intellectual and political freedom were not abstract principles that could be separated from the nature and content of social development. Nor was freedom a right to be enjoyed by intellectuals alone. Freedom was not only one of the essential ends of socialism, it also was an essential means to achieve socialist goals. Intellectual and political freedom for all the people was necessary to check the growth of bureaucracy, necessary to prevent the formation and solidification of a new bureaucratic ruling class, and necessary for genuine social equality. A privileged ruling Party attracted careerists and bureaucrats who separated themselves from the masses and stood above them. Only when special privileges were eliminated would genuine revolutionaries join the Party. They thus called for a reduction in the number of full-time officials, the abolition of special privileges, popular supervision over state and Party organs, popular control over political and economic life, and the introduction of "socialist democracy," both within and without the Party.

The critics did not confine themselves to condemning the inequities between leaders and led; they also pointed to undesirable social inequalities that had emerged among the people. The Party was criticized for ignoring the oppressive burdens under which the peasants labored and for sanctioning the growing gap between the cities and the countryside. Marxist critics deplored the lack of workers' control in the factories, the absence of free trade unions, and the new system of wage differentials which was creating divisions among the urban proletariat.

It is striking how much of this critique repeated and anticipated the Maoist critique of Chinese state and society. At the very time of the Hundred Flowers movement, Mao too was lashing out against the privileges of a Party bureaucracy that had separated itself from the masses and abandoned its revolutionary traditions of "plain living and hard work." In his February speech he had identified "bureaucratic practices" among the leaders as the principal cause of the "contradictions among the people" and declared that "we must stamp out bureaucracy." His attacks on bureaucracy were to become increasingly radical, and he soon was not only to condemn "bureaucratic practices" but to demand the elimination of what he termed "the bureaucratic class"—and, like the critics of 1957, he was to find that class imbedded in the Communist Party. Already in 1957 Mao complained that, "A dangerous tendency has shown itself of late among many of our personnel—an unwillingness to share the joys and hardships of the masses, a concern for personal position and gain."[29] And he long had been concerned with the growth of inequality in Chinese society, and especially the differences between town and countryside. He had referred to the matter briefly in his February speech, noting that "the wages of a small number of workers and some government personnel are rather too high" and thus "the peasants have reason to be dissatisfied. . . ."[30] An egalitarian drive to narrow the gap between town and countryside and to strike down urban elites was to be a major aim of Maoist policies during both the Great Leap Forward campaign and the Cultural Revolution. Even before the year 1957 was out, Mao was to lower wage differentials among urban workers, reversing the "wage reforms" of 1956.

Yet the socialist critics of the spring of 1957 soon were to be branded as "enemies of socialism" and condemned as "counterrevolutionaries" in the antirightist campaign that tragically brought the Hundred Flowers movement to an end. And Mao was to place himself at the head of the heresy-hunting campaign of the latter half of 1957 whose victims included many of those who apparently shared his view of the condition of Chinese society and its deficiencies as a socialist society. It is both ironic and tragic that Mao should have participated in the persecution of intellectuals whom he had invited to "bloom and contend" and whose social and political criticisms were similar to his own. While Mao shared the egalitarian and anti-bureaucratic aims of the socialist critics, he did not share their commitment to freedom and democracy. Mao's inability to recognize that the building of institutions of political democracy and institutional guarantees of intellectual freedom are integral parts in the building of socialism was to prove to be one of the fatal flaws in the "Maoist vision."

Beyond the attacks on bureaucracy and inequality, the Hundred Flowers campaign raised other issues that Mao was soon to take up and champion. Particularly prominent were criticisms of the Soviet Union and the uncritical adoption of Soviet methods. Some attacked the Russians for having dismantled the industrial base of Manchuria at the end of World War II, for having forced China to bear the costs of the Korean War, and for economic aid that entailed political strings and heavy interest payments. In 1957 they were to be denounced as "anti-Soviet and anti-socialist nationalists," but Mao and others were to denounce the Soviet Union in more virulent fashion three years later. Others criticized the "mechanical copying" of Soviet curricula and textbooks in schools and the "blind imitation" of Soviet theories and techniques in science and industry. And they did so on the very eve of the wholesale Maoist abandonment of "the Soviet model." Teachers and students criticized hierarchical distinctions and formalistic methods in schools and universities, anticipating the Maoist attack on the educational system during the Cultural Revolution. Complaints were heard about the neglect of preventive medicine for the masses, that doctors were spending much of their time attending to Party officials, and that traditional medicine was being ignored—complaints soon to be heard from Mao. And the government was reproached for "paying too much attention to the cities." In the summer of 1957, at the height of the antirightist campaign, the literary critic Chen Qixia was accused of having engaged in a conspiracy against the Party; the "evidence" brought to support the charge included a reported statement that peasants might rise in revolt because "living standards are so unequal in town and country." Six months later Mao was to launch the Great Leap Forward campaign, which had as one of its stated goals the closing of the gap between urban and rural areas.

University students were the most radical and least inhibited of the Hundred Flowers critics. What was called "the storm in the universities" began on May 19 at Beijing University. Classrooms were emptied as students expressed their criticisms in the form of big-character posters pasted on university buildings and in classrooms; the main arena in "the battle of posters" became known as the Democratic Wall and it was there that the first Chinese translation of Khrushchev's speech denouncing Stalin appeared, an abridged version translated from the New York *Daily Worker.* The movement expanded into rallies, demonstrations and outdoor meetings, centering at an area of the campus renamed the Democratic Plaza. Like the May Fourth Movement, the example set by the students in Beijing was emulated at universities throughout the country. The criticisms of the students were much the same as those of older intellectuals, although they put particular emphasis on reducing the power of Party committees in the universities and eliminating Soviet influences in education. The main difference was that "blooming and contending" among students took a more explicitly political character. Quasi-political organizations (such as the

Hundred Flowers Society) sprang up, distributing leaflets, organizing rallies and publishing mimeographed newspapers. Discussion meetings often turned into "struggle sessions," with Party cadres and university administrators the targets of the struggles. Some student leaders quickly acquired national reputations; among the most prominent and outspoken was Lin Xiling, a young woman who was studying at Chinese People's University, a cadre training school. She attacked the "new class" system from a Marxist perspective and argued that China could not achieve a genuine socialist society until China became genuinely democratic.

By early June, the growing student movement (which by then had spread from universities to middle schools) was becoming increasingly militant and sometimes violent; there were reports of students occupying university offices, attacking government and Party buildings, and holding school and Party officials hostage. And in emulation of their May Fourth predecessors, there was an abortive attempt to "go to the people," as some students attempted to organize workers and peasants.

Although the budding student movement was cut short in mid-June, the rapidity with which students could spontaneously organize for political action against established authority was a prophetic pointer to the future. In different political circumstances and for different political ends, the phenomenon was to be repeated in the Cultural Revolution and in the 1980s on much vaster scales. The "storm in the universities" of 1957 was not nearly so stormy as the one Mao was to unleash nine years later.

· · ·

An editorial in the *People's Daily* on June 8 signaled the end of the Hundred Flowers campaign. The Party organ hitherto had remained editorially silent, largely confining itself to reporting the criticisms of the critics. Now it announced that "right-wingers" had abused their freedom in order to attack socialism and the Communist Party. Subsequent editorials specifically rebutted the criticisms of the era of "blooming and contending," warned of the danger of anarchy, and emphasized the need for class struggle against the enemies who had revealed themselves during the campaign. By the middle of the month, the forums where intellectuals had been criticizing the Party had turned into sessions where Party officials denounced the critics. The antirightist campaign had begun and it was to continue for a year as a heresy hunt for dissidents both within and outside the Party. The slogan "let a hundred flowers bloom" remained official policy, but the policy was no longer to cultivate new flowers but to root out "poisonous weeds."

Lest Mao's unpublished February 27 speech be used to justify continued criticism of the Party, a revised version was published on June 18 to justify the suppression of the critics. The published version noted that the author had made "certain additions" to the original verbatim record. Among the additions were a list of six criteria to distinguish permissible from unpermissible ideas. The ex post facto criteria were sufficiently vague to banish virtually every critic from the ranks of "the people"—and it was solely for the Party to determine whether a particular idea tended to strengthen or weaken "the leadership of the Communist Party" or whether it was beneficial or harmful to "socialist transformation." There were other significant additions and deletions, judging from a tape recording of the original, extracts from which were then being circulated in Poland. In the February speech, for example, Mao argued that "Stalin made the mistake of substituting internal differences for external antagonism, which resulted in a rule of terror and the liquidation of thousands of Communists." This was deleted from the published version of June, for at the time the Chinese Communists were preparing to convert a variety of hitherto "nonantagonistic contradictions among the people" into antagonistic class differences. Also deleted was Mao's warning that terroristic methods in dealing with internal antagonisms might result in their transformation into "antagonisms of the nation-enemy type, as happened in Hungary." The June version referred to "certain people in our country [who] were delighted when the Hungarian events took place. They hoped that something similar would happen in China. . . ." During the antirightist drive, some Chinese intellectuals were accused of emulating the Hungarian Petofi Club with the hope of stimulating a revolt to overthrow Communist rule. In the February speech, Mao had been critical of Party officials who opposed the Hundred Flowers policy and attributed their opposition to "a fear of criticism"; there was, he said, no need to fear "that the policy of a hundred flowers will yield poisoned fruit," and added that even some of the latter might prove beneficial. In the June publication, by contrast, he emphasized the need to distinguish between "fragrant flowers and poisonous weeds." The officially published version was markedly harsher in tone than the original speech and the revisions were designed to justify repression on the grounds that the intellectuals had gone beyond the bounds of acceptable criticism.

The weight of the antirightist campaign first fell hardest on the leaders of the "democratic parties." Luo Longqi and Zhang Bojun (both heads of central government ministries) were the most publicized targets, although they had been among the most cautious critics. Subjected to endless denunciation in the press and at rectification meetings, they were forced to confess that they had organized an "invisible conspiracy" against the socialist system. When original confessions were deemed inadequate, other and more abject ones were demanded. Although the period of "blooming and contending" lasted little more than a month, the era of repentance dragged on into the spring of 1959. The public confessions were similar to those exacted during the heresy hunts in Stalinist Russia. For example, after "confessing" to a bewildering variety of political and ideological sins, Luo Longqi concluded his self-denunciation: "With contrition, I own that I have failed to live up to the expectations of Chairman Mao, the leadership of the Party, and the scores of thousands of [Democratic] League members. . . . I want to transform myself radically. And I want to work honestly for the socialist cause and the Chinese people."[31] Zhang Bojun concluded his detailed recantation of "my reactionary political program" with the following prostration:

> The whole nation is demanding stern punishment for me, a rightist. This is what should be done and I am prepared to accept it. I hate my wickedness. I want to kill the old and reactionary self so that he will not return to life. I will join the whole nation in the stern struggle against the rightists, including myself. The great Chinese Communist Party once saved me, it saved me once more today. I hope to gain a new life under the leadership and teaching of the Party and Chairman Mao and to return to the stand of loving the Party and socialism.[32]

And Qu Anping, chief editor of the *Guangming Daily* until the antirightist onslaught, was first publicly denounced by his son and then denounced himself: "I sincerely admit my mistakes, ask punishment from the people, and surrender to the people."[33]

But unlike Stalinist Russia, where flagellant "confessions" normally were presented as evidence to pronounce death sentences, in China punishment usually ended after a psychologically torturous ordeal. Luo Longqi and Zhang Bojun, removed from their ministerial posts in 1957, were reinstated as leaders of the democratic parties and in 1959 resumed their places as delegates to the People's Political Consultative Conference.

Students, who had been the most vehement critics in May and June, were treated relatively leniently and with little public fanfare. The official Party line was that the young students, who had grown to maturity in the new society, had been misled by the older bourgeois intellectuals, who were hangovers from the prerevolutionary order. Some student leaders were sent to the countryside for "reform through labor," but most students branded as rightists were permitted to remain in school under Party supervision.

The harshest treatment was reserved for left-wing writers and artists who had advocated freedom to depict actual social conditions. Their earlier experiences with Party bureaucrats had made them more suspicious than most intellectuals, and they had confined themselves to oblique criticisms of Maoist orthodoxies on art and literature. But this did not spare them the retribution of Zhou Yang, who was reestablished as China's literary dictator during the antirightist campaign. The Hundred Flowers slogan, he declared, was not meant to be a policy of "liberalization as certain bourgeois writers . . . imagine, but a militant slogan for the development of socialist culture." The militant development of "socialist culture" meant militancy in the political repression of socialist writers. Zhou Yang had scores to settle with old opponents. One victim was the Marxist Ding Ling, perhaps the most creative of China's living writers. A Communist Party member since the early days of the revolution, she had spent three years in a Guomindang prison in the 1930s for other political heresies. Ding Ling now was accused of fomenting anti-Party activities, and denounced as a rightist bent on subverting the thoughts of younger writers. She was expelled from the Party, removed from her position in the Writers Union, and dispatched to northern Manchuria for "labor reform." Her writings were removed from library shelves. Similar fates befell other literary intellectuals who were reluctant to confess political sins and the Writers Union was turned into a police organ to punish heretical writers.

The suppression of the Hundred Flowers movement thus destroyed the hope that China's "transition to socialism" might proceed on the basis of popular democracy and with some measure of intellectual freedom. It reinforced the fact that the exercise of state power was a monopoly of the Communist Party, tearing away the last shreds of the facade that the "democratic parties" could play a meaningful role in the political life of the nation. It silenced the intellectuals, Marxists and non-Marxists alike; and subjected them to harsher forms of political and intellectual repression. And it restored to absolute primacy Maoist orthodoxies on art and literature which continued to stifle Chinese intellectual and artistic life.

Why did the Party—and Mao—betray the promise of a more democratic and free society and break their solemn pledges not to retaliate against the intellectuals they had invited to freely "bloom and contend" and openly criticize the Party? Motivations are difficult to read and the passage of time has not made the task any easier. The Hundred Flowers still defies an entirely satisfactory interpretation. One view, widely held at the time both inside and outside China, was that the whole movement was a trap laid by the Communist leadership, a Machiavellian plot to "smoke out" dissenters and then punish them once they exposed themselves. With the antirightist campaign, the Hundred Flowers did in effect become that, and some Communist leaders later claimed that this had been the purpose all along. A July 12 *People's Daily* editorial suggested that the Party deliberately had permitted "poisonous weeds" to emerge in order to destroy their cultivators. And Liu Shaoqi put the same interpretation on the Hundred Flowers policy in May 1958: "we allow the anti-socialist poisonous weeds to grow and confront the people with contrasts, so that by way of comparison, the people can see clearly what they really are, and roused to indignation, rally together to up-root them."[34]

This ex post facto explanation serves well the self-image of an infallible and unified Leninist party consistently pursuing a well-charted course. But the Party was hardly a monolithic entity in 1956–1957, and the evidence of the time points to the Hundred Flowers policy as a distinctively Maoist ini-tiative taken in opposition to most Party leaders. The question of why the Party as such broke its pledge does not really arise since the Party as such never really made a pledge in the first place. The question is why Mao made the pledge and then broke it, and neither of the two parts of the question lends itself to easy explanation. There is perhaps some truth in the view that Mao was responding to the upheavals in Eastern Europe, and particu-larly in Hungary, by loosening the political reins to prevent a similar explo-sion in China; and then tightening the reins again when the Hundred Flowers seemed to threaten Communist power. A deep concern with the Hungarian Revolution is certainly evident in Mao's February 1957 speech, or at least in the revised version of June. But while events in other Com-munist countries perhaps influenced the timing and outcome of the second phase of the campaign—the February speech and the resultant "blooming and contending" of May and June—the fact remains that Mao was advo-cating the Hundred Flowers policy well before the fall 1956 upheavals in Poland (which the Chinese supported against the Soviet Union) and Hun-gary, and indeed even before Khrushchev's February 1956 speech on Stalin. Maoist motives seem more complex, and more contradictory, than the "letting off steam" theory allows.

The optimistic premise upon which the Hundred Flowers policy was based was that the people were basically united in support of the estab-lished socialist system. Certainly one of the most striking features of Mao's speeches and writings in 1955–56 is a populist conception of "the people" as an organic entity, 600,000,000 "united as one" in the task of building so-cialism. The conviction that "the interests of the people are basically the same" and that they were conscious of their identity of interests is a notion Mao repeated time and again. And despite his long-standing distrust of in-tellectuals, Mao was also convinced that even if most intellectuals were not socialists or Marxists, the overwhelming majority were "patriotic," and therefore were willing "to serve their flourishing socialist motherland."[35] The problem of "contradictions" lay not so much with the intellectuals as with Party officials who "are not good at getting along with intellectuals."[36] The vision that Mao presented in February 1957 (although there were contradictory strains) suggested a relatively peaceful transition to socialism and communism based on "the united front of all patriotic forces."[37] The Hundred Flowers policy of criticism from below and "supervision" from outside the Party would serve to prevent leaders from becoming alienated from the people, and peacefully resolve still nonantagonistic contradictions between leaders and led. Popular criticism, it was believed, would lead to ever higher levels of unity as the nation progressed through ever higher stages of socialist transformation. And it was assumed that a basically united people understood that "freedom" should not go beyond the bounds of socialist "discipline," and that "democracy" should be combined with "centralism."

Another assumption of the Hundred Flowers policy was the long-standing Maoist belief in the value of struggle, partly as an end in itself, and partly as a therapeutic device for the development of the correct ideas necessary for socialist transformation. Marxism itself, Mao emphasized,

> can only develop through struggle—this is true not only in the past and present, it is necessarily true in the future also. What is correct always develops in the course of struggle with what is wrong. The true, the good and the beautiful always exist in comparison with the false, the evil and the ugly, and grow in struggle with the latter. As mankind in general rejects an untruth and accepts a truth, a new truth will begin struggling with new erroneous ideas. Such struggles will never end. This is the law of development of truth and it is certainly the law of development of Marxism.[38]

Thus the flourishing of correct Marxist ideas was dependent on Marxists being confronted with the challenge of incorrect ideas. For, as Mao put it, "correct ideas, if pampered in hothouses without being exposed to the elements or immunized from disease, will not win out against wrong ones."[39] Without the challenge of wrong ideas, Marxism would stagnate and the revolutionary spirit would die. Thus the class struggle "in the ideological field" was both inevitable and beneficial, and it was necessary to wage it; indeed, if it did not exist, it would have to be created.

On the one hand, this tremendous emphasis on the necessity of struggle—and a never ending struggle at that—seems in conflict with the Maoist vision of a united people pursuing a peaceful path to socialism and peacefully resolving whatever nonantagonistic contradictions appear along the way. Yet it is precisely through struggle, Mao believed, that "the people" attain the proper consciousness to keep them unified, achieve ever higher levels of unity through ever higher levels of ideological transformation, and remain on the proper course of social development. The Maoist notion of a united people peacefully building socialism presupposed constant processes of struggle and ideological transformation. Nor was it only "the people" and the non-Party intelligentsia who stood in need of ideological transformation; the Party itself was badly in need of remolding and rectification. Struggle stimulated by criticism from below and outside the Party, even (and perhaps especially) if such criticism entailed incorrect thoughts, would, it was assumed, serve to revitalize a leadership grown conservative and a Party apparatus showing signs of bureaucratic stagnation.

The nature of the criticisms that burst forth in May and June, and the vehemence with which they were expressed, confirmed the worst fears of many Party leaders and cadres. And Mao's faith in a basically unified people and a basically pro-socialist intelligentsia was shaken. For he took socialist critiques of the inadequacies of socialism in China as anti-socialist attacks, even though Mao himself was later to repeat many of the criticisms he then condemned as "bourgeois rightism." Particularly disturbing was that the most outspoken critics were young students who had grown to maturity after 1949 and whose ideological errors could not be easily attributed to the influences of the old society.

It would be tempting to attribute the end of the Hundred Flowers campaign to conservative Party bureaucrats who opposed Mao's policy from the outset, who had the most to fear from freedom of criticism, and who thirsted for a pretext to suppress the movement and take retribution against their critics—and thus spare Mao the historical responsibility for having purged the critics he had called into being. But the weight of evidence suggests that Mao was little more prepared than other Communist leaders to tolerate criticism that went beyond the vague boundaries of "socialist discipline." As early as May 25 he expressed concern over the direction the campaign was taking: "Any speech or action which deviates from socialism is entirely wrong," he warned in an address to the Communist Youth League. And in June, when the campaign seemed to threaten social and political disorder, he was not reluctant to call on the full power of Party and state to launch the antirightist witch hunt. He castigated newspapers for having printed "seditious reports showing the bourgeois point of view" and his statements over the summer months increasingly emphasized the continued existence of class struggle and stressed the need for "discipline" (rather than "freedom") and for "centralism" (rather than "democracy").[40] Although most of China's leaders would not have allowed the Hundred Flowers campaign in the first place, Mao clearly does not emerge from the episode as any champion of the free expression of ideas.

If the suppression of the Hundred Flowers movement and the subsequent antirightist campaign marked a defeat for what some observers saw as Mao's "liberalizing" vision of a new united front of the whole people and a victory for Mao's conservative Party opponents, that defeat was in large measure inherent in the very premises of Mao's Hundred Flowers policy. Both the assumption that "the people" were a basically united entity and the goal of unity lent themselves to a heresy-hunting outcome. For if the people were basically united in their aims and interests, then the implicit assumption was that they would express more or less similar ideas; ideas that diverged from what were deemed to be the socialist interests of the people put their exponents outside the ranks of "the people" and sanctioned depriving them of the right of freedom of speech, a right reserved only for the people and not their "enemies." For the latter, as Mao cavalierly put it in the revised version of his speech, "the matter is easy; we simply deprive them of their freedom of speech."[41] Since the ultimate criterion for determining one's membership in the ranks of "the people" was one's conscious attitudes, the right of "freedom of speech" was a most limited and tenuous one from the outset. Moreover, the stated goal of the campaign was not the free expression of ideas as an end in itself but rather as the means to achieve higher levels of sociopolitical unity. The Maoist formula in accordance with which the movement was to proceed was "unity-criticism-unity." If criticism threatened to produce disunity, the logical and inevitable Maoist response was to bring it to an end.

• • •

While the failure of the Hundred Flowers movement marked a defeat for Mao and a victory for the established Party apparatus, Maoists soon turned the ensuing antirightist campaign into an instrument to serve their own political ends. The antirightist campaign began as a Party witch-hunt to silence and punish its critics. But at a Central Committee meeting held in Qingdao in late July, Mao announced that it was to be extended from the cities to the countryside in the form of a "socialist education" campaign. The purpose was to consolidate the collectives, combat "spontaneous tendencies toward capitalism" in the rural areas, and oppose rightist policies which had permitted the expansion of private plots and free markets. By early fall, the sale of agricultural products on the private market was virtually eliminated, peasants who had drifted away from the collectives were persuaded or forced to rejoin, and stricter political controls were established over the countryside.

The final Maoist twist of the screw was to turn the Party's antirightist campaign into a massive purge of "rightists" in the Party itself, a campaign officially sanctioned by the Central Committee in September. Invoking the principle of the mass line, Mao launched attacks against bureaucratism and conservative resistance to socialist transformation. The *xiafang* movement, underway since early 1957, was intensified, and urban administrative offices were emptied as state and Party officials and cadres were "sent down" to engage in physical labor, mostly in the countryside. By the time the purge had run its course in 1958, over a million Party members had been expelled, put on probation, or officially reprimanded. In the process, Maoists regained control of the Party apparatus. At the same time, Maoist socioeconomic policies gained the upper hand in the higher councils of the Party, for in the political atmosphere created by the growing antirightist drive it had become politically dangerous to advocate policies that might be considered conservative. Early in October the Central Committee formally approved Mao's radical twelve-year program for agriculture, thus settling the debate over economic policy that had raged over the previous two years. In effect, this meant the scrapping of the Second Five Year Plan, and this led directly to the Great Leap Forward campaign of 1958. One immediate result of the Maoist ascendancy was the reversal of the wage-reform measures of early 1956. Material incentives now were denounced as a rightist deviation. The new and more egalitarian wage policy adopted in November 1957 emphasized social mobilization and moral incentives.

· · ·

The period of the Hundred Flowers was the time when the Chinese abandoned the Soviet model of development and embarked on a distinctively Chinese road to socialism. It was the time that China announced its ideological and social autonomy from the Soviet Union and its Stalinist heritage. It is a cruel and tragic historical irony that the break with the Stalinist pattern of socioeconomic development was not accompanied by a break with Stalinist methods in political and intellectual life. The latter was precluded by the suppression of the critics who had briefly "bloomed and contended" in May and June of 1957. China thereafter was to follow a new path to socialism, but not one leading to the goals of political democracy and intellectual freedom, as the era of the Hundred Flowers seemingly had promised.

NOTES

1. Mao Tse-tung [Mao Zedong], *Socialist Upsurge in China's Countryside* (Peking: Foreign Languages Press, 1957), pp. 159–160.
2. Chou En-lai [Zhou Enlai], "On the Question of Intellectuals," January 14, 1956, in Robert R. Bowie and John K. Fairbank, *Communist China 1955–1959: Policy Documents with Analysis* (Cambridge, Mass.: Harvard University Press, 1962), p. 133.

3. Mao Tse-tung, *On the Correct Handling of Contradictions Among the People* (Peking: Foreign Languages Press, 1957), p. 24.

4. *The Eighth National Congress of the Communist Party of China: Documents* (Peking: Foreign Languages Press, 1956), 1:142.

5. Mao, *On Correct Handling,* p. 9.

6. Chou, "On the Question of Intellectuals," pp. 128–144.

7. The number of Party members officially classified as intellectuals jumped dramatically from 1,255,923 in 1956 to 1,880,000 in 1957, out of a total of 12,720,000. Workers numbered 1,740,000 in 1957. See Franz Schurmann, *Ideology and Organization in Communist China* (Berkeley: University of California Press, 1966), p. 132.

8. Mao presented his new views on economic development on April 25, 1956 in the speech "On the Ten Great Relationships." For an English translation of the text, which became available only during the course of the Cultural Revolution, see Stuart R. Schram, ed., *Mao Tse-tung Unrehearsed: Talks and Letters, 1956–71* (Middlesex, England: Penguin, 1974), pp. 61–83. The document is discussed in greater detail in Chapter 12 below.

9. "On the Historical Experience of the Dictatorship of the Proletariat" was followed by a sequel in December 1956, another and more lengthy editorial in the *People's Daily* entitled "More on the Historical Experience of the Dictatorship of the Proletariat," which also dealt with "the question of Stalin" and in a more favorable light. The second installment was written largely in response to later events, and especially the Hungarian revolution.

10. Mao Tse-tung, *The Historical Experience of the Dictatorship of the Proletariat* (Beijing: Foreign Languages Press, 1961), pp. 14–18. Mao's "private" views about Stalin were far less flattering. In a talk of 1958, for example: "The Chinese revolution won victory by acting contrary to Stalin's will. . . . If we had followed . . . Stalin's methods the Chinese revolution couldn't have succeeded. When our revolution succeeded, Stalin said it was a fake." Mao, "Talks at Chengtu," in Schram, ed., *Mao Tse-tung Unrehearsed,* pp. 102–103.

11. Mao, *Historical Experience,* pp. 7–13.

12. "Let a Hundred Flowers Blossom, a Hundred Schools of Thought Contend!" appeared in the *People's Daily* on June 13, 1956. An English translation was published in Beijing in 1958 and is reprinted in Bowie and Fairbank, *Communist China,* pp. 151–163.

13. *Ibid.,* pp. 152–153.

14. *Ibid.,* pp. 152–157.

15. *Ibid.,* pp. 157–162.

16. *Ibid.,* pp. 155.

17. Luo's speech to the Chinese People's Political Consultative Conference was delivered on March 18, 1957 and published in the *People's Daily* on March 23. For a partial translation, see Roderick MacFarquhar, *The Hundred Flowers Campaign and the Chinese Intellectuals* (New York: Praeger, 1960), pp. 20–21.

18. "Proposals of the Eighth National Congress of the Communist Party of China for the Second Five-Year Plan for Development of the National Economy," September 27, 1956, in Bowie and Fairbank, *Communist China,* pp. 204–216.

19. Chou En-lai, "Report on the Proposals for the Second Five-Year Plan for Development of the National Economy," September 16, 1956, in Bowie and Fairbank, *Communist China,* p. 228.

20. For the most accurate English translation of "On the Ten Great Relationships," see Schram, ed., *Mao Tse-tung Unrehearsed,* pp. 61–83.

21. Mao, *On Correct Handling,* p. 49.

22. *Ibid.,* p. 58.

23. *Ibid.,* p. 50 (italics added).

24. Teng Hsiao-p'ing [Deng Xiaoping], "Report on the Revision of the Constitution of the Communist Party of China," *Eighth National Congress of the Communist Party of China,* 1:213.

25. Cited in MacFarquhar, *The Hundred Flowers Campaign,* p. 28.

26. *Ibid.,* p. 49.

27. *Ibid.,* p. 87.

28. *Ibid.,* p. 75.

29. Mao, *On Correct Handling,* p. 66.

30. *Ibid.,* p. 38.

31. Lo Lung-chi [Luo Longqi], "My Preliminary Examination," statement presented to the National People's Congress on July 15, 1957. Translated in Bowie and Fairbank, *Communist China,* pp. 331–337.

32. Chang Po-chün [Zhang Bojun], "I Bow My Head and Admit My Guilt Before the People," statement presented to the National People's Congress on July 15, 1957. Translated in Bowie and Fairbank, *Communist China,* pp. 337–341.

33. From a speech delivered to the National People's Congress on July 13, 1957. *Jen-min jih-pao* [*Renmin ribao*], July 15, 1957. Translated in MacFarquhar, *Hundred Flowers Campaign,* pp. 285–286.

34. Liu Shao-ch'i [Liu Shaoqi], "The Present Situation, the Party's General Line for Socialist Construction and Its Future Tasks," report to the second session of the Eighth National Congress delivered on May 5, 1958. Translated in Bowie and Fairbank, *Communist China,* p. 434.

35. Mao, *On Correct Handling,* p. 52.

36. *Ibid.,* p. 42.

37. *Ibid.,* p. 47.

38. *Ibid.,* p. 51.

39. *Ibid.,* p. 53.

40. See, for example, Mao's comments on "The Bourgeois Orientation of the *Wen-hui Pao*" and "The Situation in the Summer of 1957" in Jerome Ch'en, ed., *Mao Papers* (London: Oxford University Press, 1970), pp. 55–56.

41. Mao, *On Correct Handling,* p. 53.

11

Permanent Revolution

The Ideological Origins of the Great Leap

THE GREAT LEAP FORWARD campaign of 1958–60 was, in part, the Maoist response to the consequences of early industrialization. In the early years of the People's Republic, Chinese Communists believed that the road to socialism in an economically backward land began with urban industrialization in order to create the necessary material prerequisites for the new society, prerequisites that an abortive capitalism had failed to provide. By 1956 Mao Zedong and others had concluded that the social costs exacted by that road was too heavy a price for socialists to pay. China's First Five Year Plan had led to the growth of bureaucracy, new social inequalities and privileged elites, a growing gulf between the modernizing cities and the backward countryside, and processes of ideological decay. The social, political, and an ideological results seemed to be moving China further away from, rather than toward, a socialist and communist future. The Maoist conclusion was that socialist ends could be attained only by socialist means. And the Maoist remedy for the evils of urban industrialization was to industrialize the countryside. In the new rural communes Maoists would find what appeared to be the ideal agency to reconcile the means and ends of socialism, agencies that would serve the needs of modern economic development while at the same time forming the basic social units for China's "leap" to a communist utopia. In the communization movement of the summer of 1958 Maoists rejected in social practice what they already had come to reject in their socialist theory: the Soviet orthodoxy that the combination of nationalized means of production and rapid industrial development automatically guaranteed the arrival of a communist society. The Second Five Year Plan, scheduled to begin in 1958, was never formally revoked, but it was left to gather dust on the drawing boards of the economic planners.

There were no detailed blueprints for the Great Leap. It was the product of a utopian social vision, not an economic plan on the order of a five year plan. When the "Great Leap Forward" slogan was set forth in January 1958, Mao outlined general guidelines for China's socioeconomic development, but it is unlikely that he had "people's communes" firmly in mind. Yet underlying the Maoist vision of the Great Leap were a set of theoretical assumptions and a distinctive theory of economic development from which the communes logically were to emerge.

The ideological impetus for the Great Leap was deeply rooted in revolutionary Maoism. Many of the intellectual predispositions that had molded the Maoist interpretation and practice of Marxism over the revolutionary years again came to the fore a decade after the revolutionary victory. A voluntaristic belief that the consciousness and moral qualities of human beings are the decisive factors in determining the course of history, a populist belief that true revolutionary creativity resides among the peasant masses, and a particular faith in the revolutionary advantages of backwardness— such are some of the elements of the revolutionary heritage that were revived and given a more radical interpretation. These beliefs, combined with lessons derived from the experiences of a decade of postrevolutionary history, received their most general theoretical expression in what was announced on the eve of the Great Leap as "the theory of permanent revolution."

Mao Zedong emerged as an advocate of "permanent revolution" in an unpublished speech delivered to the Supreme State Conference on January 28, 1958 and elaborated on his interpretation of the concept in a report on "work methods" prepared for Party circulation three days later.[1] Liu Shaoqi brought the term into the public realm in May 1958 when he declared that the Chinese Communist Party always had been guided by "the Marxist-Leninist theory of permanent revolution."[2] The concept appeared prominently in the theoretical literature of the Great Leap period, and soon was canonized as part of "Mao Zedong Thought."

The term "permanent revolution" is identified primarily with Trotsky, but it was also employed by Marx. A brief review of its earlier history might be useful for understanding how the Maoist usage establishes the place that Mao Zedong occupies in the Marxist tradition.

Marxism and the Idea of Permanent Revolution

The term "permanent revolution" or, more precisely, "The Revolution in Permanence," was set forth by Marx in 1850. The original theory was formulated with reference to comparatively backward Germany in response to the political conservatism of the German bourgeoisie in the defeated revolution of 1848. In anticipation that another European upheaval was imminent, Marx pondered the role of an embryonic proletariat in a country where the bourgeoisie could not be counted on to carry out its democratic tasks. His conclusion was that once the proletariat appeared on the political scene it could not allow a timid bourgeoisie to halt the revolutionary process in midstream; the proletariat would be compelled to achieve political supremacy, establish a "proletarian dictatorship," and more or less immediately transform the bourgeois-democratic revolution into a socialist one.[3]

If the German workers were to pursue their own class interests and not be seduced by the bourgeoisie, their battle cry was to be: "The Revolution in Permanence!"[4]

The notion of "permanent revolution" modified the Marxist orthodoxy that there are well-defined political stages that necessarily correspond to stages of socioeconomic development. For later Marxists in economically backward countries, it provided doctrinal authority for the possibility that even a small proletariat could seize the political opportunity to turn a bourgeois-democratic revolution into a socialist one, at least in the context of an international revolutionary situation.

The notion of permanent revolution does not appear explicitly in the writings of Marx and Engels after 1850, in the decades when the revolutionary situation did not develop according to their earlier expectations. After 1905, in different political and historical circumstances, it was revived and more elaborately formulated by Trotsky, with whom the theory is primarily identified.

Trotsky maintained that in the era of international socialist revolution the working classes of the backward countries (Russia, in particular, and the colonial and semicolonial countries of Asia and the Middle East by extension) were potentially more revolutionary than their counterparts in the mature nations of the West. Since the Russian bourgeoisie had proven too weak and politically timid to perform its appointed bourgeois-democratic historical tasks, those tasks would fall to the proletariat with the assistance of the peasantry. The numerical weakness of the proletariat, it was argued, was outweighed by its political militancy in economically backward lands, and thus the workers would assume the leadership of the bourgeois-democratic revolution. Once having gained political hegemony, the proletariat would find it impossible to confine the revolution to bourgeois limits; the necessary outcome would be a proletarian dictatorship and the transformation of the revolution into a socialist one. That outcome, in turn, would provide the stimulus for socialist revolutions in the advanced nations of Western Europe, which would guarantee the survival of the revolution in its backward homeland. As Trotsky declared in 1906, in his classic inversion of orthodox Marxism, it was likely that "in a backward country with a lesser degree of capitalistic development, the proletariat should sooner reach political supremacy than in a highly developed capitalist state."[5]

Thus for Trotsky the revolution would be "permanent" in two respects. First, a revolution in an economically backward land could not be confined to any distinct "bourgeois-democratic" phase, but would proceed "uninterrupted" to socialism. Second, a revolution could not be confined to a single nation; the survival of a revolution in a backward country was dependent on the timely outbreak of socialist revolutions in the advanced countries, for only in an international revolutionary context could the permanence of the revolutionary process be maintained.

These perspectives guided Lenin as well as Trotsky in the Russian October Revolution. The events of 1917–1918 dissolved all but terminological and semantic distinctions between Lenin's theory of "the democratic dictatorship of the proletariat and peasantry" and Trotsky's theory of "permanent revolution." It was not until the advent of Stalin that the notion of permanent revolution became an ideological heresy in a newly canonized Marxist-Leninist orthodoxy. Stalin's doctrine of "socialism in one country" replaced the internationalist revolutionary perspective while the notion of an "uninterrupted" revolutionary process was replaced by the dogma that all revolutions (save perhaps the Russian) must proceed through distinct and well-defined stages of sociopolitical development. Thus when Mao proclaimed in January 1958 that "I advocate the theory of permanent revolution,"[6] he invited the charge of "Trotskyism," and he soon was to hear the accusation, despite the fact that such Trotskyists as could be found in the People's Republic languished in jails. It is hardly surprising that Mao hastened to add that his theory should not be confused with Trotsky's, although between the two there are significant similarities as well as vast differences.

Maoism and the Concept of Permanent Revolution

The Maoist version of the theory begins with the view that the whole revolutionary process, until the realization of communism, is characterized by an endless series of social contradictions and struggles which can be resolved only by radical revolutionary breaks with existing reality. Progress from one phase to another "must necessarily be a relationship between quantitative and qualitative changes. All mutations, all leaps forward are revolutions which must pass through struggles. The theory of [the] cessation of struggles [in a socialist society] is sheer metaphysics." Moreover, the resolution of contradictions can only be transient, for "disequilibrium is normal and absolute whereas equilibrium is temporary and relative."[7]

Mao's emphasis on "disequilibrium" as an absolute and universal law of historical development was the very antithesis of the rational planning and calculating mentality that went into the making of five year plans of economic development—a notion profoundly unsettling to Chinese economic planners and most Party leaders. For Mao, on the other hand, the combination of rapid economic development and a continuous process of increasingly radical social and ideological transformations was necessary to fully release the latent productive energies of the masses and to prevent the ever-present danger of backsliding into capitalism. As he declared in his January 28 speech, "In making revolution, one must strike while the iron is hot, one revolution following another; the revolution must advance without interruption."[8] And the revolutionary advance was to be social as well as economic, for the central Maoist assumption was that the socialist transformation of the "superstructure" was more the precondition for modern economic development than the product of it. In setting forth the concept of "permanent revolution" in early 1958, Mao called for a "great technical revolution," but the call presupposed an already completed—or an about-to-be-completed—socialist revolution "on the political and ideological fronts."[9] And the Maoist practice of permanent revolution, as it was revealed in the policies of the Great Leap, stressed the cultivation of a popular "communist consciousness" and the creation of embryonic forms of communist social organization as much as it did the "technical revolution." In the Maoist view, the process of modern economic development begins with the seizure of state power, is followed by the transformation of social relationships, and the latter in turn opens the way for the development of productive forces.[10]

What is rejected in the Maoist version of permanent revolution is not rapid economic development but rather the Marxist-Leninist view that there are well-defined and more or less prolonged stages of sociopolitical development that correspond to stages in the development of material productive forces. What is affirmed is that changes in the "superstructure"—in social relationships, political forms, and ideological consciousness—must be accomplished as quickly as possible, "one after the other," if the goals of the revolution are to be achieved. Thus in summarizing Chinese sociohistorical development since 1949, Mao emphasized the uninterrupted character of the revolutionary process. No sooner had the bourgeois phase of the revolution been completed (with the completion of the land reform campaign), than China embarked upon the transition to socialism, a revolution "basically completed" in 1956 according to Mao. And now (in 1958) the Great Leap Forward campaign was intended not only to bring about a technological revolution but also to mark China's passage from socialism to communism. For Mao these were fundamental revolutionary "leaps" in social, political, and ideological life—and the process of social change obviously was proceeding much more rapidly than the rate of economic development. Within a decade after the revolutionary victory, China had passed through the bourgeois-democratic and socialist revolutions and, according to the Maoist perspective of the time, was prepared for a leap to a communist society. But China, as Maoists acknowledged, remained a poor and economically backward country. This, of course, invited accusations of the Trotskyist heresy of "leaping over stages." To ward off the accusations Maoists countered with a purely verbal orthodoxy: "We are advocates of permanent revolution but also believe in revolution by stages." But the "stages" of social development, at least in theory, are passed through so rapidly that in this respect Mao appears as a super-Trotskyist.

At the same time, he also was anti-Stalinist. It was, after all, a principal Stalinist orthodoxy that such contradictions as exist in a presumably socialist society could be resolved by a gradual process of evolutionary change. The Maoist view that the struggle to achieve socialism and communism demands qualitative "leaps," radical breaks with the past, and a continuous series of revolutions was an explicit theoretical rejection of Stalinism—just as the Maoist practice of the Great Leap marks a wholesale rejection of the entire Soviet pattern of socioeconomic development.

The whole vision of a continuous process of revolutionary change that would rapidly transform China into a country both economically modern and socially communist was based on a profound faith in the powers of human consciousness and the human will to bring about that transformation. Just as Maoist revolutionary strategy had rested on a faith that determined people motivated by the proper ideas and moral values could triumph over the most formidable material obstacles, so now a similar faith was brought to bear to deal with postrevolutionary problems of social and economic development. If China lacked the Marxian-defined economic prerequisites for a communist society, those objective economic conditions could be brought into existence in the very process of striving to realize ultimate communist goals, a process that the notion of permanent revolution demanded be undertaken in the here and now. The key to success was a mobilized people armed with the proper revolutionary spirit, will, and leaders. In launching the Great Leap and setting forth the utopian social and economic goals it was to achieve, Mao looked to the "subjective" factors in history, to what he called "the boundless creative powers" of the masses and their "inexhaustible enthusiasm for socialism."

If modern economic development itself did not guarantee the arrival of a communist future, a modern economy and popular prosperity were very much part of that future. Maoists did not envision a primitive communist utopia existing in perpetual conditions of economic scarcity. From the very beginning of the Great Leap, Mao emphasized the necessity for a "great technical revolution." Chinese industrial production, he declared in January 1958, would overtake England in fifteen years, and this became one of the great popular rallying cries of the time. The manner in which Mao conceived the problem of carrying out the technical revolution, which he discussed in outlining his theory of permanent revolution, reflects the decisive role of human consciousness implicit in that theory. In analyzing the relationship between economic and psychological factors, Mao described a vicious cycle in which economic stagnation and mental stagnation tend to reinforce each other. Because of China's economic backwardness, her people were still "spiritually restricted" and "unable to take much initiative." The way to break the cycle was to stimulate the consciousness of the masses, release their latent energies, and turn them to the task of economic development. The task was like fighting a never ending war: "After a victory, we must at once put forward a new task. In this way, cadres and masses will forever be filled with revolutionary fervour. . . ."[11]

Once the process started, there would be a progressive and dynamic cyclical development of ever higher levels of consciousness and economic progress, each stimulating the progressive movement of the other. As applied to economic development, "permanent revolution" meant a constant process of ideologically inspired mass activism: "Ideological work and political work is the guarantee for the completion of economic technological work and it serves the economic basis. Ideology and politics are the commanders, the soul."[12]

In the Maoist worldview, the emergence of the new society presupposed the emergence of a spiritually transformed people. The slogans that guided the Great Leap Forward campaign—"man is the decisive factor" and "men are more important than machines"—logically flowed from these views, as did Maoist theoretical treatises that concluded with the striking proposition that "the subjective can create the objective." The notion of permanent revolution was above all a formula for the continuous revolutionization of human consciousness and energies as the key to the achievement of the social and economic goals promised by the Chinese Revolution.

Another prominent aspect of the Maoist version of "permanent revolution," even though it was not explicitly formulated in the theory itself, was a populist belief that the true sources of revolutionary creativity reside in the countryside. Just as the Maoist revolutionary strategy of "people's war" was based on a profound faith in the spontaneous revolutionary strivings of the peasantry, so the emerging Maoist strategy for postrevolutionary socioeconomic development took on an equally strong agrarian orientation. In 1958, as in 1927, "the people" were defined essentially as the vast peasant masses and Maoists again looked primarily to the countryside for the sources of progress and regeneration. The potential to achieve the appropriate transformation of morality and consciousness was attributed essentially to "the pioneering peasants," not to the urban populace. The functions of proletarian dictatorship and the tasks of the transition to communism were assigned not to the urban proletariat but rather to the rural people's communes. During the Great Leap Forward, the rural people's commune was seen as the agency to eliminate the differences between town and countryside, between peasants and workers, and between mental and manual labor; and, indeed, even to eventually abolish the domestic functions of the state. The policies of the Great Leap Forward campaign emphasized "the industrialization of the countryside" and one of the prominent slogans of the time was "the urbanization of the countryside and the ruralization of the cities." Permanent revolution meant the permanence of agrarian revolution.

Closely associated with the voluntarist emphasis and the populist faith was another long-held Maoist belief revived on the eve of the Great Leap Forward campaign, which underlies the whole conception of "permanent revolution"—namely, a particular perception of the "advantages of backwardness." This was not simply the now familiar idea that economically backward nations in the modern world are offered the advantage of speeding up their development by borrowing the technologies of the industrially advanced countries. Rather, it was a more general and pervasive faith in the moral-social virtues and revolutionary political advantages of backwardness as such, a faith not dissimilar to that held by the nineteenth-century

Russian Narodniks. As early as 1919, before his conversion to Marxism, Mao deplored China's impotence and wretched backwardness but nevertheless saw in that very condition a huge reservoir of youthful creativity and revolutionary energy, which augured well for the future. "Our Chinese people possess great intrinsic energy. . . . The more profound the oppression, the greater the resistance; that which has accumulated for a long time will surely burst forth quickly."[13] And from the beginning of his career as a Marxist revolutionary, Mao was disposed to find the sources of modern revolution in those areas of society least influenced by modern economic forces—in a peasantry relatively uninvolved in capitalist relationships and in a de-urbanized intelligentsia relatively uncorrupted by the bourgeois ideas which pervaded the cities. It was this conversion of China's backwardness into a revolutionary virtue that led Mao to predict in 1930 that "the revolution will certainly move towards an upsurge more quickly in China than in Western Europe,"[14] and to draw a dichotomy between the revolutionary countryside and the conservative cities in the making of the Chinese revolution.

This tendency to celebrate the revolutionary advantages of backwardness received its most radical—and most un-Marxian—formulation in the "poor and blank" thesis, the special revolutionary virtues that Mao attributed to the Chinese people in April of 1958:

> Apart from their other characteristics, China's 600 million people have two remarkable peculiarities; they are, first of all, poor, and secondly blank. That may seem like a bad thing, but it is really a good thing. Poor people want change, want to do things, want revolution. A clean sheet of paper has no blotches, and so the newest and most beautiful words can be written on it, the newest and most beautiful pictures can be painted on it.[15]

The condition of being "poor" and "blank" not only demanded a process of "permanent revolution" to overcome that condition but it also made possible an uninterrupted development leading to communism, for it was precisely because of China's backwardness that its people possessed special revolutionary capacities and were uniquely amenable to the appropriate spiritual transformation; they could write, or could have written on them, "the newest and most beautiful words." For, as Mao later declared: "In history it is always people with a low level of culture who triumph over people with a high level of culture."[16]

Implicit in the "poor and blank" thesis is a notion strikingly similar to the nineteenth-century Russian Populist assumption that an economically backward country does not suffer from the historical "overmaturity" and the moral decadence that had stifled the revolutionary spirit in the advanced Western nations and is therefore potentially more revolutionary than other countries. Just as the Russian Populists proclaimed pre-industrial Russia to be closer to socialism than the industrialized nations of the West precisely because of the relative absence of modern capitalist economic development, so Mao proclaimed the special Chinese revolutionary virtues of being poor and blank and saw preindustrial China pioneering the way to a universal socialist and communist future. Just as Herzen had declared that "we possess nothing" to declare his faith in Russia's socialist future,[17] Mao found China "a clean sheet of paper," and in this condition he saw the promise of its future socialist greatness.

If the Chinese people in general were characterized by being "poor and blank," those virtues were especially characteristic of two special sections of the people. For the poorest of the people were the peasants and the most "blank" the youth. While poor peasants most wanted revolution, the youth of China were the most receptive to the appropriate transformation of ideology and spirit. If the "poor and blank" thesis served to reinforce Mao's belief that the peasantry was the truly revolutionary class in Chinese society, it also marked the revival of the special faith in youth that characterized the formative stages of his intellectual development, the New Youth era of 1915–1919. "From ancient times," Mao remarked in a speech in 1958, "the people who have created new schools of thought have always been young people without great learning."[18]

What relationship does the Maoist conception of permanent revolution bear to the conceptions of Marx and Trotsky? That Mao chose to adopt the Marxist term, especially in view of its heretical standing in Soviet Marxist-Leninist orthodoxy, is itself a matter of some significance. The choice dramatized Chinese political and ideological autonomy from Moscow and the Maoist determination to pursue a distinctively Chinese road to communism, and at the same time it reflected the desire of Maoists to tie themselves to the Marxist tradition and draw upon its most voluntaristic strains. But apart from the use of the term itself, the Maoist theory has rather little in common with the conceptions of either Marx or Trotsky. While the Chinese version retained (and, indeed, magnified) the general notion that a backward country might telescope stages of revolutionary development, it did so in an historical context, on the basis of ideological assumptions, and through proposed means that together constitute a wholesale rejection of many of the most fundamental premises of Marxist theory. While Marx and Trotsky raised the possibility of permanent revolution with reference to a bourgeois revolution passing over into a socialist one in an international revolutionary situation, the Maoist theory addressed itself to what was assumed to be the period of the transition from socialism to communism in China alone, without reference to any international revolutionary process. Whereas Marx and Trotsky assumed that the success of a socialist revolution in an economically backward country was ultimately dependent on successful socialist revolutions in the advanced industrialized nations, for only the latter could provide the material conditions for any genuinely socialist society, the Maoist assumption was that economic backwardness was not a barrier to either the socialist or the communist reorganization of society. Indeed, backwardness was converted into a revolutionary virtue that would yield the human energies and moral purity for the process of permanent revolution, and thus China could advance to a communist utopia on the basis of its own meager material resources. And while Trotsky as well as Marx believed that only the urban proletariat could transform a bourgeois revolution into a socialist one, the Maoist belief was that the true sources for revolutionary transformation reside in the peasantry and that the countryside is the main arena where the struggle to achieve socialism and communism will be determined.

The Maoist version of permanent revolution rests on a literal interpretation of the Marxist premise that human beings make history, an extreme voluntarist belief that human consciousness is the decisive factor in determining the course of social development. Marx, to be sure, believed that people "make their own history," but he also insisted, as did Trotsky, that "they do not make it just as they please; they do not make it under circumstances chosen by themselves, but under circumstances directly encountered, given and transmitted from the past."[19] For Mao, such Marxian historical restraints on the activation of human consciousness were largely absent, and thus dedicated people with the proper ideas and will were free to mold objective reality in accordance with their consciousness, "just as they please," in large measure, regardless of both the particular national socioeconomic conditions and the general international revolutionary conditions in which they might find themselves.

These Maoist departures from the premises of Marxism found their most radical expression in the "poor and blank" thesis with which the Maoist notion of permanent revolution is so intimately connected. People, Marx once warned (and even Trotsky's conception of permanent revolution retained the warning), "do not build themselves a new world out of the fruits of the earth, as vulgar superstition believes, but out of the historical accomplishments of their declining civilization. They must, in the course of their development, begin by themselves producing the material conditions of a new society, and no effort of mind or will can free them from this destiny."[20] For Maoists, by contrast, it was not the accomplishments of the past that were important but rather the belief that the present is unburdened by the historical weight of the past. It was the condition of being "poor and blank" that gave rise to their confidence in the emergence of the new society. Reflected in this celebration of the "advantages of backwardness" was the absence of any real Marxist faith in the objective forces of history, the lack of the Marxist conviction that socialism and communism were immanent in the progressive movement of history itself. Rather, what was decisive in determining the historical outcome were the "subjective factors," the consciousness, the moral values and the actions of dedicated people. On the basis of this most un-Marxian conviction the policies of the Great Leap were formulated and implemented.

NOTES

1. Mao Tse-tung [Mao Zedong], "Sixty Points on Working Methods," in Jerome Ch'en, ed., *Mao Papers* (London: Oxford University Press, 1970), pp. 57–76.

2. Liu Shao-ch'i [Liu Shaoqi], "The Present Situation, the Party's General Line for Socialist Construction and Its Future Tasks," May 5, 1958, Bowie and Fairbank, *Communist China 1955–1959: Policy Documents with Analysis* (Cambridge, Mass.: Harvard University Press, 1962), p. 425.

3. Karl Marx, "Address of the Central Committee to the Communist League," March, 1850, in Karl Marx and Frederick Engels, *Selected Works* (Moscow: 1950), 1:102.

4. *Ibid.*, 1:108.

5. Leon Trotsky, *Our Revolution* (New York, 1918), p. 84. Trotsky originally set fourth the theory in his *Results and Prospects* of 1906. For a recent English edition of the work, see Leon Trotsky, *The Permanent Revolution and Results and Prospects* (New York: Pathfinder Press, 1974), pp. 29–122.

6. Mao Tse-tung, "Speech to the Supreme State Conference." For an English translation, see *Chinese Law and Government*, 1, No. 4:10–14.

7. Mao, "Sixty Points on Working Methods," pp. 65–66.

8. Mao, "Speech to the Supreme State Conference."

9. Mao, "Sixty Points on Working Methods."

10. As Mao later formulated the matter in a 1961 critique of Stalinism entitled "Reading Notes on the Soviet Union's 'Political Economy,'" *Mao Zedong Sixiang Wansui*, (Taipei, n.p., 1969), pp. 319–399.

11. Mao, "Sixty Points on Working Methods," p. 63.

12. *Ibid.*, p. 64.

13. "The Great Union of the Popular Masses," *Hsiang-chiang p'ing-lun* [*Xiangjiang pinglun*], July–August, 1919. For a partial English translation, see Stuart Schram, *The Political Thought of Mao Tse-tung* (New York: Praeger, 1969), p. 163.

14. Mao Tse-tung, "A Single Spark Can Start a Prairie Fire," in *Selected Works of Mao Tse-tung* (Peking: Foreign Languages Press, 1961), 1:118.

15. *Hongqi* (Red Flag), June 1, 1958, pp. 3–4. For an English translation, see *Peking Review*, June 10, 1958.

16. Mao Tse-tung, "Reading Notes on the Soviet Union's 'Political Economy,'" *Mao Zedong Sixiang Wansui* (JPRS translation), p. 307.

17. Alexander Herzen, "The Russian People and Socialism" (1851), in Herzen, *From the Other Shore* (London: Weidenfeld & Nicolson, 1956), p. 199.

18. Mao, "Talk at Chengtu," March 22, 1958, in Stuart R. Schram, ed., *Mao Tse-tung Unrehearsed: Talks and Letters 1956–71* (Middlesex, England: Penguin 1974), p. 118.

19. Karl Marx, "The Eighteenth Brumaire of Louis Bonaparte," in Marx and Engels, *Selected Works* (1950), 1:225.

20. Karl Marx, "Die moralisierende Kritik und die kritisierende Moral," in Karl Marx, *Selected Writings in Sociology and Social Philosophy* (London: Watts, 1956), p. 240.

12

Economics of the Great Leap Forward

T HE "GREAT LEAP" strategy of development relied ultimately
on what Maoists perceived to be the "revolutionary enthusiasm"
of the masses, especially the peasant masses, but it did not assume
that moral zeal alone would bring modern economic development. The
utopian fervors of 1958 were accompanied by a distinctive Maoist theory
of economic development, which, when viewed in light of concrete Chinese socioeconomic conditions, appears not nearly as irrational as the
scheme is usually now pictured.

To understand the economic rationale of the Great Leap Forward, it is
necessary to distinguish between the Maoist theory of economic development and the manner in which it was implemented during the course of the
campaign. The distinction is partly artificial because Maoism only fully reveals itself in practice, but in this case a largely abstract exposition seems
justified because of the vast gap between what was intended and what was
actually done. In the final analysis, of course, Maoists, like all historical actors, must be judged on the basis of what they have done rather than on the
basis of what they might have intended to do.

A distinctively Maoist economic theory took shape in response to three
major problems that confronted Chinese society as the First Five Year Plan
was drawing to a close. First, there was the immediate problem of growing

unemployment in the cities and underemployment in the countryside, chronic problems which the First Five Year Plan had failed to resolve and the proposed Second Five Year Plan offered little promise of alleviating. Second, there was the more general question of how to speed up the process of "primitive socialist accumulation." With little prospect of any significant foreign investment, the question turned on how to make most efficient use of China's major resource, human labor. And that, in turn, called into question the efficacy of concentrating on the development of capital-intensive heavy industries. Quite apart from the social consequences of urban industrialization, Maoists raised the question of whether China's long-range needs of national economic development could be met by a continued reliance on the Soviet model of development. Third, the general recognition that China required a "technical revolution" raised the question of how modern technology and science could be mastered without fostering the development of a privileged technological intelligentsia.

Problems of Population, Unemployment, and Underemployment

One of the problems plaguing economically backward countries in the modern world is that urbanization has been proceeding much more rapidly than industrialization. Among the contemporary legacies of imperialism and colonialism is not only the phenomenon of "lopsided development" between modern cities and backward rural areas, but the tendency for cities themselves to grow in economically distorted and socially disfigured form. In cities resting on weak and structurally deficient industrial bases, huge populations conglomerate, the great majority living in destitution and squalor on the fringes of modern economic life. The horrendous social consequences are still painfully apparent today in many of the urban centers of Asia, Africa, and Latin America, as they were in pre-1949 China. While the Chinese Communists succeeded in alleviating the worst social abuses in the cities during the first years of their rule, they were not successful in dealing with the more fundamental problem of "overpopulated" cities. Although urban industry and the urban proletariat grew rapidly in the 1950s, the increase in the urban population from 57,000,000 in 1949 to about 100,000,000 in 1957 cannot be accounted for by the growth of the urban economy alone. Many of the new urban dwellers were peasant migrants unable to find work in urban enterprises. The result was persistent widespread unemployment and underemployment in the cities.

The government was reluctant to recognize the problem. When the First Five Year Plan began in 1953, most economic planners assumed that a rapidly growing industry would create sufficient employment for a rapidly growing urban population. On the basis of that assumption they rejected birth and population control (denounced as anti-Marxist Malthusian heresies) and did little to control rural migration to the cities.

Only in the relatively free intellectual atmosphere of the Hundred Flowers was the issue of population control seriously debated and the proponents of birth control permitted to publicly speak. Even Mao, in the original version of "On the Correct Handling of Contradictions Among the People," briefly emerged as an advocate of population control.[1] The new official interest in the matter reflected a growing recognition that industrialization would not resolve the population problem. Various *xiafang* campaigns to send urbanites to the countryside served only to compound the problem of underemployment in the rural areas.

Urban unemployment reached crisis proportions in early 1957, when the poor harvest of the previous autumn and dislocations resulting from collectivization greatly increased the flow of peasants moving to the cities. The problem was aggravated by a campaign to reduce the size of the bureaucracy, increased numbers of demobilized soldiers, and a reduction in the number of middle-school graduates permitted to enter universities. The intensified *xiafang* campaign in late 1957, partly an attempt to alleviate growing unemployment in the cities, did not address itself to the basic reasons for unemployment and underemployment in either town or countryside. By then, Chinese leaders were aware that urban unemployment was a chronic problem inherent in the economic policies of the time. Even Mao's optimistic Twelve Year Plan for Agricultural Development assumed that it would take from five to seven years to achieve full employment in the cities. And China's more orthodox economic planners, in drawing up the Second Five Year Plan, acknowledged that increasingly high levels of unemployment could be anticipated, on the order of 5,000,000 additional unemployed a year.[2] Given China's huge and rapidly growing population, a continued emphasis on large-scale, capital-intensive modern industries meant rising levels of unemployment and chronic underemployment.

The new Maoist economic strategy of 1958 implied a dramatic shift of emphasis from capital-intensive to labor-intensive projects—a shift from heavy industry to agriculture, light industry, and small-scale industries which required relatively little capital investment but rather depended on the maximum utilization of labor. In this sense, it was a policy designed to solve the problem of unemployment in both town and countryside—and to do so at one stroke. At the same time, it was a policy that announced itself as an immediate solution to China's population problem, for in the perspective of an economic strategy based on the maximal use of labor, a large and growing population was seen not as a barrier to modern development but rather an economic asset. Whereas in early 1957 Mao favored population control, in early 1958 he declared that "the more people there are the greater ferment of ideas, the greater the enthusiasm and the energy."[3] The debate on population control was thus settled and advocates of birth control once again were accused of Malthusian heresies.

Labor Power and "Primitive Socialist Accumulation"

The task of "primitive socialist accumulation" (the raising of capital to build the modern industrial base on which a future socialist society presumably would rest) was accomplished in the Soviet Union largely through the exploitation of the peasantry. Stalin made a conscious decision to extract from a "collectivized" peasantry the capital necessary to pursue a crash program of industrial development and to subordinate agriculture and consumer goods industries to the overriding goal of creating a vast heavy industrial sector. It was further assumed that an established modern industrial base would have a "spread" effect, eventually leading to the modernization of the economy as a whole.

As in the Soviet case, the capital for China's industrialization in the 1950s had been extracted largely from the countryside. Whether continuing the Stalinist strategy, as proposed in the draft of the Second Five Year Plan, would have modernized China as it partially did Russia is highly problematic in view of the fact that China had begun its "primitive socialist accumulation" on a far lower economic level and with a vast peasantry existing on the barest margins of subsistence. At the very minimum, the continued pursuit of the Soviet model would have demanded increasingly repressive and far more exploitative agrarian policies. The hope to avoid exploiting the countryside for the benefit of the cities was one factor that motivated the new Maoist strategy of economic development. Another was the belief that capital could be accumulated more rapidly and invested more equitably through the intensive mobilization of the untapped labor power of the masses, particularly the peasant masses.

The policies introduced in 1958 did not reject the development of heavy industry; still less were they a Luddite repudiation of modern economic life in general. Indeed, it was envisioned that such capital-intensive and strategic industries as steel and iron, chemicals, and machine-building would develop even more rapidly than before—but not at the expense of the development of agriculture and light industries. Rather, all sectors of the economy were to develop together and develop rapidly through the formula of "simultaneous development," the principal economic notion of the

Great Leap. Heavy capital investments in the advanced industrial sector would continue, but at the same time there would be increased investments in light industry and agriculture, and the three would grow together in dynamic fashion, with each stimulating the development of the others. The Maoist argument, simply put, was that the promotion of light industries producing inexpensive consumer goods for peasant consumption was essential to motivate peasants to increase agricultural production, while greater agricultural output, in turn, would further stimulate the development of light industry and was the essential prerequisite for the state to accumulate sufficient capital for heavy industrial development. On the basis of this concept of dynamic interaction among the three economic sectors Mao had declared that, "if you have a strong desire to develop heavy industry, then you will pay attention to the development of light industry and agriculture."[4] From this statement flowed the policy of "simultaneous development" as the most rapid road to the building of a modern economy.

While a process of "simultaneous development" clearly would be the best of all possible economic worlds, it was by no means clear that the Maoist policy was within the realm of the possible. No one questioned the desirability of developing all sectors of the economy in a manner that was "faster, better, and cheaper," as the slogan of the time went, but questions were raised as to how it could be done. It had been assumed that the modern industrial sector could be developed rapidly only at the expense of other sectors—and most Chinese Communist leaders accepted the social consequences of that assumption. If capital investments in heavy urban industry were not to be reduced, then how was a "great leap forward" in light industries and agriculture to be financed? The Maoist answer was that the key to simultaneous development was the labor power of the Chinese masses; through the establishment of new forms of social organization and through the proper ideological guidance, the hitherto underutilized labor potential of the people could be released and mobilized in a vast crusade to conquer nature. It was a principal Maoist assumption that the new labor-intensive projects in industry as well as agriculture would not require new capital but rather would generate it.

Since most of China's labor power, and an even greater proportion of its underutilized labor, resided in the peasantry, the new strategy of rapid economic development focused on the countryside rather than on the cities. The labor potential of the peasants, which could be utilized only partially in agricultural production even under the best of circumstances, was now to be fully realized by promoting the industrial development of the rural areas. The huge reservoir of surplus labor during the "slack" seasons in agriculture was to be turned to the development of small and medium-scale industries that required little capital investment. Labor-intensive industries such as crop processing, tool manufacturing, simple consumer-goods production, shale-oil production, and small chemical and fertilizer plants could grow in conjunction with agricultural production in rural areas. Such locally-based industrial projects not only would make more efficient use of the labor power of the peasant masses, but also would bring industry closer to sources of raw materials (and thus reduce strains on the fragile transportation system), exploit poorer quality raw materials not suitable for use in urban-based heavy industrial enterprises, encourage technological innovations based on local needs and conditions, and speed up capital accumulation to support large-scale construction and industrial projects.

This combination of industrial and agricultural production was seen as desirable on social as well as economic grounds. The growth of local industries would promote the economic development of the more backward regions of the country and reduce regional inequities; and rural industrialization would be an initial step in abolishing the distinctions between workers and peasants, and between town and countryside.

The new Maoist economic strategy presupposed a radical decentralization of socioeconomic life. In contrast to the form of decentralization that had been inaugurated in the autumn of 1957, when a large degree of administrative authority had been delegated by the central government and the economic ministries in Beijing to provincial and municipal administrative units and to large-scale economic enterprises (a form similar to post-Stalinist changes in the Soviet Union and many East European countries), the Maoist policies of 1958 implied a wholesale dismantling of centralized bureaucratic planning organs, and the transfer of economic decision-making to basic production units. The Maoist argument was that the full utilization of local resources and labor power demanded that economic decentralization be carried down to the localities, that the initiative and creativity of the masses in production could be brought forth fully only if the people themselves participated in economic planning in their own communities.

Decentralization and the emphasis on local development did not mean, or at least was not intended to mean, the abandonment of national economic planning, especially not insofar as the modern industrial sector was concerned. Even more ambitious plans were drawn up for the development of heavy industry. The new industrial policy of "walking on two legs" envisioned the rapid development of both the large-scale modern sector and small and medium-scale industries in the interior based on indigenous technologies and local resources. Since the latter were labor-intensive operations, it was assumed that there would be no lessening of the rate of capital investment in heavy industry.

The Technological Revolution

What is often taken as Mao's "anti-technocratic bias" was not a bias against modern technology and science as such, but rather a concern for the social consequences of modern technological development. Indeed, the grandiose economic achievements that were promised by the Great Leap presupposed an extraordinarily rapid application of both advanced and intermediate technologies as well as the general development of scientific knowledge and education. And no one more strongly emphasized the need for these than did Mao. In launching the Great Leap, he hailed the successes of China's socialist transformation but lamented the country's continued economic backwardness. "We must now start a technological revolution," he declared in January 1958, "so that we may overtake England in 15 or more years. . . . The technological revolution is designed to make everyone learn science and technology."[5]

For Mao and Maoists, however, economic goals could not be separated from social and political ones. While no one questioned the necessity and desirability of mastering modern science and technology, Maoists were concerned with the question of how they were to be mastered and by whom. Part of the Maoist concern was a widely shared anxiety that China had become far too dependent on Soviet technology. In 1956 Mao had warned that "we should not become one-sided and copy everything which comes from abroad, and introduce it mechanistically."[6] That "abroad" meant the Soviet Union was unmistakable, and the point was made more explicitly early in 1958. "Learning should be combined with creativity," he then said, and "to import Soviet codes and conventions inflexibly is to lack the creative spirit." He proceeded to level a wholesale attack on the Soviet-modeled First Five Year Plan, complaining that,

> all we could do in our ignorance was to import foreign methods. Our statistical work was practically a copy of Soviet work; in the educational field copying was also pretty bad. . . . We did not even study our own experience of education in the Liberated Areas. The same applied to our public health work, with the result that I couldn't have eggs or chicken soup for three years because an article appeared in the Soviet Union which said that one shouldn't eat them. . . . We lacked understanding of the whole economic situation and understood still less the differences between the Soviet Union and China. So all we could do was follow blindly.[7]

Having embarked upon a radically new strategy of development, it is hardly surprising that Mao was determined to break down China's reliance on the Soviet Union as well. It was not only a matter of the unsuitability of much of Soviet technology, especially to the new Maoist emphasis on small-scale rural industrialization. Also very much involved was the fear, reflecting long-standing nationalist resentments, that Chinese economic and technological dependence on Russia implied a degree of political dependence as well.[8] Moreover, economic and political dependence fostered psychological dependence, which, in turn, inhibited the initiative and activism of the masses; in the Maoist view, foreign borrowing had left the Chinese people "mentally fettered" and "passive," and their full liberation (and the liberation of their productive potential) required a spirit of "self-reliance." Thus the Maoist call for China to develop an independent and indigenous technology reflected a combination of old considerations of national pride and new economic considerations. It was a call that foreshadowed one of the main themes that emerged during the Great Leap Forward era—the principle of "self-reliance."

While Mao's desire to end copying of Soviet methods was generally shared by most Party leaders and the non-Party intelligentsia—indeed, it had been among the more prominent criticisms heard during the Hundred Flowers campaign—it is unlikely that many were receptive to the alternative program for technological development that he proposed. Mao's program, simply put, envisioned the development and application of modern science and technology without professional scientists and technocrats. To Party economic planners, this seemed an economically irrational notion, and to the technological intelligentsia a professionally threatening one as well.

But for Mao science and technology were not politically neutral matters. If left to itself, modern scientific and technological development generated technological elites and fostered bureaucracy and social inequality. Whereas in 1956 Party leaders had freed the natural sciences from any "class character," in January 1958 Mao restored the political and social links. "With the focus on technology," he warned, "[we are] apt to neglect politics. . . . Ideological and political work is the guarantee for the completion of economic and technological work. . . ."[9] In Mao's "technical revolution," politics, not technicians, were to be in command to guarantee that the means of modern science and technology were used in a fashion consistent with socialist ends.

Whereas two years earlier Zhou Enlai had posed the problem in terms of a technological intelligentsia that was insufficient in numbers and lacking in professional skills, Mao now saw the problem in terms of how China could acquire modern scientific and technological knowledge without creating a privileged technocratic elite. The Maoist solution was deceptively simple and perhaps simplistically utopian: the masses of peasants and workers themselves were to master modern technology. Moreover, they were to do so in the course of everyday productive work, learning the necessary skills and expertise in the course of doing, studying while working, and applying their newly-acquired knowledge to immediate productive needs, and in ways appropriate to suit local conditions. There were to be no "experts," but only "reds and experts," a new generation of politically conscious "jacks-of-all-trades" who were to combine mental with manual labor and who were to be capable of engaging in "scientific and cultural undertakings as well as physical labor." The result would be the creation of a whole nation of what Mao called "socialist-conscious, cultured laborers." The "red and expert" formula was thus interpreted to mean neither simply "red" cadres acquiring technical expertise nor technical experts acquiring a "red" political consciousness (although it meant that too), but rather became a universal ideal to be universally realized. Just as the Chinese nation was to become technologically self-reliant and not dependent on other nations, so too were the Chinese people to become self-reliant and not dependent on a technological elite. Technological development was conceived as a mass movement, and one of the great rallying cries of the Great Leap Forward years was the slogan "the masses must make themselves masters of culture and science." It was amid such utopian fervors that the Great Leap Forward campaign got under way.

NOTES

1. See Roderick MacFarquhar, ed., *The Hundred Flowers Campaign and the Chinese Intellectuals* (New York: Praeger, 1960), p. 273.

2. Christopher Howe, *Employment and Economic Growth in Urban China, 1949–57* (Cambridge, England: Cambridge University Press, 1971), p. 125.

3. *Hongqi* (Red Flag), June 1, 1958, p. 3.

4. Mao Tse-tung [Mao Zedong], "On the Ten Great Relationships," in Stuart R. Schram, ed., *Mao Tse-tung Unrehearsed: Talks and Letters 1956–71* (Middlesex, England: Penguin, 1974), p. 63.

5. Mao Tse-tung, "Sixty Points on Working Methods," in Jerome Ch'en, ed., *Mao Papers* (London: Oxford University Press, 1970), p. 63.

6. Mao, "On the Ten Great Relationships," p. 81.

7. Mao Tse-tung, "Talks at the Chengtu Conference," March 1958, in Schram, ed., *Mao Unrehearsed,* pp. 96–99.

8. Mao's attacks on uncritical Chinese borrowing of Soviet methods were soon to be followed by wide-ranging criticisms of the Soviet Union in general and of Stalin in particular. These appear in their most comprehensive and forceful form in Mao's 1961 "Reading Notes on the

Soviet Union's 'Political Economy,'" *Mao Zedong Sixiang Wansui* (Taipei, 1969). An English translation appears in *JPRS* document No. 61269, pp. 247–313. For a perceptive analysis, see Richard Levy, "New Light on Mao," *China Quarterly,* No. 61 (March 1975), pp. 95–117.

9. Mao, "Sixty Points on Working Methods," p. 64.

13

The People's Communes and the "Transition to Communism"

1958–1960

A T THE BEGINNING of 1958, hardly more than eight years after the birth of the People's Republic, Mao Zedong was convinced that the transition to socialism had been successfully carried out. To be sure, the "ideological" class struggle between "the proletariat" and "the bourgeoisie" had yet to be concluded (indeed he hinted that it might have to be waged indefinitely), and there remained the ever present danger of a regression back to capitalism, or at least to some presocialist state of affairs. But the fundamental tasks involved in the socialist reorganization of Chinese society had been achieved, or so Mao believed. Thus, the time was ripe for China to move to a higher stage of social development, a course dictated by the theory of permanent revolution whereby "revolutions come one after another." "Our revolutions are like battles," Mao declared. "After a victory, we must at once put forward a new task."[1] The new task was "the transition from socialism to communism."

To most Chinese Communist leaders, the call to proceed to a communist reorganization of society must have seemed a wildly utopian notion, for "socialist transformation" had begun only a few years before and industrialization was still in its infancy. Mao agreed that China remained a woefully backward country but from this fact he drew strikingly novel theoretical and practical conclusions.

If China's socialist system was still unconsolidated, then this seemed to Mao more an opportunity to move to a higher social stage than an imperative to institutionalize the existing system. For Mao had come to believe that it was precisely the relative immaturity of a social order that offered the greatest potential for radical change. And, conversely, he believed that the more consolidated a social system became, the more resistant it would be to change. Even more than ever before, Mao emphasized the decisive role of "consciousness" in sociohistorical development. As he put it in the detailed (but unpublished) critiques of Stalin and Soviet theory he then was undertaking: "We cannot go on consolidating [a social system] for all time, otherwise we will make inflexible the ideology reflecting this system and render people incapable of adjusting their thoughts to new changes."[2] In bringing about the revolutionary transformation of social relations, the guiding Maoist principle was "to strike while the iron is hot."[3] To stabilize the existing order—and thus to delay moving to a higher stage of development—was a prescription for stagnation and regression.

Nor did Mao regard economic backwardness as a barrier to "the transition to communism." Indeed, he regarded it as an asset, for it was in 1958 that he set forth publicly his remarkable thesis on the revolutionary advantages of being "poor and blank," which he soon followed with the proposition that the more backward the economy, the easier the socialist and communist reorganization of society would be.[4] To be sure, economic backwardness also was deplored—and indeed was to be overcome—but it was to be overcome simultaneously with processes of social revolutionary change leading to communism. In launching the Great Leap Forward campaign, Mao promised both a "technical revolution" and a social revolution, both an economic miracle and a social miracle—but the latter was not dependent on the prior accomplishment of the former. Indeed, it was the revolutionary transformation of social relations and consciousness that would release the latent productive powers of the masses and provide the impetus for the "technical revolution"—and at the same time guarantee that economic development would be carried out in a fashion consistent with the realization of communist social goals. Just as during the collectivization campaign of 1955 Mao had proceeded on the assumption that "the economic conditions of our country being what they are, technical reform will take longer than social reform," he now was even more firmly convinced that a social revolution was the necessary prerequisite for an economic revolution, that "proletarianization" must precede "mechanization."

In attempting to understand the rather extraordinary events of 1958–1960, it is important to keep in mind these Maoist assumptions on the relationship between social and economic change. For Mao and

Maoists, the term "great leap"—which had been used several years before, but only with reference to rapid increases in production—now had acquired a social as well as an economic meaning. It conveyed the expectation of a qualitative transformation of social relationships as well as the expectation of a "leap" in economic development. In the Maoist mentality, as it revealed itself in both the theory and the practice of the Great Leap, the pursuit of communist social and ideological goals was inextricably intertwined with the goal of rapidly developing the material forces of production—and the former was seen as the precondition for the proper development of the latter. The Great Leap was the time when Maoists explicitly rejected the Stalinist orthodoxy that the combination of state ownership of the key means of production with rapid economic development guaranteed the advent of a communist society. In the Maoist view, by contrast, the promise of a communist future demanded the introduction of communist forms of social organization and the cultivation of a communist consciousness in the here and now, in conditions of economic scarcity, and as the prerequisites for transcending those conditions. It was the time when Maoism announced itself as a doctrine that divorced communism from its Marxist-defined economic preconditions.

The Great Leap Forward campaign began at the end of 1957 and intensified in the early months of 1958 as a drive for increased productivity in both industry and agriculture. The campaign to produce "more, faster, better, and cheaper" (as the popular slogan of the time exhorted) proceeded in accordance with the new Maoist economic strategy of "simultaneous development" formally adopted by the Party in October 1957. A new emphasis on agriculture and small industries accompanied the raising of production targets in the heavy industrial sector. The centralized bureaucratic economic apparatus was partially dismantled in favor of relative autonomy and decision-making authority for localities and basic production units. Administrative offices were emptied as officials were "sent down" (*xiafang*) to engage in manual labor on farms and in factories in the name of "simple administration." Ideological exhortations and moral appeals replaced material rewards as the incentive for workers and peasants to work harder and longer, accompanied by the promise that "three years of struggle" would be followed by "a thousand years of communist happiness." The social mobilization of the masses for labor rather than the bureaucratic direction of laborers became the central organizational feature of a campaign that acquired an increasingly militaristic character—and indeed was described as one which involved "fighting battles against the natural world" analogous to the battles that had been fought during the revolutionary years, demanding the same qualities of heroism and self-sacrifice.

In industry the Great Leap was marked by the implementation of the policy of "walking on two legs" (a policy announced three years before but hitherto largely dormant), in accordance with which medium and small-scale labor-intensive industries using indigenous technologies were to be developed simultaneously with the modern industrial sector. For workers in modern factories it was a policy that meant harder and longer working hours (and for some, lower wages as well) to meet ever higher and increasingly unrealistic production quotas. The "second leg" of the new industrial policy was most spectacularly symbolized by the mobilization of tens of millions of people in urban and rural areas in the futile "backyard" iron and steel campaign; it was the most publicized and most wasteful of the new labor-intensive local industrial projects. Other small-scale undertakings, especially local chemical and fertilizer factories and coal mines in the rural areas, were less publicized but often effective.

In the countryside, the size of private family plots was reduced; the scale and intensity of collective labor expanded; millions of urban cadres and technicians arrived to assist in the organization of new local industries; and armies of peasants were mobilized for large-scale irrigation and water conservation projects. The "campaign to build water works," begun in the autumn of 1957, was expanded enormously in the early months of 1958.

If Maoists were "utopian" in their economic expectations, they were even more so in their belief that the Chinese people were prepared to carry out "the transition from socialism to communism." As the campaigns for increased productivity grew in scope and intensity, Maoists searched for a new form of social organization to accomplish both the economic revolution and the social one. The form that was discovered was the people's commune, and by the summer of 1958 Maoists were hailing the commune as the agency for China's transition to a communist society.

The Rural People's Communes

The vast communization movement, which radically transformed the Chinese countryside and the lives of its 500,000,000 inhabitants in the summer and fall of 1958, was not the product of any detailed blueprint. Much of what happened was spontaneous, and many of the most crucial policy decisions were improvised during the frenetic course of the movement or made by local leaders on the spot. The spontaneous character of the campaign was partly responsible for the remarkable dynamism that communization generated—and it contributed a good deal to the economic chaos that eventually resulted.

Although the communes can be seen as a logical outgrowth of Mao's new economic strategy, especially when that strategy became connected with utopian visions of the imminent advent of communism, there is no evidence that Maoists had communization in mind when the Great Leap Forward began. Only a few months before Mao anticipated that it would take five years or more to consolidate the existing collective farms.[5] During the early months of 1958 Mao did not use the term "commune" in his speeches and writings. Nor did he explicitly advocate the wholesale "communist" reorganization of society. Although the December 1957 Politburo meeting, which formally launched the Great Leap, called for amalgamating collectives into larger units, this was motivated more by the organizational needs of the massive irrigation and water-conservation movement (begun several months earlier) than by utopian visions of communism. It was not until the Great Leap Forward was well underway that the commune was discovered and in the late summer of 1958 seized upon by Maoists as the organizational ideal for China's "transition from socialism to communism."

The communization movement involved the complex interplay of the spontaneous radicalism of rural cadres and poor peasants from below with the radical utopianism of Mao and Maoists from above. And, just as in the collectivization campaign of 1955, the two proved mutually reinforcing, with the result that the movement acquired a fantastic momentum of its own and proceeded at a frantic tempo that far exceeded the hopes and expectations of even its most radical exponents. The first of the communes appeared on an experimental basis in Henan province in April 1958. While it is unlikely that the experiment could have been undertaken without the approval of Maoist leaders in Beijing, the initiative apparently came from radical local activists. Spontaneity and local initiatives were certainly predominant in July when (after an excellent summer harvest) the amalgamation of collectives into communes spread rapidly in Henan and Hebei provinces and certain areas of Manchuria. The movement grew without official Party sanction and with little central direction, but it received powerful ideological encouragement from Maoist leaders. In the July 1, 1958, issue of the newly established Party theoretical periodical *Red Flag,* Chen Boda, a leading Maoist theoretician and Mao's personal secretary, first used the term "people's commune" to describe an expanded and reorganized collective in Hubei. The Hubei commune, according to Chen, had succeeded in combining agricultural and industrial production, and it had produced new "all-round" people who were acquiring scientific and technological knowledge in the course of working, integrating "technological revolution" with "cultural revolution," and learning to perform essential administrative functions as well as advanced productive methods. The commune was thus in the process of realizing the Marxist goals of eliminating the distinctions between mental and manual labor, between industry and agriculture, and between town and countryside—thereby opening the road "on which our country can smoothly pass over from socialism to communism." Chen attributed these accomplishments to the heroic spirit of the working masses.[6]

In a lengthy speech delivered in early July at Beijing University to commemorate the thirty-seventh anniversary of the founding of the Chinese Communist Party, Chen Boda elaborated on these themes in an even more utopian fashion and with the support of copious quotations drawn from the writings of Marx, Lenin, and Mao. He described the movement toward communism in the countryside in almost chiliastic terms and attributed the revolutionary upsurge not only to the creativity of "the pioneering peasants" but also (and especially) to the inspiration of the thought of Mao Zedong. And he attributed the idea and the ideal of the commune to Mao as well:

> Comrade Mao Zedong said that we should steadily and systematically organize "industry, agriculture, commerce, education and soldiers into a big commune, thereby to form the basic units of society." . . . This conception of the commune is a conclusion drawn by Comrade Mao Zedong from real life.[7]

In view of the close personal and ideological relationship between Chen and Mao, the *Red Flag* articles signaled Maoist approval (if not necessarily official Party approval) of the growing communization movement. By the time Liu Shaoqi and other Party leaders set out on tours to inspect communization in the northern provinces in late July, the movement already was widespread. Mao personally added to the momentum by undertaking an inspection tour of his own early in August; his glowing praise of the commune system was prominently reported in the press, as was his call for the extension of the system throughout the country. Thus when the members of the Politburo met in "enlarged session" (a meeting which included provincial and regional Party secretaries as well as the entire Central Committee) at the seaside resort of Beidaihe August 17–30, they were faced with another Maoist *fait accompli*. Many communes already had been established, the campaign to establish new ones was proceeding at an accelerating pace, and Mao's enthusiastic approval of communization had been widely publicized in newspapers and periodicals. Despite the grave reservations of many Party leaders, they had no alternative but to formally ratify what was already taking place, although the length of the meeting suggests that they did so only after considerable debate.

Formal ratification came in the form of a resolution issued on August 29 from Beidaihe in the name of the Central Committee. Observing that "the people's communes are the logical result of the march of events," that "they are already widespread," and that "it is highly probable that there will soon be an upsurge in setting up people's communes throughout the country and the development is irresistible," the resolution sanctioned universal communization and recognized the commune as the appropriate organizational form "to guide the peasants to accelerate socialist construction, complete the building of socialism ahead of time, and carry out the gradual transition to communism." The resolution recommended that wherever possible the commune should be coextensive with the *xiang* and ideally should comprise about 2,000 peasant households. While the document accepted the Maoist demand that the commune system be universalized, at least in the rural areas, it also reflected the reservations and doubts of non-Maoist Party leaders. The resolution was replete with warnings against "compulsory or rash steps" in the organization of communes and any measures which might have an adverse effect on agricultural production. Moreover, it insisted on the socialist rather than the communist character of the new organizations. The commune system of ownership was to be "collective" rather than characterized by "ownership by the people as a whole," while the system of distribution was to be in accord with the socialist principle of "to each according to his work" and not the communist ideal "to each according to his needs." While the communes were to prepare the way for "the gradual transition to communism," the resolution was vague on when that transition might come about. Indeed, it implied that it might take many decades, for it was suggested that the conditions for the transition to communism required not only an "advance in the people's consciousness" but also an unspecified level of "the development of production" and an "increase of income."[8] The August 29 resolution was a rather moderate document in contrast to the more radical utopian Maoist writings of the time, which advocated the immediate introduction of communist forms of work and organization and promised the more or less immediate advent of a communist utopia.

Communization proceeded more rapidly and more radically than Party leaders anticipated. Before the year was out, virtually the entire rural population was organized in some 24,000 people's communes which had emerged from the hasty amalgamation of 750,000 collective farms. Much larger than officially proposed, the average commune comprised 5,000 households (approximately 30,000 people); but the populations varied greatly, ranging from less than 5,000 members to over 100,000. And in defiance of the August resolution, many communes moved immediately to introduce communist forms of social life, work organization, and distribution.

The summer and fall of 1958 was the most radical phase of the Great Leap. It was a time when hopes for economic abundance and a communist utopia were highest, and popular enthusiasm was the greatest. It was a time when postponed Marxist utopian goals became immediate ones and Maoist leaders proclaimed them to be more or less immediately realizable. The ultimate goals of classical Marxism—not excluding the most utopian of all visions, the "withering away" of the state—were popularized not as distant ends but as the immediate tasks of the day. The achievement of these historically unprecedented tasks was assigned to the people's communes, which were conceived not merely as productive organizations but also as new social organizations that "combined economic, cultural, political and military affairs" and thus merged "workers, peasants, merchants, students, and militiamen into a single entity." By combining industry with agriculture, education with productive activity, and by merging economic with political power, the communes were to perform all the social revolutionary transformations that Marxists traditionally assigned to the period of "the dictatorship of the proletariat," the time of transition from socialism to communism. In the Maoist literature of the Great Leap, the commune was seen to be "the organizer of living" as well as the organizer of production; it was conceived not only as the means to realize ultimate communist ends but also as an embryonic communist society that was taking shape in the here and now, an embryo that would grow to become the basic social unit of the future communist utopia.

The commune was also conceived as both the product and the producer of new communist people, the ideal "red and experts" who would perform a vast variety of social functions and who were the carriers of that all-important "communist consciousness" upon which the new society ultimately was dependent. Very soon, it typically was proclaimed, "everyone will be a mental laborer and at the same time a physical laborer; everyone can be a philosopher, scientist, writer, and artist." The more utopian themes and passages in classical Marxist writings were widely drawn upon to support this vision. In the early days of communization nothing was more frequently quoted than the passage in *The German Ideology* where Marx took one of his rare glimpses into the future and saw a communist society:

> [where] nobody has one exclusive sphere of activity but each can become accomplished in any branch he wishes, [a society that] regulates the general production and thus makes it possible for me to do one thing today and another tomorrow, to hunt in the morning, fish in the afternoon, rear cattle in the evening, criticize after dinner, just as I have a mind, without ever becoming hunter, fisherman, shepherd or critic.

These utopian visions of a future classless and stateless society at first evoked positive responses among the peasants and undoubtedly contributed to their willingness to sacrifice in order to bring about that future. In the chiliastic atmosphere of the early days of communization, Mao Zedong was thus able to partly bypass the regular bureaucratic channels of the Party and state and establish, for a time, a direct bond between himself and the people, a bond between his utopian visions of communism and popular aspirations for social change and economic prosperity.

Even before the communes were established, a radical change in work organization had been wrought by the vast irrigation and water-conservation campaigns begun in autumn 1957. Peasants from different villages were brought together in production brigades and work teams that functioned with military-like discipline to perform specialized tasks, with labor organized (and remunerated) as in a modern factory. With the establishment of the communes, the large production brigades (generally consisting of several thousand peasants) became more formalized and extended their functions to agricultural production as well as to the operation of newly established commune industries and large-scale construction works. Within the large brigades were a dozen or more smaller brigades (later called work teams) whose members were recruited from a single village. Coordinating the work of the brigades was the commune, which in theory functioned as a more or less autonomous and self-sufficient economic, social, and political unit.

The mobilization of peasants into production brigades demanded immediate and far-reaching changes in rural social life, changes which were celebrated as progress towards communism. The transfer of male peasants to irrigation work, large-scale construction projects, and to the new industrial undertakings created labor shortages in agriculture. The obvious solution was to draw women into full-time productive labor in the fields as well as in light industries. Although instituted to relieve an acute labor shortage, the result was hailed as a giant step toward sexual equality and proclaimed to be one of the communist aims the communes were designed to achieve. The measures necessary to free women from traditional domestic chores and thus to free them for agricultural labor—the establishment of communal mess halls and nurseries usually staffed by older peasant women—were celebrated as "the socialization of household work." Although the intensive mobilization of both male and female labor, coupled with the introduction of new communal forms of living, temporarily changed the pattern of family life, the family as such remained intact. Disruptions occurred, primarily because some male workers were assigned to projects distant from their villages and temporarily separated from their wives and children, but contrary to widespread reports in the Western press at the time, the existing family structure was not abolished. Nor was there any inclination to do so. Even the most radical Maoists remained firmly committed to the maintenance of the nuclear family, just as they remained tied to highly puritanical sexual mores.

While the family remained secure, its private property did not. As visions of communism grew, so did demands for total abolition of personal possessions and for a general social leveling. The ideological demand was reinforced by the economic logic of the universal mobilization of labor. With most able-bodied men and women organized in production brigades and working from sunrise to sunset on collective projects, little time or energy was left to tend family plots and animals. Private holdings, which accounted for about 7 percent of the cultivated land at the beginning of 1958, were virtually eliminated by the end of the year and became communal property, as did hitherto family-owned pigs and fowl. In the areas where communization was most radically pursued, everything from homes to cooking utensils, furniture, and watches were collectivized and turned over to the commune—at least in theory.

The next step was to distribute the surplus product, that which remained after state taxes and what was set aside for investment and welfare, in accordance with the communist principle of to each according to one's need. While official regulations governing the operation of the communes specified that the new organizations were to be socialist in nature and that remuneration was to be based on one's labor, the problem of determining individual labor contributions for work performed in collective fashion proved formidable—and, in the hectic circumstances of the time, impossible to resolve. It was much easier to simply distribute the surplus equally, or according to real or perceived individual needs, than calculate the quantity and quality of labor. The national formula arrived at near the end of the year recommended that 30 percent of the surplus be distributed according to labor and 70 percent according to need, although the extent to which the general formula was applied remains obscure. Indeed, the evidence is too scanty to determine how much of the widely celebrated social radicalism of early communization was actually practiced, for it was the most radical and "model" communes that were the most widely publicized, both within and outside China. In reality, the communes differed enormously, not only in size and wealth but in nature. Some involved little more than formal administrative reorganizations of existing collective farms, whereas others moved rapidly to achieve what was perceived to be a new communist order. The only universal feature was the intensive mobilization of labor and the lengthening of the working day.

Of far greater and lasting significance than the more spectacular social radicalism of the time (much of which vanished as rapidly as it had appeared) were new policies in industry and education. One was the policy of promoting "the industrialization of the countryside" and the other was the introduction of a new rural educational system based on the principle of "work and study." Maoists found theoretical support for these policies in the writings of Karl Marx. Despite Marx's aversion to drawing "utopian" blueprints of the future communist society, he did (on rare occasions) outline in general terms his conception of the "dictatorship of the proletariat" and the corresponding period of the transition from socialism to communism. In the Manifesto of 1848 he set forth ten "generally applicable" measures following the overthrow of the bourgeois state. Among them was the "combination of agriculture with manufacturing industries" and the "gradual abolition of the distinction between town and country, by a more equitable distribution of population over the country." In educational policy, he urged the general principle of the "combination of education with industrial production."[9] If Maoist policies were not necessarily directly inspired by the writings of Marx, they nonetheless were consistent with the measures Marx had proposed and theoretically justified by repeated references to the classic texts, although pursued under vastly different historical conditions from those Marx had envisioned.

The positive accomplishments of the program for establishing commune-operated industries should not be obscured by the strange spectacle of the "backyard" steel and iron production campaign of 1958. The backyard furnaces resulted in an enormous waste of labor and soon were abandoned. But other rural industries, established at the same time with less fanfare, proved viable and often innovative. Relying on local human and material resources, and using primitive technologies, they served well the immediate goals they were intended to achieve by assisting agricultural productivity and development, providing peasants with small consumer goods which otherwise would not have been produced, and utilizing surplus rural labor which otherwise would have gone unused. If there were waste, inefficiency, and false starts in the beginning, in the long run Chinese agriculture has benefited by the commune-operated shops manufacturing and repairing agricultural implements, small chemical plants producing fertilizers and insecticides, small-scale power generators, and local crop-processing industries. And both rural society and the national economy have profited from local coal-mining operations, small oil refineries, and locally produced consumer goods. These were the forerunners of the enormously successful "township and village enterprises" of the post-Mao era.

The new education policies were closely related to the new emphasis on the industrialization of the countryside. Communization was accompanied by an ambitious effort to establish locally operated part-time educational facilities: "red and expert" universities, evening schools, spare-time educational programs, and a variety of "half-work and half-study" programs. The guiding principle was the "combination of education and production" and the main purpose was to provide the peasants with the minimal technological knowledge and the basic literacy necessary for the operation of local rural industries and the future introduction of modern agricultural techniques. The program drew on a long modern Chinese tradition of radical educational concepts and experiences, which included the "half-work, half-study" ideal of young intellectuals in the May Fourth era (a program in which Mao personally had taken part) as well as the *minban* (popular-managed) schools and other educational experiments of the Yan'an years.[10]

In addition to serving immediate productive needs, the new rural school system was seen as a means to realize the Maoist ideal for "the masses to make themselves masters of technology," lessen the need for specialized urban universities and schools, forestall the growth of a technological intelligentsia, and thus contribute to the realization of the Marxist goals of abolishing the distinctions between town and countryside and between mental and manual labor. In the utopian spirit of the times, the various programs based on the combination of education with productive labor were typically described as ones "designed to foster students who are socialist-minded and cultured laborers and ensure their moral, intellectual and physical development to produce new men of communism."[11] "The red and expert and spare-time universities are not intended to meet temporary needs alone," it was proclaimed. "Coordination between education and productive labor is one of the fundamental principles underlying our socialist education," and the new institutions were not only the ideal form to achieve this combination but they also "open our eyes to the germs of the educational system in a communist society."[12] Theoretical support for the new educational program was found in Marx's statement that "an early combination of productive labor with education is one of the most potent means for the transformation of present-day society" and Engels' vision of a future communist society which would educate "well-rounded human beings" who would "pass from one branch of production to another in response to the needs of society or their own inclinations."[13]

The radical utopianism that characterized communization was not confined to social and economic policies but extended to the political sphere. The Maoist choice of the term "commune" to characterize the new forms of social organization was by no means fortuitous. The term was derived from Karl Marx's analysis of the Paris Commune of 1871 and the Marxist identification of the Paris Commune as the historical model of the dictatorship of the proletariat. As such, the term "commune," in the Marxist tradition, conveyed the notion of an entirely new form of the organization of political power—the armed community of laborers who would smash the existing centralized state apparatus (what Marx referred to as "the ubiquitous organs of standing army, police, and bureaucracy") and replace it with popular "working bodies," which would restore to society as a whole the social powers usurped by the state. In Marx's description of the Commune, standing army and police are replaced by the armed populace; the state bureaucracy is destroyed in favor of popular organs, which combine executive and legislative functions; such socially necessary administrative functions as remain are performed not by appointed officials but by popularly selected members of the working people who carry out their duties at ordinary worker's wages, without special status or privileges, and are under the constant supervision of the people; and state power is decentralized into a "free federation" of self-governed local communes.[14] It was with this conception of political power reorganized as the dictatorship of the proletariat that Marx envisioned the transition period that would lead to a classless communist society and, in the process, result in the disappearance of the state itself. It was a conception held by radical Maoists as they undertook to reorganize Chinese society into people's communes.

One way in which the Marxian model of the Paris Commune reflected itself (although in distorted form) in Maoist practice was in the general militarization of work and life. "Our revolutions are like battles," Mao had declared in January 1958, and by July peasants on communes were organized in battalions marching off to labor in the fields in step, with martial music blaring from loudspeakers. The slogans of the time called upon the masses not only to collectivize but also to "militarize," "combatize," and "disciplinize." Although the militarization of work was ideologically rationalized by Marxist references to the Commune as a community dominated by the armed masses, the purpose was increased labor productivity. But the result was to be the physical exhaustion of the peasants, who were subjected to intolerable physical demands and an increasingly unrealistic extension of the working day.

More in harmony with the Marxist concept of the Commune was the revival of the people's militia and the arming of the peasantry, measures which coincided with communization and the Taiwan Straits crisis of August 1958.[15] In the literature of the time, the internal "war against nature" was closely linked to the threat of external aggression. As an August 1958 *Red Flag* editorial put it:

Though militarization in agricultural work is not for the purpose of repulsing the enemies of mankind, but for the purpose of carrying on the struggle with nature, it makes it easy to transform one of these two kinds of struggle into the other. . . . if an external enemy should dare to attack us, all people can be mobilized and armed, and made into an army decisively, resolutely, thoroughly, and completely to destroy the enemy.[16]

Although the immediate danger of war over Quemoy and Matsu soon passed, the militia campaign continued. By the end of 1959, some 220,000,000 people had been recruited into the militia and 30,000,000 had been armed with primitive rifles.[17] The revival of the popular militia (an act presented in terms of the Commune ideal of abolishing the standing army) was soon to become an issue in a bitter political struggle over the nature and role of the regular People's Liberation Army.

Perhaps the most radically utopian aspect of communization—and when for a brief time the people's communes approached most closely the Marxist model of the Paris Commune—was the role assigned to the communes in the reorganization and exercise of political power. The Maoist theoretical literature of 1958 strongly suggests that the communes originally were conceived as organs of "proletarian dictatorship," albeit without an urban proletariat.[18] The commune's appropriation of the administrative functions of the *xiang* was interpreted as making the commune a political unit "performing the functions of state power" and "the most desirable organizational form" for the period of the transition from socialism to communism.[19] It was stressed that the communes were not merely productive organizations but ones which "combined economic, cultural, political and military affairs," and combined "workers, peasants, merchants, students and militia into a single entity." Special emphasis was placed on the role of the commune in "merging" the basic economic units of society with the basic "organs of state power," a step that was hailed as the beginning of a process in which the internal functions of the state (now assigned to the commune, at least in theory) gradually would disappear.[20] The vision of the "withering away" of the state was the most utopian of all the utopian goals proclaimed and popularized during the early period of communization and it probably struck deeply responsive chords among the peasantry, for it meshed with traditional peasant anarchist dreams of freedom from the tyranny of officials and bureaucrats.

References to the Marxian model appear frequently in the Maoist literature of the time. A Chinese Marxist theoretician writing in September 1958 typically observed that "the integration of the *xiang* with the commune will make the commune not very different from the Paris Commune, integrating economic organization with the organization of state power."[21] More important than the possible influence of Marxist precedents is that the political functions which Maoists assigned to the communes in theory, and the realities of communization, posed a grave challenge to the functioning of existing Party and state bureaucracies. Had the people's communes actually developed in the manner Maoists originally envisioned, centralized political power in China would have been fundamentally undermined—much in the way in which Marx had attributed to the Paris Commune the potential to restore to the producers those social powers which had been usurped by the state. The antibureaucratic implications of communization were unmistakable, and bureaucrats with vested interests in the pre-Great Leap order soon began to respond to the threat. Their first opportunity to blunt the radical thrust of communization came in early December, when the Party Central Committee convened at Wuhan to deal with the economic and organizational difficulties that resulted from the hasty manner in which Maoist-inspired rural cadres implemented Mao's policies.

The First Retreat

Communization began in the summer of 1958, assisted by a bountiful harvest and widespread popular enthusiasm. By late autumn, the movement was burdened by food shortages and a marked decline in peasant morale. The haste with which communes were established resulted in organizational chaos, compounded by the lack of skilled personnel to properly manage complex fiscal affairs and the new forms of communal life and work. Peasants from richer collectives resented the economic leveling that resulted from their amalgamation with peasants from poorer collectives; and they expressed their dissatisfaction by slaughtering and consuming farm animals instead of turning them over to the commune. And peasants in general came to resent arbitrary work assignments, inequities in remuneration, and inefficient management of mess halls and other communal facilities. The mobilization of peasant labor for industrial, irrigation and construction projects often led to the neglect of agricultural production and, consequently, food shortages. A general breakdown of national economic planning led to gross inefficiencies in the production and distribution of goods and materials, bottlenecks in an overtaxed transportation system, fiscal policies based on inflated production reports, and shortages of raw materials for industry. The "commandism" practiced by local cadres produced the regimentation of labor rather than communal labor, and the lengthening of the working day to meet unrealistic production quotas resulted in the general physical exhaustion of the working population. The realities of communization bore little resemblance to the principles of the rational utilization of labor upon which the Great Leap Forward originally was based, and still less to the ideal of communal life and labor voluntarily undertaken.

As economic difficulties multiplied and popular dissatisfaction grew, Party leaders met at Wuhan on November 28 to attempt to restore economic stability. They emerged on December 10 with a resolution that retained much of the utopian rhetoric of the summer and fall and reaffirmed that the rural communes would be the agency for China's eventual transition to communism,[22] but one which set forth policies designed to blunt the social and political radicalism of communization. The policies were approved and implemented over the opposition of Mao, marking the beginning of a bitter political struggle that was to come to a dramatic climax the following summer.

Among the measures adopted at Wuhan was the reestablishment of the "production brigade" as the basic unit of production, in effect, a reversion to the pre-commune collective based on the natural village, although the commune retained ownership of local industrial enterprises. The resolution discussed at great length (and in orthodox Marxist-Leninist terms) the distinction between the socialist and communist stages of development, firmly identified the commune with the former, and thus insisted that the social product be distributed solely on the basis of work rather than need. It was emphasized that the road to communism involved "a long and complicated process," that a communist reorganization of society presupposed advanced productive forces, and that this could be achieved "only after the lapse of considerable time." In the meantime, the resolution warned against "impetuous attempts" to introduce communist measures and "utopian dreams" of skipping over historically necessary stages of social development. Accordingly, it called for a restoration of individual ownership of personal property such as houses, furniture, consumer goods, small farm tools, and the restoration of small family plots for supplementary food production and individual family ownership of small domestic animals and poultry. And to undermine the influence of local rural cadres who had spearheaded radical communization, the Central Committee demanded the reestablishment of the full authority of regular Party and state organs over the countryside.

A series of other Party meetings in the early months of 1959 further moderated the operation of the communes and established stricter centralized controls over them. These meetings, as was the Wuhan Plenum of December, were dominated by Liu Shaoqi. It was reflective of the political trends of the time that Mao's presumably voluntary decision to step down as head of state was announced by the Central Committee during the Wuhan meeting and that the position of Chairman of the People's Republic formally was conferred on Liu in April 1959. Mao retained the more important post of Chairman of the Party, but he was no longer fully in command of the Party apparatus. He later was to complain that, after the Wuhan plenum, he was treated like "a dead ancestor."[23]

While Mao may have been treated like a dead man, he did not behave like one. The first half of 1959 was marked by increasingly bitter Party debates over socioeconomic policy, centering on the communes, with Maoists unsuccessfully attempting to revive the radicalism of the Great Leap. In April Mao sent a personal directive to local Party committees condemning the decisions of the Wuhan meeting. But the retreat ordered in December continued. By the summer of 1959 most of the communes were little more than hollow administrative structures. Communal mess halls were abandoned, peasants were devoting more and more of their labor to private family plots, and private rural markets (abolished in late 1957) reappeared. Despite attempts by leaders in Beijing to restore centralized planning and political controls, economic conditions continued to deteriorate. Shortages of raw materials and transportation difficulties gravely hampered industrial production. And unusually severe floods and drought in the spring and summer (affecting nearly half of the cultivated land) held ominous implications for agricultural production and the national economy in general.

As the economic situation became more critical, the political struggle between Maoists and the Party hierarchy intensified. The struggle revolved about what Maoists later called "the two roads"—one presumably leading back to capitalism and the other forward to socialism and communism—although the political lines had yet to be fully drawn. Matters reached a head (the first of many) in early August, when the Party Central Committee convened its Eighth Plenum at the mountain resort of Lushan in Jiangxi province.

The Lushan Plenum

Three momentous issues confronted Communist leaders at the Lushan meeting: the future of the communes and the Great Leap; Mao's political future; and control of the People's Liberation Army. The three issues came together (although they were to be resolved only temporarily) in the dramatic confrontation between Mao and Peng Dehuai, a veteran revolutionary who had played a major role in the history of the Red Army since joining Mao at Jinggangshan in 1928 and who had commanded Chinese forces in the Korean War.

The prelude to the drama enacted at Lushan began when Peng, in his capacity as Minister of Defense, led a Chinese military delegation on a visit to the Soviet Union and Eastern Europe in the spring of 1959. During the course of his travels, Peng expressed to Khrushchev and other foreign Communist leaders his displeasure (which coincided with Soviet displeasure) over the policies of the Great Leap and the leadership of Mao. In Peng's view, a view shared by other military leaders, China's domestic socioeconomic policies were intimately related to its military policies and its relations with the Soviet Union. China's military security required a rational plan of economic development (to modernize the professional army that Peng headed) as well as the sophisticated weapons and the nuclear shield provided by the Soviet Union. The Great Leap Forward campaign threatened both, for it was undermining industrial and technological development within China and undermining the Sino-Soviet alliance. And even more directly threatening to the professional army was Maoist talk about reviving the popular militia.

When Peng returned to China in mid-June, he launched a wholesale attack on the Great Leap, culminating a month later in a "Letter of Opinion" addressed directly to Mao. With a striking lack of subtlety, he condemned communization, the collapse of national planning, the alienation of the Party from the masses, and oppressive economic and political conditions—all of which he attributed to the "petty bourgeois fanaticism" of Maoists.[24]

Although it is most unlikely that Peng was involved with the Russians in any anti-Mao conspiracy, this may have seemed to Mao and others to be the case. For it was precisely when Peng returned from his military mission to the Soviet Union in June that Khrushchev unilaterally abrogated the 1957 agreement according to which the Soviet Union was to provide China with modern military technology, including, it was reported, a sample atomic bomb. And it was at the very time that Peng was circulating his "Letter of Opinion" that Khrushchev, in a speech delivered in Poland on July 18, first publicly denounced the Chinese communes, attributing them to the ideas of people who "do not properly understand what communism is or how it is to be built."[25] Mao, at any rate, was firmly convinced that Peng (among others) had gone "behind the back of our fatherland to collude with a foreign country."[26]

Mao was by no means uncritical of his own role in the Great Leap. On July 23, in one of the conferences preceding the Lushan Plenum, Mao criticized himself for promoting the backyard steel campaign (which he described as "a great catastrophe") and for pushing communization with undue haste. "The chaos caused was on a grand scale and I take responsibility."[27] The speech, however, was a curious combination of confessions, a defense of the Great Leap policies in general and the communes in particular, a call for the revival of communization, and political threats. Mao still found mass "enthusiasm for communism" among the peasantry, reaffirmed his own enthusiasm for the communes and their future (while acknowledging the mistakes of the past), denied that he and the Party had become isolated from the masses, and was harshly critical of comrades who "waver in times of crisis and show a lack of resolution in the great storms of history." And he put the most threatening of his political threats in the most dramatic fashion. Should the Great Leap and the communes be allowed to perish, he vowed to "go to the countryside to lead the peasants to overthrow the government. If those of you in the Liberation Army won't follow me, then I will go and find a Red Army, and organize another Liberation Army. But I think the Liberation Army would follow me."[28]

Mao hardly could have drawn the political lines more sharply. Nor could he have more narrowly limited the range of policy choices that the Politburo and Central Committee could make. Not only did he challenge the Party to choose between himself and Peng Dehuai, but he tied the question of his personal leadership of the Party to his policy on the communes and to Maoist leadership of the army. Since most Party leaders were not about to risk a major political upheaval (and perhaps even a civil war) by attempting to remove Mao, they had little choice but to reaffirm Mao's political supremacy, and in the bargain support his policies as well. While Mao sought dramatic and decisive confrontations, most of his opponents were, above all, men of order who were not about to compound a chaotic economic situation with political chaos. They did not share the boldness of a Peng Dehuai, and, however much Liu Shaoqi and others may have shared Peng's criticisms of the Great Leap, they shrank from following him into a battle that held such unpredictable consequences.

Thus when the Eighth Plenum of the Central Committee formally convened on August 2, Peng found himself politically isolated; and his criticism of the Great Leap was, for the time being, in political discredit as well. Mao insisted that Peng also be politically disgraced, a demand that Party leaders hardly could refuse in view of the widespread suspicions that Peng was involved in Khrushchev's heavy-handed attempts to interfere in internal Chinese affairs. For however great their differences on matters of domestic policy, most Chinese Communists were committed no less ardently than Mao to the principle of Chinese national independence. The Lushan Plenum, accordingly, adopted a resolution denouncing "the anti-Party clique headed by Peng Dehuai," which subsequent statements likened to the anti-Party conspiracy of Gao Gang in the early 1950s, and condemned him for having slandered the Great Leap. Peng was dismissed as minister of defense and his supporters were removed from key positions in the army. In September he was succeeded by the then eminently Maoist Lin Biao.

The official communique that emerged on August 26 from the Lushan meeting was quite candid in acknowledging the failures of the Great Leap. The communique was particularly critical of the now abandoned backyard steel production campaign and the absence of central planning and direction. Also admitted was that due to inadequate accounting procedures, the celebrated increases in production for 1958 had been grossly overestimated. The officially announced figure of 375,000,000 tons for grain production was revised downward to 250,000,000 tons. The actual figure was probably about 215 million tons.[29] Nevertheless, the Lushan resolution called for the revival of the Great Leap Forward and reaffirmed the validity and viability of the people's communes. The difficulties experienced by the communes now were attributed to "right opportunists" who underestimated achievements and overestimated defects. Communal mess halls were to be restored and private peasant plots reduced. But the Lushan Plenum formalized the Wuhan decision that the production brigade not the commune was to be the primary "unit of account." For the time being, the concept of communal ownership of property was rejected.

The revival of the Great Leap in the fall of 1959 and the winter of 1960 was a pale reflection of the original movement and Mao's political victory at Lushan soon proved hollow. Maoist ideological appeals fell on deaf ears as floods and drought ravaged much of the countryside and food shortages spread in the wake of a poor harvest. Facing the threat of a bitter winter, peasants resisted the introduction of mess halls and the abolition of their private plots—and demoralized rural Party cadres were little inclined to press the issues. The statements of Party leaders were prefaced with the radical slogans of the Great Leap, but the substance of policy was to continue the cautious retreat from communization, implicitly sanctioning material incentives, the reemergence of private markets, and the return to the small intra-village team (in effect, the old mutual aid team) as the basic unit of production. Immediate economic needs rather than radical social visions also guided policy in the urban areas as food shortages spread to the cities and industrial production was increasingly hampered by problems of supply and distribution. The previous year's utopian fervor and popular enthusiasm withered as the struggle to achieve communism turned into an elemental struggle for basic subsistence and sheer survival.

By the end of 1959 Mao had come to recognize the gravity of the economic situation and had come to accept (however reluctantly) the inevitability of dismantling the Great Leap Forward. In a letter written in late November and circulated through the rural Party organizations, he invoked not the principle of "permanent revolution," with which the Great Leap had begun, but rather uncharacteristically advised paying attention "only to real possibilities," the somber note on which the campaign came to an end. Over the following months Mao quietly withdrew from day-to-day Party affairs and political life, although without relinquishing his formal position as chairman of the Chinese Communist Party, and seemingly acquiesced in the reassertion of the power of regular Party and state organizations, personified in the growing dominance of Liu Shaoqi. Indeed, there is much to suggest that Mao no longer regarded the Party as a reliable instrument of revolutionary social change. In September of 1959 he had complained that "bourgeois elements have infiltrated our Communist Party,"[30] and by the end of the year he perhaps concluded that the "bourgeoisie" (as Mao loosely used the term) had come to dominate the Party. In 1960, at any event, Mao no longer fully commanded either the Party or the state and no longer determined the policies they pursued. What remained of his victory at Lushan was tenuous control of the army through his protégé Lin Biao.

. . .

The last act in the Great Leap, although it was enacted neither in the spirit nor for the purpose of the original movement, was an attempt to establish "communes" in the cities early in 1960. A number of urban communes had been organized in the summer and fall of 1958, but the urban movement was halted in December 1958, ostensibly because the complexities of urban life and the persistence of bourgeois ideology in the cities made urban communization more difficult than the communization of the countryside.[31] When the movement was revived in 1960, it was still accompanied by a good deal of the utopian rhetoric of the Great Leap, but the purpose was no longer social revolution but economic survival. It was a temporary expedient to cope with the shortages of food and other basic necessities by reorganizing the system of supply and distribution and organizing the unemployed, youth, and women into hastily established workshops to produce household goods and food in vegetable gardens on the outskirts of the cities. Unlike the rural communes, which remained, even though in attenuated form, the urban communes soon disappeared entirely as economic conditions improved after 1961.

Before that improvement came about, however, the people of China, in cities and countryside alike, were to endure the most difficult and calamitous year in the history of the People's Republic. In 1960 the forces of nature inflicted even crueler blows than they had the previous year. Typhoons caused unprecedented floods in South China and Liaoning, drought afflicted the middle and lower reaches of the Yellow River (whose flow was reduced by two-thirds), and pests afflicted wide areas of the countryside. More than 60 percent of the cultivated area suffered from flood or drought and agricultural production plummeted. As famine threatened the land, industrial production fell because of damage to industrial crops, disruptions in the transportation system, the transfer of labor to officially designated disaster areas, and because laborers were physically exhausted and weakened by increasingly critical food shortages.

The economic crisis was gravely compounded in the summer of 1960, when Nikita Khrushchev abruptly recalled the 1,400 Soviet scientists and industrial specialists working in some 250 Chinese enterprises. The official Soviet explanation, which came only several years later, charged that the Russian specialists had been ill-treated by their Chinese hosts. The real reasons, of course, lay in the rapid deterioration of Sino-Soviet relations. A long series of events preceded the act which, perhaps more than anything else, precipitated the final rupture between the two countries. Russian anger over the Great Leap Forward and the Chinese abandonment of "the Soviet model" coincided with Chinese resentment over the absence of Soviet support in the Quemoy-Matsu crisis of 1958 and border disputes with India in 1959. Khrushchev's visit to Beijing in late September of 1959, coming directly after his "summit" meeting with President Eisenhower at Camp David, his public ridicule of the communes, and the Peng Dehuai affair, served only to exacerbate the hostility between the two countries and between Mao and Khrushchev personally. Not even the usual pro forma communique issued from the Beijing talks. But in April 1960 the Chinese issued what was in effect a public declaration of independence from the Soviet Union in the realm of international affairs as well as domestic policy—in the form of the treatise *Long Live Leninism,* published in commemoration of the 90th anniversary of Lenin's birth and probably written by Mao himself. And in June, at the congress of the Rumanian CP in Bucharest, Sino-Soviet hostilities came into the open—or at least openly before an international Communist audience—when Khrushchev made a scathing attack on China and the Chinese delegate Peng Zhen replied in kind. Several weeks later, upon his return to Moscow, Khrushchev ordered the Russian specialists to return home, and apparently ordered them to take their blueprints with them.

The move surprised and shocked the Russian experts as much as it did the Chinese. In the words of Mikhail Klochko, a chemist who was a member of two Soviet scientific missions to China:

As one of those who was suddenly and surprisingly ordered home in 1960, I can testify that all of the anger at the move was not limited to the Chinese. Without exception my fellow scientists and the other Soviet specialists whom I knew in China were extremely upset at being recalled before the end of our contracts. Like myself, others must have had difficulty hiding their amazement when told by Soviet representatives in Peking that dissatisfaction with our living and working conditions was an important reason for our recall. In fact few of us had ever lived better in our lives than we did in China. Our Chinese hosts were even more mystified; again and again they asked why we were leaving and whether anything could be done to prevent our going.

. . . At the beginning of September not a single Soviet citizen remained in China, apart from diplomats and a few trade officials.[32]

Klochko has provided a vivid summary of the immediate economic impact of the Soviet attempt to punish the Chinese for their insubordination:

The abruptness of the withdrawal meant that construction stopped at the sites of scores of new plants and factories while work at many existing ones was thrown into confusion. Spare parts were no longer available for plants built according to Russian design and mines and electric power stations developed with Russian help were closed down. Planning on new undertakings was abandoned because the Russians simultaneously canceled contracts for the delivery of plans and equipment. A planned power and irrigation project for the Yellow River, which frequently overflows its banks, was one of those which had to be abandoned.[33]

Following two successive years of natural calamities, declining harvests, and general organizational chaos, the abrupt termination of Russian technological aid dealt yet another crippling blow to the Chinese economy. It was thus that China's "fraternal socialist ally" made its contribution to the "bitter years" of 1960–62. Hunger stalked the land as grain output dropped sharply to 170,000,000 tons in 1959 (from 200,000,000 in 1958) and further declined to 144,000,000 tons in 1960. Output increased only slightly in 1961, not returning to its 1957 figure until 1965. And it was only in the early 1970s that per capita food grain production was restored to its immediate pre-Great Leap level.[34]

It long has been known that food shortages, resulting in malnutrition and disease, took a heavy toll of lives in the early 1960s. But it also long had been generally assumed that the Communist state—through an effective system of rationing grain reserves (which were supplemented by large purchases of Canadian and Australian wheat)—managed to avert massive famine. That assumption proved erroneous. Eyewitness accounts of people starving to death sporadically began to appear in the post-Mao years as well as official statements alluding (however obliquely) to famine conditions.[35]

Moreover, government mortality statistics released in the early 1980s show a substantial rise in the death rate for the years 1959–61, which demographers calculate as indicating 15,000,000 famine-related deaths. Taking other factors into account, some scholars have concluded that as many as 30,000,000 people perished.[36]

Famine, unfortunately, has been a chronic feature of Chinese history. In the first chapter of his book on the Great Leap famine (a chapter entitled "China: Land of Famine"), Jasper Becker notes that 1,828 "major" famines were recorded during the years 108 BC–1911 AD, that their severity and frequency appear to have increased over the centuries, and that a 1876 famine in North China left 13 million dead, a higher percentage of the population than in the case of the Great Leap.[37] "For many of those [foreigners] who became involved with China in the first half of this century," Becker observes, "witnessing famine became the defining experience."[38]

For many years, both in China and abroad, it was a nearly universal belief that one of the great accomplishments of the 1949 Revolution was to definitely break with this ghastly legacy of chronic starvation. The real history of the Great Leap, not fully revealed until more than two decades after the event, has shattered this belief. While the scope of the famine still remains uncertain, there is no doubt that the Great Leap exacted a "high price in blood," in the words of the noted economist Sun Yefang.[39]

Mao Zedong, the main author of the Great Leap, obviously bears the greatest moral and historical responsibility for the human disaster that resulted from the adventure. But this does not make Mao a mass murderer on the order of Hitler and Stalin, as it is now the fashion to portray him. It was not Mao's intention to kill off a portion of the peasantry, as Becker and others imply.[40] There is a vast moral difference between unintended and unforeseen consequences of political actions, however horrible those consequences might be, and deliberate and willful genocide. The blurring of that difference does no service to the task of understanding the terrible moral ambiguities of this most genocidal of all centuries.

The political atmosphere of the Great Leap, not food shortages alone, was responsible for the famine that brought the movement to its tragic conclusion. Local rural cadres, under intense pressure from higher Party officials to produce spectacular results, responded by grossly inflating production figures. The "wind of exaggeration," as it came to be called, pervaded all levels of the bureaucracy and led state leaders to believe that far more was being produced than actually was the case. Even belated campaigns to "verify" production results yielded greatly inflated statistics. On the erroneous assumption that the countryside held a vast surplus, the state abandoned hitherto moderate procurement policies and sharply raised quotas of grain that peasants were forced to sell to government stores at low prices. In 1959, as agricultural output was falling, state procurements of food grains were rising.[41] Not until well into 1960 was the gravity of the situation fully recognized in Beijing. Government quotas were cut, but not before famine threatened many rural areas.

The crisis was compounded by local officials who concealed food shortages and famine conditions. Just as political considerations had impelled cadres to inflate output figures in the early phases of the Great Leap, fears over the political consequences of economic failure yielded reports that disguised deteriorating local conditions as the campaign neared its fateful end. In a political climate dominated by a continuing witch-hunt against "rightists," fearful local officials often simply lied to their superiors about the grave plight of the peasantry.[42] As a consequence, relief supplies were never sent to many areas suffering from natural or man-made disasters, or arrived too late. Millions perished as a result.

For many years standard Maoist accounts attributed the failure of the Great Leap (insofar as failure was acknowledged) simply to a combination of natural calamities and Soviet treachery. But Mao Zedong himself was aware early of the vast gap between intentions and results and the enormous incongruities between the policies he advocated and the way they were being implemented. In February 1959 he referred to policies and practices that oppressed the peasantry, suggesting a Stalinist infection: "With the peasants, he [Stalin] drained the pond to catch the fish. Right now, we have the same illness."[43] And at the Lushan conference later that year he was critical (and partly self-critical) of the hasty and disorderly manner communization and labor mobilization were being carried out, critical of the "commandism" of cadres, and critical of the breakdown of central planning. For the economic chaos of the time "the main responsibility was mine," he confessed, "and you should take me to task."[44] Yet for Mao, like many of the local rural cadres who looked to him for guidance, personal political consideration ultimately proved more compelling than the welfare of the peasantry. For it was at the Lushan meeting that Mao had insisted on the purge of Peng Dehuai—and, as if to justify the political deed, further insisted on reviving the radical policies Peng had criticized. Mao must bear the main responsibility for the enormous human tragedy that in large measure resulted from the renewal of the "communist wind" the Chairman previously had condemned.

The Great Leap Forward campaign, which began with such great expectations in 1958, thus ended in 1960 with an economic and human disaster for China and a political debacle for Mao Zedong. It created a legacy of bitterness and distrust between the peasantry and the Communist Party. The

Great Leap further contributed to the collapse of the Sino-Soviet alliance, adding an increasingly precarious external situation to a grave internal economic crisis. Half-surrounded by hostile American military bases (stretching from Korea, Japan, Okinawa, and Taiwan to Southeast Asia), China was now also confronted with a new Soviet threat from the north. Both the internal crisis and the external threat called for extraordinary political wisdom, but as China entered the new decade the politicians of the People's Republic were in hostile confrontation with each other.

NOTES

1. Mao Tse-tung [Mao Zedong], "Sixty Points on Working Methods," in Jerome Ch'en, ed., *Mao Papers* (London: Oxford University Press, 1970), pp. 62–63.
2. Mao Tse-tung, "Reading Notes on the Soviet Union's 'Political Economy,'" *Mao Zedong Sixiang Wansui* (Taipei: n.p., 1967, 1969), JPRS, p. 272.
3. Mao Tse-tung, "Speech to the Supreme State Conference," *Chinese Law and Government*, 1, No. 4:10–14.
4. Mao, "Reading Notes," pp. 333–334.
5. Mao Tse-tung, *On the Correct Handling of Contradictions Among the People* (Peking: Foreign Languages Press, 1957), p. 35.
6. Ch'en Po-ta [Chen Boda], "New Society, New People," *Hongqi*, No. 3, July 1, 1958.
7. Ch'en Po-ta, "Under the Banner of Comrade Mao Tse-tung," *Hongqi*, No. 4, July 16, 1958.
8. "Resolution of the Central Committee of the Chinese Communist Party on the Establishment of People's Communes in the Rural Areas," August 29, 1958, in Robert R. Bowie and John K. Fairbank, *Communist China 1955–59: Policy Documents with Analysis* (Cambridge, Mass.: Harvard University Press, 1962), pp. 454–456.
9. Karl Marx and Frederick Engels, *Selected Works* (Moscow: Foreign Languages Publishing House, 1950), 1:50–51.
10. For a discussion of the *minban* precedents, see Mark Seldon, *The Yenan Way in Revolutionary China* (Cambridge, Mass.: Harvard University Press, 1971), esp. pp. 270–274.
11. Chang Kuang-chun [Zhang Guangzhun], "Will Half-Work and Half-Study Lower the Educational Quality?" *Shih-shih Shou-ts'e (Current Events)*, No. 20, October 27, 1958. (SCMM 151; revised translation from original).
12. Chin Hao [Jin Hao], "Repudiate Criticisms of the Red and Expert Universities," *Chung-kuo Ch'ing-nien (Chinese Youth)*, No. 13, July 1, 1958. (SCMM 143; revised transl.).
13. Karl Marx, "Critique of the Gotha Program," in Marx and Engels, *Selected Works*, 2:36.
14. Karl Marx, "The Civil War in France," in Marx and Engels, *Selected Works*, esp. 1:468–475.
15. The Chinese began intensive bombardments of the Guomindang-occupied offshore islands of Quemoy and Matsu in late August 1958, following the breakdown of Sino-American talks in Geneva. The United States countered with threats of air and naval action against China itself while the Chinese spoke with increased determination of the need to liberate Taiwan. The bombardments ceased a month later and the talks were resumed in Warsaw.
16. *Hung-ch'i*, No. 7, August 1958, quoted in Franz Schurmann, *Ideology and Organization in Communist China* (Berkeley: University of California Press, 1966), p. 479.

17. Schurmann, *Ideology and Organization,* p. 478.

18. The term "dictatorship of the proletariat," it might be noted, now had replaced the formula of a "people's dictatorship" as the official designation of the nature of state power in the People's Republic.

19. As typically put by the Maoist theoretician Kuan Feng [Guan Feng], "A Brief Discussion of the Great Historical Significance of People's Communes," *Zhexue Yanjiu* (*Philosophic Research*), 1958, No. 5.

20. *Jen-min jih-pao* editorial, September 3, 1958; Wu Chih-pu [Wu Zhibu], "From APCs to People's Communes," *Hung-ch'i* (*Red Flag*), 1958, No. 8. For a translation of the latter, see SCMM No. 147, pp. 1–10.

21. Wu Zhibu, "On People's Communes," *Chung-kuo Ch'ing-nien* (*Chinese Youth*), September 6, 1958 (SCMM, No. 524, p. 5).

22. The opening paragraphs of the resolution defined the commune as an institution that "combines industry, agriculture, trade, education and military affairs" and integrates "government administration and commune management." It was further proclaimed that the communes would pioneer the way to the "final elimination of the differences between rural and urban areas, between worker and peasant, and between mental and manual labor" as well as the eventual "elimination of the domestic functions of the state." "Resolution on Questions Concerning People's Communes, Sixth Plenary Session of the Eighth Central Committee of the CCP" (December 10, 1958). New China News Agency, Beijing, December 18, 1958.

23. Mao Tse-tung, "Talk at the Report Meeting," October 24, 1966, in Stuart R. Schram, ed., *Mao Tse-tung Unrehearsed: Talks and Letters, 1956–71* (Middlesex, England: Penguin, 1974), pp. 266–267.

24. Peng Teh-huai [Peng Dehuai], "Letter of Opinion," *The Case of Peng Teh-huai, 1959–68* (Hong Kong: Union Research Institute, 1968), pp. 7–13.

25. Prior to this time, public Soviet commentaries largely were confined to veiled criticisms of the Great Leap and Mao, often in the form of attacks on the "Blanquist" heresy of Communists who failed to recognize the necessary stages of historical development. There was one notable exception. On December 1, 1958, in a private conversation with Senator Hubert Humphrey, Khrushchev voiced his disapproval of the communes. Humphrey proved incapable of keeping the news to himself and Khrushchev's comments appeared in the European edition of the New York *Herald Tribune* in late December and in the January 12, 1959 edition of *Life,* much to the embarrassment of the Soviet leader.

26. Mao Tse-tung, "Speech at the Enlarged Session of the Military Affairs Committee and the External Affairs Conference," September 11, 1959, in Schram, ed., *Mao Tse-tung Unrehearsed,* p. 151.

27. Mao Tse-tung, "Speech at the Lushan Conference," July 23, 1959, in Schram, ed., *Mao Tse-tung Unrehearsed,* esp. pp. 143–46.

28. *Ibid.,* p. 139 and pp. 131–43, passim. While Mao cataloged in some detail and with candor the errors and mistakes of both himself and others, he implicitly excused the former by noting that even Confucius and Marx had made mistakes.

29. Production fell perilously in 1959 to 170,000,000 tons and to 144,000,000 tons in 1960.

30. Mao, "Speech at the Enlarged Session of the Military Affairs Committee and the External Affairs Conference," September 11, 1959, in Schram, ed., *Mao Tse-tung Unrehearsed,* p. 148.

31. "Resolution on Questions Concerning People's Communes," December 10, 1958, *Current Background,* No. 542, p. 6. The resolution still called for the transformation of "old cities" into "new cities" but the transformation was postponed, for the reasons noted.

32. "The Sino-Soviet Split—the Withdrawal of the Specialists," *International Journal* (Toronto), Vol. XXVI, No. 3 (Summer, 1971), p. 556. Klochko, needless to say, did not write his recollections of the event in the Soviet Union. He was granted political asylum in Canada in 1961.

33. *Ibid.,* p. 559.

34. Nicholas R. Lardy, *Agriculture in China's Modern Economic Development* (Cambridge, England: Cambridge University Press, 1983), Table 4.2, p. 149.

35. For an English translation of a Chinese article describing conditions in one famine-stricken area, see "Starving to Death in China," with an introduction by Thomas P. Bernstein and an anonymous author, in *The New York Review of Books,* June 16, 1983, pp. 36–38. Other instances are recounted in Jasper Becker, *Hungry Ghosts: China's Secret Famine* (London: John Murray, 1996).

36. Judith Bannister, *China's Changing Population* (Stanford: Stanford University Press, 1987).

37. Jasper Becker, *Hungry Ghosts,* pp. 9–11.

38. *Ibid.,* p. 13.

39. Cited in Thomas Bernstein's highly perceptive analysis of the famine and its causes, "Stalinism, Famine, and Chinese Peasants," *Theory and Society,* Vol. 13, No. 3, p. 343.

40. Although never quite stated outright, the view that Mao and other Communist leaders were engaged in permanent war against the peasantry is implied throughout Becker's valuable but badly flawed and essentially undocumented account. In his concluding section, Becker manages to misinterpret and condemn both Confucius and Mao as malevolently anti-peasant in a single paragraph—although (typically) without bothering to produce supporting evidence in either case. He writes: "By the beginning of the Great Leap Forward officials are recorded in Party documents as saying that the peasants must be regarded as the enemy since they stand in the way of progress. This readiness to strip villagers of all their rights was allied to a general contempt for the peasants which may date back further, to Confucius. He had described them as 'inferior beings' who, since they cannot be educated, must be exploited." (Becker, *Hungry Ghosts,* p. 309.).

41. Lardy, *Agriculture in China's Modern Economic Development,* Table 2.1, p. 34. As food grain production fell from 200,000,000 tons in 1958 to 170,000,000 tons in 1959, the marketing of food grains (primarily to government stores) increased from 52,000,000 to 64,000,000 tons, or from about 31 percent of the total to over 45 percent in 1959. On the causes of the "wind of exaggeration" and the tragic effects of this anomaly, see Bernstein, "Stalinism, Famine, and Chinese Peasants," pp. 350–60, and William Hinton, *Shenfan* (New York: Random House, 1983), pp. 247–57.

42. On the reasons why local officials concealed food shortages and famine and for examples of the phenomenon, see Bernstein, "Stalinism, Famine, and Chinese Peasants," pp. 360–69.

43. Mao Tse-tung, "Speeches at the Chengchow Conference" (February–March, 1959), *Chinese Law and Government,* Winter 1976–77, p. 18.

44. Mao, "Speech at the Lushan Conference" (July 23, 1959), *Mao Tse-tung Unrehearsed,* pp. 131–46.

PART FOUR

THE
THERMIDORIAN
REACTION

1960–1965

14

The Bureaucratic Restoration

THE BUREAUCRATIZATION of state and society has been a
universal feature of the history of the twentieth century, but
nowhere has the process been more pronounced than in the
"post-capitalist" societies that have issued from ostensibly socialist revolutions. The gigantic Soviet bureaucracy was of course the most grotesque
example—and the prototype. But Communist China hardly proved an exception. China, where the bureaucratic state had exceptionally deep cultural roots and a sophisticated expression in ancient and medieval times,
was far from immune to the bureaucratic influences of its past and the bureaucratic imperatives of its modern political and economic development.

Although the Communist victory in 1949 destroyed a Guomindang bureaucracy that was notoriously corrupt and oppressive, it did not fundamentally change the conditions which permit bureaucracy to flourish.
Indeed, in the wake of the Revolution, as with most modern revolutions,
came a massive process of bureaucratic centralization, closely associated
with the achievement of national unification and the drive for rapid industrialization.

The Communist bureaucracy grew rapidly in the 1950s, its vast expansion hastened by the demands of the First Five Year Plan. The new and
massive Party-state apparatus penetrated society far more deeply than any

previous bureaucracy in Chinese history. Bureaucratic growth and routinization were temporarily interrupted during the period of the Great
Leap, but these processes resumed with renewed vigor in the tragic aftermath of that failed movement.

Although it is now common—on the basis of the histories of twentieth-
century Communist regimes—to associate Marxism with bureaucracy, it
needs to be emphasized that the bureaucratization of Chinese state and society in the 1950s and 1960s was wholly inconsistent with Marxist teachings
about the nature of socialism and its essential preconditions. Karl Marx saw
the state as the product of the class contradictions of society, and bureaucracy as its typical organizational form. For Marx, state and bureaucracy
were alien powers that rose above society to usurp human social powers.
The bureaucratic state was rooted in what Marx called "the unsocial nature" of social life, in "private property, trade, industry, and the mutual
plundering of different civil groups. . . . this debasement, this slavery of civil
society is the natural foundation on which the modern state rests, just as
the civil society of slavery was the foundation of the state in antiquity. The
existence of the state and the existence of slavery are indivisible."[1] Thus socialism demanded the abolition of state and bureaucracy, just as it presupposed the abolition of the class-based society which originally produced
them. The original Marxian expectation was that when the "organizing activity [of socialism] begins, where its own aim and spirit emerge, there socialism throws the political hull away."[2] For Marx, human emancipation
would be realized "only when man has recognized and organized his own
powers as social powers so that social force is no longer separated from him
as political power."[3]

Marx recognized that under certain sociohistorical conditions, especially
where social classes were weak, the state could achieve a large measure of
independence and an autonomous bureaucracy could come to dominate
society.[4] But he did not believe that such conditions would prevail in the aftermath of a genuine socialist revolution. He was convinced, as he had optimistically predicted in the *Manifesto*, that when "class distinctions have
disappeared and all production has been concentrated in the hands of a
vast association of the whole nation, the public power will lose its political
character."[5]

It was from these perspectives that Marx celebrated the Paris Commune
of 1871, and set forth a model of how political power should be reorganized in the wake of a socialist-oriented revolution. His perhaps romanticized analysis of the Parisian revolt, *The Civil War in France*, greatly
influenced Chinese Communist thought and action during the Great Leap,
as we have seen, and was to do so again in the early phases of the Cultural

Revolution. In that treatise, Marx had emphasized that the victorious working class needed to destroy (and not simply take over) what he called "the centralized State power, with its ubiquitous organs of standing army, police, bureaucracy, clergy, and judicature." He praised the antibureaucratic safeguards adopted by the Communards to restore political power to society as a whole—the performance of necessary administrative tasks by ordinary working people who were democratically elected and subject to immediate popular recall, paid prevailing workers' salaries, and barred from enjoying special status or privileges.[6] Such, in brief, was Marx's remedy for the problem of bureaucracy in a postrevolutionary society.

It one of the ironies of the history of Marxism in the twentieth century that successful Marxist-led revolutions have resulted not in the reduction of bureaucratic power, much less any process of the withering away of the state, but rather in the growth of bureaucracies more massive in scale, more powerful in function, and more independent in nature than those they replaced. That Marx, and Marxists, gravely underestimated the threat that bureaucratization might pose to a postrevolutionary society often has been noted. But equally well noted is that Marx never anticipated socialist-oriented revolutions in the economically backward lands where in fact they have occurred—indeed, they have occurred in precisely the kinds of historical situations that Marx himself believed likely to foster powerful bureaucratic states. The problem appeared soon after the first successful socialist revolution. Less than five years after the Russian Revolution, Lenin pondered why the new Soviet order had quickly become so bureaucratic and oppressive. On his deathbed he somberly concluded that he had witnessed the resurrection of the old czarist bureaucracy to which the Bolsheviks "had given only a Soviet veneer." Lenin's worst fears were soon realized with the massive bureaucratization of Soviet state and society during the Stalinist era, and the unleashing of what Isaac Deutscher called "an almost permanent orgy of bureaucratic violence."[7]

Conditions in China at the time of the Communist victory provided even more fertile soil for the growth of bureaucracy than had been the case in Russia. China was a far more economically backward land, a more predominantly peasant society, and one with a far weaker social class structure. The Chinese proletariat was far smaller and less politically mature than its Russian counterpart; it had only the most tenuous links to the ruling Communist Party. Moreover, it was a country that lacked a democratic tradition and was burdened with a deeply-ingrained bureaucratic tradition. The revolution itself took place in a profoundly nationalist environment, almost entirely lacking any internationalist dimension either in objective historical reality or in the mentality of its leaders. In short, China in 1949 suffered from the absence of most of the conditions that Marxists assumed would yield a society governed by the immediate producers rather than a new bureaucracy.

Adding to the conditions favoring bureaucratization were the imperatives of national political centralization and rapid economic development in a country long racked by chaotic political upheavals and poverty. Furthermore, the destruction of the propertied classes—the landlord-gentry elite and what remained of the bourgeoisie—however socially and perhaps economically necessary—removed the last barriers to the growth of an autonomous bureaucracy. Chinese society after 1949 was divided less by social class differences than by the elemental distinction between rulers and ruled, by what Mao Zedong referred to as the contradiction between "those in positions of leadership and the led."[8] And with the nationalization of the major means of production, Communists "in positions of leadership" not only monopolized political power but controlled the nation's economy as well.

Under such conditions, it was inevitable that a vast bureaucratic apparatus would rise above society and become the dominant social force. Yet while a new ruling bureaucracy arose in the People's Republic, its power was relatively restrained, at least compared to the Soviet bureaucracy. The restraints were imposed by two factors. One was the lingering influence of the revolutionary heritage, which passed down the egalitarian values forged during the heroic struggles of the 1930s and 1940s, values which dictated close relations between leaders and led in accordance with the antihierarchial principles of the still celebrated "mass line." A second, and perhaps more important factor, was the enormous personal authority and popular prestige of Mao Zedong, whose deep hostility to bureaucracy was coupled with a claim to a special personal relationship with the people, a relationship that transcended all formal organizational structures.

The sources and nature of Mao's antibureaucratism is a complex and controversial matter that we shall encounter again in discussing the Cultural Revolution. Here it must suffice to note briefly the two major explanations for Mao's antibureaucratism. If it is seen as a genuine antipathy to bureaucratic organization and procedures, and not simply a convenient political ploy, much weight must be given to the anarchist influences on the pre-Marxian Mao in the early May Fourth period, influences which persisted and were reinforced by Mao's attraction to the more anti-authoritarian strains in the Marxist tradition—especially the idealized model of the Paris Commune set forth in Marx's *The Civil War in France,* a text that appears prominently in the ideology of both the Great Leap and the Cultural Revolution. Many observers, on the other hand, are inclined to dismiss intellectual influences, instead viewing Mao's antibureaucratic tendencies as motivated by the eminently mundane and practical political aim of crushing any organizational threat to the arbitrary personal authority of the supreme leader. In this interpretation, Mao is essentially the Chinese Communist version of Stalin.

Mao was no doubt no less interested than Stalin in maintaining his personal supremacy over the Communist organizational apparatus, but his methods were far different. Whereas Stalin played off one bureaucratic agency against another to maintain his personal supremacy, Mao was inclined to call forth mass popular movements against his bureaucratic foes. This was clearly the case in the revolutionary revivalism that took place during the years 1955–1960. When Mao launched the drive to collectivize agriculture in 1955, for example, he did so in the populist spirit of the revolutionary years, going over the heads of Party bureaucrats and bypassing much of the formal bureaucratic structure of the new state. The Hundred Flowers campaign posed an explicit threat to the privileges and independence of entrenched bureaucratic interests, especially when Mao pointed to "the bureaucratic practices of certain state functionaries in their relations with the masses" as a principal contradiction in Chinese society and demanded that "we must stamp out bureaucracy." And the egalitarian and populist thrust of the Great Leap Forward had profoundly antibureaucratic implications—and encountered powerful bureaucratic resistance. The revolutionary revivalism of the late 1950s did not stamp out bureaucracy, but it did serve to mitigate the power of a bureaucracy standing above society.

However, the retreat from the Great Leap in 1960, and Mao's retreat from the center of the political stage, led to the reassertion of the power of Party and state bureaucracies. Faced with what was becoming a struggle for sheer survival, the mood of the masses turned sullen and apolitical. Maoist ideological appeals fell on deaf ears. A demoralized and politically apathetic population is a condition on which bureaucracy always thrives, and such was the condition of China in the aftermath of the Great Leap. The sharp decline in both agricultural and industrial production, the shortages in food and supplies, the dislocations in the systems of transportation and distribution, the breakdown of national planning, the threat of famine, and the generally chaotic conditions of economic and social life all demanded the reintroduction of centralized economic and political controls. The demand reflected itself in a renewed Leninist emphasis on the virtues of discipline, order and organization. And there was a general aversion to Maoist-style mass campaigns in favor of economic stability and sociopolitical order. A return to order was the order of the day and the mood of the times. Thus both powerful objective and subjective factors were at work to bring about the restoration of bureaucratic rule

Bureaucratization dominated all facets of Chinese economic, social, and political life in the early 1960s, but the phenomenon had its primary locus in the Chinese Communist Party, which controlled the formal state administration, the army, all mass organizations, and the basic units of social organization in both town and countryside. The history of the Party, and its 17 million members, from 1960 to 1965 was molded by the reaffirmation of fundamentalist Leninist principles of political organization, particularly the cardinal Leninist principle of the crucial role of the vanguard party. The Party was to be a highly centralized apparatus presided over by a revolutionary leadership possessing a true socialist consciousness and functioning with military-like precision; a disciplined organization in which the Party center (or the "general staff," as Lenin had phrased it) exercised the appropriate discipline over its cadres, who, in turn, disciplined and organized the masses for effective action. This conception of the nature of the Party was naturally accompanied by a typical Leninist hostility to the "spontaneity" of the masses. Nothing better describes the mentality of those who controlled the Party apparatus during those years, and their conception of the relationship between the Party and the people, than Lenin's dictum that "the Party exists for the very purpose of going ahead of the masses and showing the masses the way."[9] Just as the leaders of the Party were to train and discipline their cadres, the latter were to train and organize the masses.

It was precisely the "spontaneity of the masses," the virtue so prized by Maoists, that was blamed for undermining the stability of the postrevolutionary order in general, and the authority of the Party in particular. By the end of the Great Leap the organizational structure of the Party had been gravely weakened, and its membership had become demoralized. Party officials, who now began to look more to the leadership of Liu Shaoqi than Mao Zedong, were intent on reestablishing the Leninist authority and legitimacy of the Party, restoring firm lines of command within it, and restoring its command over society in general.[10] From the prevailing Leninist perspective, this was the immediate and essential prerequisite for dealing with the economic crisis and restoring social order.

One of their first acts was to blame the disasters of the Great Leap on lower-level Party cadres (mostly Maoist-inspired rural cadres), who were accused of a vast array of Marxist-Leninist ideological deficiencies. They also were charged with the sin of "commandism"—ignoring the desires, wishes, and complaints of the masses. It was an easy enough charge to make at a time when the masses had lost their taste for radical social action and the mood of an impoverished population favored order and stability. Many local cadres were dismissed, and those who remained were instructed to act strictly in accordance with the directives passed down from higher levels of the Party hierarchy. It was therefore not the Party as such that was to be faulted for the difficulties plaguing Chinese society but rather the errors of some of its individual members. It was thus that the myth of the infallibility of the Leninist party was maintained for the time being.

The downgrading of the role of basic-unit cadres (those in direct contact with people in factories, communes, schools, and residential organizations) was naturally accompanied by an increase in the power of the middle and higher organs of the Party, especially the authority of provincial, regional, and urban Party committees. The latter were headed by Party secretaries, usually members of the Central Committee and directly responsible to it, who became the most powerful figures in their areas of jurisdiction. The centralization of the Party apparatus was reinforced by the establishment in 1960 of new regional Party bureaus directly attached to the Central Committee and a new emphasis on the role of control commissions, which hitherto had played only a relatively limited role in Party life. New Party schools for the training of disciplined cadres appeared, and Party directives stressed more strongly than ever the Leninist virtues of a tightly knit organizational structure, strict adherence to formal Party rules and procedures, and the obedience of lower to higher-level organs—and ultimately obedience to the Central Committee and its Politburo, which stood at the apex of the ultra-centralist structure of command. A 1961–1962 campaign to restore the Leninist spirit of the Party stressed the principle of "democratic centralism," with the emphasis clearly on centralism. In view of the firm control exercised by the Party over the key organs of the state, and indeed the very considerable overlapping in key personnel, the increasingly centralized and bureaucratic character of the Party meant the increasing bureaucratization of the formal state administrative structure. It also meant increased centralized control over the rural communes by outside Party organs and the restoration of the authority of economic ministries in Beijing over urban factories and other large enterprises.

These tendencies toward bureaucratic centralization and professionalism were reflected in the Party's personnel policies in the post-Great Leap period. While the role of radical rural cadres who had spearheaded the communization movement was downgraded, many officials purged in the antirightist campaign of 1957–1958 were reinstated. New recruits tended to be people who possessed technical and administrative expertise; such matters as class background and ideological commitment were factors of decidedly lesser concern. It was an environment in which the Party tended to attract opportunists rather than revolutionaries, one that reinforced the latent careerist tendencies already present in the Party. This was hardly a new phenomenon. Bureaucratic opportunism and careerism had been among the more prominent objects of attack by the critics whom Mao briefly had invited to "bloom and contend" in the spring of 1957. In the early 1960s the tendency merely was more pronounced than it had been a half-decade earlier. Indeed, the bureaucratization of Party and state in the post-Great Leap years was largely a continuation of a trend that had dominated the 1950s and had been interrupted only temporarily by the utopianism and populism of the Great Leap. It took the form of the institutionalization of a system of thirty formal ranks for state and Party cadres, the introduction of a differentiated system of wage payments corresponding to the hierarchy of cadre ranks, and the growth of functional specialization among cadres in both governmental and Party organs. The transformation of revolutionary cadres into bureaucratic functionaries and administrators, the development of a bureaucratic caste enjoying special privileges, the growth of bureaucratic professionalism and occupational specialization, and the general growth of a bureaucracy increasingly separated from society—all were phenomena that had their roots in the pre-Great Leap era and flourished in the post-Great Leap years.

If the Chinese Communist Party was in the process of being transformed from a revolutionary organization into a professional bureaucratic apparatus with strong vested interests in its own self-preservation and perpetuation, it had an equally strong interest in preserving the society from which it had sprung and which it ruled. And preservation, in the first instance, required overcoming the grave economic crisis into which the Great Leap Forward campaign had degenerated. Whatever the evils of bureaucracy, the Party demonstrated the virtues of bureaucratic organization in rescuing China from its plight and reestablishing a viable national economy. Through a combination of the restoration of centralized controls over production and a renewed emphasis on material incentives for the producers, the leaders in Beijing, relying primarily on the organizational effectiveness of a reinvigorated Leninist party, succeeded in reviving the national economy in a remarkably short time. The ministries in Beijing reestablished centralized control and planning over the modern industrial sector of the economy, and the authority of managers and technocrats (acting according to the guidance of the Party) was greatly strengthened. Higher Party organs imposed central direction over the operation of the communes and over the rural economy in general. Centralization of economic life was coupled with a policy that allowed wide latitude for authorities in local productive units to offer financial incentives to workers and peasants in order to raise popular morale and spur production. In industrial enterprises this meant increasingly differentiated wage rates and a system of bonuses and prizes. In the rural areas it meant the encouragement of private peasant plots, the reappearance of private markets, and toleration of a growing tendency toward a market economy. By the end of 1961 conditions in both town and countryside were largely stabilized, and production began to increase after three successive years of decline. The rapidity of the recovery from near disastrous economic conditions and the renewal of growth must be attributed in large measure to the organizational effectiveness of the Chinese Communist Party and the bureaucratic precision with which it functioned.

. . .

During the early 1960s Mao Zedong occupied a most ambiguous place in the political life of the People's Republic. Mao remained the chairman of the Party, but he did not control its apparatus or determine its policies; indeed, the policies the Party pursued were increasingly repugnant to him. Maoist slogans and quotations were widely propagated, but they were used less to achieve radical Maoist social aims than to promote national unity, maintain social order, and spur production. Due homage was paid to Mao as the leader of the revolution and the Party, but he could not assume leadership of the nation. When Mao appeared at Party gatherings, his speeches were greeted with the customary "enthusiastic applause" (according to the official transcripts), but the import of his words were largely ignored by most Party leaders. The gap between Chinese Communist theory and practice widened, and the conflict between radical Maoists and Party bureaucrats grew increasingly sharp and eventually irreconcilable.

Shortly after his victory over Peng Dehuai at Lushan in August 1959, Mao removed himself from the day-to-day affairs of the Party. The withdrawal was perhaps voluntary, or at least graceful, but it was certainly motivated by Mao's awareness that Peng's criticisms of the Great Leap were widely shared by Party leaders, even if they did not share Peng's bluntness, by a recognition that he could not command a majority of the Central Committee to continue the socially radical policies of the Great Leap (even assuming that he might have been inclined to do so), and that a collapsing economy and a demoralized peasantry did not provide favorable circumstances for any attempt to override the Central Committee as he had in the past. Thus control over the Party and its policies fell into the hands of cautious leaders, the "Thermidoreans" who were less interested in social change than in political order and economic efficiency. The most prominent of the Thermidoreans was Liu Shaoqi—the formal head of state of the People's Republic, the senior Vice Chairman of the Party, Mao's informal heir apparent, and certainly the most orthodox Leninist among Chinese Communist leaders. Another was Deng Xiaoping, who, as the General Secretary of the Party, wielded vast power over its organizational apparatus. The ascendency of Liu and Deng was accompanied by the restoration of the authority of Party bureaucrats whose power had been eclipsed during the Great Leap era—such leading Party officials as Lu Dingyi, Peng Zhen, and Luo Ruiqing; and the economic planners who had been the architects of the First Five Year Plan, such as Chen Yun, Li Fuchun, and Bo Yibo. All had been critical of the policies of the Great Leap (although hitherto mostly silent critics), and they now proceeded to dismantle those policies and return China to a condition of "normalcy."

The early 1960s were undoubtedly the most frustrating years in Mao's long political life. He was the acknowledged and still celebrated leader of the revolution, but he was no longer able to determine the direction in which the new society was moving. His attempts to inaugurate new revolutionary campaigns were repeatedly thwarted, distorted or ignored. Having taken the fateful decision to withdraw from active leadership in late 1959, Mao found it impossible to regain the reins of control over an increasingly bureaucratized and routinized Party machine. They were years in which he was "treated as a dead ancestor," as he later charged. "Deng Xiaoping never came to consult me," he complained in 1966, "from 1959 to the present he has never consulted me over anything at all."[11]

With the disintegration of the Great Leap and his consequent isolation from the center of political power, Mao began to suffer from an uncharacteristic loss of confidence in the future of the revolution. He no longer entertained any hope of an imminent transition from socialism to communism. The vision of a "leap" from "the realm of necessity" to "the realm of freedom" was no longer conceived as a sudden qualitative change, but rather now was characterized by Mao as a gradual process of indeterminate length. The Great Leap Forward promise of an economic miracle vanished in similar fashion. Whereas in 1958 Mao had declared that it would take only fifteen years for China to reach the economic levels of the industrialized West, in 1962 he somberly concluded that "it will be impossible to develop our productive power so rapidly as to catch up with, and overtake, the most advanced capitalist countries in less than one hundred years." He observed that Western capitalism had developed over a period of three centuries and implied that the development of socialism and communism would take place over an equally lengthy historical era.[12]

Not only did visions of communism fade, but so did confidence in the continued viability of the existing system. Mao began to brood over the possibility that the work of the revolution would be destroyed and that he might be forced to begin anew. He speculated that the revolutionary order might "perish" and be replaced by a nonrevolutionary state. He became increasingly obsessed with the possibility of historical regression. New bourgeois elements are produced in a socialist society, he insisted much more forcefully than ever before; classes remain, the class struggle persists, and "this class struggle is a protracted, complex, [and] sometimes even violent affair."[13] Nor was it by any means assured that this "protracted" class struggle would have a favorable outcome. In the autumn of 1962 Mao raised the possibility of "the restoration of the reactionary classes" and warned that "a country like ours can still move toward its opposite."[14] In the years preceding the Cultural Revolution the sense of historical indeterminateness that generally characterized the Maoist mentality—and which hitherto generally reflected itself in a deep faith that determined revolutionaries could mold history in accordance with their ideas and ideals—began to assume darkly pessimistic overtones and implications.

While Mao was less confident about the future of the People's Republic than he had been, he did not fall into a state of political paralysis. He was unwilling to play the role of a "dead ancestor" to which he claimed he had been assigned. If he had lost faith in the Party as a reliable revolutionary instrument, or at least in the Party as it was, he remained confident in his own abilities to rekindle the flames of revolution through other means. If Mao could not control the Party bureaucracy, the Party bureaucrats were unable to control Mao. They could not physically remove him from the political scene or even from his formal position as Chairman of the Party without risking a massive political struggle and very possibly a violent civil war. Mao still enjoyed enormous personal prestige in Chinese society (which he and his followers undertook to cultivate through the form of the "Mao cult") and he retained a wide following among the Party rank and file, most of whom were probably unaware of the conflict among their higher leaders. Most importantly, he apparently commanded the loyalty of much of the People's Liberation Army (PLA) largely through the efforts of Lin Biao. Mao had lost control over the Party, but he hardly was powerless.

Nor is it likely that those who came to dominate the Party and state bureaucracies in the early 1960s were inclined to remove Mao as titular head of the Party. The Thermidoreans, above all, valued order and thus were intent on reestablishing social, economic, and political stability. They were not about to compound the chaos by precipitating a new political crisis with unpredictable consequences. They preferred to use Mao for their own ends rather than attempt to bury him. They invoked his name as a symbol of national unity and his slogans to promote the non-Maoist order they were attempting to build. Yet by invoking the authority of Mao and his "thoughts," the Thermidoreans were unwittingly contributing to their own political demise. In the meantime, they were determined to avoid an open clash. It was Mao who was to pose the political challenges and force the confrontations.

In the years 1960 and 1961 Mao apparently took little or no part in the work of the Party. His energies were turned to fortifying his political and ideological control over the PLA. He emerged from relative political seclusion in January of 1962, with a speech delivered to a national Party work conference attended by some 7,000 provincial and district Party functionaries. The speech was a wide-ranging and harshly critical attack on the bureaucratic methods and practices that had come to dominate Party life in the post-Great Leap years. Mao focused on the Leninist principle of democratic centralism, a formula much emphasized by Liu Shaoqi and other Party leaders over the previous two years. Liu had interpreted and applied the principle in a super-Leninist and ultra-centralist fashion, perhaps best described in Rosa Luxemburg's prophetic critique of the Leninist scheme of Party organization and the "bureaucratic straitjacket" it threatened to impose; writing in 1904, she characterized it as a scheme that demanded "blind subordination" to "the party center, which alone thinks, guides, and decides for all," and meant "the rigorous separation of the organized nucleus of revolutionaries" from the mass movement.[15] No better words can be found to describe the character and methods of the Chinese Communist Party in the early 1960s. Mao for his part affirmed the validity of the principle of democratic centralism, but gave it a far different interpretation. In effect, he equated the Leninist notion with his own principle of the mass line, which, he strongly implied, the Party had abandoned. Charging that "some of our comrades still do not understand the democratic centralism which Marx and Lenin talked of," he defined it for them in the fashion of a formula: "First democracy, then centralism; coming from the masses, returning to the masses; the unity of leadership and the masses."[16] The issue was not "democracy" in the conventional sense, but rather whether the impulses leading to policy decisions were to come primarily from the bottom up or to be dictated from the top down. By emphasizing democracy over centralism, Mao was expressing his abiding faith in the revolutionary spontaneity and initiative of the masses—the mass spontaneity so much distrusted in orthodox Leninist theory, and at the same time condemning Party leaders who lacked that faith. For Mao, democracy meant that the masses were to speak first, even though they were not necessarily to have the last word.

The absence of a proper Maoist understanding of "democratic centralism" was reflected in Party officials whom Mao chastised as being:

afraid of the masses, afraid of the masses talking about them, afraid of the masses criticizing them. . . . There are some comrades who are afraid of the masses initiating discussion and putting forward ideas which differ from those of the leaders and leading organizations. As soon as problems are discussed they suppress the activism of the masses and do not allow others to speak out. This attitude is extremely evil.[17]

Among the practitioners of this evil were the first secretaries of provincial, district, and county Party committees—the pillars of the Party bureaucracy—whom Mao called "tyrants" and against whom he directed some of his most bitter and sarcastic barbs.

Another proposition Mao pursued was that class struggles persist in a socialist society. It was not a new notion, but he now presented it in a qualitatively new way. The class struggle in China was no longer seen in the relatively benign form of mostly nonantagonistic contradictions that took place primarily "in the ideological field," as Mao had characterized it in 1957. "The reactionary classes which have been overthrown are still planning a comeback," he now warned. "In a socialist society, new bourgeois elements may still be produced." But it was not the fear that old reactionary classes or the bourgeoisie as such might regain state power that concerned Mao but rather the state of the Party: "There are some people who adopt the guise of Communist Party members, but they in no way represent the working class—instead they represent the bourgeoisie. All is not pure within the Party." And with his own minority position in the higher councils of the Party no doubt very much in mind, he defended the rights of a minority: "Very often the ideas of a minority will prove to be correct. History abounds with such instances." He concluded his remarks with a warning and a threat: "let other people speak out. The heavens will not fall and you will not be thrown out. If you do not let others speak, then the day will surely come when you are thrown out."[18]

Mao's speech, according to the official transcript, was greeted with the usual "enthusiastic applause." But it had no noticeable effect on the policies and practices of the Party.

Mao spoke again in September 1962 at the Central Committee's Tenth Plenum. Mao's speech at the Plenum (and his talks at the informal sessions which preceded it) largely repeated the views he had presented in his "seven thousand cadres" speech in January, stressing particularly the necessity and inevitability of class struggle to combat the growing danger of "revisionism."[19] Mao also called for a massive ideological education campaign for both Party cadres and masses to be conducted in accordance with the principles of the Yan'an rectification movement of 1942–1945. This was duly approved by the Central Committee and, in various forms and through a variety of instrumentalities, was to proceed over the next three and one-half years under the name of the "Socialist Education Movement." For Maoists, the aims of the new campaign were to revolutionize the Party and the thought and behavior of its cadres, raise the ideological consciousness and socialist spirit of the masses, and reverse what were seen as "capitalist" and "revisionist" tendencies in the social and economic life of the country—and particularly the countryside. The Maoist thrust of the movement was to be blunted, and its aims were to be subverted, by an entrenched Party bureaucracy, which wanted neither the leadership of Mao nor the disruptions of Maoist mass campaigns.

As the Socialist Education Movement foundered on bureaucratic resistance and popular apathy, the frustrations and fears of Mao and Maoists grew. Mao's own frustrations were certainly, in part, political ones; he was bitter that he was unable to control the Party that he had built and guided through more than two decades of revolutionary struggle. All the more galling was that he had lived to witness, and was powerless to prevent, the transformation of the Party from a revolutionary instrument into a conservative bureaucratic apparatus, a Party that had succumbed to all the bureaucratic practices he had so long fought against. For Mao, bureaucracy had always been among the greatest evils. He viewed bureaucracy not so much, in a Marxist sense, as a reflection and product of the evils of society, but rather more, in an anarchist sense, as an evil that is visited upon society, as a principal source of social vices and inequities. And while Marxists traditionally have been reluctant to assign a social class status to bureaucratic strata, Mao was not. As he put it in 1965:

> The bureaucratic class is a class in sharp opposition to the working class and the poor and lower-middle peasants. How can these people who have become or are in the process of becoming bourgeois elements sucking the blood of the workers be properly recognized? These people are the objectives of the struggle, the objectives of the revolution.[20]

For Mao, then, "the bureaucratic class" was virtually synonymous with "the bourgeoisie," and bureaucratic dominance was equated with "revisionism" or capitalism, or at least considered the main force leading to a "bourgeois restoration." The leaders of "the bureaucratic class" to which Mao referred were of course the leaders of the Chinese Communist Party. But the Maoist concern was more than a thirst for power, pure and simple. That Mao was struggling for political power, that he was determined to regain political supremacy, and that he was determined to remove the bureaucratic obstacles that stood in his way are all matters that may be taken for granted. But if Mao regarded bureaucracy as evil, he also viewed as evil the socioeconomic policies that Party bureaucrats were pursuing. If he found intolerable his own loss of power, he found no less intolerable the direction in which Chinese society was moving.

NOTES

1. Karl Marx, "Critical Notes on 'The King of Prussia and Social Reform,'" in *Writings of the Young Marx on Philosophy and Society,* trans. Loyd Easton and Kurt Guddat (New York: Anchor, 1967), p. 349.
2. *Ibid.,* p. 357.
3. Karl Marx, "On the Jewish Question," in *Writings of Young Marx,* p. 241.
4. Karl Marx, *The Eighteenth Brumaire of Louis Bonaparte* (Chicago: Kerr, 1919), p. 146.
5. Marx and Engels, *Selected Works,* 1:51.
6. Karl Marx, "The Civil War in France," in Marx and Engels, *Selected Works,* 1:468–481.
7. Isaac Deutscher, *Marxism in Our Time* (San Francisco: Ramparts Press, 1971), p. 201.
8. Mao Tse-tung [Mao Zedong], *On the Correct Handling of Contradictions Among the People* (Beijing: Foreign Languages Press, 1957), p. 9.
9. As Lenin put it at the Second Comintern Congress meeting at Petrograd in 1921. The concept of the vanguard party is, of course, most fully set forth in Lenin's 1902 treatise "What Is to Be Done?" See V. I. Lenin, *Selected Works* (Moscow: Foreign Languages Publishing House, 1952), 1, Part 1:203–409.
10. As Franz Schurmann has noted, it was during the years of Liu Shaoqi's dominance that the writings of Lenin were most widely propagated. Franz Schurmann, *Ideology and Organization in Communist China* (Berkeley: University of California Press, 1966), p. 520.
11. Mao Tse-tung, "Talk at the Report Meeting," October 24, 1966, in Schram, ed. *Mao Tse-tung Unrehearsed,* pp. 266–267.
12. Mao Tse-tung, "Talk at an Enlarged Central Work Conference," January 30, 1962, in Schram, ed., *Mao Tse-tung Unrehearsed,* pp. 170–175.
13. *Ibid.,* p. 168.
14. Mao Tse-tung, "Speech at the Tenth Plenum of the Eighth Central Committee," September 24, 1962, in Schram, ed., *Mao Tse-tung Unrehearsed,* p. 189.
15. Rosa Luxemburg, "Organizational Questions of Social Democracy," in *Rosa Luxemburg Speaks* (New York: Pathfinder Press, 1970), p. 118.
16. Mao, "Talk at Enlarged Central Work Conference," pp. 158–160.
17. *Ibid.,* pp. 160–162.
18. *Ibid.,* pp. 168–187.
19. The text of Mao's formal speech to the Plenum is translated in Schram, ed., *Mao Tse-tung Unrehearsed,* pp. 188–196.
20. Mao Tse-tung, "Selections from Chairman Mao," JPRS 49826, p. 23.

15

The New Economic Policy, 1961–1965

URING THE CULTURAL revolution of 1966–1969, the economic policies of the preceding half-decade were condemned for leading China on a retreat from "socialism" to "capitalism," and the Party leaders responsible for implementing those policies were purged as "capitalist-roaders" who allegedly had exercised a "bourgeois dictatorship." This, in brief, was the Maoist judgment on the early 1960s, or at least the dramatic picture of a "life-and-death struggle" between capitalism and socialism that Maoists presented to the world.

Yet the differences between what came to be known as the Maoist and Liuist roads do not appear to be nearly so sharp. It is instructive to compare the economic policies pursued by Liu Shaoqi in the early 1960s with those adopted by Lenin in the Soviet Union forty years earlier. In 1921 Lenin introduced the New Economic Policy to rehabilitate the Russian economy after the ravages of World War I, the revolution, and the ensuing civil war. The new policy, a retreat from the radical policies of the period of War Communism, encouraged capitalist forms of economic activity, as Lenin frankly acknowledged. The NEP, as the program came to be called, established a "mixed economy," partly state and partly private. While large industrial enterprises remained in the hands of the Bolshevik government, private enterprise was permitted (and indeed encouraged) in smaller industries and in commerce. Except for standard forms of agricultural taxation, the countryside was largely left to itself, that is to say, left free for the development of small-scale capitalist farming and the workings of the market. The import of foreign capital for industrial development was encouraged—and eminently capitalist methods of management and work organization (such as Taylorism) were adopted even in state-owned industrial enterprises. Lenin's immediate aim was economic recovery; his long-range expectation was that the socialist sector gradually would expand and eventually prove victorious in a process of essentially peaceful economic competition.

The economic policies adopted by Chinese leaders forty years later were in some respects similar to Lenin's NEP. They constituted a large-scale retreat (in fact if not in name) from the radicalism of the Great Leap Forward in an attempt to deal with the grave economic crisis and famine of 1960–1961. In agriculture, concessions were made to "petty capitalism," primarily by permitting an extension of the private plots worked by individual peasant households. In industry, greater emphasis was placed on the criterion of "profitability" in the operation of enterprises, and the authority of managers and technocrats was strengthened. Wider scope was given to market forces and prices, and material incentives were stressed over moral ones. Yet, as an alleged "retreat to capitalism," the Chinese program was but a pale reflection of its earlier Soviet counterpart. Agricultural production remained basically collectivized; no more than 12 percent of the tillable land was allowed to be restored as private plots. Industries, both large and small, remained under state ownership, and commerce in general remained under fairly strict centralized government control. No invitations were extended for foreign capitalist investment. If Liu Shaoqi was a "capitalist-roader," he walked a far more narrow and cautious path in the early 1960s than did Lenin in the early 1920s. Nonetheless, the differences between what came to be known as "the two roads," between "Liuism" and "Maoism," were profound, and the policies dominant in the early 1960s had significant social consequences—and ones which Maoists found repugnant.

The Chinese version of NEP began as a series of ad hoc emergency measures in 1960 to deal with the immediate crisis of widespread food shortages and the threat of famine. Part of the problem was one of distribution, and that part was handled with dispatch by a reinvigorated centralized state apparatus through an efficient system of rationing and transport. But the larger problem was the sharp decline in agricultural production over three successive years (1959–1961). Production was revived—although not before millions perished—through a combination of centralized Party control over the countryside, the virtual removal of communal controls over individual peasant producers, and urban assistance to rural areas. Hundreds of thousands of Party cadres were sent to the villages, displacing (and criticizing) the Maoist-inspired local rural cadres. They were reinforced by soldiers, students, and millions of unemployed urban dwellers who were sent to the countryside to engage in agricultural work. The small private family plots were restored, the free market in rural areas was reopened, "communized" personal and household belongings were returned, and peasants were permitted to reclaim uncultivated lands and till them on their own. From the cities came emergency aid in the form of insecticides, chemical fertilizers, and small farm tools. By the end of 1962 the agrarian economy was stabilized.

These measures proceeded under the policy of taking "agriculture as the foundation of the economy and industry as the leading sector," a slogan adopted by the Party Central Committee in January 1961. It was a recognition by Communist leaders of the central importance of a viable agricultural economy for the national economy. It meant giving priority to the agrarian sector and accepting a slower rate of industrial development than had been envisioned both in the First Five Year Plan and the Great Leap. It was a slogan that could be accepted by Maoists and non-Maoists alike, and it meant there was to be no return to a Stalinist strategy that subordinated agriculture to heavy industry.

Yet the slogan was not without ambiguities. For if agriculture was now to be granted a certain priority, it was by no means clear how agricultural production was to be socially organized. Also left ambiguous was the question of the relationship between agriculture and industry, between town and countryside, and the fate of the Maoist program of industrializing the rural areas. What "taking agriculture as the foundation" meant in terms of concrete policies was dependent upon who was determining and implementing policy.

The Decline of the Communes

The abandonment of the Great Leap did not result in the abolition of the rural people's communes, although it did result in a drastic reduction in their size. The 24,000 communes were broken down into approximately 74,000 units, each with about 1,600 households, and each corresponding roughly to the old *xiang* structure and the traditional rural marketing area.[1] The communes remained the basic administrative units in the countryside, but operated under the direction of salaried state functionaries who were responsible for the implementation of centrally determined policies.

But while the communes remained as political units, their original socioeconomic functions were emasculated. Party directives of the early 1960s denounced "egalitarianism" in the distribution of the agricultural product and encouraged the use of material incentives to promote production. Not only were private plots returned and peasants encouraged to engage in "sideline" occupations and to trade on the reopened free market, but the operation of commune industries was discouraged in favor of peasants purchasing goods produced in urban factories. Furthermore, the basic work unit was progressively reduced from the commune as a whole to the production brigade and finally to the production team. By the beginning of 1962 the team, consisting of about twenty or thirty households (the equivalent of the former "lower" agricultural producer cooperative), was established as the principal unit for the organization of labor and production.[2]

The autonomy of the commune was reduced further by transferring control of its commercial and financial affairs to the *xian* (county) governments, organs of the centralized state administrative apparatus. The *xian* administration also assumed control of the commune militia and its educational institutions and health services. The tractors and other large-scale farm machinery distributed to the communes during the Great Leap were now returned to some 2000 Soviet-style tractor stations, with the profits from the rentals going to the state.

The policies of the period facilitated the growth of petty capitalism in the countryside, although on a far smaller scale than Lenin and other Russian leaders had been willing to tolerate in the Soviet Union forty years earlier. Nevertheless, the retreat from collective production was by no means insignificant. Although private family plots officially were limited to 6 percent of the arable land, they actually came to constitute twice that percentage. Given the relatively high prices for fruits, vegetables and domestic animals that could be commanded on the free market (and even higher prices on a flourishing black market in the cities), most peasants naturally were disposed to devote more time and energy to their private holdings than to collective work. By the mid-1960s, private production probably accounted for about one-third of peasant income. Moreover, collective labor on the production team was by no means conducted along egalitarian lines. Complex workpoint systems were introduced to remunerate peasants according to their individual productivity rather than according to the amount of time or labor they contributed.

Both the workpoint system in collective production and the new opportunities for sideline production on private plots inevitably benefited the more productive, physically stronger, more experienced, and more entrepreneurial-minded peasants. The result was increasing income differentiations among the rural population. Growing inequality was exacerbated by the far greater problem of corruption among rural Party cadres. During the early 1960s, the communes were plagued by local leaders who embezzled communal funds and resources. Even more widespread was collusion between lower-level team cadres and peasants (often members of the former village elite) in the allocation of workpoints, to the economic advantage of both.

The differences between "Maoists" and "Liuists" in dealing with corruption and inequality in the countryside were not as great as they later were portrayed during the Cultural Revolution. Liu Shaoqi was no less intent than Mao on eliminating cadre corruption and blunting spontaneous tendencies towards rural capitalism. The differences centered more on the methods to be employed than on the goals to be achieved. Whereas Liu and most Party leaders were inclined to use the central Party and state apparatus to rectify the rural situation, Mao and Maoists wished to stimulate a popular movement based on the ideological and political mobilization of the poorer peasants.

The Reorganization of Industry

As in the rural areas, the new policies in the cities were initially emergency measures to alleviate a critical and rapidly deteriorating economic situation. In 1960 and 1961, some factories had closed and many were operating at reduced capacities for want of adequate raw materials and supplies. Most of the small industrial enterprises and shops, hastily established during the Great Leap, were grossly inefficient and wasteful of scarce resources. By 1962, industrial production had declined by about 40 percent from the 1958–1959 levels. The cities were filled with workers, unemployed and underemployed, their ranks swollen by millions of peasant migrants from depressed rural areas.

The first step taken by the government to reestablish a viable urban economy was stringent financial retrenchment. Thousands of small and economically inefficient factories and shops were closed and most of the workers in larger enterprises hired during the Great Leap were dismissed. A freeze was placed on new employment. In all, the total industrial work force was cut by half. A second measure was to send economically redundant urbanites to the countryside, a drive that reached its peak in the spring of 1962 in what was called the "return to the village" (*huixiang*) movement. The campaign was not motivated by any populist spirit, nor was it conducted in the manner of earlier Maoist-inspired *xiafang* movements. It was dictated by the economic necessity to relieve the strain on a precarious urban food supply, just as the industrial cutbacks were dictated by a shortage of raw materials and a scarcity of state investment capital.

The long-term problem of modernizing the industrial sector was pursued through the reintroduction of central economic planning combined with a degree of economic autonomy for individual enterprises and a reliance on semi-market forces, the strengthening of managerial authority, a renewed emphasis on technological and scientific expertise, and a heavy stress on financial incentives for the workers to spur productivity and raise the quality of what was being produced. Direction over the economy in general was returned to the economic ministries in Beijing, and the architects of the First Five Year Plan were restored to prominence. Managerial authority in individual factories and enterprises, which had virtually disappeared during the Great Leap, was reestablished. Managers and technological experts, who were closely linked to district and provincial Party organizations, regained control over the operations of industrial enterprises, although now under a more flexible and autonomous system called "independent operational authority." The traditional distinction between managers and workers reemerged, and the new emphasis clearly was on technical "expertise" rather than political "redness." If industrial workers were once again subjected to the authority of managers, they were compensated through the revival of a system of financial incentives for increased productivity and promises of a better material life. Increasing economic differentiations among the working class came about less through revisions in the formal wage structure than through the widespread introduction of piece rate work and the use of prizes and bonuses to reward workers for their individual productive performances. The reliance on material incentives was justified on the grounds of economic efficacy—the pressing need to raise productivity in a still economically backward land—and ideologically justified by the traditional Marxist principle that in a socialist society the distribution of goods necessarily would be guided by the principle "to each according to one's work" rather than the communist principle "to each according to one's needs."

While the new industrial policies restored many of the features of the First Five Year Plan, they were by no means a wholesale return to the "Stalinist model." The policy of "taking agriculture as the foundation" was in fact taken seriously, finding concrete expression in a significant shift of investment from urban industrial development to agriculture. Important sectors of modern industry were refashioned to increase production of chemical fertilizers and modern farm tools. Scientific institutes were established for the development of improved seeds, and a program for rural electrification was undertaken. While the principal formulators of the First

Five Year Plan had been restored to their posts, they now envisaged a much more modest pace of industrial development than the ambitious targets they had set in the previous decade, and now gave priority to the modernization of agricultural production. In this sense, the Liuist period was a fundamental departure from the Stalinist strategy of subordinating all to the heavy industrial push.

In light of the disastrous conditions confronting the government in 1960–1961, the rapidity of the recovery and the renewal of economic growth was quite remarkable. Agricultural production began to revive in 1962 and increased at a steady, if not spectacular rate, over the following years. Grain output rose from a low of 193,000,000 tons in 1961 to 240,000,000 tons in 1965[3] augmented by large wheat purchases from Canada and Australia. The modern industrial sector was stabilized in 1962. Between 1963 and 1965 industrial production grew at an average annual rate of approximately 11 percent, industrial employment 7 percent, and labor productivity 5.5 percent.[4]

The policies of Liu Shaoqi brought economic recovery and renewed growth, but the social and ideological results were less salutary. There was a social price to be paid for economic progress—and the price was the emergence of new forms of inequality. The tolerance of market forces and the ever present "spontaneous" tendencies toward capitalism in the countryside gave rise to a new stratum of relatively rich peasants who, often in cooperation with local cadres and officials, developed a vested interest in the new economic policies and the government that presided over them. In the cities there emerged a relatively privileged stratum of more experienced and skilled industrial workers who benefited from the system of piece rate work and incentive bonuses, measures that encouraged productivity but also made workers compete with one another, militating against a sense of collective class solidarity. The absence of a collective consciousness among the workers facilitated, in turn, an increasing differentiation between the working class as a whole and a rising technological-bureaucratic elite fostered by the emphasis on material rewards for professional competence and technical skills.

Perhaps the most glaring manifestation of inequality was a growing social, economic and cultural gap between the cities and the rural areas. While a minority of peasants prospered, the countryside as a whole remained backward and fell further behind the modernizing cities. The Great Leap Forward policy of industrializing the countryside was abandoned and most local rural industrial undertakings were closed or atrophied, thus firmly reestablishing the sharp distinctions between industrial and agricultural production and between workers and peasants. The prices of industrial goods sold to the peasants (such as chemical fertilizers, agricultural machinery, cloth, salt, kerosene, matches, and, for those few who could afford them, radios and bicycles) were kept artificially high, to the benefit of the urban economy and in defiance of the stated Maoist policy of encouraging peasant consumption by maintaining only a narrow differential between the prices of industrial and agricultural products.[5] Moreover, since productivity in industry rose far more rapidly than in agriculture, the bonus system served to further increase the already considerable differential between worker and peasant incomes. Further widening the gap between town and countryside were urban-oriented educational policies and an inequitable distribution of medical and social services. Just as during the First Five Year Plan, the countryside was being exploited for the benefit of the cities.

The growth of new forms of socioeconomic inequality was alluded to by Zhou Enlai in his report to the Third National People's Congress, which met in Beijing in late December of 1964 and reelected Liu Shaoqi as Chairman of the People's Republic. After lauding the economic gains of the previous two years, Zhou observed:

> new exploiters will be ceaselessly generated in society, in Party and government organs, in economic organizations and in cultural and educational departments. These new bourgeois elements and other exploiters will invariably try to find their protectors and agents in the higher leading organizations. The old and new bourgeois elements and other exploiters will invariably join hands in opposing Socialism and developing capitalism.[6]

Who were the "new bourgeois elements" to whom Zhou referred? Obviously they were not owners of property, but rather those who enjoyed economic privileges, social prestige, and political power within the existing "socialist" order. They were privileged not by virtue of property but by virtue of function and income. The new rich peasants and the more highly paid industrial workers hardly could be described as "new exploiters." However undesirable, such economic differentiations among the masses were no more than symptoms of a deeper social disease. The nature of the disease was hinted at (and partially diagnosed) in Zhou's statement that the "new exploiters" are "generated" in "Party and government organs." Implicit was the suggestion that the Party-state bureaucracy itself was the source and site of "new bourgeois elements."

What Zhou Enlai left implicit, Mao Zedong soon made bluntly explicit. By 1965 he began to charge that "the bureaucratic class" was the oppressor of the masses of workers and peasants, and it was this view of bureaucracy as generating a new exploiting class that lay behind Mao's increasingly strong insistence that China was racked by a sharpening conflict between "the bourgeoisie" and "the proletariat," a growing emphasis on the need for "class struggle," and the belief that the contest between "socialism" and "capitalism" was approaching a decisive stage. No doubt these Maoist perceptions were influenced by the deepening conflict with the Soviet Union—and, consequently, a heightened awareness that the pursuit of "revisionist" policies portended a regression to "capitalism." But the Maoist fears of the time grew primarily out of the concrete realities of the internal Chinese situation. For Mao, the economic policies pursued during the post-Great Leap years posed the question as to whether socialist ends could be achieved through nonsocialist means. From the sense of historical indeterminateness that characterizes the Maoist mentality—that is, the absence of any confidence in the historical inevitability of socialism—flowed the belief that people are free to choose their ends and thus the moral injunction that they must choose means which are consistent with the ends they seek. In the eyes of Mao, the means most Party leaders had chosen were seen as incompatible with socialism; instead, they were seen as leading to what Maoists chose to call "the road back to capitalism."

Of no less concern to Maoists than social inequality and bureaucratic elitism were the processes of ideological decay which accompanied them. Due homage was paid to the "Thoughts of Mao," but mostly in ritualistic fashion. If Mao was treated politically as a "dead ancestor," his ideas and ideals fared little better. The leaders who presided over the Party and state apparatus were preoccupied with social order, administrative efficiency, technological progress and economic development. The popular mood was dominated by a longing for security and a quest for a better material life. Between the Party leaders and the mostly politically apathetic masses, stood a technological intelligentsia and the cadres of state and Party who increasingly ignored the Maoist political ethic in favor of a bureaucratic vocational ethic. It was a tendency that was in harmony with the dominant policies and the general temper of the times, as was the conversion of the "red and expert" notion from a universalistic Maoist ideal of the future "all-round" communist individual into a formula that gave priority to the acquisition of professional and technological competence over political and ideological considerations. The urban masses, it was observed, responded with a most non-Maoist enthusiasm to state appeals to increase production—and thus to increase income—in order to purchase "the four good things": watches, bicycles, radios, and sewing machines. And in the countryside, Maoists observed such "unhealthy tendencies" among the peasants as the revival of traditional religious festivals, money marriages, superstitious cults, extravagant spending on holidays, and gambling, as well as a sharp decline in the ideological zeal of rural cadres.[7]

Education

In a society where stratification is based primarily on income and function, rather than on property, the educational system is a particularly powerful force for promoting socioeconomic equality—or inequality. The educational policies of the early 1960s promoted inequality.

During the previous decade there had been an enormous expansion of educational opportunities. Between 1949 and 1957 the number of primary school students increased from approximately 26,000,000 to 64,000,000, while university enrollment almost quadrupled, from 117,000 to 441,000. The early educational policies of the People's Republic, like its economic policies, were largely patterned on the Soviet model, especially in institutions of higher education. The overwhelming emphasis was on scientific and technological education to produce specialists and experts necessary for carrying out the industrial goals of the First Five Year Plan. There was a wholesale borrowing of Russian pedagogical methods, forms of organization, and textbooks. Thousands of college graduates went to the Soviet Union for advanced training in modern science and technology.[8]

While great progress was made in the 1950s in expanding educational opportunities to a much wider section of the population than under the old regime, the opportunities still remained very limited and unequal. Although the stated purpose of the new educational system was to serve workers and peasants, the criterion of formal academic achievement for admission to middle schools and universities favored both the old and new privileged groups in Chinese society—the sons and daughters of the remnant urban bourgeoisie, higher Party and government officials, and the technological intelligentsia. Moreover, educational opportunities were unevenly distributed between the cities and the rural areas. Universities were located in the cities, urban oriented in curricula, and drew most of their students from the urban classes. While children who lived in the cities were afforded the opportunity of at least a primary school education, many rural children were not, or received only the most rudimentary schooling.

The educational policies of the Great Leap were designed to correct these inequities through new programs of education, particularly in the countryside. A vast variety of "half-work, half-study" programs, "red and expert universities," and part-time evening schools for peasants and workers were hastily established in accordance with the Great Leap goals of permitting "the masses to make themselves masters of science and technology" and eliminating the distinction between mental and manual labor. Regular six-year primary schools and three-year middle schools were expanded in the rural areas under the administration of the communes so as to better serve local needs and realize the Marxian goal of combining education with productive activities.

In the early 1960s these egalitarian policies were reversed in favor of the practices of the mid-1950s. Financial retrenchment forced many poorer schools to close, thus restricting educational opportunities for children from lower income families in both town and countryside. Many of the half-study and part-time schools and programs were abandoned. Primary and middle schools in the rural areas were removed from communal control and returned to the administration of *xian* education departments, thus restoring control over the rural educational system to the central state apparatus. A renewed emphasis on standardized admissions criteria for middle schools and universities through formal examinations worked to the advantage of the children of the more privileged social groups and favored urban over rural youth. What was in effect a two-track educational system emerged, roughly divided between town and countryside. In the rural areas, children who received a primary school education (and not all did[9]) advanced, if they did at all, mostly to what were called "agricultural middle schools" for vocational training rather than to regular full-time middle schools. In the cities, special schools of high quality were favored in order to train a relatively small number of highly trained experts so as to replenish the ranks of the technological intelligentsia and the bureaucratic elite. The first duty of students was to study and acquire professional ability, it was emphasized, and in the better schools and in the universities political education and productive-labor requirements tended to become ritualistic observances. In all, the educational system in the early 1960s was probably more elitist than it had been a decade earlier, reinforcing growing socioeconomic differences.

Just as inequalities in the educational system reflected and perpetuated social and economic differentiations, so too was this the case in other state financed and operated services—most notably, public health. In the years since 1949 striking progress had been achieved in the control of infectious and parasitic diseases and in the building of a modern medical system. Beginning with an emphasis on preventive medicine and popular campaigns to raise the levels of sanitation and public hygiene, the new government soon was able to claim credit for the virtual elimination of smallpox, cholera, typhus, typhoid fever, plague, and leprosy, as well as venereal dis-

ease and opium addiction; the incidence of tuberculosis and most parasitic diseases was reduced significantly. Huge state investments funded
modern medical training and hospitals, hitherto largely dependent on foreign philanthropy. Between 1949 and 1957, over 800 Western-type hospitals were built, adding some 300,000 beds to the 90,000 available when
the People's Republic was established. The number of doctors trained in
modern Western medicine increased from 40,000 in 1949 to 150,000 in
1965, supplemented by 170,000 paramedics; by the early 1960s, medical
schools were graduating about 25,000 new doctors each year.[10] The
achievements were impressive, but the benefits were unevenly distributed.
Urban inhabitants enjoyed far greater access to modern medical services
than did peasants, and the differences between town and countryside in
this area (as in so many other areas in the early 1960s) were glaring and
growing. It was a matter that brought forth some caustic comments from
Mao Zedong in 1965:

> Tell the Ministry of Public Health that it only works for fifteen percent of the
> total population of the country and that this fifteen percent is mainly composed
> of gentlemen, while the broad masses of the peasants do not get any medical
> treatment. First they don't have any doctors; second they don't have any medi-
> cine. The Ministry of Public Health is not a Ministry of Public Health for the
> people, so why not change the name to the Ministry of Urban Health, the Min-
> istry of Gentlemen's Health, or even to the Ministry of Urban Gentlemen's
> Health? . . . The methods of medical examination and treatment used by hospi-
> tals nowadays are not at all appropriate for the countryside, and the way doctors
> are trained is only for the benefit of the cities. And yet in China over five hundred
> million of our population are peasants.[11]

The economic successes of the time, based on non-Maoist methods, thus
produced social and political results that were incongruous with the Maoist
egalitarian visions. The price for economic progress was bureaucratic and
technocratic elitism, the emergence of new forms of inequality in both the
cities and the rural areas, and a widening gap between town and countryside. The price was not one which Mao was willing to pay, and the Socialist
Education Movement, launched in 1963, was the first attempt to reverse
the course that the Thermidoreans were following.

NOTES

1. The argument that *xiang* boundaries were drawn to generally correspond to the traditional
   "standard marketing area," consisting of a dozen or so villages economically and socially ori-

ented to a market town, is presented in G. William Skinner, "Market Town and Social Structure in Rural China," *Journal of Asian Studies,* 24, 1 (November 1964): 32–43.

2. These measures were officially carried out in accordance with the "Urgent Directive on Rural Work" (the "Twelve Articles") and the "Draft Regulations Concerning Rural Communes," respectively issued by the Central Committee in November 1960 and March 1961.

3. Chao Kang, *Agricultural Production in Communist China, 1949–65* (Madison: University of Wisconsin Press, 1970), pp. 242–60. Chao's reconstructed data give the figures of 160,000,000 tons in 1961 and 200,000,000 tons in 1965 but nonetheless reflect a similar rate of increase.

4. Barry Richman, *Industrial Society in Communist China* (New York: Random House, 1969), p. 615.

5. Mao's views on the issue were set forth in his 1956 speech "On the Ten Great Relationships": "The peasants' burden of taxation is too heavy while the price of agricultural products is very low, and that of industrial goods very high. While developing industry, especially heavy industry, we must at the same time give agriculture a certain status by adopting correct policies for agricultural taxation, and for pricing industrial and agricultural products. . . . In the exchange of industrial and agricultural products we adopt in our country a policy of reducing the 'scissors' gap, a policy of the exchange of equal or near-equal values, a policy of low profit and high sales in industrial products, and a policy of stable prices." Stuart R. Schram, ed., *Mao Unrehearsed: Talks and Letters,* 1956–71 (Middlesex, England: Penguin, 1974), pp. 64, 71.

6. Chou En-lai [Zhou Enlai], "Report on the Work of the Government," December 30, 1964, *Peking Review,* 8, 1 (January 1, 1965): 6–20.

7. "Report to the Hsien Three Level Cadre Meeting," February 9, 1963, Appendix A in Richard Baum and Frederick C. Teiwes, *Ssu-Ch'ing: The Socialist Education Movement of 1962–1966* (Berkeley: University of California Press, 1968), pp. 49–57.

8. Generally reflective of the heavy emphasis on scientific and technological education is the composition of college and university graduates for the year 1962. According to official data, only 7,000, or 4 percent, of the 170,000 graduates majored in the social sciences and humanities; 59,000 of the 1962 graduates were engineers; 11,000 were graduates in science; 20,000 in agriculture and forestry; 17,000 in medicine and public health; and the remaining 56,000 were graduates of teachers' or normal colleges, where a similar technological orientation was present, as it was in the primary and middle schools.

   Of the 170,000 graduates in 1962, only 1,000 passed examinations to become research students (graduate students). Prior to 1949, it might be noted, there was not a single graduate school in China, save for a small number of medical and professional schools. Postgraduate education developed only very slowly after 1949, but on a high and rigorous academic level. Most Chinese students who went on for postgraduate study did so in the Soviet Union, and to a lesser extent in the Eastern European countries.

9. In 1965 it was reported that 30,000,000 primary school-aged children, mostly in the rural areas, were not receiving formal education of any sort. *People's Daily,* May 18, 1965 (SCMM, No. 3475, p. 14.).

10. Victor W. Sidel, "Medicine and Public Health," in Michel Oksenberg, ed., *China's Developmental Experience* (New York: Praeger, 1973), pp. 110–120. For a particularly perceptive account of the development of medical care in the People's Republic, see Joshua Horn, *Away with All Pests* (New York: Monthly Review Press, 1969).

11. "Directive on Public Health," June 26, 1965, in Schram, ed., *Mao Tse-tung Unrehearsed,* pp. 232–233.

16

The Socialist Education Movement, 1962–1965

IN LATE 1962, with the economy stabilized, Mao Zedong emerged from political seclusion to launch the "Socialist Education Movement." The new campaign aimed to counter bureaucratization, reverse socioeconomic policies that Maoists condemned as "revisionist" and believed were creating new forms of capitalism, and revitalize a collectivistic spirit within the Party and in society at large. It was to be Mao's last attempt, prior to the Cultural Revolution, to implement his vision of radical social transformation through existing Party and state institutions.

The campaign had its origins in a September 1962 speech to the Central Committee when Mao had set forth the thesis that classes and class struggles necessarily exist in socialist societies, stressed that the class struggle in China would continue for a prolonged period, and raised the spectre that the outcome of the struggle could be a "restoration of the reactionary classes." "A country like ours can still move toward its opposite," he warned. To wage the struggle between "Chinese revisionism" and "Marxism-Leninism," Mao proposed a Yan'an-style movement, based on the model of the rectification campaign of 1942–1944.[1]

While Mao was no longer in control of the Party apparatus, he was not without the power to influence formal Party policies. He still commanded enormous personal prestige and, no less important, seemed to command the People's Liberation Army as well. Thus the Central Committee, with copious quotations from Mao, agreed that the entire historical period of "the transition to communism" would be characterized by a continuing class struggle between the proletariat and the bourgeoisie, condemned revisionist tendencies within the Party, and called for strengthening the socialist life of the rural people's communes.[2] The practical (and rather pale) expression of these resolutions was a limited ideological rectification campaign to improve the work of rural Party cadres and raise the consciousness of the masses in selected rural areas during the winter of 1962–63. It was not until May 1963 that the "Draft Resolution of the Central Committee on Some Problems in Current Rural Work" concretely stated the purposes and methods of the Socialist Education Movement and launched the campaign on a nationwide basis.

The May 1963 resolution, or the "First Ten Points," was an eminently Maoist document, setting forth the two major concerns which originally motivated the Socialist Education Movement. One was the decline of the communes and the disintegration of collective farming. The second was the increasingly bureaucratic character of the Communist Party and the widespread corruption which pervaded local rural Party organs. Accordingly, the original aims of the movement were to restore collectivism in the rural areas by reestablishing the communes as functioning socioeconomic units and to cleanse the Party of corruption and bureaucratic elitism.

The most visible expression of the "First Ten Points" was the "four cleans" (*siqing*) campaign, an investigation of how cadres determined workpoints, kept accounts, distributed supplies, and handled warehouses and granaries. The aim was not only to root out corrupt practices but to expose the collusion between Party cadres and rich peasants and their exploitation of the majority of the rural population. The method to carry out the campaign was "to set the masses in motion" through the organization of "poor and lower-middle peasant associations."

To combat bureaucracy and the growing separation between leaders and masses, the resolution stressed the need for officials and cadres to labor in the fields on a regular basis to demonstrate that "the cadres of our Party are ordinary laborers . . . and not overlords who sit above the heads of the people." And to overcome the political apathy of both masses and cadres, the resolution called for new ideological reeducation campaigns and a renewed emphasis on "self-education."[3]

What marked the "First Ten Points" as distinctively Maoist was not so much the goals it announced—for all Party leaders were concerned with cadre corruption and the growth of "spontaneous" capitalist tendencies— but rather the means which Maoists proposed to restore socialist principles in the countryside. The document was permeated by populist and antibureaucratic impulses phrased in characteristically Maoist terms, stressing a far greater reliance on the grass-roots organization and initiative of the peasant masses than on the organizational apparatus of the Party. Indicative of the populist tone of the resolution was the reproduction of Mao's 1941 statement that, "We must clearly understand that the masses are the real heroes, while we ourselves are often childish and ignorant." The document concluded with a lengthy passage from a more recent directive by Mao, where he warned that the Chinese Communist Party was not only in danger of turning to revisionism but to "fascism" as well, and where he described the Socialist Education Movement in terms that foreshadowed the chiliastic fervors of the Cultural Revolution:

> This is a struggle that calls for the reeducation of man. This is a struggle for reorganizing the revolutionary class armies for a confrontation with the forces of feudalism and capitalism which are now feverishly attacking us. We must nip their counterrevolution in the bud. We must make it a great movement to reform the bulk of elements in these counterrevolutionary forces and turn them into new men. With cadres and masses joining hand in hand in production labor and scientific experiments, our Party will take another stride forward in becoming a more glorious, greater, and more correct Party; our cadres will be versed in politics as well as in business operations, become red as well as expert. They will then no longer be toplofty, no longer bureaucrats and overlords, no longer divorced from the masses. They will then merge themselves with the masses, becoming truly good cadres supported by the masses.[4]

Although Party leaders generally shared Mao's concern over cadre corruption and the retreat from collectivism, they viewed the new Maoist calls for the mass mobilization of the peasantry and an intensified class struggle as threats to maintaining agricultural productivity and to the organizational viability of the CCP—and as a threat to their own control over the Party and state apparatus. Bureaucratic resistance to carrying out the measures proposed in the "First Ten Points" was fortified by the appearance of two additional Party directives on the Socialist Education Movement; one came to be called the "Later Ten Points" and was drafted by the Party's General Secretary Deng Xiaoping in September 1963, while the second (known as the "Revised Later Ten Points") was issued by Liu Shaoqi in September 1964.[5] Both offered detailed instructions on implementing the policies set forth in Mao's original directive of May 1963. Both duly quoted the writings of Mao. But the real purpose was to blunt the radical thrust of the movement, limit its scope, and, most importantly, keep the movement under the centralized control of the Party. The device for accomplishing this was the dispatch of "work teams" (small groups of outside cadres organized by higher Party organs) to villages and communes to supervise local cadres and the masses. The work team was an old Communist organizational method, widely employed during the land reform campaigns. The method was revived to blunt the Maoist demand that the Socialist Education Movement proceed on the basis of the initiative and mobilization of the peasant masses themselves. Whereas the original Maoist directive emphasized that the first step was "to set the masses in motion," Liu Shaoqi insisted that "to launch the Socialist Education Movement at any point requires the sending of a work team from the higher level. The whole movement should be led by the work team."[6] Neither version of the "Later Ten Points" made mention of the peasant associations that figured so prominently in the "First Ten Points"; instead, it was decreed that "meetings should first be convened within the Party."[7] Rather than the peasants having their own organizations, as Mao had proposed, Deng and Liu emphasized the central importance of the Party, with higher organs rectifying the errors of local level cadres and then proceeding to lead and educate the masses: "To consolidate over 95 percent of the cadres is a prerequisite to the consolidation of over 95 percent of the masses. When the question of the cadres is properly handled, the question of consolidating the masses will also be solved."[8]

Operating from orthodox Leninist perspectives, most Party leaders— and most notably, Liu Shaoqi and Deng Xiaoping—believed that what was crucial for successful political and economic work was the organizational and ideological soundness of the CCP and the quality and discipline of its cadres. This firm Leninist belief in the Party as the sole bearer of a true socialist consciousness (and thus the only institution capable of correct political action) was epitomized in the crucial role assigned to the work team, the agency of the centralized Party apparatus that would discipline lower level Party organs and cadres and guide the masses from above.

Mao Zedong, by contrast, never had arrived at so firm a Leninist belief in the ideological infallibility of the Party. His faith in the Party as the repository of "proletarian consciousness" always had been mitigated by an equally strong faith that the true sources of revolutionary creativity resided in the masses themselves, and particularly in the peasantry. For Mao, the Party was as much the "pupil" of the masses as it was their "teacher," and particularly so in the early 1960s when his trust in the Party as a reliable instrument of revolution had all but vanished. In the Socialist Education Movement, he looked primarily to the peasants themselves, to a more or less spontaneous upsurge from below. From this essentially populist faith in

the people flowed the strong Maoist insistence that the movement to restore collectivism and revive a socialist spirit was to be based on associations comprising a majority of the peasantry, and not on "work teams"
controlled by higher Party organs.

The differences were made explicit in January 1965 when Mao convened a "national work conference" (ostensibly under the auspices of the
Politburo of the Party's Central Committee) and from that forum issued a
new directive known as the "Twenty-three Articles."[9] Beginning with the
proposition that the struggle between "socialism" and "capitalism" in society at large was reflected within the Party, the document redirected the
focus of the movement away from cadres in rural localities to "those people
in positions of authority within the Party who take the capitalist road."
Some such "capitalist-roaders" remained concealed, it ominously warned,
and some were operating at the highest levels of the Party, including the
Central Committee itself. It was, in effect, a declaration of political war
against the Party bureaucracy and its top leaders. And the war was to be
waged through a radical implementation of the principles of the mass line.
"We must boldly unleash the masses," Mao declared, and he added (reviving a metaphor made famous in his collectivization speech of a decade earlier), "we must not be like women with bound feet." There was a renewed
call for the establishment of peasant associations and an injunction that
specific problems arising during the course of the movement were to "be
judged and decided by the masses" and "not be decided from above." The
"four cleans," hitherto confined to correcting specific economic and political irregularities in the countryside, were now broadly redefined as "clean
politics, clean economics, clean organization, and clean ideology," thus
making no one immune to the campaign for purification. The document
left little doubt that Maoists regarded the Party itself, particularly its highest leaders, as the primary source of political and ideological impurities,
and it left little room for compromise.[10] With the Socialist Education
Movement now turned against "those people in positions of authority
within the Party who take the capitalist road," the battle lines for the Cultural Revolution inexorably were being drawn.

The Role of the Army

As Maoists grew increasingly disillusioned with the Party, they began to
look to the People's Liberation Army as the primary institutional repository
of revolutionary values, as a model for refashioning society, and as a political instrument to combat the conservatism of the Party bureaucracy. It is, of
course, paradoxical that a standing army, the most bureaucratic and hierar-

chical organ of the state machine, should have been seen as an instrument to serve antibureaucratic and egalitarian ends. This apparent contradiction between Maoist means and ends seems less glaring (although it by no means vanishes) in light of the rather unique history of the People's Liberation Army (PLA). During the revolutionary years, the Red Army was less a professional military organization than a highly politicized and egalitarian popular force of peasant guerrilla fighters. In a situation where revolutionary struggle primarily took the form of military struggle over a period of two decades, the function of the army could not be confined to fighting alone but necessarily encompassed political organization, economic production, and the ideological education and mobilization of the masses. The Party may have commanded the gun, as the Maoist maxim went, but the distinction between military and civilian functions, between army and Party, was a thin one or, perhaps more precisely, an overlapping one. The army was led not by professional soldiers but by eminently political men, the leaders of the CCP. The situation gave rise to the perception, particularly on the part of Mao, that the army no less than the Party was the bearer of the values and conscience of the revolution. The perception remained, even as the PLA increasingly took on the characteristics of a professional standing army in the years after 1949.

The army, now presumably refashioned and once again revolutionized according to Maoist precepts by Lin Biao in the early 1960s, first appeared on the civilian political scene early in 1963 with the launching of the "learn from the PLA" campaign. Its role, initially, was largely confined to propaganda, primarily popularizing the heroic and self-sacrificing deeds of revolutionary soldiers; the first and most celebrated of these model soldier-heroes who exemplified all the proper Maoist moral virtues was the legendary Lei Feng, typically described as "one of Chairman Mao's good warriors." By 1964 military intervention in civilian affairs became more direct when the PLA's General Political Department assigned army personnel to work in schools and in government offices and economic organizations. In the countryside, the influence of the PLA was exercised mainly through its control over the local militia, organizations composed of army veterans and young peasants, which were now revived after having fallen into disarray with the collapse of the Great Leap.

Yet military intervention was limited and its nature unique. The PLA did not take over either the functions of the Party or the government. The operations of both Party and state remained in the hands of their officially designated civilian leaders. Nor did the PLA prove decisive in the outcome of the Socialist Education Movement, the final results of which, from a

Maoist point of view, were meager at best. What made the process of military involvement unique was that the impetus for intervention came not from within the army but rather from without, from the civilian political sector itself. The army did not intervene in civilian life on its own but was called into the political arena by Party politicians or, more precisely, by the Maoist faction of the Party. And it was the latter who defined and limited the role of the army. The call was intended partly to assist Maoists in an intra-Party conflict, but perhaps in greater part to present the PLA as a model for emulation in various areas of political, economic, and ideological life. The political results, in any event, were inconclusive. In 1965 the "Liuists" remained in control of the Party and state apparatus, while the Maoist minority within the Party remained in increasingly hostile opposition, backed by the apparent support of the army.

The Mao Cult

The most curious political assignment of the army during these years was the glorification of the person and the thought of Mao Zedong. The cult of Mao was by no means an entirely new phenomenon, for the Chairman long had occupied a semi-sacred position in the eyes of his more devoted followers and among much of the peasantry. But prior to the 1960s it was a perception that developed more or less spontaneously, largely corresponding to the enormous personal role Mao played in the history of the revolution. As early as the Yan'an days, Edgar Snow reported in 1937, legends that Mao led "a charmed life" already were widespread in the Soviet areas.[11] The popularization of Mao's writings and the veritable canonization of his "thought" during the rectification campaign of the early 1940s contributed to the rapidly growing "personality cult," and perceptions of him as a "savior" and "the star of salvation" undoubtedly were reinforced by the victory of 1949. While the revolutionary triumph enhanced Mao's already vast personal power and prestige, in the early years of the People's Republic he did not attempt to go beyond the rules of the Party and state institutions he headed—although there was no lack of public praise for the creativity of his thought and the wisdom of his leadership. It was not until 1955, when Mao found it expedient to place himself above the Party in the agricultural collectivization campaign, that he began to foster the political conditions that demanded a supreme leader and a political climate conducive to the flourishing of the cult that was to be built around him. Those political conditions, briefly put, centered on the ability of a popular leader to overcome bureaucratic resistance to his policies by standing above established political institutions and by speaking to and for society as a whole. Implicit in that demonstration was the message that political wisdom resided not in the institution of the Party but in its leader and his thought.

The growth of the Mao cult was temporarily retarded by the impact of Khrushchev's 1956 speech denouncing Stalin and his "cult of the person-ality." While the official Chinese response duly denounced "personality cults," it did not truly reflect Mao's own views on the matter. In a secret speech delivered early in 1958, Mao distinguished between "correct" and "incorrect" forms of political cults: "The question at issue is not whether or not there should be a cult of the individual, but rather whether or not the individual concerned represents the truth. If he does, then he should be revered."[12] Mao's belief that he possessed the truth and that he de-served reverence was amply demonstrated during the Great Leap Forward campaign, when he appeared as a utopian prophet speaking directly to the people, partly bypassing regular institutions of Party and state. The failure of the Great Leap gravely undermined the semi-sacred posture Mao had come to assume—and indeed led to the publication of a rash of bitter satirical attacks against him, mostly in the form of historical allegories. The reassertion of the power of Party and state bureaucracies in the early 1960s, in turn, created an urgent political need for Mao to reestablish his personal and ideological supremacy. It was a task that fell to the People's Liberation Army.

In contrast to its earlier incarnations, the Mao cult fashioned in the 1960s was a rather contrived affair, although, as the events of the Cultural Revolution were soon to demonstrate, no less real a political phenomenon because of that. Following his campaign, launched in 1960, to turn the PLA into a "great school of Mao Zedong Thought," Lin Biao proceeded to use that school to educate the entire nation—and to deify Mao and his "thought" in the process. It was the Political Department of the army that published the first edition of *Quotations from Chairman Mao* in May of 1964. In his introductions to the various editions of that soon to be fa-mous—and fetishized—"little red book," Lin Biao made increasingly ex-travagant claims for the universal validity and extraordinary powers of Mao's thoughts. "Comrade Mao Zedong is the greatest Marxist-Leninist of our era" whose genius had raised the doctrine to "a higher and com-pletely new stage," Lin proclaimed. The masses of the people as well as cadres and intellectuals were advised to "study Chairman Mao's writings, follow his teachings, act according to his instructions and be his good fighters," for, once grasped by the masses, Mao's thought was no less than "an inexhaustible source of strength and a spiritual atom bomb of infinite power," Lin wrote shortly after China's first successful nuclear test in October 1964. The campaign to study Mao's writings, to the virtual exclusion of all other writings, was conducted largely by the PLA, which printed nearly a billion copies of the *Quotations* along with some 150,000,000 copies of Mao's *Selected Works* over the next three years. And the heroic figures popularized as models for emulation were mostly PLA soldiers, all of whom attributed their miraculous deeds to the inspiration of Mao's thought.

By 1965 the cult was becoming all pervasive. It was not only the "thoughts" that were being deified but their producer as well. When Edgar Snow visited the People's Republic in the winter of 1964–1965, he was puzzled by the "immoderate glorification" of Mao.

> Giant portraits of him now hung in the streets, busts were in every chamber, his books and photographs were everywhere on display to the exclusion of others. In the four-hour revolutionary pageant of dance and song, *The East Is Red,* Mao was the only hero. As a climax in that performance—presented, with a cast of 2,000, for the visiting King Mohammed Zahir Shah and the Queen of Afghanistan, accompanied by their host, Chairman Liu Shao-ch'i—I saw a portrait copied from a photograph taken by myself in 1936, blown up to about thirty feet high. It gave me a mixed feeling of pride of craftsmanship and uneasy recollection of similar extravaganzas of worship of Joseph Stalin seen during wartime years in Russia. . . . The one-man cult was not yet universal, but the trend was unmistakable.[13]

Mao apparently had few reservations about the cult. Not only had he distinguished between "good" and "bad" personality cults, but in an interview with Edgar Snow (held in January 1965) he suggested that such cults were essential political assets. Candidly acknowledging the existence of the phenomenon in China, Mao went on to suggest that Khrushchev's fall from power, which had occurred only three months earlier, might be attributed to the fact that the former Russian leader "had had no cult of personality at all."[14]

Revolutionary Successors

One of the major themes of the forthcoming Cultural Revolution was first heard in the spring of 1964: the need to train "revolutionary successors." The Maoist call was of course directed to the youth of China, for the youth were not only the bearers of the future society, it was also assumed that they were less corrupted by the traditions of the past and the pernicious "revisionist" influences of the present. Thus, youth were seen as more amenable than their elders to acquiring the proper consciousness necessary for the pursuit of revolutionary goals. It is thus hardly surprising that the problem of training "worthy successors" was first publicly discussed at a Communist Youth League congress, held in June 1964, although there was to be some historical irony in the fact that the youth organization was to be dismantled little more than two years later in the name of removing one of the obstacles to continuing the revolution. And it was wholly appropriate that the five criteria for revolutionary successors that Mao laid down were first published in the most comprehensive Chinese critique of the Soviet Union— the document entitled "On Khrushchev's Phoney Communism and Its Historical Lessons for the World"[15]—for the Soviet Union (in Maoist eyes) now had become a wholly negative example of a postrevolutionary society. In that document Mao made public his fears that China was following the same revisionist path to capitalism as Russia and his warnings (hitherto confined to Party councils) that China was threatened with the danger of "a counterrevolutionary restoration," that the Chinese Communist Party was in danger of becoming transformed into a revisionist and even a fascist party, and that the struggle between socialism and capitalism in China would span a lengthy historical era of a century or longer. The criteria Mao set forth for training "millions of successors who will carry on the cause of proletarian revolution" are not especially noteworthy, and we shall not pause to note them here.[16] What is worth noting about the campaign is that it reflected not only Mao's fears about the future and fate of the revolution but also his distrust of the Communist Party. Implicit in the campaign was the assumption that the Party could not be relied upon to continue the work of the revolution. True successors were to be trained not by the Party but directly through the study and the practice of the thought of the Chairman. Here the movement to train revolutionary successors merged with "the learn from the PLA" campaign and the growing Mao cult, the two main carriers of revolutionary values and the revolutionary alternatives to a conservative Party and state apparatus.

Mao's concern with the overriding need for ideological purity among the youth was reflected in his growing dissatisfaction over China's educational system. He complained that "book-learning" divorced from social reality and revolutionary practice was corrupting both the minds and the bodies of young people. The remedy he proposed in 1964 was to reduce the period of formal education and to "put into practice the union of education and productive labor."[17] While Mao had long harbored a certain enmity toward formal education (and especially to institutions of higher education), he had never expressed his views in so extreme a form as he did in the years immediately preceding the Cultural Revolution. "At present," he complained, "there is too much studying going on, and this is exceedingly harmful." From the history of traditional China he drew the lesson that, "when the intellectuals had power, things were in a bad state [and] the country was in disorder," and thus he concluded, "It is evident that to read too many books is harmful." True knowledge came from the practical experiences of real life and not from formal education, a point demonstrated by the fact that Confucius

> never attended middle school or university. . . . Gorki had only two years of primary school; his learning was all self-taught. Franklin of America was originally a newspaper seller, yet he discovered electricity. Watt was a worker, yet he invented the steam engine. Both in ancient and modern times, in China and abroad, many scientists trained themselves in the course of practice.

From this Mao drew the strange conclusion that "if you read too many books, they petrify your mind in the end." The Chairman also demanded the reform of the existing school system and conventional methods of teaching and examination—all of which he condemned as "exceedingly destructive of people."[18]

Debates on History and Dialectics

If Mao was concerned about the education of the youth—and whether they would be educated as bearers of the Maoist revolutionary ethic—his fears about the future deepened as he heard the ideas then being advanced by many of China's most prominent intellectuals. In the early 1960s Marxist theoreticians, scholars, and writers engaged in debates on such subjects as the inheritability of traditional Chinese culture, the role of the peasantry in Chinese history, the nature of human nature, historical materialism, Marxist literary theory, and dialectics. The discussions were erudite, for the most part, and were conducted in a relatively free and open atmosphere— and many of the views and arguments that emerged were decidedly anti-Maoist in their theoretical content and political implications.[19]

The noted philosopher Feng Yulan and the historian Wu Han (vice-mayor of Beijing as well as a professor at Beijing University) suggested, for example, that traditional Confucian thought, especially the concept of *ren* ("humanism"), offered a universally valid system of moral values and a rich cultural legacy that should be inherited by contemporary socialist society. It was not a suggestion that conformed with the increasingly antitraditionalist posture Maoism had assumed or with Maoist demands for a radical break with the vestiges of the feudal traditions of the past. At the same time other

Marxist historians, such as Liu Jie, argued that the laws of class struggle had not governed Chinese history as they had the history of the West, and this had resulted in a distinctively Chinese evolutionary process of historical development; also invoking the concept of *ren*, which allegedly had mitigated class conflict in the past, it was argued that the principle might be applied to serve the same purpose in the present. The argument appeared at the very time Mao was insisting that the survival of the revolution required intensifying class struggle. Other scholars took issue with the Maoist thesis that peasant rebellions were the motive force of historical development in traditional society, some suggesting that the peasantry constituted a social force no less conservative in the present than it allegedly had been in the past—just as Maoists, in the Socialist Education Movement, were hailing the revolutionary energies and the spirit of struggle latent in the peasant masses.

These non-Maoist historical views were echoed by literary theorists. In a remarkably explicit refutation of the Maoist emphasis on class struggle and the accompanying Maoist insistence that all forms of consciousness, including all literature and art, were expressions of particular class interests, some scholars set forth an "historicist" position to the effect that in a given historical era various forms of consciousness inevitably merged into a "spirit of the age." From this it followed that such revolutionary and non-revolutionary elements in contemporary Chinese society were more or less united in a general national spirit, and with contradictions thus naturally reconciled, there was no need to artificially foster ideological and political struggle. Other writers challenged the Maoist view that the function of literature and art in a socialist society was to popularize heroic revolutionary examples and condemn counterrevolutionary villains. Instead, it was argued, realism demanded that the masses be portrayed as they really were rather than as Maoists wished them to be—as mostly what were termed "middle people," caught up in the whirlwind of revolutionary change, standing ambiguously between the forces of the new and the old. Such, in reality, was the position of the peasants in particular, who were to be realistically portrayed as essentially politically ambivalent. It was not a very Maoist portrait of the peasantry, needless to say.

The controversies eventually came to focus on two Marxist theoretical issues: the interpretation of historical materialism and the proper understanding of dialectical materialism. On the first, the non-Maoist participants generally held to an orthodox Marxist view, invoking, often in rather deterministic fashion, the Marxist proposition that "being determines consciousness"—as opposed to the voluntaristic Maoist emphasis on the decisive role of consciousness in transforming historical and social reality. The political implications of these differences were made rather explicit in the course of the debates. Mao, with an excessive reliance on subjective historical factors, his critics suggested, had gone beyond the bounds of objective historical possibilities in the Great Leap Forward campaign, and was attempting to do so again with the Socialist Education Movement. In brief, he had violated the dictates of the objective laws of historical development as taught by Marxist theory. For Maoists, by contrast, it was a prime article of faith that "the subjective can create the objective," and they never tired of quoting Marx's statement that "once theory is grasped by the masses, it itself becomes a material force" and Marx's injunction that hitherto "the philosophers have only interpreted the world, in various ways; the point, however, is to change it." The critics of Mao were charged with failing to recognize the dynamic role of the masses in sociohistorical development, with attempting to dampen their revolutionary enthusiasm, and with propagating theories designed to prevent the people from changing the world in accordance with socialist goals.

The theoretical debates culminated in a bitter ideological controversy on dialectical materialism in 1964 which centered on the views of Yang Xianzhen, head of the Higher Party School for the training of upper level cadres and a theoretician widely regarded as an ideological spokesman for Liu Shaoqi. While the debates on dialectics produced a voluminous and rather obtuse body of literature on epistemology and other philosophical problems, the differences were popularized and oversimplified in Yang's formula that "two combine into one" constitutes the fundamental law of dialectics, as opposed to Mao's insistence that "one divides into two." Whereas Mao held that the unity of opposites was temporary while the struggle between them was eternal, Yang and his disciples stressed the mutuality of opposites and the unity of contradictions as the principal law of dialectical materialism and sociohistorical development. Yang's views provided theoretical support for the then still politically dominant Liuists and their policies of an orderly and more or less evolutionary pattern of development, whereas the views of his Maoist protagonists lent support to Mao's emphasis on the necessity of revolutionary transformations through class struggle in the present and to the Maoist notion of the ceaselessness of contradictions and struggles in the future.

The theories advanced by many intellectuals in the years 1962–1964 were seen by Maoists as ideological reflections of the "revisionist" tendencies that had come to dominate the Party; in part, they were attributed to the persistence of traditional Chinese values among the intelligentsia and the equally pernicious influences of contemporary Soviet and East European intellectuals. But for Mao ideas were more than simply reflections of social reality; consciousness was an historical force in its own right in determining the direction of society. And more than purely academic debates were required to remedy the situation. The remedy Mao first proposed (in February 1964) was both simple and drastic: "We must drive actors, poets, dramatists, and writers out of the cities, and pack them off to the country-side."[20] In June 1964 he called for a "rectification" campaign along the lines of the antirightist movement of the latter half of 1957. For the past fifteen years, he complained, the intellectuals

> have acted as high and mighty bureaucrats, have not gone to the workers, peas-
> ants, and soldiers, and have not reflected socialist reality and socialist construc-
> tion. In recent years, they have slid right down to the brink of revisionism. Unless
> they remold themselves in real earnest in the future, they are bound to become a
> group like the Hungarian Petofi Club.[21]

If Mao was concerned over the revisionist tendencies of the intelli-gentsia, he probably was even less happy about the feeble efforts of the Party to combat those tendencies. The task of conducting the rectification movement in the latter half of 1964 fell to the Party's Propaganda Depart-ment, headed by Lu Dingyi and Zhou Yang. It was a perfunctory and pale affair compared to previous ideological campaigns, and largely kept within the boundaries of polite academic debate. It was not that Lu Dingyi or Zhou Yang had become recent converts to the cause of intellectual free-dom—for Zhou Yang in particular had long established himself as the guardian of literary and cultural orthodoxy, and had acquired a well-deserved reputation as a witch-hunter of considerable ruthlessness. Rather, it was their intention to insulate the Party and the state Ministry of Culture from Maoist and PLA influences. It was hardly to be expected, in any event, that the leaders of the Party apparatus would prove especially ardent in "remolding" the thoughts of those who were providing ideological justi-fication for their policies. Nor is it likely that Mao expected much more than the little that was done. Indeed, his opinion of the Party had fallen so low that he no longer refrained from such sarcastic comments as one he made in August of 1964: "At present, you can buy a Party branch secretary for a few packs of cigarettes, not to mention marrying a daughter to him."[22] The rectification campaign, along with the historical and philosophical de-bates, quietly petered out early in 1965, as did the Socialist Education Movement as a whole.

The more heretical and heterodox voices were stilled by 1965, but the ideological issues remained unresolved, just as the political struggle be-tween Maoists and the Party bureaucracy remained a stalemate. Only in one limited area of the cultural realm did Maoists gain a symbolic victory, and that involved the curious spectacle of the army, assisted by Mao's wife Jiang Qing, engaged in the reform of the traditional Beijing opera. Otherwise, Maoism was dominant only in the realm of formal ideology. While appropriate lip service was paid to the "thought of Mao," real power over the Party and state remained in non-Maoist hands and basically conservative socioeconomic policies continued to be pursued under the cover of radical rhetoric. Maoist attempts to revolutionize thought and society were frustrated at every turn by the resistance of entrenched bureaucracies and the apparent political inertia of the masses. At no time in the history of the People's Republic was the gap between theory and practice so wide.

The sense of activism—and the impatience—that continued to characterize Mao's mentality during those years were reflected in his poem entitled "Reply to Guo Moruo," written in 1963: "Seize the day, seize the hour! . . . Our force is irresistible." These active impulses were soon to find real political expression, and on a momentous scale. If the half-decade following the Great Leap can be seen as a variant of the Thermidorean reaction, then the events that began to unfold in early 1966 marked the beginning of Mao's revolution against the Thermidoreans.

NOTES

1. Mao Tse-tung [Mao Zedong], "Speech at the Tenth Plenum of the Eighth Central Committee," in Stuart R. Schram, ed., *Mao Tse-tung Unrehearsed: Talks and Letters, 1956–71* (Middlesex, England: Penguin, 1974), pp. 188–196.

2. Of the three main resolutions which emerged from Plenum, only the general communiqué was made public at the time. *Documents of Chinese Communist Party Central Committee* (Hong Kong: Union Research Institute, 1971), pp. 185–192. The other two were secret documents circulated through intra-Party channels. *Documents of the Chinese Communist Party Central Committee*, pp. 193–205, 695–725.

3. "Draft Resolution of the Central Committee of the Chinese Communist Party on Some Problems in Current Rural Work," May 20, 1963. Text translated in Richard Baum and Frederick C. Teiwes, *Ssu-Ch'ing: The Socialist Education Movement of 1962–1966* (Berkeley: University of California Press, 1968), Appendix B, p. 68 and pp. 58–71, *passim.*

4. *Ibid.,* pp. 62–71.

5. Both documents were titled "Some Concrete Policy Formulations of the Central Committee of the Chinese Communist Party in the Rural Socialist Education Movement." (See Baum and Teiwes, *Ssu-Ch'ing,* Appendixes C and E, pp. 72–94, 102–117.)

6. "Revised Later Ten Points," Baum and Teiwes, *Ssu-Ch'ing,* Appendix E, p. 105.

7. "Later Ten Points," Baum and Teiwes, *Ssu-Ch'ing,* Appendix C, p. 91.

8. "Later Ten Points," p. 85. Liu Shaoqi's revised version elaborated on, and emphasized even more strongly, the point that the rectification of the cadres was the key to the proper development of the mass movement. "In short," he concluded, "to educate the masses we must first educate the cadres; and to solve the problems of the masses we must first solve the problems of the cadres." ("Revised Later Ten Points," p. 108.)

9. The document was formally titled "Some Problems Currently Arising in the Course of the Rural Socialist Education Movement." Baum and Teiwes, *Ssu-Ch'ing*, Appendix F, pp. 118–126.

10. In late 1964, Liu Shaoqi apparently was willing to compromise his differences with Mao, or at least paper them over, through the device of combining Mao's original directive on the Socialist Education Movement with his own "Revised Later Ten Points" and calling them the "Double Ten Points." Mao refused the offer and issued his twenty-three-point directive of January 1965. Liu, in turn, refused to accept the latter, which was aimed against the Party bureaucracy over which he still wielded firm control.

11. Snow's own impressions of the forty-four-year-old Mao in 1937, when Mao's name was hardly known outside of China and little known within China save for the still limited Soviet areas, were uncannily perceptive and prophetic: "You feel a certain force of density in him. It is nothing quick or flashy, but a kind of solid elemental vitality. You feel that whatever extraordinary there is in this man grows out of the uncanny degree to which he synthesizes and expresses the urgent demands of millions of Chinese, and especially the peasantry—those impoverished, underfed, exploited, illiterate but kind, generous, courageous and just now rather rebellious human beings who are the vast majority of the Chinese people. If these demands and the movement which is pressing them forward are the dynamics which can regenerate China, then in this deeply historical sense Mao Tse-tung may possibly become a very great man." Edgar Snow, *Red Star Over China* (New York: Random House, 1938), p. 67.

12. Mao Tse-tung, "Talks at the Chengtu Conference," March 10, 1958, in Schram, ed., *Mao Tse-tung Unrehearsed*, pp. 99–100.

13. Edgar Snow, *The Long Revolution* (New York: Random House, 1971), pp. 68–69.

14. *Ibid.*, p. 205.

15. The lengthy treatise first appeared on July 14, 1964 as editorials in the *People's Daily* and the Party theoretical journal *Red Flag*. It was the ninth and final Chinese reply to the "open letter" of the Central Committee of the Soviet Party, published July 14, 1963. An English translation published in pamphlet form by the Foreign Languages Press (Peking, 1964) is reproduced in A. Doak Barnett, *China after Mao* (Princeton, N.J.: Princeton University Press, 1967), pp. 123–195.

16. The five criteria, briefly, were that "worthy successors" must be genuine Marxist-Leninists, revolutionaries who serve the majority of the people, "proletarian statesmen" capable of uniting with the vast majority of the masses, models in applying the principles of democratic centralism and the mass line, and people who were "modest and prudent." *Ibid.*, pp. 193–194. Mao elaborated on the criteria in a revealing discussion with his nephew Mao Yüan-hsin [Mao Yuanxin]; for a transcript of the talk, see Schram, ed., *Mao Tse-tung Unrehearsed*, pp. 242–250.

17. Mao Tse-tung, "Remarks at the Spring Festival," February 13, 1964, *Mao Tse-tung Unrehearsed*, p. 206.

18. *Ibid.*, pp. 203–211.

19. For an excellent survey of the debates and the issues involved, see Merle Goldman, "The Chinese Communist Party's 'Cultural Revolution' of 1962–64," in Chalmers Johnson, ed., *Ideology and Politics in Contemporary China* (Seattle: University of Washington Press, 1973), pp. 219–254.

20. Mao, "Remarks at the Spring Festival," p. 207.

21. Mao Tse-tung, "Instructions Concerning Art and Literature," June 27, 1964, in *Mao Tse-tung Ssu-hsiang Wan-sui* (Taipei: n.p., 1967). Translated in *Current Background*, No. 891.

22. Mao Tse-tung, "Talk on Questions of Philosophy," August 18, 1964, *Mao Tse-tung Unrehearsed*, p. 217.

PART FIVE

THE CULTURAL REVOLUTION AND ITS AFTERMATH

1966–1976

17

The Concept of Cultural Revolution

AO ZEDONG'S LAST revolutionary act was to turn into the greatest tragedy of his long revolutionary career—and one with dire consequences for the Chinese people. In 1966 the seventy-two-year-old Mao staged his final revolutionary drama, stimulating a cataclysmic upheaval that he baptized "the Great Proletarian Cultural Revolution." It was his last desperate attempt to revive a revolution that he believed was dying. It was an attempt that failed, and it was a failure on a grand scale, dominating and distorting the social and political life of the People's Republic for more than a decade and tarnishing the historical image of Mao in the process. In launching the Cultural Revolution, Mao proclaimed principles and ideals he could not (or would not) sustain, and unleashed social and political forces he could not control, forces which were to exact a fearsome human and social toll. Before the drama had played itself out, it consumed, physically or spiritually, virtually all of its original promoters and supporters as well as many of its intended victims— along with a good number of unintended ones who would have preferred to stand on the sidelines of the battles that racked and nearly wrecked China during the last decade of the Maoist regime.

Mao Zedong's successors in Beijing, most of whom were among the political victims of Mao's last revolution, condemn the Cultural Revolution as a decade-long "catastrophe" (now officially dated as the period from May 1966 to October 1976), "responsible for the most severe setback and the heaviest losses suffered by the Party, the state and the people since the founding of the People's Republic," according to the official assessment. Although the most horrendous crimes of the era are blamed upon Mao's evil associates, especially Lin Biao and the "Gang of Four," the main responsibility for the movement as a whole resides with Mao himself who, it is said, "initiated and led" the movement on the basis of erroneous "leftist" ideas that were "inconsistent with the system of Mao Zedong Thought." But Mao's personal ideological and political errors are ultimately attributed to deeper historical forces inherited from the millennia, especially the persisting influences of China's long feudal past. A pernicious "petty-bourgeois ideology," deeply rooted in a two-thousand-year-long tradition of small-scale peasant production, produced the contemporary political phenomenon of "ultra-leftism," which, it is argued, first manifested itself in the utopianism of the Great Leap Forward campaign and then found its most disastrous political expression in the Cultural Revolution and its "feudal-fascist" results. It is acknowledged, however, that "it remains difficult to eliminate the evil ideological and political influences of centuries of feudal autocracy."[1]

In the years since the death of Mao Zedong, especially since 1978, much has been told and learned about the events of the "cultural revolution decade" and about the extent of human suffering those events entailed. The disclosures of recent years, from both official and unofficial Chinese sources, certainly demand a searching reassessment of the Cultural Revolution and its results, particularly on the part of those who once expressed (to greater or lesser degrees) some sympathy for the movement. But it does not demand uncritical repetitions of the version of events dispensed in Beijing in recent years. Those in post-Maoist China who are free to speak and write about the Cultural Revolution are for the most part those who were the political and sometimes physical victims of the time, and their political and emotional stake in portraying the cultural revolution decade as an unmitigated disaster is no less compelling than the political stake Maoists once had in portraying it as the most glorious of revolutionary triumphs. As Harry Harding has cautioned:

> China's official repudiation of the Cultural Revolution invites another look. This time, however, we should be skeptical. The Chinese who today preach a new gospel condemning the Cultural Revolution are its principal surviving victims, the "ghosts and monsters" so often beaten, duncecapped, and denounced by the Red Guards. If we simply translate the revised authorized version into English,

we will be repeating the mistakes we made in the late 1960s, when we took the official rationale for the Cultural Revolution at face value.[2]

Today's wholesale condemnations of the Cultural Revolution will prove little more conducive to historical understanding than did the uncritical celebrations of the event in years past.

Controversies over the nature and results of the Cultural Revolution will rage for many years to come, and it will be decades before its full history can be written with any reasonable degree of accuracy and understanding. Yet the "decade of catastrophe" obviously cannot be ignored in the interim, nor can the events of the era be conveniently dismissed as "the ten lost years." For not only was the Cultural Revolution the historical culmination of Maoism and the Maoist era, but the experiences of the time continue to dominate the political consciousness of many Chinese in the post-Mao era. An attempt to write even a brief preliminary account is a formidable task not only because of the political passions the Cultural Revolution necessarily arouses but also because of the moral and historical dilemmas it poses. There is no period in China's long history so complex and contradictory or so lacking in historical precedents, no other period where all historical analogies fail. Rarely has any society revealed itself so openly with all its contradictions and scars, and rarely have events unfolded in ways so strange, tortuous, and bizarre. Few episodes in modern history are filled with so many ironies and paradoxes, plagued by such deep incongruities between means and ends, and marred by so large a gulf between intentions and results.

The Cultural Revolution began with its leaders loudly proclaiming the principles of popular democracy, but the masses of people who heeded the proclamation subordinated themselves at the outset to the thoughts and person of Mao Zedong, "the Great Helmsman" who presented himself as the embodiment of the collective popular will. The movement announced itself (and won much of its massive popular support) as a war against bureaucratic privilege and oppression, but it soon fell under the sway of the Chinese army, the most oppressive and hierarchical organ of the bureaucratic state apparatus. Maoist leaders initially provoked a popular assault against the Chinese Communist Party, promising a more democratic political structure, but those very leaders eventually proclaimed the Cultural Revolution really had always aimed to "consolidate" the Party, and soon thereafter the movement degenerated into a ferocious struggle among Communist leaders for control of the Party apparatus. At the outset the leaders of the Cultural Revolution attacked "the four olds," especially the lingering influences of superstitions inherited from old China's feudal tradition, only to replace them with the superstitious worship of Mao Zedong and the primitive rituals performed around the Chairman's cult. One of the loudly announced intentions of the movement was to train the youth of China as "revolutionary successors" to the May Fourth generation of older revolutionary leaders, but the result of the Cultural Revolution was to breed political disillusionment and cynicism among an entire generation of young Chinese, many of whom in the wake of the catastrophe would refer to themselves collectively as "the lost generation." The Cultural Revolution politically activated China's urban working class for the first time since the proletariat had been so brutally crushed by Chiang Kai-shek's armies in 1927, but the genuine workers' organizations formed during the early phases of the movement were dissolved and suppressed from above long before the Cultural Revolution was officially concluded, with China's working class once again condemned to political passivity. The ideology of the Cultural Revolution purported to speak on behalf of the countryside against the exploitative cities, but most peasants gained little from the up-heaval, and some lost much. The leaders of the Cultural Revolution at first appealed to the intelligentsia to join a crusade against bureaucratic tyranny—and many intellectuals responded—but intellectuals as a social group would then become the principal victims of the movement's virulent anti-intellectualism. Aiming to revitalize the spirit of socialism in China, to forestall the danger of a "bourgeois restoration," and to guarantee China's "transition to socialism," the upheaval in the end only discredited the very idea of socialism in the eyes of many Chinese, creating "a crisis of faith" in Marxism and undermining such fragile foundations for socialism as existed in the People's Republic. The struggles that were unleashed, which were meant to bring ever higher levels of unity among the people in the pursuit of a better future, led only to an endless cycle of violence and vengeance that has yet to spend itself fully.

Between the intentions that motivated the Cultural Revolution and the actual results of the upheaval, there is an enormous gap. What the movement yielded in the end bore little resemblance to the ideals and aims that were proclaimed at the beginning. History, it need hardly be emphasized, must be written primarily on the basis of what people do rather than what they say. And Mao Zedong, like any other historical actor, ultimately must be judged by the results of his actions rather than by his words and intentions. Goals and intentions are not historically inconsequential, however, and certainly not morally irrelevant. Any serious attempt to understand the meaning of the events that unfolded in (and engulfed) China in the years 1966–69 must begin by confronting the yet unfulfilled task "to distinguish the intention that underlay the Cultural Revolution from the circumstances that perverted the intention into its own caricature."[3] The clash between the intentions of Mao and the circumstances he encountered lies at the heart of the tragedy of the Cultural Revolution. Thus the discussion must begin with an examination of the aims and goals of the Cultural Revolution—if for no other reason than to appreciate the magnitude of the failure.

The Concept of Cultural Revolution and the Aims of the Great Proletarian Cultural Revolution

Mao Zedong was not the inventor of either the term or the concept of "cultural revolution." The notion of "cultural revolution" is deeply imbedded in the thought of the modern Chinese intelligentsia. A half-century before Mao embarked upon the adventure of the Great Proletarian Cultural Revolution, indeed before there were Marxists in China, the Western-oriented Chinese intellectuals associated with the New Culture Movement (circa 1915–19),[4] and especially with the *New Youth* magazine, were calling for a "cultural revolution" (*wenhua geming*) to bring about a fundamental transformation of the culture and psychology of the nation. The term, as it was employed by China's radical democratic intellectuals in the second decade of the century, conveyed two notions that would prove of enduring significance in contemporary Chinese thought and politics. First, China's iconoclastic intellectuals demanded a wholesale rejection of the traditional Chinese cultural heritage, which they tended to view as not only useless for China's modern regeneration but also morally evil and inherently corrupt. Second, they placed an extraordinary emphasis on the role of human consciousness in the making of history, believing that cultural and intellectual change was the essential prerequisite for effective political action and socioeconomic progress.

Both of these ideas deeply influenced the young Mao Zedong in his formative years, and both eventually became crucial features of the Maoist variant of Marxism-Leninism. The doctrine that came to be celebrated as "Mao Zedong Thought" was above all based on the faith that people armed with the proper ideas and will could surmount all material obstacles and mold social reality in accordance with their ideals. While Mao paid ideological deference to the presumably "objective laws" of historical development set forth in orthodox Marxist texts, he clearly believed that the course of history ultimately was determined by what people thought and their willingness to engage in revolutionary action. From that belief flowed the enormous Maoist concern with developing "correct consciousness" among the people, the stress on "ideological remolding," and the emphasis on "thought reform." Just as the maxim that people are "more important than machines" was the guiding Maoist principle for the making of revolution and the fighting of war, so the Maoist strategy of postrevolutionary development relied upon the consciousness of the Chinese people, on what Mao so often celebrated as "the boundless creative powers" of the masses.

Closely associated with Mao's belief that conscious human activity is the ultimately decisive factor in history was his highly iconoclastic condemnation of traditional Chinese culture. "Correct consciousness," in the Maoist view, required the total elimination of the pernicious influences of traditional values and old ideas. That cultural iconoclasm and the belief in conscious human activity as the determining force in history were the key elements in Mao's notion of cultural revolution, a concept he had inherited from the pre-Marxian intellectuals of the New Culture era and one which retained a central place in his Marxist outlook during both the revolutionary Yan'an era and the postrevolutionary history of the People's Republic.[5]

The concept of cultural revolution is part of the Marxist tradition as well as the modern Chinese intellectual tradition, having achieved a certain prominence in Russia shortly after the Bolshevik Revolution of 1917. Among the Russian advocates of a "cultural revolution" was Lenin, who, like Mao, was concerned with maintaining the socialist spirit of the revolution during the lengthy period that would be required to carry out the modern economic transformation of a backward land. But Lenin's idea of cultural revolution was far different from Mao's later conception, and the differences suggest some measure of the ideological distance between Leninism and Maoism.[6] When Lenin called for a cultural revolution, he generally had in mind the need to bring the fruits of modern "bourgeois culture" to the masses of a backward land who remained mired in "feudal" habits, customs, and methods of work. The construction of a socialist culture was a task to be performed in the future, and it was dependent on establishing the material and social prerequisites for a socialist society. Lenin assumed that the bearers of modern culture were properly politicized and technically educated intellectuals, and to a lesser extent the more advanced sectors of the urban working class, who would bring the fruits of modern urban industrial culture to the peasants in the backward countryside. Further, Lenin believed that the modern cultural transformation of the people would proceed gradually, since it was dependent on the building of a modern industrial economy. While emphasizing the need to raise the cultural level of the masses (especially the peasantry), he emphasized even more strongly that "to be cultured we must achieve a certain development of the material means of production, [we] must have a certain material base."[7]

And Lenin took it for granted that a cultural revolution demanded inheriting the cultural legacies of the past, arguing that it was essential "to grasp all the culture which capitalism has left and build socialism from it."[8]

On all of these issues, Mao Zedong's concept of cultural revolution differed radically from Lenin's—and departed from the Western Marxist tradition generally. Whereas Lenin assumed that the cultural development of the Russian people presupposed the modern industrial development of the Russian nation, Mao Zedong, uninhibited by orthodox Marxist considerations, envisioned a China moving rapidly to socialism and communism through a process of "continuous" revolution. For Mao, neither a socialist nor a communist society was dependent on the prior development of material productive forces; rather, the essential precondition was the "proletarianization" of the consciousness of the people, and that was to be accomplished through the means of a cultural revolution. For Mao, the cultural "proletarianization" of the masses was not so much the product of modern economic development as the precondition for it, at least insofar as economic growth might contribute to a socialist historical outcome. In socialist construction, Mao emphasized time and again, "the important question is the remolding of people."[9]

While Lenin, in advocating cultural revolution, praised as historically progressive the dissemination of capitalist cultural forms and techniques among the backward populace of a largely pre-capitalist land, that certainly was not the case with Mao ruling an even more backward country. For Mao, Western bourgeois culture and capitalist methods were no less pernicious, and no less incompatible with socialist ends, than the hated feudal culture of China's Confucian past. The cultural revolution was intended to destroy the evil influences of both. Indeed, Mao eventually rejected (as Lenin never did) the Marxist proposition that capitalism is a progressive stage in historical development; instead, he came to celebrate the socialist advantages of China's backwardness, arguing that China had been fortunate to have escaped a prolonged capitalist phase of development.[10]

Mao's concept of cultural revolution also radically departed from Lenin's on the question of who were to be the bearers of modern culture. For Lenin, the role of intellectuals remained decisive. Just as Lenin's conception of the revolutionary party demanded that the "consciousness" of the intelligentsia be imposed on the "spontaneous" movement of the amorphous masses, so he assumed that technologically proficient intellectuals would spearhead the industrial transformation of Russia and bring modern culture to the masses in the process. In contrast, Mao Zedong, distrustful of intellectuals, retained a populist-type faith in popular spontaneity, believing that a cultured people would emerge from the revolutionary self-activity of the masses and thereby realize his vision of a nation of "socialist-conscious, cultured laborers." The principle of self-reliance had an internal as well as external significance for Mao. Just as the Chinese nation was to become economically self-reliant and not dependent on other countries, so the Chinese people were to become self-reliant and not dependent on an intellectual-technocratic elite. "The masses must make themselves masters of culture and science," a Maoist slogan of the Great Leap era, was to be heard again during the Cultural Revolution.

Mao's distrust of the urban intelligentsia extended to a distrust of cities in general. While Lenin retained a firm Marxist belief that the forces of modern historical progress resided in the cities, and thus naturally assumed that the cultural revolution would spread from the urban to the rural areas, Mao Zedong retained the powerful anti-urban biases bred during the long revolutionary years in the countryside. Just as Maoist revolutionary strategy took the form of mobilizing peasants to "surround and overwhelm" the conservative cities, so his vision of the proper course of postrevolutionary development centered on the countryside as the true repository of social and cultural creativity. In the postrevolutionary era, as before, the cities remained under Maoist suspicion as the breeding grounds of cultural and ideological corruptions. Whereas Lenin advocated sending members of the urban proletariat to the countryside to raise the cultural level of peasants, Mao advocated sending urban dwellers to the countryside to learn "proletarian virtues" from the peasants—and he was to do so on a massive scale during the Great Proletarian Cultural Revolution.

Perhaps the most striking difference between the Maoist and Leninist concepts of "cultural revolution" concerned the relationship of the envisioned new society to the cultural legacies of the past. Lenin, like Marx, assumed that a socialist society would inherit (and build upon) all the cultural as well as material accomplishments of its predecessors. Hence he deplored Russia's cultural backwardness, which, shortly before his death in 1924, he partly blamed for the degeneration of the Russian Revolution.[11] Mao Zedong, by contrast, seemed to celebrate the very absence of culture, or at least the absence of "high culture." "In history," he once remarked, "it is always people with a low level of culture who triumph over people with a high level of culture."[12] The remark reflected a long-standing Maoist faith in the alleged socialist advantages of backwardness, a faith which found its most extreme cultural expression in the remarkable "poor and blank" thesis announced at the beginning of the Great Leap campaign in 1958:

> Apart from their other characteristics, China's 600 million people have two remarkable peculiarities; they are, first of all, poor, and secondly blank. That may

seem like a bad thing, but it is really a good thing. Poor people want change, want to do things, want revolution. A clean sheet of paper has no blotches, and so the newest and most beautiful words can be written on it, the newest and most beautiful pictures can be painted on it.[13]

It would be difficult to invent a formula more radically opposed to the logic of the Marxist conception of history[14] and to Marx's and Lenin's belief that the new society necessarily would inherit all the accomplishments (and all the burdens) of the past. Mao Zedong, by declaring the Chinese people "blank," was driven by a utopian impulse to escape history and by an iconoclastic desire to wipe the historical-cultural slate clean. Having rejected the traditional Chinese cultural heritage, Mao attempted to fill the emotional void with an even more iconoclastic proclamation of the nonexistence of the past in the present. A new culture, Mao seemed to believe, could be created ex nihilo on a fresh canvas, on a "clean sheet of paper" unmarred by historical blemishes. In his iconoclasm and in his belief in the powers of the human consciousness to mold history, Mao's concept of cultural revolution owed far more to the May Fourth intellectual tradition than to Marxist-Leninist traditions.

Yet the "clean sheet of paper" Mao optimistically proclaimed China to be when he launched the Great Leap Forward campaign in 1958 had become a canvas marred by all manner of political and ideological blotches, he pessimistically concluded in the early 1960s. In a 1964 conversation with his longtime friend André Malraux, then France's Minister of Culture, Mao emphasized that "the thought, culture, and customs which brought China to where we found her [in 1949] must disappear, and the thought, customs, and culture of proletarian China, which do not yet exist, must appear."[15] Destruction, not inheritance—and not yet construction—was the Maoist injunction when the Great Proletarian Cultural Revolution was launched in 1966, just as it had been the injunction of the pre-Marxian Chen Duxiu when he had launched the New Culture Movement half a century before. If the Cultural Revolution was a "utopian" movement, it was (unlike the Great Leap) marked by a strangely negative utopianism, its author far more preoccupied with the weight of the past than with any positive vision of the future.

The vast upheaval that Mao Zedong set in motion in the mid-1960s, the consequences of which were to dominate the last decade of his rule, was of course not simply the product of his concept of cultural revolution. It goes without saying that the power interests and the personal political ambitions of Mao and other Communist leaders were very much involved in the outbreak of the Cultural Revolution and the tortured course the movement took. But it needs to be emphasized, especially since it is now usually ignored, that this most extraordinary of political upheavals was also undertaken with the intention of resolving a host of social problems that had emerged in the postrevolutionary years: growing social inequality, the fading of the socialist vision among leaders and populace alike, and the entrenchment of new bureaucratic elites. These tendencies raised the specter that China was becoming like the Soviet Union, where, Maoists loudly charged on the eve of the great upheaval, "a privileged bureaucratic stratum" had usurped power.[16] The social and political problems that the Maoists vowed to address were very real ones. More was involved in the making of the Cultural Revolution than Mao's "erroneous" ideas and a thirst for total power.

Social Inequality

The social inequalities bred by the Soviet-modeled First Five Year Plan (1953–57), temporarily halted by the egalitarianism of the Great Leap, resumed at an even more rapid pace in the early 1960s. The Chinese Communist Party, at least in its official ideology, was committed to narrowing and eventually eliminating what were called the "three great differences": between mental and manual labor, city and countryside, and workers and peasants. But under the policies pursued by the Liuist regime to recover from the debacle of the Great Leap, those differences clearly were widening. The strengthening of the authority of managers and technological personnel in the urban industrial sector again widened the distinction between administrators and workers in the factories—and the distinction between mental and manual labor. The latter grew increasingly conspicuous as intellectuals were restored to their customary professional and social status, bringing renewed Maoist complaints that intellectuals were behaving as "high and mighty bureaucrats." A growing reliance on piece-rate wages and bonus payments, designed to spur productivity, increased socioeconomic differences within the urban working class, while drastic reductions in the number of state employees aggravated the even more politically explosive division between relatively privileged regular factory workers with lifetime job tenure and an ever larger semi-proletariat of temporary and contract workers.[17]

In the countryside, the emasculation of the people's communes, the expansion of individual family farming on private plots, the growth of rural markets, and the decline of collective labor inevitably increased socioeconomic differentiations among the peasantry. What was condemned in official ideology as "spontaneous tendencies towards capitalism" in the rural areas was in fact tolerated and often encouraged by official policy in many parts of the countryside.

While a minority of peasants thrived in a semi-market economy, the countryside as a whole fared less well than the cities. As the nation struggled to recover from the Great Leap, when famine ravaged portions of the countryside, state fiscal and economic policies favored urban inhabitants, especially bureaucrats, intellectuals, and workers who were regular state employees. State austerity measures fell hardest on the local rural industries established during the Great Leap, many of which were forced to close, thereby undermining the most viable Maoist policy for narrowing the difference between peasants and workers. Rural and part-time schools were deemphasized in favor of urban educational institutions, including special schools reserved for the children of Party officials.[18] Many of the rural health care centers established during the Great Leap were forced to close, while urban medical facilities expanded. In the period immediately following the Great Leap, the gap between town and countryside, along with other inequalities, grew more rapidly than they had in the 1950s.

The Fading of the Socialist Vision

As social inequality grew in the early 1960s, collectivist values declined and Marxian socialist goals, although still proclaimed, became increasingly divorced from social and political practice. After the collapse of the Great Leap the citizens of China, seemingly disillusioned with politics, turned to private pursuits and familial obligations. That was particularly the case in the countryside, where the revival of private markets was accompanied by a revival of traditional religious beliefs and social customs. The apparent political apathy of the people was reinforced by the conservatism of the majority of Party leaders; who, behind facades of radical Maoist rhetoric, were concerned with economic development, technological expertise, and above all, power in an increasingly bureaucratized Party apparatus.

The conservatism of both the Party and the people was in large measure due to the debacle of the Great Leap. The movement that had aroused such heady expectations of an imminent communist utopia and economic abundance had soon turned into a desperate struggle for sheer physical survival, demoralizing the masses and making most Party leaders suspicious of Mao's utopian schemes. But apart from the immediate effects of the Great Leap, long-term forces were at work moderating the radicalism of the Chinese Revolution. One factor was the very success of that revolution, or more precisely the success of the Party that had presided over it. The Chinese Communist Party, having fashioned a new social order, now had an overriding interest in maintaining that order. The Party as an institution had no interest in Mao Zedong's demand for "permanent" revolution; rather, its interest lay in the permanence of its rule, and that presupposed the stability of the society it governed. By the early 1960s the Party had grown into an enormous organization of some 20 million members, functioning with almost military precision in accordance with the Leninist organizational principles laid down by Liu Shaoqi. The Party organization had been formed originally to achieve revolutionary ends, but now the power of the organization itself seemed to have become the principal end. A noted political theorist has observed that there is "an inverse relationship between a radical movement's organizational strength and the preservation of its radicalism,"[19] and the truth of this proposition can be abundantly documented in the conservative character of the Chinese Communist Party in the years immediately preceding the Cultural Revolution.

Mao's fears that the radical spirit of the revolution was dying were thus by no means groundless. The prevalence of what he regarded as "bourgeois," "revisionist," and "feudal" ideological tendencies, while significant in themselves, seemed symptomatic of a deeper spiritual malaise and political degeneration. His awareness that he and the other surviving members of the original May Fourth generation of revolutionary leaders would soon be passing from the political scene deepened his anxieties. For this there was good reason since a period of generational change is also typically the occasion for deradicalizing change. To carry on the revolutionary enterprise, Mao looked not to his immediate political heirs, but rather, like his May Fourth predecessors, to the youth of China. The campaign to train young people as "revolutionary successors" got under way in 1964, and the hope of creating a new generation of revolutionaries was to become one of the more prominent themes of the approaching Cultural Revolution.

For Mao, socialism in China could not long survive the absence of a vital socialist vision. The overriding Maoist aim in the Great Proletarian Cultural Revolution was to spiritually re-revolutionize a once revolutionary Party and populace.

Classes and Class Struggle

Of the multitude of issues involved in the origins of the Cultural Revolution, none had more momentous implications than the nature of postrevolutionary China's social class structure. Many of the crucial ideological battles of the Cultural Revolution were fought over this issue, and it was here that Maoist theory was at once the boldest and the most ambiguous.

What actually happened in Chinese society after 1949 seems reasonably clear, at least in broad outline. The completion of land reform completed the destruction of the traditional landlord-gentry ruling class. Rich peasants as a distinct class, as well as most other significant socioeconomic differentiations among the peasantry, were largely eliminated with the collectivization campaign of 1955–56. At the same time, the urban bourgeoisie also ceased to exist as a social class, the greater portion of the compradore bourgeoisie having put itself out of business by fleeing the country in 1949. The properties of the remaining "national bourgeoisie" were nationalized during the "socialist transformation" of 1953–56, and the survivors reduced to a vanishing group of aging pensioners collecting paltry dividends from the state bonds given them in payment for their industrial and commercial enterprises. By 1956 private ownership of the means of production had been largely abolished in both town and countryside, and the exploiting classes of the old society had been eliminated. In their place came a growing army of state and Party bureaucrats, who assumed the economic functions of the old exploiting classes, although ostensibly as representatives of the workers and peasants. As in the Soviet Union, the disappearance of the old economically based ruling classes was accompanied by the emergence of a new politically based bureaucratic ruling class, albeit one in still embryonic form whose members saw themselves as "servants of the people."

The social realities of China's "socialist transformation" were clear enough, but less clear was Chinese Marxist theory, whose authors were theoretically ill-equipped to take into account the new bureaucratic phenomenon and politically disinclined to do so. At the Eighth Congress of the Chinese Communist Party in 1956, Liu Shaoqi (who delivered the main report) celebrated the elimination of the old exploiting classes and thereby proclaimed the definitive victory of socialism.[20] With capitalism thus defeated, Deng Xiaoping declared the virtual elimination of class divisions; social differences were now "only a matter of division of labor within the same class."[21] The principal contradiction in Chinese society, it was therefore concluded, was no longer between antagonistic social groups but rather "between the advanced socialist system and the backward social productive forces,"[22] a formula that was to reappear more than two decades later as a principal ideological orthodoxy of the post-Maoist era. From this it followed that the main task facing the Party in the new socialist era was no longer the promotion of class struggle but rather the development of the economy.

Classes and class struggle, to be sure, were not completely ignored. Remnants of the expropriated classes remained, as did their ideological residues, and these hangovers from the past found continuing expression in the formalization of the system of class designations and political labels applied to each citizen and duly recorded in their dossiers kept in Party and security police files. Although classes such as the bourgeoisie, landlords, and rich peasants no longer survived in social reality, the individuals (and their offspring) who once had been members of those groups were so designated in state and Party records. Officially recorded class designations, accompanied by a complex and changing system of political labels based on the Party's evaluation of an individual's political history and behavior,[23] could be emphasized or deemphasized as political needs dictated. In the euphoria of celebrating the triumph of "socialism" in 1956, class background as well as class struggle were deemphasized.

While official ideology took into account the disappearance of the old ruling classes, the 1956 Party Congress failed to address the social status of the bureaucrats who had assumed the economic functions hitherto performed by rural landlords and urban capitalists—and who increasingly came to enjoy many of the social and economic privileges of the classes they had displaced, albeit without any claims to private property. On the question of the new postrevolutionary bureaucracy, the Eighth Congress was content to issue standard admonitions against "bureaucratic practices," ritualistically advising Party members not to estrange themselves from the masses.

China in 1956, following "socialist transformation," was essentially similar to the Soviet Union in both social structure and official ideology. As in the Soviet Union, the propertied classes of the old regime had been destroyed and a new bureaucracy had become the economic manager of society, controlling (if not legally owning) state and collective property. And, like Soviet ideology, the ideology of the CCP celebrated the elimination of the exploiting classes, declared the cessation of class struggle, and ignored (or denied the existence of) a new bureaucratic ruling group. Yet in China, as in Russia, one of the more obvious social results of the revolution and the abolition of private ownership of productive property was the rise to dominance of an autonomous and privileged bureaucracy. That the power and privileges of the bureaucracy, indeed its origins, were rooted in the monopoly of political power exercised by the Leninist Party was self-evident, and it was equally evident that the leaders of Communist Parties had a strong interest in ignoring the social class status of its bureaucratic offspring. It was far more congenial to Communist bureaucrats to concern themselves with the "class designations" of individuals once members of now nonexistent social classes of the prerevolutionary past than to entertain the possibility that the new society may have produced a new ruling class. This deception was ideologically facilitated by a crude interpretation of Marxist theory which narrowly defines classes solely in terms of ownership of private property. From this there followed the universal Communist orthodoxy (first expounded by Stalin in 1936) that no new exploiting classes could arise in a society where private ownership of the means of production has been abolished.

In 1956 Mao Zedong apparently agreed with the official Party doctrine that the triumph of socialism had done away with antagonistic class divisions (save for "bourgeois remnants" and a handful of counterrevolutionaries) and thus mitigated the need for class struggle. In December 1956 he argued that "after the elimination of classes, the class struggle should not continue to be stressed as though it was being intensified, as was done by Stalin, with the result that the healthy development of socialist democracy was hampered."[24] Not until the early 1960s, after the failure of the Great Leap and the consequent waning of visions of a classless communist utopia,[25] did a now politically weakened Mao Zedong confront the problem of analyzing social class relationships in a postrevolutionary society where private property had been abolished, particularly the problem of new classes produced by the political structures of the new society itself. He emphasized more strongly than ever before the persistence of class struggle in a socialist society, especially in his Tenth Plenum speech of September 1962, from which emerged one of the dominant slogans of the forthcoming Cultural Revolution: "Never forget class struggle." He warned that the classes overthrown by the revolution were "still planning a comeback" and added an even more significant and ominous warning: "In a socialist society, new bourgeois elements may still be produced."[26]

Mao's use of the term "bourgeois" was confusing and ambiguous, but in setting forth the notion of "new bourgeois elements" produced in a socialist society, he clearly was no longer primarily concerned with the social and ideological remnants of the expropriated classes of the old society. His attention now focused on the forms of inequality being generated by the new society created by the revolution, inequalities and social relationships based on the possession of political power rather than the ownership of property. In the early 1960s he was increasingly critical of the whole system of organized inequality rooted in the elaborate hierarchy of bureaucratic ranks and status that had grown in the Party and state administration and threatened to envelop the whole of society. He lamented the degeneration of the Chinese Communist Party from a revolutionary organization of self-sacrificing fighters for justice and equality into a conservative bureaucratic apparatus. He complained that Party cadres were becoming hedonistic and corrupt, seeking only power, status, and luxuries.[27] The next generation, Mao feared, would only perpetuate the errors of its parents: "The children of cadres are a cause of discouragement. They lack experience of life and society, yet their airs are considerable and they have a great sense of superiority."[28] Mao was also highly critical of Stalin's injunction that "cadres decide everything," a slogan identified in Soviet history with the general institutionalization of inequality.[29]

In the years immediately preceding the Cultural Revolution, Mao arrived at a conclusion that no other Marxist in power had hitherto been willing to entertain. A socialist society, he now believed, could generate a new class of exploiters; the main barriers to the "transition to socialism" were not the bourgeois residues of the past but rather the bureaucrats of the present, the onetime revolutionaries whom the revolution had transformed into rulers and who by virtue of their political power controlled the new society and appropriated much of the fruits of social labor in the process. On occasion Mao was quite explicit, indeed blunt, in setting forth this view, as when (in 1965) he condemned "the bureaucratic class" as a class "in sharp opposition to the working class and the poor and lower-middle peasants," as those becoming "bourgeois elements sucking the blood of the workers."[30] Nor did he hesitate to identify the site and source of these "new bourgeois elements" or their leaders. They were, he charged on the eve of the Cultural Revolution, "those people in positions of authority within the Party who take the capitalist road." What seemed at the time to be pure ideological bombast proved to be a remarkably accurate prognosis of the future of Chinese Communist society.

Mao Zedong was not the first to recognize that a socialist revolution could produce a new exploiting class of bureaucratic rulers. He was preceded by Max Weber, Leon Trotsky, and Milovan Djilas, among a good many others. What was unique about Mao's notion of a new bureaucratic ruling class was not his analysis of the phenomenon, which was theoretically ill-developed in any event, but rather the fact that the idea was put forth by the leader of a Communist state. It had not happened before, and it is not likely to happen again. The notion has been a highly heretical and politically explosive one in official Marxist-Leninist ideologies, calling into question the legitimacy of the Communist regimes these ideologies were designed to rationalize. From Mao's perspective, however, China's bureaucrats did indeed take on the appearance of a new exploiting class, using political power to appropriate a good share of the surplus produced by the workers and peasants. They had a vested interest not in private property but rather in "public ownership" by a state that they controlled, and from which they derived social and economic benefits for themselves and their families. They owed their status and privileges, however paltry in most cases, not to ownership of property but rather (in Marx's phrase) to their status as the de facto "owners of the conditions of production." In Mao's eyes, they were, or at least were becoming, a propertyless but functional bourgeoisie.

While Mao clearly recognized this fundamental and elemental reality of postrevolutionary "socialist societies," and on occasion expressed it, he ultimately shrank from the political implications of identifying China's bureaucrats as a new ruling class. To do so would have demanded a political revolution and not simply a cultural one, in effect, the violent overthrow of the existing Communist state and not merely its spiritual reformation. Although Mao characterized the Cultural Revolution as the most "profound" of revolutions that would "touch men's very souls," he knew well the difference between a movement for spiritual revitalization and a real revolution. No doubt there were emotional inhibitions as well as political ones. The bureaucrats with whom Mao had become so bitterly disillusioned were, after all, his onetime revolutionary comrades and cadres.[31] To condemn them *in toto* would be to condemn the revolution he had led and the new society he had been so instrumental in creating. He preferred to believe that most could be reformed and ideologically remolded, to become again what they once had been. For all its verbal thunder and fury, the Cultural Revolution was thus intended more as a reformist than a revolutionary movement—and a nonviolent one. That it came to involve massive violence had more to do with the condition of Chinese society than the state of Mao's mind.

Having drawn back from the implications of the view that China was under the domination of a new bureaucratic ruling class, Mao eventually arrived at a conception of class based on the criterion of individual political behavior. One's class status was to be determined not so much by such reasonably objective criteria as economic status or political position but rather by more subjective factors: the evaluation of one's ideological proclivities, level of "political consciousness," and political activities. What decided who belonged to which class in a socialist society, Mao concluded, was not economic or political position, past or present, but rather one's "class standpoint."[32] This definition had the advantage of retaining the notion that classes and class struggle persist in a socialist society (including "new bourgeois elements") while superseding the old system of class designations, which after 1956 no longer conformed to social reality—but without condemning the Party bureaucracy *in toto* as an enemy class. It was a conception of class in keeping with Mao's long-standing proclivity to define class less in terms of a group's (or individual's) place in the socioeconomic structure than by a political evaluation of their potential for revolutionary action or, as in the 1960s, for counterrevolutionary action. But it was also a conception of class whose subjective criteria easily lent themselves to arbitrary classifications of political foes as "class enemies" and to a greater concern with the political behavior of individuals than of social groups.

Chinese Communist ideology thus conveyed three different theories of class on the eve of the Cultural Revolution: first, the image of China's pre-1956 social class structure, inherited from the old regime, which lingered on in the official system of "class designations"; second, the theory of a new bureaucratic ruling class generated by the new society itself, a notion abortively put forward by Mao and pursued by some of his more radical followers;[33] and third, the notion that class status was determined by individual political consciousness and behavior. The first had conservative political implications, sanctifying the post-1956 sociopolitical order, and was naturally favored by most Party officials and cadres. The second implied the necessity of a revolution against the existing political order. The third, essentially reformist in nature, was the one held by Mao at the beginning of the Cultural Revolution, and it supported his belief that 95 percent of the cadres were basically good and that the Party as a whole could be politically and ideologically reformed and purged of bourgeois influences, but only through the radical means of mass mobilization and class struggle.

Yet all three versions of class—conservative, revolutionary, and reformist—had become part of the political consciousness of the Chinese people, who were told that the Cultural Revolution involved an acute class struggle between the "bourgeoisie" and the "proletariat." But how was one to identify "the bourgeoisie"? Against whom was the class struggle to be directed? The conflicting and ambiguous views of class and class struggle emanating from Beijing over the years offered no clear answers to these questions. Or, rather, they suggested different answers, depending on which version of class analysis one adopted. It is hardly surprising that each of the multitude of political groups and actors in the Cultural Revolution adopted the version best suited to its particular political and social interests. The theoretical confusion over the matter of class and class struggle would contribute to the chaos into which the Cultural Revolution soon degenerated and to the indiscriminate persecution of groups and individuals who could all too easily be labeled "class enemies" on a variety of theoretical and political grounds.[34]

NOTES

1. The official Chinese Party verdict on Mao and the Cultural Revolution is set forth in "Resolution on Certain Questions in the History of Our Party Since the Founding of the People's Republic of China," Sixth Plenary Session of the 11th Central Committee of the Communist Party of China, June 27, 1981, *Beijing Review,* July 6, 1981, pp. 10–39.

2. Harry Harding, "Reappraising the Cultural Revolution," *The Wilson Quarterly,* Autumn 1980, p. 137.

3. Arif Dirlik, "The Predicament of Marxist Revolutionary Consciousness," *Modern China,* 9, No. 2 (April 1983): 188.

4. On the New Culture Movement of 1915–19, see Chapter 2 above, especially pp. 14–16.

5. The concept of "cultural revolution" received special emphasis in Mao's seminal 1940 treatise "On New Democracy," where he argued that the building of a new "revolutionary culture" was essential for political success. *Selected Works of Mao Tse-tung* (Peking: Foreign Languages Press, 1967), Vol. II, pp. 339–84. "Destruction before construction," one of the maxims of the Cultural Revolution of 1966, was also set forth in this essay with respect to the need to sweep away the culture of the past, echoing the injunction of Chen Duxiu and his New Culture Movement followers of the second decade of the century.

6. For a fuller discussion of the differences between Lenin's and Mao's conceptions, see Maurice Meisner, "Iconoclasm and Cultural Revolution in China and Russia," in Abbott Gleason, Peter Kenez, and Richard Stites (eds.), *Bolshevik Culture* (Bloomington: Indiana University Press, 1985), pp. 279–93. Portions of the present discussion are drawn from this essay.

7. V. I. Lenin, "On Cooperation," in V. I. Lenin, *Selected Works* (Moscow: Progress Publishers, 1967), Vol. III, p. 764.

8. Cited in Richard Stites, "Iconoclastic Currents in the Russian Revolution: Destroying and Preserving the Past," in Gleason, Kenez, and Stites (eds.) *Bolshevik Culture,* p. 17. Not all Russian Marxists shared Lenin's views on the economic prerequisites for cultural change. Some Bolshevik advocates of "cultural revolution," such as Alexander Bogdanov and some of the leaders of the "proletarian culture" movement, gave primacy to the factors of "culture" and "consciousness" in a manner that is remarkably similar to Mao's later conceptions. On Bogdanov's views on the role of culture in social and economic development, see James C. McClelland, "Utopianism versus Revolutionary Heroism in Bolshevik Policy: The Proletarian Culture Debate," *Slavic Review,* 39, No. 3 (September 1980): 403–25.

9. As, for example, in his critique of the Stalinist pattern of development written a few years before the Cultural Revolution: "Reading Notes on the Soviet Union's 'Political Economy,'" *Mao Tse-tung ssu-hsiang wan-sui,* p. 182.

10. On the relationship between socialism and backwardness, Mao was bluntly explicit in rejecting Lenin's views—and conventional Marxist teachings in general. In the early 1960s Mao wrote: "Lenin said: 'The more backward the country, the more difficult its transition from capitalism to socialism.' Now it seems that this way of speaking is incorrect. As a matter of fact, the more backward the economy, the easier, not the more difficult, the transition from capitalism to socialism." "Reading Notes on the Soviet Union's 'Political Economy,'" *Mao Tse-tung ssu-hsiang wan-sui,* pp. 333–34.

11. For a fascinating essay on Lenin's last somber views on the bureaucratic degeneration of the Bolshevik Revolution, which he tended to blame on the Bolsheviks' low level of civilization, their lack of *kulturnost,* see Isaac Deutscher, "The Moral Dilemmas of Lenin," in Deutscher, *Ironies of History* (London: Oxford University Press, 1966), pp. 167–73.

12. *Mao Tse-tung ssu-hsiang wan-sui,* p. 240.

13. *Hongqi (Red Flag),* June 1, 1958, pp. 3–4. English version in *Peking Review,* June 10, 1958.

14. As formulated by Marx in an oft-quoted passage that expressed a central notion of the materialist conception of history: "Men make their own history, but they do not make it just as they please; they do not make it under circumstances chosen by themselves, but under circumstances directly encountered, given and transmitted from the past. The tradition of all dead

generations weighs like a nightmare on the brain of the living." *The Eighteenth Brumaire of Louis Bonaparte,* Marx and Engels, *Selected Works,* Vol. I, p. 225.

15. André Malraux, *Anti-Memoirs* (New York: Holt, Rinehart & Winston, 1968), pp. 373–74.

16. "On Khrushchev's Phony Communism and Its Historical Lessons for the World," *Peking Review,* July 17, 1964, pp. 7–28. One of the major documents in the Sino-Soviet dispute, and probably largely authored by Mao, the treatise was originally published as a joint editorial by *People's Daily* and the main Party theoretical journal *Red Flag.*

17. Contract workers, drawn from the urban unemployed and from under-employed peasants in villages close to urban centers, were hired for limited periods to work in factories or on construction or other projects. Unlike regular state-employed workers, they enjoyed no job security or social benefits. They were (and are) in fact a *lumpenproletariat* and constitute what Marx called "the reserve army of unemployed."

18. John Gardner, "Educated Youth and Urban-Rural Inequalities, 1958–66," in John W. Lewis (ed.), *The City in Communist China* (Stanford, Calif.: Stanford University Press, 1971), pp. 235–86.

19. Robert C. Tucker, *The Marxian Revolutionary Idea* (New York: Norton, 1969), p. 187.

20. Liu Shao-ch'i [Liu Shaoqi], "Political Report of the CCP Central Committee," *Eighth National Congress of the Communist Party of China* (Peking: Foreign Languages Press, 1956), Vol. I, p. 15.

21. Teng Hsiao-p'ing [Deng Xiaoping], "Report on the Revision of the Constitution of the CCP," *ibid.,* p. 313.

22. "Resolution on the Political Report of the CCP Central Committee to the Eighth National Congress of the Party," *ibid.*

23. For a perceptive discussion of the system of political labels and its relationship to the system of class designations, see Richard Curt Kraus, *Class Conflict in Chinese Socialism* (New York: Columbia University Press, 1981).

24. "More on the Historical Experience of the Dictatorship of the Proletariat," an editorial originally published in *People's Daily* on December 29, 1956. In his April 1956 speech "On the Ten Great Relationships," Mao barely mentioned either classes or class struggle. Several years later, in the early 1960s, Mao was critical of Stalin (who had made contradictory pronouncements on classes and class struggle, as political needs dictated) for having neglected class struggle.

25. As Richard Kraus has pointed out, the Great Leap, although a pristine expression of Maoism, was relatively unconcerned with classes and class struggle—partly, perhaps, because it promised to bring about the transition from socialism to a classless communist society. See Kraus, *Class Conflict in Chinese Socialism,* pp. 65–66. On the Maoist view of class and on the whole question of classes in both theory and reality in the People's Republic, Kraus's volume is a gold mine of information and insight.

26. Mao Tse-tung, "Talk at an Enlarged Central Work Conference," January 30, 1962, and "Speech at the Tenth Plenum of the Eighth Central Committee," September 24, 1962, in Stuart R. Schram (ed.), *Mao Tse-tung Unrehearsed: Talks and Letters, 1956–71* (Harmondsworth, Middlesex, England: 1974): pp. 170–75 and 188–96.

27. Mao Tse-tung, "Twenty Manifestations of Bureaucracy," in "Chairman Mao's Selected Writings," JPRS, No. 49829, February 12, 1970, pp. 42–43.

28. Mao Tse-tung, "Reading Notes on the Soviet Text 'Political Economy,'" translated by Moss Roberts in Mao Tse-tung, *A Critique of Soviet Economics* (New York: Monthly Review Press, 1977), p. 71.

29. As Mao wrote in 1962: "Stalin's book from first to last says nothing about the superstructure. It is not concerned with people; it considers things, not people. . . . They [the Soviets] believe that technology decides everything, that cadres decide everything, speaking only of 'expert,' never of 'red,' only of the cadres, never of the masses." Mao Tse-tung, "Critique of Stalin's *Economic Problems of Socialism in the USSR,*" in *A Critique of Soviet Economics,* p. 135.

30. Mao, "Selections from Chairman Mao," JPRS, No. 49826, p. 23.

31. See Kraus, *Class Conflict in Chinese Socialism,* p. 150.

32. For a detailed analysis of Mao's conception of class as political behavior and its relationship to the Marxist theory of class see Kraus, chapter 5, pp. 89–114.

33. Although held and theoretically elaborated by some during the "cultural revolution decade" and after, it was not until the last year of his life (in 1975–76) that Mao returned to the notion of a bureaucratic ruling class. By then, however, he had no time left to act upon it.

34. For an unusually perceptive and informative analysis of the practical political results of the clash between conflicting theories of class during the Cultural Revolution, written by a one-time Red Guard, see Weiran Lin, "An Abortive Chinese Enlightenment—The Cultural Revolution and Class Theory," Ph.D. dissertation, Department of History, University of Wisconsin-Madison, 1996.

18

The Great Proletarian Cultural Revolution, 1966–1969

T HE FIRST PUBLIC RUMBLINGS of the "Great Proletarian Cultural Revolution" were heard in November 1965, when a minor literary critic, Yao Wenyuan (later condemned as one of the "Gang of Four"), wrote a critique of the popular play *Hai Jui Dismissed from Office*. Written five years before by the historian and Party official Wu Han, the allegorical drama set in the Ming dynasty celebrated the heroism of a virtuous official deposed by a tyrannical emperor for having protested the seizure of peasant lands by rapacious landlords and corrupt bureaucrats. It took little imagination on the part of the politically astute Chinese reader to identify the tyrannical emperor as Mao Zedong, the virtuous official as Peng Dehuai, and the confiscation of peasant lands as an allusion to the policies of the Great Leap, which Peng had vehemently opposed, resulting in his political demise in 1959.

Wu Han's play was one of many anti-Maoist historical allegories and political satires written during the "bitter years" following the collapse of the Great Leap. The writers were not simply isolated intellectuals, but people who enjoyed the patronage of Mao's most prominent political foes, including Liu Shaoqi, Deng Xiaoping, and Peng Zhen. Among the more noteworthy examples of this literary genre were several series of essays entitled "Evening Chats at Yenshan" and "Notes from Three-Family Village," in which it was suggested that Mao, among other failings, was an amnesiac who had forgotten his promises and suffered from a severe mental disorder.[1]

Most of the satirical attacks ceased with Mao's Tenth Plenum speech of September 1962, the launching of the Socialist Education Movement, and the general tightening of the political-ideological reins. At the time Mao, aware of the intimate tie between literature and politics in China, sarcastically remarked that "the use of novels for anti-Party activity is a great invention" and entirely without sarcasm went on to observe that "anyone wanting to overthrow a political regime must create public opinion and do some preparatory ideological work."[2] While open literary attacks on Mao ended in 1962, they were not forgotten, despite Mao's alleged amnesia. It was at Mao's personal direction (and with the assistance of Mao's wife, Jiang Qing) that Yao Wenyuan's critique of Wu Han was published in November 1965. Not only did Wu Han distort the Ming historical record, Yao charged, but the play's message of "returning the land" to the peasants offered ideological support for those who wanted to "demolish the people's communes and to restore the criminal rule of the landlords and rich peasants." All of this was no less than "the focal point of bourgeois opposition to the dictatorship of the proletariat."[3] The opposition, as events would soon reveal, was more Leninist than bourgeois.

Although Maoists later dated the beginning of the Cultural Revolution with the appearance of Yao's article, it seemed a matter of little significance at the time. Nor did anything exceptional occur during the debates in literary and ideological circles that ensued over the next six months. If the Cultural Revolution was under way, it seemed to be confined mostly to academic and literary circles.

But Mao was bent on more than just another ideological cleansing of the cultural realm. Beneath the symptoms of cultural and ideological decay he saw lurking much graver social and political maladies, which the established Party apparatus seemed little inclined to remedy. Indeed, he had already identified the principal enemy of socialism in China as "those people in authority *within the Party* who are taking the capitalist road." At the January 1965 Politburo meeting from which Mao had emerged with this politically ominous thesis, he had prevailed on Party leaders to undertake a "cultural revolution." Delegated to implement that still vague and seemingly innocuous concept was a "Five-Man Group" chaired by Peng Zhen, the fifth-ranking member of the Politburo, head of the Beijing Party organization and mayor of the capital city as well. Of the five, only one, Kang Sheng, could be counted as a supporter of Mao. The Group was dormant until the November appearance of Yao Wenyuan's article. Then Peng Zhen was moved to action, but only to blunt the political thrust of the Maoist attack. In February 1966 Peng censured Yao and other Maoists for "treating a purely academic question in political terms." Despite the obvious political issues involved, Peng and the Party apparatus managed to keep the debate confined to largely academic and historical questions well into the spring of 1966. In the meantime, Mao disappeared from public view, having embarked in November 1965 on a six-month tour of the provinces to rally support for his policies.

With Mao's return to Beijing in the spring, events began to unfold at a dizzying pace. The attacks against Wu Han and other literary-political foes of Mao—the "Black Gang," as they were called—became more shrill and increasingly political. The army, now more firmly under the command of Lin Biao following the purge of its Chief of Staff, Luo Ruiqing, earlier in the year (the former secret police head was accused of having given priority to military affairs rather than to the thoughts of Mao), declared itself "the mainstay of the dictatorship of the proletariat" and announced that it would play an important role in the unfolding Cultural Revolution. Editorials in *Liberation Army Daily* in early May demanded not only a purge of "anti-socialist elements" in cultural circles but the elimination of "right-opportunist elements within the Party." On May 16 a directive drafted by Mao (and issued in the name of the Party Central Committee) dissolved the Five-Man Group, condemned Peng Zhen for having obstructed the Cultural Revolution, charged that "representatives of the bourgeoisie" had infiltrated the Party at all levels (not excluding the Central Committee itself), and were preparing to establish a "dictatorship of the bourgeoisie." "Persons like Khrushchev," the document ominously warned, "are still nestling beside us."[4]

The Cultural Revolution was thus quickly turning explicitly political, and the first high-ranking Party leader to fall was Peng Zhen. It was soon revealed that Peng and his followers had been dismissed from their official posts and that the Beijing Party committee and municipal government had been reorganized around loyal Maoists, headed by Li Xuefeng. A wholesale purge of the propaganda and cultural apparatus in the capital immediately followed; the most notable victims were Lu Dingyi, chief of the Party's propaganda department (who also controlled the authoritative *People's Daily*), and Zhou Yang, China's longtime literary and cultural czar. Under the direction of the newly created "Cultural Revolution Group" Maoists now controlled Beijing and the country's principal organs of communication. The Cultural Revolution Group, headed by Jiang Qing and Chen Boda and composed mostly of radical intellectuals, was a quasi-official agency established to guide the Cultural Revolution, and in the process it assumed many of the powers of the Party Central Committee and Politburo.

But Mao's purpose was not simply to achieve ascendancy in Beijing. The Maoist aim was to bring about the total reformation of the country's political structure and the social life of the nation—and, moreover, the spiritual transformation of the people. Indeed, the factors of revolutionary spirit and consciousness were regarded as decisive in determining the eventual outcome of what was now being described as a "life-and-death struggle" between socialism and capitalism. The underlying Maoist assumption in the Cultural Revolution was that the existing state and Party apparatus was dominated by "bourgeois ideology" and thus was producing capitalist-type socioeconomic relationships in society at large. Only by raising the political consciousness of the masses, revitalizing the socialist spirit and ideals of the revolution, and refashioning a state structure guided by "proletarian ideology" could the danger of a regression to capitalism be forestalled. And by both Maoist preference and objective political necessity, those aims could be accomplished only by the mobilization of the people for Maoist-inspired revolutionary action. In the course of revolutionary struggle, it was believed, the people would spiritually transform themselves while transforming their objective social world. What Mao called for was no less than a "profound" revolution "that touches people to their very souls." If Marx believed that social being determines consciousness, Mao seemed to believe that it was consciousness as such (mediated through political action and the state apparatus) that ultimately determines social being.

The Red Guards

The spontaneous mass movement from below was not long in coming, although it came with the generous assistance of Mao's Cultural Revolution Group and Lin Biao's army. University and middle school students were the first to respond to the Maoist call to rebel against established authority—some genuinely inspired by the announced ideals and goals of the Cultural Revolution, others in pursuit of their particular social interests in the academic and political hierarchies, and still others organized as "rebels" by the regular Party apparatus to deflect the radical thrust of the Maoist attack. That diversity of intermingling motives and aims was to result in a youth movement that was not only massive but also extraordinarily complex and fractionalized.

The chaos that soon engulfed the schools was signaled on May 25, when students at Beijing University led by a young philosophy instructor, Nie

Yuanzi, posted on the campus walls a manifesto denouncing the university president for having suppressed student discussion of the Wu Han affair and calling upon "all revolutionary intellectuals" to "go into battle." The first of the "big-character posters," (which were to become the main form of popular political communication during the Cultural Revolution) was immediately torn down by Party authorities, and those involved in the incident were duly punished. But a week later, when Mao hailed the poster as "the manifesto of the Beijing commune of the 1960s" (predicting, in apparent reference to the Paris Commune of 1871, that China soon would see "a wholly new form of state structure") and had it broadcast on Beijing radio and published in *People's Daily,* rebel student groups were organized with extraordinary rapidity and in bewildering variety at schools throughout the country. Encouraged by a June 18 decree postponing university entrance exams for six months in order to refashion the entire educational system, student activists mounted political—and sometimes physical—attacks against school administrators, teachers, and especially school Party committees.

The student rebels not only fought political and educational authorities, they also soon became locked in battle with each other. For at the very beginning of the student turmoil in early June, Liu Shaoqi hastily dispatched Party work teams to the campuses in an effort to keep the burgeoning movement under the Party's organizational control. The work teams organized "rebel" student groups, led primarily by the sons and daughters of Party officials, which supported the school Party committees and attempted to deflect the Cultural Revolution attack away from the Maoist target, the "power holders," to "bourgeois authorities" and those with "bad" class backgrounds. "Bourgeois authorities" were most obviously intellectuals, individual professors, teachers, writers, and others who were virtually defenseless against political attack. Contrary to the current version of events, the terrible persecution of intellectuals during the Cultural Revolution was begun not by Maoist radicals but rather by Party-organized "rebels" intent on protecting Party bureaucrats from Maoist assaults. One of the first victims was Gao Yisheng, the president of the Steel Institute in Beijing, who was driven to suicide by the local Party work team in July 1966.[5] Many others were to suffer similar fates over the months and years that followed. Intellectuals, the most vulnerable group in Chinese society and the most conveniently identifiable as "bourgeois," would be indiscriminately attacked from virtually all political quarters over the course of the Cultural Revolution, but at the outset the principal culprits in this unsavory business were groups operating under the sponsorship of the established Party apparatus, which was itself under Maoist attack.

Besides persecuting intellectuals, student groups organized by Party work teams attacked fellow students with "bad" class backgrounds—the sons and daughters of former landlords, former rich peasants, and former capitalists, and those whose parents were intellectuals. They found it politically useful as well as socially advantageous to perpetuate those outmoded class designations and to invent as well the "bloodline theory" (or the theory of "natural redness"), by which they claimed to have inherited the revolutionary virtues of their once revolutionary parents, who were now mostly officials in the Party-state apparatus. The political intentions behind that arcane "class analysis" and behind the attack on intellectuals in general were of course the same: to protect the existing Party machine.

One of the ironies of China's postrevolutionary history, fully apparent during the Cultural Revolution, is that the revolutionaries drawn from the oppressed classes under the old regime tended to be socially and politically conservative under the new order (increasingly so as the years went on), whereas the social and political radicals in "liberated" China tended to be the children of families who made up the privileged classes in pre-1949 China. It takes no great sociological insight to unravel the paradox. The onetime revolutionaries, who came mostly from the poorer peasantry and the working class, were, along with their children, favored for political positions, educational opportunities, and employment after 1949. They enjoyed an unaccustomed high social status under the new regime. The children of former capitalists, ex-landlords, and intellectuals, on the other hand, labored under various forms of social, economic, and political discrimination—and nowhere more than in the educational system. Whereas those who could claim lowly class origins (at least those among them with access to political power) had a conservative stake in the postrevolutionary order and its new inequalities, the offspring of the former ruling classes were the new underprivileged. It is hardly surprising that the latter responded so enthusiastically to radical Maoist critiques of bureaucratic privilege and calls for greater equality, while the former rallied to the defense of the Party and channeled their "revolutionary" energies into assaults against the offspring of the formerly privileged social classes. The political divisions that appeared in the student movement in the summer of 1966—which were to remain throughout the Cultural Revolution and beyond—were eminently rational expressions of conflicting social interests, however irrational the student movement became in other respects. Students from worker and peasant families whose fathers were not Party cadres and who had a disproportionately low representation in the middle schools and universities tended to divide more or less equally among the radical and conservative "rebel" groups.[6]

The struggle, verbal and often physical, between vaguely "Maoist" and "Liuist" student groups continued through much of the summer of 1966, with Party work teams largely successful in manipulating events in their favor. Both groups loudly shouted Maoist slogans and proclaimed their loyalty to Mao and his "thought," but they interpreted the Chairman's thoughts differently to suit their own purposes, especially his thoughts about social class. It was not until late July that Mao, over the opposition of Liu Shaoqi, ordered the withdrawal of the work teams from the schools, condemning the previous "fifty days of White Terror." Student rebels were now free to organize themselves solely on the basis of the authority of Mao's thought, unhampered by the dictates of the Party organization. They quickly did so, reincarnating themselves as Red Guards, but not without reproducing in their new guise the social and political divisions that had marked the student movement of June and July.

The name "Red Guards" occupies a hallowed place in the Marxist revolutionary tradition. The original Red Guards were the armed Russian workers and soldiers who seized power in the Bolshevik Revolution of 1917. In the Chinese Communist revolutionary movement during the 1930s and 1940s, the local peasant militias who supported the soldiers of the regular Red Army were called Red Guards. In early August of 1966, young students wearing armbands bearing the characters for "Red Guard" appeared on the streets of Beijing. Within a few weeks, and with the encouragement of Maoist leaders in the capital, Red Guard groups were organized at virtually every university and middle school in the land. Rallying under the slogans "it is justified to rebel" and "destruction before construction," rebellious youth numbering in the millions soon were marching in the streets of cities and towns throughout the country, conveying the Maoist injunction to destroy all "ghosts and monsters." They flocked to Beijing to receive the Chairman's personal blessing, which was bestowed in dramatic fashion on August 18, when a million youths crowded into the square beneath the Gate of Heavenly Peace, the symbolic site of revolutionary upheaval since the May Fourth incident of 1919. Mao appeared atop the gate at sunrise in a godlike posture and solemnly donned a red armband, thereby becoming the "Supreme Commander" of the Red Guards as well as their "great teacher," "great leader," and "great helmsman." A month earlier the seventy-two-year-old Chairman had performed another dramatic act in his self-deification, announcing his political supremacy as well as his physical virility through a much-publicized swimming exhibition in the Yangzi, reportedly covering a distance of nine miles in sixty-five minutes.

Both the deified presence of an aging Mao and the rebellious energies of the young Red Guards were essential for carrying out the program of the Cultural Revolution, for the latter were the chosen instruments to implement the various "directives" and "instructions" issued by the former. The program itself was set forth in "Sixteen Articles" approved at a heated twelve-day meeting of the Party Central Committee (the Eleventh Plenum) at the beginning of August, from which many non-Maoist Party leaders were excluded, their places taken by Red Guard representatives. The "Sixteen Articles" explicitly defined the purpose of the movement as the overthrow of "those within the Party who are in authority and taking the capitalist road." A second, closely related purpose was to destroy what soon was known as "the four olds." "Although the bourgeoisie has been overthrown," the document read, "it is still trying to use the old ideas, culture, customs, and habits of the exploiting classes to corrupt the masses, capture their minds, and endeavor to stage a comeback."[7] The "bourgeoisie" was thus to be identified as those deemed to be carriers of "old ideas," while "old ideas" were all ideas not conforming to "Mao Zedong Thought," which had now replaced the organized authority of the Party as the sole source of political legitimacy.

As it had been made abundantly clear that the danger of a "bourgeois restoration" resided primarily within the Party itself and among its highest-ranking leaders, the tasks of cleansing the Party and eliminating bourgeois influences in society as a whole plainly were not to be left to the Party in the fashion of earlier rectification campaigns. Rather, the cultural revolutionary means was "boldly to arouse the masses." Time and again it was proclaimed that "the only method is for the masses to liberate themselves, and any method of doing things in their stead must not be used." It was stipulated that the agents for stimulating the mass movement were to be the Red Guards, whom their elders hailed as those "large numbers of revolutionary young people, previously unknown [who] have become courageous and daring pathbreakers." The burgeoning of the "pathbreakers" was facilitated, in turn, by the newly proclaimed principle of "the free mobilization of the masses," which had now replaced mass mobilization under the customary auspices of Party work teams.

If all of this had not given regular Party leaders enough cause for anxiety, the "Sixteen Articles" by no means made it entirely certain that the ultimate political result of the revolution from below would be simply a rectified Communist Party in its old Leninist form. It was hinted that in the future political power would be reorganized more in accordance with Marx's description of the Paris Commune than with Lenin's concept of the vanguard party. The new political organizations that had come into being early in the upheaval, the "cultural revolutionary groups, committees, and congresses," it was declared, "should not be temporary organizations but permanent, standing mass organizations." They were proper organizational forms not only for schools and economic enterprises but also for government organs in cities and villages. It was further stated that "it is necessary to institute a system of general elections, like that of the Paris Commune." Indeed, Mao personally endorsed the original Marxist model of proletarian dictatorship, having proclaimed in July that Nie Yuanzi's celebrated big-character poster was the "manifesto of the Chinese Paris Commune" of the twentieth century. Its significance, he added, surpassed that of the Paris Commune itself.[8]

While the leaders of the Cultural Revolution left ambiguous their vision of the new political order—and the place of the Party in it—there was nothing ambiguous (although there was much that was astonishing) about Mao Zedong's call for the masses to rebel against the existing Party and its organizations, albeit a call made in the name of the Party and its Chairman. On August 5 Mao had put his own big-character poster on the door of the room where the Central Committee was meeting, urging his student followers to "bombard the headquarters" of his Party opponents who, he alleged, were exercising a "bourgeois dictatorship." Three days later the "Sixteen Articles" was publicly promulgated as the charter of the Cultural Revolution. On August 18 the Red Guards, presumably guided by the thoughts of Mao and acting in accordance with his personal instructions, were anointed as the vanguard of the rebellion against Party and state authorities. At the same time, Lin Biao, now described as Mao's "closest comrade in arms," was informally named the Chairman's successor. From then on, the Maoist attack was directed against the entire Party apparatus and most of its highest-ranking leaders, especially Liu Shaoqi, now variously referred to as "the leading person in authority taking the capitalist road" and "China's Khrushchev,"[9] and Deng Xiaoping, the Party General Secretary, now known as "the second leading person in authority taking the capitalist road." In official publications, Liu Shaoqi was not referred to by name (although his name appeared in wall posters often enough) until the autumn of 1968, when China's premier Leninist was branded a "counterrevolutionary" and formally expelled from the Party he had devoted his life to organizing. But after November 1966 Liu was no longer seen in public; placed under arrest, he died of pneumonia in 1969 (it was revealed a decade later) while being transported from Beijing to Hefei. With the political demise of the Chairman of the People's Republic in late 1966, such ceremonial functions as China's head of state performed during the Cultural Revolution were assumed by Soong Qingling, widow of Sun Yat-sen and Vice Chairperson of the People's Republic.

What makes this so remarkable a phenomenon in the history of post-revolutionary societies is that the call for rebellion against the existing political order came from those who had built that order. It came from some among the veterans of the revolution—and Mao was certainly the most venerable and venerated of the veterans—who had created state and Party institutions they now had come to regard as obstacles to, rather than as instruments of, the revolutionary social changes they sought. But the more important question about the Cultural Revolution is not so much why Mao issued his rebellious call but rather why and how so many tens of millions of ordinary Chinese citizens responded to it.

. . .

Following the spectacular August 18 rally in Tiananmen Square, the Red Guards took to the streets of Beijing and other cities in a frenzied crusade against "the four olds." They did so in far more violent and indiscriminate fashion than their elders anticipated or wanted. Although the "Sixteen Articles" had enjoined them to "put daring above everything else," it also cautioned that "contradictions among the people" were to be resolved "by reasoning, not by coercion or force" and that even "anti-socialist rightists" were to be "given a chance to turn over a new leaf." It was further stipulated that "both the cultural revolution and production [should be carried on] without one hampering the other." Indeed, it was emphasized that the movement aimed to revolutionize popular consciousness in order to increase production, not disrupt it. But in their initial assaults the Red Guards paid little heed to such distinctions and restraints. The young rebels acted more in the mystically anarchistic spirit of an early Red Guard manifesto, which proclaimed that the "supernatural powers" and "magic" derived from "Mao Zedong's great invincible thought" were to be used "to turn the old world upside down, smash it to pieces, pulverize it, create chaos and make a tremendous mess, the bigger the better."[10]

During the remaining chaotic months of 1966 millions of Red Guards, carrying portraits of Mao (who was "the reddest sun in our hearts," they chanted) and waving copies of the Chairman's "little red book" (to which some attributed semimagical properties), marched through the streets of the cities and traveled over the country and through the countryside in a campaign against all symbols of the feudal past and the bourgeois influences of the present. Museums and homes were ransacked, and old books and works of art were destroyed. Everything from ancient Confucian texts to modern recordings of Beethoven were sought out and thrown into dustbins. New revolutionary names were pasted on street signs and buildings, along with portraits of the Chairman and his sayings. Hapless citizens wearing Western-style clothes or Hong Kong-style haircuts were attacked and humiliated, as were those possessing old Buddhist and Daoist relics. The Cultural Revolution soon began to destroy people as well as culture. As the Red Guard assault moved from uprooting the "four olds" to attacking "power-holders," Party officials and administrative cadres were "arrested" and paraded through the streets in duncecaps, forced to confess their "crimes" at public rallies, and often physically as well as psychologically abused at struggle sessions. Not a few were beaten to death or driven to suicide. The brunt of the attack was borne by intellectuals, who were the most vulnerable and the most defenseless. One of the earliest victims was Lao She, China's most renowned playwright and the author of the famed *Rickshaw Boy*. He was repeatedly ordered to "study" and "struggle" meetings by middle school Red Guards; his house was pillaged and his books burned. Finally, the body of the sixty-seven-year-old author was found in Taiping Lake near Beijing in late August of 1966, a suicide by drowning, it was reported.[11]

Red Guard activities did not go wholly unchallenged. Bloody battles sometimes ensued when the young militants entered factories and communes and were confronted by rival rebel groups of workers and peasants. Even bloodier battles were fought among the Red Guards themselves, for the social and political divisions that marked the student movement from the outset became deeper and more bitter as time went on, escalating into a seemingly endless cycle of violence and revenge between "conservative" and "radical" factions within the movement. The ranks of the Red Guards swelled, and the violence and factionalism of the movement were exacerbated, as increasing numbers of urban youths who had been sent to work in the countryside in earlier years returned to the cities to participate in the Cultural Revolution. Denied educational and employment opportunities in the cities, they were the most discontented of all youth, harboring particularly bitter grievances against the Party and especially against the children of Party cadres and PLA officers who managed to exempt themselves from *xiafang* and enjoyed preferential treatment in the universities. The "returned youth" usually joined the more radical Red Guard organizations.[12]

The older cultural revolutionaries in Beijing simultaneously attempted to restrain and encourage the actions of their youthful "pathbreakers." The Red Guards were exhorted not to use force; ordered not to interfere with the productive activities of workers and peasants; admonished for indiscriminate attacks on local and provincial Party organizations rather than on individual "capitalist-roaders"; and criticized for fomenting differences among the masses rather than uniting with them in common struggle. Futile efforts were made to bring the swelling (and increasingly factionalized) movement under some sort of central control. At the same time, the PLA was ordered to assist the Red Guards, who were given free use of railroads, buses, and trucks and provided with food and lodging wherever they went. Such privileges hardly were conducive to inhibiting the wanderlust of the Red Guards, nor did the announcement at the end of October that schools would remain closed for the academic year do anything to dampen their rebellious proclivities. Before the year was out, some 12,000,000 Red Guards had journeyed to Beijing to see (and be seen by) Chairman Mao. The massive rallies beneath the Gate of Heavenly Peace (the eighth and last of which took place November 26), and the magnetic presence of Mao, did nothing to restrain the movement, especially since the speeches of Lin Biao and others conveyed more praise of their revolutionary zeal than criticism of their "leftist excesses." The Red Guards continued to embark on "long marches" through the countryside to steel themselves as "revolutionary successors"; they freely traveled across the land to "exchange revolutionary experiences"; they intensified their "bombardments" of the headquarters of local Party organizations and continued to hound individual cadres, intellectuals, ex-capitalists and others who might be branded with derogatory political labels or class designations.

By the end of 1966, in the view of most members of the Cultural Revolution Group in Beijing, the Red Guards had outlived their political usefulness. They had more than fulfilled their assigned task to "expose" Party leaders "taking the capitalist road," and indeed had put the entire Party apparatus on the defensive, but their attacks on all authority threatened anarchy and was hardly in accord with the Maoist goal to "achieve the unity of more than 95 percent of the cadres." They had carried out the Maoist injunction to "boldly arouse the masses," but they often only aroused workers and peasants to defend the existing order of things against the youthful and often arrogant interlopers. Moreover, the almost total lack of discipline, the violent factionalism, the vandalism and sometimes outright hooliganism that characterized the movement led Maoist authorities in Beijing to conclude that the Red Guards had become a political liability. In 1967 various and increasingly stringent measures were taken to remove "the vanguard" of the Cultural Revolution from the political stage. But the Red Guards were not to be dispersed as easily as they had been called into being.

The Cultural Revolution would not be terminated with attempts to end the political life of the Red Guards. In 1967 the Great Proletarian Cultural Revolution moved to a new stage—the move to "seize power" from local, provincial, and regional Party authorities—and new political actors moved to the center of the political arena: workers and soldiers. The new stage was to prove far more turbulent than that of the previous six months, when the Red Guards had dominated the stage.

The Rise and Fall of the Shanghai Commune

As the Cultural Revolution spread from Beijing to other urban centers and the provinces in the summer and fall of 1966, it became apparent to Maoist leaders that they had underestimated both the disorders the movement would bring and the power of local Party organizations to resist the movement. At a work conference in late October, Mao Zedong acknowledged that "the Great Cultural Revolution wreaked havoc after I approved Nie Yuanzi's big-character poster" and "I myself had not foreseen that . . . the whole country would be thrown into turmoil. . . . Since it was I who caused the havoc, it is understandable if you have some bitter words for me."[13] At the same time, Chen Boda, head of the Cultural Revolution Group, attempted to explain why the mass organizations had failed to achieve unity and fashion a new political structure; he blamed local Party leaders who were "afraid of losing their positions and prestige" and thus had "instigated workers and peasants to fight the students."[14] Chen, of course, failed to note that he and other Maoist leaders in Beijing were no less active than non-Maoist Party officials in seeking to manipulate the mass movement for their own political ends.

There was another factor Maoists had underestimated: the spontaneous social and political radicalism of the urban working class, which soon was to acquire a dynamic of its own. But at the end of 1966 the Maoist concern was with the resilience of the old Party bureaucracies in the cities and the provinces, which had managed to maintain themselves by playing upon the divisions within the growing mass movement. As a functioning national organization, the Party had virtually ceased to exist. In Beijing, Mao and the Cultural Revolution Group held sway, issuing directives in the name of the Central Committee. But in the provinces, districts, and cities outside the capital, local Party organizations survived and functioned within their own spheres of jurisdiction. Everywhere the old bureaucratic apparatus was under attack, but almost everywhere the separate parts of the old structure remained more or less intact, their leaders paying homage to the thoughts of Mao while fending off the onslaughts of the Chairman's local supporters. To break the political stalemate, the leaders in Beijing called for the immediate implementation of one of the aims announced in the "Sixteen Articles," the "seizure of power by proletarian revolutionaries." The first attempt was made in Shanghai, and the events in that city of 11,000,000 in the early months of 1967 were to prove decisive in determining the future course of the nationwide struggle, revealing both the objective limits that the Cultural Revolution confronted and the subjective limitations of the cultural revolutionaries.

. . .

Shanghai was not only the most populous city in China but also the most highly industrialized. In the huge and modern factories of the sprawling metropolis there labored the largest and most concentrated part of China's proletariat, heir to a militant working class tradition forged in the bloody revolutionary struggles of the 1920s. Shanghai was the most culturally cosmopolitan of Chinese cities and also the most politically radical, the home of a mature working class and long the center of modern China's radical intelligentsia. The Chinese Communist Party was officially born in Shanghai in 1921, and Mao Zedong had called upon its radical intellectuals to begin the Cultural Revolution in 1965. If China was to have a "proletarian cultural revolution," Shanghai was its natural starting point. The dramatic events that unfolded in the gigantic city in late 1966 and early 1967 foreshadowed what would occur, albeit on a smaller scale, in many other urban areas.

Inspired by the Maoist upheaval in Beijing, the Cultural Revolution in Shanghai began in the summer of 1966 with students organizing Red Guard groups in emulation of their counterparts in the capital. As elsewhere, the Shanghai Red Guards were rent by bitter internal disputes, partly of their own making and partly manufactured by Party officials. But however factionalized, the movement grew and acquired an increasingly radical momentum, rapidly escalating from attacks against Party authorities on wall posters and at mass rallies to physical attacks on government offices, from the criticism of "bourgeois authorities" in schools to a massive challenge to the authority of the established Party-state bureaucracy headed by the mayor of the city, Cao Diqiu, and the regional first secretary of the Party's East China bureau, Chen Peishen.[15]

A particularly explosive political issue that arose early in the Shanghai movement, as it did elsewhere, and one which clearly revealed the deep resentments of the people against those who governed them, was the "black files," political dossiers on citizens compiled by Party and police functionaries in schools, factories, neighborhood associations, and mass organizations. The files inhibited political action on the part of many inclined to heed the Maoist call to rebel, especially workers who feared economic as well as political retribution should the Party be restored to its customary preeminence. Student rebels demanded that the files be destroyed, encouraged by an October 5 directive from Beijing ordering that they be burned in public. But Party officials refused to release materials they labeled "state secrets," and in early November some of the more militant Red Guards staged nocturnal raids on Party offices and attempted to seize the files, resulting in violent clashes with Party cadres and police. A new directive from Beijing on November 16 again called for destruction of the files but stipulated that the matter be settled by persuasion and not by force. Party authorities proved less than amenable to persuasion, and the result in the end was not the elimination of political dossiers but increased hostility between rebel citizens and Party cadres, leaving a legacy of distrust that was to remain long after the Cultural Revolution ended.

While the prestige of the Shanghai Party apparatus was undermined by the struggle over the "black files," the power of the apparatus was destroyed by Shanghai's working class. By mid-autumn of 1966 the rebellion had spread from the schools to the factories, thus marking the appearance of the actual proletariat in the drama of the "Great Proletarian Cultural Revolution." But the workers did not join the battle as a united body. It was a class divided between older and more skilled workers, who benefited from the prevailing wage and bonus system and generally wished to preserve the existing sociopolitical order, and younger unskilled and apprentice workers, whose conditions of life and work made them more inclined to rebel against the Party bureaucracy. A far greater gap separated regular workers, who were permanent state employees, and a vast semi-proletariat of temporary and contract workers, drawn mostly from peasants on nearby communes (and, to a lesser extent, from the urban unemployed), who were hired for limited periods and were subject to immediate dismissal. The contract workers lived on the barest margins of subsistence, not only laboring at meager wages but lacking even the most elementary social welfare benefits and the job security enjoyed by regular workers. Originally conceived, or at least ideologically justified, as a means to reduce the distinction between workers and peasants (one of "the three great differences"), the contract system became no more than a source of cheap labor for state enterprises—and of profit for the Communist state. The system had been greatly expanded in the years immediately preceding the Cultural Revolution, as were other forms of labor exploitation.[16]

The ranks of the Shanghai working class grew as young workers and students who had been involuntarily dispatched to the countryside in earlier years returned to the city demanding jobs and housing. Also seeking jobs were demobilized soldiers, along with a variety of temporary and part-time manual laborers.

From those disparate groups of Shanghai's working class and urban poor came different and often conflicting socioeconomic demands, which soon found expression in rival political organizations. The Cultural Revolution, for the first time in the history of the People's Republic, brought discontented workers and others the freedom to voice their grievances and the freedom (albeit short-lived) to establish their own organizations, unhampered by the organizational and ideological restraints imposed by the Communist Party. The result was the spontaneous emergence of a bewildering variety of popular rebel organizations, all proclaiming fidelity to Mao and Maoist principles but interpreting those principles to suit their own particular interests. At the beginning of November several of the rebel groups formed a loose alliance under the name Headquarters of the Revolutionary Revolt of Shanghai Workers, which came under the leadership of Wang Hongwen, a young textile worker and mid-level Party functionary. The Workers' Headquarters was largely the self-creation of the Shanghai workers, owing little to instructions from Beijing. Indeed, the Maoist instructions then coming from the capital were stressing the productive over the revolutionary role of the workers, instructing them to fulfill their eight-hour working day before participating in the Cultural Revolution. What was vaguely envisioned in the capital was a peaceful transformation of productive relationships in the factories, with workers' committees (created during spare time, it was emphasized) cooperating with managerial cadres. Fearful of disrupting production, Beijing waited until the beginning of the new year before calling upon workers to organize themselves as "revolutionary rebels."

But the revolutionary upsurge in Shanghai was proceeding more rapidly than Maoist leaders anticipated. On November 8 the Workers' Headquarters presented its demands to the Shanghai Municipal Party Committee, and they clearly portended the replacement of the old bureaucratic administration by new popular organs of government. The workers demanded that the Headquarters be recognized as a legal organization under "the dictatorship of the proletariat," thereby challenging the Party's monopoly of political power; they insisted that the workers be provided with the means to organize all factories in the city; and they called for the municipal government to give a public accounting of its administration. When the demands were refused, some of the more radical workers were determined to present them to Mao himself, and on November 10 they attempted to do so by commandeering a train bound for Beijing. Party authorities halted the train at Anding, a small town on the outskirts of Shanghai, but half the workers defied orders to return to the city and settled in for a three-day siege.

The leaders in the capital reacted to the crisis at Anding with hesitation and uncertainty. The first response was a telegram from Chen Boda warning that "it is a serious matter to disobey Party instructions." The main job of workers was to work, he added, while "joining the Revolution is only secondary." "They must therefore go back to work," he decreed.[17] But before the Shanghai authorities could implement the order, new instructions arrived from Beijing, personally conveyed by Zhang Chunqiao, who had been secretary of the Shanghai Party Committee until July, when he had left to become a leading member of the Cultural Revolution Group in the capital. On November 14 Zhang declared the Workers' Headquarters a legitimate revolutionary organization, signed their demands in the name of the Party Central Committee, and forced the reluctant Mayor Cao to sign as well. Maoist leaders in Beijing apparently had concluded that the time had come to permit the proletariat, at least in Shanghai, to participate in what was hailed as a "proletarian" revolution. Mao Zedong to that point had had little to say about the role of the actual proletariat in the Great Proletarian Cultural Revolution; as events in Shanghai and elsewhere were soon to demonstrate, his faith in the urban working class was transient.

With the victory of the Workers' Headquarters in mid-November, the power of the Shanghai Party and government apparatus rapidly disintegrated as rebel groups freely roamed the city to organize workers and others. The mass movement grew at a frenetic pace and on a vast scale, as a growing variety of working-class organizations, loosely allied with Red Guard groups, competed for popular support and for power. Among the more prominent of the revolutionary organizations, most initially allied with the Workers' Headquarters but organizationally separate and politically more radical, were the Workers' Second Regiment (a 500,000-strong organization of manual laborers led by the fiery Geng Jinzhang), the Workers' Third Army (a group of several hundred thousand radical workers and students who had split away from the Workers' Headquarters), and the Red Flag Army, part of a loose nationwide confederation of demobilized soldiers.[18] Opposing the radical workers was an organization that called itself the Workers' Scarlet Guards for the Defense of Mao Zedong Thought. The Scarlet Guards, a relatively conservative organization composed mainly of skilled workers and technicians and claiming a membership of 800,000, was probably originally organized by the old Party machine to counter the attacks of the radicals, but the Scarlet Guards soon began condemning the Shanghai Municipal Party Committee for having capitulated to the political and economic demands of the rebels. It rallied under its banner the not inconsiderable number of Shanghai workers and other citizens who wished to preserve the pre-Cultural Revolution order of things, although loudly proclaiming fidelity to Mao and his thought while doing so.

By mid-December Shanghai was roughly divided into two huge rival coalitions, one led by the conservative Scarlet Guards and the other by the original Workers' Headquarters, although neither was monolithic. The rivalry erupted into large-scale violence in the last week of the year, virtually halting production in the factories and gravely disrupting municipal services. The economy of the huge metropolis was paralyzed when the Scarlet Guards declared a general strike on December 31 amidst a wave of strikes, political demonstrations, marches, and escalating violence. The chaos was compounded when the old bureaucracy, in a desperate effort to save itself, expended the last of the financial resources of the city and its factories. Partly in response to economic demands made by virtually all sectors of the working population, partly in an attempt to bribe the workers into political passivity, the Municipal Committee authorized the payment of bonuses, retroactive wage increases, and cash handouts. What later was condemned as "the ill wind of economism" was the last gasp of the old Shanghai Party apparatus, whose officials, having exhausted their economic as well as political capital, now could only stand by helplessly and watch the rise of the popular movement that was preparing to overthrow them.

The overthrow, which would be celebrated as the "January Revolution," was accomplished during the first week of the new year. On January 5 a dozen rebel organizations loosely allied with the Workers' Headquarters (and with the encouragement and assistance of members of the Cultural Revolution Group in the capital) published a "Message to All the People of Shanghai" in the city's leading newspaper *Wenhuibao,* which had been taken over by insurgents two days before. The message deplored the divisions within the surging mass revolutionary movement (and condemned the Scarlet Guards and Party authorities for creating them), appealed to workers to return to the factories, and called for the unity of workers, students, intellectuals and cadres. That call for unity received dramatic expression the next day, January 6, when more than a million citizens gathered to hold a mass meeting in the central city square, with the proceedings observed on television by millions of others. Mayor Cao and other high Party officials were denounced, removed from their positions, and forced to make public confessions. Over the next few days lesser officials were similarly humiliated and paraded through the streets wearing placards and duncecaps. The old regime had fallen.

However, the place of the old Municipal Party Committee was taken not by the workers who had carried out the "January Revolution" but rather by Zhang Chunqiao, who again appeared in Shanghai on January 6—not only to place himself at the head of the victorious mass movement but also to control it and to reestablish order in the city.[19] Along with his assistant from the Cultural Revolution Group in Beijing, Yao Wenyuan, Zhang struck a political deal with Wang Hongwen, the leader of the Workers' Headquarters, an alliance that brought together three of those who a decade later were jailed as the "Gang of Four." The Workers' Headquarters was now Zhang's main base of popular support, but he did not rely on the masses alone to restore order in Shanghai. He also took over the local Party apparatus, using his old organizational connections to win the cooperation of basic-level cadres. Zhang further had at his disposal the city's secret police agencies and local units of the PLA, which he freely employed in urging workers to return to the factories, rejecting "economist" demands for higher wages, suppressing strikes, and reestablishing political order. Before the end of January, Shanghai was functioning in more or less normal economic and administrative fashion.

Zhang Chunqiao was less successful in maintaining the unity of the mass movement briefly achieved in early January. While the Scarlet Guards disbanded, many of its members apparently joining the Workers' Headquarters, the more radical groups that had taken part in the January Revolution went into opposition. Fearing that Zhang's new regime would differ little from the one it had replaced, organizations representing manual laborers and the *lumpenproletariat* (especially Geng Jinzhang's Second Regiment) challenged the revolutionary legitimacy of Zhang's rule. Factional fighting resumed during the last two weeks of January, sometimes erupting into violence.[20]

What provided the mass movement with a semblance of unity was Zhang's promise that the new order would be constructed in accordance with the democratic principles of the Marxist model of the Paris Commune, principles loudly proclaimed since the beginning of the Cultural Revolution. Those principles enjoyed almost universal support among Shanghai's political activists, in large part, no doubt, because of their distaste for the old Party dictatorship. "All power to the Commune," if not necessarily to Zhang, was the slogan heard throughout the city early in 1967.

The Shanghai People's Commune, after some delay due to factional bickering, was formally proclaimed on February 5. Its birth was accompanied by a massive rally of a million workers to celebrate "the greatest day in the history of proletarian and revolutionary Shanghai." But the attempt to establish a "proletarian dictatorship" based on the principles Marx set forth in 1871 was flawed from the outset. Whereas the Marxist model demanded a "self-government of the producers," with officials democratically elected and subject to mass supervision and immediate popular recall, the leaders of the Shanghai Commune—Zhang Chunqiao and Yao Wenyuan—were appointed by Beijing. Such authority and legitimacy as Zhang and Yao possessed derived not from the workers of Shanghai but from the supreme authority of Chairman Mao. Whereas Marx had called for the abolition of the standing army and the police, Zhang used the PLA and the security police to enforce his rule in the name of the Commune and to suppress dissent; indeed, at the inauguration of the new government he emphasized that it had the support of the army. Moreover, Zhang excluded his political opponents from the planning, organization, and leadership of the Commune, driving some of them to announce a rival "New Shanghai People's Commune" and to send delegations to Beijing protesting Zhang's repressive policies.[21]

Yet the Commune and its hallowed principles had been proclaimed in Shanghai. More important, the Marxian ideals of the Commune had taken root among the people of the city. Given the opportunity and freedom, the embryonic organization, however unpromising its origins, might have grown to maturity on its own base of popular support and participation.

But that was not to be. While the people of Shanghai waited for Beijing to hail the Commune with the same enthusiasm as the January Revolution, Mao Zedong now was attracted to very different political models. During the month of January two other "power seizures" had taken place, one in Shaanxi Province and the other in the city of Harbin in northern Manchuria. In both instances, a most prominent part in the "revolutionary movements" had been played by the People's Liberation Army. In both cases the political outcome of the overthrow of local Party leaders was not a commune but a "revolutionary committee" based on what came to be called the "triple alliance" of mass revolutionary organizations, Party cadres, and the army—with the last clearly the dominant partner. Within a month, Maoist leaders in Beijing were declaring the "revolutionary committee" the only appropriate structure for the reorganization of political power. In the meantime nothing was said publicly about the Shanghai Commune. But the decision was conveyed privately to Zhang Chunqiao and Yao Wenyuan in mid-February when Mao summoned them to an audience in Beijing, where they remained ten days. Having heard that some Shanghai revolutionaries were demanding the abolition of all "heads," Mao informed Zhang and Yao of his thoughts on the matter: "This is extreme anarchism, it is most reactionary. . . . In reality there will always be heads." As for the Shanghai Commune itself, Mao doubted that its radical principles could be implemented anywhere else in China but Shanghai and wondered whether such a form of political organization could exercise the necessary revolutionary vigilance even in Shanghai: "Communes are too weak when it comes to suppressing counterrevolutionaries. People have come and complained to me that when the Bureau of Public Security arrest people, they go in the front door and out the back." Thus Mao suggested—and a suggestion from the Chairman at the time was a supreme command—that the Shanghai Commune transform itself into a "revolutionary committee."[22] In a prophetic pointer to the future course of the Cultural Revolution, Mao also wondered whether the Commune structure left any political place for the Communist Party, insisting that China would require the Party and its experienced cadres for the foreseeable future.[23]

Upon his return to Shanghai, Zhang Chunqiao was forced to explain to the people of the city in a televised speech on February 24 why the Commune had ceased to exist, not an easy task in view of the widely publicized claims by Maoist theoreticians that Chairman Mao had not only inherited but also "developed and enriched" the experience of the Paris Commune, not to mention Mao's own lavish praise of the original Marxian model of proletarian dictatorship. In any event, the Shanghai People's Commune, after an undistinguished nineteen-day existence, became the "Revolutionary Committee of the Municipality of Shanghai." The decision was made in Beijing, not by the workers of Shanghai. Plans to establish communes in other cities immediately were abandoned in favor of the "triple alliance," and the Shanghai Commune itself became a non-event; nowhere is its birth or death recorded in official accounts of the Great Proletarian Cultural Revolution.

Although the proclamation of the Shanghai People's Commune had done nothing to change the realities of political power in Shanghai, more than a change of names was involved in the demise of the Commune. Its disappearance symbolized an abandonment of principles and a crushing of hopes. For the "revolutionary committees," in Shanghai as elsewhere, were not organs of popular democratic rule but essentially bureaucratic instrumentalities. Initially dominated by the army, they eventually were to come under the control of, and merge with, a refashioned but still very Leninist Communist Party.

The events of February 1967 signaled the first of a long series of Maoist retreats from the original aims of the Cultural Revolution. Those events also revealed that all political power in China ultimately resided in, and was attributed to, one man and his "thought," a phenomenon akin to that once described by Karl Marx as one where the political power of the people "finds its ultimate expression in an Executive power that subjugates the commonweal to its own autocratic will."[24] The cult of Mao Zedong had now become so pervasive that the Chairman could decide not only the fate of individuals but the destiny of social movements. The workers of Shanghai who had won political power on their own, and for a brief moment in early January had made a reality of the much-celebrated Cultural Revolution aim of creating a "great alliance of proletarian revolutionaries," now surrendered that power to a "higher authority." The Cultural Revolution right "to dare to rebel," it was now clear, was not a right inherent in the people but one granted them by the authority of the deified Mao, and thus one that could be revoked by him. For the workers of Shanghai, in February 1967, Mao defined the limits of rebellion and determined its political outcome.

Power Seizures, the Army, and the Ultra-Left (March–August 1967)

The pattern of events in Shanghai that culminated in the January Revolution was repeated, with considerable variation, elsewhere in China in 1967. But in most other cities and provinces the power of local Party organizations was greater, while the mass movement was weaker, even more factionalized, and guided by less experienced leaders than in Shanghai. Moreover, the now officially sanctioned movement to "seize power from below" was restrained by the decree that the only acceptable political outcome of a "power seizure" was a revolutionary committee based on the "triple alliance"; in practice there were to be no more radical experiments with the Paris Commune model, even though its Marxian principles might still be praised in theory. Moreover, on January 23 Lin Biao, on orders from Mao, had instructed the People's Liberation Army to enter the political struggles, to support "the revolutionary left" and maintain order at the same time.

The decision in favor of military intervention was both momentous and incongruous, for now the army, the most bureaucratic agency of the state apparatus, was called upon to promote what was supposed to be a popular revolutionary movement against bureaucratic elitism. Yet for Mao, this fateful step perhaps did not appear as inconsistent as it did to later observers—and indeed to many Chinese involved in the battle at the time. Mao no doubt looked upon an army made up mostly of peasants as a more reliable and certainly more effective revolutionary force than the urban masses, who seemed utterly incapable of self-discipline and unity. Moreover, he always had regarded the army as the main repository of the revolutionary heritage of struggle and egalitarian values. Under Lin Biao's direction, the PLA presumably had undergone "living ideological indoctrination" in the "thought of Mao Zedong" in the years prior to the Cultural Revolution and therefore, it was thought, was fully prepared to play its appointed revolutionary role. These views were not shared by all of the Chairman's followers.

Mao did not call on the army to impose a revolution from above, nor did the PLA attempt a takeover in the name of "order." For the most part, the army remained obedient to the civilian authority of Mao, if not necessarily to the Cultural Revolution Group as a whole. Yet in an increasingly chaotic situation where the Party had ceased to function as a national organization and the mass movement was hopelessly divided, it was inevitable that the army would become the arbiter of the struggles of the Cultural Revolution. As conditions became ever more chaotic, the army came to play an increasingly prominent role not only in the political but also the economic life of the nation. Soldiers entered factories and communes, and it was largely due to the discipline enforced by the PLA that production in both cities and countryside was maintained during those turbulent times. Where revolutionary committees were established, it was usually the military that assumed the dominant position in the tripartite alliance, more often than not siding with the old cadres rather than the representatives of mass organizations. Faced with the dilemma of determining who was "the revolutionary left" among a multitude of groups claiming to be the true followers of Chairman Mao, the army usually supported the less radical rebel organizations in the interests of stability. Charged with the often conflicting tasks of assisting the revolutionary efforts of the masses and maintaining social and economic order, army commanders usually preferred order.

The preference for order frequently led to the military suppression of the more radical mass organizations. In February and March of 1967, in what some later condemned as the "March Black Winds," the army forcibly disbanded (and sometimes militarily attacked) radical student and worker organizations in the provinces of Sichuan, Anhui, Hunan, Hubei, and Fujian. Many thousands of activists were arrested, killed, and wounded.[25] While groups of virtually all political orientations resorted to violence during the Cultural Revolution, most of the lives taken during the upheaval were not the work of "radical Maoists," as conventionally assumed, but rather the work of the army, with radicals as their usual victims. Where the PLA did not employ force, it preferred to define the Cultural Revolution as a mass movement to study Mao Zedong Thought. As Hong Yung Lee has observed, making Mao's thought an object of study rather than a guide to action served to dampen revolutionary activism and was intended to resolve the army's dilemma between "its rhetorical commitment to revolution and its conservative institutional interests."[26] In many areas following the January Revolution, Maoist aims were obstructed by de facto alliances between the PLA, Party cadres, and the more conservative mass organizations.

If military intervention blunted the radical thrust of the Cultural Revolution, the actions of the PLA were largely in accord with the relatively moderate course Mao was pursuing at the time. Having declared in February 1967 that the slogan "doubt everything and overthrow everything" was reactionary, Mao moved to eliminate the more anarchistic tendencies he had unleashed the year before. Nationwide organizations of contract workers, apprentices, demobilized soldiers, and students returned from the countryside—now deemed excessively radical and violent—were branded as "counterrevolutionary" and officially banned. New efforts were made to restrain the activities of Red Guards, if not to remove them from the political scene entirely. Students were urged to return to their schools, which, it was prematurely announced, would reopen in March. Draconian punishments were decreed for attacks on government offices, seizures of official files, and physical assaults on state and Party cadres. In April a new drive was launched against the already silenced Liu Shaoqi, now accused (although not yet by name) of being a national traitor as well as a capitalist-roader. The purpose was to unify the factionalized movement by "narrowing the target." More significant was the attempt to reestablish the functioning of the state apparatus headed by Zhou Enlai, and to a lesser extent the legitimacy of the Party, excepting, of course, those still very large segments of the organization controlled by alleged followers of Liu Shaoqi. The effort centered on the rehabilitation of Party cadres, the overwhelming majority of whom, it was said, were good and loyal revolutionaries, or at least amenable to rectification. Cadres were now described as the "backbone of the struggle to seize power." Zhou Enlai made Herculean efforts to persuade the mass organizations to end their indiscriminate attacks on cadres and to unite with them in common struggle.

Despite the efforts to unify the mass movement and the presence of the PLA on the political scene, the drive to "seize power" and establish revolutionary committees was a slow and arduous process. Many attempts failed, and others were denounced as "false power seizures," cases where existing Party committees simply changed their names. In other cases, the PLA prevented mass organizations deemed too radical from coming to power, calling the attempts "sham power seizures."[27] At the end of April 1967, apart from Shanghai and Beijing,[28] only four of China's twenty-seven provinces and autonomous regions had set up officially approved revolutionary committees: Shaanxi, Heilongjiang, Guizhou, and Shandong. Elsewhere the old Party organizations remained entrenched, besieged by a variety of rebel organizations. The latter, in turn, were in conflict with each other as well as with army units ostensibly dispatched to support them. The chaotic struggle seemed to have reached a stalemate, and the Cultural Revolution seemed to be grinding to an inconclusive if bloody end.

The revolutionary flames soon were rekindled by radical Maoist leaders and organizations who were later condemned as "ultra-leftists." Hostility to the army grew in the spring of 1967 as local military commanders came down on the side of "order," which in most places meant protecting what remained of the old Party machine, supporting conservative mass organizations, and preserving the political status quo. Popular resentments over the intrusion of the army were exacerbated by a concurrent campaign for the restoration of cadres, orchestrated from Beijing by Zhou Enlai. The opposition was by no means confined to a few radical extremists, for the whole history of the Cultural Revolution clearly reveals that workers, students, and peasants harbored bitter resentments against Party cadres in general, and not simply against the mere "handful" officially termed "anti-socialist rightists." Without that widespread popular resentment against bureaucratic privilege, it would be difficult to explain why millions responded to the Maoist call to rebel.

Opposition to military intervention and to the resurrection of old cadres meant an implicit rejection of the revolutionary committees, the now orthodox Maoist political formula. The rejection soon became explicit when it was charged that the masses were being excluded from the triple alliance. Indeed, almost everywhere political power gravitated to the army, which in turn relied on experienced civilian cadres to maintain administrative order and production.

In May these resentments burst forth in a radical drive to reverse what was called the "February adverse current" and the "black wind" of the previous months. The drive soon exploded into a frenzy of popular violence against all authority. In Beijing, where wall posters denouncing Zhou Enlai as the leader of the "red capitalist class" had begun to appear in late April, the leftist attack centered on the state bureaucracy and its ministries, particularly the Ministry of Foreign Affairs. Red Guard organizations conducted a series of raids on its offices, seized and destroyed secret documents in its archives, and demanded the ouster of the foreign minister, the veteran Red Army Marshal Chen Yi. From provincial cities came an ominous stream of reports of armed struggles between contending mass organizations in factories, schools, and streets. Despite orders from the Cultural Revolution Group in Beijing forbidding violence, illegal arrests, and the seizure of arms from PLA arsenals, the scale and scope of the battles escalated. By July, against a background of nationwide violence and chaos, there were new demands to implement the old Maoist call for a "Commune of China."

In an attempt to reconcile the warring factions, high government and military leaders were sent from Beijing to the provinces to forge "great revolutionary alliances." A particularly perilous situation existed in Wuhan, a major industrial center and the heart of China's railroad system. From the beginning of July, much of the paralyzed city on the Yangzi had become a battleground for two huge rival mass organizations. One, the "Million Heroes" (made up of some 500,000 skilled industrial workers, state office employees, and militiamen), was supported by the local Party organization and the regional military commander, General Chen Zaidao, who long had ignored official instructions to refrain from attacking rebel organizations. The other, an alliance of more radical (and younger) workers and student Red Guard organizations, the Wuhan Workers' General Headquarters, which had made an abortive attempt to seize power in January and claimed a membership of 400,000, was besieged by the Million Heroes, who had been supplied with weapons and troops by General Chen.[29] When Chen refused to obey orders from Zhou Enlai to lift the siege, two prominent members of the Cultural Revolution Group, Wang Li and Xie Fuzhi, were dispatched to Wuhan. The emissaries from Beijing arrived on July 16 and ordered Chen and other local commanders to withdraw their support of the Million Heroes in favor of the Workers' Headquarters and make public self-criticisms. The response of the Wuhan military leaders was swift. In the early morning hours of July 20, soldiers of the mutinous PLA division detained Xie Fuzhi while Wang Li was kidnapped by the Million Heroes, with PLA encouragement. Xie, who was Minister of Public Security, was held under house arrest while Wang Li, a radical intellectual, was taken to a military headquarters and brutally beaten. The response from Beijing was equally swift when the news reached the capital—and after Zhou Enlai failed in an attempt to mediate the dispute, his plane unable to land at an airfield surrounded by hostile troops and tanks. Three infantry divisions and an airborne unit converged on Wuhan, along with navy gunboats sailing up the Yangzi. It was only under the threat of superior military force that Chen Zaidao capitulated. Wang Li and Xie Fuzhi returned to Beijing to receive a hero's welcome at a massive rally held at Tiananmen Square on July 25. The Wuhan military leaders were arrested and returned to the capital in disgrace. No one could have foreseen that within a few months Wang Li would be purged as a "counterrevolutionary," whereas a year later the leader of the mutiny, General Chen, would be standing on public podiums alongside the top leaders of the People's Republic, as if he had been a loyal supporter of Mao and the Cultural Revolution all along. It was an ironic turn of events, yet perhaps not out of keeping with the inexorable political logic of the retreat from the principles of the Cultural Revolution that had begun in February.

The Wuhan mutiny raised the specter of civil war, for it revealed that the one apparently cohesive force that remained in the country, the PLA, was something less than monolithic. That specter loomed ominously larger during the critical month of August 1967, as leftist leaders vociferously questioned the revolutionary credentials of the army and rebel masses attacked it physically, thus threatening to bring to the army the same political differences that already had torn the Party asunder and had divided the mass movement into a multitude of warring factions. While Chairman Mao remained publicly silent Jiang Qing did not. Referring to the Wuhan incident in a July 24 speech, she angrily advised Red Guards to "attack with words, but defend yourselves with weapons." Rebel groups throughout the country thereupon promptly proceeded to seize such weapons as they could. (It was observed that the PLA, briefly bowing to the Cultural Revolution Group, permitted radical Red Guard and workers' organizations to "seize" old weapons while supplying more sophisticated arms to conservative organizations,[30] thereby ensuring even bigger and bloodier battles between the rival groups.) An editorial in the July 31 issue of *Red Flag*, provocatively entitled "The Proletariat Must Firmly Grasp the Barrel of the Gun," called for the overthrow of "persons in authority taking the capitalist road" in the army as well as in the Party. On August 9 Lin Biao criticized unnamed military commanders for "suppressing the masses," demanded that they make public self-criticisms, and advised them to take "revolutionary rebels" as their teachers—although he took care to treat the Wuhan incident as a political error amenable to the proper ideological rectification, not as a mutiny.[31] But Wang Li and other radical leaders of the Cultural Revolution Group gave public speeches demanding the ouster of the "handful of revisionists" who had usurped power in the army, just as their counterparts allegedly had done in the Party.

Individual army leaders had been criticized earlier in the Cultural Revolution, not excluding Zhu De, the "father of the Red Army," who on one occasion was characterized as "a big warlord who has wormed his way into the Party." But this was the first time that leading luminaries of the movement suggested that the model Maoist instrument as a whole, the "pillar of the dictatorship of the proletariat" itself, was suffering from "bourgeois" and "revisionist" infections and therefore should be subjected to the same processes of cultural revolutionary purification as all other organizations and institutions.

In Beijing the new leftist offensive of August, fueled by the passions aroused over the Wuhan affair and the fiery speeches of left-wing leaders, focused on the central state apparatus. Tiananmen Square was occupied for a week by hundreds of thousands of demonstrators demanding that Liu Shaoqi be turned over to the people for public trial. Angry crowds besieged the offices of Zhou Enlai. And in one of the more bizarre episodes of the Cultural Revolution, the Foreign Ministry was taken over by rebels for two weeks. Installed as de facto foreign minister in place of Chen Yi was Yao Dengshan, a diplomat who had won popular acclaim for his heroic attempt to defend the Chinese Embassy in Jakarta when it had been sacked in April. Chinese foreign policy had been largely dormant since the beginning of the Cultural Revolution, but now a new "revolutionary internationalist" program was proclaimed, based on a literal reading of Lin Biao's 1965 treatise, "Long Live the Victory of People's War." Cables bearing new "revolutionary" instructions flowed from Beijing to Chinese embassies abroad; foreign diplomats were harassed in the Chinese capital, and an ultimatum was presented to the British government demanding the release of Communist journalists imprisoned in Hong Kong. The brief era of "proletarian internationalism" in foreign policy culminated—and ended—with the burning of the British Chancery in Beijing on August 22.

The functioning of the central government soon was restored, but in other cities and provincial centers the situation was far more difficult. Rebel organizations, armed with weapons seized from military depots—and in some cases from convoys of war materials bound for Vietnam—were locked in pitched battles with PLA soldiers throughout much of the country. In some areas, armed peasants marched into cities and towns to attack government buildings. The PLA now not only had to defend itself against the masses who had "dared to rebel" but had to protect such civilian administrations as still functioned in the local areas, whether they were new revolutionary committees or old Party organizations. The battles, often bloody and usually inconclusive, were spreading and threatened total economic and political chaos.

In late August China seemed to be sinking into anarchy. Mao, having returned to Beijing from an "inspection tour" of the provinces, was now convinced that to continue the Cultural Revolution as a movement based on the initiative of the masses was to run the risk of a massive civil war. He opted for order and, in effect, the end of the Cultural Revolution.

The Thermidor of the Cultural Revolution

On September 5, 1967, the army was instructed to restore order. The masses were instructed to turn in their arms and forbidden to interfere with the mission of the PLA, which was hailed as a "peerless people's army" that was "personally formed and led by our great leader Chairman Mao and commanded by Vice Supreme Commander Lin Biao." Lest there be any question that the order was definitive, the directive was jointly issued by the Party Central Committee, the Cultural Revolution Group, the State Council of the central government, and the Central Military Affairs Committee of the PLA—and signed by Mao Zedong. The directive was addressed to all mass organizations the Cultural Revolution had spawned as well as to all governmental and military organs. The restoration of order under PLA direction was accompanied by efforts to rebuild the Party and reestablish the authority of the state bureaucracy under the leadership of Zhou Enlai. The process was protracted and difficult, but it proceeded with an inexorable logic, which dictated that the political power that had fallen to the army would eventually pass to a revived and refurbished Communist Party.

The whole process of the "return to normalcy" was decorated with an abundance of revolutionary rhetoric, which retained many of the slogans and battle cries of the Cultural Revolution, but it was made abundantly clear that the right of the masses to rebel had been withdrawn. The task of publicly announcing that decision fell to Jiang Qing, who took advantage of the occasion to hastily renounce her own past views and leftist comrades, declaring that it was no longer permissible to attack either the army or the government and that even verbal criticisms would be considered counterrevolutionary. Attacks were now to be directed against the "ultra-left" plotters with whom she had been intimately associated but now had discovered were really members of "a very typical counterrevolutionary organization" to whose machinations all the factionalism and violence of the summer months were to be attributed.[32]

The message that order was the order of the day was forcefully conveyed by public executions of alleged instigators of violence. That the army was now inviolable, at least as far as the masses were concerned, was symbolically demonstrated on National Day, October 1, 1967, when most of the old generals denounced so vehemently earlier in the year stood prominently alongside Mao atop the Gate of Heavenly Peace. That the Red Guards were no longer wanted was made clear two weeks later in a directive ordering the youth to return to their studies. And the demise of the Cultural Revolution Group itself was signaled in November, when *Red Flag,* the Party theoretical journal which had become the radical voice of the Cultural Revolution, was ordered to suspend publication.

According to the official Maoist version of events, the chaos of the "hot summer" of 1967 resulted from plots hatched by a small group of leaders in

Beijing who had formed a clandestine organization known as the "May Six-teenth Corps," a name taken from the famous circular that had launched the Cultural Revolution. The plotters, it is said, playing on the divisions within the revolutionary movement (especially among the gullible Red Guards), instigated the violence for the ultimate purpose of overthrowing the "proletarian headquarters" of Mao Zedong and seizing state power. Once exposed as "anarchists," "neo-Trotskyists," and "ultra-leftists" they were duly disposed of. But in the Orwellian world of official mythology, and aided by a bit of dialectical magic, the "ultra-leftists" were converted into counterrevolutionary rightists, who, subsequent investigations revealed, were really tied to Liu Shaoqi. "Ultra-left in form, but ultra-right in essence" was the official verdict.[33]

The leaders of the alleged conspiracy turned out to be most of the leading members of the central Cultural Revolution Group, especially those who in the years before and during the Cultural Revolution were most closely identified with Mao Zedong. Initially they included such eminently radical Maoist theoreticians as Wang Li, Guan Feng, and Qi Benyu, and eventually, some years later, even Chen Boda and Lin Biao.[34]

Revolutionary movements typically produce extremists and radical excesses, and the Cultural Revolution certainly produced more than its fair share. In mid-1967 there were no lack of "cultural revolutionaries" literally practicing the slogan Mao had condemned some months earlier: "Doubt everything and overthrow everything." But that nihilistic tendency had been present in the Cultural Revolution from the beginning, from the time of the inception of the Red Guards a year before. More important for understanding the events of the summer of 1967 is another common phenomenon in the history of revolutions: leaders who adhere to the original aims of the revolution appear as "extremists" when higher leaders compromise those aims and moderate the radical thrust of the movement. The fact of the matter is that in February Mao had embarked on a more moderate course—perhaps more because of what he perceived to be objective limitations than because of natural inclination—and those who were branded as "ultra-leftists" were those who did not move as rapidly as the Chairman or who were unwilling to do so. Moreover, the mass movement that Mao had called into being had acquired a radical life of its own, and much of it was no longer under anyone's control or direction.

To be sure, members of the Cultural Revolution Group did manipulate Red Guard groups and other mass organizations in their struggles with the PLA and the state bureaucracy, as PLA commanders and other bureaucratic leaders did in their turn, usually with greater success. The divisions at the top no doubt perpetuated the factionalism that plagued the mass movement below. Radical intellectuals such as Wang Li, Guan Feng, and Qi Benyu actually did organize a faction within the now divided Cultural Revolution Group itself, using the name of "May Sixteenth" to symbolize their commitment to the original goals of the Cultural Revolution, which, as it happened, coincided with their personal political interests. In the streets of Beijing in late May of 1967 young militants calling themselves the "May 16 Armed Corps" were observed marching, and they undoubtedly took their direction from the more radical leaders in the capital, including Mao's wife Jiang Qing, who was particularly noted for her inflammatory speeches to young rebels. But there is no evidence of any organized plot to seize state power, much less to overthrow Mao. Even less credible is the view that a few "ultra-leftist" intellectuals in Beijing, utterly lacking an organizational structure of any sort, could have incited and directed the massive violence that appeared virtually everywhere over the vast land during the summer. Save for providing ideological inspiration for those prepared to receive it, the influence of the Cultural Revolution Group intellectuals was largely confined to Beijing. A far more plausible explanation for the events of the "hot summer" is that they were largely spontaneous reactions, among rebel leaders and rank and file alike, to widespread fears that the promises of the Cultural Revolution were being betrayed.

The construction of the post-Cultural Revolution order and the preservation of such gains as could be salvaged from the wreckage of the upheaval required both a united leadership at the top and the obedience of the masses below. Neither was easy to achieve. Some of the more prominent of the radical leaders of the Cultural Revolution Group, such as Wang Li and Guan Feng, were arrested on Mao's orders early in September. But the counter-Cultural Revolution thrust against the seemingly hydra-headed "ultra-left" became a permanent purge that continued until virtually all the original leaders of the Cultural Revolution (save Mao himself) were removed from the political scene, for as Mao moved to the right, or at least to the center, most of his disciples found themselves too far to the left. In a sense, the continuing purge of ultra-leftists would eventually reach Mao himself, although not until several years after his death.

Purges in the increasingly Byzantine political atmosphere of Beijing were not directed exclusively against leftists. In March 1968 Yang Chengwu, acting chief of staff of the PLA since the dismissal of Luo Ruiqing in 1965, was arrested and replaced, along with the commander of the Beijing garrison and the political commissar of the air force. Reportedly, Lin Biao personally arrested Yang in the presence of 10,000 PLA officers meeting in the Great Hall of the People, despite the fact that the two men had been close comrades since the Long March. Yang had been in the forefront of PLA opposition to the Cultural Revolution Group, which brought him into a particularly acrimonious encounter with Jiang Qing. But Mao probably ordered his arrest not to defend the Cultural Revolution Group but because he feared that the army was moving too rapidly into the political vacuum and acquiring too large a share of power. The Chairman preferred to keep some semblance of balance between conservatives and radicals at the top of the political hierarchy. However that may have been, the incident suggested that the PLA was not necessarily the most stable pillar of "the dictatorship of the proletariat" and thus provided impetus to a campaign, now being quietly promoted by Mao as well as Zhou Enlai, to reestablish the supremacy of the Party and the central state apparatus as the most appropriate institutions to guide the country back to stability and order.[35]

While continuing political differences and intrigues among the leaders in Beijing hindered the stabilization of the post-Cultural Revolution order, the state of the mass movement posed more formidable barriers. The desired Maoist solution presupposed a "great alliance" of the popular revolutionary organizations whose members harmoniously and enthusiastically would integrate themselves into the "triple alliance." But there was little real unity among the people and even less enthusiasm. By the spring of 1968 most of the working class, having grown weary of the strife and struggles of a movement whose goals they could no longer easily define, turned politically passive, and many of their organizations disintegrated or became dormant. The mood of the urban populace was noted in Beijing by two American teachers who had perceptively observed the Cultural Revolution:

> [A] pall hung over the capital city of the revolution. As we took long walks down the back lanes of Peking and rode the buses from here to there, silently observing the people who had learned about revolution by making it, there could be no question that the joy had gone out of the movement. The spirit of adventure had been replaced by a grimness reflected in the faces of a people who still marched behind crimson banners and portraits of the Chairman, but who did so out of habit.[36]

Rebels who continued to be politically active in what remained of the mass revolutionary organizations were often distrustful of the Party cadres and PLA soldiers with whom they were enjoined to unite. The reconciliation was difficult at best and usually enforced by the army, which bore the ultimate responsibility for establishing the tripartite revolutionary committees from provinces down to factories, communes, and neighborhoods. But some of the more militant factions of the remnant mass movement continued to fight battles, in a war that was all but over, well into the summer of 1968. Among them were the surviving members of a coalition of radical

Red Guard organizations formed in Hunan province late in 1967, the *Shengwulian*. One of the most critically radical and theoretically sophisticated organizations produced by the Cultural Revolution, the *Shengwulian* combined the original ideals of the Cultural Revolution with the theory of a new bureaucratic ruling class, a notion Mao had briefly entertained but abandoned in the mid-1960s. The *Shengwulian* advocated Mao's theory of "continuous revolution under the dictatorship of the proletariat" but saw its purpose as the overthrow of China's "Red capitalist class" personified by Zhou Enlai. They praised the Cultural Revolution for having awakened the masses and for having stimulated popular democracy but criticized its leaders' proclivity to attack individuals instead of searching for the social class roots of China's social and political problems. They found those roots in China's "new bureaucratic bourgeoisie," which still controlled the old state machine and had usurped the power of the new revolutionary committees. Their proposed remedy was "smashing" the existing state apparatus in favor of a "People's Commune of China" based on the popular democratic principles of the Paris Commune.[37] The *Shengwulian*, or at least its leaders, were radical Maoists—but too radical for Mao in 1968. In January they were denounced by Minister of Public Security Kang Sheng and others as "anarchists" and "Trotskyists" and brutally suppressed over the following months by the army and secret police.

The final popular radical upsurge of the Cultural Revolution came in the spring and early summer of 1968. Rage against the heavy-handed intervention of the army, combined with a brief official campaign against "rightist trends," led to new outbursts of violence in various parts of the country, particularly between rival Red Guard groups and between students and soldiers. In Guangzhou old factional disputes flared into fighting so intense that the army was forced to impose a dawn-to-dusk curfew in the city, even while supplying arms to the conservative faction.[38] But the bloodiest fighting took place in the more remote provinces, and nowhere was the bloodshed greater than it was in Guangxi, where Wei Guoqing, political commissar of the provincial military district and future ally of Deng Xiaoping, carried out massacres and mass executions of radical Red Guards that were shocking even by the bloody standards of the time.[39] There had been much persecution and bloodshed earlier in the Cultural Revolution, coming from a variety of political quarters, and more was to come later, but the greatest toll in human lives probably was taken by the PLA in its general repression of Red Guards and other radicals in the summer of 1968.

The last battles of the Cultural Revolution were fought where the struggle had begun two years before: on university campuses in Beijing. For three months the campuses were turned into armed camps by student rebels, partly repeating the factional struggles of the previous summer (but now with more lethal weapons), partly in inchoate rebellion against the new authoritarian order being imposed from above. Finally, at the end of July, Mao summoned the student leaders to a personal audience and informed them (with tears in his eyes, it was reported) that the time had come for the Red Guards to pass from the historical scene.[40] Less gently, PLA-directed "Workers' Mao Zedong Thought Propaganda Teams" were sent to the campuses to end the fighting and discipline the students. Throughout the country, where Red Guard groups failed to dissolve themselves, they were swiftly crushed by the army, and not without further bloodshed. The death of the Red Guard movement thus came at the hands of the force that had assisted its birth. Many student rebels were dispatched to the countryside to be "reeducated by the poor and lower-middle peasants," while some were permitted to remain in school to study as best they could under the supervision of soldiers and workers.

Also sent to the countryside—to balance the political ledger, as it were—were hundreds of thousands of Party officials and cadres who had been among the more intransigent in their resistance to the Cultural Revolution. Tilling virgin lands and living a spartan life for several years, it was hoped, would cure them of their bureaucratic habits before they were returned to their official posts. The May Seventh Cadre Schools, as they were called, were to become a prominent feature of Chinese political life in the years after the Cultural Revolution, celebrated as a remedy for bureaucratism. At the time, in 1968, the removal of the more conspicuous bureaucrats from the cities was a way to ease tensions between masses and cadres and to ease the way for the reappearance of a presumably purified Party.

However, before the supremacy of the Party could be fully reestablished it was necessary to complete what was called the "phase of broad unity," now the desired political result of the Cultural Revolution. Progress toward unity was measured by the establishment of officially approved provincial revolutionary committees, which in turn were responsible for setting up similar "three-in-one" committees at district, county, and municipal levels of administration. The process went more slowly than was anticipated, but it was finally completed in September 1968, when revolutionary committees were established in the southwestern provinces and finally in Xinjiang and Tibet. In all cases the committees were formed largely under the auspices of the army, and indeed most provincial committees were headed by military commanders or PLA political commissars. Civilians chaired revolutionary committees only in the provinces of Hebei and Shaanxi. The masses, or more precisely those selected as their representatives, participated, but the representatives were drawn less from the mass organizations that had come into being during the Cultural Revolution than from what could be salvaged from the ruins of the mass movement. The revolutionary committees were hardly the "permanent mass standing organizations" instituted by "a system of general elections" that had been promised in 1966.

With the political situation more or less stabilized and the radicalism of the popular movement tamed, the Central Committee convened its Twelfth Plenum in October—in customary secrecy. The main business was the formal expulsion of Liu Shaoqi from the Party, a decision publicly announced at the end of the month. It was announced further that Liu had been removed from all his official posts, including that of Chairman of the People's Republic (a position he formally owed not to the Party but rather to the National People's Congress). The charge was that Liu not only had followed a "capitalist road" but also that he was a "renegade, traitor, and scab" and, moreover, a secret agent of the Guomindang who had consistently betrayed the Party since 1922. The purpose of those absurd accusations, so reminiscent of those leveled at the Old Bolsheviks by Stalin during the purge trials of the 1930s, was painfully obvious: to restore the revolutionary image of a more or less infallible Leninist Party. Now it could be suggested to the more gullible that the Liuist deviation was not one that grew naturally within the Party, but rather was an alien intrusion. The struggle between the "two lines" could now be reduced to a struggle between revolutionaries and counterrevolutionaries, between a proletarian Party that on the whole had maintained its revolutionary purity and enemy agents who had infiltrated its ranks from without.

As the Cultural Revolution waned in 1968, the cult of Mao, paradoxically, grew more extravagant. The writings of the Chairman were printed and distributed in ever greater volume. Portraits, statues, and plaster busts of Mao increased in both size and number. But whereas in the early days of the Cultural Revolution the cult had inspired, and had flourished on the basis of, the spontaneous revolutionary fervor of the people, it now manifested itself in a form resembling the established rituals of an orthodox church. It was observed, for example, that "PLA teams fostered group therapy sessions all over Peking, at which members of opposing factions sat together and embroidered portraits of the Chairman."[41] In households there were often "tablets of loyalty" to Mao's thought around which family members gathered to pay reverence. Schoolchildren no longer began the day by saying "good morning" but by chanting, "May Chairman Mao live ten thousand times ten thousand years." Throughout the land exhibition halls, decorated with traditional religious symbols, were built to chronicle the life and commemorate the deeds of the Chairman, and people came on organized pilgrimages to pay homage at what the official press termed "sacred shrines." The test of loyalty to Mao was no longer measured by revolutionary acts inspired by his thought but by the ability to recite his sayings and by the size of portraits carried in streets or hung in homes. In 1966 the Mao cult had stimulated iconoclasts; in 1968 it produced icons.

Both the person of Mao and his personality cult were essential for the birth of the Cultural Revolution, but the cult reached its strange apogee as the movement was being buried. It was perhaps inevitable that the people, having surrendered the power they briefly had grasped with declarations of eternal loyalty to the all-embracing wisdom of "Mao Zedong Thought," should now subordinate themselves to its author. Yet the phenomenon of the Mao cult flourishing on the wreckage of the mass movement was neither paradoxical nor unwelcome to the commanders of the PLA, for they long had favored "ideological transformation" under the aegis of Mao's Thought as a substitute for any real political movement directed against established institutions. And the army was now the dominant institution in the People's Republic.

The last official campaign of the Cultural Revolution, and the prelude to the full restoration of the Chinese Communist Party, was a 1968–69 movement to "purify class ranks." Its ostensible purpose was to investigate the political reliability of Party cadres and other leaders who had been attacked in the Cultural Revolution, as well as those who had risen to positions of authority during the upheaval. The criteria employed in the purge marked a further Maoist retreat on the question of defining class in a presumably socialist society. Whereas at the beginning of the Cultural Revolution Mao had settled on defining class in terms of political behavior, he now compromised with old-line bureaucrats who found it politically expedient to emphasize social class origins. Thus the investigative teams were instructed to inquire into not only the political histories of those who came under scrutiny but also their possible social ties to what were called the "five black categories"—those who once were (or were labeled) landlords, rich peasants, reactionaries, bad elements, or rightists. In keeping with the political temper of the times, the purge fell hardest on intellectuals and leaders of radical organizations formed during the Cultural Revolution. It was observed that conservative political leaders responded enthusiastically to the "purification" campaign.[42] The rectification movement spread from cadres to citizens in general, many of whom suffered persecution and discrimination because of their allegedly "bad" class backgrounds. With social origins again a principal standard of political judgment, those with less than pure family histories became fair game for others who had old political or personal grudges to settle, to say nothing of the multitude of new animosities generated by the Cultural Revolution.

The Cultural Revolution came to its anticlimactic end when the CCP opened its Ninth Congress on April 1, 1969, the first held since 1958 and the first to which observers from foreign Communist Parties were not invited. Lin Biao, now at the height of his power and prestige, delivered the main political report, generally assessing the Cultural Revolution (which he now redefined as a movement for "Party consolidation") and the international situation. At the time there seemed nothing exceptional about his remarks. The Congress' resolutions stressed the need to study "Mao Zedong Thought" (as it was officially canonized) as the sole guide for correct revolutionary action; the need to emphasize agriculture in economic development; and especially the need to rebuild the Party, which now was to be fully restored to its customary vanguard position. Mao underscored the latter point in a talk delivered shortly after the close of the Congress, adding that the Party should continue to be "rectified" by the masses in the process of its reconstruction. He also added that "after a few years maybe we shall have to carry out another [Cultural] revolution."[43]

The predominant role that the army had assumed in the political life of the People's Republic was reflected in the composition of the new Central Committee elected at the Ninth Congress. Of the 170 full and 109 alternate members named to the enlarged body, 49 percent were PLA soldiers, while the remainder were equally divided between old Party officials and representatives of mass organizations. The five-member Standing Committee of the Politburo, the locus of power, included, in addition to Mao and Lin Biao, Zhou Enlai, Chen Boda, and Kang Sheng. Perhaps reflecting doubts that even a rebuilt and rectified Party would remain faithfully Maoist, and perhaps even more reflecting the influence of the army, it was written into the new Party constitution that "Comrade Lin Biao is Comrade Mao Zedong's close comrade-in-arms *and successor.*"[44] The public communiqué released at the conclusion of the closed-door meeting on April 24 duly condemned Liu Shaoqi as a "counterrevolutionary revisionist," hailed the "great victories" of the Great Proletarian Cultural Revolution, and proclaimed that it had been "a congress of unity and a congress of victory."

Yet unity was to prove an elusive goal, and the nature of the victory was difficult to define. The Cultural Revolution had begun with a wholesale attack on the Communist Party; it ended with the resurrection of the Party in its orthodox Lenninist form, albeit shorn of Mao's more prominent opponents. In 1966–67 a massive popular movement had flourished on the basis of the principle that "the masses must liberate themselves"; by 1969 the mass movement had disintegrated, and selected remnants of it had been absorbed by old bureaucratic apparatuses. Much blood had been shed, but what had changed? That question must have been on the minds of many Chinese in the spring of 1969.

NOTES

1. Besides Wu Han, who was vice mayor of Beijing, the best known satirists were Deng Tuo and Liao Mosha, both leading officials in the Beijing Party Committee. The essays, including Deng's "Special Treatment for Amnesia," originally appeared in leading Beijing newspapers, one of which, *Frontline,* was edited by Deng.
2. Mao Tse-tung [Mao Zedong], "Speech at the Tenth Plenum of the Eighth Central Committee," September 24, 1962, in Stuart R. Schram (ed.), *Mao Tse-tung Unrehearsed: Talks and Letters, 1956–71* (Harmondsworth, Middlesex, England: Penguin, 1974), p. 195.
3. Yao Wen-yuan [Yao Wenyuan], "On the New Historical Play 'Dismissal of Hai Jui,'" Shanghai *Wen-hui-pao,* November 10, 1965. For an English translation, see *The Case of P'eng Teh-huai, 1959–68* (Hong Kong: Union Research Institute, 1968), pp. 235–61.
4. The May 16 circular was not published until a year later, on May 16, 1967. For an English translation of the text, see *Peking Review,* No. 21 (May 19, 1967), pp. 6–9.
5. The incident is described by Hong Yung Lee, *The Politics of the Chinese Cultural Revolution* (Berkeley: University of California Press, 1978), pp. 215–16. Lee's richly documented and analytically insightful volume is by far the most important study for understanding the social class dimensions of the Cultural Revolution. On the role of the Party work teams in the student movement, see *ibid.,* ch. 2, pp. 26–63. As Lee concludes: "While the members of underprivileged social groups became the victims selected by the Party organization, the most privileged groups, the children of cadres, became the major allies of the Party organization." *Ibid.,* p. 63.
6. The social basis of Red Guard political factionalism is explored in perceptive and detailed fashion in Stanley Rosen, *Red Guard Factionalism and the Cultural Revolution in Guangzhou (Canton)* (Boulder, Colo.: Westview Press, 1982), and in Lee, *The Politics of the Chinese Cultural Revolution.* For a representative sampling of the class origins of radical and conservative Red Guards, see Rosen, Table 4.2, pp. 148–49.
7. *Decision of the Central Committee of the Chinese Communist Party Concerning the Great Proletarian Cultural Revolution* (Peking: Foreign Languages Press, 1966), pp. 1–13.
8. Mao Tse-tung, "Talk to Leaders of the Centre," July 21, 1966, in Schram (ed.), *Mao Tse-tung Unrehearsed,* p. 253.
9. For a detailed account of Liu's politics and policies, see Lowell Dittmer, *Liu Shao-ch'i and the Chinese Cultural Revolution,* revised edition. (Armonk, N.Y.: M.E. Sharpe, 1998.)
10. "Long Live the Revolutionary Rebel Spirit of the Proletariat," *Peking Review,* September 9, 1966, pp. 20–21. The injunction to "turn the old world upside down" was probably derived from last line of the poem "Two Birds: A Dialogue," written by Mao in 1965.
11. For a graphic description of Lao She's ordeal, see Jonathan D. Spence, *The Gate of Heavenly Peace* (New York: Viking Press, 1981), pp. 343–49.
12. Lee, *Politics of the Cultural Revolution,* pp. 54–55.
13. Mao Tse-tung, "Talk at Central Work Conference," October 25, 1966, in Schram (ed.), *Mao Tse-tung Unrehearsed,* p. 271.
14. "A Summary of the Last Two Months of Progress in the Cultural Revolution," *Tung-feng chan-pao* [*Dongfeng zhanbao*] *(East Wind Combat News),* December 11, 1966, JPRS No. 40488, p. 13.

15. Among the more noteworthy of the many accounts of the Cultural Revolution in Shanghai are Neale Hunter, *Shanghai Journal* (Boston: Beacon Press, 1969); Andrew G. Walder, *Chang Ch'un-ch'iao and Shanghai's January Revolution* (Ann Arbor: Center for Chinese Studies, University of Michigan, 1978); Gerald Tannebaum, "The 1967 Shanghai January Revolution Recounted," *Eastern Horizon,* May-June 1968, pp. 7–25; Parris Chang, "Shanghai and Chinese Politics: Before and After the Cultural Revolution," in Christopher Howe (ed.), *Shanghai: Revolution and Development in an Asian Metropolis* (Cambridge: Cambridge University Press, 1981), pp. 66–90; Lynn T. White III, "Shanghai's Polity in the Cultural Revolution," in John W. Lewis (ed.), *The City in Communist China* (Stanford, Calif.: Stanford University Press, 1971), pp. 325–70.

16. Another perversion of a social ideal wrought by Liuist economic and educational policies involved young workers and students in "half-work and half-study" programs. Originally designed to reduce the distinction between mental and manual labor and provide educational opportunities for disadvantaged workers, it simply functioned as another source of cheap labor. When the program's participants rebelled at the beginning of the Cultural Revolution, they were denounced by Party officials as "riffraff." Lee, *Politics of the Cultural Revolution,* pp. 132–33.

17. Quoted in Hunter, *Shanghai Journal,* pp. 139–40.

18. For detailed information on the multitude of rebel groups active in Shanghai during the Cultural Revolution, see *ibid., passim.* Eighteen of the more prominent Shanghai organizations are listed on pp. 300–301.

19. For a detailed account of Chang's manipulation of the Shanghai revolutionary movement in January and February 1967, see Walder, *Chang Ch'un-ch'iao and Shanghai's January Revolution,* ch. 7, pp. 51–63.

20. Among the more prominent groups opposing Chang, in addition to Keng's Second Regiment, were the Workers' Third Army (which had broken away from the Workers' Headquarters), the Red Flag Army of demobilized soldiers, and several radical student groups, including the largest of the student organizations, the Red Revolutionaries, previously closely allied with the Workers' Headquarters. On the opposition to Zhang, see *ibid.* pp. 58–63; Lee, *The Politics of the Chinese Cultural Revolution,* pp. 146–50; and Hunter, *Shanghai Journal,* pp. 221–67.

21. The leading figure in the "New Shanghai People's Commune" was Geng Qinzheng, leader of the Second Regiment, who claimed the support of forty-eight revolutionary organizations and greater popular support than that enjoyed by Zhang Chunqiao. On Geng Qinzheng's role in Shanghai politics, see Hunter, *Shanghai Journal,* chapters 11–13.

22. Mao Tse-tung, "Talks at Three Meetings with Comrades Chang Ch'un-ch'iao and Yao Wen-yuan," in Schram (ed.), *Mao Tse-tung Unrehearsed,* pp. 277–78.

23. *SCMP,* No. 4147.

24. Karl Marx, *The Eighteenth Brumaire of Louis Bonaparte* (Chicago: Kerr, 1919), p. 146.

25. Lee, *The Politics of the Chinese Cultural Revolution,* pp. 189–91. On the generally conservative role of the army, see pp. 168–203, 234–43.

26. *Ibid.,* p. 183.

27. As, for example, in Guangxi. See *ibid.,* p. 160.

28. Beijing, Shanghai, and Tianjin are autonomous cities administered directly by the central government rather than by provincial authorities.

29. More than a thousand were killed in the battles of June and July, while industrial production was reduced to half of capacity. Thomas W. Robinson, "The Wuhan Incident: Local Strife and Provincial Rebellion During the Cultural Revolution," *The China Quarterly,* No. 47 (July-September 1971), pp. 413–18.

30. Lee, *The Politics of the Chinese Cultural Revolution,* p. 249.

31. Lin Biao's speech was delivered to a meeting of high-level military and political leaders in Beijing. For a translation, see *SCMP* No. 4036, pp. 1–6. Lin, as commander of the PLA, obviously had a strong interest in preserving the institution, unlike the radical intellectuals of the Cultural Revolution Group.

32. For an English translation of the text of Jiang Qing's speech, see *SCMP* No. 4069, pp. 1–9.

33. For the more or less official Maoist version, see William Hinton, *Turning Point in China* (New York: Monthly Review Press, 1972), especially pp. 71–78.

34. The purge of Chen Boda in 1970 and the fall of Lin Biao in 1971 are discussed in Chapter 20.

35. Conflicting, and sometimes absurd, explanations of the Yang Chengwu incident emanated from Beijing over the years, not excluding a 1972 charge that Yang had been involved with the infamous "May Sixteenth" group in a plot against Mao. On the latter, see Hinton, *Turning Point in China,* pp. 76–77 and footnote on pp. 39–40. Yang reemerged on the political and military scene in 1974.

36. David Milton and Nancy Dall Milton, *The Wind Will Not Subside: Years in Revolutionary China 1964–1969* (New York: Pantheon Books, 1976), p. 330.

37. For some of the principal *Shengwulien* documents, including its "Program" and the treatise "Whither China?" see Klaus Mehnert, *Peking and the New Left* (Berkeley, Calif.: Center for Chinese Studies, 1969). The organization's ideological inspiration may well have come from one of the last "ultra-leftist" intellectuals in the Cultural Revolution Group, Qi Benyu, who was purged in February 1968 as the *Shengwulien* was being suppressed.

38. On the Red Guard movement in Guangzhou, see Rosen, *Red Guard Factionalism.*

39. Victor Falkenheim, "The Cultural Revolution in Kwangsi, Yunnan and Fukien," *Asian Survey,* IX, No. 8 (1969): 580–85; Stanley Karnow, *Mao and China: From Revolution to Revolution* (New York: Viking, 1972), pp. 434–35, 438; *Far Eastern Economic Review,* July 4, 1968, p. 13.

40. The text of the tape-recorded talk, "Dialogue with the Capital Red Guards," widely distributed in China at the time, is translated in JPRS No. 61269-2 (February 20, 1974). On the struggle between the Red Guard "Heaven" and "Earth" factions in Beijing, see Lee, *The Politics of the Chinese Cultural Revolution,* chs. 7–9 passim; William Hinton, *Hundred Day War: The Cultural Revolution at Tsinghua University* (New York: Monthly Review Press, 1972); and Milton and Milton, *The Wind Will Not Subside,* pp. 317–29. In reply to student protests that their suppression was being directed from behind the scenes by a "black hand," Mao acknowledged that "The black hand is nobody else but me" (Milton and Milton, p. 321).

41. Milton and Milton, *The Wind Will Not Subside,* p. 335.

42. Lee, *The Politics of the Chinese Cultural Revolution,* p. 291. For a description and analysis of the campaign, see pp. 287–96.

43. Mao Tse-tung, "Talk at the First Plenum of the Ninth Central Committee of the Chinese Communist Party," April 28, 1969, in Schram (ed.), *Mao Tse-tung Unrehearsed,* pp. 282–89.

44. "The Constitution of the Communist Party of China," adopted April 14, 1969, text in *Peking Review,* April 30, 1969. Italics added.

19

Social Results of the Cultural Revolution

I N 1969 IT APPEARED that the Cultural Revolution had come full circle, returning the People's Republic to its pre-Cultural Revolution starting point. Political power resided where it had been three years before—in the closely intertwined trinity of Party, army, and state bureaucracy. The Party was being rebuilt on its traditional Leninist foundations and was being restored to its old preeminence. To be sure, new revolutionary committees had come into being at all levels of political administration and economic life, but it took little political foresight to know that such committees soon would become instruments to carry out policies decided upon within the inner councils of the Party, whose supreme authority was now being reestablished.

Yet, for both better and worse, the Cultural Revolution did bring important changes in the social character and political climate of life in China, even if not in its formal institutions. One immediately apparent change was that the reins of political power were firmly in Maoist hands. More precisely, they were largely in the hands of Mao himself, for many eminent "Maoists" had fallen by the wayside in the course of the upheaval, and others were soon to follow them to political oblivion. That power now rested with Mao was a basic political fact, and it had enormous social consequences in an historical situation where political power was crucial in determining the direction of social development. The power Mao gained from the Cultural Revolution was employed to pursue relatively egalitarian socioeconomic policies in the late 1960s and the early years of the new decade, reversing many of the "Liuist" policies and practices dominant in the years just before the great upheaval. Yet the Maoist program that emerged from all the revolutionary fury and thunder of the Cultural Revolution was essentially reformist in character, intended to mitigate the more glaring manifestations of inequality and elitism rather than to fundamentally change the social and political structure of the People's Republic. The post–Cultural Revolution Maoist program did not bring about any revolutionary transformation of existing social relationships, as advertised at the time by Maoist ideologists.[1] Moreover, much of what might have proved positive in Mao's socioeconomic strategy was largely vitiated by the increasingly despotic and arbitrary exercise of political power at both the highest and the lowest levels of the state apparatus during the last years of the Maoist regime, one of the many unintended consequences of the Cultural Revolution and a phenomenon that some post-Maoist leaders would later condemn as "feudal-fascism." But the changes wrought by the upheaval, both positive and negative, profoundly affected the lives of the vast majority of the Chinese people. Among surviving victims and participants alike, the traumatic experiences of the Cultural Revolution shaped all political concerns and consciousness through the remainder of the Maoist era and well into the Deng era that followed. However one chooses to judge the nature and results of the Cultural Revolution, the three turbulent years that make up its history cannot be dismissed as simply another case of *plus ça change, plus c'est la même chose.*

The most obvious result of the Cultural Revolution, and perforce the starting point for any evaluation of the upheaval and its consequences, is that it took a fearsome toll of human lives. Of the number killed, no official count was taken at the time. Such official figures as have emerged from the post-Mao regime are fragmentary at best. The estimates of outside observers vary greatly, depending on the political proclivities of the observer. But even official statistics, however incomplete and scattered, suggest killings on a massive scale. When the Gang of Four was brought to trial in 1980,[2] the official indictment charged that the Gang and its supporters were responsible for the deaths of 34,000 innocent people during what is now called the "cultural revolution decade," 1966–1976. The indictment itself suggests a far greater toll. In providing such details as it did on specific incidents, it reported 14,000 deaths in the southwestern province of Yunnan alone and more than 16,000 in sparsely populated Inner Mongolia.[3]

A more independent and probably more reliable calculation was made by Li Zhengtian, one of the ideological forerunners of the Democracy Movement of the late 1970s. According to Li's investigation, some 40,000 people were killed in the province of Guangdong during the Cultural Revolution, with the greatest number of lives taken during the PLA suppression of the Red Guard movement in 1968.[4] Li's estimate for Guangdong is roughly consistent with a widely accepted nationwide figure of 400,000 Cultural Revolution deaths, a number first reported in 1979 by the Agence France Presse correspondent in Beijing based on estimates of unofficial but "usually reliable" Chinese sources.[5] The toll may well have been higher. It is unlikely that it was less.

Besides the dead, millions of Chinese limped away from the battles and repression of the Cultural Revolution physically and psychologically scarred. Many were beaten and tortured in endless "struggle" sessions, and others were wounded in factional battles that grew ever more violent in direct proportion as they became devoid of political purpose. Children were persecuted for the alleged political sins (or social origins) of their parents, and parents were denounced by their children. Millions were arbitrarily arrested and sent to prisons and labor camps, and many more millions were shipped off to labor or to idle away their days in the more remote areas of Manchuria and Xinjiang. Lives were broken and careers destroyed. Whatever else it may have been, the Cultural Revolution was a time of enormous human suffering.

The persecution of intellectuals and cadres has been widely publicized both within and outside China. It is less well known that while virtually all factions involved in the Cultural Revolution engaged in violence and committed atrocities in what became a seemingly endless cycle of violence and revenge, the greatest atrocities and a heavy share of the killings appear to have been the work of the PLA, especially in the general repression of radical Red Guard and workers' organizations in the summer of 1968. It is hardly surprising that this should have been the case when an armed, organized military force was given (or assumed) a free hand to rid the country of an anarchistic and poorly armed popular movement whose members had perhaps taken too literally the Maoist slogan "Dare to rebel." It was an army, moreover, made up mostly of young peasants who were inherently suspicious of rebellious urban students. Nor is it surprising that leaders in Beijing, both in the Maoist and post-Mao eras, should wish to obscure the role of the PLA in the atrocities of the Cultural Revolution, for the "people's army," if not necessarily the "pillar of the dictatorship of the proletariat," is certainly the pillar of the Chinese Communist state. Rather than tarnish the image of the PLA, whose commanders are so closely politically intertwined with the leaders of the Party, the latter find it more convenient to blame their political foes for the evils of the time. Thus the 1980 indictment of the Gang of Four, which chronicles the 14,000 deaths in the province of Yunnan, attributes the tragedy to "ultra-leftists" who, it is said, slandered the provincial Party leader—while failing to mention the well-known fact that the great majority of the dead were radical Red Guards massacred by local units of the Chinese army. Nor have post-Mao authorities acknowledged the bloody reign of terror against radical organizations and alleged "leftists" in Jiangsu province and the city of Nanjing carried out by General Xu Shiyu, commander of the powerful Nanjing Military Region. Beginning in the early months of 1967, General Xu's repression of radicals reached its apogee in 1970. In a year-long "Drag Out May 16" campaign directed against alleged "ultra-leftists," over 100,000 people were accused of leftist heresies; many were executed, imprisoned, or exiled to labor reform camps.[6]

If Beijing's distortions are politically understandable, even though disquieting, eyebrows might well be raised when foreign writers perpetuate the fiction. While the sufferings of intellectuals during the Cultural Revolution have been described in grisly detail, the massacres carried out by the PLA are rarely mentioned. Rather, the atrocities of the era are vaguely attributed, at least in the more popular literature, to "radical Maoists." The radical Maoists, however, were as much the victims of Mao's Cultural Revolution as were China's intellectuals—and in far greater numbers.

Nonetheless the Cultural Revolution yielded inhumanities in sufficient quantity for all groups and institutions involved to share some part of the blame. And one of the products of the years 1966–69 was a bitter legacy of grief, distrust, hatred, and a thirst for revenge. Such was the gruesome background for the politics and policies of the 1970s.

The Peasantry and the Relationship between Town and Countryside

The Cultural Revolution was a distinctly urban movement. Its great political battles were fought in the cities, and its main revolutionary actors were urban workers, students, and intellectuals. But such meager social gains as it yielded went to the countryside.

During the years that the cities were in turmoil, most of the countryside remained politically quiescent. Villages on the outskirts of cities sometimes were drawn into the struggles of the Cultural Revolution. Old Party organizations and new rebel groups both attempted to recruit peasants for the urban battles. In the relatively few cases where peasants acted on their own between 1966 and 1968, they did so for mostly "economist" ends, marching into the cities and towns to demand an extension of private family plots and free markets. But the vast majority of the peasantry never became directly involved in the main political struggles of the Cultural Revolution. That was in keeping with the desires of the leaders in Beijing, whose policy was to insulate the countryside from the urban battles. Red Guards were forbidden to enter the villages, and although the prohibition was not always heeded, the student radicals rarely found rural audiences responsive to revolutionary appeals. Directives issued from Beijing, to be sure, called for poor peasants to wage their own "class struggle" and to struggle against the "four olds," but above all the directives emphasized the need to maintain and increase productivity. While temporary disruptions in the factories could be tolerated, this clearly was not the case in agriculture, a precarious enterprise even in the best of times in China. When token forces of PLA soldiers were sent to the countryside in the summer of 1967 to "aid agriculture" and assist the "poor and lower-middle peasants," they found that many villagers had never heard of the Cultural Revolution, while most of the remainder were indifferent to the battles being waged in the cities. The task of the soldiers, in any event, was less to promote class struggle than to ensure that such struggles as there were did not hinder production.

Only when the Cultural Revolution was waning in the cities in 1968–69 was the movement extended to the countryside. There were political and social conflicts in the villages, but they were relatively benign in comparison to the struggles that had racked the cities. The situation varied enormously from region to region and from village to village. Some villages split into political factions, mimicking those in the cities or in nearby middle schools, but the divisions often were based more on old clan and neighborhood differences than on political ones.[7] In many areas there was an intensification of class antagonisms, but this usually involved "poor and lower-middle peasant associations" reenacting old hatreds against former landlords and rich peasants, based on the memory of class divisions that had long ago ceased to exist. One result was often the persecution of individuals stigmatized with "bad" class labels, but it was hardly the "life and death" class struggle depicted in the official press. In the countryside, as Richard Kraus has pointed out, there was a particularly strong tendency to translate old class designations into new caste categories.[8] In many villages the Cultural Revolution "struggle between two lines" was largely confined to PLA-organized ideological campaigns against Liu Shaoqi's "revisionist" policies and the organization of sessions for the study of the thoughts of Mao Zedong. The one universal feature of the Cultural Revolution in the rural areas was a grotesque burgeoning of the cult of Mao, with villages erecting communal "rooms of loyalty" dedicated to Mao's thought and peasant families paying reverence to the Chairman before household "tablets of loyalty," much in the fashion they traditionally venerated their ancestors. Almost equally widespread was the degeneration of village political life into a brutal struggle for power behind a façade of "class struggle" and the use of Cultural Revolution political slogans as a pretext for settling old personal and kinship grudges.

Nonetheless, the Cultural Revolution did yield significant changes in rural social and economic policies, although they resulted less from such political and social struggles as took place in the villages than through the commands of a state-Party apparatus now under Maoist control. Thus Liu Shaoqi's rural policies, now condemned as "capitalist" and "revisionist," were replaced by those advocated by Mao during the abortive Socialist Education Movement of the early 1960s. If there was somewhat greater participation by poorer peasants in the socioeconomic life of the villages and communes, the rural areas in general were subjected to greater political control and economic coercion by higher Party organs and the state administration in the 1970s than had been the case in the 1960s. The Cultural Revolution, in any event, certainly did not result in peasant control over the institutions that governed their lives.

Maoist rural policies were mainly directed toward halting the "spontaneous tendencies toward capitalism" that appeared to have been developing so rapidly in the early 1960s. Private household plots, which had grown to 15 percent or more of the cultivated land, were now limited to 5 percent. Free rural markets, while not entirely abolished, were severely restricted, and peasants were subjected to strong political and ideological pressures to sell privately produced "sideline" goods to state commercial organizations at government-determined prices. Renewed efforts were undertaken to curb the endemic problem of cadre corruption in the allocation of workpoints for collective labor, one of the main sources of growing socioeconomic inequalities in the years prior to the Cultural Revolution. But the workpoint system remained the same, resting (at least in theory) on the inherently non-egalitarian socialist principle "to each according to one's labor" rather than the communist principle "to each according to one's need."

Although egalitarianism was rejected in practice in most areas of the countryside, much emphasis was given to a campaign to "learn from Dazhai," a brigade that epitomized the Maoist ideals of collectivism and self-reliance. Here, in a rather remote and barren area of Shaanxi province, it is said that a group of selfless peasants organized spontaneously to build a flourishing socialist community from the fruits of the earth. Rejecting private cultivation of household plots, they evolved a new system of collective work and remuneration known as "self-assessment and public discussion," with workpoints determined by such criteria as political consciousness, honesty, and spirit of dedication to work performed for the good of the community as a whole. Inspired by the teachings of Mao, it was said, they constructed a largely self-sufficient community through the full mobilization of the labor power of previously underemployed peasants, with the brigade rather than the production team as the unit of account. The Dazhai experiment was first set forward as a model by Mao in 1964, and with the Cultural Revolution it became a national model to emulate. The Dazhai brigade's peasant leader, Chen Yonggui, became a national political figure, elevated to the Party's Central Committee in 1969 and to its Politburo in 1973. But Dazhai, however socially progressive and economically successful, always remained a romanticized model, an example of the spartan and egalitarian principles around which Maoists believed rural communities should be organized, but not necessarily what Chinese rural life really was or was becoming.[9]

Probably the most socially significant and economically successful of the new-rural policies resulting from the Cultural Revolution was the regeneration of the program to build industrial enterprises in the countryside. Rural industrialization had been announced as one of the goals of the Cultural Revolution at the outset of the movement. "While the main task of the peasants in the commune is agriculture," Mao wrote in May of 1966, "they should at the same time study military affairs, politics, and culture, [and] where conditions permit, they should collectively run small plants."[10] The goal was not new. Many local rural industries had been established during the Great Leap Forward campaign, but most proved nonviable or atrophied during the ensuing economic crisis, and the effort was largely abandoned. In the aftermath of the Cultural Revolution the program was revived, and thereafter it thrived as one of the main innovations of the Maoist developmental strategy foreshadowing the enormous growth of the township and village industries in the post-Mao years. The Maoist aims were social as well as economic: social in their promise to diminish two of the "three great differences"—between workers and peasants, and between town and countryside; and economic in their use of local labor and resources that otherwise would go to waste, thus contributing both to rural development and the national economy in general.

Most rural industries initially were established to assist agricultural production. The emphasis was on the building of small enterprises for the production and repair of farm machinery and tools, the manufacture of chemical fertilizers, the processing of locally produced agricultural products, and small technical centers to develop improved seeds and popularize new agricultural techniques. By the end of the Maoist era in 1976, half of China's chemical fertilizer was being produced by local rural industries, as was a large portion of the country's rapidly growing output of farm machinery. In addition, many small factories in the countryside were producing cement, pig iron, construction materials, electricity, chemicals, pharmaceuticals, and a variety of small consumer goods. By the mid-1970s, it was not unusual for a single county (*xian*) to have a hundred or more such small factories producing several hundred different products.[11]

The program of rural industrialization was part (and probably the most successful part) of a larger Maoist design to achieve local socioeconomic self-sufficiency in rural areas and to narrow the gap between town and countryside. At the end of the Maoist era, the program could claim a good many accomplishments: the transformation of almost 20,000,000 peasants into full-time or part-time industrial workers in the countryside; some amelioration of the chronic problem of rural underemployment; and, in the case of the more successful enterprises, the generation of new capital for agriculture and for further investment in the expanding rural industries. Moreover, rural industry contributed to the regeneration of the communes as vital socioeconomic organizations in the years following the Cultural Revolution, with some of the more advanced communes becoming mini-technological centers disseminating scientific knowledge and technical skills to surrounding agricultural areas. Although the development of industry in the countryside did not have any statistically significant impact on the gap between urban and rural income levels, which remained as wide after the Cultural Revolution as before, it was a program that proceeded, by and large, in accordance with the dictum Mao had set forth in 1961:

> Don't crowd into the cities. Vigorously develop industry in the countryside and turn peasants into workers on the spot. This is a very important question of policy; and that is that rural living standards must not be lower than in the cities. They can be more or less the same or slightly higher than in the cities. Every commune must have its own economic center and its own institutions of higher education to bring up its own intellectuals. Only in this way can we truly resolve the problem of excessive population in the rural areas.[12]

The Cultural Revolution also resulted in a shift of emphasis, from the cities to the countryside in two other vitally important areas of Chinese life: medical care and education. In the early 1960s, with the retrenchment following the disasters of the Great Leap, more than 200,000 of China's 280,000 rural health clinics were closed, while the number of urban clinics nearly doubled.[13] In 1965 Mao Zedong, complaining that doctors were being trained "only for the benefit of the cities" in a country where the vast majority of the population lived in the rural areas, proposed some radical measures to remedy the situation:

> In medical education there is no need to accept only higher middle school graduates. . . . It will be enough to give three years [of medical training] to graduates from higher primary schools. They would then study and raise their standards mainly through practice. If this kind of doctor is sent down to the countryside, even if they haven't much talent, they would be better than quacks and witch doctors, and the villages would be better able to afford to keep them.

Mao also suggested a greater emphasis on preventive medicine and the treatment of "commonly seen, frequently occurring, and widespread diseases" rather than the study of "rare, profound, and difficult diseases at the so-called pinnacle of science." He concluded, "We should leave behind in the city a few of the less able doctors who graduated one or two years ago, and the others should all go into the countryside. . . . In medical and health work put the emphasis on the countryside!"[14]

The policies pursued after 1969 followed these proposals, by and large. When medical schools resumed functioning after the disruptions of the Cultural Revolution, the program of formal study was reduced from six to three years in order to graduate doctors to meet immediate needs, and the curriculum was revised to deal with the problems for which, as Mao had put it, "the masses most need solutions." The new classes admitted for study in 1971 included a far greater number of students from rural areas, many of them younger "barefoot" doctors who lacked formal education but who possessed a wealth of practical knowledge and experience. The entire national health care system was radically decentralized, with urban hospitals and medical schools establishing clinics and local teaching institutes on the rural communes and providing doctors to staff them. More mobile medical teams were dispatched to the countryside by urban medical centers and the PLA (which has its own system of medical schools and hospitals), and all city medical personnel were required to serve on such teams or at commune medical centers on a rotating basis. In 1969 the training program of barefoot doctors was greatly accelerated and systematized. By the mid-1970s more than a million such paramedics (the number having increased more than fourfold since 1965) were engaged in preventive medicine; providing health education and birth control information and devices; and treating common illnesses while referring more seriously ill patients to commune or city hospitals. Although the new health care system in the countryside was financed primarily by local funds from communes, brigades, and production teams, central government support was essential. Professional medical personnel working in the countryside were on state salaries, mobile medical teams were state financed, and the costs of training barefoot doctors were largely borne by the state. In all, this entailed a significant transfer of resources from urban to rural areas, although the level of medical services still remained far lower in the countryside than in the cities.

The radical restructuring of the educational system during and after the Cultural Revolution benefited the countryside much in the same fashion as the reforms in health care. The deficiencies and inequities in the system that prevailed in the years before 1966 were glaring and growing. Educational resources were concentrated in the urban areas, not only in universities and middle schools but in the quantity and quality of primary schools as well. Entrance exams and a conventional grading system, the enforcement of rigid age limits for attendance, and the imposition of tuition fees severely limited educational opportunities for the urban poor and even more so for rural youth. In large measure, the system and the content of education were oriented to train students for professional careers in the cities and served to perpetuate the privileges of urban elites. It was certainly partially intentional; in the early 1960s, the number of rural and part-time schools declined, while urban special preparatory schools designed for the children of Party and government officials expanded.[15] Moreover, the entire educational system was both costly and inefficient. Universities produced an abundance of specialized graduates for already overstaffed government and urban industrial bureaus, but few with the technological skills so much needed in the countryside.

The educational system had come under criticism in the years prior to 1966. The severest critic was Mao Zedong, who in 1964 concluded that "the present method of education ruins talent and ruins youth." He advocated that the period of formal schooling be shortened and that a new system based on "the union of education and productive labor" replace the old system of book learning divorced from real life. Mao emphasized his long-held belief that the best and most creative form of education is that which comes from self-teaching in the course of practice. To support the argument he converted Confucius into a poor peasant, an "all-round" person, and even a forerunner of the "mass line":

> Confucius was from a poor peasant family; he herded sheep, and never attended middle school or university either. He was a musician, he did all sorts of things. . . . He may also have been an accountant. He could play the lute and drive a

chariot, ride a horse and shoot with bow and arrow. He produced seventy-two sages, such as Yen Hui and Tseng-tzu, and he had 3,000 disciples. In his youth, he came from the masses, and understood something of the suffering of the masses.[16]

But significant educational reforms did not come until the Cultural Revolution shattered the established Party apparatus. When schools reopened, after having largely ceased to function during the Cultural Revolution, they did so in accordance with new Maoist educational policies. Certainly the most positive feature of those policies was the expansion of education in the rural areas. State aid to relatively well-off urban districts was reduced, and funds were redirected to the poorer areas, primarily in the countryside. Although local self-reliance was proclaimed the guiding principle, state financial aid and policies remained critical in determining how and where education was provided. The new policies placed a priority on primary schools; and since primary education was already universal in the cities, the aim was to introduce at least five years of primary schooling even in remote rural areas. During the now condemned "cultural revolution decade" (1966–76) there was a dramatic increase in primary and secondary enrollments in the countryside, with primary enrollments increasing from about 116,000,000 to 150,000,000 over the decade and secondary enrollments (including the addition of two-year junior middle school classes to village primary schools) rising from 15,000,000 to 58,000,000.[17]

The expansion of rural schools was accompanied by attempts to dismantle the state educational bureaucracy and decentralize the school system. Whereas prior to the Cultural Revolution rural schools were administered by county governments (organs of the state bureaucracy) in accordance with standardized national policies, the new policy called for local community control. Primary schools were generally to be managed by production brigades and middle schools by communes, with the aim of providing peasants a greater voice in selecting teachers and teaching materials, in recommending students for admission to middle schools and universities, and in refashioning the curriculum to meet particular local needs.[18] In addition, tuition fees, entrance examinations, and age limits on student attendance were abolished. Many of the spare-time and work-study educational programs introduced during the Great Leap Forward were revived. Changes in admissions criteria and curricula in middle schools and universities enhanced opportunities in higher education for rural youth. For admission to universities, entrance examinations were downgraded in favor of a system of recommendation from local production units and selection on the basis of political criteria as well as academic ability, with priority given to poorer peasants, workers, soldiers, and lower level cadres. University students were admitted only after having completed several years of productive labor and were required to return to work in their home areas after graduation.

The vigor with which the new rural education programs were pursued in the early 1970s was in striking contrast to the dismal state of education (especially higher education) in the cities in the post-Cultural Revolution era. Yet if the peasantry generally benefited from the social reforms yielded by the Cultural Revolution, they derived few if any economic gains from the upheaval. Contrary to speculation at the time, the Cultural Revolution did not significantly disrupt agricultural production, which continued to grow at a modest rate of about 3 percent annually in the late 1960s and early 1970s.[19] But peasant incomes remained essentially stagnant, in view of a 2 percent per annum rate of population increase, and there was no rise in rural living standards or per capita food consumption. After the Cultural Revolution, as before, the countryside was economically exploited by the cities and remained the main source of state capital accumulation for investment in urban industry. The rural surplus that might otherwise have gone to raise peasant living standards continued to be drained into state coffers through taxes, forced grain deliveries, and state pricing policies. Even though a good many peasants benefited from the program of rural industrialization and from reforms in education and health care, the Cultural Revolution did not bring any fundamental change in the relationship between town and countryside.

The Working Class and the Division of Labor in Industry

While the Cultural Revolution brought a small measure of social, if not economic, gains for the peasantry, it yielded nothing for the urban workers who had been the principal actors in the revolutionary dramas of 1966–68. There were, of course, widely publicized Maoist claims that the Cultural Revolution resulted in a revolutionary transformation in the industrial division of labor, changes that presumably found expression in what one writer termed "the gradual elimination of the distinction between performance tasks and administrative tasks [and] between manual labor and intellectual labor."[20] There is little to support these rather grandiose claims; indeed, all evidence suggests that productive relationships in the factories remained much the same after 1969 as they were in the years prior to 1966.

During the Cultural Revolution, to be sure, a wholesale attack against the existing system of industrial organization was launched by rebel workers' groups, sometimes supported by the more radical leaders in Beijing.

Demands were heard for the immediate producers to assume control over the means of production; elimination of wage differentials and bonuses in favor of a more egalitarian system of remuneration; abolition of the system of temporary and contract workers; workers' freedom to work in factories and enterprises of their own choosing rather than in places assigned by the state; and the abolition of Party-controlled trade unions.

These demands were not wholly ignored in the new industrial policies pursued after the Cultural Revolution.[21] The trade union bureaucracy, having collapsed along with local Party organizations between 1966 and 1968, was formally abolished along with the central Ministry of Labor. Individual bonuses and piecework rate wages were eliminated as part of a general policy that aimed to establish the primacy of moral and political incentives over material ones. The bureaucratic and hierarchical character of enterprises was mitigated by reductions in administrative personnel and the abolition of "unreasonable rules" governing work organization and factory operations—the "10,000 rules," which proliferated over the years and were attributed to the bureaucratic practices of the Liuist regime. Attempts to reduce the status and functional differences between workers and administrators, and between manual and mental labor, were undertaken through the revival of the old tradition of cadre participation in productive labor and worker participation in management. Whereas administrative cadres and technicians were instructed to spend at least a third of their time on the factory benches, elected workers' management teams were to play a role in planning and decision making. The responsibility for managing enterprises was lodged in factory revolutionary committees (based on the "three-in-one" combination of workers' representatives, cadres, and soldiers), which were to replace the old authoritarian management system. And an attempt was made to decentralize the state industrial establishment by transferring control of many enterprises from ministries in Beijing to provincial administrations.

Many of these innovations, if they survived at all, were partially reversed in the early 1970s, or were far less than they seemed to be. Meanwhile, the more fundamental demands that emerged from the Cultural Revolution were either ignored or denounced as "ultra-leftist." Indeed, the most striking feature of industrial organization in the post-Cultural Revolution era were not the changes introduced but what remained the same. External controls over the movement of laborers—more stringent than those ever practiced in the Soviet Union—remained in force, officially justified as necessary to control peasant migration to the cities. Freedom of job choice was listed among the heresies of Liu Shaoqi, who also was accused of having planned to introduce a capitalist-type free labor market.[22] The highly exploitive system of temporary and contract workers, who made up nearly half of the non-agricultural work force, was retained despite the fact that it had been widely denounced as a particularly pernicious form of exploitation during the Cultural Revolution and the expansion of the system in the early 1960s was attributed to the "capitalist" policies promoted by Liu Shaoqi. The basic wage system remained intact, modified only by the elimination of individual bonuses and prizes (some of which, in fact, had been abolished prior to 1966, while others were retained under new names) and by politico-ideological campaigns denouncing monetary incentives and celebrating the moral virtues of selfless and collectivistic work in behalf of the people. Salary differentials for employees in state enterprises were approximately the same as before the Cultural Revolution, with a national eight-grade wage system for factory workers ranging from 30 to 108 *yuan* per month (excluding apprentices and temporary and contract workers whose wages fell below the minimum), a fifteen-grade system for technicians, and a thirty-grade system for administrative and other cadres. In 1972 at a model factory in Beijing, for example, workers' wages ranged from 30 to 102 *yuan*, with an average of 54 *yuan*, whereas the average for technicians, engineers, and cadres was about 150 *yuan*.[23] Despite the radical Maoist rhetoric of the time, proposals for a more egalitarian wage system were condemned as "ultra-leftist," while the whole hierarchy of worker and cadre work grades was left untouched.

Moreover, the drive to reestablish labor discipline in the factories after the disruptions of the Cultural Revolution (particularly aimed at younger workers who had been the most politically radical) was followed in the early 1970s by the gradual revival of many of the old factory rules and regulations previously abolished and by a growing emphasis on specialist administrators and technical criteria.[24] Radical critiques of prevailing factory work regulations were considered manifestations of the ubiquitous "ultra-left line." Even the demise of the trade unions proved to be temporary. By mid-1973, new official unions emerged on the provincial level, replacing or absorbing the "workers' representative congresses" organized during the Cultural Revolution, and the reappearance of a national federation soon followed. The functions of the new Party-controlled trade unions were not significantly different from those of their pre-Cultural Revolution predecessors.

However, crucial for measuring changes in industrial organization is the question of the nature and role of the factory revolutionary committees. The revolutionary committees, after all, were loudly hailed as the principal organizational achievement of the Cultural Revolution and the main institutions for workers to participate in the making of economic and political decisions. Here the essential fact was that factory revolutionary committees soon came under the control of the Party. With the 1969 decision to rebuild the Party, the reestablishment of the authority of provincial and municipal Party organizations was quickly followed by the reestablishment of Party committees in the factories. It was clear in 1969—and it became even clearer in subsequent years—that factory revolutionary committees would be subordinated to factory Party committees, which, in turn, were ultimately responsible to higher levels of the Party. The majority of the members of factory revolutionary committees were Party members and the secretary of the Party committee almost invariably was also the head of the revolutionary committee and simultaneously the director of the factory. The power to make economic and managerial decisions resided, in the final analysis, in the Party committees, and the revolutionary committees were little more than instruments to carry out those decisions.

In China, during the Maoist era and after, collective work did not come under collective control. Whatever the climate may have been in Chinese factories in the 1970s, the basic structure of productive relationships was no different from what it had been in earlier decades. The claim that the Cultural Revolution brought a fundamental change in the position of the urban working class, much less the beginnings of a revolutionary transformation of the division of labor, cannot stand the test of serious scrutiny. For the urban workers, who manned the battalions of "revolutionary masses" during the years 1966–68, life and work remained much the same in the years that followed. And it cannot be assumed that the whole of the urban working class was gravely dissatisfied with the result. For while the Cultural Revolution revealed a society seething with socioeconomic and political discontents, it also revealed that the majority of the established proletariat (that is, state workers with lifetime job tenure) supported the established Party apparatus and had a conservative stake in the existing industrial order.

Intellectuals, Students, and Culture

No social group or institution in Chinese society escaped unscathed from the Cultural Revolution, but none were as badly scarred as China's intellectuals. Ironically, many members of the intelligentsia regarded themselves as the intellectual heirs of China's first "cultural revolution" of 1915–19, a movement for modern enlightenment that broke many of the shackles of a millennial tradition of cultural and political despotism—and gave birth to the Chinese Communist movement. Half a century later, the leader of that victorious movement, himself a product of the first cultural revolution, launched a new Cultural Revolution that made intellectuals its principal victims. The second cultural revolution became a caricature of the first; political persecution, intellectual repression, and cultural obscurantism soon became its trademarks—and the marks cut most deeply on those whom Mao called "the stinking ninth category," the intellectuals.

In an ostensibly "proletarian" revolution, which placed so extreme an emphasis on "class" and "class standpoint," intellectuals were suspect from the beginning. Their knowledge separated them from the masses of workers and peasants, as did their relatively privileged material status. In a movement directed against "the bourgeoisie," intellectuals seemed the most obviously "bourgeois" in a society that no longer had a bourgeoisie. They became easy targets of opportunity, and often of opportunists. Relatively defenseless, intellectuals became the political scapegoats of all factions involved in the Cultural Revolution, radical and conservative alike. They were hounded by Red Guards zealously seeking out the "bourgeoisie" and attacked by Party officials seeking to deflect the political assault away from themselves. Along with Party cadres, intellectuals were among the first victims of the Cultural Revolution, their homes frequently ransacked, their books burned and manuscripts destroyed, their alleged political sins visited upon their children and families, while they themselves were often subjected to physically as well as psychologically agonizing "study and criticism" sessions. They were more vulnerable than Party officials, having no organizational structure to provide protection. Although many intellectuals were Party members—indeed, they were represented in the Party in far greater proportion than any other social group—they rarely were in positions of real political power. Being the most defenseless, they were the most persecuted. And the era of persecution was prolonged. The attacks on Party officials largely ceased with the Maoist decision to rebuild the Communist Party in late 1967, and many cadres "overthrown" in the early phases of the Cultural Revolution were restored to their positions after 1969. The witch-hunt against intellectuals continued, however, with varying degrees of intensity, through the remainder of the Maoist era. A good many were arrested and jailed or sent off to labor camps in the barren reaches of Xinjiang and northern Manchuria, often the victims of old personal and political vendettas. Millions were sent to do menial labor in the countryside, where they languished for years and sometimes were subjected to further humiliations by local rural cadres and peasants. Strangely, they usually retained their formal ranks in the institutions where they once worked and received their salaries in the interim. The bureaucracy functioned more or less normally, even if life was abnormal. Those who remained in the cities or were allowed to return after presumably being "proletarianized" by laboring in the fields and cow-sheds often found themselves with little to do. Research in the social sciences and humanities had all but ceased while scientific and technological institutes were paralyzed by political fears and by a lack of equipment and supplies. In 1975 Deng Xiaoping commented on the continuing stagna-tion of science and technology: "Out of the 150,000 scientific and techni-cal cadres in the Academy of Sciences, no one dares go into the research laboratories. They are all afraid of being disparaged as 'white' specialists. The young are frightened and the old are frightened. . . . Research person-nel no longer read books nowadays."[25]

The state of higher education was little better. Emptied of students, uni-versities resumed functioning on a limited basis in the years 1970–72, usu-ally under the political supervision of soldiers. By the mid-1970s college enrollments were only about one-third of what they had been a decade be-fore. University campuses were lifeless and somber places, largely devoid of any intellectual or even genuine political life, their demoralized (and often academically ill-prepared) students and faculty listlessly performing only the required political and academic rituals. Official statements re-ported that the universities were undergoing a long-term process of exper-imentation and reform, and there were heated debates on educational policy, but little was actually done to remedy the languor. Maoist cultural revolutionaries had destroyed the old elitist educational establishment, but, with the exception of elementary education in the rural areas, the Cultural Revolution yielded no viable system to take its place.

Cultural as well as educational life seemed to descend to a dark and ob-scurantist age. Writers could not write or could not publish what they did write, for little was being published save for the writings of Mao and the po-litical polemics involved in the ideological campaigns of the time. Artists did not paint and actors and musicians did not perform, save for those few involved in Jiang Qing's "revolutionary" ballets and operas, the main "cul-tural" product of the Cultural Revolution. Few new films were produced, and those made prior to 1966 were not shown. Most museums holding tra-ditional or modern works of art were closed to the public. Bookstore shelves were largely empty, having been purged of most Chinese as well as foreign literature. Virtually all academic, scientific, and cultural journals had been suspended in 1966, and few were permitted to resume publica-tion during the remainder of the Maoist era. The study of Marxism was re-duced to ritualized commentaries on a relatively small number of officially approved classic texts or portions of texts. Even the use of libraries was re-stricted. For intellectuals, the period of 1966–76 was truly the "ten lost years," and for the country as a whole it was a tragic waste of talent and experience which added to the somberness of life, especially in the cities. For this state of affairs, much of the blame rests with the powerful anti-intellectual and anti-urban impulses that long had characterized Maoism, which reached their zenith on the eve of the Cultural Revolution. When Mao declared in 1964 that "we must drive actors, poets, dramatists, and writers out of the cities, and pack them off to the countryside," few could have predicted that the injunction actually would be carried out.

Urban students fared little better than intellectuals—and worse, in the long run. When Maoist leaders in Beijing decided to end the Cultural Revolution in the cities in late 1967 and disband the Red Guards, Mao Zedong urged educated urban youth to "go to the countryside to be reeducated by the poor and lower-middle peasants." The revived "rustification" program,[26] which was conducted on a massive scale through the remainder of the Maoist era, was cloaked with the revolutionary ideal of narrowing the gap between town and countryside. But it served eminently practical political and economic purposes at the time, removing from the cities the politically disruptive Red Guards and relieving the urban areas of millions who would otherwise have been added to the unemployment rolls. Demobilized Red Guards were soon followed by ordinary middle school graduates, and over the years 1967–76 some 17,000,000 urban youth, willingly or not, were sent to live in the villages. Such revolutionary idealism as may have originally facilitated the migration to the countryside soon gave way to feelings of betrayal and political cynicism. Deprived of the possibilities of higher education or urban employment, and subjected to the unanticipated hardships and poverty of rural life, the "rusticated" youth eventually came to view themselves as "the lost generation." Such was the fate of the great majority of those who had been the first to heed Chairman Mao's call "to dare to rebel."

Political Power and Social Classes: The Domination of State over Society

The great failure of the Great Proletarian Cultural Revolution was not that it did not bring fundamental social changes. In conditions of economic scarcity, any attempt to radically transform the existing division of labor and abolish class distinctions surely would have resulted in economic chaos and social regression. The real failure of the Cultural Revolution was that it did not produce democratic political institutions that might have permitted the working population to acquire control over the means of production and eventually, as they developed modern productive forces, bring about their own socioeconomic emancipation and the emancipation of society as a whole.

At the beginning, the Cultural Revolution seemed to promise fundamental political changes. The "Sixteen Articles" of August 1966 had called for the establishment of "permanent, standing mass organizations" as "organs of power" at all levels of political, social, and economic life and, moreover, the institution of "a system of general elections like that of the Paris Commune." At the same time Mao himself had predicted that China would soon see the emergence of a "wholly new form of state power" and implied that it would be organized in accordance with the principles of the Marxist model of the Commune. But the history of the Cultural Revolution was in very large part a history of retreats from these socialist ideals. The retreat began with Mao's rejection of the Shanghai Commune in 1967 in favor of military-dominated revolutionary committees and concluded in 1969 with the restoration of the authority of the Party, which soon turned the revolutionary committees into bureaucratic organs to carry out its policies. Whatever may have been Mao's intention at the beginning of the Cultural Revolution, in the end he settled for the reestablishment of a presumably ideologically rectified Party and a presumably reformed state bureaucracy.

The failure of the Cultural Revolution to produce new political institutions is particularly striking in view of the Maoist argument that it was precisely the political superstructure that was crucial in the struggle between "socialism" and "capitalism." Maoists began the Cultural Revolution with the assumption (a remarkably prophetic one, it would now seem) that the existing Party-state apparatus was leading China on the road back to capitalism. The assumption flowed from two key, if sometimes implicit, Maoist beliefs. The first was that officials in the upper echelons of the Party bureaucracy, by virtue of their power and prestige in the state apparatus, were acquiring material privileges and exploiting society as a whole; in effect, they were becoming a functional bourgeoisie, albeit one whose privileges derived from political power rather than from property. The second proposition was that an entrenched bureaucracy had acquired a vested interest in preserving the social order over which it ruled and from which it derived its privileged position, and thus was opposed to radical social changes and willing to tolerate (and perhaps even promote) capitalist forms of socioeconomic relations and ideologies in society at large.

Yet the end result of the Cultural Revolution was the restoration of the very political structure identified as the main source of the "revisionist" tendencies threatening to bring about a "bourgeois restoration." To be sure, the political apparatus underwent reforms in the wake of the Cultural Revolution, but they were not significantly different from earlier attempts to rectify and control the bureaucracy. In accordance with the Maoist preference for "simple administration," it was said that government organs and functionaries were reduced in number, at least at the upper levels of the state administration. In 1970 Zhou Enlai claimed that ninety central government bureaus had been consolidated into twenty-six, and their administrative personnel reduced from 60,000 to 10,000. Yet at the same time Zhou reported that 95 percent of Party officials dismissed during the Cultural Revolution had been reinstated,[27] and many more were restored to their posts in the years that followed. Clearly, the old bureaucratic apparatus emerged from the Cultural Revolution largely intact, albeit with some changes in personnel and organization.[28] Not only did the bureaucracy survive, it did so in bloated form. Many of the political activists of the Cultural Revolution had to be rewarded, and the usual reward was appointment to an official position. Millions were added to the membership of the Communist Party and to the rolls of those holding bureaucratic posts. One of the ironic results of the Cultural Revolution, ostensibly a movement against bureaucracy and bureaucratic privilege, was to swell the numbers of China's bureaucrats, especially at the lower and middle levels of the political hierarchy.

There were of course much-publicized campaigns against bureaucratic arrogance and bourgeois habits, as well as a renewed emphasis on the virtues of the mass line. More significant, however, was the fact that no change was made in the highly formalized cadre system, based on a hierarchy of twenty-four official ranks with salary levels far higher than those enjoyed by workers and peasants. Nor was there any serious attempt to eliminate the many privileges traditionally enjoyed by those occupying official positions, such as free meals and expenses provided in the performance of official duties—and for high-level leaders, houses, servants, chauffeur-driven cars, access to special stores and goods, and vacations at official resorts. That half-hidden but well-established system of bureaucratic privileges and benefits survived the Cultural Revolution and its egalitarian ideology along with the bureaucracy itself, although the material rewards bestowed on those occupying official posts may have been somewhat less conspicuously displayed for a time than in years past.

The Maoist remedy for "bureaucratism" demanded that officials and all "brain workers" regularly participate in productive labor so as not to become "divorced from the masses." The Cultural Revolution produced a more or less institutionalized means for the practice in the form of "May Seventh" rural cadre schools. Some 3,000,000 officials found themselves in these newly built communes during their first year of existence (the first was established on May 7, 1968), and millions more experienced this process of "ideological revolutionization" in subsequent years. Dividing their day between self-sufficient productive labor and intensive study of Marxism-Leninism and the thoughts of Mao for periods ranging from six months to two years, officials were allegedly cured of their bureaucratic proclivities by "learning from the peasants" and "integrating themselves with the masses." Yet, however admirable it may be to have bureaucrats leave their offices to labor in the fields, particularly in a country where the gap between mental and manual labor traditionally was so wide, the system left a great deal to be desired as a remedy for bureaucracy. If the purpose was to teach officials to "integrate themselves with the masses," it was strange that the "May Seventh" schools often were physically separated from neighboring communes of peasants. The peasants remained peasants, in any event, while the officials remained officials. While engaged in work and study in the countryside (for which, it was claimed, they volunteered, regarding it as an honor), they retained their official titles and continued to receive the salaries appropriate to their rank. After having taken the cure, they usually were returned to their original positions, or equivalent posts. Even if the experience had salutary effects on the behavior and attitudes of cadres in their relations with the masses, as was claimed, it left untouched the basic structural and functional distinction between rulers and ruled. If the political reforms that resulted from the Cultural Revolution mitigated some of the more glaring manifestations of bureaucratic elitism, they did not fundamentally alter the relationship between state and society. And that relationship, bluntly put, was one where the state (and the bureaucrats who are its representatives) exercised an overwhelming dominance over society.

The phenomenon of the dominance of political over social power was of course hardly new. It had characterized the whole history of the People's Republic and indeed modern Chinese history in general. But rarely had it manifested itself so forcefully as during and after the Cultural Revolution, and rarely had the problem cried out so urgently and so obviously for a solution. In Marxist terms (which were not the terms preferred by Maoists or favored by their successors) it is the age-old problem of "alienated social power," that is, the process by which the state, the product of society, rises above society, becomes estranged from it, and comes to dominate social life. The Cultural Revolution yielded no solution to the problem but only perpetuated it. Indeed, it exacerbated it. The bitter factionalism engendered by the Cultural Revolution and the general breakdown of established political procedures created a situation in the last years of the Maoist era where the exercise of state power became increasingly arbitrary and despotic.

The Cultural Revolution not only failed to produce permanent institutions of popular self-government but also failed to resolve the more immediate problems of political succession. One of the original aims of the Cultural Revolution was to "train revolutionary successors." But in the summer of 1968, when Mao summoned Red Guard leaders to his "proletarian headquarters" to inform them that the time had come to end their rebellions (and then dispatched most of their followers to the countryside), it was an admission that the young generation had failed the political test. Nor did the Cultural Revolution yield an answer to the short-term question of political succession at the top—in effect, the question of who would (or who possibly could) succeed Mao. If the masses were politically quiet after 1968, that was not the case in the Politburo, where the unresolved issues of the Cultural Revolution were to erupt into fierce political struggles in the 1970s and throw its participants into a Byzantine world of political intrigue.

NOTES

1. The most sophisticated argument that the Cultural Revolution really did have socially revolutionary results is presented by Charles Bettelheim, *Cultural Revolution and Industrial Organization in China* (New York: Monthly Review Press, 1974).

2. The trial of the "Gang of Four," ostensibly "radical" disciples of Mao arrested shortly after their patron's death in 1976, is briefly discussed in Chapter 22 below.

3. *Beijing Review,* No. 48 (1980), pp. 9–28.

4. Qi Hao (ed.), *Guanyu Shebuizhuyi de Minzhu yu Fazhi* (Hong Kong: Bibliothèque Asiatique, 1976), pp. 3, 167; Zi Chuan, "Li Yizhe yu Wo," *Bei Dou,* No. 4 (1977), p. 15. Cited in Stanley Rosen, "The Democracy Movement in Guangzhou," paper presented at the April 1982 meeting of the Association for Asian Studies, pp. 10–12. For references to PLA massacres of Red Guards in Guangdong province and Hainan island, see also Stanley Rosen, "Guangzhou's Democracy Movement in Cultural Revolution Perspective," *China Quarterly,* No. 101 (March 1985), p. 5.

5. Agence France Presse, Beijing, February 3, 1979; FBIS-CHI 79-25 (February 5, 1979), p. E2. Also see Roger Garside, *Coming Alive: China After Mao* (New York: Mentor, 1982), pp. 45*n.,* 47.

6. Xu Shiyu's repression in Nanjing and Jiangsu is described in Barrett McCormick, "Political Reform in Post-Mao China: Democracy and Due Process in a Leninist State" (Ph.D. thesis, Department of Political Science, University of Wisconsin-Madison, 1985), pp. 61–63. General Xu was transferred from Nanjing in the early 1970s and appointed commander of the Guangzhou Military Region. Xu Shiyu and Wei Guoqing (First Secretary of the Guangdong Party Committee in the 1970s, notorious for his murderous military suppression of radical Red Guards in Guangxi in 1968) were among the more prominent military and political allies of Deng Xiaoping, and both were to occupy high positions in the post-Mao regime. For addi-

tional information on PLA repression in Nanjing and elsewhere during the Cultural Revolution, see Chang Ping and Dennis Bloodsworth, *Heirs Apparent* (London: Secker & Warburg, 1973), p. 94.

7. William Hinton reports that this occurred in Longbow village in Shaanxi province. William Hinton, "Village in Transition," in Mark Selden and Victor Lippit (eds.), *The Transition to Socialism in China* (Armonk, N.Y.: M. E. Sharpe, 1982), p. 107. For a detailed account of the Cultural Revolution in Longbow village, see Hinton's superb *Shenfan* (New York: Random House, 1983), parts VI through IX.

8. On the transformation of class into caste after 1956, see Kraus, *Class Conflict in Chinese Socialism,* chapter 6. In the rural areas this often extended to a reluctance to marry the offspring of former landlords and rich peasants.

9. On the Dazhai model and its political history, see Tang Tsou, Marc Blecher, and Mitch Meisner, "National Agricultural Policy: The Dazhai Model and Local Change in the Post-Mao Era," in Selden and Lippit (eds.), *The Transition to Socialism in China,* pp. 266–99.

10. Letter from Mao to Lin Biao, text translated in *Current Background,* No. 891, p. 56. The following discussion on the industrialization of the countryside is partially drawn from Jon Sigurdson's excellent article "Rural Industry and the Internal Transfer of Technology," in Stuart R. Schram (ed.), *Authority, Participation and Cultural Change* (Cambridge: Cambridge University Press, 1973), pp. 199–232.

11. See Mark Selden, *The People's Republic of China: A Documentary History of Revolutionary Change* (New York: Monthly Review Press, 1979), p. 125. For a comprehensive report on rural industrialization as of the summer of 1975, see Dwight Perkins (ed.), *Rural Small-Scale Industry in the People's Republic of China* (Berkeley: University of California Press, 1977).

12. Mao Tse-tung [Mao Zedong], "Reading Notes on the Soviet Union's 'Political Economy,'" *Mao Tse-tung ssu-hsiang wan-sui* (Taipei: n.p., 1969), pp. 389–90.

13. Byung-joon Ahn, *Chinese Politics and the Cultural Revolution* (Seattle: University of Washington Press, 1976), p. 155.

14. Mao Tse-tung, "Directive on Public Health," June 26, 1965, in Stuart R. Schram (ed.), *Mao Tse-tung Unrehearsed: Talks and Letters, 1956–71* (Harmondsworth, Middlesex, England: Penguin, 1974), pp. 232–33.

15. John Gardner, "Educated Youth and Urban-Rural Inequalities, 1958-1966," in John W. Lewis (ed.), *The City in Communist China* (Stanford, Calif.: Stanford University Press, 1971), pp. 235–86.

16. Mao Tse-tung, "Remarks at the Spring Festival," February 13, 1964, in Schram (ed.), *Mao Tse-tung Unrehearsed,* pp. 197–211.

17. Suzanne Pepper, "Chinese Education After Mao: Two Steps Forward, Two Steps Back, and Begin Again?" *The China Quarterly,* No. 81 (March 1980), pp. 6–7. Primary education was cut from six to five years, while two-year junior middle school classes were added to village primary schools, thus accounting for the extraordinarily rapid increase in secondary enrollments. *Ibid.,* p. 11.

18. Local management of schools was accompanied by local financing of education from commune and brigade funds, with state assistance for the payment of teachers' salaries. *Ibid.,* p. 7. Local autonomy was of course limited by a national policy demanding that the curriculum at all levels include political education, particularly the study of "Mao Zedong Thought," military training, and regular participation in productive manual labor. For an analysis of the effects of the Cultural Revolution on educational policies and practice, see John Gardner and Wilt Idema, "China's Educational Revolution," in Schram (ed.), *Authority, Participation and Cultural Change,* pp. 257–89.

19. Some of the problems under which the agrarian economy labored in the 1970s are briefly discussed in Part VI below.

20. Bettelheim, *Cultural Revolution and Industrial Organization,* p. 11.

21. For three different interpretations of the nature and results of the industrial policies yielded by the Cultural Revolution, see Stephen Andors, *China's Industrial Revolution* (New York: Pantheon Books, 1977), chapters 7–9; Andrew Walder, "Some Ironies of the Maoist Legacy in Industry," in Selden and Lippit (eds.), *The Transition to Socialism in China,* pp. 215–37; and Andrew Watson, "Industrial Management: Experiments in Mass Participation," in Bill Brugger (ed.), *China: The Impact of the Cultural Revolution* (London: Croom Helm, 1978), pp. 171–202.

22. Christopher Howe, "Labor Organization and Incentives in Industry, Before and After the Cultural Revolution," in Schram (ed.), *Authority, Participation and Cultural Change,* p. 242.

23. Bettelheim, *Cultural Revolution and Industrial Organization,* pp. 15–16. Similar and sometimes wider differentials were reported from other factories in different areas of the country in the early 1970s.

24. For concrete examples of these tendencies, see Howe, "Labor Organization and Incentives in Industry," esp. pp. 248–50, and Watson, "Industrial Management: Experiments in Mass Participation," pp. 180–99.

25. Cited in Roger Garside, *Coming Alive: China After Mao* (New York: Mentor, 1982), p. 64.

26. On the "rustification" of urban youth, see Thomas P. Bernstein, *Up to the Mountains and Down to the Villages* (New Haven: Yale University Press, 1977).

27. Edgar Snow, *The Long Revolution* (New York: Random House, 1972). pp. 13–14.

28. Even changes in personnel were limited. By the mid-1970s, for example, the great majority of leaders of the new provincial revolutionary committees were people who had held provincial bureaucratic positions prior to the Cultural Revolution. On the establishment, nature, and demise of provincial revolutionary committees, see David S. G. Goodman, "The Provincial Revolutionary Committee in the People's Republic of China, 1967–1979: An Obituary," *The China Quarterly,* No. 85 (March 1981), pp. 49–79.

20

The Aftermath of the Cultural Revolution
and the Close of the Maoist Era, 1969–1976

HARDLY HAD THE Ninth Congress of the Chinese Communist Party closed in April 1969, having proclaimed the Great Proletarian Cultural Revolution a glorious triumph and having declared itself a congress of "unity and victory," when new political struggles erupted to shatter such "unity" as had been achieved. The struggles revolved around the issues the Cultural Revolution had raised—and left unresolved—and were inflamed by the political passions that the great upheaval continued to arouse. But unlike the days of the Cultural Revolution itself, when the masses were involved in battles against bureaucratic authority, Chinese politics now reverted to factional strife among Communist leaders of the bureaucracy, entirely hidden from public view.

The Fall of Lin Biao

Two issues dominated Chinese politics in the years after the Ninth Congress seemingly had written the closing chapter on the Cultural Revolution. One was the question of the place of the People's Republic in an international arena presided over by two hostile "superpowers," the United States and the Soviet Union. The other was the question of the place of the Party in the internal post-Cultural Revolution order. The two questions were curiously interrelated, for both derived from the experience of the Cultural Revolution, an experience whose meaning was perceived differently by its surviving leaders.

At first sight, it is difficult to see any significant relationship between the Cultural Revolution and questions of foreign policy. Between 1966 and 1969 China seemed to withdraw into itself, as its leaders reinforced the national isolation imposed first by a hostile United States and then by an equally hostile Soviet Union. Preoccupied with internal conflicts, Maoist leaders seemed content to allow China's foreign relations to remain dormant. They even recalled most Chinese ambassadors in 1967. When the Cultural Revolution was launched in 1966, United States military intervention in Vietnam was being massively escalated, bombs were being dropped very near the Chinese border, and the United States was threatening to extend the war to China itself. But the Cultural Revolution was undertaken not because of the threat posed by American intervention in Vietnam, as some observers speculated at the time,[1] but rather in spite of it. As far as the "world revolution" was concerned, Maoists attached far more importance to the internal struggle in China than to the struggle raging in Vietnam. It had been Liu Shaoqi, not Mao, who had issued the strongest warnings that China was prepared to assist the Vietnamese people in their resistance to American imperialism. In fact, Mao candidly told Edgar Snow in 1970 that one of his main reasons for deposing Liu Shaoqi was Liu's proposal to revive the Sino-Soviet alliance to ward off the American threat in Vietnam, which would have delayed the Cultural Revolution.[2]

An enormous measure of national egoism was reflected in the Maoist belief that the fate of the world revolution was dependent on the fate of the Chinese revolution. What the Chinese took to be "proletarian internationalism" had received its most fulsome expression in Lin Biao's 1965 treatise "Long Live the Victory of People's War," an eminently Maoist document that projected the Chinese revolutionary experience into a global vision of a revolutionary process in which the "revolutionary countryside"—the economically backward lands of Asia, Africa, and Latin America—would surround and overwhelm the advanced "cities" of Europe and North America. Although more a hopeful description of the world situation than a prescription for Chinese action in the world, it was nonetheless the world view held by the leaders of the Cultural Revolution. It was assumed that the success of socialism in China, to be ensured by the success of the Cultural Revolution, would serve as the model for successful socialist revolutions elsewhere. A socialist China would thus become the "revolutionary homeland," replacing a morally bankrupt and "capitalist" Soviet Union, whose revisionism at home and opportunism abroad were leading the forces of world revolution astray.

Chinese national isolation during the Cultural Revolution, then, was spuri-
ously undertaken in the name of "proletarian internationalism." From Beijing in those years came fervent declarations of solidarity with popular
revolutionary movements throughout the world,[3] accompanied by wholesale denunciations of reactionary governments and leaders everywhere,
from the "fascist" Ne Win in Burma to de Gaulle in France, and of course
Lyndon Johnson and Leonid Brezhnev. In 1967 Mao not only called China
"the political center of world revolution" but also proposed that it become
"the military and technical center of the world revolution."[4]

Before the Cultural Revolution came to an end, however, the actions of
the Soviet Union rudely intruded on this "internationalist" revolutionary vision. In August 1968 Soviet armies invaded Czechoslovakia, an action
more harshly denounced in Beijing than in any other of the world's capitals.
While the Chinese Communists had precious little sympathy for Dubcek's
experiment in democratic socialism, they have always insisted on the right
of national sovereignty, as both a matter of principle and a matter of national self-interest. The occupation of Czechoslovakia raised the specter of
war with the Soviet Union, for along with it came the infamous "Brezhnev
doctrine" of "limited sovereignty" for socialist countries, that is, the "right"
of the Soviet Union to militarily intervene in the countries belonging to
what was once known as the "Communist camp." For China the threat was
ominous and immediate, for the Russians already had made thinly veiled
warnings about a "preemptive" attack (preferably in concert with the
United States) against Chinese nuclear installations, which since 1967 included hydrogen bombs. More than a million Russian troops were deployed along the 5,000-mile Sino-Soviet border; hundreds of Soviet
nuclear missiles were targeted against Chinese cities; and border clashes
were growing in frequency and intensity. When the CCP's Ninth Congress
opened in April 1969, Chinese and Soviet troops had just fought bloody
battles on the frozen Ussuri River in northern Manchuria.

At that Congress, through the medium of Lin Biao's main report, the
Chinese Communists first placed Soviet "social imperialism" on the same
footing as American imperialism, both principal enemies of the oppressed
nations and of China. While American imperialism was typically denounced as "the most ferocious enemy of the peoples of the world," Lin
had equally harsh words for the Soviet Union. The "new czars," he
charged, were establishing colonies "on the model of Hitler's 'New
Order'" and were engaged in "fascist acts of banditry." But both imperialism and social imperialism, Lin optimistically concluded, would inevitably
meet their doom at the hands of the popular forces of world revolution.[5]

For Mao and Zhou Enlai, merely condemning the Soviet Union and the

United States as equally evil and relying on the *deus ex machina* of world revolution were insufficient to deal with the peril from the north. Zhou, undoubtedly with the strong support of Mao, was advocating a new global diplomatic strategy based on the rather traditional principles of national sovereignty, peaceful coexistence, and the establishment of friendly relations "between states with different social systems." It was a strategy that defined the Soviet Union as the principal enemy, and correspondingly, dictated a tactical accommodation with the United States. As it happened, the strategy coincided with American interests that would soon bring Henry Kissinger and Richard Nixon to Beijing. This new diplomacy was of course wholly inconsistent with the proclaimed principle of "proletarian internationalism" (which might better be termed a spirit of messianic revolutionary nationalism) that briefly had held sway. To Lin Biao it seemed, if not necessarily so much a betrayal of principle, then certainly a politically damaging repudiation of the vision of a worldwide "people's war" with which he had been so intimately identified. On the question of China's foreign policy, particularly the policy of rapprochement with the United States, one of the battle lines between Mao and his designated "successor" was drawn.

Another battle line was drawn on a second and closely related question: the pace and manner that Mao and Zhou proposed for rebuilding the Communist Party and reestablishing its authority. At issue was not whether the Party should be rebuilt—the Cultural Revolution had produced no viable institutions to take its place—but rather whether it would be rebuilt on its old Leninist foundations, reassume its former monopolistic position, and retain most of its pre-Cultural Revolution leaders. For Mao, and especially for Zhou Enlai, the rapid restoration of the Party was the first and most essential domestic order of business, particularly to correct the anomalous political result of the Cultural Revolution, which had made the army the dominant force in the political life of the nation. No matter how much proletarian virtue the PLA might possess, the situation gave rise to Bonapartist fears, and Mao began to criticize the rule of the military commanders as "arrogant." Moreover, the growing preoccupation with the Russian menace made all the more urgent the fashioning of a stable internal political order. The Maoist emphasis was on national unity and reconciliation under the leadership of a revived and rebuilt Party, and Mao now was openly sanctioning the return of most former Party leaders and the wholesale rehabilitation of its cadres who had been so harshly denounced (and often "overthrown") during the Cultural Revolution. Indeed, Mao now claimed that from the beginning of the Cultural Revolution he had disapproved of the "maltreatment" of Party members and pointed to that unhappy legacy as a major impediment to the rebuilding of the Party.[6]

In the eyes of remaining radical leaders in Beijing who had thusfar managed to escape the continuing purge of "ultra-leftists," most notably Chen Boda, old "capitalist-roaders" were being returned to prominence with unseemly haste. New leaders were being selected less in accordance with the Cultural Revolution criterion of political virtue than on the basis of administrative competence and political convenience. Lin Biao was also opposed to the restoration of old cadres, less one suspects out of any attachment to the principles of the Cultural Revolution he invoked, than because the Leninist rebuilding of the Party posed a threat to his political ambitions. The more the Party was strengthened through the return of pre-Cultural Revolution officials, the less was the power of Lin Biao to determine the course of policy and events. Thus at the Ninth Congress, Lin proposed that the Cultural Revolution Group, which had been headed by Chen Boda since its inception three years earlier, should continue to function. It was not that Lin had political support in the Cultural Revolution Group; indeed, he had been locked in bitter conflict with most of its members since 1968, when the PLA under his command had so brutally suppressed the radical Red Guards. But, he apparently calculated that the Group could serve as a counterweight to the Party Politburo and slow the process of Party rebuilding. Lin's proposal, in any event, was unsuccessful, and in December 1969 the Cultural Revolution Group was abolished.

The political struggles that followed the Ninth Congress, or at least the conflict between Lin Biao and Mao Zedong, cannot easily be interpreted as simply a struggle between military and civilian authority, between army and Party, however tempting it might be to do so to dispose of an episode that still remains shrouded in mystery. As that secret struggle unfolded between 1969 and 1971, it is unlikely that Lin spoke for the army as a whole or even perceived himself as its spokesperson. When the PLA had come under attack from the Cultural Revolution Left in the summer of 1967, Lin partially joined the attack, thereby earning the wrath of a good many army commanders. It was Zhou Enlai, more than Lin, who had come to the defense of the PLA at the time. To be sure, Lin had his followers among PLA leaders, and frantically attempted to acquire others to maintain his position as Mao's putative "successor," but they remained far fewer and less powerful than those who owed their loyalty to Mao and Zhou. Lin's challenge to the Chairman was not a military challenge to civilian authority, but a political one.

Yet it was a political challenge of a most ambiguous and dubious sort, involving issues that had more to do with questions of power and expediency than of real political or social substance. There is little evidence to support the view that the conflict between Lin and Mao was a clash between "radicals" and "moderates." It strains credulity to cast Lin as an exponent of the principles of the Cultural Revolution, vainly protesting the Maoist betrayal of those principles in the period after the Ninth Congress. Although the post-Mao leaders of China would find it politically convenient to lump together "Lin Biao and the Gang of Four" as "ultra-leftists" and charge them with the responsibility for most of the evils of the "cultural revolution decade," the truth is that Lin and those who later were to be branded the "Gang" were the bitterest of political rivals. One of the future members of the Gang, Jiang Qing, formed a coalition with Zhou Enlai (despite all the differences between them) to oppose Lin Biao in 1968, a coalition that was instrumental in Lin's political downfall in 1971.[7] And Zhang Chunqiao, another member of the ill-fated quartet, was one of the intended victims of Lin Biao's abortive 1971 coup d'état.[8] Among the many charges eventually leveled against Lin Biao, and they included virtually everything on the Chinese Communist Party's long list of ideological and political heresies, the accusation that he was a "careerist" and a "conspirator" out for supreme political power seems the most plausible. It is difficult to escape William Joseph's conclusion that Lin Biao was simply "a political opportunist who supported whatever line and policies furthered his own power."[9]

Among the policies that furthered his power was his opposition to the wholesale rebuilding of the Party and to the rapprochement with the United States. The issues dividing Mao and Lin, along with Mao's growing suspicion of Lin's personal ambitions and conspiratorial ways, led to an open confrontation between the two when the Central Committee of the Ninth Congress convened its Second Plenum at Lushan in late August 1970. Or more precisely, the conflict was then openly revealed to the members of the Central Committee; the Chinese people were not told of the political struggle among their leaders until two years later, and then only the victors' version of the events and issues involved. In contrast to the days of the Cultural Revolution, public debate of public policy was no longer in fashion.

According to Mao's later account, Lin Biao and Chen Boda (who were at least temporarily and tactically allied at the time) carried out a "surprise attack" at the Lushan meeting. Mao described the "program" of his opponents as twofold: first, the appointment of a State Chairman to fill the post from which Liu Shaoqi had been removed, and second, the addition of a provision in the draft of the new state constitution extolling Mao as a "genius."[10] The "surprise attack" consisted of speeches critical of the foreign and domestic policies of Zhou Enlai, surprising only because their content was not discussed with Mao beforehand. The proposal to appoint a State Chairman was contrary to Mao's decision of several months earlier to omit mention of the position in the new constitution—in effect, to abolish the office—probably because he did not want his "successor" Lin Biao to obtain it for fear of undermining Premier Zhou Enlai's supremacy over the state administration. The proposal to proclaim Mao a "genius" was a somewhat more enigmatic matter. Mao later called it a "theoretical question." At the time, it would seem, it was an eminently practical political question. To praise Mao as a genius was very much in the spirit of the Cultural Revolution, especially the spirit long favored by the PLA, when Mao stood high above all institutions as supreme leader and utopian prophet with direct links to the masses. To celebrate the genius of Mao in 1970 was an attempt to recreate the Cultural Revolution situation when all political wisdom and authority resided in Mao and his thought rather than in the Communist Party, and thus to attempt to blunt the current drive to restore the Party to its pre-Cultural Revolution Leninist preeminence. Mao was quick to recognize the political implications of this belated attempt to use the cult of Mao against his now Leninist policy on the Party. He refused the accolade and later commented on its political import: "Genius does not depend on one person or a few people. It depends on a Party, the Party which is the vanguard of the proletariat."[11]

The Central Committee neither appointed a Chairman of the republic nor proclaimed Mao a genius. Instead, Lin Biao and Chen Boda were criticized for obstructing the process of Party rebuilding. Moreover, after apparently heated debate, the new foreign policies designed by Zhou Enlai were endorsed. The official communiqué that emerged from the two-week closed-door meeting announced that China's foreign policy was based on the principle of "peaceful coexistence between countries with different social systems."[12] It was the first time in more than five years that this phrase had been heard in public.

The Lushan Plenum also marked the downfall of Chen Boda, Mao's longtime personal secretary, confidant, and Maoist theoretician par excellence. The Cultural Revolution had elevated Chen to the apex of power as one of the five members of the Standing Committee of the Politburo, standing alongside Mao, Lin Biao, Zhou Enlai, and Kang Sheng. He now became the victim of a brief campaign of vilification. Accused of various "ultra-leftist" deviations, he was excommunicated as "China's Trotsky."

The problem of deposing Lin Biao was a more formidable task. For Lin was not only Mao's official heir apparent and China's Minister of Defense, he had emerged from the Cultural Revolution with a popular prestige seemingly second only to that of the Chairman himself. From the time of the Nanchang uprising of 1927, he had been one of the great heroes of the Chinese Revolution and, since their first meeting in 1928, one of Mao's closest comrades in arms. Moreover, the extent of military support Lin could command was unknown in the fall of 1970. The strategy that was to bring his downfall would take a year to unfold.

The conflict between Mao and Lin was of course totally hidden from public view. To the Chinese people, Lin still appeared to be Mao's chosen successor. He continued to make public speeches and preside at official gatherings. His picture was displayed in newspapers almost as prominently as Mao's. On May Day, 1971, Lin and Mao stood together on the reviewing stand above Tiananmen Square. But behind the façade of public unity, the political struggle was intensifying, with Mao removing from power a variety of political and military leaders thought to be sympathetic to Chen Boda or Lin Biao, including Li Xuefeng, the political commissar for the Beijing Military Region. Mao also ensured the loyalty of the PLA units in and around the capital by transferring (in January 1971) troops under Lin Biao's direct command from Beijing to their original base in northern Manchuria, ostensibly to counter a Soviet threat.

While the fall of Lin Biao was being prepared, the policies he opposed were being implemented. The process of rebuilding the Party machine was greatly accelerated. For eighteen months after the Party's Ninth Congress it had proved impossible to establish provincial Party committees. The Lushan Plenum served to remove the political obstacles. Between December 1970 and August 1971, Party committees were set up in all provinces, effectively subordinating the provincial revolutionary committees. In the meantime, Zhou Enlai's new diplomacy was beginning to bear its anticipated fruits. In November 1970 Zhou told Edgar Snow that the Chinese government had responded affirmatively to overtures from Washington to resume Sino-American discussions that had been suspended in Warsaw a year before, although preferably at a different site.[13] The new site was to be Beijing. In December Mao advised Snow that Richard Nixon would be welcomed in China as either tourist or president.[14] The invitation was quickly relayed to Washington, and Snow received permission to publish his interview with Mao. It appeared in *Life* magazine in April 1971, at the very time Lin Biao and his supporters were making their final appeal before the Politburo to reverse the course of Chinese foreign policy. But the era of "ping-pong diplomacy"[15] already had begun, and it soon gave way to an era of *realpolitik*. On July 11 came the startling announcement that Secretary of State Henry Kissinger had been in Beijing for two days of discussions with Premier Zhou Enlai, preparing the way for President Nixon's dramatic visit the following February. It was a diplomatic triumph for both sides.

In September, two months after Kissinger's visit, Lin Biao vanished from the public scene. No explanation for his absence was forthcoming for ten months. Finally, on July 28, 1972, the first official account of what would be called "the tenth major struggle between the two lines in the history of the Communist Party of China" was issued. Lin Biao, it was said, had plotted a coup d'état that involved an attempt to assassinate Mao Zedong. When the plot failed, he attempted to flee to the Soviet Union on a jet aircraft along with his wife and son and other accomplices. But the plane crashed in the People's Republic of Mongolia, killing all aboard.

There is, of course, no way to either verify or disprove the official story. As in most such cases, one is left with little more than such versions and documents as the survivors and victors choose to provide. All that can be said with any reasonable degree of certainty is that a major political crisis took place in September 1971, which involved a wholesale purge of the upper echelons of both the military and civilian administrations, including the dismissal of eleven of the twenty-one members of the Politburo, and that Lin Biao perished in the process, whether on the Trident jet that crashed in Outer Mongolia on September 13 or by other means at another time.[16]

In recent years myriad "revelations" about Lin Biao have issued from Beijing and elsewhere, but save for details about the alleged plot to seize state power, they have revealed little more about the origins and nature of the crisis of September 1971 than was known in the summer of 1972. That there were plots and counterplots at the very highest levels of the Party-state apparatus in the year following the Lushan Plenum cannot be doubted—and they make for a sad commentary on the effects of the Cultural Revolution on the character of political life in the People's Republic. But it cannot be taken for granted that Lin and his supporters were the original plotters. It seems likely that it was Mao who took the political initiative, determined to eliminate Lin and his faction for reasons of both power and policy. In the last months of 1970 Mao began to purge Lin Biao's military and political supporters, and in early 1971 he reorganized the Beijing Military Region around PLA units upon whose support he could count. When the Chairman embarked on his "inspection tour" of the provinces on August 18, 1971, he clearly did so for the purpose of mobilizing the support of local PLA commanders in the campaign against Lin and to prepare the denouement that was to take place the following month. At the time Mao claimed that he had been shielding Lin and following the policy of "curing the disease to save the patient." He held out the possibility that Lin still might be reformed but ominously added: "It is difficult for someone who has taken the lead in committing major errors of principle . . . to reform."[17]

Clearly, Mao intended to bring the conflict to a decisive end, having little expectation that Lin Biao would prove amenable to "reform." And it is likely that Lin Biao responded to Mao's threatening political maneuvers by planning what proved to be an abortive coup d'état and assassination plot that Chinese authorities alleged were devised a year earlier and set forth in a document known as "Outline of the '571 Project.'" In early September 1971, according to a later Beijing account, the plotters planned to attack Chairman Mao's special train with flamethrowers and bazookas, dynamite the railway bridge near Suzhou over which the train was to pass, bomb the train from the air or blow up the oil depot in Shanghai. If these elaborate measures failed, there was a further plan to have the Chairman shot by a member of his own bodyguard when he reached Shanghai.[18] However, as Zhou Enlai acknowledged in a meeting with a group of American newspaper editors in late 1972, the "571 Project" was never put into operation. There was in fact no attempt on Mao's life and no effort to carry out the alleged coup; instead, fearing the plot had been discovered, Lin hastily fled on the ill-fated plane that crashed in Mongolia.[19] But whatever Lin Biao's motives and activities may have been, his demise—and the purge of his supporters in the Party, army, and revolutionary committees[20]—removed the last barriers to the consolidation of the post-Cultural Revolution order as Mao and Zhou wished to have it.

The fall of Lin Biao was followed by a host of "ultra-leftist" charges leveled against Mao's onetime designated "successor." In addition to allegations that he had conspired to assassinate Mao and establish a military dictatorship, had conducted "illicit relations" with the Soviet Union, and had opposed Mao's policy on the rehabilitation of Party cadres and his "revolutionary line" in foreign policy, Lin also was accused of having exaggerated the spontaneity of the masses, overemphasized the human and spiritual factors in production, undermined rural stability by attempting to hastily universalize the Dazhai model and by advocating a more or less immediate transition to communism, and having fostered too zealously the Mao cult and the rote memorization of the Chairman's sayings in lieu of serious study of his works. In 1972 it appeared to a number of foreign observers that Lin Biao had been unmasked as the most prominent of the "ultra-leftists."[21] Indeed, high-ranking Chinese officials told visitors at the time that Lin had been the "backstage boss" of the radical May Sixteenth group during the Cultural Revolution.[22] The alleged ultra-leftist heresies were perhaps less revealing about Lin Biao than about the continuing retreat from Cultural Revolution policies then being led by Mao Zedong and Zhou Enlai.

The deradicalization of the Cultural Revolution accelerated markedly in the two years after the fall of Lin Biao. It was a process above all marked by the reestablishment of the authority of the Chinese Communist Party, which soon was no less dominant in the political and economic life of the nation than in the years before the Cultural Revolution. It was not only the institution that was restored but also the great majority of its old leaders. Officials and cadres denounced and overthrown as "capitalist-roaders," "demons," and "monsters" were returned to positions of power and prominence in ever increasing numbers—and without official explanation, save for charges that the "excesses" of the Cultural Revolution were largely due to the evil machinations of Lin Biao. Most of the old provincial Party leaders and their deputies were reappointed to high offices, although, to save embarrassment, stationed in provinces other than those they had governed in 1966.[23] In general, the older and more conservative cadres prevailed over the younger and more radical ones who had risen to prominence during the Cultural Revolution. The process of "rehabilitation" did not exclude such prominent "monsters" as Chen Zaidao and Zhong Hanhua, the leaders of the 1967 Wuhan mutiny, who reappeared at public forums in 1972 and were assigned to new military commands. The old Party-controlled mass organizations also reappeared; a reorganized Communist Youth League in lieu of the disbanded Red Guards, and a reconstructed official trade union federation replacing the workers' congresses.

As the Party was rebuilt, the political role of the revolutionary committees and the army declined. The revolutionary committees had in fact become anachronistic, for their purpose in large part had been to represent the popular mass organizations, which now had disappeared. They nevertheless continued to exist, partly as an administrative convenience, partly as an ideological necessity, lest their formal abolition be taken as a renunciation of the Cultural Revolution. At the same time the PLA, purged of leaders who were alleged supporters of Lin Biao, gradually withdrew from the dominant political position it had been called upon to assume during the Cultural Revolution. That the Party would again command the gun was a point that Mao had made clear in the course of his 1971 provincial tour, advising army commanders: "You should pay attention to military affairs. . . . It would be putting the cart before the horse if matters already decided by regional Party committees were later turned over to army Party committees for discussion."[24] A decade earlier Maoists had established the PLA as the model for universal emulation, but now the slogans of the day enjoined the PLA to learn "the fine work style" of the Party and to "learn from the people of the whole country."

The rebuilding of the Party was logically accompanied by the partial dismantling of the cult of Mao. This had been a Janus-faced phenomenon. On the one hand, it was an extreme expression of the alienation of the social power of the people, for it was not simply a matter of the masses worshiping the authority of a state that stood above them but totally subordinating themselves (and their power) to the higher authority of a single man, perceived as the embodiment of their collective will and the source of all wisdom. Yet during the Cultural Revolution the cult had been the main instrument that encouraged citizens to attack the bureaucratic apparatus which ruled over them and to legitimize that rebellion against authority. Mao was certainly acutely aware of the political utility and functions of the cult, even if not of its alien and alienating character. In his December 1970 talk with Edgar Snow, he again candidly acknowledged the existence of a "cult of personality" (as he had in 1965) and, moreover, argued that it had been a necessary weapon to dismantle a Party bureaucracy that was no longer under his control. Now that the situation had been rectified, the time had come for the cult to be "cooled down," although Mao implied that this might take some time. It was difficult, he said, for people to overcome the habits of "3,000 years of emperor-worshiping tradition."[25] Mao's association of his "personality cult" with that ancient tradition suggests that he was well aware of the social roots of the phenomenon, aware that the cult flourished because China was still basically a peasant land dominated by old rural traditions. The thrust of his remarks was that he took advantage of this condition of cultural backwardness to mystify his own authority in order to demystify the authority of the Chinese Communist Party.

The cult was in fact "cooled" in the years after 1971. Although neither Mao nor his thought suffered any lack of public and official adulation, the emphasis was now on the supreme authority (if not necessarily the absolute infallibility) of the Party. The Party itself, of course, was still led by a now more Leninist-inclined Mao and presumably guided by his thought. The excesses and more irrational aspects of the cult were blamed on Lin Biao. Lin, to be sure, had been the most ardent promoter of the cult, but there is no evidence that Mao had any objections to the efforts of his onetime "closest comrade in arms" before 1970.

In the years after Lin Biao's death, the new foreign policy designed by Zhou Enlai began to pay great nationalist dividends, but at an enormous cost for China's proclaimed principles of "proletarian internationalism." In October 1971 the People's Republic triumphantly entered the United Nations, the United States no longer willing or able to continue the obstructionist policies it had pursued for more than two decades. The "Shanghai Communiqué" that concluded President Nixon's celebrated visit to China in February 1972 essentially endorsed the positions the Chinese had been setting forth since 1949; it promised the eventual normalization of diplo-

matic relations between the two countries, called for the progressive withdrawal of United States military forces from Taiwan, and recognized that
the future of Taiwan was an internal Chinese matter. The implementation
of these agreements was to be long delayed by Watergate and the other in-
scrutabilities of both Chinese and American domestic politics. In the
meantime, the policy of "peaceful coexistence between countries with different social systems" was practiced with a vengeance elsewhere. Entirely
"peaceful relations" were maintained with the government of Pakistan during the Bengali revolt and with Madame Bandaranaike during the revolutionary uprising in Ceylon in 1971. The notorious "Christmas bombings" of
North Vietnam in 1972 brought forth verbal protests from Beijing, but they
were sufficiently restrained to preserve cordial relations with Henry
Kissinger and Richard Nixon. All manner of feudal monarchs and military
dictators (many formerly denounced as fascist or worse) embarked upon
pilgrimages to Beijing and were received with all due honors. Normal
diplomatic and trade relations were established with the Franco regime in
Spain and with the fascist military junta in Greece. In the last years of the
Mao period China emerged as one of the great champions of the North At-
lantic Treaty Organization and was one of the few countries in what was
once known as "the socialist bloc" to maintain formal diplomatic and trade
relations with the Chilean militarists who so brutally overthrew the Marxist
government of Salvador Allende. And in early 1976 China found itself involved in Angola on the same side as the United States and apartheid
South Africa.

These more embarrassing developments which followed from China's
new diplomacy and its entrance into the world of international power politics flowed from a policy that subordinated all other considerations to the
overriding struggle against "Soviet social imperialism." The tactics, motivated by considerations of national self-interest in general, and by the very
real threat of the Soviet Union in particular, were elevated to the level of a
doctrine proclaiming that the interests of revolutionary movements everywhere were identical with the national interests of "socialist China." It was
a doctrine that bore the imprint of Stalin's doctrine of "socialism in one
country" as well as one that reflected the profoundly nationalist content of
Maoism.

If there were new departures in foreign policy in the early 1970s, at least
as far as relations with the United States were concerned, this was not the
case with domestic policy, which for the most part was characterized by a
cautious retreat from the radicalism of the Cultural Revolution. A brief attempt to revive the economic policies of the Great Leap in 1968–69 had
proved abortive, and by 1970 the dominant policies (largely formulated

under Zhou Enlai's guidance) were stressing stable and orderly economic growth. In agriculture, the Dazhai model was broadened to mean "Dazhai-type counties," less a model for social change than for improvements in productive techniques. In industry, factory managers dismissed during the Cultural Revolution were restored to their former posts, accompanied by calls to strengthen managerial authority, labor discipline, and factory rules and regulations—and to struggle against "anarchism" and "ultra-leftism." There were dramatic increases in foreign trade and in imports of foreign technology.[26] Veteran Party leaders attacked during the Cultural Revolution were "rehabilitated" at an increasingly rapid pace; by 1973, it has been noted, "the pre-Cultural Revolution cadres were running the government ministries."[27] And there was a perceptible loosening of the cultural strait-jacket, with performances by several Western symphony orchestras in Shanghai and Beijing and the reappearance of numerous books and movies previously banned. Except for the realm of education, where attempts to implement the radical reforms of the Cultural Revolution continued (although university entrance exams were partially reinstituted in 1972), the general tendency was to return to the pre-Cultural Revolution order of things. The tendency was not universally embraced by all factions of the Party, as events soon were to reveal.

Nonetheless, the foreign and domestic policies Mao and Zhou were pursuing received formal ratification at the Tenth National Congress of the Chinese Communist Party held in Beijing from August 24 to 28, 1973. The Congress met without prior public announcement and was convened with more than the usual secrecy. But it had the eminently public purpose of attempting to demonstrate to Party members and non-Party masses alike that, despite the demise of Lin Biao, the surviving leaders remained true to the spirit and principles of the Cultural Revolution, and to show that Lin had not adhered to those principles and, indeed, had never represented them. The concern to document continuity with the Cultural Revolution doubtless was largely responsible for the decision to have one of the two main reports to the Congress delivered by Wang Hongwen, a former Shanghai factory worker and youthful Party activist whom the Cultural Revolution had catapulted to a position of national political leadership. The other report was presented by Zhou Enlai. Mao presided over the Congress but apparently did not address the gathering, although he was clearly attempting to balance, if not necessarily reconcile, the "radical" and "moderate" factions of the Party, respectively represented at the Tenth Congress by Wang Hongwen and Zhou Enlai.

Both Zhou and Wang took pains to emphasize the correctness of the general political lines laid out at the Ninth Congress, and from there the lines that linked the present leadership to the Cultural Revolution, however tenuous those lines had become. Both emphasized the total supremacy and indispensable vanguard role of the Party. "We should further strengthen the centralized leadership of the Party," Zhou stressed. "Of the seven sectors— industry, agriculture, commerce, culture and education, the army, the government, and the Party—it is the Party that exercises overall leadership."[28] Wang Hongwen presented an even more fundamentalist conception of the Leninist party. "The Party must exercise leadership in everything," he insisted. To be sure, Wang also stressed the old Maoist maxim that Party cadres must accept "criticism and supervision from the masses." And he struck a faintly cultural revolutionary note when he declared that "a true Communist must act without any selfish considerations and dare to go against the tide, fearing neither removal from his post, expulsion from the Party, imprisonment, divorce nor guillotine."[29] However, in the wake of the Lin Biao affair it was most unlikely that many were eager to take up the challenge. The main thrust of the Congress, in any event, was to sanction the reestablishment of the Party in its orthodox Leninist form; the documents that emerged from the meeting in the Great Hall of the People stressed time and again (and always in bold black characters) that "it is the Party that exercises overall leadership."

The restoration of the system of total Party dominance, now fully laid down in theory as well as in fact, required an absurd rewriting of the history of the Cultural Revolution. Thus the revised Party constitution solemnly declared that the "great victories in the Great Proletarian Cultural Revolution" had occurred under the leadership of the Chinese Communist Party.[30] And Wang Hongwen proclaimed that the Cultural Revolution had really been a "Party consolidation movement."[31]

Zhou Enlai discussed the international situation ("one characterized by great disorder on earth")[32] in general and familiar terms, but his specific policies of *realpolitik* received concrete approval with the election to the Central Committee of Foreign Minister Ji Pengfei and his chief deputies. At the same time, the number of PLA representatives in the Central Committee was significantly reduced.

The most difficult task confronting the Congress was to explain the fall of Lin Biao. In 1972 Lin and Chen Boda had been depicted as "ultra-leftists." It was soon realized, however, that such accusations against two of the most prominent leaders of the Cultural Revolution might create doubts about the validity of the whole enterprise or doubts about whether the present leaders truly represented its now canonized spirit and principles. Thus Lin and Chen were hastily converted into "ultra-rightists" and formally expelled from the Party—Lin posthumously, as a "bourgeois careerist, conspirator, counter-revolutionary double dealer, renegade and traitor," and Chen as a "principal member of the Lin Biao anti-Party clique, anti-Communist Guomindang element, Trotskyite, renegade, enemy agent and revisionist." Zhou Enlai went to fantastic lengths to connect Lin with Liu Shaoqi.[33] Lin was charged with opposing the doctrine of "continuing the revolution under the dictatorship of the proletariat," holding that the main contradiction in Chinese society was between "the advanced socialist system and the backward productive forces" (rather than the Maoist thesis that it was between the "proletariat" and the "bourgeoisie"), and therefore advocating the heinous view that the main task was to "develop production." His aim was no less than to turn the CCP into "a revisionist, fascist party . . . subvert the dictatorship of the proletariat and restore capitalism . . . institute a feudal-compradore-fascist dictatorship, [and] capitulate to Soviet revisionism and social imperialism." As if that were not enough, Zhou charged that Lin's crimes could be traced back to his earliest days as a Communist. Mao, it was claimed, had been "trying seriously and patiently to educate" Lin since 1929, but, as matters turned out, "Lin Biao's bourgeois idealist world outlook was not at all remolded. At important junctures of the revolution he invariably committed Right opportunist errors and invariably played double-faced tricks, putting up a false front to deceive the Party and the people."[34] Why it took more than forty years for Mao to uncover the false front was not explained. Such was the verdict of a Congress that proclaimed its faith and trust in the masses—but the masses certainly were not to be trusted with the truth about their leaders. While few mourned the death of Lin Biao, the whole episode—and the Party's explanation of it—only served to deepen the political cynicism festering in Chinese society since the latter days of the Cultural Revolution.

The Party constitution was revised, most notably of course by deleting that most embarrassing paragraph which declared Lin Biao to be Mao's chosen successor. The new constitution also took a further step in "cooling" the Mao cult by omitting some of the more grandiose statements on the powers of Mao Zedong Thought that appeared in the 1969 document and were identified with the attack on the Party during the Cultural Revolution. However, continuity with the Cultural Revolution was expressed in retaining the Maoist thesis that class struggles persist in a socialist society, the theory of "continued revolution under the dictatorship of the proletariat," and the prediction that other cultural revolutions would take place "many times in the future." In 1973 these propositions seemed glaringly incongruent with the Maoist emphasis on political unity, centralization, and consolidation.

Finally, the Congress duly confirmed the political leadership of the Party that had emerged after the fall of Lin Biao, emphasized the urgency of training revolutionary successors, and, in the interim, established a system of more or less collective leadership under Mao by appointing five Vice Chairmen: Zhou Enlai, Wang Hongwen, Kang Sheng, Ye Jianying, and Li Desheng.[35] The Chairman and the five Vice-Chairmen, along with Zhu De, Zhang Chungqiao, and Dong Biwu, made up the ruling Standing Committee of the Politburo, presiding over a Party whose membership had now swelled to 28,000,000.

The Anti-Confucius Campaign

Soon after the Tenth Congress closed, after an unusually brief five-day session, it became apparent that the problem of politically burying the dead Lin Biao was more difficult than the disposal of Liu Shaoqi during the Cultural Revolution. Liu had been the principal target of the great upheaval, while Lin had been one of its main leaders. The difficulties in providing a credible explanation for the fall of Lin Biao were compounded when it was decided to add to the long list of charges already made the fantastic allegation that he also had been a disciple of Confucius.

In 1972 a seemingly academic debate had been initiated by the Maoist historian and ideologist Guo Moruo on the periodization of ancient history, particularly the nature and timing of China's transition from a slave to a feudal society in the first millennium B.C. The historical discussion soon came to focus on the role of Confucius during that transitional era, with general agreement not only that Confucianism was a reactionary philosophy in modern times but that Confucius himself had been a reactionary in his own time, the author of a doctrine that had impeded the historically progressive transition from "slavery" to "feudalism." In the summer of 1973 articles attacking Confucius and Confucianism began to appear in more popular newspapers and magazines. And after the Tenth Party Congress in August, the crusade against Confucius, dead for more than 2,000 years, was linked with the campaign against Lin Biao, dead a mere two years.

The "Pi Lin, Pi Kong" ("Criticize Lin, Criticize Confucius") movement dominated the official press and public life for more than a year. The writings of most of those involved in this strange campaign were filled with obtuse historical allusions and complex literary allegories, but the main thrust was to celebrate the historically progressive character of the Qin dynasty (which had unified China in 221 B.C.), its first emperor (Qin Shihuangdi), and its authoritarian Legalist doctrines; and, correspondingly, to condemn as historically reactionary the Confucian opposition, which represented the interests of the dying slave-owning aristocracy, clinging to ancient political and territorial divisions. The First Emperor of the Qin (who had burned Confucian books, and buried alive Confucian scholars) traditionally had been regarded as the greatest tyrant in Chinese history, but now he was depicted as China's great unifier. However ruthless his methods, he had acted in accordance with the progressive movement of history. The contemporary political message was clear: Mao Zedong, the modern Qin Shihuangdi,[36] recognized and acted upon the objective forces of historical change by promoting national unity, political centralization, and modern economic development. Lin Biao, by contrast, was the modern personification of the old Confucian scholars (particularly the reincarnation of the traitorous, pro-Confucian official Lu Buwei) who had set themselves against the progressive forces of history, promoting political factionalism, territorial separatism, outmoded ideas, and antiquated social relationships. Lin was thus portrayed as the heir of a reactionary 2,500-year-old ideological tradition. As if to seal the historical case, the official press solemnly reported the shocking discovery that old Confucian scrolls had been found hanging in Lin Biao's home.

Yet the "criticize Lin, criticize Confucius" campaign had less to do with Lin Biao or Confucius than it did with conflicting evaluations of the Cultural Revolution and with the question of who was to lead China into the post-Cultural Revolution era and in what direction. The campaign assumed a significance far beyond its dubious contributions to historiography because it became the occasion to fire the opening salvoes in what would prove the final, climactic political battle of the Maoist era. On one side stood the veteran officials and cadres, mostly old revolutionaries, who had been attacked and criticized during the Cultural Revolution—and who looked to Premier Zhou Enlai for leadership and guidance. Across the battle line were cadres who had gained political prominence during the Cultural Revolution and who sought to defend the fruits of the upheaval, which they called the "socialist newborn things." Their most prominent leaders were those who soon would be known as the "Gang of Four": Jiang Qing, Yao Wenyuan, Zhang Chunqiao, and Wang Hongwen, all members of the Party's Politburo, with the latter two on its ruling Standing Committee as well. The conflict between the veteran Party leaders and the Cultural Revolutionaries was in part a struggle over power in the bureaucracy, in part a conflict over policy in society at large. The two factions had more or less united, albeit briefly, against Lin Biao in 1971, and both had gained from Lin's demise. Mao had attempted to keep the bureaucratic struggle within bounds, striving to balance if not necessarily reconcile the contending groups. At the Tenth Party Congress in 1973, for example, equal time had been given to Zhou Enlai and Wang Hongwen. But the anti-Confucius campaign, whatever its origins and original purpose may have been, soon became the vehicle for the intensification of the political conflict. Both factions seized the opportunity to attack the policies of their rivals, albeit under the cloak of scholarly investigations into antiquity. In the ostensibly historical debates that ensued, the person and policies of Zhou Enlai loomed particularly large, although the Premier usually appeared in a third-century B.C. disguise. Zhou's supporters portrayed his main historical analogue—Li Si, the loyal minister of the First Emperor of the Qin dynasty—as an economic modernizer, a technological innovator, and the architect of a centralized state that suppressed military separatism and operated according to the rule of law. Zhou Enlai's critics, on the other hand, emphasized Li Si's uncompromising stand against the seditious Confucian opposition (he favored burying them alive and burning their books), implicitly and reproachfully contrasting it with Zhou's policy of restoring officials felled during the Cultural Revolution. The wholesale rehabilitation of cadres, it was thus suggested, was restaffing state organs with potentially seditious counterrevolutionaries. Other contemporary issues that became involved in the historical controversies—the reforms in education, the social status of women, and the importation of foreign technology—were treated in similarly veiled (and often even more obtuse) historical analogies. It was a debate conducted by and for the highly educated and probably was largely unintelligible to the great majority of the Chinese people, whose participation was confined to attendance at ritualized criticism sessions condemning half-forgotten Confucian pieties.

By the autumn of 1974 the anti-Confucian literature was becoming ever more obscure, and the campaign in general was fading into well-deserved oblivion. Its promoters and participants would have been hard pressed to explain what had been accomplished. Whichever side had gotten the best of the historical debate, and it mattered little, Zhou Enlai and the veteran bureaucrats clearly held the better political hand, as was to be demonstrated at meetings of the Party Central Committee and the National People's Congress in January 1975. But before the anti-Confucian campaign had come to its murky and inconclusive end, Zhou Enlai had fallen mortally ill. Suffering from lung cancer, he was hospitalized in May 1974. From his sickbed he valiantly continued to conduct affairs of state. As Zhou lay dying, so too did Mao. At the end of 1974 the eighty-one-year-old Chairman was in visibly failing health and, as he frequently told visitors, "preparing to see God." The effects of Parkinson's disease,which had afflicted him for a decade, could no longer be concealed.[37] With the passing of the two great leaders of the People's Republic now anticipated, both of whom were in fact to die in the same fateful year of 1976, the question of political succession assumed a new urgency and inflamed the factional strife that erupted into furious political and ideological battles over the final eighteen months of the Maoist era.

A new actor who was to play a most prominent role in those battles had quietly slipped onto the political stage a few years earlier. Among the many pre-Cultural Revolution officials returned to office during the early 1970s was Deng Xiaoping. When the former General Secretary of the Party appeared at official banquets in the spring of 1973, no one noted, at least publicly, that a few years before he had been condemned to apparent political purgatory as "the second leading person in authority taking the capitalist road." In a rapid series of political leaps, whose historical import could hardly be fully appreciated at the time, Deng was appointed a Vice Premier of the State Council under Zhou and, at the Tenth Party Congress in August 1973, reelected to the Party's Central Committee and Politburo after an absence of seven years. In the spring of 1974 he headed the Chinese delegation to a special session of the United Nations, where he announced that the post-World War II "socialist bloc" no longer existed and that henceforth China was to be considered part of the Third World.[38] At a meeting of the Party's Central Committee in early January 1975 Deng was elevated to the Politburo's Standing Committee and, it was soon revealed, appointed chief of staff of the PLA as well. When the Fourth National People's Congress met later that month, Deng seemingly became Premier Zhou's heir apparent with his appointment as the first of twelve new Vice Premiers.

Zhou Enlai's final bequest to the revolution, to which he had devoted himself for more than a half a century, was an impassioned call for the "modernization of agriculture, industry, national defense, science and technology" to put China "in the front ranks of the world" before the end of the century. The policy of the "Four Modernizations" was soon to be inherited and pursued by Deng Xiaoping, but it also harkened back to the vision Mao Zedong had set forth when the People's Republic was founded in 1949, the hope that by the year 2000 China would be "a powerful country with a high degree of socialist industrialization." Zhou's reaffirmation of that eminently nationalist goal came at the long-delayed Fourth National People's Congress, which convened in Beijing January 13–17, 1975. That was the first meeting since 1964 of what is formally "the highest organ of state power" in the People's Republic. Some 2,800 deputies gathered to ratify the enormous changes that had taken place in the country since the body had last met, to promulgate a new state constitution, and, as customary, to approve the policies and the changes in personnel already decided by the Party's Central Committee, which had met the week before. A dying

Zhou Enlai left his hospital bed to deliver the report on the work of the government, summing up the accomplishments of the past twenty-five years (for which Zhou could rightly claim a good share of the credit) and expressing his hopes for a future China that would be a "powerful modern socialist country," foreshadowing the program (if not necessarily all the policies) that soon would proceed under the slogan of the "Four Modernizations." Mao Zedong did not attend the Congress, remaining in his native province of Hunan, perhaps for reasons of health, perhaps to register his disapproval of the proceedings, perhaps simply to underscore his gradual withdrawal from the political stage.[39]

Zhou Enlai's report, which emphasized China's past economic progress and even more the need for modernization in the future, revealed that the disruptions of the Cultural Revolution had not gravely undermined the ongoing program for rapid industrialization. Total industrial output for 1974, he reported, was 190 percent greater than in 1964, including a 120 percent increase in steel production, 91 percent in coal, 650 percent in petroleum, 200 percent in electric power, 330 percent in chemical fertilizers, and a fivefold increase in tractor production. Agricultural output in 1974 was estimated to be 51 percent higher than ten years before. Zhou also claimed that since the founding of the People's Republic, grain production had increased by 140 percent while the population had grown by 60 percent.[40] These claims are generally supported by the estimates of most foreign economic specialists, although the statistics on gross output, however impressive, do not reveal the increasingly grave structural and other problems in the Chinese economy that post-Mao leaders would be forced to confront.[41]

The new and relatively succinct state constitution approved by the Fourth Congress, replacing the one of 1954, was a significantly revised document that attempted to take into account the vast social and economic transformations of the preceding twenty years as well as the postrevolutionary transformations of Maoist ideology. On the assumption that the "bourgeois" stage of the revolution successfully had been completed (an assumption that soon would be challenged), the People's Republic no longer was described as a "people's democratic State," but rather as "a socialist State of the dictatorship of the proletariat." The total supremacy of the Party over the state administration was made a matter of law as well as fact. Whereas the 1954 constitution proclaimed that "All power . . . belongs to the people," the new document added: "The Communist Party of China is the core of the leadership of the whole Chinese people. The working class exercises leadership over the state through its vanguard, the Communist Party of China." Further, it was explicitly laid down that the National People's Congress and state power in general were under the direction of the Party.[42] Also written into the constitution was the dictum that "Marxism-Leninism-Mao Zedong Thought is the theoretical basis guiding the thinking of our nation," along with several specific Maoist propositions, particularly the notion of the persistence of class struggle under socialism and the theory of "continuous revolution." The rural communes were formally institutionalized as the primary form of both economic and political organization in the countryside, although the production team was to remain "the basic accounting unit" and the right of commune members to farm small private plots for personal needs was constitutionally recognized. The revolutionary committees were made permanent institutions, although they were described more as administrative bodies than policy-making organs. The "three-in-one" principle upon which the revolutionary committees presumably rested was redefined as the "combination of the old, the middle-aged, and the young," a formula doubtless reflecting concerns over political stability and succession. The problem of filling the position of Chairman of the Republic, vacated by the purge of Liu Shaoqi, was resolved by simply abolishing the office. The ceremonial duties of China's formal head of state now fell to the aged Marshal Zhu De in his capacity as Chairman of the Standing Committee of the National People's Congress. Reflecting the generally more repressive character of the time, some of the freedoms formally granted in the 1954 constitution were deleted from the 1975 document, most notably "the freedom of citizens to engage in scientific research, literary and artistic creation, and other cultural pursuits" and the "freedom of residence and freedom to change residence." On the other hand, striking a faintly Cultural Revolution chord, it was stated that the people had the right to speak out freely, hold "great debates," and write big-character posters. One new freedom was added at the personal direction of Mao: the right of workers to strike. There were no great expectations that these rights would be honored any more fully than such other constitutionally guaranteed rights as freedom of speech, press, assembly, association, and demonstration.

Yet if the prospects for greater freedom were no brighter than they had been, it appeared in January 1975 that Zhou Enlai had succeeded in establishing a stable post–Cultural Revolution political order and had arranged for a smooth transition to the era when neither he nor Mao would be on hand. Zhou and the veteran bureaucrats clearly had dominated both the Party Central Committee meeting and the National People's Congress. The overwhelming majority of the twenty-nine ministers appointed to the State Council were pre-Cultural Revolution officials, most of them personally and politically close to Zhou. Only the Ministry of Culture had been left in the hands of the leftists. And Deng Xiaoping, whose spectacular political resurrection had come to symbolize the restoration of old cadres, seemed firmly entrenched as Zhou's successor—and perhaps Mao's as well.

The Rise and Fall of the "Gang of Four"

The unity that Zhou Enlai appeared to have fashioned in January 1975 was shattered within a month of the closing of the Fourth National People's Congress. In February left-wing Party leaders made their final bid for power, launching a campaign to study the Marxist concept of the dictatorship of the proletariat. The leftist attack was directed against Zhou Enlai or, more precisely, against Deng Xiaoping, who was the de facto head of the government during the long months that Zhou lay dying in the hospital.

The most prominent of the leftists were Zhang Chunqiao (the self-appointed leader of the abortive Shanghai Commune), the polemicist Yao Wenyuan (whose celebrated article had announced the opening of the Cultural Revolution), Wang Hongwen (the onetime Shanghai textile worker whom the Tenth Congress of 1973 had placed near the top of the Party hierarchy), and Jiang Qing (Mao's wife and China's would-be cultural czar). They later were to be known as "the Gang of Four," but before they were banished as the "Gang" (in October 1976), they were among the highest leaders of the Chinese Communist Party. All four were members of the Party's Politburo, and two (Zhang and Wang) were members of its Standing Committee as well, both bodies being more or less equally divided in 1975 between veteran revolutionaries and cultural revolutionaries. Yet the leftists had considerably less power than they appeared to have, and certainly far less than their opponents were to attribute to them after their purge. The influence of the Four and their supporters was largely confined to the cultural realm and to the official media, of which they made good use to magnify their importance well beyond its actual proportions. The real levers of power in the state bureaucracy and the army remained firmly in the hands of veteran officials of pre-Cultural Revolution vintage. The political prominence of the "Gang," indeed their political survival, was ultimately dependent on the patronage of an ailing and increasingly feeble Mao Zedong.

Mao's patronage, however, was ambiguous, and the relationship between the Chairman and those who claimed to be his true disciples remains murky. Mao himself is credited with coining the term "Gang of Four" when he advised his would-be disciples at a May 1975 Politburo meeting not to act as a "gang" after having admonished them for their conspiratorial activities a year earlier.[43] It seems likely that Mao was in general agreement with the policies and ideology advocated by the Four but not with their political methods. As events would demonstrate, he certainly did not regard them as worthy, or even acceptable, successors. Rather than the Gang manipulating a declining Mao for their own advantage, as some suppose,[44] it may well have been the case that Mao knowingly encouraged them to raise issues about social class and political power that would eventually bring about their political downfall, but would nevertheless have the effect of placing those issues on a future Chinese Marxist agenda.[45]

However that may have been, the Four were not simply puppets suspended on strings pulled by Mao. They represented more than themselves and their personal ambitions, although not the workers and peasants whose interests they claimed to champion. About the countryside they knew little, and among the peasants they were little known. Among the urban working class they could claim only scattered pockets of support; the mass organizations of the Cultural Revolution where they once had had influence had long since been suppressed, while the conservative mass organizations that represented the bulk of the working class long had supported the veteran leaders of the Party and the PLA. What the Four did represent was a sector of the post-Cultural Revolution bureaucracy, especially the millions of younger and lower-level cadres who had been admitted to the Party or had risen in rank by virtue of the Cultural Revolution. These were not the genuine radicals of the Cultural Revolution era, all of whom had now vanished in the continuing purge of the ultra-left that had begun in 1967, but rather more the careerists and the opportunists who (like the Four to whom they looked for leadership) had wound their way upward in the political hierarchy by faithfully following all the twists and turns of the Maoist line. They were tied to what one observer has aptly termed "the established left."[46] If Deng Xiaoping represented the veteran officials and personified the restoration of the old cadres, the Gang represented the interests of the new cadres. In very large measure, the increasingly Byzantine political struggles of 1975–76 were a conflict between old and new bureaucrats for control over the Party and state apparatus. Save for Mao Zedong, whose continued presence provided an aura of palace intrigue to the proceedings, the veteran bureaucrats held most of the political and military advantages.

Yet if the final round of political struggle of the Maoist era was essentially a struggle between conflicting bureaucratic interests, the accompanying ideological battles raised issues of wider social importance. The campaign to study the Marxist theory of the dictatorship of the proletariat, which was begun in February 1975 on Mao's personal instructions, focused on the politically explosive question of the relationship between social inequality and political power. Leftist theoreticians maintained their emphasis on the crucial importance of the political superstructure and the revolutionary transformation of social relationships as the keys to pursuing the correct path of economic development, but they now combined that with a search for a more orthodox Marxist explanation for persisting social inequality. Here they took as their main text one of Karl Marx's rare commentaries on the transitional era of the dictatorship of the proletariat, his 1875 *Critique of the Gotha Program.* In the *Critique* Marx had distinguished between the lower and higher phases of communism, with the former inevitably "stamped with the birthmarks of the old society from whose womb it emerges." Among those birthmarks was "the narrow horizon of bourgeois right," which bequeathed to the new society wide differentials in individual income (based on the unequal productive capacities of individuals) and other socioeconomic inequalities. Ignoring much else in Marx's *Critique,* Maoist ideologues seized on the concept of "bourgeois right," treating it not so much as the inevitable legacy of the capitalist past but as a threat to the socialist and communist future. "Bourgeois right," it was argued, especially by Zhang Chunqiao, who had written on the concept almost two decades earlier,[47] manifested itself in China's commodity economy, in the eight-grade wage system, in various aspects of private and semi-collective forms of ownership in the countryside, and in the widening status differences in productive processes, among other manifestations. Such were the material sources, it was further argued, for revisionist tendencies in the Party, for the production of "new bourgeois elements," and for class polarization in society at large. Thus the restriction of "bourgeois right" by the "dictatorship of the proletariat" (i.e., the Communist state) was necessary to protect what were called "the socialist newborn things," that is, the egalitarian fruits of the Cultural Revolution (of which there had been precious few to begin with and even fewer that remained). It was further necessary to reduce "the three great differences" (between mental and manual labor, town and countryside, worker and peasant) and thereby forestall the emergence of a new class of capitalist exploiters. Restricting "bourgeois right," simply put, meant state policies favoring more egalitarian forms of remuneration and distribution.

The leftists' critique of "bourgeois right" led to lengthy and inconclusive debates between the contending political factions—conducted within the ideological boundaries of the campaign to study the dictatorship of the proletariat—on the chief policy issues of the time: economic development strategy; the prevailing wage system; educational policy, especially the issue of university entrance examinations; the import of foreign technology; policy toward intellectuals; private plots and markets in the countryside; and the restoration of old cadres denounced during the Cultural Revolution. As the ideological debates raged throughout 1975, Deng Xiaoping, in his capacity as First Vice Premier and thus de facto head of government, pursued as best he could the modernization program Zhou Enlai had set forth in January. While paying formal ideological deference to the Maoist orthodoxies of the time and the desirability of restricting "bourgeois right," Deng was quite blunt in stating that all policies were to be judged mainly by economic criteria or, as he put it, "whether they restrict or release the productive forces." To this end, he had the State Council issue three policy documents in the autumn of 1975 calling for the rationalization of industry through the strengthening of managerial authority and labor discipline, the rapid development of modern science and technology partially to be brought about through large-scale borrowing from abroad, and the need to win the support of the intellectuals by raising their status and revitalizing the system of higher education.[48] The social implications of Deng's policy proposals, whatever their economic virtues, were clearly the expansion, not the restriction, of "bourgeois right."

On the issue of "bourgeois right," and most other issues as well, the ideologists of both factions invoked the textual authority of Marx, but both offered only one-sided and mechanistic interpretations of Marxist theory, although, of course, from different sides. But the debate between the old revolutionaries and the cultural revolutionaries would ultimately be settled not by the degree of Marxist theoretical sophistication demonstrated by the contending factions but rather by military force. Before that verdict was to be rendered, however, the political and ideological struggle was to continue for another year, through the latter months of 1975 and much of 1976. And it was conducted in an increasingly repressive and terroristic political environment. As established Party norms and state legal procedures broke down under the strains of the factional struggle, political power was employed in an increasingly coercive fashion. Arbitrary arrests and unrestrained secret police activities became more common, and an atmosphere of fear and terror pervaded the land, especially the urban areas. For this, the members and supporters of the future Gang of Four bore much of the responsibility. Although they hardly exercised a brutal "feudal-fascist" dictatorship, as was later charged, for the simple reason that they never really controlled the state, they were not reluctant to use coercive and terroristic political methods where they had the power to do so. That was particularly so in the realm of cultural affairs, the one area where the Gang was clearly dominant, and thus the repression fell particularly hard on intellectuals. It was also the case in the city of Shanghai, the main political stronghold of the Four, and in the practice of secret police agencies under the control of Kang Sheng and Wang Dongxing.

But if the political actions of the Gang were limited by the limitations of their actual power, the ideology they dispensed contributed greatly to the repressive character of the politics of the time. One of the more striking features of their treatises on the "dictatorship of the proletariat" was an enormous emphasis on the more authoritarian aspects of the Marxist concept. The need to strengthen "proletarian dictatorship" and further centralize state power was justified by the alleged gravity of the class struggle. As Zhang Chunqiao argued: "The class struggle between the proletariat and the bourgeoisie, the class struggle between the different political forces, and the class struggle in the ideological field . . . will continue to be long and torturous. . . . Even when all landlords and capitalists of the old generation have died, such class struggles will by no means come to a stop, and a bourgeois restoration may still occur."[49] With the prospect of an endless class struggle, it was necessary to exercise what Zhang termed "all-round dictatorship over the bourgeoisie," which meant an increasingly dictatorial and oppressive state. There was also the prospect that the state would act in an ever more arbitrary fashion, for the "leftist" ideology of the time celebrated violence as a necessary and desirable attribute of the dictatorship of the proletariat. "Instead of opposing revolutionary violence which conforms to the direction of historical development, Marxists acclaim it," it was said.[50] The glorification of "revolutionary violence" also dominated discussions of the Paris Commune, which was still praised in the literature as the model for proletarian dictatorship but, in striking contrast to the early days of the Cultural Revolution, no longer praised as a model of "mass democracy" and "the self-government of the producers" but rather for its repressive features. Indeed, the model was now viewed as partially flawed, because the Communards, it was said, had indulged in excessive "benevolence" toward class enemies and had failed to employ the full power of the state.

The general theoretical conclusion Maoist ideologists derived from their study of the concept of the dictatorship of the proletariat was the centrality of the "superstructure"—the state, its leaders, and their ideology—in determining the course of historical development and especially in promoting transitions from one mode of production to another. The emphasis on the decisive role of the state (and its repressive functions) had of course been one of the main themes of the earlier anti-Confucius campaign, with its glorification of the centralized Qin state of ancient times, the First Emperor, and Legalism. But the emphasis on the role of a strong and centralized state power reached its apogee during the campaign to study the dictatorship of the proletariat. It was, at best, a grotesquely perverted version of Marxism.

Along with the debilitating factional political conflict, the dictatorship of the proletariat campaign dragged on through the end of 1975, only briefly interrupted in the autumn of that year by a strange, short-lived movement dealing with the popular historical novel *Water Margin,* one of Mao's favorite works in traditional Chinese literature.[51] Written in the fourteenth century, the novel describes the exploits of a group of rebel bandits during the Song dynasty, one of whose members had betrayed the rebels and gone over to the Imperial court. People were told that criticisms of the fictional "capitulationist" would prove salutary as a safeguard against the contemporary danger of national and class betrayal. While Mao probably had Lin Biao in mind, some attempted to turn the movement against Deng Xiaoping—guilty, it was implied, of class capitulationism by advocating trading China's natural resources (coal and oil) for foreign technology.

The *Water Margin* campaign, whatever may have been the intentions of its promoters, had no noticeable effect on either China's foreign policies or the domestic political struggle. What broke the internal political stalemate, although in ways that could not have been anticipated, was the death of Zhou Enlai, which ushered in the final chapter in the political history of the Maoist era. Having valiantly attempted to conduct affairs of state from his hospital bed for more than a year, Premier Zhou succumbed to cancer on January 8, 1976, at the age of seventy-eight. His accomplishments and leadership were widely lauded in the Western press as his death was mourned by the people of China. Zhou's successor as Premier was neither Deng Xiaoping (as Zhou had planned and as was generally anticipated) nor Zhang Chunqiao, who was Second Vice Premier after Deng. Mao, apparently, trusted neither the leader of the veteran revolutionaries nor the leader of the cultural revolutionaries. Appointed acting Premier was the relatively obscure Minister of Public Security, Hua Guofeng. A loyal Maoist, or at least unquestionably loyal to Mao, Hua's chief virtue was that he had kept a respectable political distance from both of the contending factions, satisfactory for the time being to the veteran bureaucrats, but not to the Gang. His task in any event was to hold the government together and keep the factional conflict within bounds.

Little was heard from Deng Xiaoping after he delivered the eulogy at Zhou Enlai's funeral on January 15. But much was heard about him on wall posters and in newspapers, which revived old Cultural Revolution accusations about "China's new Khrushchev" and a "leading person in authority taking the capitalist road." It was left to Jiang Qing to add a new disclosure: Deng, she charged, was "an international capitalist agent." The leftists' opportunity to cast Deng into political oblivion for a second time came in April.

In the early days of April, with the approach of the Qing Ming festival, the traditional time to mourn the dead, groups of Beijing citizens marched into Tiananmen Square to lay wreaths at the Monument of People's Heroes in honor of Zhou Enlai. They came from factories, schools, government ministries, and nearby communes—and they came in defiance of the government, which had declared Qing Ming an outmoded feudal custom and had forbidden the placing of wreaths in the Square. Yet people came in increasing numbers over a period of four days, not only with wreaths but also with poems, wall posters, and speeches eulogizing Zhou Enlai, and in many cases making veiled criticisms of the Gang of Four. On Sunday, April 4, the day before Qing Ming, hundreds of thousands of citizens came to Tiananmen to pay respects to their dead Premier, and by nightfall the huge Square was filled with both wreaths and wall posters. In the darkness of the early morning hours, workers dispatched by the municipal government hastily gathered up the wreaths and posters and carted them off in trucks. The next day, tens of thousands of enraged citizens marched into the Square in demonstrations of protest. Disorder followed, but the violence was minor, in part because many members of the police and security forces sympathized with the demonstrators. Most of the protesters were persuaded to leave peacefully, but several thousand who remained at nightfall were attacked by the urban militia. Some were wounded, many arrested, and several hundred imprisoned.[52]

The "April Fifth Movement," as it came to be called, became a powerful political symbol over the years to come—symbolic of the spirit of popular resistance to a despotic state. But the immediate result was a meeting of the Party Politburo on April 7, which declared the Tiananmen demonstrations a "counterrevolutionary incident," even though the more militant of the demonstrators were seen raising their right fists in the Communist salute and heard singing the *Internationale*.[53] The incident was blamed on Deng Xiaoping, who was removed from all his official posts in both the Party apparatus and the state administration, although he was permitted to keep his membership in the Communist Party "so as to see how he will behave in the future." Benefiting from Deng's second fall from power was Hua Guofeng, who was confirmed as Premier of the State Council by the Party Politburo (although this had yet to be formally ratified by the National People's Congress) and also elevated to first Vice Chairman of the Party, making him Mao's apparent successor.

There followed a campaign to criticize Deng Xiaoping, now best known to readers of the official press as "an unrepentant capitalist-roader." His leadership of the State Council in 1975, when Zhou Enlai lay dying, was condemned as a "right deviationist wind" and his policy documents on modernization were labeled "the three poisonous weeds." The campaign against Deng, which was advertised as a mass criticism movement, was marked by a singular lack of popular participation. But it was accompanied by a new wave of secret police repression, as tens of thousands were arrested as alleged "counterrevolutionaries."

As the campaign against Deng Xiaoping dragged on into the summer of 1976, Mao Zedong lay dying, and the society he had founded seemed to be disintegrating. Industrial production plummeted as the cities were swept by a wave of workers' strikes, factory slowdowns, and absenteeism. Among a demoralized population, the old factional conflicts of the Cultural Revolution were resumed, accompanied by an upsurge in crime and social disorder. On July 28, 1976, one of the most massive earthquakes in Chinese history struck North China, its epicenter about 100 miles east of Beijing, leveling the newly-industrialized city of Tangshan and killing nearly a quarter of its one million inhabitants. To counteract the lingering influence of the traditional belief that natural disasters were portents of dynastic collapse, the leftist leaders in the capital instructed the survivors to begin a movement to criticize the notion of the Mandate of Heaven, and the superstitions associated with it, all the while exhorting them to continue the campaign against Deng Xiaoping. International assistance was rejected in the name of "self-reliance" and relief efforts were left to the PLA, which did in fact coordinate a remarkably effective medical and economic rehabilitation operation that drew upon the resources of many provinces. By early autumn, many of Tangshan's coal mines and steel mills had resumed production.

Mao Zedong had made his last official appearance at the Party's Tenth Congress in 1973 and then retired to the seclusion of his study. Ailing, increasingly feeble, and at times not entirely lucid, he largely confined himself to brief meetings with visiting foreign dignitaries, mostly at his residence in the old imperial section of Beijing once called the Forbidden City. Mao's role in the political events of his last years remains obscure at best, although it is probable that he rendered the final judgments on most important questions of policy until the early spring of 1976. That certainly was not the case by June, when it was officially announced that the Chairman could no longer receive foreign visitors. Mao Zedong died on September 9, 1976, at the age of eighty-two.

The leaders of China's political and military bureaucracies, which had risen phoenix-like from the ashes of the Great Proletarian Cultural Revolution, wasted little time in severing such tenuous links as remained with the radical Maoist tradition, although they invoked the name of Mao and his slogans while doing so. Early in October, with the period of mourning for the late Chairman barely concluded, the Politburo purged itself of its more radical members. Those who thereafter were to be known as the Gang of

Four were arrested in a military coup and accused of having conspired to seize state power, among a vast array of other charges.[54] Hua Guofeng, having already assumed Zhou Enlai's place as Premier of the State Council, now was also selected to replace Mao as Chairman of the Chinese Communist Party. Hua made his appearance on the political stage as neither revolutionary leader nor statesman, but rather as caretaker for the bureaucracy.

The year 1976 marks not only the close of the Maoist era but also the departure of virtually all of the original generation of Chinese Marxist revolutionaries who had grown to intellectual and political maturity during the May Fourth Movement. The Cultural Revolution and its turbulent aftermath already had taken an enormous toll of the old revolutionaries (and of the country's leadership), first among the "capitalist-roaders" against whom the movement originally was directed and then among those Maoist leaders who originally directed the movement and then fell victim to the various purges of "ultra-leftists." For very different reasons, neither of Mao's putative successors, Liu Shaoqi and Lin Biao, survived the upheaval. Age and illness removed other old revolutionaries who had politically survived a revolutionary process that consumed so many of its leaders and children. Dong Biwu, one of the few remaining founders of the Chinese Communist Party, died in April 1975. In December, death took Kang Sheng, who had served Mao as "China's Beria" since the Yan'an days. Zhou Enlai, who served him far better, died in January 1976. The ninety-year-old Zhu De, the father of the Red Army and a towering symbol of revolutionary legitimacy and unity, died in July 1976. Deng Xiaoping, the youngest of the old revolutionaries, had been banished to political purgatory for a second time, this time seemingly beyond redemption.

With Mao's death, the May Fourth generation of Communist revolutionaries had all but vanished. For more than half a century they had been the carriers of the most modern of revolutionary doctrines in the oldest of nations. Historians surely will record them among the most remarkable and illustrious of revolutionary intelligentsias, for they were the leaders of the greatest and most dynamic revolution in the history of the modern world and then presided over the beginnings of the modern transformation of the world's most populous country—and also one of the most backward. The victory of 1949 earned them power, but in a country that was utterly destitute and inhabited by a people racked by the most wretched poverty and despair. With only the most meager of material resources they fashioned China into a unified and modern nation-state and laid the foundations for a modern industrial economy.

The legacies of the Maoist era, both positive and negative, will be further considered in several of the chapters which follow. What needs to be emphasized here is that the aim of the generation of old revolutionaries was to make China both modern *and* socialist. However bitterly they became divided in their later years over means and methods, the first generation remained firmly committed to pursuing the Marxist goals they had embraced in their youthful days. New generations of leaders will continue to promote the modern economic and political development of China and might well prove successful in achieving those long elusive and eminently nationalist goals of "wealth and power" (*fu jiang*). But whether post-Maoist leaders would continue to strive for a socialist future as ardently as their predecessors was one of the questions that hung over China at the close of the Mao era.

NOTES

1. For example, Franz Schurmann, "What Is Happening in China: An Exchange," *New York Review of Books,* January 12, 1967.
2. Edgar Snow, *The Long Revolution* (New York: Random House, 1972), pp. 17–20.
3. Chinese support for armed revolutionary struggles was of course largely verbal. It was also highly selective; the death of Che Guervara, for example, was not even mentioned in the Chinese press.
4. From remarks made by Mao in the summer of 1967 and widely disseminated throughout China in pamphlet form. For a translation of the text, see Jean Daubier, *A History of the Cultural Revolution* (New York: Vintage Books, 1974), Appendix 4, pp. 307–13.
5. Lin Piao [Lin Biao], "Report to the Ninth Congress of the Communist Party of China," *Collection of Important Documents of the Great Proletarian Cultural Revolution* (Peking: Foreign Languages Press, 1970), pp. 94–107.
6. As related to Edgar Snow in December 1970. Snow, *The Long Revolution,* p. 174.
7. On the Zhou Enlai–Jiang Qing coalition against Lin Biao, see Hong Yung Lee, *The Politics of the Chinese Cultural Revolution* (Berkeley: University of California Press, 1978), Ch. 8 and Conclusion.
8. As set forth in the "Outline of '571 Project.'" See note 18 below.
9. William Joseph, in his perceptive study *The Critique of Ultra-Leftism in China,* 1958–1981 (Stanford, Calf.: Stanford University Press, 1984), p. 145. For other accounts and interpretations of the fall of Lin Biao, see Michael Y. M. Kau (ed.), *The Lin Piao Affair: Power Politics and Military Coup* (White Plains, N.Y.: International Arts and Sciences Press, 1975); Jaapvan Ginnekan, *The Rise and Fall of Lin Piao* (New York: Avon Books, 1977); Livio Maitan, *Party, Army, and Masses in China* (London: New Left Books, 1976), ch. 14; and Philip Bridgham, "The Fall of Lin Piao," *The China Quarterly,* No. 55 (1973), pp. 427–49.
10. "Summary of Chairman Mao's Talks with Responsible Comrades at Various Places during his Provincial Tour," August-September 1971, in Stuart R. Schram (ed.), *Mao Tse-tung Unrehearsed: Talks and Letters,* 1956–1971 (Harmondsworth, Middlesex, England: Penguin, 1974), pp. 292–93.
11. *Ibid.,* p. 293.
12. "Communiqué of the Second Plenary Session of the Ninth Central Committee of the Communist Party of China," *Peking Review,* September 11, 1970.

13. Snow, *The Long Revolution,* pp. 10–12. Chinese and American ambassadors had held more than one hundred fruitless meetings in Warsaw since the mid-1950s.

14. *Ibid.,* pp. 171–72.

15. So named when in early April of 1971 a Chinese table tennis team in Japan invited a touring American team to visit the People's Republic. The U.S. players were accompanied by a large number of American journalists.

16. A Chinese Trident jet did crash near Under Khan in Mongolia on September 13, but Chinese and Russian accounts differ as to the identity of the victims.

17. "Summary of Chairman Mao's Talks with Responsible Comrades at Various Places during his Provincial Tour," August-September 1971, in Schram (ed.), *Mao Tse-tung Unrehearsed,* p. 294. Mao listed the principal figures in the first nine of the "major struggles" in the history of the CCP, from Chen Duxiu in 1927 to Liu Shaoqi in 1966. Lin Biao, of course, was soon to be the tenth.

18. New China News Agency, November 17, 1980 (*The New York Times,* November 18, 1980). For a partial English translation of the "Outline of the '571 Project,'" regarded as more or less authentic by most observers, see *Issues and Studies,* VIII, No. 8 (May 1972): 79–83.

19. *The New York Times,* October 12, 1972, p. 3.

20. Arrested as accomplices in the plot were a number of top military leaders, including Huang Yongsheng, PLA Chief of Staff, and Wu Faxian, commander of the Air Force.

21. See, for example, William Hinton, *Turning Point in China* (New York: Monthly Review Press, 1972), pp. 39–40, and Charles Bettelheim, *Cultural Revolution and Industrial Organization in China* (New York: Monthly Review Press, 1974), pp. 118–22.

22. For example, Parris H. Chang, "Political Rehabilitation of Cadres in China: A Traveller's View," *The China Quarterly,* April–June 1973, p. 333.

23. One observer visiting the People's Republic in the autumn of 1972 was able to identify at least fifty Party secretaries and deputy secretaries who had been returned to office. The number undoubtedly was greater and grew in subsequent years. *Ibid.,* p. 335, note 11.

24. "Summary of Chairman Mao's Talks with Responsible Comrades at Various Places during his Provincial Tour," in Schram (ed.), *Mao Tse-tung Unrehearsed,* p. 296.

25. Snow, *The Long Revolution,* pp. 18–19, 169–70.

26. China's foreign trade, which had declined in 1967–68, had returned to its pre-Cultural Revolution levels by the end of 1968. From 1969 to 1975, the value of foreign trade increased from about US$4 billion to $14 billion per annum. Joseph Cheng, "Strategy for Economic Development" in Bill Brugger (ed.), *China: The Impact of the Cultural Revolution* (London: Croom Helm, 1978), pp. 140–41. From the end of 1972 until the spring of 1975, the People's Republic imported whole industrial plants valued at US$2.8 billion, primarily from Japan and Western Europe. Kojima Reiitsu, "Accumulation, Technology, and China's Economic Development," in Mark Selden and Victor Lippit (eds.), *The Transition to Socialism in China,* (Armonk, N.Y.: M. E. Sharpe, 1982), pp. 248–49.

27. Hong Yung Lee, "Deng Xiaoping's Reform of the Chinese Bureaucracy," in *The Limits of Reform in China* (Washington: The Wilson Center, 1982), p. 31.

28. Chou En-lai [Zhou Enlai], "Report to the Tenth National Congress of the Communist Party of China," August 24, 1973, in *The Tenth National Congress of the Communist Party of China (Documents)* (Peking: Foreign Languages Press, 1973), p. 34.

29. Wang Hung-wen [Wang Hongwen], "Report on the Revision of the Party Constitution," August 24, 1973, *ibid.,* pp. 48–54.

30. "Constitution of the Communist Party of China," *ibid.,* p. 61.

31. Wang Hung-wen, "Report," p. 44.

32. Chou En-lai, "Report," p. 21. The more picturesque and literal translation of the phrase—much favored by Mao at the time—is "great disorder under Heaven."

33. Before Lin Biao's demise was publicly revealed, he and his associates were referred to in official pronouncements by the phrase "swindlers like Liu Shaoqi."

34. Chou En-lai, "Report," pp. 5–20.

35. Ye Jianying (1898–1986), an instructor at the Whampoa Academy in the mid-1920s, became one of the principal leaders of the Red Army after 1927, serving under Zhu De and Peng Dehuai as chief of staff of the main Communist army during the Yan'an era. After the fall of Lin Biao in 1971, he emerged as the most powerful military figure in the People's Republic. Li Desheng (1916–   ) joined the Red Army in 1935 at the age of nineteen. Primarily a professional soldier, he rose rapidly through the ranks to become a divisional commander in the postrevolutionary years. An unwavering supporter of Mao Zedong during the Cultural Revolution, he was elected an alternate member of the Party's Politburo in April 1969 and was appointed director of the PLA General Political Department in 1970.

36. In the "Outline of Project 571," the document allegedly setting forth Lin Biao's plot against Mao, which was widely circulated for internal study after Lin's death, Mao was condemned as "a contemporary Qin Shihuangdi." The Chairman proved eager to accept the historical analogy.

37. Mao's physical decline was apparent to the foreign visitors he continued to receive in his official residence in 1975 and through the early months of 1976. He apparently had suffered a stroke sometime in 1974, partially paralyzing the left side of his body and impairing his speech. He often was forced to communicate through cryptic written notes.

38. What Deng enunciated later was called the "Three Worlds theory," sometimes attributed to Mao Zedong. According to the "theory," the first world consists of the two superpowers, the United States and the U.S.S.R., the second comprises the developed capitalist and socialist countries of Eastern and Western Europe, and the third includes the developing countries of most of the rest of the world. Presupposed is a potential degree of unity of the second and third worlds against the first.

39. Mao attended neither the Party Central Committee Plenum nor the National People's Congress. His health, however fragile, nevertheless did not prevent his receiving Franz Josef Strauss, the West German opposition leader, while the Congress was in session.

40. Chou En-lai, "Report on the Work of the Government," January 13, 1975, *Peking Review,* January 24, 1975, pp. 21–25.

41. On the economic successes and failures of the Maoist era, see Chapter 21 below. Most data suggest that industrial production increased at a 10 percent annual rate during the "cultural revolution decade," 1966–76.

42. This point received special emphasis in Zhang Chunqiao's speech presenting the constitution to the Congress, where he stressed the "Party's centralized leadership over the structure of the state." For an English translation of the text of the 1975 constitution, see *Peking Review,* January 24, 1975, pp. 12–17.

43. *Peking Review,* January 14, 1977, pp. 28–29.

44. For example, Roger Garside, *Coming Alive: China After Mao* (New York: Mentor, 1982), p. 57: "In the Cultural Revolution [the Gang] had acted as [Mao's] agents, but in his declining years they appeared at times to manipulate him for their own advantage. Mao had no one else to turn to, but he was not deceived."

45. As suggested by Richard Kraus, *Class Conflict in Chinese Socialism* (New York: Columbia University Press, 1981), p. 163.

46. The term is used by Kjeld Erik Brodsgaard, "The Democracy Movement in China, 1978–1979," *Asian Survey,* XXI, No. 7 (July 1981), p. 751.

47. In 1958, at the height of the Great Leap, Zhang had written an article entitled "Break Away from the Idea of Bourgeois Right." Elaborating on a brief commentary written by Mao, Zhang advocated that the relatively egalitarian supply system of the revolutionary years should replace the system of wage differentials introduced in the postrevolutionary era, suggesting that it should apply to bureaucrats and cadres as well as communized peasants. For a discussion of the article and its political import, see Harry Harding, *Organizing China: The Problem of Bureaucracy, 1949–1976* (Stanford, Calif.: Stanford University Press, 1981), pp. 190–93.

48. The three documents drafted in accordance with Deng's instructions in 1975 are "On the General Program for All Work of the Whole Party and the Whole Country," "Some Questions on Accelerating the Development of Industry" ("The Twenty Articles"), and "Report on the Work of the Chinese Academy of Sciences." For English translations of the original texts, see Chi Hsin, *The Case of the Gang of Four* (Hong Kong: Cosmos Books, 1977), pp. 203–95.

49. Chang Ch'un-ch'iao [Zhang Chunqiao], "On Exercising All-Round Dictatorship over the Bourgeoisie," *Peking Review,* April 4, 1975, p. 8. This was Chang's principal theoretical contribution to the campaign to study the dictatorship of the proletariat. It originally appeared in *Red Flag* on April 1. See *Peking Review,* pp. 5–11 for a full English translation. Yao Wenyuan's best-known piece, "The Social Basis of the Lin Piao Anti-Party Clique," had appeared in *Red Flag* a month before. For an English translation, see *Peking Review,* March 7, 1975, pp. 5–10.

50. Yu Tung [Yu Dong], "Programme for Consolidation of the Dictatorship of the Proletariat," *Peking Review,* January 18, 1974, p. 6.

51. The novel is best known in the West in Pearl Buck's English translation under the title *All Men Are Brothers.*

52. For a moving and detailed eyewitness account of the events in Tiananmen Square in early April, see Garside, *Coming Alive,* pp. 101–26. As Garside notes, similar if smaller demonstrations honoring Zhou Enlai took place in cities and towns throughout much of the country (p. 105).

53. *Ibid.,* pp. 107 and 109.

54. The arrest of the "Gang" (Zhang Chunqiao, Yao Wenyuan, Wang Hongwen, and Jiang Qing) was plotted by Hua Guofeng and Minister of Defense Ye Jianying in concert with most top commanders of the PLA. The actual deed was performed in the early morning hours of October 6 by soldiers of the elite "8341 Unit," commanded by the eminently Maoist Wang Dongxing.

PART SIX

DENG XIAOPING AND THE ORIGINS OF CHINESE CAPITALISM

1976–1998

21

The Legacies of the Maoist Era

T HE CHINESE COMMUNISTS came to power in 1949
promising not one revolution but two; a bourgeois revolution to
be followed in due historical course by a socialist one. The bourgeois revolution, left unfinished (indeed, hardly begun) by Chiang Kai-
shek's Nationalist regime, was accomplished swiftly by China's new
Marxist rulers. In the early 1950s the Communists rapidly fashioned the
decaying fragments of the old Chinese empire into a modern nation-state
and instilled in its enormous population powerful feelings of national identity and a strong sense of social purpose. The long-delayed agrarian revolution was completed with the conclusion of the Land Reform campaign in
1952, finally removing the archaic gentry-landlord class from the historical
scene and liberating the great majority of the Chinese people from ancient
modes of economic exploitation and social oppression. The territorial unification of the country, the establishment of a strong centralized state, the
emergence of a national market, and the abolition of pre-capitalist social
relations in the countryside created, in turn, the necessary conditions for
the development of modern productive forces. The immense human and
material resources latent in the vast land could now be harnessed to bring
about the transformation of a backward and long-stagnant economy into a
modern industrial one.

What was achieved during the early years of the People's Republic essentially was the program Sun Yatsen, the founder of the Guomindang and "the father of the country," had set forth at the beginning of the century: national unification, independence from foreign imperialism, "land to the tiller," and a plan for modern industrial development. And the Communists, to whom the task of implementing that program fell, can justly claim to be the rightful heirs of that most eminent of China's bourgeois revolutionaries. The fruits of Mao's "New Democratic" revolution of the early 1950s are now apparent. China, long (and not long ago) among the most wretched and impoverished of countries, has indeed "stood up" in the world, as Mao Zedong so proudly proclaimed in 1949, and today stands as an independent, powerful, and rapidly modernizing nation.

The bourgeois phase of the Chinese Revolution did not resemble any classic Western model of a capitalist-type revolution. China's bourgeois revolution was carried out under the auspices of a Marxist political party proclaiming socialist and communist goals. The remaining members of a weak Chinese bourgeoisie were neither its leaders not its beneficiaries. Moreover, the distinguishing feature of Western bourgeois revolutions— the creation of conditions conducive to the flourishing of private property and capitalist development—hardly distinguished the Maoist version. "National capitalism" in the cities and individual peasant proprietorship in the countryside were limited in scope and duration; the limitations were imposed by a state presided over by Marxists who aimed to abolish private property. And when Beijing's Communist leaders decided (perhaps prematurely, it would now seem) that the essential "bourgeois" historical tasks had been accomplished, they were determined to bring about the second of the two revolutions they had promised. The era of "the transition to socialism" was announced in 1953, less than four years after the establishment of the People's Republic, and it began at a very low level of economic development, indeed amid conditions of general scarcity and poverty. Over the remaining two decades of the Mao era, modernization and socialism were to be pursued simultaneously—in accordance with the dictates of "permanent revolution."

Among the distinguishing features of the Mao period, many observers once believed, was a unique attempt to reconcile the means of modern industrialism with the ends of socialism. That, no doubt, was Mao's aim, and it certainly was the Maoist claim. But, in the end, Mao Zedong was far more successful as an economic modernizer than as a builder of socialism. This judgment, of course, does not accord with the conventional wisdom of the day, which tells us that Mao sacrificed "modernization" to "ideological purity" and that economic development was neglected as the late Chairman embarked on a fruitless quest for a socialist spiritual utopia. The actual historical record conveys a rather different story, and it is essentially a story of rapid industrialization. The post-Mao critiques of the Maoist economic legacy, which dwell less on the accomplishments than on the deficiencies of the era, nonetheless reveal that the value of gross industrial output grew thirty-eight-fold during the Mao period, and that of heavy industry ninety-fold, albeit starting from a tiny modern industrial base whose output had been halved by the ravages of foreign invasion and civil war. But between 1952 (when industrial production was restored to its highest pre-war levels) and 1977, the output of Chinese industry increased at an average annual rate of 11.3 percent, as rapid a pace of industrialization as has ever been achieved by any country during a comparable period in modern world history.[1] Over the Mao era, the contribution of industry to China's net material product increased from 23 percent to over 50 percent while agriculture's share declined from 58 to 34 percent.[2] As a noted Australian economist has observed:

> This sharp rise [of almost 30 per cent] in industry's share in China's national income is a rare historical phenomenon. For example, during the first four or five decades of their drive to modern industrialization, the industrial share rose by only 11 percent in Britain (1801–41); and 22 percent in Japan (1878/82–1923/27). In the postwar experience of newly industrializing countries, probably only Taiwan has demonstrated as impressive a record as China in this respect.[3]

China's transformation from a primarily agrarian country to a relatively industrialized nation was reflected in dramatic increases in the production of the products associated with modernization, at least prior to the "information age." Between 1952 and 1976, the output of steel grew from 1.3 to 23 million tons; coal from 66 to 448 million tons; electric power from 7 to 133 billion kilowatt-hours; crude oil from virtually nothing to 28 million tons; chemical fertilizer from 0.2 to 28 million tons; and cement from 3 to 49 million tons.[4] By the mid-1970s China was manufacturing jet airplanes, heavy tractors, and modern ocean-going vessels in substantial quantities. The People's Republic was also producing nuclear weapons and long-range ballistic missiles; it first launched a satellite in 1970, six years after its first successful atomic bomb test.

Industrialization began to bring significant changes in China's social structure. Although 75 percent of a working population that totaled about 400,000,000 remained employed in agriculture during the Mao era, the industrial working class grew from 3,000,000 in 1952 to about 50,000,000 in the mid-1970s, a figure that includes 28,000,000 peasants who had become workers in commune or brigade factories under the policy of small-scale rural industrialization. In addition, nearly 20 million workers were employed in transport and construction work closely linked with industry.[5] A new technological intelligentsia was created. The number of Chinese scientists and technicians increased from 50,000 in 1949 (and 425,000 in 1952) to 2,500,000 in 1966 and five million in 1979, 99 percent of them trained in the post–1949 years.[6] And mammoth irrigation and water control works were constructed during the Mao era, which greatly facilitated the upsurge in agricultural production and productivity in the early 1980s.

. . .

Many blunders were committed in the Maoist industrialization drive, and the process was indeed marred by the "irrationalities" and "imbalances" that Mao's successors were to diagnose. Some of the blunders, especially the Great Leap, were on a monumental scale and took a heavy human as well as economic toll. Other economic failings became chronically imbedded in the postrevolutionary pattern of economic development, at least in practice if not in intent, stubbornly defying all Maoist remedies and ideological exhortations. Certainly the most serious of these failings was the agonizingly slow growth of agriculture, making a mockery of the enormous Maoist ideological emphasis on developing the countryside. While industrial production grew rapidly at an annual rate of 11 percent between 1952 and the close of the Mao period, agricultural output increased by only 2.3 percent per annum,[7] barely keeping pace with the average yearly population increase of 2 percent—which resulted in a near doubling of the Chinese population over the twenty-five-years of the Mao era.

Nor was the modern industrial sector itself free of serious deficiencies. If Maoist policies mitigated many of the more appalling social inequities generated by Stalinist-style industrialization, they did not succeed in fundamentally changing the Soviet-modeled industrial structure originally built in the 1950s. At the close of the Mao era, consequently, Chinese industry was suffering from many of the same problems that were plaguing its Soviet and East European counterparts and that would soon contribute to their collapse. Waste, inefficiency, overstaffing, bureaucratic inertia, low productivity, and petty corruption had become chronic features of China's industrial life. Popular living standards were sacrificed to achieve ever higher rates of capital accumulation for investment in heavy industry. Trade and service enterprises were neglected, as were consumer goods industries. And a demoralized working class was left in the wake. Although industrial output continued to increase by 10 percent per annum during the last years of the Maoist regime (with the exception of the fateful year of 1976), this rate of growth was not maintained without sacrificing the quality of what was produced and not without increasing state capital investment in the modern industrial sector. The accumulation rate (that is, the proportion of the material product withheld from consumption and invested to expand productive capacity) increased from about 23 percent in the early 1960s to 33 percent in the early 1970s, reaching an unsustainable peak of 36.7 percent in 1978.[8] State funds were allocated primarily to finance the growth of heavy industry; only 12 percent of state investment went to agriculture during the Mao years, and barely 5 percent to the development of consumer goods industries.[9] These policies facilitated very high rates of national economic growth but depressed consumption and popular living standards.

The problems in industry were compounded by technological backwardness. While the policy of self-reliance limited (although by no means entirely precluded) access to foreign technology, the Cultural Revolution had devastating effects on higher education, basic research, and the morale of the technological intelligentsia—contributing to the obsolescence of the industrial plant built in the 1950s and to a grave shortage of qualified scientists during the last years of the Maoist regime.

Yet despite all the failings and setbacks, it is an inescapable historical conclusion that the Maoist era was the time of China's modern industrial revolution. Starting with an industrial base smaller than that of Belgium's in the early 1950s, the China that for so long was ridiculed as "the sick man of Asia" emerged at the end of the Mao period as one of the six largest industrial producers in the world. National income grew five-fold over the 25-year period 1952–1978, increasing from 60 billion to over 300 billion *yuan,* with industry accounting for most of the growth. On a per capita basis, the index of national income (at constant prices) increased from 100 in 1949 (and 160 in 1952) to 217 in 1957 and 440 in 1978.[10] Over the last two decades of the Maoist era, from 1957 to 1975 (a period held in low esteem by Mao's successors), even taking into account the economic disasters of the Great Leap, China's national income increased by 63 percent on a per capita basis during this period of rapid population growth, more than doubling overall.[11]

The Maoist economic record, however flawed, is nonetheless the record of an era when the basic foundations for modern industrialism were laid. Indeed, it is a record that compares favorably with comparable stages in the industrialization of Germany, Japan, and Russia—hitherto the most economically successful cases (among major countries) of late modernization. In Germany the rate of economic growth for the period

1880–1914 was 33 percent per decade. In Japan from 1874–1929 the rate of increase per decade was 43 percent.[12] The Soviet Union over the period 1928–58 achieved a decadal increase of 54 percent. In China over the years 1952–72 the decadal rate was 64 percent.[13] This was hardly economic development at "a snail's pace," as foreign journalists persist in misinforming their readers.[14]

This economic achievement was all the more remarkable in that it was accomplished by the Chinese people themselves on the basis of their own meager material resources, with little outside assistance or support. Save for limited Soviet aid in the 1950s, which was repaid in full (and with interest) by the mid-1960s, Maoist industrialization proceeded without benefit of foreign loans or investments. It was as much a hostile international environment as the once hallowed principle of "self-reliance" that imposed conditions of virtual autarky until the late 1970s. At the close of the Maoist era, China was unique among developing countries in being able to claim an economy burdened by neither foreign debt nor internal inflation.

Although it has become unfashionable to recall the accomplishments of Mao's time, it remains the case that the Maoist regime made immense progress in bringing about China's modern industrial transformation, and it did so under adverse internal and external conditions. Without the industrial revolution of the Mao era, the economic reformers who rose to prominence in the post-Mao era would have had little to reform.

Of the Chinese people, Mao's industrial revolution demanded hard labor and great sacrifices, as had been the case in the industrialization of Japan and Russia in earlier times. Popular consumption and living standards suffered as the Communist state appropriated ever larger shares of the surplus to finance the expansion of the modern industrial plant. The state, simply put, exploited the people it ruled, especially the peasantry, in order to build a heavy industrial base and to support the growing bureaucracy that presided over it. But it is not the case, as some of the more zealous champions of the market have suggested, that the Chinese people did not materially benefit during the years of Maoist industrialization. To be sure, China's sharply rising national income did not translate itself into corresponding increases in income for the working population, whose labor was responsible for the rise. Some of the increase was absorbed by a rapidly growing population, partly the result of the ineffectiveness of belatedly implemented birth control policies. However, most of the surplus flowed into state coffers (and from there to the modern industrial sector and its bureaucracy), leaving only enough for meager increases in popular income over the last two decades of the Maoist regime. While the income of state employees, including regular factory workers, rose significantly during the late Mao period, the income of peasants, who made up 75 percent of the laboring population, increased little, if at all, after 1957.[15] Yet among gains not easy to quantify in economic calculations, but vital for measuring popular welfare, one must note the vast expansion of schools and educational opportunities during the Mao era, the transformation of a largely illiterate population into a mostly literate one, and the building of a relatively comprehensive health care system where none existed before. The near doubling of average life expectancy over the quarter-century of Mao's rule—from an average of thirty-five in pre-1949 China to sixty-five in the mid-1970s—offers dramatic statistical evidence for the material and social gains that the Communist Revolution brought to the great majority of the Chinese people.

Upon completing his monumental history of the Soviet Union, the great English historian E. H. Carr warned: "The danger is not that we shall draw a veil over the enormous blots on the record of the Revolution, over its cost in human suffering, over the crimes committed in its name. The danger is that we shall be tempted to forget altogether, and to pass over in silence, its immense achievements."[16]

Carr's words deserve to be pondered by students of modern Chinese history as well as Russian history, for revolutions do not easily lend themselves to balanced appraisals. Great social upheavals typically arouse great and unattainable expectations, and when those high hopes are dashed long periods of disillusionment and cynicism inevitably follow, while the actual historical achievements are ignored or forgotten. It usually takes several generations, far removed from the political and ideological battles of the revolutionary epoch, to bring the historical picture back into focus. It is the blots on the Maoist record, especially the Great Leap and the Cultural Revolution, that are now most deeply imprinted on our political and historical consciousness. That these adventures were failures colossal in scope, and that they took an enormous human toll, cannot and should not be forgotten. But future historians, without ignoring the failures and the crimes, will surely record the Maoist era in the history of the People's Republic (however else they may judge it) as one of the great modernizing epochs in world history, and one that brought great social and human benefits to the Chinese people.

• • •

More questionable than Mao Zedong's historical status as a modernizer is his lingering, if tarnished, image as the builder of a socialist society. If Maoism laid the foundations for China's modern industrial revolution, did it also bring about a socialist reorganization of Chinese society, as once was so loudly claimed and many still assume—especially those who today applaud post-Mao China's embrace of the market as an abandonment of "socialism"? To what social result did the much-heralded Maoist "transition to socialism" actually lead?

The social and economic transformation of China during the Maoist era cannot be understood simply as a version of "the modernization process," however broadly one chooses to define that rather vague term. Modernization, after all, does not typically entail the abolition of private property. Yet it was precisely the absence of private ownership of the means of production that came to crucially define Chinese society only a few years after the Communist victory of 1949. By 1956 virtually all that remained of the private sector of the urban economy had been effectively nationalized and agriculture had been collectivized, putting the economies of both the cities and the countryside under state control. If state (and "collective") ownership of productive property, along with the proclaimed principle of "payment according to work," are the defining features of socialism—and such was the definition that prevailed in Beijing and elsewhere at the time—then China had become a socialist society very early in the Maoist period. In 1956, when Chinese Communist leaders from Mao Zedong to Deng Xiaoping were celebrating the triumph of socialism, China was in fact no less "socialist" than the Soviet Union.

As had been the case in the Soviet Union, nationalization and collectivization in China were accompanied by an intensive drive for industrialization, and the latter of course is the essence of all versions of modernization. But the industrial development of the People's Republic, proceeding wholly under state auspices, was originally conceived not as an end in itself but as a means to socialist ends. The postrevolutionary regimes of both Russia and China sought to bring about socialism and modern industrialism simultaneously, abandoning (in their different fashions) the orthodox Marxist belief that socialism presupposed industrial capitalism. But in many respects the socialist experiment was pursued far more vigorously in Maoist China than in the Soviet Union, for Mao, unlike Lenin and Stalin, was unwilling to entrust the socialist future to the impersonal forces of modern technology alone. Maoism demanded that economic development be accompanied (and indeed preceded) by a "permanent" process of radical transformations in social relationships and popular consciousness. Socialist institutions and communist values, Mao taught, had to be created in the very process of constructing their Marxian-defined material prerequisites. Rejecting the easy Soviet orthodoxy that the development of the productive forces would more or less automatically guarantee an eventual communist utopia, Maoism insisted that the means of modern economic development be reconciled with the ends of socialism and that this take place in the here and now. It was a doctrine that taught that the new society presupposed new people and that the cultivation of socialist human beings was no less important in the building of a socialist society than the construction of its technological base. Thus Maoism insisted that progress toward socialism was to be measured not simply by the level of economic development but also by reductions of "the three great differences"—by progress in pursuing the classic Marxist goals of eliminating the age-old distinctions between mental and manual labor, between workers and peasants, and between town and countryside.

Yet the Maoist attempt to construct a socialist society in an economically backward land, notable though it was in many ways, in the end was overwhelmed by the contradictions between Mao's modernizing aims and his socialist aspirations—offering fresh historical evidence to support Karl Marx's insistence that socialism could be built successfully only on the material and social foundations provided by capitalism. In China, as elsewhere, industrialization imposed its own imperatives, generating new forms of social inequality that were incongruous with socialist visions. As industrial development proceeded, new bureaucratic and technological elites emerged. The rural areas were exploited for the benefit of the industrializing cities in an accelerating process of "primitive accumulation." And the industrial values of economic rationality and bureaucratic professionalism became the dominant social norms, subordinating the socialist goals that China's industrialization was originally intended to serve. If the Maoist regime mitigated these inegalitarian tendencies, at least in comparison with its Soviet predecessor, it by no means halted them. Industrialization demands an increasingly specialized division of labor, and in China, as elsewhere, the new division of labor served to widen rather than narrow the "three great differences," Maoist ideological exhortations and claims notwithstanding.[17] Reducing the gap between town and countryside was the most cherished of Maoist goals, yet the actual economic differences between the cities and the rural areas grew wider, both relatively and absolutely, during the Mao era. Between 1952 and 1975, annual per capita consumption among the rural population increased from 62 to 124 *yuan* (in current prices) whereas among the non-agricultural population it increased from 148 to 324 *yuan*.[18]

A graver flaw in the Maoist socialist enterprise was the contradiction between the Communist state and Chinese society. One obvious result of the revolutionary victory of 1949 was the establishment of a powerful centralized state and an enormous expansion of its bureaucratic apparatus. Ironically, in a Marxian sense (although quite in keeping with the logic of

Stalinism), as China became more "socialist," the state became all the more dominant. For with the expropriation of the propertied classes, the nationalization of industry, and the collectivization of agriculture, not only was the state the political master of society, but it became its sole economic master as well. While Maoist ideologists celebrated the spontaneity and creativity of the masses, the Maoist state machine became increasingly separated from the society it ruled, its bureaucracy grew ever larger and more alien, and the division between rulers and the ruled became ever more pronounced. Before the power of the bureaucratic state, society lay prostrate. In response to this degrading spectacle of social power totally subordinated to political power, Maoism offered no remedies—save for fabricating the cult of a leader who claimed to personally embody the collective will of the people. The cult of Mao Zedong was one of history's most extreme examples of the alienation of social power into fetishized political authority. At the end, all the monuments to Mao stood as grotesque reminders of a monumental political failure.

While some of the socioeconomic preconditions for socialism were created during the Maoist era, it certainly was not an era that saw the creation of socialism's no less essential political preconditions. For socialism requires more than the abolition of private property and the building of a nationalized industry. Socialism means, if it is to have a genuine meaning, a system where political power is exercised by the whole of the working population, permitting them to control both the conditions and the products of their labor. The distinguishing feature of socialism is not state property but rather what Marx termed the "property of the associated producers." And "the dictatorship of the proletariat," so often invoked during the Mao era to justify political despotism, is actually the period (according to Marxist theory) when the social powers usurped by the state are returned to society as a whole, the time when the state is transformed into what Marx called "the self-government of the producers." In Maoist China these elemental Marxian socialist political conceptions were absent in both theory and practice. Maoism was a doctrine that confronted (even if it did not resolve) the dilemma of reconciling the means of modern economic development with the ends of socialism, but it was not a doctrine that recognized popular democracy as both the necessary means to achieve socialism and one of its essential ends as well.

There were two crucial periods in the Mao era when the problem of the relationship between the Communist state and Chinese society were explicitly raised and presented for solution. During the Hundred Flowers campaign Mao himself initially posed the question of the contradiction between "the leadership" and "the led," and from the movement itself came demands for political democracy and intellectual freedom. But these demands were suppressed in the "antirightist" witch-hunt that followed, and the contradiction between rulers and ruled remained unresolved. The Cultural Revolution began with a wholesale attack against Party and state bureaucracies, and at first seemed to promise the democratic reorganization of political power in accordance with the Marxian principles of the Paris Commune. But the promise was soon betrayed, and the upheaval concluded with the total reestablishment of the rule of the Leninist party. Mao Zedong initiated both the Hundred Flowers movement and the Cultural Revolution, and he thus bears the principal responsibility for the failure of their promises to make the state the servant instead of the master of society—as well as the responsibility for the human suffering that these failed movements caused.

For many years, in the 1960s and 1970s, Maoists pointed to the Soviet Union as a "negative example" of the building of socialism. Yet they ignored the obvious lesson that the Soviet historical experience imparts—that "the transition to socialism" is impossible without freedom and popular democracy, and that conditions of economic backwardness and a hostile international environment cannot indefinitely be invoked to justify their absence. The old Marxist dream of the "withering away" of the state may be no more than a utopian hope for any foreseeable historical future, but there is nothing at all utopian about the demand of the Chinese people to enjoy such elementary democratic liberties as freedom of expression and freedom of association. Without that modest beginning, slogans such as "socialist democracy," however ardently proclaimed, remain hollow ideological rationalizations for the continuing dominance of state over society. Such a beginning was not made during the Maoist era.

. . .

The legacy that Mao Zedong left for his successors was thus a most ambiguous and contradictory one, marked by a deep incongruity between the Maoist regime's progressive socioeconomic accomplishments and its retrogressive political characteristics. On the one hand, Mao "created a nation," as Deng Xiaoping said, completing in the early years of the People's Republic many of the unfinished tasks of the Guomindang's abortive bourgeois revolution. The Maoist regime also established some of the preconditions for socialism. It began China's modern industrial revolution; it abolished private ownership of the means of production, a necessary if by no means sufficient condition for socialism; and it kept alive (far longer into the postrevolutionary era than might have been anticipated) a vital socialist vision of the future. On the other hand, Maoism retained essentially

Stalinist methods of bureaucratic political rule; it generated its own cults, orthodoxies, and dogmas and it consistently suppressed all intellectual and political dissent. Mao Zedong, to be sure, looked upon the Communist bureaucracy as a great evil, but the only remedy he could devise to control his own creation was to rely on his personal prestige and the force of his own personality. Neither in theory nor in practice does the Maoist legacy include meaningful institutional safeguards against bureaucratic domination.

Thus at the end of the Mao era China resided in that misty historical realm of bureaucratically dominated socioeconomic orders that are neither capitalist nor socialist—and which, for want of any better term, have sometimes been called "post-capitalist" or simply "postrevolutionary." Maoist China was not capitalist because it had abolished an essential condition of capitalism—private ownership of the means of production. It was not genuinely socialist because the masses of producers, workers and peasants alike, were denied the means to control the products and conditions of their labor—and also denied the means to control the state, which increasingly stood above them as both the economic and political manager of society. If the Maoist regime was by and large successful in carrying out the bourgeois phase of the revolution, it proved incapable of achieving the proclaimed "transition to socialism." At the end of the Mao period it was as if China was

> Wandering between two worlds, one dead,
> The other powerless to be born.[19]

It is most unlikely that the impasse would have been broken, and that socialism would have flowered, had Mao and Maoism survived longer than they did. Well before Mao's death, Maoism had exhausted its once great creative energies. Its method of financing modern industrial development—essentially the exploitation of the villages—could not long have been sustained without pauperizing the peasants who had given the Communists their power in the first place. The Cultural Revolution, the last of Mao's popular campaigns, had failed in its professed aims, leaving only a politically disillusioned population in the wake of the debacle. Disillusionment was soon followed by cynicism, as a weary people observed from afar the Byzantine political struggles and palace intrigues that raged above them in the 1970s and lent so grotesque a cast to the last chapter in the political history of the Mao era. In response to the popular political malaise and the looming economic crisis Maoism proved incapable of offering effective remedies. A population grown cynical and politically apathetic could no longer be easily inspired by old revolutionary slogans and ideological exhortations. The condition of China in the last years of the Maoist era clearly demanded a new course, but an enfeebled Mao Zedong and a dogmatized Maoism were unable to provide the ideas and the inspiration needed to regenerate the revolution.

In a sense, Maoism sowed the seeds of its own demise. What came to be celebrated as Mao Zedong Thought was a doctrine forged in the most backward rural areas of one of the world's most backward lands; it had been under a Maoist banner that the forces of peasant revolt had been organized to carry out the greatest of modern revolutions. Having achieved political success, the victorious revolutionaries set out to both modernize and socialize the vast land they had come to rule. As modernizers they must be credited with many striking successes, especially in view of the enormity of the task they confronted. They created a modern nation-state, established a modern educational system, and inaugurated the beginnings of China's modern industrial and technological transformation.

But Maoist political methods and ideology continued to reflect many of the features of the backward environment in which the doctrine was born—and those methods and habits of thought became ever more anachronistic in a modernizing China increasingly populated by new generations further and further removed from the primitive rural conditions that had molded the revolution and the mentality of many of its leaders. In many respects, Maoism continued to bear the birthmarks of the very backwardness it strove to overcome. And insofar as the Maoist regime was successful in modernizing China, Maoism seemed more and more unsuited to modern Chinese conditions. It was thus inevitable that Mao's successors, sooner or later, would discard much of what was most distinctively "Maoist" in the politics and ideology of the founder of the People's Republic.

NOTES

1. Ma Hong and Sun Shangqing, eds., *Studies in the Problems of China's Economic Structure* (Beijing, 1981), Vol. I, JPRS-CEA-84-064-1 (August 3, 1984), pp. 25–26; Nicholas R. Lardy, *Agriculture in China's Modern Economic Development* (Cambridge, England: Cambridge University Press, 1983), p. 3.

2. Y. Y. Kueh, "The Maoist Legacy and China's New Industrialization Strategy," *The China Quarterly*, No. 119 (September 1989), p. 421. See also Lardy, *Agriculture in China's Modern Economic Development*, p. 1. Other methods of calculation show the value of industrial production as a proportion of total production increasing from 30 to 72 percent during the Mao period; Ma and Sun, pp. 25–26.

3. Kueh, "The Maoist Legacy," p. 421.

4. Data drawn from U.S. Central Intelligence Agency, *People's Republic of China: Handbook of Economic Indicators* (Washington, D.C., 1976); U.S. Department of Commerce, *The Chinese Economy and Foreign Trade Perspectives* (Washington, D.C., 1977); and Joint Economic Committee of Congress, *China: A Reassessment of the Economy* (Washington, D.C., 1975), as compiled by Mark Selden, *The People's Republic of China: A Documentary History* (New York: Monthly Review Press, 1979), Tables 13 and 14, pp. 135–136.

5. K. C. Yeh, "Macroeconomic Changes in the Chinese Economy During the Readjustment," *The China Quarterly,* No. 100 (December 1984), Table A2, p. 716.

6. Tong Dalin and Hu Ping, "Science and Technology," in Yu Guangyuan, ed., *China's Socialist Modernization* (Beijing: Foreign Languages Press, 1984), p. 644.

7. Lardy, *Agriculture in China's Modern Economic Development,* p. 3.

8. Dong Furen, "On the Relation between Accumulation and Consumption in China's Development." Paper presented at the U.S.-China Conference on Alternative Strategies for Economic Development, Racine, Wisconsin, November 21–24, 1980, p. 26. Cited in Carl Riskin, *China's Political Economy: The Quest for Development Since 1949* (New York: Oxford University Press, 1987), p. 271.

9. Lardy, *Agriculture in China's Modern Economic Development,* Table 3-7, p. 130.

10. *Ibid.,* Table 1.1, p. 2.

11. *Ibid.*

12. Simon Kuznets, *Economic Growth of Nations: Total Output and Production Structure* (Cambridge, Mass.: Harvard University Press, 1971), Table 4, pp. 38–39.

13. Gilbert Rozman, *The Modernization of China* (New York: The Free Press, 1981), Table 10.2, p. 350.

14. As the economic history of the Mao period is typically characterized, e.g., John Burns in *The New York Times,* March 31, 1985, p. E-4.

15. Available statistics on collectively distributed income indicate significant per capita growth during the last two decades of the Mao era. But after taking into account other factors, especially restrictions on private plots and markets after 1966, most observers agree with Nicholas Lardy's conclusion that "real per capita farm income at best grew very modestly between 1956–57 and 1977." For a discussion of the difficulties in determining the truth of the matter, see Lardy, *Agriculture in China's Modern Economic Development,* pp. 160–63.

16. Quoted in Tarik Ali, ed., *The Stalinist Legacy: Its Impact on Twentieth-Century World Politics* (Harmondsworth, Middlesex, England: Penguin Books, 1984), p. 9.

17. For Mao's views on the division of labor, see Maurice Meisner, "Marx, Mao and Deng on the Division of Labor in History," in Arif Dirlik and Maurice Meisner, eds., *Marxism and the Chinese Experience* (Armonk, N.Y.: M. E. Sharpe, 1989), pp. 79–116.

18. Riskin, *China's Political Economy,* Table 10.8, p. 241.

19. Matthew Arnold, "Stanzas from the Grand Chartreuse," *The Poems of Matthew Arnold*, ed. Kenneth Allott (New York: Barnes & Noble, 1965), p. 288.

22

The Rise of Deng Xiaoping and the Critique of Maoism

THE POST-MAO era began under cover of a Maoist facade. Hua Guofeng, having presided over the "smashing of the Gang of Four" in the early autumn of 1976,[1] was immediately installed as the new Chairman of the Chinese Communist Party; the installation was legitimized solely by what were claimed to have been "arrangements" made by Mao Zedong on his deathbed. The official press repeatedly reproduced the scrap of paper the dying Mao allegedly had given Hua. "With you in charge, I am at ease," Mao was said to have scribbled. During his brief tenure, Hua went to great lengths to imitate his predecessor, not only in political style and rhetoric but also in dress and physical appearance. Portraits of Hua appeared in all public places, always hung alongside those of the late Chairman. And the new regime spared no public expense in constructing a huge mausoleum in Tiananmen Square, where the embalmed corpse of Mao Zedong was to reside permanently in a crystal box, so that, as the macabre announcement put it, "the broad masses of the people will be able to pay their respects to his remains."

To demonstrate continuity with Mao's economic policies, Hua convened a series of conferences on agriculture, the realm where he had made his initial political mark during the "socialist high tide" of 1955–56. The conferences proceeded under the old slogan "learn from Dazhai," the brigade that Mao had set forth as the model which exemplified the virtues of egalitarianism and self-reliance. And in early 1977 Hua somewhat rashly vowed, along with other Maoist loyalists, "to support *whatever* policy decisions were made by Chairman Mao" and "unswervingly follow *whatever* instructions were given by Chairman Mao." The pledge was to earn Hua Guofeng and his associates the name of the "Whatever" faction, the pejorative label that their political opponents were soon to bestow.

But Hua Guofeng was selective in following the late Chairman's "instructions." Having constructed an elaborate Maoist political facade, he moved, however slowly and cautiously, to abandon the policies of the late Maoist era and to return in large measure to the Maoism of the 1950s. The first such changes came in cultural and educational policies, where the influence of the now imprisoned Gang of Four had been the strongest. Reviving the old Maoist slogan to "let a hundred flowers bloom," the new regime did away with the more obscurantist policies of the Cultural Revolution period. Hitherto banned plays, operas, and films once again appeared in theaters. Literary and scholarly journals dormant since 1966 resumed publication, joined by a growing variety of new periodicals and magazines. An especially notable product of the post-Mao cultural thaw was the outpouring of short stories by young writers describing their experiences during the Cultural Revolution—"the literature of the wounded generation" as it came to be called. Invoking the hallowed Maoist injunction to "make foreign things serve China," the government promoted international cultural exchanges and encouraged the publication of new translations of Western literary classics, repudiating the xenophobic fears of foreign "bourgeois" contamination that had stifled artistic life for more than a decade. Intellectuals who had been jailed, sent to labor in remote rural areas, or otherwise silenced during the Cultural Revolution or before, were quietly rehabilitated. They slowly returned to the cities to resume their work in 1977 and 1978.

Along with cultural liberalization came new educational policies, or more precisely, a return to old ones. Even as he continued to celebrate the accomplishments of the Cultural Revolution in his speeches, Hua began to undo many of the egalitarian educational reforms that had issued from the upheaval, beginning a process that would soon result in the full reestablishment of the elitist educational system built in the 1950s. Special attention was given to reviving the universities and the higher research institutes, which soon were functioning much as they had in the years prior to the Cultural Revolution. The new cultural and educational policies were intended to win the support of intellectuals for the Hua regime and for the "Four Modernizations," a term officially enshrined in newly promulgated

Party and state constitutions. But Hua Guofeng, a beneficiary of the Cultural Revolution who had clothed himself in Maoist garb, won few new political adherents. His policies, however, did reinvigorate the urban intelligentsia, most of whom harbored anti-Maoist sentiments and would soon articulate them.

The Hua government sought to mitigate discontent among workers and peasants as well as intellectuals. Employees of state enterprises were given a 10 percent wage increase on October 1, 1977, the twenty-eighth anniversary of the People's Republic. This was intended as compensation, in part, for the imposition of stricter forms of "scientific management" and a more stringent labor discipline. And while the Maoist Dazhai model was lauded in official ideology, in practice state agricultural policies permitted larger private family plots for subsidiary production and encouraged the expansion of rural markets.

It was as an economic modernizer that Hua Guofeng attempted to make his mark on the history of the People's Republic. Hua's economic proposals were embellished with an abundance of Maoist rhetoric, especially emphasizing Mao's pre-Great Leap writings. The image of Zhou Enlai was continually invoked to popularize the Four Modernizations. But Hua's economic program was largely based on the policy documents Deng Xiaoping had drawn up for the State Council in the autumn of 1975, although the debt to Deng went unacknowledged. In 1977, as Deng had proposed two years before, the Hua government greatly expanded the purchase of modern technology from the advanced capitalist countries, financed largely by Chinese coal and oil exports. Great emphasis was placed on the rapid acquisition of modern scientific knowledge and the training of a technological intelligentsia, for which the restoration of the pre-Cultural Revolution system of higher education was a prerequisite. Plans were drawn up for the mechanization of agriculture. Both industrial productivity and production were raised through a combination of stricter work rules in the factories and greater material rewards for the workers.

Reflective of the tenor of the times was the reappearance of the economic planners of the 1950s, who had been in eclipse during the late Maoist era. The most politically important among them was Chen Yun, one of the designers of the First Five Year Plan of 1953–57, who favored the use of market mechanisms to supplement state planning.

Hua Guofeng's most ambitious effort to achieve the Four Modernizations was his proposed Ten Year Plan—for the years 1976–85—belatedly unveiled in February 1978. A somewhat revised version of a document drafted by the State Council in 1975 (when that body was operating under the direction of Deng Xiaoping), the Plan called for a new heavy industrial push on the frenetic order of the First Five Year Plan. By 1985, some 120 mammoth industrial projects were to be constructed, including gigantic steel and iron complexes, oil and gas fields, coal mines, power stations, railroads and harbors.[2] By the year 2000, Hua predicted, China's industry would approach that of the world's most advanced nations. But Hua failed to explain how the enormous sums required to finance the new industrialization drive would be raised. Nor did he address the imbalances and other economic problems inherited from the Mao era. Hua's modernization program proved financially unviable and soon had to be abandoned.

The abortiveness of the Ten Year Plan was one factor in Hua Guofeng's political demise. Another was the growing power and popularity of Deng Xiaoping, who in his third political ascent (and second resurrection) was determined to make the post-Mao era definitively post-Maoist.

The Triumph of Deng Xiaoping

Deng Xiaoping was the last important member of the remarkable May Fourth generation of Chinese Communist leaders.[3] A Party activist since the early 1920s, his not inconsiderable contributions to the Communist revolution—and his membership in the Maoist faction—won him a high place in the postrevolutionary order. In 1956 he stood alongside Liu Shaoqi and delivered one of the two main reports to the Eighth CCP Congress, the one post-1949 Party Congress whose spirit and ideology were to be celebrated in the post-Mao era. In the same year Deng was also appointed Party General Secretary, giving him considerable control over the CCP's organizational apparatus and permitting him to strengthen the close ties with political and military leaders that he had forged during the revolutionary period. But a decade later, during the Cultural Revolution, Deng Xiaoping was branded "the second leading person in authority taking the capitalist road" and dispatched to labor in a tractor factory in Jiangxi province, far from Beijing. In 1973, under Zhou Enlai's patronage and with Mao Zedong's consent, he was recalled to Beijing and restored to his high official posts—and without the customary requirement of confessing past political errors. Deng soon established himself as the dying Zhou's apparent successor—only to be once again dismissed from office as "an unrepentant capitalist roader" several months after Zhou's death, blamed for instigating the Tiananmen incident of April 1976.[4] Pursued by the Gang of Four during the last dreary months of Mao's reign, Deng fled to South China, where his old PLA allies provided sanctuary. His political will undiminished, the seventy-two-year-old Deng plotted his return to Beijing, reportedly contemplating civil war if necessary.[5] But with the death of Mao

Zedong in September 1976 and the "smashing of the Gang of Four" in October, a peaceful way was opened for Deng's second political rehabilitation.

The restoration of Deng Xiaoping to his high Party and government positions, and the rise to dictatorial power that was to make him China's "paramount leader," required breaking apart the political coalition that had brought down the Gang of Four. That uneasy alliance was led by Hua Guofeng, who had presided over the October 1976 coup and who had installed himself as Chairman of the Communist Party and Premier of the State Council, making him the official successor to both Mao Zedong and Zhou Enlai. The events that were to result in Deng's ascendancy and Hua's demise unfolded over a period of two years, and were carried out by Deng in a manner both sophisticated and ruthless, without provoking those "large-scale and turbulent" political and social struggles that he now so deplored.

More than the force of his personality and clever tactics were responsible for Deng's political success. He had the backing of most senior Party leaders, many of them longtime associates. No less important was the widespread support he enjoyed among military commanders, partly the political fruit of the close ties he had cultivated with Red Army officers during the revolutionary years. Deng's belief that the Communist Party should adhere strictly to its Leninist organizational principles and that political promotions should take place in orderly fashion—"step by step" and not "by helicopter," as he put it—appealed to both the ideals and the self-interest of veteran Party and PLA leaders. After the turmoil of the Cultural Revolution and its aftermath, the promise of bureaucratic regularity and social stability was enormously attractive to senior officials, both civilian and military, and increasingly they looked upon Deng as their natural leader.

In addition to high-level bureaucrats, old cadres, and PLA generals, Deng could add most intellectuals to his list of supporters. He had championed the social interests of intellectuals since the Eighth Party Congress of 1956.[6] And in his 1975 policy documents, Deng had offered intellectuals a prominent and lucrative role in bringing about the Four Modernizations, promising them higher status and greater professional autonomy. Consequently, most intellectuals saw Deng as the legitimate successor to the venerated Zhou Enlai.

Deng Xiaoping's political ambitions thus rested on a powerful and articulate base of social and political support. But what gave dynamism to Deng's political coalition was the issue of the Cultural Revolution—and the burning desire of its surviving victims to seek justice and retribution. That Deng himself had been among the victims of the upheaval, indeed twice victimized, won him the sympathy and support of millions who had suffered during the previous decade. Drawn to him were Party cadres who had been attacked, humiliated, and "overthrown"; intellectuals who had been silenced and persecuted; disillusioned former Red Guards who had been betrayed by Mao's torturous political course and found themselves members of "the lost generation"; millions of urban youth who had been shipped off to the countryside; and millions more ordinary citizens who had suffered a variety of physical and psychological abuses. All looked to Deng to bring about a "reversal of unjust verdicts."

. . .

Precisely where Deng Xiaoping possessed enormous political assets, Hua Guofeng was burdened with fatal political liabilities. Whereas Deng enjoyed the support of senior leaders of China's powerful military and civilian bureaucracies, Hua, having risen to prominence during the Cultural Revolution, could only call upon a far less important sector of the bureaucracy—the amorphous group of mostly lower-level officials who had benefited from that chaotic period. Deng won wide popular support, at least in the cities, on the promise that he would right the wrongs of the Cultural Revolution era, but Hua had neither a real base of power in the bureaucracy nor any significant popular support in society at large. Indeed, it was precisely his lack of power and prestige that had made him a more or less acceptable candidate to preside over the general interests of the factionalized bureaucracy during the perilous days following Mao Zedong's death—and to preside over the purge of the Gang of Four, who seemed to threaten established bureaucratic interests. The temporary occupant of the positions vacated by Mao and Zhou Enlai, he possessed few of the qualities of either, ill-cast to play the role either of revolutionary or of statesman. Attempting to cling to the high offices he had fortuitously acquired, Hua laid claim to Mao's legacy and the legacy of the Cultural Revolution—but he did so at a time when Mao's aura was fading and when the Cultural Revolution was coming under public criticism. The legacy of the late Maoist era, Hua Guofeng's sole claim to political legitimacy, hung on him like a millstone; he could neither do without it nor, in the post-Mao era, could he survive with it.

Hua Guofeng's political demise was hastened by his political blunders. Hua stubbornly continued to promote a campaign (initially organized by the Gang of Four) to criticize Deng Xiaoping's "counterrevolutionary revisionist line," until the end of December 1976—well after it had become politically anachronistic. After bringing down the Gang of Four, he began a purge of their alleged "hidden followers," thereby weakening his potential support in the Party and government bureaucracies. Hua's "Hundred

Flowers" policy facilitated the emergence of an articulate source of anti-Maoist (and pro-Deng) opinion in the cities. His ill-conceived and soon abandoned Ten Year Plan suggested ineptitude. Neither Hua's bland personality nor his thin political credentials could add the substance of power to the high official titles he had inherited. He was thus unable to resist the demands of senior Party leaders, supported by the growing force of public opinion in the major cities, that Deng Xiaoping be invited to rejoin the government. In the summer of 1977 Deng was formally restored to the Party and state positions he had occupied prior to his second fall from power in April 1976, and he soon established himself as one of China's top three leaders—along with Hua and Defense Minister Ye Jianying.

Once having regained a place near the top of the political hierarchy, Deng Xiaoping was unwilling to share power with Hua Guofeng—who, he had not forgotten, had risen to prominence during the Cultural Revolution, when Deng himself had been humiliated and purged. He was now determined to secure supreme power for himself. Behind the usual public facade of "unity and stability" a new struggle in the Politburo erupted between Deng's self-styled "Practice" faction, which had adopted the somewhat banal but politically potent slogan "practice is the sole criterion of truth," and the pejoratively labeled "Whateverists," led by Hua Guofeng.

Throughout 1978 Deng Xiaoping's power and popularity grew. A continuing purge of "leftists" in the bureaucracy created places for Deng's old and new political allies. He successfully cultivated the support of intellectuals, promising them greater material benefits and higher social status, an end to political suspicions, the rapid development of science and technology, professional autonomy, and greater authority in a modernized system of higher education.[7] He also hinted at sweeping economic reforms and political democratization.

Deng's power was further augmented by the reappearance of veteran cadres who had held official positions in the 1950s, their ranks and confidence fortified by the "rehabilitation" of many of Mao's old political foes who had been felled during the Cultural Revolution and before. Among the rehabilitated were 100,000 political prisoners—intellectuals, Party cadres, and others—who had been in detention or political disgrace since the anti-rightist campaign of 1957.[8] They were quietly released from bondage in June 1978; it was not publicly mentioned that Deng Xiaoping had been the chief witch-hunter during the 1957 repression.

During 1978 there were many "reversals of verdicts," but none was more dramatic and of greater political significance than the Party's new judgment on the Tiananmen incident of April 5, 1976. Officially con-

demned as a "counterrevolutionary act" at the time, it had been the pretext
for the dismissal of Deng Xiaoping from the government, his second fall
from power. But in the autumn of 1978, Wu De, the mayor of Beijing who
had ordered the militia into the square beneath the Gate of Heavenly
Peace in 1976, was ousted from office and the Tiananmen demonstration
was rechristened a "revolutionary event." The official press now lauded the
heroism of the demonstrators who had gathered in Tiananmen Square two
and a half years before. In the time between the two Party judgments, the
Tiananmen incident had acquired enormous symbolic significance as the
expression of the democratic yearnings of the people against a despotic
state. What had been enshrined as the "April Fifth Movement" by youthful
dissidents in 1976 reappeared in the form of wall posters along the streets
of Beijing early in 1978. Calling democracy "the fifth modernization," the
ranks of the youthful activists (mostly ex-Red Guards and young workers)
were swelled by the Party's reversal of its "verdict" on the Tiananmen incident. The democratic activists were further encouraged by the apparent
support of Deng Xiaoping and his allies. In the last months of 1978 the
streets of downtown Beijing were filled with political meetings and rallies.
Ever bolder wall posters denounced the injustices of the Mao period, especially the Cultural Revolution, demanded the ouster of "Maoists" who still
sat in the Politburo, and called for human rights, socialist legality, and a democratic political system. It was a time of great exhilaration and hope.

. . .

As the Democracy Movement, as it came to be called, grew around the
square beneath the Gate of Heavenly Peace, Party leaders gathered in their
meeting halls above Tiananmen Square in a "work conference" to prepare
the Third Plenum of the Party's Eleventh Central Committee, which formally convened December 18–22, 1978. It was to prove a critical convoca-
tion in the history of the People's Republic.

The Third Plenum was a decisive, if not yet total, triumph for Deng
Xiaoping and his "practice faction." A sufficient number of Deng's supporters were elevated to the Central Committee and the Politburo to give
Deng effective control over both bodies, and thus over the Party as a
whole. Most of those who had been branded "Whateverists" were not dismissed from their formal Party offices for the moment, but they were re-
lieved of their more important political and economic responsibilities.
Party Chairman Hua Guofeng emerged from the December 1978 Party
meetings with his titles intact but not his power. Forced to engage in a "self-
criticism," Hua now would perform little more than ceremonial functions

under Deng's direction—until he was forced to surrender his political titles in 1981, long after he had surrendered his authority.

What came to be the most celebrated result of the Third Plenum was the decision to "shift the emphasis of the Party's work to socialist modernization." Socialist modernization was not a new term but it was imbued with a new meaning: it now meant, simply put, the subordination of all other considerations to the task of modern economic development. Accordingly, the Central Committee decreed an end to class struggle, or at least to struggles of a "turbulent" and "mass" character, hoping thereby to bring about the social and political stability that would facilitate the pursuit of the Four Modernizations. The Third Plenum also enjoined combining "adjustment by the market" with "adjustment by the plan," thus providing the initial political sanction for the capitalist-style reforms that were to dominate the history of the Deng era.

. . .

Deng Xiaoping followed his triumph at the Third Plenum in Beijing with a triumphal tour of the United States at the end of January 1979 to mark the official establishment of diplomatic relations between the two countries, three decades after the founding of the People's Republic. Deng was the fortuitous political beneficiary of the *realpolitik* diplomacy begun by Mao Zedong and Zhou Enlai (together with Richard Nixon and Henry Kissinger) seven years earlier, and this added to his already considerable prestige both at home and abroad. Less flattering were Deng's arrogant public threats to "teach Vietnam a lesson." On February 17, shortly after his return from the United States, the Chinese army invaded Vietnam. The pretext was the Vietnamese occupation of Kampuchea (Cambodia) and the ouster of the Chinese-backed (and genocidal) Pol Pot regime. After several weeks of bloody but inconclusive fighting, the Chinese troops ignominiously withdrew. China's Vietnam war took a heavy human and economic toll on both sides and tarnished the international image of the new Deng regime. The only lesson that the invasion imparted was that the military effectiveness of the PLA had declined markedly.[9]

The Democracy Movement of 1978–1981

Deng Xiaoping soon discovered that he had foes at home as well as in Vietnam. The democratic activists who had assisted Deng in his rise to power in the last months of 1978 increased in both numbers and militancy during the early months of 1979. Many were former Red Guards now in their late twenties or early thirties, self-educated members of the "lost generation" who worked at a variety of ordinary jobs. Few were students; virtually no older intellectuals joined or openly supported the movement. Yet the youthful activists, encouraged by the Deng faction's promises of "socialist democracy" and "socialist legality," demonstrated extraordinary intellectual powers and organizational skills, quickly establishing their own quasi-political societies and publishing a growing variety of mimeographed journals. The democratic ferment spread rapidly from Beijing to other large cities and provincial centers.

Although most members of the Democracy Movement had supported Deng Xiaoping's drive for power in 1978, and still looked to Deng in the early months of 1979 to bring about a process of democratization, the eminently Leninist leaders of the post-Mao regime were not about to sanction a movement that operated beyond the organizational control of the Communist Party. And they certainly would not tolerate independent groups that were potential vehicles for the expression of broader social grievances, especially not at a time when millions of jobless and discontented "rusticated" youth were illegally returning to the cities. Unlike the older intellectuals, who benefited from the cultural and intellectual liberalization of the time, most of the youthful democratic activists maintained an uncompromising anti-authoritarian stance, rejecting the Party's insistence on a monopoly of political leadership and its claim to ideological infallibility. Some revived the old "ultra-left" theory of Cultural Revolution vintage that China was ruled by a privileged "bureaucratic class."

The repression began early in the spring of 1979, when the government banned unofficial journals and organizations, and began to arrest their leaders. One of the first to be arrested was Wei Jingsheng, editor of the journal *Explorations,* a critic of both Deng Xiaoping and Mao Zedong, and the author of the celebrated wall poster treatise "The Fifth Modernization—Democracy and Others." In addition to political and ideological crimes, he was accused of having passed military secrets on the PLA's invasion of Vietnam to foreign newspaper reporters. Wei, in fact, was one of only a handful of Chinese citizens who had protested the invasion of Vietnam. After a one-day trial in October 1979, he was sentenced to fifteen years imprisonment. Many others followed him to prison over the next two years.

In the course of the repression, Deng Xiaoping, now firmly established as the country's "paramount leader," denounced his onetime democratic allies as anarchists and criminals and, most damningly, accused them of having revived the pernicious political methods of the Cultural Revolution. Accordingly, Deng demanded the abolition of the "four great freedoms"—

the right to "speak out freely, air views freely, hold great debates, and write big-character posters"—which had been added to the state constitution at Mao's recommendation in January 1975. Although these constitutionally proclaimed rights had rarely been honored in practice, even on paper Deng found them uncomfortably reminiscent of the attack on the Communist Party during the Cultural Revolution.[10] Even as the government was busily promulgating new legal codes in 1979 and 1980, evidence of "socialist democratization," it was officially said, many of those who had been active in the Democracy Movement were being sent to labor camps by administrative decree.

In place of Mao's "four great freedoms" Deng proclaimed the "Four Cardinal Principles: "upholding the socialist road, the dictatorship of the proletariat, the leadership of the Communist Party, and Marxism-Leninism-Mao Zedong Thought."[11] Of these, the leadership of the Party was the most important principle, Deng emphasized; indeed, it was to prove the only enduring one.

By the spring of 1981 the once flourishing Democracy Movement had vanished from public view. Most of the leaders were in jail and the few surviving activists had been reduced to a precarious underground existence. The movement, in fact, had never acquired a significant popular following, in part because of the general depoliticization of social life fostered by the post-Mao regime. To fill the ideological and political void among a population grown cynical during the "cultural revolution decade," the Deng government set forth no new social and political ideals to strive for, but rather simply promised a better material life, encouraging citizens to purchase the many new consumer goods appearing on department store shelves and advertised on the billboards that formerly displayed revolutionary slogans. Little public protest, or even public interest, accompanied the demise of the Democracy Movement. It was the victim of both state repression and popular political apathy. Most conspicuously silent were China's intellectuals.

. . .

As the Democracy Movement was being suppressed below, Deng Xiaoping was consolidating his control over the Party and state bureaucracies at the top, methodically removing from positions of authority all those who were considered Mao loyalists and replacing them with members of his own faction. Most of the remaining "Whateverists" were purged at a February 1980 meeting of the Central Committee. Among them were Wang Dongxing, the former head of the elite 8341 military unit that had arrested the Gang of Four in 1976, and Chen Yonggui, the peasant leader of the once-celebrated Dazhai brigade whom Mao had elevated to the Politburo during the Cultural Revolution. The places of the departing "leftists" were taken by veteran Party leaders who had been branded as "rightists" during the Cultural Revolution. For good measure, and reflecting the political temper of the times, Liu Shaoqi, the Leninist par excellence in the history of Chinese Communism, was posthumously readmitted to the CCP in a well-publicized ceremony that featured a speech by Deng Xiaoping. Liu's purge during the Cultural Revolution was denounced as "the biggest frameup our Party has ever known."

The political burial of Hua Guofeng was accomplished in a courteous but pragmatically efficient fashion. As a reward for his political cooperation (and to present a public facade of unity), Hua had been permitted to retain the official titles he had inherited from Zhou Enlai and Mao Zedong for several years after real power had passed to Deng Xiaoping. In September 1980, however, he was forced to resign his position as Premier of the State Council in favor of Zhao Ziyang, whom Deng had elevated to the Politburo in January.[12] Also in 1980, Hua's long powerless position as Chairman of the CCP became purely titular when Deng Xiaoping decided to revive the Secretariat as the leading Party organ, an office Deng himself had headed in the 1950s before Mao abolished it. Named General Secretary (and thus formal head of the Party) was Deng's closest disciple, Hu Yaobang.[13] Hua Guofeng quietly resigned from the now figurehead position of Party Chairman in June 1981, at the same Central Committee meeting that produced the official assessment of Mao Zedong. A year later Hua was dropped from membership in the Politburo, but he was allowed to remain one of 348 members of the Central Committee, an honorably obscure resting place for Mao's first and rather undistinguished successor.

The new political order fashioned in the wake of the Third Plenum was formally consecrated when the Chinese Communist Party (whose membership had grown to 40 million) held its Twelfth Congress in September 1982. The Congress, which Deng Xiaoping described as the most important in the Party's history since 1945, when Mao's leadership had been celebrated, was largely devoted to ratifying Deng's new economic policies (which will be considered in the following chapter) and his revamping of the Party leadership. Hu Yaobang's position as General Secretary was confirmed and the now redundant office of Party Chairman was abolished. The Congress placed unusual emphasis on the Leninist virtues of a tight centralized organizational structure and the discipline of Party members, many of whom at the lower levels of the hierarchy were suspected of lingering "leftist" proclivities. The term "leftist" was now broadly defined to include any lack of enthusiasm for the new regime's reformist economic policies. Although

Deng preferred to rule mostly from behind the scenes, having installed proteges as heads of Party and state, by the early 1980s there was no question—and certainly no one dared question—that Deng Xiaoping was indeed China's "paramount leader."

The Question of Mao and the Reinterpretation of "Mao Zedong Thought"

Deng Xiaoping's construction of the post-Maoist order required more than the removal of his leftist political foes and their replacement by officials loyal to the new leader. It also required the demystification of Mao Zedong, whose ghost dominated the political consciousness of the new era almost as much as his person had dominated the politics of his own time. The legitimacy of the Deng regime, presided over by men who shared the trauma of having been purged during the Cultural Revolution, could best be established by reducing the still semi-sacred stature of the late Chairman, who had purged them. And Maoist policies and doctrines could more easily be abandoned by demonstrating the fallibilities of their author.

More than a thirst for revenge or pragmatic considerations of power motivated the reassessment of Mao Zedong and his era. Among the surviving victims of the Cultural Revolution, especially intellectuals and Party bureaucrats, there was a moral need to honor those of their friends and colleagues who had not survived. This need dictated not only posthumous "rehabilitations" but also was a dramatic demonstration that the appropriate historical lessons had been learned and that the evils of the Maoist era would not be repeated. Mao had predicted many future cultural revolutions, but his successors were intent on demonstrating that there would never be another.

Yet any serious evaluation of Mao Zedong's historical role was a most precarious political enterprise, and not only because the image of the late Chairman occupied an almost sacred place in popular consciousness. More important was the fact that Mao also loomed large in the consciousness *and the lineage* of China's post-Maoist leaders. Whatever their personal feelings about their former Chairman, Communist leaders could not do without an historically redeemable Mao in tracing their own line of political descent. Mao, after all, was both the Lenin and the Stalin of the Chinese Revolution, albeit vastly different from his Russian counterparts in ideology, political practice, and personality. Like Lenin, Mao had been the acknowledged leader of the revolution and the founder of the new society; like Stalin, he had been the supreme ruler of the postrevolutionary regime for over a quarter century. Simply to denounce Mao as a tyrant and usurper, as

Khrushchev had denounced Stalin in 1956, would have cast doubt not only on the political legitimacy of the Chinese Communist state but also on the moral validity of the revolution that produced it. In condemning Stalin, Khrushchev could invoke the authority of Lenin. But for Mao's successors, there was no Chinese Lenin to call on other than Mao himself. It was with these elemental historical and political considerations in mind that Deng Xiaoping observed, in the summer of 1980 when the official assessment of Mao was being prepared, that: "It isn't only his [Mao's] portrait which remains in Tiananmen Square, it is the memory of a man who guided us to victory and built a country."[14]

Deng's comment suggests that not only considerations of political legitimacy were involved in the Party's assessment of Mao Zedong, but also the mantle of modern Chinese nationalism. For Mao was twentieth-century China's great patriotic hero as well as the leader of its Communist revolution. He had, as Deng Xiaoping said, "built a country," enabling a long humiliated and impoverished China to "stand up in the world." Moreover, the enormous popular prestige Mao had acquired during his lifetime—as both a revolutionary and a nationalist leader—lingered on long after his death, especially among the peasantry, many millions of whom continued to venerate the deified Chairman. Nor did the dead Mao lack worshippers among living members of the Communist Party, particularly among the old cadres who had fought alongside him during the revolutionary years and the millions of young activists who had been recruited during the Cultural Revolution.

Deng Xiaoping was keenly aware of these elemental facts of Chinese political life. In one of the more perceptive expressions of his celebrated political pragmatism, Deng counseled that it was necessary to make "an appropriate evaluation" of Mao's merits, warning that otherwise "the old workers will not feel satisfied, nor will the poor and lower-middle peasants of the period of land reform, nor will a good number of cadres who have close ties with them."[15] In preparing the public evaluation of Mao, his official assessors knew that they would have to proceed with great political caution.

Long before the Party's formal assessment of Mao Zedong's historical role was released in June 1981, the reputation of Mao was being gradually undermined by a long series of politically symbolic acts and ideological changes. Although the Third Plenum of December 1978 abandoned many of Mao's ideas and policies—and clearly inaugurated the post-Maoist era—it did so without issuing any formal judgment on either Mao or the Mao period. Indeed, the official communiqué that concluded the Third Plenum fulsomely invoked the authority of Mao's writings and announced that an assessment of the Cultural Revolution could wait until an "appropriate time" in the future. But the Plenum did call for a sweeping "reversal of verdicts," including the rehabilitation of many of Mao's old political opponents. Of these, none had greater symbolic political import than the reversal of the verdict on Peng Dehuai. Mao's dismissal of the popular general in 1959 was widely regarded as one of the greatest injustices of the Maoist era, and calls to rectify the wrong had been heard from many quarters for nearly two decades. Peng died in 1974, but the case of Peng Dehuai remained among the many festering sores in Chinese political life. In accordance with the Plenum's decision, Peng was publicly rehabilitated on December 25, 1978, with Deng Xiaoping delivering the official eulogy, lauding the dead marshal as one of the great heroes of the revolution and restoring him to the honored place in history that he had occupied prior to 1959. The ceremony was rife with political meaning, for it was impossible to honor Peng without suggesting that Mao had been something less than honorable. Nor was it possible to laud Peng without implying criticism of the Great Leap Forward campaign, which Peng had so vigorously opposed, leading to his purge.

The Third Plenum was followed throughout the year 1979 by a torrent of implicit criticism of Mao in official publications—and explicit critiques by Democracy Movement activists, which appeared in unofficial journals and on wall posters. The "rehabilitations" of those who had been branded "rightists" and "capitalist-roaders" during the late Mao era accelerated, restoring to high places in political and cultural life many once purged officials and intellectuals and thus fortifying anti-Maoist opinion in the major cities. Prominent among the rehabilitated was the conservative bureaucrat Peng Zhen, the first of the high-ranking Party leaders felled during the Cultural Revolution, whom Deng now put in charge of drafting new legal codes. The implicit critique of Mao was intensified by a Party campaign against "ultra-leftism," which was to remain the principal (although not the sole) ideological and political heresy of the Deng era. While the campaign was ostensibly directed against the long-dead Lin Biao and the imprisoned Gang of Four, the stigma of ultra-leftism was soon employed to generally characterize most of the last two decades of Mao's rule, as scores of scholars and Party theoreticians put forth increasingly elaborate explanations of the "petty-bourgeois" social basis and "feudal" ideological roots of the Great Leap Forward campaign and the Cultural Revolution.[16] The critique of ultra-leftism, and of the late Mao era in general, gained considerable political momentum when the venerable PLA Marshal (and Politburo member) Ye Jianying commemorated the thirtieth anniversary of the People's Republic in a speech delivered on October 1, 1979. In an address approved in detail beforehand by the Party Central Committee, Ye attributed the disasters of the Great Leap to "leftist errors" that violated "objective economic laws" and condemned the Cultural Revolution as a decade long calamity (1966–76) visited on China by those who had pursued an "ultraleft" line.[17] Ye placed the blame on Lin Biao and the Gang of Four, as was the official political custom of the time, but it was clear to all that many others also bore responsibility for the Cultural Revolution, and that Mao Zedong was chief among them.

In the official critique of Maoism that emerged in 1979 and 1980, Mao Zedong was rarely mentioned by name. Indeed, on other political and policy matters, his writings were still authoritatively (if selectively) quoted when it proved politically convenient to do so. But there were increasingly harsh denunciations of "the personality cult," a term that performed the same euphemistic function in China at the time as it had a quarter-century before during the de-Stalinization years in the Soviet Union. The official remedy for the evils fostered by "the personality cult," sometimes referred to as "modern superstition," was adherence to Leninist norms of "inner party democracy" and "collective leadership," although these loudly proclaimed principles did little to hinder the concentration of power in the hands of Deng Xiaoping. "Collective leadership" did find expression, however, in the redefinition of the official ideology of "Mao Zedong Thought," which, increasingly purged of its more radical ideas, was now proclaimed to be the collective wisdom of the Party, not simply the creation of one man. Performing a similar function were new accounts of the sixty-year history of the Chinese Communist Party which emphasized the contributions of revolutionaries who had been neglected in the historiography of the Mao period. By the middle of 1980, although the question of the historical role of Mao himself had yet to be publicly confronted, the last two decades of the late Chairman's rule had been opened to critical scrutiny.

To undermine Mao's popular prestige, the new government looked to the televised trial of the Gang of Four, which opened on November 20, 1980, four years after their arrest. Over a period of two months in the Ministry of Public Security building in Beijing, the Four were tried together with Mao's onetime secretary, Chen Boda, before a special tribunal of thirty-five judges. A separate panel simultaneously tried five PLA generals implicated in Lin Biao's 1971 plot against Mao, although the relationship between the two proceedings was never clarified. The lengthy indictment charged the accused with forty-eight criminal offenses, including plots to overthrow the government, attempts to assassinate Mao Zedong, illegal arrests, torture, and the persecution of 700,000 people, resulting in 34,000 deaths.[18] Although advertised as a criminal trial conducted in accordance with a modernized legal code, the trial was of course eminently political. The judges paid far less attention to the new legal codes than to the Party Politburo, which dictated the proceedings in detail from the original indictment to the final verdicts.

If the trial of the Gang of Four failed to convince foreign observers that the Deng government had embraced internationally-accepted legal norms—indeed, to many it seemed uncomfortably reminiscent of a Stalinist-style show trial—it did serve the internal political purposes for which it was staged. The highly publicized trial made for a powerful condemnation of political life during the last decade of the Mao era, with nightly television broadcasts of selected segments of the proceedings featuring witnesses who related in often grisly detail horrifying incidents of torture and death during the "cultural revolution decade." For urban intellectuals and workers who had been victimized during what was now being called the "feudal-fascist" reign of the Gang of Four and who could now watch a manacled Jiang Qing and others on exhibit in an iron cage, the trial served as a partial "settling of accounts" and an emotional catharsis. For Deng Xiaoping and his associates, the trial was a satisfying act of political revenge and also served the eminently pragmatic function of facilitating the ongoing purge of "leftists" in the Party, state, and military bureaucracies. The trial in Beijing was in fact the model for a long series of less-publicized trials of alleged "followers of the Gang of Four" in the provinces. But the most important political purpose of the highly ritualized spectacle was to raise the question of the role of Mao Zedong in the events for which his widow and onetime comrades stood condemned as criminals.

It was of course clear from the outset that Mao Zedong was the unnamed defendant on trial with the Gang of Four. In the course of the proceedings, a defiant Jiang Qing unwittingly (but predictably) served Deng Xiaoping's political purpose by continually invoking the authority of her late husband in her defense, at one point declaring: "I was Chairman Mao's dog. Whomever he told me to bite, I bit." And the chief prosecutor, in a closing statement drafted by the Politburo, noted (while ritualistically lauding Mao) that the Chinese people "are very clear that Chairman Mao was responsible . . . for their plight during the Cultural Revolution."[19]

But Deng's aim was not to condemn Mao to historical oblivion together with the Gang of Four. Rather it was to rescue Mao *for* history by separating him from the Gang, although it was a humanly fallible Mao who was rescued, considerably diminished in historical stature and moral authority. The separation was accomplished by distinguishing between "political errors" and "criminal offenses," a distinction Deng had laid down in the summer of 1980. The distinction was taken up by the official press during and after the trial of the Gang, and it was repeatedly emphasized that there was "a difference in principle between Mao's mistakes and the crimes of Lin Biao, Jiang Qing, and their cohorts."[20] In accordance with this perhaps historically dubious distinction, the Party publicly set forth its official historical verdict on Mao Zedong, five months after a Party-controlled court had passed its verdict of guilty on the Gang of Four.

The Resolution on Mao Zedong

On June 27, 1981, one day after accepting Hua Guofeng's resignation as Party Chairman, the Sixth Plenum of the CCP's Eleventh Central Committee issued the long awaited assessment of the place of Mao Zedong in the history of the Chinese Revolution. The "Resolution on Certain Questions in the History of Our Party Since the Founding of the People's Republic of China" had been prepared over a period of fifteen months. Four thousand Party leaders and theoreticians, it was claimed, helped draft the document, which was repeatedly revised in accordance with detailed "suggestions" made by Deng Xiaoping. Many of Deng's suggestions stressed the need to "affirm" Mao's contributions to the revolutionary cause, in addition to criticizing his political and ideological errors. While most senior Party leaders, virtually all purged during the Cultural Revolution, were eager to avenge themselves on Mao's ghost, Deng Xiaoping appreciated the political need to preserve Mao as a symbol of both revolutionary and nationalist legitimacy.

As Deng had insisted, the final version of the Resolution generously praised Mao's leadership in the long revolutionary struggle and lauded his "brilliant successes" in economic development and "socialist transformation" in the early years of the People's Republic. Yet while praising Mao as a great revolutionary and modernizer, the Resolution was severe in criticizing the late Chairman's "mistakes" during the last two decades of his rule. Among the mistakes was the decision to broaden the scope of the antirightist campaign in 1957, resulting in the persecution of many innocent cadres and intellectuals, although the original phase of that witch-hunt (which had been led by Deng Xiaoping) was judged "necessary" and "correct." More serious were Mao's "leftist" errors, which were responsible for the economic disasters of the Great Leap, although it was acknowledged that most Party leaders (including Deng Xiaoping and Liu Shaoqi) had initially supported the ill-fated venture with considerable enthusiasm. Moreover, it was charged that Mao had undermined Leninist principles of "democratic centralism in Party life" by ruling with "personal arbitrariness" and by fostering a "personality cult" during his later years. Even more serious was his invention of the "erroneous left theses" that sanctioned the Cultural Revolution, which was now unambiguously condemned as a decade-long catastrophe "responsible for the most severe setback and the heaviest losses suffered by the Party, the state and the people since the founding of the People's Republic." Although the worst evils of the era were attributed to Lin Biao and the Gang of Four, Mao was not spared blame. "Chief responsibility for the grave left error of the Cultural Revolution, an error comprehensive in magnitude and protracted in duration, does indeed lie with Comrade Mao Zedong," the Resolution concluded.[21]

The aging Mao's "leftist" errors, which loom so large and so ominously in the Party's critique, are ideological tendencies that Marxists traditionally have denounced as "utopian" and "unscientific." The Resolution elaborated on these. Mao, according to his official assessors, "overestimated the role of man's subjective will and efforts," indulged in theories and policies "divorced from reality," and raised entirely unrealistic expectations of the imminent advent of a communist utopia amid conditions of material scarcity. He thus violated what his more orthodox Marxist-Leninist successors took to be "the objective laws" of history. Yet however harsh the official critique was in this and many other respects, the Resolution, in its overall historical assessment, concluded that Mao's "contributions to the Chinese Revolution far outweigh his mistakes" and that because of those contributions over so many decades "the Chinese people have always regarded Comrade Mao Zedong as their respected and beloved great leader and teacher." In the years following the promulgation of the Resolution, it came to be a popularized orthodoxy that Mao had been 70 percent correct and 30 percent wrong.

Private assessments of Mao by many intellectual and political leaders of the post-Maoist order were less generous than those publicly set down in the Central Committee document of June 1981. But the praise for Mao in the official Resolution, which uneasily accompanied the critique of his "leftist" mistakes, represented more than a search for revolutionary continuity and political legitimacy by the new leaders of the Chinese Communist Party. The praise also reflected the genuine respect and admiration (if not necessarily affection) felt by surviving senior Party leaders for the early Mao—the Mao who was the leader of the Revolution, the Mao who was the liberator of the Chinese nation, and the Mao who had been an economic modernizer—before he had been infected with "erroneous leftist" ideas. Veteran Party officials, now restored to power after years of humiliation and sometimes persecution, nostalgically looked back to the Mao who was the revolutionary leader of the Party during their own youthful days as revolutionaries. And they looked back to the Mao who presided over the new state in the early and mid-1950s, a time they now viewed as a golden age in the history of their land. For Deng Xiaoping and many of his associates, more than pragmatic political considerations were involved in their praise of Mao, for they sought to recapture the "uncorrupted" Maoism of the years prior to 1957, before Mao succumbed to what they regarded as pernicious radical and utopian notions.

In the years after the Resolution of 1981 had settled the Mao question, at least officially, the remaining artifacts of the cult of Mao were quietly removed from public display, although some were soon to make strange reappearances in popular culture and in unofficial political life. But in 1981, in official Communist Party ideology and political ritual, Mao was retained as a revolutionary, nationalist, and modernizing symbol. The purpose, of course, was to reinforce the legitimacy of the post-Mao regime by tying it to the Chinese Communist revolutionary tradition, a tradition in which Mao of course had played the largest and longest part. Consequently, Mao's writings continued to be frequently quoted in official publications, albeit highly selectively, and the much de-radicalized image of the dead Chairman continued to be utilized and sometimes celebrated over the post-Mao years, as political circumstances dictated.

Yet perhaps more important than the preservation of Mao Zedong as a political symbol was the simultaneous repudiation of the social and ideological radicalism of the last two decades of the Maoist era. That, together with the reduction of Mao from a demigod to a leader of humanly fallible proportions, capable of errors "comprehensive in magnitude," provided a necessary ideological sanction for the abandonment of Maoist socioeconomic policies in favor of the market-oriented economic reforms that Deng Xiaoping and others were preparing.

NOTES

1. On the demise of the Gang, see chapter 20 above.
2. Hua Kuo-feng [Hua Guofeng], "Report to the Fifth National People's Congress" (February 26, 1978), *Peking Review,* March 10, 1978, pp. 7–40. Hua's "Report" outlined the Ten Year Plan in general terms, with subsequent government announcements providing more specific targets and goals. For a perceptive and detailed analysis of the plan, see Chu-yuan Cheng, "The Modernization of Chinese Industry," in Richard Baum, ed., *China's Four Modernizations: The New Technological Revolution* (Boulder, Colorado: Westview Press, 1980), pp. 21–48.
3. Born into a well-to-do gentry family in Sichuan province in 1904, Deng barely qualified for membership in the illustrious May Fourth generation. Still a young teenager at the time of the May Fourth incident of 1919, he nonetheless was influenced by the radical political and intellectual currents of the era, journeying to France as a work-study student in 1923. There he joined the French branch of the Chinese Communist Party, then led by Zhou Enlai.
4. See Chapter 20 above.

5. Deng is said to have told his supporters at the time: "Either we accept the fate of being slaughtered and let the Party and the country degenerate, let the country which was founded with the heart and soul of our proletarian revolutionaries of the old generation be destroyed by those four people [i.e., the Gang of Four] . . . or we should struggle against them. . . . If we win, everything can be solved. If we lose, we can take to the mountains for as long as we live or we can find shield in other countries to wait for another opportunity. At present, we can use at least the strength of the Canton Military Region, the Fuzhou Military Region, and the Nanjing Military Region to fight against them . . ." Cited in Roger Garside, *Coming Alive: China After Mao* (New York: Mentor, 1982), p. 130.

6. See Chapter 17 above.

7. For the prototypical example of his appeals to intellectuals, see Teng Hsiao-p'ing [Deng Xiaoping], "Speech at the Opening Ceremony of the National Science Conference" (March 18, 1978), *Peking Review,* March 24, 1978, pp. 9–18.

8. For a vivid account of the odyssey of one of the more illustrious of these victims, the well-known writer Ding Ling, see Jonathan Spence, *The Gate of Heavenly Peace* (New York: The Viking Press, 1981), especially pp. 335–69.

9. For a brief but excellent account of the causes and results of the invasion, see Daniel Tretiak, "China's Vietnam War and Its Consequences," *The China Quarterly,* No. 80 (December 1979), pp. 740–67.

10. Deng's demand for the abolition of the "four greats" came in a speech to a Party work conference in January 1980. See "The Present Situation and the Tasks Before Us," *Selected Works of Deng Xiaoping,* pp. 224–58. In August 1980, the Fifth National People's Congress duly obliged, deleting the "four greats" (*sida*) from the state constitution. For good measure, the Congress also eliminated the clause granting workers the right to strike, another constitutional "right" that was rarely exercised. Deng resumed his vitriolic attack against the remnants of the Democracy Movement in a speech to a Party meeting on December 25, 1980, taking special pains to denounce the notion that China was ruled by a privileged "bureaucratic class." FBIS *Daily Report,* May 4, 1981, p. W8, and *Issues and Studies* (Taipei), July 1981, pp. 115–16.

11. Deng Xiaoping, "Uphold the Four Cardinal Principles" (speech of March 30, 1979), *Selected Works of Deng Xiaoping,* pp. 166–191.

12. Zhao Ziyang (born 1919), a political cadre in the Red Army during the last decade of the Communist Revolution, rose rapidly in the postrevolutionary bureaucratic hierarchy, becoming Party Secretary for Guangdong province in the early 1960s. Purged during the Cultural Revolution, he was among the many veteran officials Mao restored to power in the early 1970s. When he was Party chief in Sichuan province in the late 1970s, his market-oriented economic experiments brought him to Deng's attention—and to Beijing.

13. Hu Yaobang (1915–1989) joined the CCP in 1933 and served as a political cadre under Deng in the Second Field Army. He remained a member of Deng's entourage after 1949 and his postrevolutionary political career waxed and waned together with the fortunes of his mentor. He was elected to the Politburo at the Third Plenum in December 1978.

14. Deng interview with Oriana Fallaci, *The Washington Post,* August 31, 1980, p. D4.

15. Deng Xiaoping, "Suggestions on the Drafting of the 'Resolution on Certain Questions in the History of Our Party Since the Founding of the People's Republic of China,'" *Beijing Review,* July 25, 1983, p. 18.

16. For an exceptionally perceptive analysis of this important strand in the history of Chinese Communism, see William Joseph, *The Critique of Ultra-Leftism in China, 1958–1981* (Stanford, California: Stanford University Press, 1984).

17. "Comrade Ye Jianying's Speech" (September 29, 1979), *Beijing Review,* October 5, 1979, pp. 7–32. Ye spoke on behalf of the Central Committee of the Party, the Standing Committee of the National People's Congress (which he chaired) and the State Council. That Ye, not Hua Guofeng, still the nominal Chairman of the Party, delivered the main 30th anniversary speech was a telling political sign of the time.

18. For the text of the indictment, see *Beijing Review,* No. 48 (December 1, 1980), pp. 9–28.

19. Jiang Qing and Zhang Chunqiao were sentenced to death but the sentences were commuted to life imprisonment shortly after the trial. Both died in prison. Jiang Qing, reportedly suffering from throat cancer, was said to have commited suicide in May 1991. Wang Hongwen, sentenced to life imprisonment, died of liver disease in 1992. Yao Wenyuan, sentenced to a lengthy prison term, was released from jail in 1996.

20. For example, *Beijing Review,* No. 1, (January 5, 1981), p. 4. The distinction had been set forth well before the trial of the Gang. See, for example, Deng's interview with Oriana Fallaci, *Washington Post,* August 31, 1980, p. D4.

21. For the official text of "Resolution on Certain Questions in the History of Our Party Since the Founding of the People's Republic of China," see *Beijing Review,* No. 27 (July 6, 1981), pp. 10–39.

23

Market Reforms and the Development of Capitalism

DENG XIAOPING came to power at the end of 1978 on a platform championing "socialist democracy." The promise of a democratic socialism struck deeply responsive chords in Chinese society, especially among intellectuals and the urban working class, winning Deng enthusiastic popular support in the cities. The Deng regime was to preside over one of the most extraordinary episodes of economic growth in world history that was to bring relative (if very unequal) prosperity to the Chinese people—but neither socialism nor democracy were to prosper in post-Maoist China.

Democracy was the first of Deng's promises to be broken. Hardly three months after his victory at the Third Plenum in December 1978, Deng turned against the most vulnerable members of the political coalition that had brought him to power—the young activists who wrote the passionate political treatises and the poignant poetry that appeared on Democracy Wall, and who had supplied much of the elan for the pro-Deng movement during the last months of 1978. The suppression of the Democracy Movement, signaled by the arrest of Wei Jingsheng in March 1979, was a depressingly prophetic pointer to the political future of post-Mao China.

During Deng Xiaoping's reign, to be sure, the Communist state generally relaxed its control over Chinese society, freeing hundreds of thousands of political prisoners and loosening ideological controls. These were by no means insignificant political gains for the Chinese people. But their democratic potential was severely limited. For by "political reform," which the new regime repeatedly said would accompany "economic reform," Deng did not mean the process of democratization that he seemingly had promised and that many assumed to be his aim. Rather, by political reform he meant, first and foremost, the restoration of Leninist organizational norms in the Chinese Communist Party, whose discipline had been undermined by the disruptions of the Cultural Revolution. Secondly, he meant the rationalization of bureaucratic rule by making the Communist bureaucracy (in Deng's words) "younger on the average, better educated, and better qualified professionally."[1] In short, there were to be no substantive changes in the Communist political system, however far-reaching the economic transformation. The Chinese Communist Party, its Leninist character refurbished and refined, was to retain its monopoly of political power. And the essentials of the Stalinist political system were to be preserved.

If there was little democratic content in the Dengist conception of "socialist democracy," there was even less socialist substance. When Deng Xiaoping and his politically victorious colleagues began to consider economic reform policies in late 1978 and early 1979, they favored various economic decentralization measures and were increasingly attracted to market solutions to break down the rigidities of China's Soviet-style system of central economic planning. But they had little interest in any real socialist reorganization of production, wherein the producers themselves would gain a measure of control over the conditions and products of their work.

The reasons for this failure to consider a socialist solution are worth pondering. Confusion over the definition of socialism played a part. In its distorted Stalinist (and Maoist) forms, in both theory and practice, "socialism" tended to be measured by the degree of state control over production, hardly appealing to reformers who attributed the problems of the Chinese economy to an overly centralized and bureaucratized system of state planning. But even those who properly understood socialism to be control of productive processes by the immediate producers rather than by the state were reluctant to propose socialist solutions. For such genuinely socialist solutions presupposed political democracy, and thus posed a direct challenge to the power of the Chinese Communist Party. Indeed, true socialism was viewed as doubly challenging, threatening the economic as well as the political power of the Communist bureaucracy. Moreover, socialism in the form of actual worker and peasant control would have been an historical novelty, never having existed before in China or elsewhere; thus it inevitably raised fears of the unknown. China's reformers, however bold and innovative they might have appeared at first, confined themselves to actually existing economic models.

Thus, in the discussions among Communist leaders and intellectuals in the politically victorious Deng camp around the time of the Third Plenum, a genuinely socialist alternative to the command economy was never seriously considered. Only reformist measures which could be accommodated within the existing political system were discussed. These included various schemes for economic decentralization and the introduction of market mechanisms. The latter seemed particularly intriguing to many Communist leaders and theoreticians, for it was presented to them at a time when the worldwide neo-liberalist celebration of the "magic of the market" was reaching a crescendo.

The decentralization of economic administration and decision making, experimented with earlier in the People's Republic (most radically and disastrously during the Great Leap Forward campaign of 1958–60), posed no general threat to Communist rule—although, depending on the particular scheme, decentralization could favor some sectors of the bureaucracy and weaken or limit others. Nor was the market the mortal threat to the Communist political system that it was assumed to be by many foreign observers. Chinese Communist leaders, in part inspired by seemingly successful "market socialist" models in Hungary and Yugoslavia, calculated that market mechanisms could be utilized to improve the quantity and the quality of both industrial and agricultural production without the Party relinquishing political power or the state losing control over the "commanding heights" of the economy. By and large, these calculations proved correct. The Communist Party-state remained politically dominant and retained a large measure of control over vital sectors of the economy. Moreover, Communist bureaucrats, many initially suspicious of market relationships (partly because of ideological principle, partly out of material self-interest), soon discovered that they were uniquely well situated to profit handsomely from a market economy. Many, of course, hastened to do so, in myriad ways that will be explored shortly.

. . .

In modern world history, the market is of course intimately identified— economically, socially, and ideologically—with industrial capitalism.[2] That a market economy inevitably breeds capitalist social relationships, and all the inequitable consequences of capitalism, was well known to China's Communist leaders in the late 1970s. But Deng Xiaoping and his reformist associates did not envision a capitalist future for China. Although some of the more zealous of the reformers tended "to disseminate a naive view of the wonders of the market," as Carl Riskin has observed,[3] most did not champion a market economy or a capitalist regime because of their intrinsic virtues. Rather, they saw the mechanism of the market as a means to eventual socialist ends, as the most efficient way to break down the stifling system of centralized state planning and to speed up the development of modern productive forces, thereby creating the essential material foundations for a future socialist society. The belief that they were pursuing eventual socialist ends was reinforced by the experiments in "market socialism" then under way in Communist Hungary and Yugoslavia, whose modest accomplishments had been greatly exaggerated by sympathetic Western commentators.

The use of capitalist means and methods to attain future socialist ends was ideologically sanctioned by a more orthodox interpretation of Marxist theory than had been fashionable in the Mao period. Deng's theoreticians placed special emphasis on the Marxian thesis that socialism presupposed capitalism, the belief that distinguished original Marxism from other nineteenth-century socialist theories. A truly socialist society, Marx had argued, could be constructed only on the material and social foundations of capitalism, only where there existed large-scale industry and, correspondingly, a mature urban proletariat, the indispensable social agent of the socialist future. Thus capitalism, however socially destructive and inhumane, was a necessary and progressive stage in history, Marx taught. Indeed, many of the classic Marxian texts, not excluding the *Communist Manifesto,* could be read (and were in fact now read in China), as celebrations of the extraordinary productive powers of capitalism. Chinese Communist reformers, therefore, invoked the authority of Marx to support the capitalist methods they favored, and also frequently quoted Lenin, especially such well-known statements as, "the only socialism we can imagine is one based on all the lessons learnt through large-scale capitalist culture."[4]

In their search for a Marxian rationale for market-reform policies, Deng's ideologists placed an enormous emphasis on the pernicious influences of China's feudal tradition. Because of the abortiveness of capitalism in modern Chinese history, they argued, pre-capitalist forms of socioeconomic life and consciousness had survived into the socialist era, making the "remnants of feudalism," not capitalism, the greatest barrier to China's modern economic development—and thus the greatest obstacle to the true development of socialism over the long term. The deleterious effects of a weak and distorted capitalism were perpetuated by the brevity and incompleteness of Mao Zedong's "New Democratic" revolution, burdening the People's Republic with a persisting "feudal consciousness" that was, they argued, largely responsible for the negative developments of the late Mao era, especially the Great Leap and the Cultural Revolution. Since capitalism is feudalism's natural historical antagonist, according to Marxist theory, it followed that capitalism still had a necessary and progressive role to play in China. On the question of whether the capitalist means they advocated were consistent with the socialist ends they sought, the reformers were perhaps troubled but for the most part silent.

Another ideological construct that was used to provide a quasi-Marxist rationale for the market was a proposition Deng Xiaoping had set forth more than two decades before. At the Eighth Party Congress in September 1956, Deng had argued that with "socialist transformation," that is, the nationalization of industry and the collectivation of agriculture, class divisions (and class struggle) had been virtually eliminated. Therefore the principal contradiction in Chinese society was no longer between antagonistic social groups but rather between "the advanced socialist system and the backward productive forces."[5] The remedy, of course, was to concentrate on developing the productive forces in order to bring the economic base in alignment with the presumably socialist political and social "superstructure."

Mao Zedong had little use for the formulas of the Eighth Congress, which he soon scrapped in favor of a renewed emphasis on class struggle. But when Deng Xiaoping came to power in 1978, his 1956 Eighth Congress thesis was resurrected to become the principal ideological orthodoxy of the early post-Mao era, sanctioning the subordination of all social (and socialist) concerns to a nationalist pursuit of rapid economic development—to be accomplished by the most expedient means, not excluding the means of the capitalist market. In the 1980s, as we shall see, Deng's thesis was refined and elaborated upon to become the theory of "the primary stage of socialism," an economically deterministic notion (in rather threadbare Marxist guise) which served to give priority to national economic development, regardless of social cost.[6]

. . .

Deng Xiaoping's economic reform program began in 1979, officially sanctioned by the Third Plenum's rather ambiguous injunction to combine "market adjustment" with "adjustment by the plan." The ambiguity of the formula was designed to satisfy both the advocates of market-type reform and those who wished to preserve the primacy of central state planning while allowing a supplementary role for the market. The initial reforms, in any event, which were designed to correct the economic imbalances inherited from the Mao period, were essentially administrative measures and required no major concessions to the market. In the spring of 1979, unceremoniously scrapping Hua Guofeng's Ten Year Plan, the new government slashed investment in heavy industry and construction in favor of light industry and agriculture. Successful efforts were undertaken to lower the "accumulation rate," that is, the proportion of the social product appropriated by the state to expand productive capacity. The rate had risen rapidly during the late Mao era and even more rapidly under the Hua Guofeng regime, thereby depressing consumption. This trend was now reversed. Prices paid to peasants for agricultural products were increased substantially, including a 20 percent rise in prices for compulsory grain deliveries to state stores and a 50 percent premium for above-quota sales. In addition, the limit on private household plots was raised from 5 to 15 percent of the cultivated land, and state restrictions on rural marketing activities were greatly eased. Urban workers also benefited, although far less than did peasants, by new bonus and profit-sharing schemes in state enterprises that rewarded gains in productivity.

The Deng regime's initial economic policies stimulated sizable increases in both agricultural and light industrial production, while at the same time providing both rural and urban inhabitants with greater incomes to purchase consumer goods, which were now being produced and imported in ever-increasing quantities. The marked improvement in popular living standards and the boom in consumption so evident in the early 1980s resulted directly from the policy changes of 1979.

Although rising consumption was due primarily to rising incomes, it was aided by the Deng government's vigorous encouragement of what proved to be an astonishingly rapid revival of private entrepreneurship in both city and countryside. In addition to thriving rural markets and fairs, in the early 1980s city streets were quickly transformed by the reappearance of peddlers and vendors selling various wares and foods, the opening of private restaurants and inns, and the establishment of many new retail and service businesses—from barbers and beauticians to television repair shops. There was also a revival of traditional handicrafts production, sometimes organized in loosely structured cooperatives, while clothes and sundry household goods were produced in hastily erected workshops and by women working in their homes on the putting-out system.

Government encouragement of these private and vaguely collective entrepreneurial endeavors was intended, in part, to fill a long-standing void in the retail and service sectors of the economy. With even small private shops and markets condemned as "capitalist tails" and mostly banned during the late Mao period, people often had to travel long distances to obtain needed goods and services at government stores, which were frequently staffed (and usually overstaffed) by indifferent employees. In larger part, the government's promotion of private enterprise was intended to mitigate the social strains of unemployment. By 1984, according to official figures, nearly 4,000,000 people were employed or self-employed in the burgeoning private sector of the urban economy and more than 32 million worked in urban "collective" enterprises, which more and more operated in a capitalist fashion in an increasingly market-driven economy.[7] The numbers were to multiply rapidly as the government removed restrictions on the numbers of workers who could be employed by private capitalist enterprises; by the mid-1980s private and "collective" endeavors had come to be the most rapidly growing sectors of the urban economy.

The attractiveness to the government of self-employment and employment by private entrepreneurs was made quite clear at the outset of the reform period by one of the leading advocates of the market, who candidly observed of such workers that "the state will not be required to pay them wages."[8] Nor was the state required to pay wages to the ever-growing numbers of people who hired themselves out as servants in private homes. Servants were by no means unknown in the Maoist period, but most were state employees working in the offices and homes of high-ranking government officials. In the post-Mao years, maids, cooks, gardeners, and nannies became commonplace in the residences of the growing elite of technocrats, intellectuals, and mid-level bureaucrats as well as in the homes of the more successful of China's new capitalist entrepreneurs and those of its many new foreign residents.

The reappearance of petty private enterprise contributed to the liveliness of Chinese cities in the early Deng era, which foreigners contrasted to the austere and drab character of urban life in Maoist China—a comparison invariably made even by those who never visited China during the Mao period. Peddlers, hawkers, and tiny open-air restaurants were soon followed by high-rise hotels, nightclubs, and luxury boutiques—as well as by beggars and prostitutes. Chinese cities thus began to resemble large cities in most of the world, displaying those stark and painful contrasts between ostentatious wealth and grinding poverty that mark most contemporary capitalist societies.

In the early 1980s, the revival of petty commerce in the cities was hailed by many Western observers as a sign of the birth of a vigorous Chinese capitalism. There were, of course, no lack of stories of entrepreneurs who did in fact heed the government's injunction to "get rich," and these were widely advertised in both the Chinese and foreign press. But the great majority of those who worked in the new private sector achieved very modest success at best or were able to eke out only a marginal existence, much like their counterparts in the cities of other Third World lands. The real origins of Chinese capitalism were to be found not in the petty commercial capitalism of the cities but in the foreign trade and investment that passed through Deng Xiaoping's "open doors" along the South China coast—and in the Chinese Communist state and its bureaucrats who controlled passage through those doors.

The Open Door Policy

When the policy of "the Four Modernizations" was set forth by Zhou Enlai in January 1975, China's Communist leaders assumed that the pursuit of the ambitious economic goals Zhou proposed would require a vast expansion of China's international trade, the acquisition of the latest technology from the advanced capitalist countries, and probably borrowing foreign capital. This would mean the abandonment—in fact if not in name—of the Maoist policy of national "self-reliance."

The principle of self-reliance had acquired an almost sacred status in Maoist China. In part, however, the celebration of self-reliance was a matter of making a virtue out of necessity. Largely isolated from the world capitalist market by a hostile United States for more than two decades, and then cut off from most of the Communist world as well when relations with the Soviet Union deteriorated in the late 1950s, China had little choice but to rely on its own resources during most of the Mao period. That necessity was perhaps made more palatable, and certainly ideologically rationalized, by the Maoist revolutionary legacy, especially the Yan'an ideal of economic self-sufficiency.[9] No doubt some Communist leaders, and certainly Mao Zedong among them, were willing to pay the economic price that self-reliance demanded in order to immunize socialist China from the corrosive effects of the world capitalist market. In any event, Mao and his colleagues, consciously or not, were partially imitating the protectionist strategy that Friedrich List devised in late nineteenth-century Prussia, a strategy which kept industrially backward Germany relatively isolated until it was able to compete with industrialized England. Whether deliberate or not, the fact remains that when China entered the world capitalist market in the late 1970s it did so on terms far more favorable than would have obtained in the 1950s.[10]

Yet whatever their conscious strategy and principles may have been, when the opportunity presented itself the leaders of the People's Republic acted rapidly to move China into the capitalist world of international trade and finance. The move began in the last years of the Mao period, following the rapprochement with the United States and Richard Nixon's February 1972 visit to Beijing and Shanghai. Between 1971 and 1974, China's foreign trade more than trebled, most of it with non-Commmunist countries.[11] The pace of trade quickened under the interim Hua Guofeng regime, and, as has been noted, Hua's abortive Ten Year Plan called for the massive importation of foreign capital and technology. Deng Xiaoping's market-oriented strategy of development and his "open door" policies greatly accelerated China's integration into the world capitalist market. From 1978 to 1988, foreign trade more than quadrupled, and then quadrupled once again over the next six years, with Japan, Hong Kong, and the United States emerging as China's leading trading partners.

This burgeoning trade has been conducted, on the whole, in accordance with the proclaimed Chinese principle of "equality and mutual benefit" and it is safe to assume that participants on all sides have profited from their various ventures. What has come under critical scrutiny by the Chinese is not the "open door" to trade but the opening of China to foreign investment—and, in order to attract foreign capital, the revival of practices uncomfortably reminiscent of life in the foreign-dominated treaty ports during semi-colonial times. The most conspicuous examples of the latter phenomenon are to be found in the "special economic zones," the first four of which were established on the South China coast in 1979 near Hong Kong and opposite Taiwan. Others followed, and within a decade virtually the whole of the Chinese coast, as well as selected inland regions, were "opened," which is to say they were offering foreign capitalists favorable conditions for the exploitation of Chinese labor and the making of quick profits—along with the amenities of life that foreign residents expect in a quasi-colonial setting.[12]

The special economic zones were embarrassments from the outset, on both socialist and nationalist grounds. At a time when the Beijing regime still felt a serious need to claim socialist credentials, the economies of the zones were frankly and indeed savagely capitalist—and to compound the ideological dilemma, the government had proclaimed that the zones would be models for the "reform" of all of urban China. Moreover, the zones were places where Chinese workers were exploited by foreign capital and where Chinese servants catered to privileged foreign residents. And the zones were breeding grounds for official corruption, both on the part of local governments and for the entrepreneurial-minded sons and daughters of high Communist Party officials who used their political influence to enrich themselves in the import-export trade and other business dealings.

Yet, apart from the still controversial question of whether the special economic zones as such have proved their economic worth, which is to say, whether they have generated more capital than the Chinese state has invested in their construction, there can be little doubt that Deng's "open door" policies in general have yielded most of their anticipated economic benefits: the influx of foreign capital to finance industrial enterprises and various other modernization projects, the alleviation of chronic shortages of foreign exchange, greater access to the advanced scientific and industrial technology of Japan and the Western countries, and employment for Chinese workers who would otherwise be unemployed.

The accumulation of capital for productive investment has certainly been the most important result of the "open door" policy. It is one of the curiosities of the development of Chinese capitalism under the Deng regime that a significant portion of these initial capital accumulations were the fruits of official corruption. Prominent among the members of China's new postrevolutionary "bourgeoisie," for example, were local officials (and their friends and relatives) who were able to buy goods and materials at low state prices and sell them at higher market prices. Equally prominent, especially in popular political consciousness, were the children of high Communist Party leaders who, in the early 1980s, were politically well positioned to play lucrative compradore roles in establishing ties between foreign capitalists and state enterprises. While some of these fruits of bureaucratic corruption no doubt found their way into secret Swiss bank accounts, as rumor had it, most was invested in a vast variety of highly profitable domestic financial, industrial and commercial enterprises in what became an extraordinarily rapid process of capital accumulation and economic growth.

Foreign investment in productive enterprises was also substantial, growing steadily if not spectacularly throughout the 1980s, then exploding into a frenzy of profit-seeking in the early 1990s. More foreign capital was invested in China in the year 1994 alone (US$ 34 billion) than in the entire decade ending in 1989.[13] Much of the imported capital has come from overseas Chinese investors, funneled largely through Hong Kong. And despite the political barriers, by the mid–1990s Taiwanese capitalists alone had invested more than US$ 25 billion on the mainland, mostly in Fujian province.

The attractiveness of China to foreign investors is not simply an endless supply of cheap labor, which of course is readily available (and often even cheaper) in many other parts of the world. Rather, it is an inexpensive labor force that is disciplined and relatively well-educated—and, not least attractive to potential investors, workers who are barred from organizing free trade unions by their Communist government, which also stands ready to insure "labor peace" in other respects as well. Deng and his successors' insistence on "stability and unity," the official euphemism for a Leninist dictatorship, is well appreciated by foreign investors. A further attraction to foreign capitalists is the possibility of direct access to the internal Chinese market, now well on the way to realizing its long-heralded potential as the largest market in the world.

The obvious economic benefits of Deng's "open door" policies have, of course, exacted costs. Among them has been the conversion of China from a debt-free into a major debtor nation—although China's foreign debt, while large in absolute terms, remains relatively modest by world standards when measured either on a per capita basis or in terms of the size of the Chinese economy.[14] China has, of course, become increasingly dependent on the fluctuations of the world capitalist market (which has not always been kind to developing countries), as well as subject to pressure from "international" (but U.S.-controlled) lending organizations such as the World Bank and the International Monetary Fund. Moreover, the "open door" has created vast new opportunities for official and unofficial corruption—although, as has been noted, in the peculiar circumstance of emergent Chinese capitalism, bureaucratic corruption is also a major source of capital accumulation. Not the least of the costs to China has been the loss of a certain (if unmeasurable) degree of national self-confidence. For the Maoist policy of self-reliance, whatever its economic price, served to instill in popular consciousness the conviction that the Chinese people could make their own distinctive future by their own efforts. That sense of confidence, the significance of which hardly can be overestimated in a land so long dominated and humiliated by foreigners, began to erode in the last years of the Mao regime. But it was more seriously undermined when post-Maoist leaders presented Western capitalist methods and techniques as a panacea for all Chinese problems—and unwittingly fostered what Simon Leys lamented as a "sudden rebirth of blind admiration for the West."[15] In response to that "blind admiration" there predictably have been reactionary nationalist responses, which probably will increase in intensity and virulence in the years to come.

Yet the burial of the Maoist policy of self-reliance did not signal a new era of dependency, as some feared at the inauguration of the "open door" policy. Unlike pre-1949 China, between the ambitions of foreign powers and the Chinese nation there now stands a strong Chinese state presided over by highly nationalistic leaders who, materially and psychologically, are more than capable of preserving China's sovereignty. An independent China, however lacking in social and political virtue, will remain one of the permanent achievements of the Chinese Communist Revolution. Nonetheless, the world capitalist market, with which China is increasingly integrated, has been (and will remain) a powerful force for the capitalist restructuring of the Chinese economy.

The Decollectivization of Agriculture

It was the countryside, where the majority of the Chinese people live and work, that was first to feel fully both the economic dynamism and the social destructiveness of a market economy. The agrarian reforms of the Deng regime in 1979–80, which at first seemed a cautious return to the "re-adjustment" policies promoted by Liu Shaoqi in the early 1960s to recover from the disaster of the Great Leap, soon became a torrent of deradicalizing change that swept away the collective rural institutions built during the 1950s and after. By the early 1980s, the communes had been dismantled, and collective agricultural production had been largely replaced by individual family farming.

This radical transformation of peasant work and life, which proceeded far more rapidly than the leaders in Beijing anticipated, just as had been the case with the other upheavals that had kept the rural population in flux over the preceding quarter-century, was in this case not inspired by a new social vision. Rather, it was motivated by the old economic need of the state to extract the surplus from the villages to finance the modern economic development of the nation, now known as the Four Modernizations. State exploitation of the countryside had been the main source of capital accumulation during the Mao period, and this remained the case in the post-Mao years. But it soon became apparent to Mao's successors that the agrarian economy, burdened with a growing population and declining productivity, was now incapable of supplying the needed capital. The essential first step, then, was to motivate peasants to increase production substantially, and thereby raise capital to support modern economic development. The new means to achieve that old end was to be the commercialization of the rural economy, albeit under a large measure of state guidance.

The first measures to encourage peasant production followed immediately from the Third Plenum, as has been noted. These included substantial price increases paid by the state for grain and other agricultural products and the removal of restrictions on rural markets. These policy "adjustments" easily could have been accommodated within the existing Maoist agrarian system—but China's market reformers wanted no such accommodation since they believed that China's real problems resided in Maoist institutions as such, not simply the way they functioned. Thus, the policy changes of early 1979 were accompanied by a wide-ranging and well-publicized critique of collective agriculture in general, undertaken by reformist intellectuals who served as policy advisers to the new Deng regime.

According to the critique, in the collectivization movement of 1955–56, the so-called "socialist high tide," Mao Zedong had ignored basic Marxist teachings on the necessary material conditions for socialism and imposed quasi-socialist relations of production on an economic foundation too weak to support them. Moreover, agricultural collectivization involved massive cadre coercion against the "middle peasants," thus alienating the most efficient producers. The result was rural economic stagnation for over two decades, with little or no increase in per capita income from the mid–1950s to the late 1970s, thus discrediting socialism in the eyes of the majority of peasants. The general critique of collectivized agriculture was reinforced when the much publicized Dazhai brigade, the Maoist model of local rural self-sufficiency and social equality, was officially denounced as a "leftist deviation" and its once-celebrated peasant leader, Chen Yonggui, was purged from the Party Politburo. The Party's charges against the Dazhai brigade, which included allegations of falsifying production figures and financial irregularities, seemed less than entirely plausible to those familiar with the history of this extensively-studied commune.[16]

In undertaking the critique of collectivization, Party ideologists invoked Deng Xiaoping's old 1956 formula, now the state orthodoxy, to the effect that the main contradiction in Chinese society was not between antagonistic social groups but rather between China's "advanced socialist system" and its backward productive forces. Deng's proposition hitherto had been used to justify a single-minded pursuit of economic development, to the neglect of other considerations, in order to bring the productive forces in harmony with the "socialist system." But the critics of collectivized agriculture gave Deng's formula a new twist, suggesting that a retreat to pre-collective forms of social organization would also contribute to resolving the contradiction between seemingly incompatible levels of social and economic development. Thus they advocated a return to family farming, arguing that a commercialized capitalist system based on individual peasant proprietorship would not only be more appropriate to China's present level of economic development but also would release the dynamism of the market to stimulate the rapid growth of rural productive forces.

The first major institutional change promoting capitalism in the Chinese countryside was officially sanctioned in September 1980, when the Party Central Committee recommended adoption of what generally came to be called the "household responsibility system" (HRS). Under the "responsibility" system, individual peasant households concluded contractual agreements with the production team for the use of given portions of the team's "collective" land, in return for which the households paid the team contractually stipulated portions of their output to meet state tax and grain quota obligations, along with small sums to support the waning collective and welfare functions the team still performed. Farm tools and draft animals, until now collectively held by the team, were divided among the households, which now engaged in individual family farming. Save for its financial obligations to the team, the household was free to work the land in whatever fashion it wished and to dispose of the surplus as it chose.

Although there had been earlier experiments with various versions of the "responsibility" system, and while in some areas peasants had acted on their own to divide the land, it was not until its official Party approval in the autumn of 1980 that the new arrangement began to be widely adopted. And although it was originally said that the contract system was to be voluntary and primarily applicable to poorer areas where collectivized farming had failed, in fact the HRS soon became mandatory and was rapidly universalized in the early 1980s: local rural Party cadres, fearful of being purged as "leftists," were zealous in promoting the new policy (and sometimes imposing it on reluctant peasants) to demonstrate their political loyalty to the Deng regime. By the end of 1983, 98 percent of peasant households had converted to one form or another of the responsibility system. As had been the case in the collectivization campaign of 1955–56, decollectivization was accomplished with "one stroke of the knife," presumably a leftist error, and little more was heard about the once loudly proclaimed principle of policy variation according to differing local conditions.

What initially replaced collective agriculture was a system Carl Riskin has aptly characterized as "tenant farming with the production team and the state as landlord."[17] But the "tenants" did not long remain an undifferentiated mass of tillers of equal parcels of the soil. New economic and social divisions among the rural population developed with extraordinary rapidity as capitalist relationships spread through the countryside. The sources of the new socioeconomic differentiations were many. First, not all the contracts concluded under the responsibility system were made for the purpose of ordinary farming. Encouraged by government policies promoting specialization and marketing, a good many peasants turned to potentially more lucrative pursuits such as the cultivation of cash crops, food-processing enterprises, small workshops and repair shops, and the operation of a variety of new businesses in commerce and transportation. In general, such "specialized households," as they were designated, and owners of businesses fared far better than ordinary peasant households, whose members continued to grow crops such as grain and other essential foods. Secondly, differentiation was promoted in 1983 when the government, in order to accommodate the needs of households lacking sufficient labor power, and especially to encourage the ambitions of the more entrepreneurially-minded rural inhabitants who held promise as potential accumulators of capital, permitted contracted lands to be rented and wage laborers to be hired. A new underclass of subtenants and hired laborers grew rapidly as government limits on the exploitation of labor were ignored and eventually all but removed,[18] while those better endowed with physical and entrepreneurial skills and ambition vigorously strove to prove the truth of the Dengist maxim that "some must get rich first," now the official rationale for growing inequality.

Finally, perhaps the most significant source of differentiation between rich and poor stemmed from the advantages enjoyed by rural Party cadres in the newly commercialized economy. Most rural officials initially opposed the return to individual family farming, partly out of ideological conviction and partly because they feared loss of power and income. However, many soon discovered that their political positions and influence were uniquely valuable assets in pursuing their private economic interests. Presiding over the process of decollectivization, many Party cadres were able to secure the best lands and the lion's share of farm tools and machinery for themselves, their relatives, and their friends. And their old political connections served them well in acquiring goods and materials in short supply for lucrative dealings on the rapidly expanding black market.[19]

Decollectivization was greatly facilitated by the dismantling of the commune system. A new state constitution adopted at the end of 1982 transferred the administrative functions of the communes to township or county (*xiang*) governments, units of the central state administration. With the demise of the political power of the communes, their collective economic and social welfare functions atrophied or were transformed into private undertakings operated for profit by individuals, families, or small corporate groups.[20] Even medical services and educational facilities were caught up in the commercialization of the countryside. Private doctors and private schools began to appear in many rural localities by the mid-1980s, and have become available to those who can afford them.

An essential prerequisite for the development of capitalism in the Chinese countryside was the privatization of land use, even if the question of formal ownership has been left ambiguous. Land originally acquired by family farmers under the household responsibility system was leased for short periods from the production teams (an organizational structure left over from the collective period) and legally remained collective property. To allay peasant fears that the new system might prove temporary, and to discourage predatory use of the land, a 1984 government regulation permitted fields to be contracted for periods of up to fifteen years. That was soon extended to half a century, and it became generally understood that land could be passed on to one's heirs for several generations. This effectively established a de facto free market in land, with "contracted" lands rented, bought, sold and mortgaged as if they were fully alienable private property.

The new rural policies yielded remarkable economic results in the early 1980s. From 1978 to 1984 the gross value of agricultural output grew at an average annual rate of 9 percent.[21] There were striking gains in labor productivity in the countryside, rural per capita income nearly doubled over those six years, and there was a visibly dramatic rise in living standards in most of the countryside. This was particularly evident in the widespread construction of new houses, an enormous increase in the purchase of consumer goods, and marked improvement in diet. Although the economic upsurge in the countryside could in part be attributed to the incentives provided by the household responsibility system and the marketization of the rural economy, in part (and probably in greater part) it resulted from the 1979 price increases for agricultural products and the general relaxation of state pressure that preceded them, both of which took place within the institutional framework of the old system of collectivized agriculture. It is instructive that the upsurge in agricultural production began under the Hua Guofeng regime in 1978 (an 8.9 percent increase) and continued in 1979 (8.6 percent), whereas the household responsibility system was not widely adopted until the early 1980s.[22] Whatever the reasons, and they no doubt vary from place to place, the early Deng era undoubtedly will be recorded as one of the most economically successful periods in the history of Chinese agriculture.

The progress in agricultural production, however, could not be sustained. In 1985 there was a sharp and unanticipated decline in grain output—from a record 407 million metric tons the previous year to 379 tons—that sent economic and psychological shock waves throughout Chinese society. It was the largest annual decline since the Great Leap, and it evoked memories and fears of famine. Grain shortages and wild fluctuations in agricultural prices followed in China's increasingly market-driven economy, a market which offered fewer and fewer rewards for those who actually worked the land. This, in turn, gave rise in many rural areas to bitter and continuing hostility between peasants and government officials, the latter intent on enforcing grain purchase contracts—and sometimes further angering peasants by paying for grain with "white slips" (*baitiao*), or IOUs, in lieu of cash. The hostility was exacerbated by a plethora of extra-legal taxes and newly invented fees which corrupt officials began to exact from peasants in the late 1980s. Since 1985, in any event, agricultural production has tended to stagnate, barely keeping pace with a relatively low rate of population growth.

Rural household income, and the relative prosperity of much of the countryside, has been sustained since the mid-1980s not by increases in agricultural production or productivity but rather by the astonishingly rapid growth of industry in the form of "township and village enterprises" (TVEs). The program for rural industrialization, a distinctively Maoist policy inaugurated during the Great Leap Forward campaign (as was noted in Chapter 12), originally was conceived not only as a way to utilize surplus labor and local materials that would otherwise go unused but also as a means to promote broader social goals, especially the reduction of the gap between city and countryside. The program was modestly successful during the Mao era. By the mid-1970s, small and mostly technologically primitive factories operated by communes and brigades employed 28 million workers, almost 10 percent of the rural labor force. It was not until the market reform period, however, that rural industry became a really dynamic force in the Chinese economy. With the encouragement of the Deng regime and with the influx of capital—from local governments, private capitalists, foreign investors, and various sorts of cooperative groupings—rural industrial enterprises grew with extraordinary rapidity, not only in numbers but also in size, diversity of output, and technological sophistication. Through much of the 1980s, the output of the TVEs grew by 35 percent per annum, and after a brief period of retrenchment at the close of the decade, high rates of growth (averaging about 30 percent per annum) again were recorded in the 1990s. By 1995, more than 125 million workers were employed in rural industries, which remained the most rapidly growing sector of a generally dynamic Chinese economy. It is the wages (however comparatively low) of these mostly younger members of peasant families who labor in the TVEs that sustains household income in much of the Chinese countryside.

The TVEs are officially classified as part of the "collective" sector of the Chinese economy, and they make up by far the largest part of what falls under that rather ambiguous designation. Yet most of the industrial enterprises in the countryside are owned and managed by private capitalists and local governments, and all perforce operate on a capitalist basis in a national and international market economy. Whether the TVEs hold the socialist potential that is sometime attributed to them is questionable—but perhaps it is not yet a closed question.[23]

The rural economic progress of the Deng era did not come about without great social and other costs—and not without creating new barriers to future progress. One of the adverse consequences of decollectivization was a marked increase in the rural birth rate in the early 1980s as the return to individual family farming made farm families want to raise more sons, so as to provide adequate labor power in the near future and to provide security for aging parents in the long term. It was an eminently rational (if also very traditional) peasant response to decollectivization and the restoration of the family farm, but not one easy to reconcile with the also eminently economically rational government policy of the one-child family, originally designed to stabilize the population at 1.2 billion by the year 2000. Forced abortions ordered by zealous government officials and female infanticide on the part of desperate peasants determined to have at least one son have been among the human sorrows caused by this clash between state and individual interests, a clash which is itself the product of contradictory state policies. In 1985 the government modified the implementation of the one-child policy, effectively allowing rural couples to have two children, thereby easing the tension between state and peasantry but jeopardizing the hope for zero population growth in the twenty-first century.

Decollectivization undermined other long-term goals and programs. The fragmentation of farming units that came with the return to family farms, especially acute in villages where lands of unequal quality were divided proportionally, made large farm machinery useless in many areas, frustrating long-standing hopes for the mechanization of Chinese agriculture. Further, as the old communes and brigades atrophied in a new market-driven society, collective funds were depleted, resulting in a contraction of welfare services for the elderly, the handicapped, and the indigent; the closing of brigade medical clinics in some areas; and a decline in the number and quality of local schools. School enrollments fell, due to the need of peasant families to keep young children at home to assist in farm work, now carried on as a family enterprise. And with the demise of the communes and the brigades, it became increasingly difficult to organize peasant labor for large-scale public works projects, such as the construction and repair of irrigation facilities and dams, a factor that aggravated the terrible floods that ravaged central and northern China in the summer of 1998.

Decollectivization has also added to China's massive environmental problems. Deforestation (and consequent flooding), for example, has become a serious problem in many regions due to the unplanned construction of new houses and the often indiscriminate felling of trees in order to build them. The boom in housing, partly due to the restoration of family farming and partly to the relative prosperity of many villages, also has contributed to reducing the amount of arable land, accelerating an alarming decline that began in 1957.[24]

The demise of collective institutions has of course undermined such collectivistic values the peasants once held, and the resulting ideological void was quickly filled by traditional customs, beliefs, superstitions, and rituals. It is ironic that "rural reform," pursued under the banner of the Four Modernizations, has revived the very "feudal" values that Deng Xiaoping and his market-reform theorists have condemned as so historically pernicious and to which they attribute many of the political evils and economic failures of the Mao era. But government leaders have been less concerned about the reappearance of old beliefs and values in the countryside than about what they describe as "extravagant" spending on traditional marriages, funerals, and festivals—for such expenditures drain the capital available for financing land improvements, the purchase of new farm equipment, and water conservation. The paucity of such long-term productive investment is one of the factors responsible for the stagnation of agricultural production since 1985 and China's increasing reliance on imported food.

The most disturbing social consequence of decollectivization has been the extraordinarily rapid growth of economic inequalities in the countryside and the creation of new rural class divisions. Inequality is hardly a novelty in rural China. But in the Mao period the greatest gaps were regional, reflecting long-standing ecological and other differences between comparatively well-off and impoverished areas of the country, whereas economic differentials within localities were rather small.[25] In the post-Mao reform era, regional inequalities have increased, especially between the coastal areas and the interior, accentuating an old prerevolutionary pattern that persisted throughout the Mao era. What is new is the emergence of ever greater and ever more visible distinctions between wealthy and poor families *within* villages, townships, and other localities, further confirming the Dengist prediction that "some will get rich first."

Those who have in fact gotten rich are a minority of the population but a still very substantial number of rural inhabitants who have been best able to take advantage of the new market mechanisms. It is a system that favors the entrepreneurially-mined, the ambitious, the physically strong, the skilled, the clever, and the families with the greatest labor power. Especially favored have been those who hold political power, or those with access to it. It was local Party cadres, overcoming such socialist ideological inhibitions as they may have had, who initially benefited most from the privatization of collective assets and who were able to contract the best lands and the most lucrative business operations for themselves, their relatives, and their friends. Rural Party officials make up the nucleus of a new rural bourgeoisie, who operate an expanding variety of profit-making enterprises. This new class includes the heads of the more successful "specialized households" who hire wage labor and operate their farms and fisheries on a capitalist basis; the owners or contractors of various service, commercial, and industrial enterprises; the professional managers and technicians who run the township and village enterprises; the local government and Party officials who manage the TVEs and are also often engaged in other legal and extra-legal money-making activities; and a new group of petty landlords who sublease contracted lands to the poorer peasants who actually till the soil. Although they are a diverse and still amorphous class, the members of the various groups who comprise the emerging rural bourgeoisie are defined by one essential characteristic: they live on the exploitation of others' labor while they themselves largely avoid manual work. In this they perpetuate that most ancient of social divisions—that between mental and manual labor—in an increasingly modern capitalist environment.

Alongside the new rural bourgeois elite resides the oldest and most populous of rural social classes, the peasantry, whose perhaps 200,000,000 working members still till the soil, now mostly on individual family farms. Differentials in income and status are enormous, ranging from prosperous "new rich peasants" (many of them favored with the government's "specialized household" designation) to the most impoverished of rural families, who are often forced to sell or mortgage their leaseholds and driven into the growing ranks of tenant farmers, wage laborers, and the unemployed.

It is noteworthy that while the majority of the Chinese people still live in the countryside, fewer and fewer are actually engaged in agricultural production. During the late Mao period, the communes had provided at least minimal security for most of the rural population, but the abolition of the commune system in the early 1980s revealed that nearly half the rural labor force of approximately 400 million was redundant. Of the 200 million farmers of working age who could no longer subsist on the land in the newly commercialized rural economy, perhaps half eventually found employment as wage laborers in the rapidly growing TVEs and other rural-based but non-agricultural enterprises. The remainder, about 100 million people (although the number fluctuates greatly depending on economic conditions), were thrust into the ranks of a new rural *lumpenproletariat*, some reduced to irregular menial labor in the countryside, others forced into criminal activities, but most eventually forming the "floating population" (*youmin*) of migrant laborers who travel to and from the cities in search of such temporary work as they can find. Living in shantytowns and working for pitiful wages, they supply much of the labor for the construction boom that has made Chinese cities appear modern and seemingly prosperous.

Decollectivization and the spread of a market economy has thus given rise to a new rural social structure, composed of four increasingly distinct and differentiated social groups: a bourgeois elite of de facto owners of various commercial and industrial enterprises, commercial farmers and landlords, local Party and government officials, and professional managers and technical personnel; a much reduced but still sizable peasantry engaged in family farming; a much expanded and rapidly growing class of wage laborers, primarily engaged in industrial work; and an underclass of migrant laborers. It is a social structure conducive to the further development of rural capitalism—and to the disappearance of the traditional peasantry.[26]

While Chinese Communist leaders promote the commercialization of the rural economy and celebrate its economic successes, they nonetheless still on occasion envision (at some unspecified time in the future) the recollectivization of agricultural production.[27] This will come about, they emphasize, not by bureaucratic decree but through the workings of "objective economic laws" and the development of production.[28] And indeed in the mid–1990s there were reports from several northern provinces of a peasant movement, apparently proceeding with the government's blessings, to partially recollectivize village property and work. Yet it is difficult to foresee a collectivistic transformation naturally issuing from a market economy that is generating such great socioeconomic differentiations and creating powerful vested interests in the present order of things. In such a polarized rural society, with much of the population now schooled in the competitive values of the market, it is most unlikely that collective farming can be reintroduced, either from above or from below, without igniting violent social conflict. It would be most ironic if a regime which so prizes social harmony, and which has condemned Maoist theories of class struggle, should have created social conditions that make real class struggles inevitable.

Urban Industry and the Commodification of Labor

As soon as the Third Plenum adjourned in December 1978, having sanctioned "adjustment by the market," the economic reformers in Deng Xiaoping's coalition presented the paramount leader with concrete proposals for the capitalist restructuring of China's huge but inefficient and technologically backward state-managed urban industrial plant. The reformers argued that the economic growth of the nation and the material well-being of the people would best be served, at least at China's current stage of development, if the production and distribution of goods were determined more by "unfettered" market forces than by central planners in Beijing. Thus the reformers proposed the decentralization of economic decision making to individual enterprises, which would operate on a profit-making basis, with nonprofitable factories allowed to fail and close, although the latter eventuality was not much emphasized. This enterprise autonomy meant that factory managers, operating within broad state guidelines, would determine production schedules, wages, and prices in accordance with changing market conditions. They would also decide how the profits of the enterprise (if any) would be utilized. Further, and most socially significant, managers would have the power to hire and fire workers in accordance with market conditions and the criterion of economic efficiency. This "smashing the iron rice bowl," as the terminology of the time had it—that is, ending the system of lifetime job security for regular state employees— would discipline a lackadaisical work force and increase labor productivity, the reformers claimed.[29]

Such, in brief, were the main features of the essentially capitalist model of urban industrial reorganization proposed in 1979. And Deng Xiaoping and other Communist leaders found it attractive, not because they found capitalism as such appealing, but rather because of the model's nationalist appeals. For the market promised economic efficiency, and that, in turn, inspired hope of a quicker route to national "wealth and power." Thus, in modified and limited form, the market model was experimentally adopted in late 1979, when the government selected several thousand enterprises to operate on a profit-making basis, as more or less autonomous capitalist units. The program was expanded in early 1980 to cover about 16 percent of the factories and other urban enterprises included in the state budget.[30]

The initial attempt at capitalist industrial restructuring proved short-lived. At the end of 1980, confronted with a host of unanticipated fiscal and social problems, the government was forced to suspend the program. Among the unintended consequences of the market-oriented policies, recently introduced in the rural areas as well as the cities, was a burst of inflation. Although the officially stated rate of price increases (about 7 percent nationwide, somewhat higher in the cities, according to probably understated official figures) was relatively modest by world standards, inflation came as a shock to a population accustomed for nearly three decades to virtually total price stability; over the 27-year Mao period, consumer price increases had averaged less than 0.5 percent per annum. Growing state budget deficits were also alarming, especially for a government that hitherto had scrupulously adhered to a balanced budget. Measures to control the deficit included sharp reductions in capital construction and the closing of inefficient factories; these remedies, in turn, aggravated the chronic problem of unemployment in the cities, now officially acknowledged to be more than 20 percent of the urban labor force.[31]

As the government grappled with inflation, unemployment, and deficits in 1980, it was also confronted by an alarming drop in the output of heavy industry. This was partly the result of overzealous efforts to correct the imbalance between producer and consumer goods production, but also in part to the new emphasis on enterprise profitability—and the fact that many essential heavy-industrial enterprises could not show a profit in a market economy. In 1981, the output of heavy industry declined by almost 5 percent according to official figures, and by more than 8 percent according to the calculations of foreign observers.[32] The government responded to the economic crisis with a policy that it called "readjustment," which reimposed strict central state controls over prices, wages, investment, and the allocation of raw materials—in effect, the reestablishment of the "command economy" in urban industry. With the central planning system restored, industrial growth resumed. In 1983, the output of heavy industry increased by 12.4 percent while light industry grew by 8.7 percent.[33] These were approximately the same rates of growth—and the same ratio between heavy and light industry—that were recorded during the late Mao era.

While the "readjustment" of the urban industrial sector was taking place in the early 1980s, the regime turned its attention to the decollectivization of agriculture in the countryside and the promotion of foreign trade and investment in the coastal areas, as we have seen. Nonetheless, the effort to bring market prescriptions to the urban economy was not entirely abandoned. At the same time that the regime was reimposing central controls over state industries, it was also encouraging the expansion of private and "collective" enterprises as well as promoting foreign-financed joint ventures in the cities and the special economic zones. Ownership and managerial patterns varied greatly in the enterprises of this rapidly expanding nonstate sector of the urban industrial economy, but they shared one essential feature: their work forces were drawn from a rapidly expanding free labor market. Wage laborers employed in urban "collective" enterprises (where employment increased by 7 million from 1981 to 1984) and in the new private sector (where employment grew from 1 to over 3 million in the early 1980s) worked for significantly lower wages than workers in state industries and enjoyed neither the job security nor the welfare benefits (such as health care and retirement pensions) guaranteed by the "iron rice bowl." Members of a "free" labor market (which is to say that they sold their labor for whatever it would fetch on the market), they could be hired or fired at the will of the managers, depending on the fluctuations of the economy. Together with the much larger numbers of wage earners being employed in the rural township and village enterprises on a contractual basis, they became members of a rapidly expanding capitalist labor market. That labor market was further expanded when many of the peasants made economically redundant by decollectivization swelled the ranks of the migrant laborers who roamed from city to city, searching for such temporary work as they could find. Thus, even though plans for comprehensive urban industrial reform had been temporarily set aside, the "iron rice bowl" already had begun to shrink in the early 1980s, partially satisfying one of the reformers' key demands.

In 1984, with industrial production stabilized and with the government emboldened by the success of the rural reforms, an ambitious new effort was undertaken to bring about the capitalist restructuring of urban industry. Deng Xiaoping personally provided the impetus for this when early in that year he embarked on a well-publicized tour of the Shenzhen special economic zone and pronounced a grand success what the official press said was the model for urban reform for the whole of China. The government's restructuring program that followed was similar to the abortive effort that had been made in 1979, save that it was now more comprehensive and pursued with greater vigor and determination.

The program consisted of three main parts. First, there was promulgated the eminently capitalist principle of enterprise profitablity. Accordingly, some 400,000 state enterprises were accorded a large measure of autonomy over wages, prices, and investment. In theory at least, they were to thrive or fail on the basis of whether they showed profits or losses in the marketplace.

Second, the 1984 reform program aimed to universalize a market in labor. Over the previous five years, China had already moved a long way toward the creation of a capitalist labor market. Now the Deng regime proposed to "smash the iron rice bowl" (to borrow the reformist rhetoric of the time) among regular workers in state factories, who in 1984 made up about 40 percent of China's industrial working class. To this "reform," however, there was intense and bitter opposition, not only among the relatively privileged workers who would have been directly affected but also from a good many veteran Communist Party officials who regarded the guarantee of lifetime job tenure as one of the great accomplishments of the Revolution. In the end, the government compromised: regular workers then employed in state factories would retain their job security and welfare guarantees but new workers would be hired on a contractual basis. A bewildering variety of contractual arrangements were worked out over the years that followed, gradually replacing the shrinking "iron rice bowl."[34]

The third part of the 1984 program was "price reform," which introduced a three-tiered price structure in place of the old system of officially-set government prices. The prices of certain key industrial products (such as steel and oil) remained fixed by the state; prices of other industrial products were allowed to fluctuate within higher and lower government-determined price ranges; and the prices of most consumer goods and agricultural products were freed from all government controls and permitted to fluctuate according to the dictates of the market.

The urban reform program, coupled with the marketization of the rural economy, ushered in five chaotic years which saw spectacular industrial growth and intense social disruption. In 1985 alone, the output of China's already huge industrial plant grew by almost 20 percent, and high rates of industrial growth, in both urban and (especially) rural areas, continued over most of the rest of the decade. Living standards in the cities rose markedly, if very inequitably, throughout the 1980s, although it has been suggested that this resulted more from the agricultural successes of the early 1980s (and the relatively low cost of foodstuffs and other products of rural origin) than from any improvement in the efficiency of urban industry.[35] However that may be, average real wages of urban workers more than doubled during the first decade of the Deng regime. There were significant improvements in diet, especially in increased consumption of meat, and also in the quantity and quality of clothing. The ownership of household goods—television sets, sewing machines, and refrigerators—grew at spectacular rates. And per capita housing space nearly doubled in the cities, whose landscapes were being transformed by a seemingly permanent boom in construction.

But this material progress, while real enough and certainly heartily welcomed by the Chinese people, was accompanied by social and psychic devastation of epic proportions. The boom-and-bust cycles (officially known as "overheating" and "retrenchment") came quickly and sharply, bringing hardship and insecurity to much of the urban working population. Adding to the hardships, especially in the "boom" phases of the cycles, were bursts of inflation, which became chronic after the partial implementation of "price reform" in 1985. By the early months of 1989, inflation had soared to an officially acknowledged national rate of 25 percent per annum, although it was considerably higher in Beijing and other large cities. A working population buffeted by unruly market forces was shocked by the growth of obvious and grotesque inequalities in economic and social life. Between a monied elite of entrepreneurs and bureaucrats who profited lavishly from the "free market" (and who were increasingly uninhibited in ostentatious displays of their new wealth in cities that were hastily spawning luxury boutiques and nightclubs), and a pauperized *lumpenproletariat* of migrant day laborers who lived in shantytowns, there was opened as wide a gulf between rich and poor as existed in any of the great cities of the capitalist world. And citizens were appalled and angered by the sudden pervasiveness of bureaucratic corruption, by officials and cadres, high and low, who were enriching themselves (and their families and friends) by using their political influence to manipulate the new market mechanisms.

. . .

In the late 1980s the economy passed through a series of rather quick boom-and-bust cycles, and the urban population experienced the painful and unsettling vicissitudes typical of an early capitalist regime. Growth rates in industrial production remained high, but so did inflation and government budgetary deficits. By the end of the first decade of the Deng regime—even though "socialist market economy" was its official designation—few could seriously doubt that an essentially capitalist economy had been fashioned in the cities of China. A free market in labor had been created, and only a shrinking minority of workers clung to the "iron rice bowl"; administrative controls had been removed over the prices of many commodities, which now fluctuated in accordance with market conditions; and most economic units operated in accordance with the capitalist principle of enterprise profitability. All that was lacking was formal, legal private ownership of property. But if China had become essentially capitalist, it was a special kind of capitalism, whose distinctive features should briefly be outlined.

Bureaucratic Capitalism

Bureaucratic capitalism, that is, the employment of political power and influence for private gain through capitalist methods of economic activity, is not an uncommon phenomenon in history, having appeared in various forms in many societies in both ancient and modern times. It certainly has not been uncommon in Chinese history. An alliance between powerful officials and a dependent bourgeoisie in profit-making commercial and industrial activities was a prominent feature of Chinese society and economy throughout the more than 2000-year imperial era.[36] And in modern times, the subordination of the bourgeoisie to high officials of the Guomindang regime of Chiang Kai-shek in the 1930s and 1940s is one of the classic examples of bureaucratic capitalism in modern world history.[37]

The origins of bureaucratic capitalism in Communist China are quite unusual, however. In the case of the People's Republic, bureaucratic capitalism emerged only after a lengthy quasi-socialist period, which had eliminated the Chinese bourgeoisie as a functioning social group. By the mid-1950s, as we saw in chapter 6, what remained of the Chinese bourgeoisie (the so-called "national bourgeoisie" in the terminology of the time) had been bought out by the Communist state, and the remnants of that class lingered on only as a small group of aging pensioners collecting modest dividends on noninheritable state bonds. The dwindling members of this dying social class were too few and too elderly to take up the bourgeois functions that Deng Xiaoping's market policies demanded. It thus fell to the Communist state to create the capitalist class that was necessary for the functioning of a market economy. In a country in which the bourgeoisie had been eliminated, and capitalist activities long distrusted and suppressed, the most likely candidates for recruitment into such a new class were the cadres of the bloated Communist bureaucracy.

Many, probably most, Communist bureaucrats were initially hostile to, or at best ambivalent about, Deng's market policies. The devolution of economic control from state and collective organizations to families and private entrepreneurs seemed to threaten bureaucratic power, status, and income. Nor could a market economy easily be reconciled with the socialist values and goals Communist leaders habitually proclaimed and many no doubt still cherished. It was a rare instance where bureaucratic self-interest and socialist principles appeared to coincide.

Nonetheless, whatever their initial reservations, the bureaucrats performed their duty, carrying out Party and central government policies under the banners of "Reform" and the "Four Modernizations." And it was not long before officials and cadres discovered that they were in uniquely favorable political positions to personally profit from the new opportunities the market offered—in effect, to take the place of an absent bourgeoisie. A good many hastened to fill the social void. The lead was taken by the middle-aged sons and daughters of the highest leaders of the Communist Party, including the children of Deng Xiaoping and Premier Zhao Ziyang, who used their political influence to play lucrative compradore roles. Operating in the coastal cities and the special economic zones, they brought together foreign capital and the Chinese market, receiving handsome commissions for arranging deals between foreign firms and state trading organizations. Beginning as influence peddlers, they soon established their own import-export companies, and from there some of their number evolved into international financiers and investment bankers, sometimes establishing ties with huge capitalist conglomerates in Hong Kong and elsewhere. Some of the wealth that they acquired by virtue of the political power and influence of their families no doubt went into luxury living and overseas investments, but most of the capital they accumulated appears to have been profitably invested in China itself, helping to finance the extraordinary growth of the Chinese economy in the late 1980s and the 1990s. The "crown princes and princesses," as the entrepreneurially-minded and avaricious sons and daughters of the Communist ruling elite were called, became the most prominent symbols of the official profiteering and corruption that overwhelmed the Communist bureaucracy in the late 1980s—and provoked the profound popular disgust with the Deng regime that found political expression in the Democracy Movement of 1989.

Local rural Party cadres also discovered that their political power and influence was useful in acquiring private wealth. Although most cadres initially opposed agricultural decollectivization—partly because of ideological conviction, partly because they feared loss of power and income—many soon came to appreciate the virtues of Deng's program to commercialize the countryside. For with the breakup of collective institutions and the establishment of the household responsibility system, local officials found themselves with the power to determine who would benefit from the contracting of land and the privatization of collective assets and functions. Thus, in much of the countryside, the best lands and the rights to operate the most lucrative businesses were acquired by Party cadres, their relatives, and their friends.[38] They often became the heads, or the patrons, of the well-to-do "specialized households"; they acquired lands and materials to build large and sometimes luxurious houses; and they (and their relatives and associates) enjoyed enormous advantages in the establishment and operation of business and industrial enterprises. In short, Party officials and their relatives became the most prominent members of the new rural bourgeoisie.

As a new rural bourgeoisie with a strong bureaucratic component was establishing itself in the countryside in the early 1980s, the government's market-oriented policies were also proving favorable to the pecuniary and entrepreneurial ambitions of urban bureaucrats, particularly after the resumption of industrial reform in 1984. Especially lucrative opportunities were offered by price reform, which allowed the prices of many commodities to fluctuate according to market conditions—but which retained a parallel system of state prices. This, in effect, legalized the black market and greatly expanded the most common and simplest form of bureaucratic enrichment—schemes whereby well-placed officials bought goods and materials at low state prices and sold them for several times the purchase price on the free market.

Urban bureaucrats also profited from government efforts, pursued with renewed vigor after 1984, to encourage the establishment of private businesses operated by individuals and households. Although it was not common until the 1990s for officials themselves to become private capitalists—to *xia hai,* or "plunge into the sea," as it came to be called—in the 1980s it was not infrequently the case that officials became patrons of business ventures formally run by their relatives and friends. Often initially funded by capital obtained through official profiteering, bureaucratic patronage was good for business and a further source of bureaucratic enrichment. In some cases de facto bureaucratic ownership of profit-making enterprises was disguised by having the enterprises officially designated as "collectives." And Premier Zhao Ziyang's "coastal strategy," which loosened central financial controls over local governments after 1985 and encouraged regionalism, vastly expanded opportunities for official profiteering and the growth of bureaucratic capitalism, especially along the southern coast and in the Yangzi delta.[39]

A new urban bourgeoisie thus began to take shape in the mid-1980s, a class which in addition to bureaucratic capitalists included the rapidly growing number of large and small private entrepreneurs, and the technical and managerial personnel of state, private, and "collective" enterprises. It was, and remains, a rather amorphous group whose members have little consciousness of their common interests as a class. Nonetheless, they are socially and economically distinct from the great majority of the urban population—wage workers in factories and commercial enterprises, lower and mid-level government personnel, small tradespeople, and migrant laborers. But if the new bourgeoisie has not yet acquired a class consciousness, its members certainly have acquired an appetite for the universal bourgeois pleasures. If nothing else, their distinctiveness as a class in Chinese society expresses itself in a taste for luxury—and the means to satisfy those tastes in expensive restaurants and nightclubs, in new and spacious apartments, and in exclusive boutiques, making China known in international trade circles as the world's most rapidly growing market for luxury goods. And the contrast between wealth and poverty in Chinese cities today is probably as great, and certainly as glaring, as it is in the metropolitan areas of most Western and Third World capitalist countries. The Dengist prediction that "some must get rich first" has come to pass with a vengeance.

It is one of the pecularities of bureaucratic capitalism in the People's Republic that not only do individual officials, and groups of officials, use their political influence to operate or sponsor private profit-making businesses, but entire bureaucracies have plunged, willingly or not, into the marketplace, where they perforce function as capitalist enterprises. With their budgets slashed by central authorities, state agencies from elementary schools to secret police agencies attempt to make up budgetary shortfalls by operating a bewildering variety of businesses—from small retail shops to large factories manufacturing goods for export, from tiny neighborhood restaurants to huge luxury hotels catering to foreign visitors and tourists. The most spectacular example of this curious phenomenon is the People's Liberation Army, now a major power in international trade and finance, which, in addition to the manufacture and export of armanents, operates through its many civilian subsidiaries an assortment of more than 20,000 profit-making industrial, commercial, and service enterprises.[40]

. . .

What are the political implications of the market economy that has grown so rapidly in China during the era of Deng Xiaoping? It is of course widely assumed in the West that a capitalist economy and political democracy are more or less inseparable, that free markets yield not only economic miracles but political freedom as well. As the distinguished British political economist and China scholar, the late Gordon White, once predicted, the long-term results of post-Mao China's market reforms would be processes of "socio-economic pluralism and political democratization."[41] Yet one need not inquire far into the modern historical record to know that the relationship between capitalism and democracy is an extraordinarily complex and tortured one,[42] and that capitalism has proved compatible with a wide variety of political regimes, not excluding fascism. Indeed, *late* capitalist industrialization tends to follow the sociopolitical route that Barrington Moore termed "conservative modernization," for which Meiji Japan and Bismarckian Germany are the prototypes, and has proved highly conducive to fascist political outcomes.[43]

Nonetheless, it thus far remains the historical case that a vigorous and independent bourgeoisie, especially one whose interests are in conflict with the existing political order, has been an indispensable element in the development of parliamentary democracy. "No bourgeoisie, no democracy," as Moore sums it up.[44] If that in fact is the general lesson that modern history teaches, it is not a lesson that augurs well for Chinese democracy. For the contemporary Chinese bourgeoisie bears little resemblance to the classic early bourgeois classes of the Western countries. The "post-Maoist" Chinese bourgeoisie, while certainly a vigorous class, is clearly not an independent one. Rather, it is a class that was created by the Communist state. It is a class that is in large measure composed of Communist officials, their relatives and their friends who were politically well-positioned to take advantage of the new opportunities the market offered. Further, it is a class that is dependent on the Communist state for its economic functioning. And it is a class whose members look to the state for political protection from the working classes and from free trade unions. In short, it is not a class with great democratic potential. Rather, serious challenges to the dictatorship of the Chinese Communist Party will likely come from the victims, not the beneficiaries, of China's state-sponsored capitalism. This is a point that will be further pursued in the following chapter, which traces the political history of China from the early 1980s to the close of the Deng era in the mid-1990s.

NOTES

1. Deng Xiaoping, "On the Reform of the System of Party and State Leadership" (August 18, 1980), *Selected Works of Deng Xiaoping* (Beijing: Foreign Languages Press, 1984), p. 308.
2. On the social and ideological history of the market in its nineteenth-century English homeland, see Karl Polanyi's classic study, *The Great Transformation* (Boston: Beacon Press, 1957).
3. Carl Riskin, "Market, Maoism and Economic Reform in China," in Mark Selden and Victor Lippit, eds., *The Transition to Socialism in China* (Armonk, N.Y.: M. E. Sharpe, 1982), p. 318.
4. Quoted, for example, by Hu Ch'iao-mu [Hu Qiaomu], "Observe Economic Laws, Speed Up the Four Modernizations," *Peking Review,* November 10, 1978, pp. 10–11.
5. "Resolution of the Eighth National Congress of the Communist Party of China on the Political Report of the Central Committee" (September 27, 1956), *Eighth National Congress of the Communist Party of China, Vol. I: Documents* (Peking: Foreign Languages Press, 1956), p. 116.
6. See Chapter 24 for a brief discussion of the notion of the "primary stage of socialism."
7. Riskin, *China's Political Economy,* Table 14.1, p. 355.
8. Xue Muqiao in a July 1979 radio interview. Cited in Roger Garside, *Coming Alive,* p. 358.
9. See Mark Selden, *The Yenan Way in Revolutionary China* (Cambridge, MA: Harvard University Press, 1971).
10. On the parallel between the People's Republic and Prussia, see Wolfgang Deckers' insightful article, "Mao Zedong and Friedrich List on De-Linking," *Journal of Contemporary Asia,* Vol. 24, No. 2 (1994), pp. 217–26.
11. Riskin, *China's Political Economy,* Table 9.1 "China's foreign trade, 1965–1975," p. 208.
12. For an excellent and succinct summary of the origins and early history of the special economic zones, see Harry Harding, *China's Second Revolution* (Washington, D.C.: Brookings Institution, 1987), pp. 163–171. For a superb critique of the zones, see Suzanne Pepper, "China's Special Economic Zones: The Current Rescue Bid for a Faltering Experiment," 1986 University Field Staff Report reprinted in *Bulletin of Concerned Asian Scholars,* Vol. 20, No. 3 (1988), pp. 1–20.
13. *China Daily News,* April 21, 1989, p. 1 and January 19, 1995, p. 1. In 1996, foreign investment increased to U.S. $40 billion, and that figure was equaled in 1997. *The Wall Street Journal,* December 15, 1997, p. A10.
14. In 1995, China's per capita foreign debt was about US $1000. In comparison, the foreign debt of Mexico was approximately US $17,000 per capita, Brazil's US $9000 per capita,

Hungary US $31,000, and Poland US $11,000. The World Bank, *Trends in Developing Economies, 1996* (Washington, D.C.: The World Bank, 1997). Figures calculated from tables on pp. 60, 109–110, 236–237, 340–341, and 430–431.

15. Characterizing the new Chinese infatuation with things Western as an "unhealthy psychology," Simon Leys, one of the severest critics of Maoism, concluded: "It is sad to see one of the most positive achievements of the [Maoist] regime suffer such a setback." *The New York Times,* op-ed article, January 3, 1979.

16. On the actual history of Dazhai in the Mao and post-Mao eras, there are many excellent first-hand studies. See, for example, Tang Tsou, Mark Blecher, and Mitchell Meisner, "Organization, Growth and Equality in Xiyang County," *Modern China,* April 1979, pp. 139–86; Tang Tsou, et al., "National Agricultural Policy: The Dazhai Model and Local Change in the Post-Mao Era," in Mark Selden and Victor Lippit, eds., *The Transition to Socialism in China,* pp. 266–299; Tang Tsou, et al., "The Responsibility System in Agriculture: Its Implementation in Xiyang and Dazhai," *Modern China,* January 1982, pp. 41–103; and William Hinton, *Shenfan* (New York: Random House, 1983).

17. Carl Riskin, *China's Political Economy,* p. 288.

18. All limits on the number of workers a private enterprise could employ were removed in 1987.

19. See, for example, Anita Chan, Richard Madsen, and Jonathan Unger, *Chen Village: The Recent History of a Peasant Community in Mao's China* (Berkeley: University of California Press, 1984), pp. 265–84.

20. On decommunization, see Vivienne Shue's insightful analysis in "The Fate of the Commune," *Modern China,* 10, No. 3 (July 1984), pp. 259–283.

21. Kenneth R. Walker, "Chinese Agriculture During the Period of Readjustment, 1979–83," *The China Quarterly,* No. 100 (December 1984), Table A1, p. 803; Carl Riskin, *China's Political Economy,* Table 12.1, p. 291.

22. As several observers have pointed out, the upsurge in agricultural production in the late 1970s and early 1980s would not have been possible without the vast irrigation, flood control, and technological infrastructure built during the Mao period. See Carl Riskin, *China's Political Economy,* p. 296; William Hinton, "A Trip to Fengyang County: Investigating China's New Family Contract System," *Monthly Review,* 35, No. 6 (November 1983), p. 14.

23. See the writings of MIT professor Cui Zhiyuan, one of the most articulate and convincing advocates of the socialist potential of the TVEs—for example, his "China's Rural Industrialization: Flexible Specialization, Moebius-Strip Ownership and Proudhonian Socialism" (unpublished University of Chicago research paper). For a fascinating study of recent cooperative and democratic developments in rural Henan province, see Cui Zhiyuan, et al., *Transformation from the Pressurized System to The Democratic System of Cooperation: Reform of Political System at the County and Township Levels* (Beijing: Central Compilation and Translation Press, 1998).

24. According to official statistics, arable land declined 15 percent between 1949 and 1992. Some foreign observers calculate an ever greater decline. See Vaclav Smil, *China's Environmental Crisis* (Armonk, N.Y.: M. E. Sharpe, 1993), pp. 57–58.

25. On egalitarianism and inequality in the late Mao period, see Riskin, *China's Political Economy,* pp. 223–256.

26. In this China joins a worldwide trend. On "the death of the peasantry," see Eric Hobsbawm's interesting discussion in *The Age of Extremes: A History of the World, 1914–1991* (New York: Pantheon Books, 1994), pp. 289–95.

27. As predicted by Party General Secretary Hu Yaobang, for example, in his report to the Twelfth Party Congress in 1982. *Beijing Review,* 25, No. 37 (September 13, 1982), pp. 18–19.

28. For example, see Deng Xiaoping, "Build Socialism with Chinese Characteristics," *Fundamental Issues in Present-Day China* (Beijing: Foreign Languages Press, 1987), pp. 53–58.

29. See, for example, Joseph Kahn's report in *The Wall Street Journal,* March 10, 1995, pp. AI and A4.

30. For detailed information on this initial effort at industrial restructuring, see Edmund Lee, "Economic Reform in Post-Mao China: An Insider's View," *Bulletin of Concerned Asian Scholars,* Vol. 15, No. 1 (January-February 1983), pp. 16–25; and Robert Michael Field, "Changes in Chinese Industry since 1978," *The China Quarterly,* No. 100 (December 1984), pp. 742–761.

31. The number of unemployed workers in the cities in 1979 was estimated to be 20,000,000 in a speech delivered by Vice-Premier Li Xiannian, the veteran Red Army commander and economic planner. The speech was published in the Hong Kong newspaper *Ming Bao* on June 14, 1979. While urban unemployment has been a chronic, if disguised, problem since the 1950s, it was exacerbated in the post-Mao years by the return of "rusticated" youth to the cities and the closing of inefficient factories.

32. Dorothy J. Solinger, "The Fifth National People's Congress and the Process of Policy Making: Reform, Readjustment, and Opposition," *Asian Survey,* Vol. XXII, No. 12 (December 1982), p. 1263.

33. State Statistical Bureau, "Communique on the Fulfillment of China's 1983 National Economic Plan," *Beijing Review,* Vol. 26, No. 14 (April 4, 1983), pp. 20–24.

34. For an enlightening discussion of the complex forms of contractual industrial labor in the Mao and Deng eras, as observed in a county in Hebei province, see the splendid study by Marc Blecher and Vivienne Shue, *Tethered Deer: Government and Economy in a Chinese County* (Stanford, CA: Stanford University Press, 1996), pp. 109–121.

35. As argued by Carl Riskin in *China's Political Economy,* p. 372.

36. For perceptive commentary on the operation of bureaucratic capitalism in traditional China, see Etienne Balazs, *Chinese Civilization and Bureaucracy* (New Haven: Yale University Press, 1964), 1–4; and Frederic Wakeman, *The Fall of Imperial China* (New York: The Free Press, 1975), chapter 3.

37. The literature on Guomindang bureaucratic capitalism is vast. For a sampling of English-language works, see Lloyd E. Eastman, *The Abortive Revolution: China under Nationalist Rule, 1927–1937* (Cambridge, Mass.: Harvard University Press, 1974); Lloyd E. Eastman, *Seeds of Destruction: Nationalist China in War and Revolution 1937–1949* (Stanford: Stanford University Press, 1984); Parks M. Coble, *The Shanghai Capitalists and the Nationalist Government, 1927–1937* (Cambridge, Mass.: Council on East Asian Studies, Harvard University, 1980); and Marie-Claire Bergere, *The Golden Age of the Chinese Bourgeoisie, 1911–1937* (Cambridge: Cambridge University Press, 1989).

38. A striking example of this is related in the highly regarded study of a village in Guangdong province, where the local Party Secretary got the lion's share of the best land and equipment parceled out during decollectivization. See the Epilogue to Anita Chan, Richard Madsen, and Jonathan Unger, *Chen Village: The Recent History of a Peasant Community in Mao's China* (Berkeley: University of California Press, 1984), pp. 265–84.

39. On Zhao Ziyang's premiership, and his brief tenure as Party General Secretary, see chapter 24.

40. See, for example, Eric Hyer, "China's Arms Merchants: Profits in Command," *The China Quarterly,* No. 132 (December 1992), pp. 1101–1118. In July 1998, Party General Secretary Jiang Zemin ordered the PLA to relinquish its businesses. There was considerable skepticism

about whether the order would be carried out. See Seth Faison, "China Moving to Untie Its Military-Industrial Knot," *The New York Times,* July 28, 1998, p. A1.

41. Gordon White, *Riding the Tiger: The Politics of Economic Reform in Post-Mao China* (Stanford, CA: Stanford University Press, 1993), p. 256.

42. For a most insightful analysis of the complexities, see Ellen Meiksins Wood, *Democracy Against Capitalism* (Cambridge: Cambridge University Press, 1995).

43. Barrington Moore, *Social Origins of Dictatorship and Democracy* (Boston: Beacon, 1966), especially chapters 5 and 8.

44. *Ibid.,* p. 418.

24

The Struggle for Democracy

F ROM THE TIME of his triumph at the Third Plenum in December 1978 until early 1994, when the ninety-year-old patriarch had become too feeble to appear in public, Deng Xiaoping was unchallenged as China's "paramount leader." He was, to put it plainly, the dictator of a Leninist Party-state and the arbiter of virtually all important decisions.

Yet during the fifteen years that he ruled China, Deng, unlike his predecessors, never assumed the high political titles that corresponded to his real power. Instead, he selected his proteges to occupy the highest offices of Party and state. Of these, the first, and certainly the most appealing was Hu Yaobang (1915–1989), who had joined the Red Army in 1930, at the age of fifteen. A survivor of the Long March, Hu became politically associated with Deng Xiaoping during the long civil war, serving as a political commissar under Deng's command in the Communist Second Field Army. After 1949, his political fortunes fluctuated along with those of his mentor. In 1980 when Mao Zedong's first successor, Hua Guofeng, was forced to relinquish his power (and then his titles), Deng selected Hu Yaobang to fill the revived post of General Secretary, the formal head of the Chinese Communist Party. The post of Party Chairman, so long occupied by Mao Zedong (and so briefly by Hua Guofeng), was abolished.

Hu Yaobang was one of those rare leaders of a Leninist party who had come to champion democratic values and procedures. Drawn to the more libertarian aspects of the Marxist tradition, he played a key role during the early Deng era in bringing about the "rehabilitations" of intellectuals and officials who had been victims of the political witch-hunts of the Mao period, especially the antirightist campaign and the Cultural Revolution. Although perforce constrained by Deng Xiaoping's policies and preferences, he did what he could to protect intellectuals from the paramount leader's periodic (but short-lived) campaigns against "bourgeois liberalization," especially in the 1983–84 campaign to combat "spiritual pollution." And Hu Yaobang was the silent patron of the *People's Daily* during that brief period in the early 1980s when the official Party newspaper promoted democratic reform and exposed official corruption—largely through the efforts of such democratic Marxists as Wang Roshui, the managing editor, and Liu Binyin, the famed investigative journalist. If these efforts did not necessarily win Hu Yaobang the mass popularity he sought, it did gain him the genuine respect of many intellectuals and students.

Less widely respected, at least until fortuitous circumstances made him into something of a martyr at the end of his political career, was another of Deng Xiaoping's disciples, Zhao Ziyang (1919–). The son of a Hunanese landlord, Zhao joined the Communist movement in the mid–1930s, when still a teenager, and served as a political cadre with the Red Army during the last decade of the civil war. As was common among the more able members of the revolutionary generation, Zhao rose rapidly in the postrevolutionary bureaucratic hierarchy after 1949, only to be ousted during the Cultural Revolution. But in 1972, when Mao was rebuilding the Party he had shattered during the Cultural Revolution, Zhao was restored to his post as Party Secretary for Guangdong province, where he cautiously assisted the young democratic activists known by the acronym "Li-Yi-Zhe."[1] However, it was not Zhao's cautious patronage of youthful democrats but rather the innovative market-reform policies he pursued as head of Sichuan province in the late 1970s that brought him to Deng Xiaoping's attention. In 1980, Deng elevated Zhao Ziyang to the Party Politburo in Beijing and installed him as Premier of the State Council, the office so long occupied by Zhou Enlai. From that lofty position, Zhao established himself as the most ardent and effective promoter of Deng's policies for the capitalist restructuring of agriculture and industry, and especially for the "opening" of China to foreign trade and investment.

By 1985 China was experiencing both the economic dynamism and the social destructiveness of a market economy. Industry, commerce, and foreign trade were booming in the expansionist phase of the "boom-and-bust" cycle that is typical of an early capitalist economy. In 1985 alone, industrial production increased by an astonishing 20 percent. But at the same time much of the population began to feel some of the more painful effects of capitalist development. In Beijing and other major cities, bursts of inflation increased the cost of basic necessities by 30 percent in the early months of 1985, depressing the living standards of the less affluent sectors of the urban population, especially factory workers and lower-level government employees. Moreover, with the rapidly increasing volume of money and goods, bureaucratic corruption grew in scope and scale—and public consciousness of official profiteering grew even more rapidly, spurred by several spectacular financial scandals.[2] Further, as noted earlier, there was a sharp and unanticipated drop in grain production in 1985 as many farmers gave up the unrewarding business of growing grain in favor of the cultivation of relatively lucrative specialized crops in an increasingly commercialized rural economy. The fall in grain output, perhaps more psychologically and politically than economically significant, sent shock waves throughout Chinese society, contributing to the growing unease and restlessness that marked the remainder of the decade. Indeed, many Chinese look back to the year 1985 as the time when the hope and optimism of the early Deng era gave way to growing doubt and pessimism.[3] And it was the time that Deng Xiaoping's personal popularity began to decline—so much so that by the early months of 1989 the paramount leader, who had enjoyed such great prestige at the beginning of the reform period, had become an object of ridicule and scorn in the cities.[4]

Opposition to the pace and social effects of marketization was reflected in splits in the Communist leadership. The divisions were particularly apparent in the tension between Deng Xiaoping and the veteran economic planner Chen Yun, who favored only a supplementary role for market forces. Chen had become the principal spokesman for those sectors of the bureaucracy that had a stake in maintaining state industry and the system of central planning. In any event, the increasingly chaotic economic situation—an "overheated" economy, in the terminology of the day—forced the government to impose austerity measures in late 1985, resulting in closed factories and unemployed workers.

Nonetheless Deng, and especially Premier Zhao Ziyang, pushed ahead with their program of capitalist restructuring. In 1986, in what was soon to be known as his "coastal strategy," Zhao promoted foreign trade and investment in China's most economically advanced areas along the Pacific, from Manchuria and Shandong in the north to Guangdong in the south. He also called for the expansion of the special economic zones. Factories and other economic enterprises were enjoined to operate as independent units responsible for their own profits and losses; in effect, they were to conduct their businesses in accordance with the capitalist principle of profit maximization. And there was a renewed emphasis on doing away with the system of job security popularly known as the "iron rice bowl," thus creating a more fully capitalist labor market. Indeed some of the more ardent reformers associated with Zhao lauded the virtues of a "reserve army of labor," that is, a large mass of unemployed workers who could be hired cheaply and fired quickly.

. . .

In the history of the Deng era, as had been the case during the Mao years, periods of relative intellectual and political liberalization alternated in cyclical fashion with periods of repression. In the spring of 1986, presumably to commemorate the thirtieth anniversary of Mao's "Hundred Flowers" policy, Deng Xiaoping inaugurated a period of political relaxation, encouraging ideological flexibility and stressing the need for "political reform." Leading Marxist intellectuals responded by emphasizing the nondogmatic character of original Marxism, arguing that Marxism was based on the assumption that the theory would be in a process of constant change as it interacted with changing social realities. Much was heard about Marx's concept of alienation, which had been revived in the early 1980s as a tool to critically analyze postrevolutionary Chinese society and politics—until discussion of alienation was suppressed by the Party's campaign against "spiritual pollution." In the course of the suppression, Wang Ruoshui, the best known of the "alienation school" theorists, was dismissed from his post as managing editor of the *People's Daily.* In the summer of 1986, Wang Ruoshui was restored to public prominence when his treatise "On the Marxist Philosophy of Man" was published in a Shanghai newspaper. Here, as in his writings during the earlier alienation debate, Wang stressed the democratic and humanitarian strains in the Marxist tradition.

Deng Xiaoping's call for "political reform" received concrete, if very limited, expression in November 1986 when the National People's Congress promulgated an electoral law for selecting delegates to local people's congresses. The first test of the electoral law, and of the democratic intentions of the Dengist regime, came on the campus of the University of Science and Technology in the provincial capital of Hefei.

The University of Science and Technology, a highly prestigious institution, had been moved during the Cultural Revolution from Beijing to the relative tranquility of Hefei (the capital of Anhui province), where it remained in the post-Mao years, enrolling an elite group of students, mostly the offspring of high officials and prominent intellectuals. On December 5, 1986, 3,000 students demonstrated to protest the lack of any real choice in forthcoming local elections. The student calls for democracy won the vigorous support of university vice-president Fang Lizhi, the well-known astrophysicist, and the covert support of various intellectuals associated with Party General Secretary Hu Yaobang. Other issues soon became involved in the continuing demonstrations, including nationalist resentments against Japan, which burst forth on the anniversary of the famous "December Ninth Movement" of 1935, when an earlier generation of students had taken the lead in protesting the failure of the Chiang Kai-shek regime to oppose Japanese aggression.[5]

The 1986 student pro-democracy demonstrations quickly spread from Hefei to some dozen cities in the Yangzi valley, culminating in Shanghai where 50,000 protesters filled People's Park in the city center on December 20, following minor clashes with the police. By this time, Deng Xiaoping and the mostly retired but still influential Party elders who surrounded him were determined to bring the demonstrations to an end. The students had begun to attract the support of workers (albeit in small numbers) in Shanghai and elsewhere; they appeared to have ties to some of the democratic Marxists in Hu Yaobang's camp; and the whole movement was escalating beyond the organizational control of the Communist Party, indeed in opposition to it. Drawing strained parallels with the Cultural Revolution, and raising the specter of "chaos," the student movement was condemned in official publications; municipal authorities were ordered to prevent further demonstrations. Under the threat of government repression, and with the beginning of semester exams, the student movement faded away early in January 1987.

Nonetheless, there were reprisals. Although the relatively few students who had been arrested were released—hoodwinked by bourgeois intellectuals, it was said—many of the workers who had been jailed during the demonstrations remained in prison on various charges, including "counter-revolution." A new campaign against "bourgeois liberalization" was launched against intellectuals, the third such witch-hunt of the Deng era. Among the victims were Fang Lizhi, who was expelled from the Communist Party and dismissed from his post as vice-president of the University of Science and Technology. Another was Liu Binyan, the investigative journalist whose exposés of official corruption had earned him the enmity of Party bureaucrats. Liu was removed from the staff of the *People's Daily,* and also, for the second time, expelled from the Party.[6]

But the most prominent casualty of the repression was Hu Yaobang, who was ousted from his post as General Secretary of the Communist Party in January 1987. Deng Xiaoping had decided months earlier to remove Hu as Party head, in part because Hu's efforts to curb corruption among the children of senior Party leaders and his close ties to democratic intellectuals had angered Party elders. The purge was to be carried out in accordance with formal Party rules at the Thirteenth Party Congress, scheduled to convene in the autumn of 1987. But the timetable was moved up, and the procedure became irregular in response to the student protests of the winter of 1986–87; Hu Yaobang was forced to accept responsibility for the disturbance, blamed for insufficient vigiliance in combating "bourgeois liberalization." The decision to remove Hu, announced as an action of the Party Politburo, which in fact never convened, was actually made at an informal meeting of Deng Xiaoping and a group of Party elders, later dubbed "the Gang of Old." The ambitious Premier Zhao Ziyang probably participated in the meeting, although Zhao later denied that he was involved in the ouster of Hu Yaobang. Zhao, in any event, was the political beneficiary. He was named to succeed Hu Yaobang as acting General Secretary of the CCP in late January 1987, and his position was formalized at the Thirteenth Party Congress in the autumn of that year. Hu Yaobang was allowed to retain his seat on the Politburo, and also on its six-member Standing Committee, but he was shorn of power and influence. Li Peng, a Soviet-trained engineer who easily accommodated himself to the interests and the style of the established Party-state bureaucracy, was named to fill the premiership that Zhao Ziyang had vacated. A technocrat who was an implementer rather than a formulator of policy, Li Peng was ideally suited to faithfully carry out Deng Xiaoping's orders.

. . .

The pace of capitalist development accelerated during Zhao Ziyang's stewardship of the Chinese Communist Party. Under Zhao's "coastal strategy," designed to promote an export-oriented economy, foreign trade flourished and favorable conditions were created for foreign investors. New vigor was brought to the eminently capitalist tasks of creating markets for labor and land. And "price reform" was further pursued, with the prices of an increasing number of commodities left to the determination of the market. All of these developments—the influx of vast sums of foreign capital, the growth of a real estate market, and commodity prices left to easily manipulated "market forces"—encouraged official profiteering and created vast new opportunities for bureaucratic enrichment.

Yet Zhao Ziyang still felt the need to claim a socialist lineage. Thus, an economic system that was rapidly on its way to becoming capitalist, as was clear to all, was officially called "socialism with Chinese characteristics." Multitudes of intellectuals associated with Zhao and Deng were brought forth to construct a Marxian ideological rationale for the regime's market policies. They drew upon the rather prominent strands in the original writings of Marx that celebrated the economic dynamism of capitalism and its historical progressiveness. They repeated Deng Xiaoping's celebrated 1956 thesis that the main contradiction in Chinese society was between its "advanced socialist system" and "backward productive forces," a formula that sanctioned the most rapid possible route to modern economic development by any means available without regard to immediate social consequences. And they invented for Zhao Ziyang's use the theory of the "primary stage of socialism," the main ideological construct of the time.

The notion of the "primary stage of socialism" held that China was already essentially a socialist society by virtue of the predominance of "public ownership" of the means of production and a system of "payment according to work." Both of these presumably socialist principles were of course fictitious, and were now even further removed from reality than they had been in the Mao period. According to the Dengist definition, China was socialist—but still immaturely socialist due to the nation's continuing economic backwardness. Only with the growth of modern productive forces to a sufficiently high level would a fully developed socialism flower. This, however, would take time, indeed the better part of a century.[7] In the meantime, all energies were to be devoted to the task of economic modernization, pure and simple, by the most efficient means possible.

The theory of the "primary stage of socialism" served as an ideological rationale for capitalist borrowing. It was assumed, not unreasonably, that a market economy, under favorable political and international conditions, offered the best chance for rapid economic modernization—and thus was the most efficacious way to establish the necessary material foundations for a developed socialist society. However, the arrival of that "developed" socialism was set so far in the future that it could not easily be related to the efforts of those who lived in the present. Socialism, the task and destination of generations not yet born, thus became unimaginable and irrelevant to those who lived in the here and now. Moreover, in the process of postponing almost indefinitely the arrival of the good society, the very definition of socialism became meaningless, and the means and ends of socialism were hopelessly confused. As originally conceived, the means of modern economic development were to serve eventual socialist ends, but as time went on socialism itself was defined as economic progress, pure and simple. Deng Xiaoping, the paramount leader, was the principal source of this confusion. One of his final comments, made in 1992, summed up his thoughts about socialism over the years: "Socialism's real nature is to liberate the productive forces, and the ultimate goal of socialism is to achieve common prosperity."[8] These were laudable sentiments, to be sure, but one might well use the same words to characterize the "real nature" of capitalism.

On other occasions, Communist leaders simply equated socialism with the political dominance of the Chinese Communist Party, presumably on the theory that the Party was the one institution that guaranteed the development of socialism and the eventual arrival of communism, whatever social detours might be necessary along the way. Such were the views expressed by Deng Xiaoping and Zhao Ziyang, both of whom, one strongly suspects, were always far less concerned with the good society of the future than the Communist Party's domination of the present. And it was also common to confuse socialism with Chinese nationalism, as when Deng Xiaoping said in 1980 (and he repeated it many times in different ways) that "the purpose of socialism is to make the country rich and strong."[9] In the end, as the Deng era came to its economically triumphant and socially destructive conclusion, what remained of socialist aims and values were subordinated to the eminently nationalist goal of making the Chinese nation "rich and strong," for which modern economic development and a powerful state apparatus were the essential elements.

Zhao Ziyang's position as General Secretary of the Chinese Communist Party was formalized at the Party's Thirteenth Congress, which convened the last week in October, 1987.[10] The Congress also officially sanctioned the policies that Zhao had pursued since succeeding Hu Yaobang in January—policies that were hastening China's transition to capitalism, even though they were officially described as part of the program of building "socialism with Chinese characteristics." But the proceedings were mostly devoted to celebrating the accomplishments of Deng Xiaoping, who was praised in an extravagant fashion not heard since the days of the Mao cult. Indeed, Zhao Ziyang characterized Deng's ideas much in way the thought of Mao Zedong had once been celebrated, as "a model in the integration of the universal truth of Marxism with Chinese reality."[11] The Third Plenum of 1978 was equated in historical significance with the revolutionary victory of 1949, the second of the "two major historic leaps" in adapting Marxism to Chinese historical conditions.[12] And the Congress contributed generously to the construction of a new cult of personality—with speeches, books, and plays glorifying the life and thought of the paramount leader from the time of the revolutionary battles of the 1930s and 1940s to the building of "socialism with Chinese characteristics" in the 1980s.

It was generally assumed that the Thirteenth Congress would be the occasion for Deng (and other veteran Party leaders of his generation) to retire from such official positions they still held and remove themselves from active involvement in Party and state politics. Deng did in fact resign from the Party Politburo, as did other elderly Communist leaders. Of the five members of the new Standing Committee of the Politburo, only Zhao Ziyang remained after the Thirteenth Congress; the newly selected members (Qiao Shi, Li Peng, Hu Qili, and Yao Yilin) were considerably younger than their predecessors, so that the average age of the body plunged from 77 to 63 years. The members of the new Standing Committee appeared in public attired in Western-style suits and ties (instead of the "Mao suits" many of the older leaders favored)—signs of "virility" and "modernity," it was said in the Western press.

Yet despite all the personnel changes, Deng Xiaoping retained supreme power after the Thirteenth Congress, indeed no less power than he enjoyed prior to the Party meeting. In large measure, Deng's continuing political dominance flowed from the great personal prestige he enjoyed as China's "paramount leader." In part, it resulted from the one formal office Deng unexpectedly decided to retain after the Thirteenth Congress—the chairmanship of the Party's Military Affairs Commission, which gave him effective control of the PLA.[13] And Deng's continuing political dominance was also perpetuated through a group of "retired" Party elders who gathered around him; dubbed "the Gang of Old," they exercised enormous influence on official policy and practice through informal political networks based on longstanding personal relationships.

• • •

Encouraged by the decisions of the Thirteenth Congress, and by Deng Xiaoping's advice to proceed with greater "speed" and "boldness," Zhao Ziyang again accelerated the process of capitalist restructuring early in 1988. The "coastal development strategy" was more fully implemented, opening to foreign investment seaboard areas (from Manchuria to Guangdong) with a total population of 200,000,000. The resulting influx of foreign capital, along with expansionist monetary policies, fueled an extraordinarily high rate of industrial growth (21 percent in 1988) but also contributed to the tide of bureaucratic corruption that was to engulf the Deng regime in the closing years of the decade.

Zhao Ziyang's market-oriented policies also included "enterprise reform," a mostly abortive effort to remove government control over the finances and management of state-owned factories. To that Zhao added, with the vigorous assistance of Deng Xiaoping, another attempt at "price reform," the gradual abolition of state-fixed prices for many commodities, both finished goods and raw materials, in favor of a reliance on market forces. But the mere anticipation of decontrolled prices brought economic and financial chaos. Fears of inflation in an economy already suffering from strong inflationary pressures resulted in a rush to withdraw funds from bank accounts, panic buying, hoarding, wild speculation in commodities, and a flurry of price increases by industrial and commercial enterprises. By the early autumn of 1988, inflation in the major cities had reached a per annum rate of 30 percent. The economy was out of control and the government was forced to adopt severe austerity measures to avert a disastrous crash. "Price reform" was abandoned even before it had been officially instituted, credit was severely tightened, the money supply and capital investment were cut, and central government controls were reestablished over many enterprises and regions which had gained de facto autonomy.

Both inflation and the retrenchment policies necessary to restrain price increases brought hardship to much of the urban population, especially workers in state factories, minor officials and clerks in government offices, intellectuals, students, and others dependent on state salaries and subsidies. Peasants, especially those engaged in grain and other basic food production, also suffered due to shortages of ever more expensive fertilizers, low government purchase prices for grain, and the extra-legal exactions of corrupt officials.

The ravages of inflation on living standards were exacerbated by the austerity measures that the government introduced in the autumn of 1988 to "cool" the "overheated" economy. These included strict controls on credit, which resulted in closed factories and unemployed workers. Particularly hard hit were the township and village enterprises (TVEs), the most dynamic sector of the Chinese economy, which had been increasing industrial output at rates near 30 percent per annum and which employed nearly 100,000,000 workers in the late 1980s. Rural industry, however, was heavily dependent on easy credit, and the government's austerity program of late 1988 forced some TVEs to close and most others to reduce production. Millions of young workers (especially young female workers) lost their jobs, some of them joining destitute peasants in a "floating population" (*youmin*) of migrant workers who moved from the rural to urban areas, and then wandered from city to city in search of such temporary work as they could find. In the spring of 1989, it was estimated that over 50 million people had been thrown into the ranks of this wandering *lumpenproletariat*.

Yet despite inflation, or sometimes because of it, some prospered, at least during the 1988 boom phase of the economic cycle. Among those who enriched themselves were those involved in foreign trade, especially politically influential traders who were able to acquire goods and materials at low state prices and export them at world market prices; the managers and employees of the rapidly expanding private and collective industries; rural entrepreneurs and even urban street vendors; and especially corrupt bureaucrats who had access to relatively cheap state-priced goods and raw materials. But for most, in a society where the gap between rich and poor was already widening with alarming speed, living standards deteriorated due to inflation—and then fell even more rapidly because of the austerity measures the government adopted in late 1988 to stem inflation. Eroding living standards, combined with growing anger over profiteering bureaucrats and others who flaunted wealth obtained by dubious means, expressed itself in widespread social unrest in the winter and spring of 1989. Signs of popular dissatisfaction with the Deng regime were everywhere: workers' strikes and slowdowns in factories; an alarming upsurge in crime (which increased by 50 percent in 1988 over 1987, according to official figures); the appearance of youth gangs in both cities and countryside; the rapid spread of old social vices such as drug addiction, prostitution, gambling, and pornography; growing student political activism, which spread from the campuses to city streets where illegal "big-character posters" began to appear; and peasant unrest, which was expressed in physical clashes with local officials and the swelling of the "floating population" of migrant laborers.

The social unrest did not escape official notice. Mobile armed police forces were organized in anticipation of disorder and police officials were dispatched abroad to learn the latest anti-riot techniques.

Neo-Authoritarianism

Physical preparations to protect the Communist state were supplemented by new ideological defenses. A revealing sign of the times was the effort of intellectuals associated with Party General Secretary Zhao Ziyang to provide an ideological rationale for combining a capitalist market economy with a Stalinist political dictatorship—the strange union that had in fact resulted from Deng Xiaoping's economic reforms. The "new authoritarians," as they came to be called, argued that the historical experience of the successful modernizing countries of East Asia—Meiji Japan, Taiwan, Singapore, and South Korea—demonstrated that the imperatives of modern economic development, especially the need to tame the masses and discipline the working population, demanded a strong state and a powerful (and enlightened) ruler. The existing Leninist political apparatus under the guidance of Deng Xiaoping eminently fulfilled these requirements, needless to say. But in addition to a wise and powerful leader, the neo-authoritarians self-servingly argued, China's economic success required a "decision-making group" composed of intellectuals such as themselves, intellectuals who could design the future and advise the leader on how to arrive there. In the meantime, China could not afford democracy, which would bring the chaos of Party politics and disruptive protests by the victims of the transition to a market economy, thus delaying China's modernization. Political democracy was not ruled out entirely, but the neo-authoritarians said that it presupposed a highly developed economy and a viable capitalist class. These did not yet exist, and thus democracy was put off until an indefinite time in the future.

Neo-authoritarian doctrines, tacitly endorsed by Party General Secretary Zhao Ziyang and based on the ideas of Deng Xiaoping, or so its proponents claimed, brought criticism from democratic Marxist intellectuals. Many democratic Marxists, such as Su Shaozhi, had been associated with ousted Party head Hu Yaobang, and thus now found themselves in political limbo, increasingly in opposition to both Deng Xiaoping and Zhao Ziyang. A lively debate ensued.[14] The critics contended that dictatorial means, whatever their economic efficacy, would not likely lead to democratic ends and they doubted the relevance of the histories of the smaller East Asian countries to the enormity of China's political and economic needs.

While the content of the debate was rather unremarkable, it did reveal how much political perspectives and social ideals had changed over the first decade of the market-reform era. In 1978, intellectuals, inspired by the promise of "socialist democracy," had flocked to join Deng Xiaoping's camp. Ten years later, in the debate on neo-authoritarianism, socialism was barely mentioned by either Zhao Ziyang's ideologists or their democratic critics. Both sides embraced the market reforms that were rapidly producing a capitalist economy, differing only over whether the process should proceed under the auspices of an authoritarian or a democratic political regime, although they agreed that in either case intellectuals were to play the crucial historical role. Marxism was largely ignored—in favor of conservative Western political science theories in the case of Zhao's most prominent ideologists, and conventional Western liberalism in the case of their democratic opponents. In the space of a decade, the intellectuals who remained the supporters and theoreticians of the Deng regime had abandoned the goal of a socialist democracy in favor of a neo-authoritarian doctrine that advocated a capitalist autocracy. The intellectual change was striking, almost as sweeping as the socioeconomic transformation itself.

Heshang (River Elegy)

As some intellectuals debated neo-authoritarian doctrines, another controversy was raging over a widely viewed film entitled *Heshang (River Elegy)*, which had been broadcast nationally on China Central Television (CCTV) in June 1988. While seemingly unrelated, the two debates had much in common. Both were centrally concerned with the political role of intellectuals, that most enduring preoccupation of the modern Chinese intelligentsia. Both were very much involved in the factional political struggles that revolved around Communist Party General Secretary Zhao Ziyang. And, most importantly, both debates revealed the ideological as well as material triumph of capitalism—and how irrelevant socialist ideas had become in Chinese intellectual life only a decade after Deng Xiaoping had achieved power on a platform championing "socialist democracy."

Heshang, visually stunning and passionately narrated, was a bitterly iconoclastic critique of traditional Chinese culture. Inspired by the radical anti-traditionalism of the May Fourth era, the producers of the film suggested that the pernicious influence of traditional values was mainly responsible for China's millennial inertia and its modern backwardness. The Yellow River, both stagnant and destructive, was *Heshang*'s metaphor for Chinese history, a history marked by the periodic and violent collapse of the socio-political order, which is then inevitably reconstructed on its old foundations in accordance with an archaic and unchanging value system. This "ultra-stability" of China's 2,000-year feudal society is the curse of Chinese history, stifling creativity and inhibiting economic development, especially the development of capitalism. The Yellow River, the cradle of Chinese culture and civilization, symbolizes the profound conservatism and backwardness of this peasant-based and inward-looking society, which, on its own, is capable only of reproducing itself and its stifling traditions.

The antithesis of the Yellow River in *Heshang* is a vibrant blue sea, symbolic of the outward-looking oceanic cultures of the capitalist West, the dynamic homeland of modern science, industry, and democracy. Like some of their May Fourth predecessors (see chapter 2) who advocated "wholesale Westernization" in 1919, the producers of *Heshang* discovered in the Western countries all that they found lacking in China and Chinese culture. A romanticized image of "the West" for China to emulate was thus constructed. But the May Fourth parallel, while tempting, is far from exact. Although the May Fourth intelligentsia lauded Western science and democracy, they were also very much aware of the threat of Western imperialism and the social ravages of Western capitalism. That awareness stimulated their often agonizing efforts to distinguish between the progressive and reactionary features of the Western countries, efforts which led many to look to socialist and Marxist theories to resolve the dilemma. Seven decades later, by contrast, their would-be successors ignored the anguishing dilemma that the West was oppressor as well as teacher in modern Chinese history. Instead, the long and exploitative history of foreign imperialism in China was reduced to a "cultural conflict" between a dynamic "blue" civilization and a stagnant "yellow" one.

Just as the intellectuals who promoted *Heshang* no longer shared the May Fourth generation's concern with imperialism, so too they differed on the question of capitalism. Although the May Fourth intellectuals admired the material and intellectual achievements of the advanced Western countries, their embrace of modern Western civilization did not typically extend to the capitalist economic system with which Western science and democracy were so intimately associated. Indeed, it was widely assumed by the May Fourth intellectuals that socialist societies would soon emerge as the most advanced expression of modern Western culture. In the late 1980s, by contrast, the "West" was seen in a more holistic and unproblematic fashion. It was widely assumed by China's intellectuals that the genuine flowering of modern science and democracy in China presupposed the building of a developed capitalist economy, a prospect which many seemed to welcome in any event—and one which Deng's market reforms and official ideology (which, in good Marxist fashion, lauded the progressiveness of capitalism) did little to discourage. A revealing moment in *Heshang* is the narrator's comment: "The death knell of capitalism long ago predicted by Karl Marx has still not sounded."[15]

It is cultural iconoclasm that seems to tie the intellectuals of the late Deng era, at least those who shared the views expressed in *Heshang,* to the May Fourth intelligentsia. In both cases, the social and political evils of the present were attributed to the baneful influences of traditional values. But the meaning of cultural iconoclasm had changed. At the time of the May Fourth movement, tradition was associated with social conservatism and employed for reactionary political ends. Cultural iconoclasm thus had radical implications. But in the postrevolutionary era of Deng Xiaoping, it was not tradition that was burdening China so much as it was the Stalinist bureaucratic apparatus that had been imposed by the Communist Revolution. To attribute China's ills to the pernicious influences of "feudal" culture was an ideological maneuver that absolved the postrevolutionary order of blame for the problems that afflicted Chinese society. Thus cultural iconoclasm, which had been socially radical during the May Fourth era, was reincarnated seventy years later, intentionally or not, as a conservative defense of the Communist regime. In finding in traditional culture the source of the ills of contemporary China, the producers of *Heshang,* whose patron was Communist Party General Secretary Zhao Ziyang, were repeating one of the prominent themes in the official ideology of the Dengist state, the assertion that the problems of the Communist present stemmed primarily from the lingering influences of China's feudal past rather than from the new sociopolitical order produced by the Communist revolution. Unlike Zhao Ziyang, not all the high bureaucrats of the Communist regime (many of whom were culturally conservative) were sufficiently astute to appreciate the political utility of cultural iconoclasm.

While the year 1919 appears prominently in *Heshang,* the year 1949 is ignored. Virtually nothing is said about the Chinese Communist Revolution or the history of the People's Republic—save to praise the efforts of Zhou Enlai, Deng Xiaoping, and Zhao Ziyang to "open" China to the West. By implication, the Maoist revolution is viewed as bringing no positive change to China's stagnant history, at best simply reflecting and perpetuating its "feudal" backwardness.

Just as the Communist revolution is largely ignored or portrayed negatively, so too are those who made the revolution, the peasants who are condemned as the social carrier of backward traditions and "feudal" ideas. A noted foreign scholar observed of *Heshang:* "For agrarian society there is open despair. The sole farmer interviewed responds briefly to a question on how prolific he has been as a father, condemned out of his own mouth for overpopulating China."[16]

Yet despite the dismal state of modern China and all the burdens of history and tradition it bears, *Heshang* concludes with the hope that China is finally prepared to break away from its millennial "ultra-stability." For one thing, there is now a clear and universal model to emulate, the utopia of the advanced capitalist countries of the West, which are so attractively portrayed in the final episode, entitled "The Color Blue." Furthermore, China now has leaders who recognize the necessity of pursuing that model through the Dengist policy of capitalist market reforms. Especially praised, implicitly but quite obviously, is Zhao Ziyang and his coastal development strategy.

But the greatest hope for China's future, according to the authors of *Heshang,* is the wisdom of intellectuals, the natural social agents of modernization who truly understand democracy and science and are thus able to provide proper guidance to the Communist Party in carrying out its market-reform program. Intellectuals, the TV narrator enthusiastically says, are "an entirely unique group" whom history has given to the Chinese people. It is the intellectuals who "hold in their hands the weapon to destroy ignorance and superstition; it is they who can conduct a direct dialogue with 'seafaring' civilization; it is they who can channel the 'blue' sweetwater spring of science and democracy onto our yellow earth."[17]

Heshang was not purely an intellectual and artistic effort. The production was intimately involved in the factional politics of the Communist Party following the Thirteenth Congress of October 1987. Party head

Zhao Ziyang was the chief political patron of the writers and producers of *Heshang,* and, not surprisingly, Zhao and his economic policies were praised in the film. Moreover, Zhao went to great lengths to ensure that *Heshang* was seen on television sets throughout the country. Following the initial broadcast in mid-June 1988, members of the "Gang of Old" and other conservative Party leaders denounced the film for preaching "cultural nihilism," and in July Party propaganda chief Hu Qili prohibited additional showings. The decision was reversed by the personal intervention of Zhao Ziyang, permitting a second nationwide broadcast in mid–August. It was not until September that the Party Central Committee convened to definitively ban the film. By that time, videotapes of *Heshang* and a book reproducing the script had been widely circulated. It was even reported that a copy of the video had been presented by Zhao Ziyang as a gift to Lee Kuan Yew, the dictator of Singapore, who personified the doctrine of "neo-authoritarianism."

It was widely assumed, by both the leaders of the Deng regime and its critics, that the televising of *River Elegy* encouraged political activism by students and intellectuals, and thus contributed to the Democracy Movement of 1989. Liu Binyan, for example, wrote that the 1988 documentary (along with an earlier TV dramatic series *New Star*) "reverberated throughout Chinese society, proving that intellectuals were capable of doing a great deal more than they had done so far."[18] And after the tragedy of June 4, 1989, Communist leaders repeatedly condemned *River Elegy* for provoking what was officially called a "counterrevolutionary rebellion," and sought to arrest its producer, Su Xiaokang, who fled into exile.

It was the intention of the authors of *Heshang* to promote democratic political change. They attempted to do so in part by launching a thinly veiled attack on conservative Communist officials who opposed the economic as well as political reforms proposed by Zhao Ziyang, however limited the latter were. Politically conservative bureaucrats were usually culturally conservative as well, and thus *Heshang,* by linking the dictatorial character of political life in modern China to authoritarian elements in traditional Chinese culture, seemed doubly outrageous to most Communist leaders—an anti-patriotic affront to the national cultural heritage as well as a manifestation of the political heresy of "bourgeois liberalization."

Yet *River Elegy* did not convey an unambiguous democratic message. The democratic credentials of the filmmakers were compromised from the beginning because of the patronage of General Secretary Zhao Ziyang. Zhao, after all, was the leader of a Leninist party, he had consistently supported Deng Xiaoping's Four Cardinal Principles (among which the leadership of the Communist Party was foremost), and he promoted neo-authoritarian doctrines. Moreover, the film itself communicated not so much the virtues of democracy as such as a glorified image of the wealth and power of the West. And what was most powerfully conveyed was the self-serving message that intellectuals were the natural leaders of Chinese society, entrusted with the mission of bringing about the capitalist regeneration of China in accordance with models of the "blue civilizations" of the advanced Western countries. It was a message that reinforced the many traditional and modern forces that fostered intellectual and political elitism, a message more consistent with Leninism and neo-authoritarianism than with popular democracy. The romanticization of the West and the elitism of China's intellectuals were to be among the more glaring weaknesses of the great Democracy Movement of 1989.

The Democracy Movement (1989)

Yet a few intellectuals, especially those who had been shunted aside after the ouster of Hu Yaobang as Party chief in 1987, did contribute to the intellectual origins of the Democracy Movement of 1989. Several well-known intellectuals, including Fang Lizhi (who had been expelled from the Party as well as dismissed from his university post following the student demonstrations of the winter of 1986–87), lectured at informal seminars organized by students at Beijing University and other colleges in the summer and fall of 1988. The best known of the "democracy salons," as they came to be called (in imitation of the radical ferment among young aristocrats that ushered in the French Revolution of 1789), was organized by Wang Dan, an undergraduate history major at Beijing University and a future leader of the Democracy Movement.

In December 1988, Su Shaozhi, a prominent Marxist theoretician and economic policy-maker in the post-Mao era—until his dismissal as head of the Marx-Lenin-Mao Institute following the fall of Hu Yaobang—boldly attacked the official ideology of the Deng regime as "ossified dogma" divorced from the changing socioeconomic realities of China and the world. To help revitalize ideology and policy, Su called for the free discussion of the many Western Marxian schools of thought that long had been beyond the pale of acceptable political discourse in China.

Early in January 1989, Fang Lizhi wrote an open letter to Deng Xiaoping suggesting that the release of Wei Jingsheng and other political prisoners would be an appropriate way to commemorate both the fortieth anniversary of the People's Republic and the seventieth anniversary of the May Fourth Movement—and, for good measure, the bicentennial of the French Revolution of 1789 and its universal principles of "liberty, equality, fraternity, and human rights."[19] Fang's letter emboldened other prominent intellectuals, who over the next two months followed with an unprecedented stream of petitions to Party and government leaders calling for a general amnesty for all political prisoners.

Ferment among the intelligentsia (or, more precisely, a tiny number among them) was soon overshadowed by growing student political activism. In the early months of 1989, the "democracy salons" which had been held erratically in 1988 had developed into discussion groups which met regularly on the campuses of several universities in Beijing. Operating under such innocuous sounding names as the "Confucius Study Society," the students met to discuss democratic theories and other heterodox ideas. In addition, secret quasipolitical groups were organized on campuses in Beijing and other cities, where students planned demonstrations to commemorate the seventieth anniversary of the May Fourth Movement of 1919 and its hallowed principles of "democracy and science"—in defiance of the official ceremonies that were to be held under the auspices of governmental organizations.

But unanticipated events dictated swifter and more dramatic political acts. On April 15, 1989 the ousted Party chief, Hu Yaobang, suffered a fatal heart attack while attending a meeting of the Politburo, where he had been permitted to retain a seat even after falling out of favor with Deng Xiaoping. Politically astute students, beyond wishing to show their genuine respect for the democratically inclined Hu, also recognized the political opportunity. They knew that the death of a high Party leader was a time when the authorities would briefly tolerate a degree of political dissent, an opportune moment to revive the tradition of "mourning the dead to criticize the living." Thus, late in the night on April 15, graduate students in the Party History Department at People's University, many of them from high official families, bicycled to Tiananmen Square to lay wreaths at the Monument to the Heroes of the Revolution in memory of Hu Yaobang. Students from other universities in Beijing soon followed their daring example, embarking on "long marches" through the streets of the capital singing the "Internationale" and other revolutionary songs on their way to the Square and to government buildings.

The marches and demonstrations spontaneously grew larger and more militant day by day. Some students staged a sit-in at the Great Hall of the People, demanding that representatives to the National People's Congress receive their petitions calling for such elementary democratic rights as freedom of organization and freedom of the press, and condemning bureaucratic corruption and nepotism. Other students, joined by unemployed youth, clashed with police when they attempted to storm the walled compound in the old Forbidden City where top Communist Party leaders had their homes and offices. The numbers in Tiananmen Square grew as workers and other citizens began to demonstrate alongside the student pioneers of the Democracy Movement.

In response to the growing popular unrest, the government barred the public from Tiananmen Square on April 22, the day of Hu Yaobang's funeral. But the authorities were outwitted by student organizers, and when Deng Xiaoping and other Communist leaders left the Great Hall of the People following the official memorial services for Hu Yaobang, they saw 100,000 people standing in the Square in silent defiance of the Deng regime. More than a million citizens lined the route of the funeral procession to Babaoshan, the cemetery on the Western outskirts of the capital. Once the hallowed ground for the burial of revolutionary heroes and martyrs, it now mainly had become the official cemetery for Communist bureaucrats.

In the days following Hu Yaobang's funeral, student leaders announced the establishment of an "Autonomous Federation" to coordinate student activities at twenty-one Beijing area universities and colleges; they formalized the boycott of classes by declaring a student "strike"; and some student activists began to appeal directly to the people of Beijing through street-corner speeches calling for democracy and denouncing official corruption. Deng Xiaoping was enraged, perhaps not least of all because of the ridicule heaped upon the increasingly unpopular "paramount leader," now often compared with the reactionary Empress Dowager, Ci Xi, who had presided over the decay of the Qing dynasty in the late nineteenth century. For his part, Deng compared the student activists of 1989 to the rebels of the Cultural Revolution, both having as their aim the creation of "chaos under the heavens."[20] The paramount leader's anger found fulsome expression in an editorial that appeared in the *People's Daily* on April 26, apparently authored by Deng himself, which attributed the student demonstrations to a "planned conspiracy" to "plunge the whole country into chaos" in order to "negate the leadership of the Chinese Communist Party and the socialist system." Henceforth, the editorial warned, the ban on illegal organizations and unauthorized demonstrations would be strictly enforced, and students were forbidden to associate with workers, peasants, and students at other schools.[21]

The *People's Daily* editorial outraged students (and others) who had taken special pains over the previous two weeks to demonstrate their loyalty to the nation, to the Communist Party, and to socialism. Rather than frightening students into quiescence, as Deng had intended, the effect of the editorial was to politically activate and unify students into what was soon to become a massive social movement. Throughout the night of April 26—a time emotionally charged with feelings of heroic self-sacrifice—students at two dozen Beijing colleges labored feverishly to organize the next day's defiance of the Deng regime. In the early morning hours of April 27, students moved out through the gates of their schools, pushing away the bewildered police and militia who had been dispatched to keep them on the campuses, and joined together in an 80,000-strong march through the streets of the city to Tiananmen Square. There they broke into smaller groups and, waving banners and singing revolutionary songs, they marched through the streets of the capital all day, seeking public support. Some citizens joined the student marchers and others offered food and money in spontaneous and often affectionate displays of solidarity.

The government, its leaders divided over how to deal with the rebellious students, retreated from the uncompromising position Deng Xiaoping had set forth on April 26, agreeing to meet with student leaders. Over the next three weeks, the Democracy Movement grew while the faction-ridden Communist Party seemed confused and impotent. The disarray of the Deng regime was compounded on April 30, when Party General Secretary Zhao Ziyang returned to Beijing after a week-long visit to North Korea.

Zhao Ziyang's relations with Deng Xiaoping had been deteriorating since the beginning of the year, when Deng became suspicious of his erstwhile protege's tolerance for "bourgeois liberalization" among intellectuals. At the same time, Zhao's popularity in society at large had evaporated; his free-wheeling market policies were blamed for the inflation which was ravaging the cities. And with his two sons conspicuously enriching themselves in the lucrative import-export trade, the Zhao family became the personification of the official profiteering that now pervaded the Communist bureaucracy and that had aroused enormous popular resentment. Zhao feared, no doubt for good reason, that Deng planned to make him the scapegoat for the economic troubles of the time—and depose him just as he had purged Hu Yaobang two years earlier.

Partly motivated by considerations of political self-preservation, partly following his natural inclinations, Zhao sided with those Party leaders who favored a conciliatory policy toward the rebellious students. This pitted Zhao against his longtime patron, Deng Xiaoping, in an internal political struggle that immobilized the Party apparatus for half a month, thereby permitting the Democracy Movement to grow.

On May 4, 1989, Zhao Ziyang characterized the students' demands as "reasonable" and urged that they be implemented in democratic fashion and through legal means.[22] On the same day, in commemoration of the seventieth anniversary of the May Fourth Movement, more than 60,000 students from thirty universities and colleges in Beijing peacefully marched from their campuses to a rally in Tiananmen Square. Although the march defied Party-dictated municipal regulations banning unapproved demonstrations, the police did not impede the columns of arm-linked, banner-waving students. The Beijing students were joined by delegations of university students from cities across the land, and more significantly, by nonstudent groups—older intellectuals, journalists from Party-controlled newspapers, workers, and other citizens. In all, more than 300,000 people gathered in the Square that day to hear speeches lauding the democratic and patriotic spirit of May Fourth, with many speakers taking pains to couple their pleas for democracy with proclamations of support for the Communist Party and the "socialist system." It was the largest demonstration thus far, and observers marveled at the extraordinary self-discipline of the participants and the organizational skills of the students.

Yet the massive May 4th rally, although clearly a triumph for the student movement, seemed anticlimactic and changed nothing. Over the week that followed, demonstrations were smaller and less frequent as many striking students returned to classes. There appeared to be a return to normalcy. But beneath the apparent calm a fierce struggle was raging within the inner councils of the Chinese Communist Party. The outcome would determine the fate of the Democracy Movement.

The inner-Party battle pitted Party General Secretary Zhao Ziyang, the disciple, against the "paramount leader" Deng Xiaoping, Zhao's erstwhile mentor. Zhao, struggling for political survival, championed many of the students' demands, although he took care to keep a safe distance from the students themselves so as not to further anger Deng. But Zhao endorsed the students' demand for a retraction of the now notorious *People's Daily* editorial of April 26, which Deng had authored. Zhao praised the patriotism of the students and supported many of their demands, including guarantees for freedom of the press and the establishment of an independent judicial system. Zhao also called for negotiations between the government and the student leaders, to be conducted on a democratic basis. But Deng Xiaoping rejected all compromise. He heard echoes of the Cultural Revolution in the spontaneity of the student movement, and he was determined to punish a new generation of youth for their rebellion against the authority of the Communist Party and their subversion of the sacrosanct "stability" of the post-Maoist order. He thus gathered around him "the Gang of Old"—veteran and mostly conservative Party leaders (virtually all of whom, like Deng, had been victims of the Cultural Revolution), and most of the generals of the PLA. Even so, it was to take Deng almost two weeks to fully reassert his authority as "paramount leader."

Deng Xiaoping's eventual triumph over Zhao Ziyang in the Politburo in mid-May was greatly facilitated by divisions among the students. In a movement so spontaneous and so youthful, chaotic factional conflicts were inevitable. While the ideological and organizational divisions were many, and often trivial, there was one fundamental difference that had momentous implications for the goals and tactics of the Democracy Movement. On the one hand, there were the older graduate students (and their followers) who had initiated the movement in mid-April and who sought to influence the internal politics of the CCP by attempting to work with Zhao Ziyang and the intellectuals associated with him. Increasingly distinguished from them, and far more numerous, was an amorphous mass of politically and culturally radical undergraduates; distrustful of authority and established institutions, they sought their own place in society, free from the organizational control of the Communist Party. They saw little difference between Zhao Ziyang and Deng Xiaoping, and were largely unconcerned with the internal struggles then raging among the senior leaders of of the Party. After the massive May 4th march, and the calm that followed, the leaders of the younger and more radical students—such as Wang Dan (a Beijing University undergraduate history major) and Wuer Kaixi (a Beijing Normal University undergraduate)—became the most prominent leaders of the Democracy Movement.

The new student leaders were impatient. Frustrated by the divided and paralyzed government's delays in responding to student demands for a "dialogue," the young leaders endorsed calls for a hunger strike to break the impasse and reenergize the movement. On the afternoon of May 13, 500 students marched into Tiananmen Square. Surrounded by thousands of supporters, they began a hunger strike in the center of the Square, encamped before the Monument to the Heroes of the Revolution. Not coincidentally, it was precisely the spot where the Soviet leader Mikhail Gorbachev was scheduled to be officially welcomed by the Chinese government two days later.

In 1989 Mikhail Gorbachev was a towering figure in world affairs. He was particularly popular in China, where his policy of *glasnost,* his outgoing personality, and his promises to democraticize a Communist regime were often contrasted with the personal remoteness of Deng Xiaoping and his political conservatism. Moreover, Gorbachev was to be the first Soviet leader to visit China since Nikita Khrushchev's stormy meeting with Mao Zedong in 1959, and his trip was intended to mark the end of the long and bitter period of Sino-Soviet hostility. The visit was widely anticipated as a major event in twentieth-century history, and thus television journalists from around the world converged on Beijing to record the meeting between Mikhail Gorbachev and Deng Xiaoping. It was because of this long-anticipated diplomatic spectacle that so many television cameras fortuitously happened to be in Beijing to broadcast to the world the rise and demise of the Chinese Democracy Movement.

On the day of Gorbachev's arrival, the student hunger strikers and their supporters remained in the Square, defying the threats of the Public Security Bureau and ignoring the pleas of Zhao Ziyang. Therefore, much to the embarrassment of Deng Xiaoping, who so prized "stability" and "order," the official welcoming ceremony for Gorbachev was hastily performed at the airport on May 15 and the Soviet leader was confined to indoor meetings and banquets during his stay in Beijing, and kept out of public view until his departure for Shanghai on May 18. Over those three days, popular support for the Democracy Movement grew enormously—as did Deng Xiaoping's determination to use military force to crush the movement, a decision reluctantly approved by the Party Politburo over the objections of General Secretary Zhao Ziyang.

The hunger strike had brought the students widespread sympathy from the citizens of Beijing, and, together with the excitement of Gorbachev's visit, had politically activated a good portion of the population. On May 15, the day Gorbachev arrived, more than half a million people came to the Square to demonstrate their support for the students. On May 17, well over a million citizens filled (and spilled out from) the vast hundred-acre expanse beneath the Gate of Heavenly Peace in what was probably the largest mass rally since the founding of the People's Republic forty years earlier.[23] What was remarkable about the demonstrations of mid–May was not only the number of those who marched but the variety of social and occupational groups that were represented—and their eagerness to identify their institutions and work units by hoisting clearly-marked banners. Intellectuals and journalists from the official press had actively supported the students earlier, but they now marched in greater numbers and were joined by hundreds of thousands of factory workers, Party cadres, government office workers, and schoolteachers. Among the marchers were editors from the government's central television and radio stations, teachers from the Central Party School for the training of Communist officials, uniformed police, and even a thousand PLA cadets. "These were not masses of anonymous demonstrators but well-labelled groups acting in an orderly (although not regimented) fashion," a visiting Australian scholar observed.[24]

The seriousness of the challenge to the Deng regime by so massive and socially broad a movement, indeed one that had attracted the support of even a good many government officials and Party cadres, was partially masked by the disciplined behavior and joyful demeanor of the demonstrators. In the square itself, the growing number of students who camped out in support of the hunger strikers created an iconoclastic carnival-like environment that obscured the deadly seriousness of the political drama that was being played out. In what seemed like a counterculture festival that some American observers called "a Chinese Woodstock," the young Chinese imitated Western radical youth of the 1960s. They danced and sang ballads, joined by several popular folk singers and rock stars; they gave spontaneous speeches and engaged in heated political debates; they wore colored headbands in emulation of radical Japanese and Korean students; they irreverently chanted slogans ridiculing Communist leaders, especially Deng Xiaoping and Premier Li Peng; and they organized essential services for their temporary municipality in the Square, acquiring supplies of food and water, organizing rudimentary waste disposal and medical systems, and operating an ambulance service that conveyed dehydrated hunger strikers to city hospitals.

As the Democracy Movement grew in scope and scale in mid-May, Deng Xiaoping intensified his efforts to suppress the "turmoil." Party elders, formally retired from their official positions but still influential in state and military bureaucracies, had been meeting at Deng's home since early in the month to discuss how to deal with the "rebellion." Alarmed by the participation of Party-state cadres and industrial workers in the massive demonstrations of mid-May, the "Gang of Old" demanded the imposition of martial law in Beijing. The decision was conveyed to Party General Secretary Zhao Ziyang when he was summoned to Deng's home on May 18, the day Gorbachev flew from Beijing to Shanghai. That evening a hastily called meeting of the Politburo's Standing Committee endorsed the martial law recommendation. Zhao Ziyang, his relationship with Deng now completely shattered, cast the lone dissenting vote. Although several other Politburo members were said to have grave reservations over the deployment of PLA soldiers in the capital, none were willing to defy China's "paramount leader." The martial law proclamation, covering key districts in Beijing, was announced by Premier Li Peng in a televised speech on the evening of May 19, after pro forma approval by the Party Central Committee and the State Council. Zhao Ziyang, in the meantime, was making a most unusual exit from Chinese Communist politics. After having unsuccessfully opposed the Politburo recommendation to impose martial law at its late night meeting on May 18, the General Secretary of the CCP embarked on a lonely journey to Tiananmen Square. Over the previous week, Zhao had praised the students for their patriotism and expressed support for many of their demands while imploring them to end the occupation of the Square. But he had refrained from talking directly with student representatives. Now, in the early morning hours of May 19, as his Party career was ending, he wandered aimlessly among the hunger strikers. "I have come too late," he tearfully acknowledged. And he added: "We were once young too, and we all had such bursts of energy. We also staged demonstrations . . . [and] we also did not think of the consequences."[25]

This act of contrition, perhaps the most humanly memorable episode in Zhao Ziyang's long political career, was one of the charges brought against him in late June during the proceedings that formalized his dismissal as General Secretary of the Chinese Communist Party. During the remainder of the Deng era, Zhao was kept under house arrest, living comfortably but silently in a villa in central Beijing.

. . .

The immediate popular response to the declaration of martial law in Beijing was defiance. Students in Tiananmen Square, who had suspended the hunger strike shortly before Li Peng decreed martial law on May 19, resumed the fast on May 20. On Sunday, May 21, more than a million citizens gathered in the Square to protest, and another demonstration of a million defiant citizens took place on May 23. In some working class residental areas, citizens erected barricades to defend the city against the PLA units that had begun to surround the capital. Factories were closed by strikes and public transportation was disrupted. The Democracy Movement spread sporadically across the country, from cities in Manchuria to Canton and Hong Kong. The Standing Committee of the customarily docile National People's Congress declared its support for the student demands and called for the repeal of martial law. And a highly prestigious group of retired PLA generals wrote an open letter to Deng Xiaoping recalling the army's popular revolutionary traditions and reminding the paramount leader that: "The People's Army belongs to the people . . . and cannot stand in opposition to the people." Indeed, the first groups of young soldiers who entered the capital intuitively fraternized with the population they had been dispatched to control, and some welcomed student invitations to join together in singing revolutionary songs.

The young soldiers were quickly withdrawn and replaced by divisions made up of veteran professional soldiers. By the last days of May, Beijing was surrounded by more than 200,000 troops unquestionably obedient to the commands of Deng Xiaoping. The Democracy Movement disintegrated under the pressure. Large-scale marches and demonstrations ceased. The hunger strike was called off for the second time. The number of occupants of the Square rapidly dwindled as most students returned to their campuses, or in some cases joined a belated "go-to-the-people" movement. By the end of May no more than 5,000 people remained in the Square, most students from universities located far from the capital.

As the student activists faded away, the heart of the Democracy Movement moved to the working-class neighborhoods of Beijing, districts several miles to the east of the Square and on the outskirts of the city. After a decade of market reform, the grievances of workers were many, even though material conditions of life had improved. The inflation that plagued the country, and especially the urban areas, since 1987 had eroded the gains in living standards achieved in the early reform period. Proposals for a "free labor market" by the neo-liberal economic advisers who surrounded Deng Xiaoping and Zhao Ziyang, and especially their increasingly shrill calls to "smash the iron rice bowl," made state workers fear loss of their job tenure and welfare benefits. Anxiety over the insecurity of their own positions sometimes turned to anger as they witnessed an orgy of official profiteering by high Communist leaders and their offspring, from Deng Xiaoping and Zhao Ziyang down to the lowest levels of the political hierarchy. And workers continued to resist bureaucratic control of their daily lives carried out by the hated work unit (*danwei*) system inherited from the Mao era.

The grievances of the urban working class, a combination of resentments over the oppressiveness of the old political system and new discontents over the unjust social consequences of the market, were expressed in growing worker support for the Democracy Movement, evident in the massive demonstration of May 17 in which workers prominently participated. That event did much to rekindle the "Polish fear" among Party leaders, their decade-old obsession about the rise of a Solidarity-type alliance between workers and intellectuals in opposition to the Communist state. And that fear, in turn, contributed to the fateful decision to impose martial law.

Communist leaders need not have worried about a worker-intellectual alliance. The elitism of most Chinese intellectuals precluded such a development. About the condition of the working class, little had been heard from Chinese intellectuals save for complaints that workers were comparatively better paid than intellectuals.[26] Some of these class prejudices had filtered down to students as well, many of whom opposed participation of workers in the Democracy Movement on the grounds that workers were undisciplined and prone to violence. The participation of workers, it was suggested, would provide the government with an excuse to use force to suppress the movement. Thus, in the early weeks of the movement, student demonstrators often marched with arms linked to exclude workers and other citizens, thereby, they thought, preserving the "purity" of their uniquely nonviolent crusade. By mid-May, however, as the now enormous movement clearly was nearing the climactic point in its struggle with the Communist state, students welcomed workers who offered their support— and protection.

Deng Xiaoping, in any event, was determined to "teach lessons" to those he regarded as the ungrateful beneficiaries of his reforms, and to use massive military force to do so. Due to divisions over tactics among Party and military leaders, the reluctance of the young soldiers of the 38th Army (the first to enter the city) to fire on unarmed civilians, and logistical problems involved in the transfer of other army groups from their bases to the vicinity of the capital, it took the Deng regime nearly two weeks to enforce its martial law decree. But by the beginning of June, Deng had assembled an overwhelming military force. Two hundred thousand troops surrounded Beijing, poised to strike on command. It was as if the capital of China was besieged by a foreign army.

In a heroic response, workers and other citizens undertook an extraordinary effort to defend the city—and to defend the students who remained in Tiananmen Square. Barricades were erected along the roads that PLA tanks and personnel carriers would need to travel to reach the center of the city. And at key intersections around Tiananmen Square, overturned buses and heavy trucks blocked the streets. In an effort to mobilize the people to defend Beijing, workers and students covered walls with posters, distributed leaflets, and gave passionate street-corner speeches to groups of citizens engaged in unaccustomed free political debates. Bicycle and motorcycle brigades were organized (the latter by sympathetic small entrepreneurs) to report on troop movements and alert citizens to danger. The police and other municipal authorities having vanished, workers and students assumed responsibility for maintaining public order and directing traffic. For many citizens of the capital, a new sense of solidarity and independence was briefly experienced.

. . .

The invasion of Beijing began at dusk on June 3. An initial PLA force of 40,000 troops, equipped with tanks and armed personnel carriers, smashed through the barricades in the eastern and western suburbs of the city and moved along the streets that led to Tiananmen Square. The advance of the army was temporarily halted in heavily populated residential districts several miles east of the Square, where large crowds blocked the way. In the less heavily populated districts just west of the Square—an area dominated by official buildings—workers, students and other citizens from various parts of the city rushed to block the advance of the army. Armed (if armed at all) with bricks, sticks, and Molotov cocktails, the civilian defenders were cut down by the PLA's tanks, machine guns, and AK-47s, in the first of many instances of indiscriminate killing that marked what was to be a night of terror. A similar fate befell the defenders in the residential neighborhoods to the east of the Square. Shortly after midnight, PLA forces reached Tiananmen, leaving long trails of death and destruction in their wake. Most of the killing had taken place in residential neighborhoods (far removed from the eyes of the television cameras trained on the Square) and in the downtown streets near Tiananmen, as the army blasted its way through human barricades and hunted down civilian resisters on its bloody drive to the Gate of Heavenly Peace. Although there were many student casualties, the great majority of dead and wounded were workers and other residents who had barricaded the streets in a futile attempt to block the army's advance.

There were few casualities in the Square itself. Much of the credit for averting further bloodshed belongs to several unlikely heroes—notably the rock star Hou Dejian[27] and the literary critic Liu Xiaobo, who began a hunger strike on June 2 to demonstrate solidarity with the students and who negotiated with PLA commanders the safe passage of the remaining 5,000 occupants. In the early morning hours of Sunday, June 5, the last of the student rebels filed out of the debris-filled Square under the menacing gaze of helmeted soldiers. They found themselves in a city that seemed to be under foreign military occupation. They wandered along streets in downtown Beijing strewn with rubble and burned-out military vehicles, past buildings pockmarked by the previous night's gunfire. The streets were patrolled by heavily armed soldiers and helicopter gunships hovered above, their searchlights ominously trained on the streets below. This eerie dawn-hour evacuation of Tiananmen Square effectively marked the end of the Democracy Movement, although scattered resistance to the PLA occupation continued in various parts of Beijing for several days and there were futile (and quickly suppressed) demonstrations in a dozen other cities protesting the massacre in the capital.

On June 9 Deng Xiaoping appeared on television to congratulate the military and police forces who had crushed what he called "the counterrevolutionary rebellion" and to offer condolences to the families of the several dozen soldiers who had been killed during the fighting. Deng had no words of regret about the civilian victims, however, whom he reviled as "the dregs of society." According to later government statements, the number of civilian deaths was less than 300. The absurdity of the official figure was pointed out by several eyewitnesses, some of whom observed that the number of unclaimed bodies in several hospitals in central Beijing was alone greater than the government's figure for the total number of people killed.[28] Although the actual count can never be known with any degree of certainty, independent observers in Beijing at the time estimated that civilian deaths ranged from 2,000 to 7,000 people, with the wounded numbering several times those figures. But no less chilling than the killings themselves was the cold and calculating manner that the employment of massive military force was decided upon—by Deng Xiaoping and a small group of elderly Party leaders who, determined to punish the youthful demonstrators and terrorize a population they regarded as insufficiently grateful, deliberately ignored all opportunities to resolve the crisis peacefully.

A nationwide wave of arrests followed the military suppression. Over the months of June and July, it is estimated that 40,000 people were arrested by various secret police agencies. Of these, several thousand were sentenced to jail terms and several hundred were executed. Most of those imprisoned and all who were executed were workers or other ordinary citizens. Students, many of whom had relatives in high places, were treated relatively leniently—save for selected leaders of the movement, whose twenty-one names appeared on a highly publicized "most-wanted" list; most of the young dissidents either fled into exile or were hunted down and jailed.

. . .

In the years following the Beijing massacre, well into the new decade, Chinese political and intellectual life was markedly more repressive than it had been during most of the 1980s. Persecution of political dissenters was harsher, the activities of the secret police more pervasive, jailings were more frequent, and Party censorship of newspapers, journals, books, and movies was more stringent. Yet despite the political repression—and perhaps partly because of it—social and economic life returned to "normalcy" with unseemly haste. China's market reformers went about the business of promoting capitalist development as if nothing unusual had happened in 1989, and indeed with renewed ardor in the 1990s. It was remarkable, and remarkably depressing, how rapidly the intense political and moral passions that had gone into the making of the Democracy Movement faded and dissipated—submerged under government-promoted waves of consumerism and nationalism.

NOTES

1. The acronym "Li-Yi-Zhe" consists of the first, second, and third characters, respectively, of the names of three democratic activists in Guangdong province in the 1970s—Li Zhengtian, Chen Yiyang, and Wang Xizhe. They became nationally known for their influential treatise,

"On Socialist Democracy and the Legal System," which covered a hundred yards of wall on a street in Canton in November 1974.

2. One of the most spectacular occurred on Hainan island, which, in 1983, in accordance with then Premier Zhao Ziyang's plan to make the island a showcase for a market economy whose development would rival Taiwan, had been granted considerable economic autonomy. Hainan's officials lost no time in taking advantage of the island's privileged status by importing duty free almost 100,000 cars and trucks and a million television sets and VCRs, which were then sold on the mainland at three or four times the purchase price. The scheme was in full operation for a period of 15 months, from January 1984 to March 1985. For accounts of the Hainan operation, see Suzanne Pepper, "China's Special Economic Zones," *Bulletin of Concerned Asian Scholars*, Vol. 20, No. 3 (1988); and Lau Shinghou and Louise de Rosario, "Anatomy of a Scam," *China Trade Report*, October 1985, pp. 8–10.

3. As noted by Liu Binyan, for example, in *China's Crisis, China's Hope* (Cambridge, Mass.: Harvard University Press, 1990), p. 103.

4. While Deng's popularity in China began to decline, he continued to be celebrated in the West for his market reforms. For example, he was named *Time*'s "Man of the Year" at the end of 1985 for a second time as well as *National Review*'s "Man of the Year." The Western celebration continued until the very eve of June 4, 1989—and was cautiously resumed in the early 1990s.

5. On the "December 9" movement, see the excellent study by John Israel and Donald W. Klein, *Rebels and Bureaucrats: China's December 9ers* (Berkeley: University of California Press, 1976).

6. It is a reflection of the moral decline of the Chinese Communist Party that Liu's 1987 expulsion from the Party was a far less traumatic experience than his first expulsion thirty years earlier. See Liu, *China's Crisis, China's Hope*, pp. xv–xvi.

7. The year 2050 was the date Zhao and Deng frequently mentioned as the time when "socialist modernization" would be more or less complete.

8. "Central Document No. 2" (1992), FBIS-CHI-91-063-S.

9. Remarks to a visiting Romanian delegation in November 1980. *The New York Times*, December 30, 1980, p. 1.

10. In January 1987 Zhao had become "acting" General Secretary of the Party. The 13th Congress formally appointed him to the position, permitting him to drop the term "acting" from his title. At the same term, Zhao resigned as Premier of the State Council, a position he had held concurrently for ten months. Li Peng was formally named to the premiership.

11. This was one of the main themes in the Congress' celebration of Deng, announced beforehand in a speech delivered by Zhao Ziyang on May 13, 1987. See *People's Daily*, July 10, 1987.

12. Zhao Ziyang, "Advance Along the Road of Socialism with Chinese Characteristics," Report to the 13th CCP Congress, October 25, 1987, *Documents of the Thirteenth National Congress of the Communist Party of China (1987)* (Beijing: Foreign Languages Press, 1987), p. 70.

13. Since Deng was no longer a member of the Politburo after the 13th Congress, the Party constitution had to be revised to accommodate Deng's decision to retain control of the Military Affairs Commission.

14. For a cogent survey of the debate, see Merle Goldman, *Sowing the Seeds of Democracy in China: Political Reform in the Deng Xiaoping Era* (Cambridge, Mass.: Harvard University Press, 1994), pp. 275–82.

15. Su Xiaokang and Wang Luxiang, *Deathsong of the River: A Reader's Guide to the Chinese TV Series Heshang* (Ithaca, N.Y.: Cornell University East Asian Program, 1991), p. 183.

16. Edward Gunn, "The Rhetoric of *Heshang*: From Cultural Criticism to Social Act," *Bulletin of Concerned Asian Scholars*, Vol. 23, No. 3 (1991), p. 19.

17. Su Xiaokang and Wang Luxiang, *Deathsong of the River,* p. 218.

18. Liu Binyan, *China's Crisis, China's Hope,* p. xxii.

19. Fang Lizhi, "Letter to Deng Xiaoping" (January 6, 1989), in Fang Lizhi, *Bringing Down the Great Wall,* pp. 242–43.

20. FBIS, May 31, 1989, pp. 35–36 for an English translation of Deng's April 25 remarks.

21. For an English translation of the April 26 editorial, see "Quarterly Chronicle and Documentation," *The China Quarterly,* No. 119 (September 1989), Appendix A, pp. 717–19.

22. In a speech to the governors of the Asian Development Bank then meeting in Beijing. For the text, see Han Minzhu, ed., *Cries for Democracy: Writings and Speeches from the 1989 Chinese Democracy Movement* (Princeton: Princeton University Press), pp. 132–34.

23. For a vivid description of the May 17 demonstration, see Lee Feigon, *China Rising* (Chicago: Ivan Dee, 1990), p. 205. Feigon's book is undoubtedly the best of the many accounts of the origins and course of the Democracy Movement, and much of my discussion of the Democracy Movement is based on it.

24. Geremie Barme, "Beijing Days, Beijing Nights," in Jonathan Unger, ed., *The Pro-Democracy Protests in China* (Armonk, N.Y.: M. E. Sharpe, 1991), p. 49.

25. Quoted in Feigon, *China Rising,* pp. 209–210.

26. As Anita Chan observed shortly after the suppression of the Democracy Movement: "If one sifts carefully through the writings of Chinese intellectuals of all persuasions of the past few years, one is hard pressed to find any mention of working class grievances." Anita Chan, "China's Long Winter," *Monthly Review,* Vol. 41, No. 8 (January 1990), p. 5.

27. Hou Dejian, a Taiwanese who had emigrated to the People's Republic in 1983, was a highly popular singer and composer of rock music.

28. For example, William Hinton, an eyewitness to the suppression, has written: "People [wounded by PLA soldiers] were afraid to stay in the hospital. They thought the troops might come and arrest them, so they got a little first aid and then went home. So many people died at home. By Wednesday [June 7] of that first week there were close to a hundred unclaimed bodies in the PUMC [Peking Union Medical College] hospital and sixty-seven unclaimed bodies in the Fuxing Hospital and similar high numbers in other hospitals around. So just the number of unclaimed bodies in the morgues of the hospitals outnumbered the total number of people the government claimed had been killed, and of course those numbers include only the ones who died in the hospital after coming for treatment. Many people were killed in the street and other people went through the hospital and died at home." William Hinton, *The Great Reversal* (New York: Monthly Review Press, 1990), p. 183.

25

The End of the Reign of Deng Xiaoping:
China in the 1990s

IN THE WEEKS following the Beijing massacre of June 3–4, 1989, it was widely predicted that economic stagnation would be the price China would have to pay for the brutal political acts of its leaders. It was a time when many Western commentators were celebrating the victories of Western capitalism and political liberalism over European Communism, some of the celebrants proclaiming that the triumph of the "free market" was the culmination of human progress and that it heralded "the end of history."[1] This utopian celebration reinforced a long-standing belief that capitalism and liberal democracy went hand in hand. And from that assumption it followed that the Chinese Communist "hard-liners" who ordered the military suppression of the Democracy Movement would also terminate the market reforms that had stimulated the economic successes of the past decade. That Deng Xiaoping was at once the most prominent of the hard-liners in 1989 (indeed, he was called "the butcher of Beijing" at the time), *and* at the same time the most ardent promoter of Chinese capitalism was an apparent contradiction that was conveniently ignored.

Deng Xiaoping, for his part, saw no incongruity between capitalist economic methods and the Stalinist political system over which he presided. In his June 9th speech congratulating the soldiers who had crushed the

Democracy Movement, or what he called "the counterrevolutionary rebellion," he vowed that the policies of market restructuring and the "open door" to the world capitalist market would not be abandoned; indeed, he suggested that they should be pursued at an even "faster pace."[2] This would not only strengthen the nation and the power of the Communist state but also raise the living standards of the people, thereby dulling memories of the "Beijing Spring," Deng reasoned. The interests of the nation, the Party, and popular welfare would be equally well served by speeding up capitalist development. Thus in a secret speech to top Communist officials delivered on June 28, 1989, Deng advised that the difficult question of fixing political responsibility for the traumatic events of the spring of 1989 be set aside for several years to enable Party leaders to fully devote their efforts to promoting economic growth.[3]

Nonetheless, the years following Tiananmen were a period of harsh political repression. Thousands of Party cadres in Beijing and elsewhere who had supported the Democracy Movement, or were suspected of having sympathized with its aims, were expelled from the Communist Party or demoted. Purges also struck intellectuals, who instantly lost the limited degree of free expression they had painstakingly gained during the 1980s. Newspapers and periodicals, some of which had acquired a small if precarious degree of autonomy, were again reduced to their customary status of official organs of Party and state. Witch-hunts seeking out religious and political heretics were intensified, and dissenters were often jailed, sometimes under brutal conditions that brought international protests.

Yet it was during this time of harsh political repression in the early 1990s that China made its most spectacular economic gains, which, it was soon revealed, gave the PRC the world's third largest economy (in terms of gross output)[4] and raised the specter of a new superpower in the making.

In 1989, to be sure, China had suffered severe economic difficulties during the "bust" phase of a typically capitalist economic cycle, enduring a painful combination of inflation and recession. Inflation, rising to a rate of 30 percent per annum in the major cities, resulted from Premier Zhao Ziyang's expansionary market policies of 1987–88—and recession resulted from the austerity measures Zhao had been forced to adopt in late 1988 to control inflation. Both had contributed to economic hardship in the cities, which in turn had generated popular support for the student movement of 1989. Production declined and unemployment increased during the dreary last six months of the year and into early 1990. However, with inflationary pressures subsiding, the government's austerity policies were eased in the summer of 1990 and growth resumed. In 1991, China's GDP increased by

7.5 percent. And following Deng Xiaoping's "southern tour" of January 1992, China achieved extraordinarily high rates of growth over a sustained and crucial period in the mid-1990s.

The "Southern Tour"

At the beginning of 1992 Deng Xiaoping no longer occupied a formal position in China's political hierarchy. In the autumn of 1989, just a few months after the PLA's suppression of the Democracy Movement, he had surrendered the last of his official titles, the chairmanship of the Party's Military Affairs Commission. Yet even without holding any Party or state office Deng remained politically dominant, meeting informally with retired Party elders of his own generation to decide the most important affairs of state, decisions which the elders implemented through their proteges in the Party and state bureaucracies. Deng's new protege was Jiang Zemin, the former Party chief of the Shanghai region, who succeeded the purged Zhao Ziyang as Party General Secretary in June 1989 and who faithfully carried out Deng's policies.

But it was mainly by virtue of his own prestige and personality—and by the aura of mystery that had come to surround him and his movements—that Deng remained China's "paramount leader" in the early 1990s. Armed with a mini-personality cult that his supporters had constructed, especially after 1989, Deng began to hover over the Party apparatus in Mao-like fashion, bypassing formal Party procedures and personally intervening from above to turn policy in the direction he favored. Deng's most dramatic Mao-like intervention was his remarkable "southern tour," which transformed the pace and nature of China's economic development.

On January 18, 1992, the 87-year-old Deng Xiaoping embarked on a five-week journey through southern China, visiting the cities of Canton (Guangzhou), Wuchang, and Shanghai as well as the special economic zones of Shenzhen and Zhuhai. At each stop along his highly publicized tour, Deng exhorted local officials to accelerate economic development and to "deepen" market-oriented restructuring, praising the capitalism of the Shenzhen economic zone and the freewheeling market policies of Guangdong province as models for national emulation. "Low-speed development is equal to stagnation or even regression," Deng warned, one of the many sometimes cryptic comments made during the course of his journey, comments that were almost immediately translated into official policy and practice—in this case, the abandonment of the post-Tiananmen policy of limiting economic growth to 6 percent per annum to avoid inflation and social unrest.

Other pronouncements by the "paramount leader" encouraged a more rapid and thoroughgoing process of market reform. To those who feared that greater marketization would result in a fully capitalist China, Deng replied that the existence of the Communist state guaranteed that economic development by whatever means ultimately would have a socialist outcome. "Political power is in our hands," he reassured the critics.

But Deng sought not simply to assuage the skeptics but to remove their leaders from power and influence. To this end, during the course of his "southern tour," he proclaimed that the main danger confronting the Party was no longer the rightist heresy of "bourgeois liberalization," presumably the source of the "counterrevolutionary rebellion" of 1989, but rather once again "leftism," which was broadly defined as a lack of sufficient enthusiasm for capitalist restructuring and the more rapid pace of economic development that Deng favored. Thus was set the ideological stage for the final Party battle between the Deng faction and the "conservatives," who favored retaining a significant role for central economic planning and the state industrial sector. The main spokesman for the latter was Chen Yun, long Deng's most prominent and tenacious foe, whose ideological capitulation in the spring of 1992 marked the definitive victory of "Dengism" in the Chinese Communist Party.

In May 1992, the comments and speeches Deng made during his "southern tour" were collected in "Central Document No. 4" in the form of concrete policy guidelines issued to Party and state officials throughout the land. There followed a swift movement toward a more fully capitalist economy amid frenetic economic growth. State enterprises were allowed a wide degree of autonomy to operate on both the domestic and international capitalist markets, including conducting foreign trade on their own. Moreover, inaugurating a complex and prolonged process of semiprivatization, a limited number of state enterprises were permitted to modify their ownership status by issuing stocks which could be purchased by individual investors as well as by institutions. Such stocks were sold on newly established exchanges in Shanghai and Shenzhen, both stops on Deng's tour, and later some of these became the much sought-after "red chips" on the Hong Kong stock exchange. In addition, more generous terms and additional "open" cities were offered to foreign banks and investors who wished to conduct business in China. And a massive effort was undertaken to make the city of Shanghai the largest trade and financial center in East Asia, one which, it was predicted, would eventually eclipse Hong Kong.

These measures, along with expansionist monetary policies, and the political sanction Deng's tour gave local officials and Party bureaucrats to increase investment and take financial risks (and to enrich themselves in the process), combined to set off an economic boom unprecedented in Chinese history and perhaps in world history. Starting from an already substantial economic base, China's GDP increased 12 percent in 1992, voiding the post-Tiananmen government decision to the effect that China's social and natural environment could accommodate no more than a 6 percent per annum rate of economic growth. In 1993 the GDP grew by an astonishing 14 percent, and by 12 percent again in 1994. Extraordinarily high rates of growth continued through the mid-1990s, despite government austerity policies that aimed (with considerable success) to control inflation. By the mid-1990s, the once seemingly utopian goal (set at the beginning of the Deng era) of quadrupling the size of the Chinese economy over the twenty-year period 1980–2000 already had been exceeded. From 1991 to 1997, the average per annum increase of China's GDP was 11 percent, by far the most rapid rate of growth of any major economy in the world.

Deng Xiaoping's policies—and Deng himself—were celebrated when the Chinese Communist Party convened its Fourteenth Congress in Beijing in October 1992. The Congress ratified the virtually unlimited adoption of capitalist methods and ideas to accelerate economic growth, although the social result was officially called a "socialist market economic system." For inventing this oxymoron, Deng was extravagantly praised for making yet another "great theoretical breakthrough" in the development of "Marxism-Leninism-Mao Zedong Thought," which incongruously remained the title of official state ideology. The Fourteenth Congress marked not only the definitive triumph of Deng's market-based economic policies and his ideology but also his definitive political triumph in the Chinese Communist Party, even though he no longer occupied any political office. The Dengist political victory was symbolized by the Congress' abolition of the Central Advisory Commission, chaired by Chen Yun. This body had been created in 1982 (and orginally headed by Deng) and served as a forum that allowed retired Party leaders to intervene in affairs of state—in addition to ensuring them the material luxuries and special privileges to which the higher leaders of the Chinese Communist Party had long been accustomed. A more substantial political victory was the wholesale revamping of the personnel of the central organs of the Party, which were now almost totally dominated by members of the Deng faction. Almost half the members of the Fourteenth Central Committee were newly selected, virtually all from among Deng's staunchest supporters. This not only ensured that the Party would remain firmly loyal to the paramount leader and his policies but also reduced the average age of members of the Central Committee to a relatively youthful 56 years, more than 80 percent of whom were college graduates in engineering and the natural sciences. The Fourteenth Congress thus progressed toward realizing Deng's goal of "political reform"—for by political reform he essentially meant not popular democracy but rather simply the technocratic rationalization of bureaucratic rule. As he had said at the beginning of the reform period, the aim was to make Communist leaders "better educated, professionally more competent, and younger."[5]

But it was his economic program, not his political policies, that really mattered, at least in most Western minds. Throughout the 1980s Deng had been celebrated in the foreign press as a great modernizer who had put Maoism to rest. When he ordered the PLA to crush the Democracy Movement in 1989, however, he was widely condemned as a brutal Communist dictator. But with his ardent promotion of capitalism during his 1992 "southern tour" and after, Deng was rehabilitated in the Western media, and was now once again praised as an enlightened market reformer.

The resumption of rapid market-based economic growth in 1992 soon brought consequences familiar to those who had experienced the boom and bust cycles of the 1980s. The first result was inflation, which by the summer of 1993 was approaching a 25 percent per annum rate in several major cities—and in 1994, according to probably conservatively compiled official statistics, was 24 percent nationwide, but considerably higher in key urban areas. Inflation—combined with a new upsurge in official corruption and bureaucratic profiteering, speculation in real estate and stocks by local governments and private individuals, and the loss of central government economic controls over some of the more booming areas, especially Guangdong province—inflicted hardship on much of the working population.

To deal with this chaotic situation, Deng Xiaoping called upon another of his proteges, Vice Premier Zhu Rongji, who had been the mayor of Shanghai in June 1989 and had managed to keep order in China's largest city without unduly antagonizing either the local population or the authorities in Beijing. Zhu, who had been promoted to the Standing Committee of the Politburo at the Fourteenth Party Congress in October 1992, had been frequently praised by Deng for his economic expertise. He was now appointed governor of the People's Bank of China, with a mandate to bring the economy under control and to counter the regionalist tendencies that the economic reforms had fostered. Emulating central bankers in capitalist countries, Zhu imposed an austerity program that relied on fiscal and monetary restraints (i.e., limits on credit and reductions in government spending and investment) to bring down inflation without plunging the economy into a deep recession. His aim, in addition to reestablishing central government control over the financial affairs of the provinces, was to dampen inflation by lowering the rate of growth from more than 12 percent to what he believed was a socially and environmentally sustainable rate of 8 percent per annum.

Deng Xiaoping objected, however. In October 1993 he issued a brief but potent declaration: "Slow growth is not socialism." As a result, Zhu Rongji's austerity plan was modified, permitting the economy to again expand by 12 percent in 1994. But enough of Zhu's tight fiscal policies remained to dramatically reduce the rate of inflation from 24 percent in 1994 to a surprisingly low 6 percent in 1996—while the GDP continued to grow at a rate of about 10 percent per annum. Zhu Rongji's policies had achieved the desideratum of central bankers in capitalist countries around the world—a "soft landing" which yielded the happy combination of low inflation and high rates of growth. Zhu was duly celebrated in international banking circles and by Western journalists[6]—and in China he became the leading candidate to succeed Li Peng as Premier of the State Council when Li's term expired in March 1998.

Deng Xiaoping made his last public appearance in February 1994 during the Lunar New Year celebrations, when a five-minute segment on national television showed the paramount leader greeting Communist officials in Shanghai. It was on that occasion, according to the official account, that Deng made his final call for a more rapid pace of economic growth. During the televised segment, however, Deng was not heard to speak, and indeed his obvious frailty and dazed expression were taken as signs of his imminent departure. Deng lingered on for another three years, although he was too physically and mentally incapacitated by Parkinson's disease and other ailments to continue to play a significant role in Chinese political life. Deng Xiaoping died on February 19, 1997 at the age of 92. The country that he had launched on so frenzied a course of economic development barely paused to note the passing of the onetime paramount leader.

Deng was the last of China's old revolutionaries, the final important survivor of that remarkable group of Communist leaders who could claim membership in the May Fourth generation of revolutionary intellectuals. Those who followed were essentially products of the post-1949 People's Republic. Deng, by contrast, had come to political maturity during the early 1920s when as a young work-study student in France he had joined the French branch of the embryonic Chinese Communist Party. He had returned to China to participate in the great revolutionary upsurge of 1925–27. After the defeat of the urban revolution he fled to the countryside and soon became one of the leaders of a peasant army during the Maoist phase of the revolutionary civil war. After 1949 he was among the leading half-dozen members of the Maoist ruling group—at least until he was temporarily felled by the Cultural Revolution.

Although Deng Xiaoping could claim a long revolutionary lineage, he will best be remembered as the father of Chinese capitalism. Capitalism was not his aim, to be sure, and he preferred to believe that the economic system he fashioned was the initial stage of socialism, which would fully flower in the middle of the next century. Nonetheless, he found capitalist economic methods the most efficient way to bring about rapid modernization—and it was a nationalist vision of the wealth and power of China in the world that was always at the the heart of his world view, as was the case with many other Chinese Communist leaders.

· · ·

In a somewhat macabre sense, Deng died in a way that facilitated the "stability and unity" he so prized in life. For his lingering death, over a period of three years, enabled his handpicked successor Jiang Zemin to consolidate his power and that of the post-Deng ruling group. During that time, Jiang removed potential sources of opposition within the Party and jailed or exiled such dissidents as remained in the land. In the process, Party General Secretary Jiang acquired several new titles—the honorific title of President of the People's Republic and the more than honorific Chairman of the Party's Central Military Commission—making him simultaneously the head of the civilian state bureaucracy, the PLA, and the Chinese Communist Party.

Jiang Zemin continued the essential elements of Deng's policies: rapid economic growth, capitalist restructuring, and the preservation of a Leninist party dictatorship. Even during the three years when semi-austerity measures were in effect (1994–96), the increase in GDP averaged nearly 10 percent per annum. Direct foreign investment boomed, with major multinational groups (in which U.S. and Japanese firms had major stakes) beginning to eclipse overseas Chinese investments funneled through Hong Kong and Taiwan.[7]

Jiang Zemin's boldest economic proposal, an entirely logical step in the progression of Deng Xiaoping's market reform plan, was to call for the partial privatization of the state industrial sector. State-owned factories and related enterprises, which still accounted for over 40 percent of industrial production in 1997 and employed 120 million workers, were of course essential for the functioning of the Chinese economy, especially in the spheres of heavy industry (such as steel, petrochemicals, mining, and machine building) and in the application of advanced technologies.[8] However, according to the reformist criterion of enterprise profitability, which had now become a sacrosanct principle, more than two-thirds of state enterprises were losing money. According to the market precepts that the Communist leaders now embraced, this was ideologically heretical as well as a drain on the state budget. Efforts to "reform" (which is to say, to apply capitalist methods to) the state industrial sector had been under way for over a decade, beginning in the mid-1980s with ideological assaults against "the iron rice bowl," the system of lifetime job tenure and social welfare benefits. But the reformers had been able to do little more than nibble at the edges of the huge state sector, detaching only a few smaller and obviously failing enterprises from direct central government control. Party leaders were reluctant to confront the problems of the state sector, in part because they feared that relinquishing government ownership would be interpreted as an abandonment of socialism. But even more, Communist leaders feared unrest among the urban working class, who would have been the main victims of "reform." For the "unprofitability" of state industries was due less to poor management than it was to the relatively generous treatment of state workers, who enjoyed considerably higher wages and much greater security than workers in the private and "collective" sectors. It is, after all, mainly cheap and expendable "free labor" that makes non-state factories so profitable.

But despite the political risks, the inexorable and insistent demands of a growing market economy made Jiang Zemin an advocate of privatization, although the term was not officially used. In the spring of 1997, beginning with a blast against the "ossified" thinking of "leftists," General Secretary Jiang set forth his plan for the reform of state enterprises in a speech to senior Party leaders. While the state was to retain ownership of a number of key defense-related and high-technology industries as well as the grain trade, most enterprises were to be privatized or at least partially denationalized. Under the slogan *"Zhua da, fang xiao"* ("grasp the big, let go of the small"), all but the largest and most essential enterprises were to be turned over to various forms of non-state ownership at a more rapid pace than hitherto had been the case. And even most large enterprises were to have diverse forms of ownership, including substantial shareholdings by both foreign and domestic investors, with both individuals and institutions (such as pension funds and local governments) participating. Moreover, the term "state ownership" was liberally redefined so that enterprises where the government's share was only thirty percent could be classified as "public."

Over the summer, Jiang's speech was widely circulated for discussion among Party cadres and then published in the *Guangming Daily* in late July.[9] Jiang's privatization proposal was formally adopted by the Fifteenth Congress of the CCP, which convened in Beijing on September 12, 1997.

The Fifteenth Congress

The main business of the first Communist Party Congress of the post-Deng era was to legitimize the leadership of Deng's handpicked successor, Jiang Zemin. This was duly accomplished without debate and by unanimous vote by the 2,000 delegates to the Fifteenth Congress. In the process, the only conceivable rival of Jiang, Qiao Shi, the Chairman of the National People's Congress, was dropped not only from the Party Politburo but from its 193-member Central Committee as well. According to some rather strained interpretations, Qiao Shi, a onetime secret police head, was an advocate of democracy and the rule of law, and thus his fall from power set back the prospects of democratization.[10] Also removed from the top leadership was General Liu Huaqing, leaving the ruling seven-member Standing Committee of the Party Politburo without a PLA representative. The three most powerful politicians in China after the Fifteenth Congress, listed in the customary hierarchical order, were General Secretary Jiang Zemin, Premier Li Peng (who soon was to succeed Qiao Shi as Chairman of the National People's Congress), and the financial specialist Zhu Rongji (who was to succeed Li Peng as Premier). Jiang Zemin emerged from the Congress with his power and prestige greatly augmented, having demonstrated that there was some substance to the high titles he had accumulated, titles which made him, simultaneously, the head of the Party, the head of state, and leader of the military. But while Jiang had collected more official titles than his predecessors, he possessed less personal power, ruling more as the head of a committee than in the individual dictatorial fashion favored by his mentor Deng Xiaoping, and before him, Mao Zedong. Nonetheless, there was little doubt after the Fifteenth Congress that Jiang was politically dominant, and he capped his internal political victory with an eight-day visit to the United States and a summit meeting with President Clinton—in a quite conscious and sometimes embarrassingly obvious imitation of Deng Xiaoping's triumphant American tour of January 1979. Clinton reciprocated with a state visit to China in the summer of 1998. Traveling in truly imperial fashion, with a retinue of more than 1,000 people, Clinton's trip proved surprisingly productive for Sino-American relations—although the event was marred by accusations of "high treason" directed against the American president by some of his domestic critics.[11]

The main policy business of the Fifteenth Congress was to approve the plan for the privatization of state enterprises, which Jiang Zemin had set forth in his May 1997 speech and which then had been circulated for discussion at Party branches over the summer. The approval of the Congress came without serious debate or discussion and, as was customary, by unanimous vote. But it was not accomplished without embarrassing a good many Communist leaders who had been schooled in the Stalinist orthodoxy that state ownership of productive property is the essence of socialism—and who were reluctant to surrender the Party's claim to be the bearer of socialism. Thus, the whole issue of privatization was clothed in layers of ideological disguise, with much emphasis on continuing "public ownership" under a vaguely defined "joint stock program" and repeated invocations of the hazy doctrine of "socialism with Chinese characteristics."

It was clear, however, that whatever new forms of ownership eventually emerged, the privatization of state property would proceed in a relatively gradual manner, perhaps over a period of a decade or longer. There was much concern in the Party about the social and political unrest that might result from the mass unemployment that surely would be a consequence of the shrinkage of the state sector—for it was acknowledged that at least one-third of the more than 100 million state workers were redundant. Moreover, the disastrous Russian experience with privatization of state enterprises remained very much on the minds of China's Communist leaders. As it turned out, the timing of the privatization program was less than propitious, for the convening of the Fifteenth Congress coincided with the deepening of a financial and economic crisis that was spreading through Southeast Asia and would soon reach Hong Kong. While the economic effects on China of the Southeast Asian crisis were yet to be felt, its psychological impact was immediate and profound, casting doubt on the wisdom of further plunging China into a chaotic world capitalist market and of relying on foreign capital invested in open stock markets to assume the burden of financing newly privatized state industries.

The Fifteenth Congress was not without its incongruities. Jiang Zemin's main report, highlighted by his proposal to sell most state-owned enterprises to private investors—certainly a major step in the construction of a fully capitalist economy by any standard of judgment—was delivered on a stage whose backdrop was a gigantic red flag embossed in yellow with a huge hammer and sickle. If any of the 2,000 delegates noticed the incongruity, none were willing to comment on it. Nor was there any comment on the Beijing massacre of 1989, which cried out for official reexamination but which remained beyond the pale of permissible political discussion.[12]

. . .

The vast expansion of private ownership of productive property portended by Jiang Zemin's plans for the sale of state enterprises struck yet another blow at the socialist claims of the Beijing regime. Those claims, long fragile and perhaps spurious to begin with,[13] had rested largely on the predominance of public ownership of the means of production. The proposed privatization of state property undermined what little remained of Chinese socialism, as socialism was conventionally understood.

To fill the deepening ideological void created by the decline of socialism, the Communist regime since the early 1980s had been devoting enormous efforts to promoting nationalism and patriotism. Those efforts were intensified by Jiang Zemin in the 1990s, when an increasingly chauvinistic nationalism became virtually the sole ideology of the Chinese Communist state.

Nationalism, of course, had always been a powerful force in the Chinese Communist movement. From the founding of the CCP in the May Fourth period throughout the revolutionary era, nationalist motivations were almost always involved in conversions to Communism. In the great urban revolutionary upsurge of the mid-1920s and the Maoist rural-based revolution that followed in the 1930s and 1940s, nationalism and social revolution had been closely intertwined.[14] Indeed, in many respects the Maoist revolution, coinciding with the Japanese invasion of China, necessarily took the form of a war of national independence as well as a social revolution. During the Mao period, both before and after 1949, nationalist and social revolutionary goals were combined in ways that were usually reinforcing, although the inherently unstable combination became more difficult to maintain after the assumption of state power in 1949.

It was not until the reign of Deng Xiaoping (1978–97), however, that nationalism definitively triumphed over revolutionary aspirations and values. After 1978, socialist goals rapidly receded, and soon were entirely overwhelmed by a single-minded nationalist pursuit of "wealth and power." Indeed, socialism had been rendered quite meaningless at the beginning of the Deng era, for the paramount leader had early erased the distinction between socialism and nationalism. "The purpose of socialism is to make the country rich and strong," he declared in 1980.[15]

It was entirely logical that the cultural iconoclasm that the Chinese Communists had inherited from their May Fourth predecessors, and which had been closely identified with popular revolutionary strivings over the decades, would now give way to a conservative nationalism that celebrated the traditional cultural and historical heritage. One reflection of this phenomenon was in official historiography, where the old Maoist emphasis on class struggles and peasant wars was largely abandoned in favor of praising the accomplishments of great emperors in traditional history and great modernizing nationalist leaders in modern history—not excluding Zeng Guofan, the suppressor of the Taiping Rebellion in the nineteenth century, and even Chiang Kai-shek. This has been accompanied by an increasingly chauvinistic celebration of the glories of traditional culture, which reached its apogee during the years that Jiang Zemin was General Secretary of the Chinese Communist Party. Manifestations of this conservative cultural nationalism included a highly publicized international conference held in 1994 to celebrate the 2,545th birthday of Confucius, the reintroduction of Confucian teachings in the schools, and the establishment of an "International Association of Confucian Studies" in Beijing—which, appropriately, selected as its honorary president Lee Kuan-yew, the neo-Confucian dictator of Singapore. And perhaps even more bizarre were the quasi-official ceremonies of worship, including kowtowing and the burning of incense, performed at the "tomb" of the mythical Yellow Emperor.

The Recovery of Hong Kong

Chinese Communist nationalism has not been confined to the hazy realm of cultural nationalism. It found more concrete expression in the return of Hong Kong to Chinese sovereignty on July 1, 1997, an event which produced an outpouring of celebratory patriotic fervor—in the People's Republic and in overseas Chinese communities—not seen since the defeat of the Japanese invaders at the end of World War II.

For Chinese of virtually all political persuasions, there was no more potent symbol of China's humiliation at the hands of foreign imperialist powers than the British Crown Colony of Hong Kong. Acquired by the English as booty at the conclusion of the Opium War of 1839–42 (a war undertaken to protect British dope smugglers and to preserve the revenues of the East India Company—the de facto colonial government of India), British Hong Kong was the product of the first of the many "unequal treaties" imposed on the old Chinese empire. It soon became the archetype of the Western colonial regimes imposed on much of Asia and Africa in the nineteenth century. Since much mythmaking about "democracy" and "autonomy" was fabricated during the waning days of English rule, it should be remembered that through most of its British history, Hong Kong was ruled by an appointed governor with autocratic powers who was responsible only to the Foreign Office in London, that it was a typical colonial society where a small foreign elite ruled over and exploited a subservient native population, and that it was a society where a virulent anti-Chinese racism pervaded virtually all aspects of life.[16]

The unification of China under the Communist regime in 1949 sounded the death knell for colonial rule in Hong Kong—as also would have been the case had Chiang Kai-shek's Guomindang won the Chinese civil war. Indeed, the Chinese Communist victory probably prolonged the life of the

British Crown Colony beyond what likely would have been the case had a non-Maoist regime unified China. For during the period of Mao Zedong's rule (1949–76), the pursuit of economic "self-reliance" left China largely isolated in the world, thereby making a *British-ruled* Hong Kong economically essential to China as a source of foreign exchange and as a link to the world economy and advanced technology. Thus, the question of Hong Kong's political future was allowed to remain dormant, however great the cost to the militantly anti-imperialist image the Maoist regime wished to display.

However, in the post-Mao era, with the ascendancy of Deng Xiaoping and his "open door" policy on foreign economic relations, a British Hong Kong became as economically redundant as it was politically anachronistic. Thus, in the early 1980s, Deng Xiaoping summoned British Prime Minister Margaret Thatcher to Beijing and informed her that the colonial era was over. Negotiations, which were dictated by Beijing, soon led to Sino-British "Joint Declaration" of 1984, which stipulated that Hong Kong (the last significant part of the once mighty British empire) would be returned to China in 1997. It was also agreed that Hong Kong's economic system would remain unchanged for 50 years and that the former colony would enjoy a degree of autonomy as a "special administrative region" of the People's Republic under Deng's formula of "one country, two systems."

Deng Xiaoping died four months before he could savor the formal restoration of Chinese sovereignty over Hong Kong, and it was thus Jiang Zemin's political good fortune to preside over that nationalist triumph on July, 1997. Despite much speculation about financial and political disorder, the transfer of governmental authority proceeded without incident, although it was accompanied by much ceremony—and, on the Chinese side, by gigantic patriotic demonstrations and great nationalistic satisfaction. The patriotic feelings were very real, given the dramatic historic significance of the occasion played out before a vast international audience, but patriotic expressions of loyalty to the "motherland" had of course long been cultivated by Beijing. In 1984, Deng Xiaoping had defined patriotism liberally, at least as far as Hong Kong was concerned. Patriotism simply meant "respect for the Chinese nation" and "sincere support for the motherland's resumption of sovereignty over Hong Kong." Beyond these principles, Deng said, patriots could hold any social or political views they wished, free to believe in "capitalism or feudalism or even slavery."[17]

Beijing's nationalist appeals found their most ardent response among wealthy Hong Kong Chinese businessmen, who hastened to join various "patriotic societies." Many wealthy Hong Kong capitalists already had substantial investments in mainland enterprises and strong financial ties to the

Communist regime. Some of these, such as the shipping tycoon Tung Chee-hwa, were placed in leading positions in the new Hong Kong government, now a "special administrative region" ruled from the capital of China. The "patriotism" of wealthy Hong Kong Chinese capitalists, and their easy fusion with the Chinese Communist elite, are suggestive of the vast social transformation that had taken place in the People's Republic during the reform era of Deng Xiaoping.

Taiwan

The reestablishment of Chinese sovereignty over Hong Kong left Taiwan as the last significant barrier to full national unification. The separation of Taiwan from the mainland, however, is a far more complex matter, historically and politically, than was the termination of British colonialism in Hong Kong. And it is fraught with danger.

Most conventional measurements of nationality in the modern world leave little doubt that Taiwan is part of the Chinese nation. Ethnically, culturally, and linguistically, the inhabitants of Taiwan are overwhelmingly Chinese. Save for a small aboriginal population, which has now virtually disappeared as a distinct ethnic group, Taiwan has been populated (although lightly for many centuries) by emigrants from the mainland, who began to arrive around the year 1000 A.D. The island was formally incorporated into the Qing empire in 1683 and governed as a prefecture of Fujian province. Most of the present inhabitants of Taiwan are descendants of migrants from Fujian who crossed the Taiwan Straits in the eighteenth and nineteenth centuries.

Contemporary ambiguities and controversies over the status of Taiwan derive from several fortuitous historical events. One was the Sino-Japanese War of 1894–95, as a result of which Taiwan was seized as war booty and made a colony in the Japanese empire. It remained a Japanese colony for half a century—isolating the people of Taiwan from the main political and intellectual currents of modern Chinese history—until it was returned to China at the end of World War II. In 1945 the government of China was the Nationalist (Guomindang) regime of Chiang Kai-shek, whose armies treated Taiwan more as a conquered territory than a liberated colony.[18] The defeat of Chiang in the civil war with the Communists ended with the flight to Taiwan of the remnants of the Nationalist army and bureaucracy—almost 2 million mainlanders who superimposed themselves on a native Taiwanese population of 10 million. The Nationalist regime in Taipei claimed to be the legitimate government of all of China; it was supported in this claim by the United States, which had established a de facto military protectorate over the island with the outbreak of the Korean War in 1950 and which generously supported Taiwan economically and diplomatically as well as militarily.

While the Nationalist government in Taiwan owed its survival to the U.S. Seventh Fleet, its legitimacy rested on the fiction that it was the government of all of China. Thus it was logical (although it may seem a bit curious today), that the Guomindang regime arrested, and sometimes executed, advocates of an independent Taiwan. Indeed, in the 1950s and 1960s, for Taiwanese to favor the separation of Taiwan from China was no less politically heretical than being sympathetic to the Communist regime in Beijing.

The artificial legitimacy of Nationalist rule in Taiwan could not of course be maintained indefinitely, and the ideological props began to crumble when President Nixon began the process of normalizing U.S. relations with the People's Republic in the early 1970s.[19] The "Shanghai Communiqué" of February 1972 provided for the gradual withdrawal of U.S. military forces (although not military aid) from Taiwan and recognized that the future of the island was an internal Chinese affair. The full normalization of Sino-American relations in 1979 was accompanied by a U.S. government acknowledgement of the "Chinese position" that there is one China and that "Taiwan is part of China." However, new ambiguities and the seeds of future conflict were sown when Deng Xiaoping, eager to establish formal diplomatic relations with the U.S., agreed to the American insistence on retaining "unofficial" U.S. political and cultural ties with Taipei as well as a continuing supply of sophisticated military technology to the island.

The potential for conflict, indeed for war, in this arrangement revealed itself in frightening fashion almost two decades later, in 1995, when the Deng era was drawing to a close. Beijing's policy toward Taiwan, demanding the reunification of the island with the mainland—by peaceful means if possible, by military force if necessary—remained essentially unchanged during the Deng era. But much changed in Taiwan during those years. After the death of Chiang Kai-shek in 1975, and the death of his son and successor Chiang Ching-kuo in 1988, democratic reforms speeded up the political "Taiwanization" of the now modernized and prosperous island. Indeed, the ruling Nationalist Party itself was increasingly dominated by native Taiwanese, a transformation dramatically highlighted in 1988 when the Taiwanese vice president, Lee Teng-hui, succeeded the younger Chiang as President of the Republic of China and as Chairman of the Nationalist Party as well. President Lee, elected on his own in 1996 in Taiwan's first democratic presidential election, duly paid lip service to the goal of one China, as was demanded by the platform of the party he headed as well as by the international situation in which Taiwan found itself. But Lee slowly began to abandon the "one China" policy and gradually attempted to move Taiwan to the status of an independent nation-state. He did so in part (and it was the cleverest part) by improving relations with the Communist regime in Beijing—allowing Taiwanese to visit the mainland (which they did in large numbers), encouraging trade with the People's Republic, and allowing Taiwanese investment on the mainland, which soon exceeded U.S. $ 25 billion. Talks were held with representatives from Beijing on such practical matters as establishing direct air service between the mainland and Taiwan, fishing rights, and emigration. But trade, investment, and discussions on questions of common interest did less to promote "peaceful unification," as Beijing desired, than to project an image of Taiwan as a small but independent nation-state bravely making its way in a world dominated by large and powerful nation-states.

However, Lee Teng-hui's veiled campaign for an independent Taiwan (which included a fruitless and embarrassing offer of one billion dollars in exchange for membership in the United Nations) came to a grinding halt, and the dangers to international stability lurking in Taiwan's separateness were revealed to the world when Lee visited the United States in June 1995. Since 1972, when President Nixon began the process of normalizing relations with China, it was understood by all sides that a "one China" policy precluded visits to the U.S. by Taiwan's top government officials, although not by private citizens. That restriction had been observed by both Republican and Democratic administrations for more than two decades. President Lee, however, accepted an invitation to speak at his alma mater, Cornell University, on the occasion of his class reunion, and thus applied for a visa. Both houses of Congress, where the old China Lobby had been reincarnated among both liberal Democrats and conservative Republicans, passed resolutions demanding that Lee be welcomed to the U.S. President Clinton, facing what seemed at the time a difficult reelection bid, quickly succumbed, and the visa was granted, despite the reservations of the State Department.

Beijing's reaction to Lee's "private" visit, a journey which of course was very public and highly publicized, was quite predictable. An indirect dialogue between Lee and Jiang Zemin on "peaceful reunification" was suspended as were seemingly promising talks on disputes over fishing rights and immigration. The Chinese ambassador to Washington was recalled. In July and August, 1996, China conducted tests of advanced missiles off the shores of Taiwan. The missile tests resumed in the autumn in a crude attempt to influence the Taiwanese presidential elections. In response, two U.S. nuclear-armed aircraft carrier battle groups were dispatched to waters near China. The potential for war was frighteningly clear to all, and both China and the U.S. retreated, with President Clinton and Jiang Zemin agreeing to exchange state visits by the year 1998 and resuming lower-level military and diplomatic exchanges in the meantime.

It would not be difficult to make a reasonable historical case for an independent Taiwan. During the half-century of Japanese colonial rule (1895–1945), the people of Taiwan were cut off from China during a crucial era in its modern history and developed a distinctive Taiwanese national identity, one that was reinforced by the different historical experiences of Taiwan and the mainland after 1949.[20] The case for independence, however, cannot easily be made by the ruling Nationalist Party, whose very presence in Taiwan is testimony to Chinese unity and an affirmation of the principle of "one China." Moreover, an historical case for nationhood based on the argument that the "nation" was created as a result of foreign colonial rule is not likely to be a persuasive nationalist argument in a post-colonial age.

In the end, however appealing the historical and moral arguments that might be invoked in favor of Taiwanese independence, the hard fact of the matter is that an independent Taiwan is not militarily or politically viable. Taiwan's quasi-independence thus far has been guaranteed by a de facto American military protectorate. But U.S. military dominance in East Asia will not last forever; indeed most military specialists believe that it will not outlive the first decade of the new century and perhaps will be withdrawn well before. That China is the dominant power in East Asia is taken for granted by virtually all Asian countries, none of whom support Taiwan or the ambiguous American policy on Taiwan. As one respected Asian "elder statesman" replied to a *New York Times* correspondent's query as to why Asian countries failed to come to the assistance of the U.S. in the 1996 crisis over Taiwan:

> China has been around here for 3,000 years. The U.S. has been out in Asia for about 50 years. We figure you're maybe good for another 20 years. But after that you'll be gone, and we'll be left alone with China. We can't afford a confrontation.[21]

"Peaceful unification" with the mainland, in one fashion or another, is thus the only rational option for Taiwan. That this is the case was reinforced in the summer of 1998 when President Clinton, during the course of his state visit to the People's Republic, made unambigious what had in fact been America's "one-China" policy since President Nixon signed the "Shanghai Communiqué" in 1972: "We don't support independence for

Taiwan; or two Chinas; or one Taiwan, one China. And we don't believe that Taiwan should be a member in any organization for which statehood is a requirement."[22]

Although the pursuit of rationality cannot be guaranteed, one must assume that the governments involved (in Taipei, Washington, and Beijing) will seek to avoid a war that could have disastrous consequences on both sides of the Pacific. Hopefully, the course that reunification takes (and it is likely to be a long-term process) will provide a meaningful measure of autonomy for Taiwan in recognition of its unique modern history. It might also be hoped that reunification will take place with a China which has decisively broken with its Stalinist past and embarked on a meaningful program of democratic reform.

Capitalism, Socialism, and Democracy

The economic results of the market-reform era inaugurated by Deng Xiaoping have been stunning. Since 1978 the Chinese economy has grown at an average of over 10 percent per year, by far the most rapid economic advance over a prolonged period of time by any major nation in modern world history. The Chinese economy has quadrupled in less than two decades—and if present rates of growth continue, China will approach the United States in total industrial output by the early decades of the new century.

The social results of Chinese capitalism have been less salutary. Certainly, the great majority of the Chinese people have materially benefited from the economic upsurge, and generally enjoy a higher standard of living than they did prior to the Deng era: better housing, improved diets, and greater means to purchase consumer goods, now available in plentiful variety.[23] These gains, for a people so long impoverished and deprived of the fruits of their labors, have a moral as well as material significance that should not be underestimated.

Nonetheless, economic progress has exacted a fearful social price. Among the costs and consequences of capitalist development in post-Mao China has been environmental destruction on the most massive scale in human history, including an alarming shrinkage of cultivated land as well as industrialization's universal proclivity to poison the air and water.[24] China's market-driven growth has generated an orgy of bureaucratic profiteering and corruption, with the extra-legal demands of rapacious officials falling most heavily on the poorest and most politically defenseless members of the population, especially in the countryside. Indeed, illegal exactions by corrupt local officials has been the main catalyst for the peasant riots that have grown in frequency and intensity throughout the 1990s.[25]

Further, general material progress has been accompanied by increasingly insecure conditions of life for the majority of the working population as the market demands labor "efficiency." This, in turn, requires the elimination of many of the social welfare and job guarantees of the Mao period, raising the threat (and increasingly the reality) of mass unemployment. Those who are employed often suffer from physically dangerous conditions of work, especially young and women workers who labor in hastily constructed private and "collective" factories, where accidents and fires kill and maim workers in numbers unprecedented in modern industrial history. The abuses suffered by workers in China, as summarized by the respected Australian scholar Anita Chan, include: "forced and bonded labor; control of workers' bodily functions and physical mistreatments; subsistence or below-subsistence wages; and a pervasive climate of violence."[26]

Furthermore, the social dislocations that rapid economic growth inevitably entails have contributed to a frightening upsurge in common crime (which increased eleven-fold between 1978 and 1990, according to official statistics), the proliferation of criminal gangs in both city and countryside, and the execution of 3,000 criminals (or alleged criminals) in 1997, more than the rest of the world combined.[27] And the cities have suffered a resurgence of the social evils that were chronic in pre-1949 China—prostitution, drug addiction, gambling, and a criminal underworld—which, it had been too easily assumed, the Communist regime had decisively eliminated in the 1950s.

The most distressing result of China's "socialist market system" has been the frighteningly rapid growth of extreme social and economic inequality. In less than two decades, China has been transformed from a relatively egalitarian society to one where the gap between the wealthy and the impoverished is among the widest and most visible in the world, a land far more inequitable than such celebrated models of Asian capitalism as Taiwan or South Korea. Old inequalities inherited from the Mao period—between town and countryside, between coastal and inland regions, and between rulers and ruled—have increased greatly in the reform period. But of far greater significance are sharp socioeconomic differentiations *within* localities and regions, a reflection of the new social class divisions that state-promoted market relations so swiftly generated. The commercialization of the countryside, for example, has yielded a new rural bourgeoisie made up of capitalist-type farmers who control relatively large tracts of land worked by hired laborers or tenant farmers, private entrepreneurs who operate a vast variety of commercial and service enterprises, and rural Communist Party cadres—with whom the new rural bourgeoisie is closely intertwined and from whose ranks many members of the new class come.[28]

At the same time, the workings of the new market mechanisms have driven from the land more than 200 million "redundant" peasants, or almost half the rural work force. Their fate, the fate of peasants in all countries undergoing capitalist development, has been proletarianization, undoubtedly the most massive and most rapid process of proletarianization in world history. A good portion, perhaps half of the displaced peasants, have found jobs as low-paid wage laborers in the township and village factories and other enterprises. Most of the remainder have been reduced to migrant laborers, members of the growing "floating population" of 100 million or more peasants who roam from city to city in search of such temporary work as they can find. Needless to say, they are victims of merciless exploitation—and their numbers are expected to increase to 200 million when they are joined by unemployed workers from state factories that are slated to be closed or sold.

Economic and social disparities are even more glaring in the urban areas than in the countryside. China's cities, whose inhabitants were accustomed to relatively small differences in living standards and visible consumption in a spartan Maoist social order, are now under the dominion of a gluttonous elite made up of high and often corrupt Communist officials and their relatives who profit from myriad market activities, private industrial and commercial entrepreneurs, financiers, and highly paid technological specialists and managers. Substantial in numbers, but only a tiny percentage of the urban population, these *nouveaux riches* support the world's most rapidly growing market in luxury goods[29]—and some among them crudely boast that they can spend more on imported wine for a single dinner than the annual salary of a factory worker. As for those who labor in factories, members of the world's largest industrial proletariat, many are finding that their "iron rice bowls"—the modest degree of security traditionally enjoyed by state workers and so long disparaged by zealous market reformers—have indeed been "smashed" due to the market restructuring and sale of state enterprises. As a result, increasing numbers of urban workers are being driven into the ranks of the new *lumpenproletariat* of migrant laborers, the world's largest and most rapidly growing army of unemployed. The social and economic gap between China's new urban bourgeois elite, who so ostentatiously display themselves in fashion salons and imported luxury automobiles, and the underclass of migrant laborers who live in shantytowns or sleep in railway stations, is as wide and disgraceful a social division as can be found in any of the cities of the capitalist world. For glaring extremes of wealth and poverty, Shanghai and Guangzhou (Canton) now vie with New York, London, Rio de Janeiro, Mexico City, and Calcutta.

The inequalities that the market has generated were not entirely unanticipated. The reform era was carefully inaugurated, after all, with a ferocious ideological campaign against Maoist "egalitarianism," denounced by Deng's intellectuals as a heinous sin to which economic backwardness and the resulting social evils were attributed. A most prominent part of this process of ideological preparation for a market society, it will be recalled, was Deng Xiaoping's crude appeal to individual acquisitiveness and greed, and his a priori sanctioning of inequality, summed up in the two maxims: "to get rich is glorious" and "some must get rich first." But while socioeconomic differentiations were expected, it is inconceivable that either the proponents (or even the opponents) of the market foresaw the extremes of wealth and poverty that actually have come to pass.

Inequality, and the other social consequences of post-Maoist China's economic development, are of course, not unique to China. They are typical features of capitalism the world over. But in China they appear in exaggerated form, having emerged more swiftly and on a more massive scale than ever before in world history, the products of a capitalism that is both more economically dynamic and more socially disruptive than any of its earlier incarnations. Indeed, Chinese capitalism, the latest comer, seems the apogee of what Marx prophetically called capitalism's "constant revolutionising of production, [its] uninterrupted disturbance of all social conditions, [its] everlasting uncertainty and agitation. . . ."[30] It is a bitter historical irony that this unruly process of capitalist development, and all of its inevitable social consequences, is taking place under a Communist regime whose ideological roots are to be found in a century-old Chinese intellectual tradition that sought to avoid the social evils of capitalism.[31]

Yet amidst the savage processes of capitalist development which they initiated and promote—and from which they profit—China's Communist leaders still feel the need to claim a Marxian socialist lineage. At the Fifteenth Communist Party Congress, the very conclave that ratified the privatization of state-owned industries, General Secretary Jiang Zemin variously proclaimed that China was advancing along the road of "socialism with Chinese characteristics," announced that the country remained in "the primary stage of socialism" (a phrase that had been dormant since the fall of Zhao Ziyang in 1989),[32] placed himself in a long line of revolutionary leaders from Karl Marx to Mao Zedong and Deng Xiaoping, and spoke glowingly (if obscurely) about "socialist democracy," the same phrase his one-time patron, Deng Xiaoping, had so artfully employed in his own rise to power two decades earlier.

It is fruitless to speculate about what intellectual and psychological significance, if any, these murky ideological terms and formulae might have for Jiang and other post-Deng Communist leaders. But the political purpose is clear enough. The appearance of some measure of ideological continuity with the Marxist tradition and its main Chinese disciples provides a facade of legitimacy for Jiang as the guardian of the Revolution of 1949, which produced the state over which he now presides. Moreover, that ideological veneer, however thin, provides a sanction for "the leading role" (i.e., the dictatorship) of the Chinese Communist Party, for it was under the guidance of the Party that the revolution was victorious and the People's Republic created—and it is the Chinese Communist Party that still claims to be the institutional repository of the revolution's socialist goals.

Socialism and Democracy

The revival of the term "socialist democracy" by Jiang Zemin is curious. After nearly two decades of intensive state-promoted capitalist development, coupled with (and intimately tied to) severe political repression, it would seem that even the idea of democratic socialism is well beyond the realm of official comprehension. Jiang Zemin, after all, has firmly tied himself to the legacy of Deng Xiaoping. Indeed, he has raised Deng's ideas and policies, what he calls "Deng Xiaoping Theory," to the status of an official state ideology. By "Deng Xiaoping Theory" he can only mean the combination of rapid capitalist development and political dictatorship. In this conception of China's development, there is much nationalist content but little place for socialism.

Nonetheless, a socialist future is still vaguely promised by the Beijing regime, apparently on the basis of an ultraorthodox Marxist belief that socialism will be the automatic result of advanced levels of economic and technological development. As Deng Xiaoping repeatedly emphasized—and this is presumably a principal tenet of what his successors understand as "Deng Xiaoping Theory"—socialism will necessarily emerge from the development of production, although he did not explain how.[33] According to Deng, however, the material preconditions for the transition from "the primary stage of socialism" to a "developed" socialism would not be present until the year 2050. His successors have enriched the theory by postponing the arrival of socialism for another half-century. Jiang Zemin has predicted that a socialist society will be built at the end of the twenty-first century.[34] In either case, socialism is postponed to a future time that is effectively severed from the hopes and actions of the present, and thus rendered meaningless.

The real sources of any conceivable Chinese socialism are to be found not in the economic maturation of the Communist system at some distant time in the future but rather in a democratic struggle against the Communist regime in the here and now. Socialism requires both a vision and a social agent. The vision cannot be imposed from above by a Great Helmsman but will develop naturally as the struggle against the social ravages of capitalism inevitably unfolds. And the social agent will likely be the proletariat, not because of any Marxian doctrinal orthodoxy, but rather because industrialization is rapidly making China's workers the most numerous, most exploited, and most politically vital social class—and the class that the Communist regime most fears.

It is no peculiarity of Chinese history that the proletariat, the class that the Chinese Communist Party still ritualistically claims to represent, has turned out to be the main threat to the Communist regime. Such, after all, was the case in many of the Eastern European Communist countries (and to a lesser extent, in the Soviet Union) from the 1950s to the 1980s. What is paradoxical in China, a paradox which participants and observers alike will be forced to confront, is that any socialist movement in China perforce will be anti-Communist and anti-capitalist at the same time. This apparent incongruity grows out of the fact that Chinese capitalism is largely a creation of the Communist state, and the Communist Party leaders and officials are centrally involved in the workings of China's "socialist market economy," relying on the power of the Communist state to protect the capitalist system from which many of them profit so handsomely.

This seemingly strange association of Communism with capitalism (which perhaps is not too surprising a union when one recalls the origins of China's state-promoted capitalism) makes it most unlikely that the new Chinese bourgeoisie will be an ardent promoter of democratic change. Rather the challenge to the Communist state will come from the victims, not from the beneficiaries, of Chinese capitalism. It will come primarily from China's greatly expanded and increasingly exploited working class and their allies. Thus the question of the freedom to organize independent trade unions emerges as one of the most crucial issues in contemporary Chinese politics, one central to the struggle for democracy and human rights.

What are the prospects for democratic change in post-Deng China? Few still cling to the once popular image of the Chinese Communist regime as an unchanging totalitarian monolith, incapable of inner movement. While the economic transformation since 1978 has been dazzling, the post-Mao political changes are not insignificant. To be sure Deng Xiaoping, once in power, lost little time in betraying his promise of "socialist democracy," and also betraying (and sometimes jailing) his onetime allies in the Democracy Wall Movement of 1978–81. Nonetheless, the early Deng regime dramatically ameliorated the repressive and totalitarian practices of the Maoist state. During the years 1978–81, hundreds of thousands of political prisoners, mostly victims of the antirightist campaign of 1957 and the Cultural Revolution, were released from prisons and labor camps and were "rehabilitated" and sometimes honored. Throughout the 1980s, although the situation varied greatly from time to time and place to place, the diversity of intellectual and cultural expression was unprecedented in the history of the People's Republic. While the actual numbers cannot be verified, all observers agree that in the early 1980s there was a "spectacular reduction" (in the words of a *Human Rights Watch* report) in the number of people imprisoned for political crimes.[35] In all, state control over everyday life was significantly eased.

Nonetheless, the essentials of the Stalinist political system were retained. And the system was ideologically reinforced by Deng's "Four Cardinal Principles,"[36] which were treated as sacrosanct by Deng's successors as they had been by Deng himself. Rule by a single party (or, more precisely, by a small committee that stood at the apex of the Leninist hierarchy) remained, and no political organization of any sort was allowed to emerge to challenge the "leading role" of the Chinese Communist Party. The Party itself, which claimed nearly 60 million members (still only 5 percent of the population), resisted any process of democratization within its own ranks. At the Fifteenth Congress in 1997, there were no open debates or controversies over any issue of significance, no delegate criticized Jiang Zemin or any other leader, and all resolutions were passed by unanimous vote, as was customary. It was all in the best Stalinist tradition.

The monopolization of political power by the Communist Party, its continued viability as a national organization with bureaucratic tentacles radiating from the capital to the virtually all localities, and the undiminished power of the political police (consisting of myriad secret police organizations), counsel skepticism about the much discussed democratic potentialities of village-level elections. The direct election of local "people's congresses" was a provision of the 1979 Electoral Law promulgated at the beginning of the Deng era, and then modified by the National People's Congress in 1986. However, the experiment was twice aborted when democratic activists attempted to impart a degree of democratic content to local elections held in 1980 and 1986.[37] The process was revived in the early and mid-1990s with the holding of village elections, followed by a promise from Jiang Zemin that the electoral process would be soon extended to townships (i.e., small cities with populations up to 100,000). While village and township elections might serve to express popular sentiment on local issues and perhaps facilitate a degree of citizens' control over local governments, local elections, however desirable, are hardly the harbinger of any general process of democratic evolution. The continued presence of national Party and police organizations in the villages and townships ensures that local elections probably will be confined to issues of purely local significance.

More promising than central government-sanctioned village elections have been unheralded local democratic initiatives quietly undertaken in scattered (and partially industrialized) areas of the countryside since the mid-1980s. These have fostered a degree of popular supervision of local Party and government officials, and simultaneously have promoted semi-collective forms of economic life, developments which some intellectuals who have become associated with the movement have termed a "democratic system of cooperation."[38]

Although the grip of the Communist state on society was greatly relaxed in the 1980s, the military suppression of the Democracy Movement in June 1989 ushered in a new and prolonged period of political repression. Beyond the massive wave of arrests by secret police agencies that immediately followed the PLA assault on Beijing, stringent political controls and ideological orthodoxies reminiscent of the pre-Deng days were reimposed on society at large. Intellectuals, journalists, and college students were targeted by the political police, but purges also struck the Communist Party itself, resulting in the expulsion or disciplining of thousands of cadres who were suspected of having sympathized with the youthful democratic activists. Workers who participated in the "Beijing Spring" were treated in a particularly cruel and arbitrary fashion, with summary executions and lengthy prison terms not uncommon. Strict censorship was once again imposed on newspapers, magazines, and books.

The Democracy Movement of 1989 and its violent suppression was of course the immediate occasion for these ultrarepressive policies in the last years of the Deng era and the early years of the "collective leadership" of Jiang Zemin. Also contributing to the repressive climate were the fears generated by the disintegration of Communism in Eastern Europe and the Soviet Union. From the demise of the Soviet Union, Deng Xiaoping and other Chinese Communist leaders derived the lesson that it was necessary to strengthen the dictatorial power of the Leninist state and party, and that democratizing policies such as those pursued by Gorbachev were terribly dangerous to the survival of Communist power. They also drew the lesson that it was necessary to "deepen" market reform in order to speed up economic development, raise living standards, and thereby mitigate popular dissatisfaction. It is this combination of capitalist development with political dictatorship that became the guiding principle of the Chinese Communist regime after 1989, in some respects foreshadowed by the neo-authoritarian doctrines that had influenced important segments of the intelligentsia in the late 1980s . It was a principle that satisfied Deng Xiaoping's obsessive fear of chaos (*luan*), which he indiscrimately identified with both Mao's Cultural Revolution and the post-Maoist democracy movements. As it happened, the capitalist economic boom of the early and mid-1990s fortuitously arrived to prop up what Deng and his successors incongruously insisted on calling "the socialist system."

The most prominent of the many thousands of victims of the political repression of the 1990s was Deng Xiaoping's old foe Wei Jingsheng, who in 1979 had prophetically warned of Deng's "metamorphosis into a dictator."[39] For that and other impolitic comments, Wei had been arrested by public security agents on March 29, 1979, inaugurating the suppression of the Democracy Wall movement. Tried on charges of criminal "counterrevolutionary" activities, Wei, after a one-day trial, was sentenced to fifteen years' imprisonment. He was the first prominent victim in what was to become a long line of victims of a permanent witch-hunt against political dissent, one that was to wax and wane in intensity as the varying political interests and inclinations of Communist leaders dictated.

Wei Jingsheng was released from jail in September 1993, six months before the conclusion of his fifteen-year sentence. But the period of "freedom" for the 44-year-old democracy activist in China's now frenetic capitalist world was short-lived. Despite new threats of a harsh imprisonment, Wei was no more inclined to bow before the authority of the state in 1993 than he had been in 1979. He wasted little time in publishing articles calling for political freedom and democratic reforms. For this he once again was arrested, and in December 1995 was sentenced to a prison term of fourteen years for having engaged in a "conspiracy to subvert the government." Wei Jingsheng served less than two years of his second sentence. Under growing international criticism, the Beijing regime released Wei in November 1997 and sent him into exile, shortly after Jiang Zemin's state visit to the United States.

During the brief interval between his two prison terms, Wei Jingsheng wrote to Wang Dan to propose "mutual assistance" among China's isolated dissidents, a suggestion that the state prosecutor was to cite as evidence of a conspiracy to subvert the government by both Wang and Wei. Wang Dan, the Beijing University undergraduate who had been a leader of the 1989 Democracy Movement, had himself only recently been released from prison, paroled after serving most of a four-year sentence for disseminating "counterrevolutionary propaganda." Once freed from his jail cell, Wang devoted himself to providing humanitarian assistance to the families of other political prisoners. He also wrote articles calling for democratic reform, several of which were published in Hong Kong and Taiwan. Wang Dan was accused of collusion with "hostile overseas forces in order to carry out the criminal act of conspiring to subvert the government."[40] He was placed under "residential surveillance" in May 1995 and held incommunicado for more than a year before being formally charged with "subversion" in October 1996. Wang Dan was then sentenced to prison for eleven years but released and forced into exile less than two years later, in April 1998, shortly before President Clinton's visit to China.

In their second prosecutions, neither Wei Jingsheng nor Wang Dan were accused of the customary crime of "counterrevolution," as they had been at their first trials. Rather, they now were imprisoned on the charge that their activities endangered the security of the state. The terminological change resulted from a Communist Party decision to remove "counterrevolution" from the criminal code, in part to avoid the appearance of political persecution in the face of widespread international criticism, in part simply because of a belated legal recognition that the revolution had ended long ago. The revision was formalized in March 1997 when the National People's Congress promulgated a new criminal code, which abolished the crime of "counterrevolution" but created a new category of prisoners called "state security offenders." The change was little more than semantic. Those who were already imprisoned as "counterrevolutionaries" remained in jail while the new "state security" laws were interpreted in sufficiently broad fashion to include all those who previously would have been charged with "counterrevolutionary activities."

This legalistic change did not alter the long-standing practice of jailing political dissidents for alleged common criminal offenses, especially on such vague charges as "hooliganism" and "theft." Nor did the removal of "counterrevolution" from the criminal code lessen the number of political prisoners jailed through administrative procedures without the dubious benefit of a trial. Such was the fate of Liu Xiaobo, the well-known literary critic who had negotiated with PLA commanders for the safe passage of 5,000 students from Tiananmen Square in the early morning hours of June 4, 1989.[41] This had earned him nearly two years in prison for "counterrevolutionary incitement." In the mid-1990s, Liu was active in writing petitions and open letters calling for democratic reforms, peaceful unification with Taiwan, and negotiations with the Dalai Lama over the status of Tibet. As a consequence, on October 7, 1996 he was arrested at his Beijing home and sentenced by the Public Security Bureau to a three-year term of "reeducation through labor," which is to say, he was dispatched to a labor camp.

Many dissidents fled into exile to avoid imprisonment, especially after June 1989. One exile was Wang Xizhe, who had already endured almost two decades in prison before he escaped to the U.S. in late 1996. Wang was one of the three young intellectuals, using the acronym "Li-Yi-Zhe," who in the early 1970s wrote the influential treatise "Socialist Democracy and the Legal System" which provided much of the intellectual inspiration for the Democracy Wall Movement of 1978–81. But before that came to pass, the three authors of the work were arrested. In March 1975, caught up in the byzantine factional political struggles of the last years of the Mao regime, Wang Xizhe and his two colleagues were shipped off to a penal colony.

In February 1979, with Deng Xiaoping now in power, the "Li-Yi-Zhe" were released and rehabilitated. Two of the three members of the group accommodated themselves to the post-Maoist order of things, taking advantage of the new opportunities the Deng regime offered. But Wang Xizhe continued on his independent course as a democratic Marxist, his voluminous writings critical of the absence of socialism as well as democracy in both the Mao and the post-Mao periods. After the arrest of Wei Jingsheng, Wang became increasingly critical of Deng Xiaoping and soon arrived at the conclusion that the Chinese Communist Party had transformed itself into a new bureaucratic ruling class. His conclusion was the most heretical of the ideological sins of the Deng era. He was arrested as a "counterrevolutionary" in April 1981 and sentenced to a fourteen-year term in jail. His health broken by the harsh conditions of his imprisonment, Wang Xizhe was paroled in 1993. Fearing rearrest because of his continuing expression of democratic socialist ideas, although his views struck few responsive chords in an increasingly depoliticized China, he went into hiding and eventually into exile, fleeing to the United States in late 1996.

. . .

The post-1989 political repression fell hardest on the urban working class. Throughout the 1980s, China's political leaders were haunted by the "Polish fear," the prospect of a Solidarity-type alliance between workers and intellectuals that might pose a serious political threat to the Communist regime. Although precious few intellectuals harbored thoughts of such an alliance, the government was quick to take repressive actions against workers at the first sign of dissent or unrest. Workers who participated in the 1989 Democracy Movement were treated far more harshly than student activists. A good many workers were summarily executed in June 1989 for alleged acts of violence.[42] And workers, who were arrested in far greater numbers than students, were invariably sentenced to far longer jail terms than students tried on similar charges. Even students on the government's "most wanted" list were treated with comparative leniency. For example Wang Dan, who headed that much-publicized list, was sentenced to four years in prison, whereas workers arrested as Democracy Movement activists were usually condemned to terms from fifteen years to death.[43]

The state was especially ruthless in punishing workers who had taken part in the abortive effort to organize trade unions during the Democracy Movement. Several organizers were publicly executed in June 1989, and others who had engaged in entirely peaceful union activities were charged with violent criminal acts and sentenced to lengthy jail terms. In some cases, union organizers were jailed without formally being charged with any offense. Such was the case with Han Dongfang, a maintenance worker at the Beijing Railway Bureau who was one of the organizers of the Beijing Workers Autonomous Federation. Imprisoned in June 1989, Han was held without charge until April 1991, when he was released for fear that he would die in jail of tuberculosis. Following his release, although he suffered chronic illness, economic deprivation, and police harassment, Han Dongfan continued his campaign to organize workers. He explained that it was Deng Xiaoping's economic reforms that made the establishment of free trade unions necessary: "If China now allows all these capitalist organizations to spring up, how can it not allow free trade unions to arise to protect the workers' interests? I wish the party unions could protect the workers, but their actions have left me disappointed. They have not done their job well."[44]

In May 1992, the Beijing regime, having gained a good deal of adverse international publicity, granted Han Dongfan an exit visa to study in the United States. But when Han attempted to return to China in the summer of 1993, he was turned back at the border, in effect condemned to permanent exile.

In no area of basic human rights has the Chinese Communist state been more ferociously vigilant than in the suppression of labor activists who strive (thus far unsuccessfully) to organize free trade unions. Vital political and economic interests are involved in the special attention that secret police and state security organs have devoted to "the labor question." The political concern is an old one, namely the Leninist fear of any group that is not under the Party's organizational control. From this obsessive anxiety there springs the determination of Communist leaders to crush any potential threat to the monopoly enjoyed by the official All-China Federation of Trade Unions, which is firmly controlled by the Party. The economic interest derives from Deng Xiaoping's market reforms, which have made the Communist state dependent on the success of the bureaucratic capitalist system it has created. Chinese capitalism, in turn, relies on the Communist state to provide an ample supply of labor, to keep wages low, and to discipline the workers. These functions are the essence of those "special Chinese characteristics" that make the People's Republic so attractive to both domestic and foreign investors—and fuel rapid economic growth. These "special characteristics" are not compatible with free and independent labor unions—and thus labor activists are treated as the most dangerous of dissidents.

In all, the Communist state has served well the interests of Chinese capitalism (and the pecuniary interests of entrepreneurial bureaucrats) by outlawing independent trade unions, suppressing such embryonic labor organizations that appear, and jailing (or sending into exile) labor activists.

The assault against labor comes at a time of great distress for China's urban working class. It is a time when the precepts and realities of a capitalist economy dictate a smaller and even lower-paid work force. It is a time when government plans for the partial privatization of state industries threaten to add as many as 40 million additional workers to the already burgeoning unemployment rolls. It is a time when "the market" demands the dismantling of most of what remains of the old Mao-era social welfare system, leaving economic enterprises and the government with increasingly meager resources to fund unemployment relief, pensions, and health care. It is a time when the income of many urban working-class families are shrinking, due in part to draconian layoffs suffered by female members of the family, especially women over age 30.[45] Moreover, adding to the burdens of working-class families are new bureaucratic exactions, such as the imposition of tuition fees at public elementary schools. And a glut of office space in modern buildings has slowed construction in the big cities, resulting in fewer jobs for migrant laborers even as the "floating population" grows into the largest "reserve army of labor" in world history.

The economic distress of the working people in both urban and rural areas, growing for several years due to the inevitable slowing of the domestic economy, has been exacerbated by the financial crisis that so suddenly engulfed the world in the last years of the millenium. Having joined the world economy in the early 1980s to gain the economic advantages of foreign trade and capital, the People's Republic must now also experience some of the less pleasant vicissitudes of the world system. The crisis of global capitalism, which was first manifested in Thailand and South Korea in the spring of 1997, soon reached China's shores. Faced with declining exports, cuts in direct foreign investment, and competition from ever cheaper goods produced by other Asian countries, economic growth fell to a per annum rate of 7 percent in the first half of 1998, and further declined thereafter.[46] This was still a high rate by world standards but a far cry from the 12 to 14 percent increases recorded just a few years earlier—and significantly less than the 8 percent rate that Zhu Rongji and other Chinese leaders have repeatedly said is the minimum needed to mitigate the effects of unemployment and preserve social stability.

Faced with this triple onslaught—from China's domestic "market," its Communist state, and the fluctuations of the world economy—China's workers, deprived of the freedom to build their own organizations, are virtually defenseless and can offer only spontaneous and sporadic resistance. Such resistance has grown rapidly over the 1990s, taking the form of local strikes, work slowdowns, and street-corner demonstrations by the growing number of unemployed, those threatened by loss of jobs, workers owed wages, and retirees owed pension payments. Whether these thus far scattered expressions of discontent will coalesce into an organized movement of opposition to the Communist state remains to be seen—and indeed remains difficult to imagine. But it is clearly the urban working class that Communist leaders fear most as the gravest threat to their profitable monopoly of political power. Perhaps they dimly recall from their youthful readings Karl Marx's prophecy that capitalism creates its own gravediggers in the form of the modern proletariat. It would be supremely ironic if that now seemingly ancient and half-forgotten prophecy, having failed to come to pass in the Western capitalist countries, were to be fulfilled in China—in opposition to a ruling Communist Party that still claims to embody the interests, the aspirations, and the historical mission of the modern industrial working class.

NOTES

1. Most famously, Francis Fukuyama, *The End of History and the Last Man* (New York: The Free Press, 1992).
2. "Speech by Deng Xiaoping, Chairman of the Central Military Commission, delivered in Beijing to commanders above corps level of the martial law enforcement troops on 9 June 1989," Quarterly Chronicle and Documentation, *The China Quarterly*, No. 119 (September 1989), p. 726.
3. *Far Eastern Economic Review*, August 10, 1989, p. 13.
4. According to an International Monetary Fund report released in the summer of 1993 and employing the new standard of "purchasing power parity," China's economy then was the world's

third largest in total economic output, barely behind Japan, although still far behind the U.S. According to the CIA's annual report to the U.S. Congress, made available at the same time, China had equalled and was on the verge of overtaking Japan, whose economy had been largely stagnant since 1990. Tim Weiner, "CIA Says Chinese Economy Rivals Japan's," *The New York Times,* August 1, 1993, Section 1, p. 6. The Chinese economy is variously ranked as the second, third, and fourth largest in the world—depending on differing standards of measurement and changing assumptions.

5. Deng Xiaoping, "On the Reform of the System of Party and State Leadership" (August 18, 1980), *Selected Works of Deng Xiaoping* (Beijing: Foreign Languages Press, 1984), p. 308. For English translations of the principal documents of the 14th CCP Congress, see *Beijing Review,* October 26–November 1, 1992.

6. For example, Seth Feison, "China Economy's Class Act," *The New York Times,* November 14, 1996, p. C18. Craig Smith, "China Expects GDP to Expand 10.5% over Coming Year," *The Wall Street Journal,* December 31, 1996, p. 4. In 1997, China's GDP actually grew 8.8%, significantly below official expectations.

7. Marcus W. Brauchili, "Foreign Investment in China Still Climbs," *The Wall Street Journal,* January 14, 1997, p. A14.

8. For an insightful and unusually balanced appraisal of China's state industrial sector, see Ajit Singh, "The Plan, the Market and Evolutionary Economic Reform in China," UNCTAD Discussion Papers, No. 76 (December 1993).

9. Jiang Zemin, "Upholding The Banner of Deng's Theory," *Beijing Review* (Aug. 25–31, 1997), pp. 10–13.

10. For example, Liu Binyan, "Jiang's Gain, the CCP's Loss," *China Focus,* Vol. 5, No. 10 (October 1, 1997), p. 1.

11. For a brief account of the Clinton visit, see Maurice Meisner, "Beyond the Rhetoric on China," *Los Angeles Times,* July 5, 1998, p. M1.

12. A letter that Zhao Ziyang wrote to the 15th Party Congress calling for a reappraisal of the 1989 Democracy Movement reportedly was suppressed by Jiang Zemin. Liu Binyan, "Jiang's Gain, the CCP's Loss, *China Focus,* Vol. 5, No. 10 (Oct. 1, 1997), p. 1.

13. For a discussion of "socialism" in Maoist and post-Maoist China, see chapter 21 above.

14. See chapters 3 and 4 above.

15. As Deng informed a visiting Rumanian delegation in November 1980. *The New York Times,* December 30, 1980, p. 2.

16. Racism was particularly apparent in social life and housing. For example, in 1904 the British colonial regime made housing segregation in Hong Kong a matter of law as well as fact when it promulgated the Hill District Reservation Ordinance, which prohibited Chinese (however wealthy) from living on "the Peak," the upper levels of the the beautiful mountain that rises from the center of Hong Kong Island.

17. Deng Xiaoping, "One Country, Two Systems," in Deng Xiaoping, *Fundamental Issues in Present-Day China* (Beijing: Foreign Languages Press, 1987), p. 52.

18. The harshness of Nationalist Chinese rule provoked a week-long Taiwanese uprising which began on February 28, 1947 in Taipei and spread throughout the island. The revolt was bloodily suppressed by the Guomindang army, which killed several thousand Taiwanese and jailed many thousands more. In the process much of the middle-class Taiwanese leadership was eliminated. See George Kerr, *Formosa Betrayed* (Boston: Houghton Mifflin Co., 1965), especially chapters 12–16. Also, Ong Joktik, "A Formosan View of the Formosan Independence Movement," in Mark Mancall, ed., *Formosa Today* (New York: Praeger, 1964), pp. 163–170.

19. See chapter 20 above.

20. I have outlined this case in greater detail, in an earlier and different political era. See Maurice Meisner, "The Development of Formosan Nationalism," in Mark Mancall ed., *Formosa Today,* pp. 147–62.

21. Quoted in Thomas L. Friedman, "Help Wanted: Deal Makers," *The New York Times,* March 24, 1996, Sect. 1, p. 15.

22. Jackie Calmes and Craig S. Smith, "Clinton Backs China on Taiwan, Loud and Clear," *The Wall Street Journal,* July 1, 1998, p. A13.

23. Abundant statistical evidence for the human gains that have resulted from economic development in recent decades can be found in UNDP, *China: Human Development Report, 1997* (Beijing, 1998).

24. For an informative and most incisive critique of the environmental consequences of China's market economy, see Richard Smith, "Creative Destruction: Capitalist Development and China's Environment," *New Left Review,* No. 222 (March–April, 1997), pp. 3–41.

25. For a description of such peasant protests in the summer of 1997, see Cheng Mu, "Peasant Riots Erupt in Hubei and Jiangxi," *China Focus,* Vol. 5, No. 10 (October 1, 1997), p. 1.

26. For details based on first-hand observation and investigation, see Anita Chan, "Workers Rights are Human Rights," *China Rights Forum* (Summer 1997), pp. 4–7.

27. Amnesty International Report, summarized in AP dispatch, *Wisconsin State Journal,* September 4, 1998, p. 8A.

28. On the rapid growth of inequality in recent years, see Azizur Rahman Khan and Carl Riskin, "Income and Inequality in China: Composition, Distribution and Growth of Household Income, 1988–1995," *The China Quarterly,* No. 154 (June 1998), pp. 221–251.

29. As reported in *The Wall Street Journal,* January 13, 1993, p. A10.

30. Karl Marx and Friedrich Engels, *Manifesto of the Communist Party,* in Robert C. Tucker ed., *The Marx-Engels Reader* (New York: Norton, 1978), p. 476.

31. One of the major themes in the thought of the modern Chinese intelligentsia since the 1890s was a belief that the fruits of modern science and industry could be acquired by China without subjecting the country to the social agonies of a capitalist regime. A closely related theme was a belief in China's "advantage of backwardness." For a brilliant analysis of these intellectual tendencies, see Wang Yaan-iee, "The Chinese Idea," Ph.D. thesis, Dept. of History, University of Wisconsin-Madison, 1997.

32. The theory of the "primary stage of socialism" is discussed in chapter 24 above.

33. See, for example, "Build Socialism with Chinese Characteristics" (June 30, 1984), Deng Xiaoping, *Fundamental Issues in Present-Day China* (Beijing: Foreign Languages Press, 1987), pp. 53–58.

34. Jiang Zemin, "Hold High The Great Banner of Deng Xiaoping Theory for an All-Round Advancement of the Cause of Building Socialism with Chinese Characteristics into the 21st Century," (September 12, 1997), *Beijing Review* (October 6–17, 1997) pp. 10–33.

35. Although statistics on political prisoners generally are kept secret, data obtained on one province gives some idea of the dramatic change that occurred. In late 1959 Heilongjiang Province had a prison population of 97,332, of whom 57,933 (about 60 percent) had been jailed as "counterrevolutionaries." In 1981, the prisoner population in the province was 23,685, among whom only 577 (less than 3 percent) were classified as " counterrevolutionaries." *Heilongjian Jiancha Zhi,* [Heilongjiang Provincial People's Procuracy] (Harbin: Heilongjiang People's Press, 1988). Cited in *Human Rights Watch/Asia,* Vol. 9, No. 4 (April 1997), p. 31.

36. See chapter 22 above.

37. On the 1980 elections, see Andrew Nathan, *Chinese Democracy* (Berkeley: University of Cal-

ifornia Press, 1985), pp. 193–223. On the 1986 elections, see Meisner, *The Deng Xiaoping Era,* pp. 360–61.

38. For a detailed study of democratic change in Xinmi county in Henan Province, see Rong Jing-ben, Cui Zhiyuan, *et al., Transformation from the Pressurized System to a Democratic System of Cooperation: Reform of the Political System at the County and Township Levels* (Beijing: Central Compilation and Translation Press, 1998). It is also noteworthy that the ambiguous owner-ship status of many rural industrial enterprises have permitted a degree of worker and com-munity participation in their management in some areas.

39. Wei Jingsheng, *"Yao minzhu haishi xin de ducai?"* ("Democracy or New Dictatorship"), JPRS No. 73421, pp. 28–30.

40. Sub-Procuratorate of Beijing Municipal Procuracy, "Bill of Indictment against Wang Dan" (October 7, 1996), translated and printed as Appendix I in *Human Rights Watch/Asia,* Vol. 8, No. 10(c), November 1996, pp. 11–13.

41. See chapter 24.

42. The number of workers *known* to have been executed in connection with the Democracy Movement is sixty. The actual number is undoubtedly considerably greater. *Asia Watch,* Vol. 4, No. 17 (May 28, 1992), p. 2.

43. See, for example, the list of 104 persons arrested in connection with the events of June 4, 1989 who were known to have been in Beijing No. 2 Prison in 1994, the overwhelming ma-jority of whom were officially identified as *gongren* [workers] serving long terms. *Human Rights Watch/Asia,* Vol. 6, No. 11 (October 3, 1994), pp. 7–13.

44. UPI, March 25, 1992. Cited in *Asia Watch,* Vol. 4, No. 17 (May 28, 1992), p. 6.

45. While women make up 39 percent of the workforce in the state sector, 60 percent of laid-off state workers were women (most over the age of 35) in the spring of 1998, according to the semi-official All-China Women's Federation. Jennifer Lin, "About Face: China's Economic Reforms Hit Hardest against Women," *Chicago Tribune,* April 26, 1998, Section 13, p. 9.

46. *The Wall Street Journal,* July 20, 1998, p. A 15.

Selected Bibliography

MUCH OF THE best literature on the history of Chinese Communism and the People's Republic is to be found in periodicals. Of special interest are *Asian Survey, Asia Watch, Australian Journal of Chinese Affairs, Bulletin of Concerned Asian Scholars, China Quarterly, China Focus, Contemporary China, Far Eastern Economic Review, Human Rights Watch/Asia, Issues and Studies, Journal of Asian Studies, Modern China,* and *Pacific Affairs.* Articles relevant to the history related in this book that have been published in these and other journals are too numerous to list individually in this brief bibliography, although many appear in the endnotes. The titles listed below include only books cited in the text and others that were considered in preparing this volume. While the bibliography is thus far from complete, it hopefully might prove of some assistance to readers who wish to pursue particular topics in greater depth or who seek interpretations different from those offered in the preceding chapters.

Ahn, Byung-joon. *Chinese Politics and the Cultural Revolution.* Seattle: University of Washington Press, 1976.

Ali, Tarik, ed. *The Stalinist Legacy.* Harmondsworth, Middlesex, England: Penguin Books, 1984.

Andors, Phyllis. *The Unfinished Liberation of Chinese Women, 1949–1980.* Bloomington: Indiana University Press, 1983.

Andors, Stephen. *China's Industrial Revolution: Politics, Planning, and Management, 1949 to the Present.* New York: Pantheon Books, 1977.

———, ed. *Workers and Workplaces in Revolutionary China.* White Plains, N.Y.: M.E. Sharpe, 1977.

Arkush, R. David. *Fei Xiaotung and Sociology in Revolutionary China.* Cambridge, Mass.: Harvard University Council on East Asian Studies, 1981.

Arnold, Matthew. *The Poems of Matthew Arnold.* Edited by Kenneth Allott. New York: Barnes & Noble, 1965.

Bachman, David M. *Bureaucracy, Economy, and Leadership in China: The Industrial Origins of the Great Leap Forward.* New York: Cambridge University Press, 1991.

——————. *Chen Yun and the Chinese Political System.* Berkeley: University of California Press, 1985.

Bahro, Rudolf. *The Alternative in Eastern Europe.* London: Verso, 1981.

Balazs, Etienne. *Chinese Civilization and Bureaucracy.* New Haven: Yale University Press, 1964.

Banister, Judith. *China's Changing Population.* Stanford, Calif.: Stanford University Press, 1987.

Bardenson, R.D. *Half-Work Half-Study Schools in Communist China.* Washington, D.C., 1964.

Barme, Geremie and John Miniford, eds. *Seeds of Fire: Chinese Voices of Conscience.* New York: Hill and Wang, 1989.

Barnett, A. Doak. *Cadres, Bureaucracy and Political Power in China.* New York: Columbia University Press, 1967.

———. *China After Mao.* Princeton, N.J.: Princeton University Press, 1967.

———. *China on the Eve of Communist Takeover.* New York: Praeger, 1963.

———. *Communist China: The Early Years 1949–1955.* New York: Praeger, 1964.

———, ed. *Chinese Communist Politics in Action.* Seattle: University of Washington Press, 1969.

Baum, Richard. *Chinese Politics in the Age of Deng Xiaoping: The Cycles of Reform.* Princeton, N.J.: Princeton University Press, 1994.

———. *Prelude to Revolution: Mao, the Party and the Peasant Question.* New York: Columbia University Press, 1975.

———, ed. *China's Four Modernizations: The New Technological Revolution.* Boulder: Westview Press, 1980.

———, and Frederick C. Teiwes. *Ssu-Ch'ing: The Socialist Education Movement of 1962–1966.* Berkeley: University of California Press, 1968.

Becker, Jasper. *Hungry Ghosts: China's Secret Famine.* London: John Murray, 1996.

Bennett, Gordon A. *Huadong: The Story of a Chinese People's Commune.* Boulder: Westview Press, 1978.

——————, and Ronald H. Montaperto. *Red Guard: The Political Biography of Dai Hsiao-ai.* New York: Doubleday, 1971.

Benton, Gregor, ed. *Wild Lilies, Poisonous Weeds: Dissident Voices from People's China.* London: Pluto Press, 1982.

Bergere, Marie-Claire. *The Golden Age of the Chinese Bourgeoisie, 1911–1937.* Cambridge: Cambridge University Press, 1989.

Bernstein, Richard. *From the Center of the Earth: The Search for the Truth About China.* Boston: Little Brown, 1982.

——————, and Ross H. Munro. *The Coming Conflict with China.* New York: Knopf, 1997.

Bernstein, Thomas P. *Up to the Mountains and Down to the Villages: The Transfer of Youth from Urban to Rural China.* New Haven: Yale University Press, 1977.

Bettelheim, Charles. *Cultural Revolution and Industrial Organization in China.* New York: Monthly Review Press, 1974.

——————, and Neil Burton. *China Since Mao.* New York: Monthly Review Press, 1978.

Bialer, Seweryn. *Stalin's Successors: Leadership, Stability, and Change in the Soviet Union.* New York: Cambridge University Press, 1980.

Blecher, Marc, and Vivienne Shue. *Tethered Deer: Government and Economy in a Chinese County.* Stanford, Calif.: Stanford University Press, 1996.

Bodde, Derk. *Peking Diary.* New York: Henry Schuman, 1950.

Borg, Dorothy, and Waldo Heinrichs, eds. *Uncertain Years: Chinese-American Relations, 1947–1950.* New York: Columbia University Press, 1980.

Bowie, Robert, and John K. Fairbank, eds. *Communist China 1955–1959: Policy Documents with Analysis.* Cambridge, Mass.: Harvard University Press, 1962.

Brandt, Conrad. *Stalin's Failure in China, 1924–1927.* Cambridge, Mass.: Harvard University Press, 1958.

————, Benjamin Schwartz, and John K. Fairbank, eds. *A Documentary History of Chinese Communism.* Cambridge, Mass.: Harvard University Press, 1952.

Brinton, Crane. *The Anatomy of Revolution.* New York: Vintage, 1965.

Brugger, Bill. *China: Liberation and Transformation, 1942–1962.* London: Croom Helm, 1981.

————. *China: Radicalism to Revisionism, 1962–1979.* London: Croom Helm, 1980.

————. *Contemporary China.* London: Croom Helm, 1977.

————, ed. *China Since the "Gang of Four."* New York: St. Martin's Press, 1980.

————, and David Kelly. *Chinese Marxism in the Post-Mao Era.* Stanford, Calif.: Stanford University Press, 1990.

Bulletin of Concerned Asian Scholars, ed. *China from Mao to Deng.* Armonk, N.Y.: M.E. Sharpe, 1983.

Butterfield, Fox. *China, Alive in the Bitter Sea.* New York: Times Books, 1982.

Cell, Charles. *Revolution at Work: Mobilization Campaigns in China.* New York: Academic Press, 1977.

Central Committee, Communist Party of China. *Resolution on Certain Questions in the History of Our Party since the Founding of the People's Republic of China.* Beijing: Foreign Languages Press, 1981.

————. *Socialist Upsurge in China's Countryside.* Peking: Foreign Languages Press, 1957.

Chan, Anita, Richard Madsen, and Jonathan Unger. *Chen Village.* Berkeley: University of California Press, 1984.

————, Stanley Rosen, and Jonathan Unger. *On Socialist Democracy and the Chinese Legal System: The Li Yizhe Debates.* Armonk, N.Y.: M.E. Sharpe, 1985.

Chang, Kuo-t'ao. *The Rise of the Chinese Communist Party.* 2 vols. Lawrence: University of Kansas Press, 1971–72.

Chang, Parris H. *Power and Policy in China.* University Park: State University of Pennsylvania Press, 1978.

————. *Radicals and Radical Ideology in China's Cultural Revolution.* New York: Research Institute on Communist Affairs, Columbia University, 1973.

Chao, Kang. *Agricultural Production in Communist China, 1949–1965.* Madison: University of Wisconsin Press, 1970.

————. *Man and Land in China.* Stanford, Calif.: Stanford University Press, 1986.

Chao, Kuo-chun. *Agrarian Policies of Mainland China: A Documentary Study (1949–1956) .* Cambridge, Mass.: Harvard University Press, 1957.

Chen, Erjin. *China: Crossroads Socialism.* London: Verso, 1984.

Ch'en, Jerome. *China and the West.* Bloomington and London: Indiana University Press, 1979.

————. *Mao and the Chinese Revolution.* London: Oxford University Press, 1965.

————, ed. *Mao Papers: Anthology and Bibliography.* London: Oxford University Press, 1970.

Chen, Johsi. *The Execution of Mayor Yin and Other Stories from the Great Proletarian Cultural Revolution.* Bloomington: Indiana University Press, 1978.

Ch'en, Theodore H. E. *Thought Reform of the Chinese Intellectuals.* Hong Kong: Hong Kong University Press, 1960.

Cheng, Chester J. *Documents of Dissent: Chinese Political Thought Since Mao.* Stanford: Hoover Institute Press, 1980.

Cheng, Chu-yuan. *China's Economic Development: Growth and Structural Change.* Boulder: Westview Press, 1982.

—————. *Communist China's Economy 1949–1962: Structural Change and Crisis*. South Orange, N. J.: Seton Hall University Press, 1963.

Cheng, Peter. *A Chronology of the People's Republic of China*. Totowa, N.J.: Littlefield, Adams, 1972.

Chesneaux, Jean. *The Chinese Labor Movement, 1919–1927*. Stanford, Calif.: Stanford University Press, 1968.

—————. *Peasant Revolts in China, 1840–1949*. London: Thames and Hudson, 1973.

Chi Hsin. *The Case of the Gang of Four*. Hong Kong: Cosmos Books, 1977.

Chow, Tse-tsung. *The May Fourth Movement: Intellectual Revolution in Modern China*. Cambridge, Mass.: Harvard University Press, 1960.

Ci, Jiwei. *Dialectic of the Chinese Revolution: From Utopianism to Hedonism*. Stanford, Calif.: Stanford University Press, 1994.

Clark, Anne B., and Donald W. Klein. *Biographic Dictionary of Chinese Communism, 1921–1965*. Cambridge, Mass.: Harvard University Press, 1971.

Coble, Parks M. *The Shanghai Capitalists and the Nationalist Government, 1927–1937*. Cambridge, Mass: Council on East Asian Studies, Harvard University, 1980.

Cohen, Jerome Alan. *The Criminal Process in the People's Republic of China, 1949–1963*. Cambridge, Mass.: Harvard University Press, 1968.

—————, ed. *Contemporary Chinese Law: Research Problems and Perspectives*. Cambridge, Mass.: Harvard University Press, 1968.

Cohen, Warren I. *America's Response to China: A History of Sino-American Relations*. New York: Columbia University Press, 1990.

Collection of Important Documents of the Great Proletarian Cultural Revolution. Peking: Foreign Languages Press, 1970.

Committee of Concerned Asian Scholars. *China, Inside the People's Republic*. New York: Bantam, 1972.

Compton, Boyd, ed. *Mao's China: Party Reform Documents, 1942–44*. Seattle: University of Washington Press, 1966.

Croizier, Ralph C., ed. *China's Cultural Legacy and Communism*. New York: Praeger, 1970.

Croll, Elisabeth. *Chinese Women Since Mao*. London: Zed Books, 1983.

—————. *Feminism and Socialism in China*. London: Routledge & Kegan Paul, 1978.

—————. *The Politics of Marriage in Contemporary China*. Cambridge: Cambridge University Press, 1981.

—————, ed. *The Women's Movement in China: A Selection of Readings*. London: Anglo-Chinese Educational Institute, 1974.

Cui, Zhiyuan, Rong Jingben, Wang Shuanzheng, et al. *Transformation from the Pressurized System to a Democractic System if Cooperation: Reform of the Political System at the County and Township Levels*. Beijing: Central Compilation and Translation Press, 1998.

Cumings, Bruce. *Origins of the Korean War*. 2 vols. Princeton, N.J.: Princeton University Press, 1981, 1990.

Davin, Delia. *Woman-Work: Women and Party in Revolutionary China*. London: Oxford University Press, 1976.

Daubier, Jean. *A History of the Chinese Cultural Revolution*. New York: Vintage, 1974.

Decision of the Central Committee of the Communist Party of China Concerning the Great Proletarian Cultural Revolution. Peking: Foreign Languages Press, 1966.

Deng, Xiaoping. *Fundamental Issues in Present-Day China*. Beijing: Foreign Languages Press, 1987.

—————. *Selected Works of Deng Xiaoping (1975–1982)*. Beijing: Foreign Languages Press, 1984.

—————. *Speeches and Writings*. Oxford: Pergamon Press, 1984.

Dernberger, Robert F., ed. *China's Development Experience in Comparative Perspective.* Cambridge, Mass.: Harvard University Press, 1980.

Deutscher, Isaac. *Ironies of History: Essays on Contemporary Communism.* London: Oxford University Press, 1966.

————. *Marxism in Our Time.* San Francisco: The Ramparts Press, 1971.

————. *The Unfinished Revolution: Russia 1917–1967.* London: Oxford University Press, 1967.

Dirlik, Arif. *After the Revolution: Waking to Global Capitalism.* Hanover, N.H.: University Press of New England, 1994.

————. *Anarchism in the Chinese Revolution.* Berkeley: University of California Press, 1991.

————. *The Origins of Chinese Communism.* New York: Oxford University Press, 1989.

————. *Revolution and History: The Origins of Marxist Historiography in China.* Berkeley: University of California Press, 1978.

————, and Maurice Meisner, eds. *Marxism and the Chinese Experience.* Armonk, N.Y.: M.E. Sharpe, 1989.

Dittmer, Lowell. *Liu Shaoqi and the Chinese Cultural Revolution,* revised edition. Armonk, N.Y.: M.E. Sharpe, 1998.

Domes, Jurgen, ed. *Chinese Politics After Mao.* Berkeley: University of California Press, 1979.

————. *The Internal Politics of China.* London: C. Hurst, 1973.

————. *Socialism in the Chinese Countryside.* London: C. Hurst, 1980.

Donnithorne, Audrey. *China's Economic System.* London: George Allen & Unwin, 1967.

Draper, Hal. *Karl Marx's Theory of Revolution, Vol. I: State and Bureaucracy.* New York: Monthly Review Press, 1977.

Dreyer, June. *China's Forty Million: Minority Nationalities and National Integration in the People's Republic of China.* Cambridge, Mass.: Harvard University Press, 1976.

Dunayevskaya, Raya. *Philosophy and Revolution.* New York: Dell, 1973.

Dunn, John. *Modern Revolutions.* London: Cambridge University Press, 1972.

Eastman, Lloyd E. *The Abortive Revolution: China under Nationalist Rule, 1927–1937.* Cambridge, Mass.: Harvard University Press, 1974.

————. *Seeds of Destruction: Nationalist China in War and Revolution, 1927–1937.* Stanford, Calif.: Stanford University Press, 1984.

Eckstein, Alexander. *China's Economic Revolution.* Cambridge: Cambridge University Press, 1977.

————. *Quantitative Measures of China's Economic Output.* Ann Arbor: University of Michigan Press, 1980.

————, Walter Galenson, and Ta-chung Liu, eds. *Economic Trends in Communist China.* Edinburgh: Edinburgh University Press, 1968.

The Eighth National Congress of the Communist Party of China (Documents). Peking: Foreign Languages Press, 1956.

Encausse, Helene Carrere, and Stuart Schram. *Marxism and Asia.* London: Allen Lane, 1969.

Esmein, Jean. *The Chinese Cultural Revolution.* New York: Anchor, 1973.

Fairbank, John K. *China: The People's Middle Kingdom and the U.S.A.* Cambridge, Mass.: Harvard University Press, 1967.

————. *China Perceived: Images and Policies in Chinese-American Relations.* New York: Knopf, 1974.

————. *The United States and China.* Fourth Edition. Cambridge, Mass.: Harvard University Press, 1979.

Fang Lizhi. *Bringing Down the Great Wall.* New York: Norton, 1992.

Fei Hsiao-t'ung (Fei Xiaotong). *China's Gentry: Essays in Urban-Rural Relations.* Chicago: University of Chicago Press, 1953.

—————. *Toward a People's Anthropology*. Beijing: New World Press, 1981.

Feigon, Lee. *Chen Duxiu: Founder of the Chinese Communist Party*. Princeton, N.J.: Princeton University Press, 1983.

—————. *China Rising*. Chicago: Ivan R. Dee, 1990.

—————. *Demystifying Tibet*. Chicago: Ivan R. Dee, 1996.

Feuerwerker, Albert, ed. *History in Communist China*. Cambridge, Mass.: Harvard University Press, 1968.

Fewsmith, Joseph. *Dilemmas of Reform in China: Political Conflict and Economic Debate*. Armonk, N.Y.: M.E. Sharpe, 1994.

Fokkema, D. W. *Literary Doctrine in China and Soviet Influence, 1956–60*. The Hague: Mouton, 1965.

Friedman, Edward. *Backward Toward Revolution: The Chinese Revolutionary Party*. Berkeley: University of California Press, 1974.

—————, and Mark Selden, eds. *America's Asia*. New York: Vintage, 1971.

—————, Paul Pickowicz, and Mark Selden. *Chinese Village, Socialist State*. New Haven: Yale University Press, 1991.

Frolic, B. Michael. *Mao's People: Sixteen Portraits of Life in Revolutionary China*. Cambridge, Mass.: Harvard University Press, 1980.

Fukuyama, Francis. *The End of History and the Last Man*. New York: The Free Press, 1992.

Fung, K. K. *Social Needs versus Economic Efficiency: Sun Yefang's Critique of Socialist Economics*. Armonk, N.Y.: M.E. Sharpe, 1982.

Gao Yuan. *Born Red: A Chronicle of the Cultural Revolution*. Stanford, Calif.: Stanford University Press, 1987.

Gardner, John. *Chinese Politics and the Succession to Mao*. London: Macmillan, 1982.

Gargan, Edward A. *China's Fate: A People's Turbulent Struggle with Reform and Repression*. New York: Doubleday, 1991.

Garside, Roger. *Coming Alive: China after Mao*. New York: Mentor, 1982.

Gasster, Michael. *China's Struggle to Modernize*. New York: Knopf, 1983.

Ginnekan, Jaap van. *The Rise and Fall of Lin Biao*. New York: Avon Books, 1977.

Gittings, John. *China Changes Face*. New York: Oxford University Press, 1990.

—————. *The Role of the Chinese Army*. New York: Oxford University Press, 1967.

—————. *Survey of the Sino-Soviet Dispute, 1963–67*. London: Oxford University Press, 1968.

—————. *The World and China, 1922–72*. New York: Harper & Row, 1974.

Gleason, Abbott, Peter Kenez, and Richard Stites, eds. *Bolshevik Culture*. Bloomington: Indiana University Press, 1985.

Goldman, Merle. *China's Intellectuals: Advise and Dissent*. Cambridge, Mass.: Harvard University Press, 1981.

—————. *Literary Dissent in Communist China*. Cambridge, Mass.: Harvard University Press, 1967.

—————. *Sowing the Seeds of Democracy in China: Political Reform in the Deng Xiaoping Era*. Cambridge, Mass.: Harvard University Press, 1994.

Goodman, David S. G., ed. *Beijing Street Voices*. London, 1981.

Gramsci, Antonio. *Selections from the Prison Notebooks*. New York: International Publishers, 1971.

Gray, Jack and Patrick Cavendish. *Chinese Communism in Crisis: Maoism and the Cultural Revolution*. London: Pall Mall, 1968.

Gray, Jack and Gordon White, eds. *China's New Developmental Strategy*. London: Academic Press, 1982.

A Great Trial in Chinese History. Beijing: New World Press, 1981.

Grieder, Jerome. *Hu Shih and the Chinese Renaissance: Liberalism in the Chinese Revolution, 1917–1937*. Cambridge, Mass.: Harvard University Press, 1970.

————. *Intellectuals and the State in Modern China: A Narrative History*. New York: The Free Press, 1981.

Greider, William. *One World, Ready or Not: The Manic Logic of Global Capitalism*. New York: Simon & Schuster, 1997.

Griffith, William E. *The Sino-Soviet Rift*. Cambridge, Mass.: MIT Press, 1964.

Grunfeld, A. Tom. *The Making of Modern Tibet*. Armonk, N.Y.: M.E. Sharpe, 1996.

Guillermaz, Jacques. *The Chinese Communist Party in Power, 1949–1976*. Boulder: Westview Press, 1976.

————. *A History of the Chinese Communist Party, 1921–1949*. New York: Random House, 1972.

Gurley, John G. *China's Economy and the Maoist Strategy*. New York: Monthly Review Press, 1976.

Hamrin, Carol Lee. *China and the Challenge of the Future*. Boulder: Westview Press, 1990.

Han Minzhu, ed. *Cries for Democracy: Writings and Speeches from the 1989 Chinese Democracy Movement*. Princeton, N.J.: Princeton University Press, 1990.

Harding, Harry. *Organizing China: The Problem of Bureaucracy, 1949–1976*. Stanford, Calif.: Stanford University Press, 1981.

————. *China's Second Revolution: Reform After Mao*. Washington, D.C.: Brookings Institution, 1987.

Harris, Nigel. *The Mandate of Heaven: Marx and Mao in Modern China*. London: Quartet Books, 1978.

Harrison, James P. *The Communists and Chinese Peasant Rebellions*. New York: Atheneum, 1969.

————. *The Long March to Power: A History of the Chinese Communist Party, 1921–1972*. New York: Praeger, 1972.

Heilbroner, Robert I. *The Nature and Logic of Capitalism*. New York: Norton, 1985.

Herzen, Alexander. *From the Other Shore*. London: Weidenfeld & Nicolson, 1956.

Hinton, Harold C., ed. *The People's Republic of China, 1949–1979: A Documentary Survey*. Wilmington, Del.: Scholarly Resources, 1980.

Hinton, William. *Fanshen: A Documentary of Revolution in a Chinese Village*. New York: Vintage, 1966.

————. *The Great Reversal*. New York: Monthly Review Press, 1990.

————. *Hundred Day War: The Cultural Revolution at Tsinghua University*. New York: Monthly Review Press, 1972.

————. *Shenfan: The Continuing Revolution in a Chinese Village*. New York: Random House, 1983.

————. *Turning Point in China*. New York: Monthly Review Press, 1972.

Hobsbawm, Eric. *The Age of Extremes: A History of the World, 1914–1991*. New York: Pantheon, 1994.

Hoffman, Charles. *The Chinese Worker*. Albany: State University of New York Press, 1974.

Hofheinz, Roy. *The Broken Wave: The Chinese Communist Peasant Movement, 1922–1928*. Cambridge, Mass.: Harvard University Press, 1977.

Honig, Emily. *Sisters and Strangers: Women in the Shanghai Cotton Mills, 1919–1949*. Stanford, Calif.: Stanford University Press, 1986.

————, and Gail Hershatter. *Personal Voices: Chinese Women in the 1980s*. Stanford, Calif.: Stanford University Press, 1988.

Hopkins, Terrence K., and Immanuel Wallerstein, eds. *Processes of the World System*. Beverly Hills, Calif.: Sage Publications, 1980.

Horn, Joshua. *Away with All Pests*. New York: Monthly Review Press, 1969.

Houn, Franklin. *To Change a Nation: Propaganda and Indoctrination in Communist China*. Glencoe, Ill.: The Free Press, 1961.

Howe, Christopher. *Employment and Economic Growth in Urban China, 1949–1957.* Cambridge: Cambridge University Press, 1971.

————, ed. *Shanghai: Revolution and Development in an Asian Metropolis*. Cambridge: Cambridge University Press, 1981.

Hsia, Adrian. *The Chinese Cultural Revolution*. New York: Seabury Press, 1972.

Hsiung, James C. *Ideology and Practice: The Evolution of Chinese Communism*. New York: Praeger, 1970.

Hsu, Immanuel C. Y. *China Without Mao*. New York: Oxford University Press, 1983.

Hsueh, Chun-tu, ed. *Revolutionary Leaders of Modern China*. New York: Oxford University Press, 1971.

Huang, Philip C. C. *The Peasant Family and Rural Development in the Yangzi Delta, 1350–1988*. Stanford, Calif.: Stanford University Press, 1990.

————, ed. *The Development of Underdevelopment in China: A Symposium*. White Plains, N.Y.: M.E. Sharpe, 1980.

Hunter, Neale. *Shanghai Journal.* Boston: Beacon Press, 1971.

Isaacs, Harold. *The Tragedy of the Chinese Revolution*. Stanford, Calif.: Stanford University Press, 1951.

Israel, John. *Student Nationalism in China*. Stanford, Calif.: Stanford University Press, 1966.

————, and Donald W. Klein. *Rebels and Bureaucrats: China's December 9ers.* Berkeley: University of California Press, 1976.

Joffe, Ellis. *Between Two Plenums: China's Intraleadership Conflict, 1959–62*. Ann Arbor: Center for Chinese Studies, University of Michigan, 1975.

————. *The Chinese Army after Mao*. Cambridge: Harvard University Press, 1987.

————. *Party and Army: Professionalism and Political Control of the Chinese Officer Corps.* Cambridge, Mass.: Harvard University Press, 1965.

Johnson, Chalmers. *Peasant Nationalism and Communist Power*. Stanford, Calif.: Stanford University Press, 1962.

————, ed. *Ideology and Politics in Contemporary China*. Seattle: University of Washington Press, 1973.

Johnson, Kay Ann. *Women, the Family, and Peasant Revolution in China.* Chicago: University of Chicago Press, 1983.

Joint Economic Committee of the U.S. Congress. *An Economic Profile of Mainland China*. Washington, D.C.: Government Printing Office, 1967.

Joseph, William A., ed. *China Briefing 1995–1996.* Armonk, N.Y.: M.E. Sharpe, 1997.

————. *The Critique of Ultra-Leftism in China, 1958–1981.* Stanford, Calif.: Stanford University Press, 1984.

Karnow, Stanley. *Mao and China: From Revolution to Revolution.* New York: Viking, 1972.

Karol, K. S. *China: The Other Communism.* New York: Hill & Wang, 1967.

————. *The Second Chinese Revolution.* New York: Hill & Wang, 1974.

Kau, Michael Ying-mao, ed. *The Lin Piao Affair*. White Plains, N.Y.: International Arts and Science Press, 1975.

————, and Susan H. Marsh, eds. *China in the Era of Deng Xiaoping: A Decade of Reform*. Armonk, N.Y.: M.E. Sharpe, 1993.

Kerr, George H. *Formosa Betrayed.* Boston: Houghton Mifflin Co., 1965.

Klein, Donald W., and Ann B. Clark, eds. *Biographical Dictionary of Chinese Communism.* Cambridge: Harvard University Press, 1971.

Knight, Nick. *Li Da and Marxist Philosophy in China.* Boulder: Westview Press, 1996.

Kraus, Richard Curt. *Brushes with Power: Modern Politics and the Chinese Art of Calligraphy.* Berkeley: University of California Press, 1991.

——————. *Class Conflict in Chinese Socialism.* New York: Columbia University Press, 1981.

——————. *Pianos and Politics in China.* New York: Oxford University Press, 1989.

Kung, Chi-keung. *Intellectuals and Masses: The Case of Qu Quibai.* Ph.D. dissertation. University of Wisconsin-Madison, 1995.

Kuznets, Simon. *Economic Growth of Nations: Total Output and Production Structure.* Cambridge, Mass.: Harvard University Press, 1971.

Lardy, Nicholas. *Agriculture in China's Modern Economic Development.* Cambridge: Cambridge University Press, 1983.

——————. *Economic Growth and Distribution in China.* Cambridge: Cambridge University Press, 1983.

——————, and Kenneth Lieberthal. *Chen Yun's Strategy for China's Development: A Non-Marxist Alternative.* Armonk, N.Y.: M.E. Sharpe, 1983.

Lee, Bennet, and Geremie Barme, eds. *The Wounded: New Stories of the Cultural Revolution.* Hong Kong: Joint Publishing Co., 1979.

Lee, Hong Yung. *From Revolutionary Cadres to Technocrats in Socialist China.* Berkeley: University of California Press, 1991.

——————. *The Politics of the Chinese Cultural Revolution.* Berkeley: University of California Press, 1978.

Lee, Leo Ou-fan. *The Romantic Generation of Chinese Writers.* Cambridge, Mass.: Harvard University Press, 1973.

Lenin, V. I. *Collected Works.* 45 vols. Moscow: Foreign Languages Publishing House, 1946–1967.

——————. *Selected Works.* 2 vols. Moscow: Foreign Languages Publishing House, 1952.

Levenson, Joseph R. *Confucian China and Its Modern Fate: A Trilogy.* Berkeley: University of California Press, 1968.

——————. *Liang Ch'i-ch'ao and the Mind of Modern China.* Cambridge, Mass.: Harvard University Press, 1959.

——————. *Revolution and Cosmopolitanism.* Berkeley: University of California Press, 1971.

Levine, Steven I. *Anvil of Victory: The Communist Revolution in Manchuria, 1945–1948.* New York: Columbia University Press, 1987.

Lewis, John W. *Leadership in Communist China.* Ithaca, N.Y.: Cornell University Press, 1963.

——————, ed. *The City in Communist China.* Stanford, Calif.: Stanford University Press, 1971.

——————, ed. *Party Leadership and Revolutionary Power in China.* Cambridge: Cambridge University Press, 1970.

——————, and Litai Xue. *China Builds the Bomb.* Stanford, Calif.: Stanford University Press, 1988.

Leys, Simon. *Broken Images: Essays on Chinese Cultural Politics.* New York: St. Martin's Press, 1980.

——————. *The Chairman's New Clothes.* London: Alison & Busby, 1981.

——————. *Chinese Shadows.* New York: Viking, 1977.

Li, Choh-ming. *The Economic Development of Communist China.* Berkeley: University of California Press, 1959.

Li, Zhisui. *The Private Life of Chairman Mao.* New York: Random House, 1994.

Liang, Heng, and Judith Shapiro. *Son of the Revolution.* New York: Knopf, 1983.

Lichtheim, George. *Marxism: An Historical and Critical Study.* New York: Praeger, 1961.

Lieberthal, Kenneth. *Governing China.* New York: Norton, 1995.

——————. *Revolution and Tradition in Tientsin, 1949–1952.* Stanford, Calif.: Stanford University Press, 1980.

Lifton, Robert Jay. *Revolutionary Immortality.* New York: Random House, 1968.

——————. *Thought Reform and the Psychology of Totalism.* New York: Norton, 1961.

Lin Chun. *The British New Left.* Edinburgh: Edinburgh University Press, 1993.

——————. *Marx's Conception of the Non-Capitalist Route.* Beijing: Institute of Marxism-Leninism-Mao Zedong Thought, 1984.

Lin, Weiran. *An Abortive Chinese Enlightenment—The Cultural Revolution and Class Theory.* Ph.D. dissertation. Madison: Department of History, University of Wisconsin-Madison, 1996.

Lin, Yu-sheng. *The Crisis of Chinese Consciousness: Radical Antitraditionalism in the May Fourth Era.* Madison: University of Wisconsin Press, 1979.

Lindbeck, John, ed. *Management of a Revolutionary Society.* Seattle: University of Washington Press, 1971.

Link, Perry. *Evening Chats in Beijing.* New York: Norton, 1992.

——————. *Roses and Thorns: The Second Blooming of the Hundred Flowers in Chinese Fiction, 1979–1980.* Berkeley: University of California Press, 1984.

——————, ed. *Stubborn Weeds: Popular and Controversial Chinese Literature After the Cultural Revolution.* Bloomington, Ind.: Indiana University Press, 1983.

Lippit, Victor. *The Economic Development of China.* Armonk, N.Y.: M.E. Sharpe, 1987.

Liu Binyan. *China's Crisis, China's Hope.* Cambridge, Mass.: Harvard University Press, 1990.

——————. *People or Monsters and Other Stories and Reportage from China After Mao.* Bloomington: Indiana University Press, 1992.

——————, with Ruan Ming and Xu Gang. *Tell the World.* New York: Pantheon, 1989.

Liu Shaoqi. *Collected Works of Liu Shao-ch'i.* 3 vols. Hong Kong: Union Research Institute, 1968–69.

Liu, T. A. and K. C. Yeh. *The Economy of Mainland China: National Income and Economic Development, 1933–1959.* Princeton, N.J.: Princeton University Press, 1965.

Luxemburg, Rosa. *Rosa Luxemburg Speaks.* New York: Pathfinder Press, 1970.

Ma, Hong, and Sun Shangqing, eds. *Studies in the Problems of China's Economic Structure.* Beijing: n.p., 1981.

Macciocchi, Maria Antionietta. *Daily Life in Revolutionary China.* New York: Monthly Review Press, 1972.

MacFarquhar, Roderick. *The Origins of the Cultural Revolution, Vol. I: Contradictions Among the People.* London: Oxford University Press, 1974.

——————. *The Origins of the Cultural Revolution, Vol. II: The Great Leap Forward, 1958–1960.* New York: Columbia University Press, 1983.

——————, ed. *China Under Mao: Politics Takes Command.* Cambridge, Mass.: MIT Press, 1966.

——————, ed. *The Hundred Flowers Campaign and the Chinese Intellectuals.* New York: Praeger, 1960.

Madsen, Richard. *Morality and Power in a Chinese Village.* Berkeley: University of California Press, 1984.

Maitan, Livio. *Party, Army and Masses in China.* London: New Left Books, 1976.

Malraux, André. *Anti-Memoirs.* New York: Holt, Rinehart & Winston, 1968.

Mancall, Mark. *China at the Center.* New York: The Free Press, 1984.

——————, ed. *Formosa Today.* New York: Praeger, 1964.

Mandell, Ernest. *Power and Money: A Marxist Theory of Bureaucracy.* London: Verso, 1992.

Mao Zedong. *A Critique of Soviet Economics.* Translated by Moss Roberts. New York: Monthly Review Press, 1977.

——————. *Mao Papers.* Edited by Jerome Ch'en. London: Oxford University Press, 1970.

——————. *Mao's Road to Power: Revolutionary Writings, 1912–1949.* ed. by Stuart R. Schram. Armonk, N.Y.: M.E. Sharpe, 1992.

——————. *Mao Zedong sixiang wansui* (Long Live the Thought of Mao Zedong). 2 vols. Taipei: n.p., 1967, 1969.

——————. *On the Correct Handling of Contradictions Among the People.* Peking: Foreign Languages Press, 1957.

——————. *Poems of Mao Tse-tung.* Edited by Wong Man. Hong Kong: Eastern Horizon Press, 1966.

——————. *Selected Works of Mao Tse-tung.* 4 vols. London: Lawrence & Wishart, 1954.

——————. *Selected Works of Mao Tse-tung.* Peking: Foreign Languages Press, 1961.

——————. *Selected Works of Mao Tse-tung.* Vol. V. Peking: Foreign Languages Press, 1977.

Marks, Robert B. *Rural Revolution in South China: Peasants and the Making of History in Haifeng County, 1570–1930.* Madison: University of Wisconsin Press, 1984.

Martin, Helmut. *Cult and Canon: The Origins and Development of State Maoism.* Armonk, N.Y.: M.E. Sharpe, 1982.

Marx, Karl. *Capital.* Vol. I. Chicago: Kerr, 1906.

——————. *Selected Writings in Sociology and Social Philosophy.* Edited by T. B. Bottomore and Maximilien Rubel. London: Watts, 1956.

——————. *Writings of the Young Marx on Philosophy and Society.* Edited by Lloyd D. Easton and Kurt H. Guddat. New York: Anchor, 1967.

——————, and Frederick Engels. *Selected Correspondence.* Moscow: Foreign Languages Publishing House, 1953.

——————. *Selected Works.* 2 vols. Moscow: Foreign Languages Publishing House, 1950.

——————. *Werke.* Berlin: Dietz, 1964.

McCormick, Thomas J. *America's Half-Century: United States Foreign Policy in the Cold War and After.* Second Edition. Baltimore: The Johns Hopkins University Press, 1995.

McCough, James P., ed. *Fei Hsiao-tung: The Dilemma of a Chinese Intellectual.* White Plains, N.Y.: M.E. Sharpe, 1979.

McDonald, Angus W., Jr. *The Urban Origins of Rural Revolution: Elites and Masses in Hunan Province, China 1911–27.* Berkeley: University of California Press, 1978.

Mehnert, Klaus. *Peking and Moscow.* London: Weidenfeld & Nicolson, 1963.

——————. *Peking and the New Left: At Home and Abroad.* Berkeley: Center for Chinese Studies, 1969.

Meisel, James H. *Counter-Revolution.* New York: Atherton, 1966.

Meisner, Maurice. *The Deng Xiaoping Era: An Inquiry into the Fate of Chinese Socialism.* New York: Hill and Wang, 1996.

——————. *Li Ta-chao and the Origins of Chinese Marxism.* Cambridge, Mass.: Harvard University Press, 1967.

——————. *Mao's China: A History of the People's Reoublic.* New York: The Free Press, 1977.

——————. *Marxism, Maoism and Utopianism.* Madison: University of Wisconsin Press, 1982.

Michels, Robert. *Political Parties.* Glencoe, Ill.: The Free Press, 1949.

Milton, David, and Nancy Dall Milton. *The Wind Will Not Subside: Years in Revolutionary China, 1964–1969.* New York: Pantheon, 1976.

Moody, Peter R. *Chinese Politics After Mao: Development and Liberalization, 1976–1983*. New York: Praeger, 1983.

Moore, Barrington. *Social Origins of Dictatorship and Democracy*. Boston: Beacon Press, 1966.

——————. *Soviet Politics: The Dilemma of Power*. Cambridge, Mass.: Harvard University Press, 1959.

Mosher, Steven. *Broken Earth: The Rural Chinese*. New York: The Free Press, 1983.

Munro, Donald J. *The Concept of Man in Contemporary China*. Ann Arbor: University of Michigan Press, 1977.

Murphey, Rhoads. *The Fading of the Maoist Vision: City and Countryside in China's Development*. New York: Metheun, 1980.

Myrdal, Jan. *Report from a Chinese Village*. New York: Pantheon, 1965.

——————. *Return to a Chinese Village*. New York: Pantheon, 1984.

——————, and Gun Kessle. *China: The Revolution Continued*. New York: Pantheon, 1970.

Nathan, Andrew. *China's Crisis*. New York: Columbia University Press, 1990.

Nathan, Andrew. *Chinese Democracy*. Berkeley: University of California Press, 1985.

National Program for Agricultural Development, 1956–1965. Peking: Foreign Languages Press, 1960.

Nee, Victor. *The Cultural Revolution at Peking University*. New York: Monthly Review Press, 1969.

——————, and David Mozingo, eds. *State and Society in Contemporary China*. Ithaca, N.Y.: Cornell University Press, 1983.

Oksenberg, Michael, ed. *China's Developmental Experience*. New York: Praeger, 1973.

——————, and Robert Oxnam, eds. *Dragon and Eagle: United States–China Relations, Past and Future*. New York: Basic Books, 1978.

On the Historical Experience of the Dictatorship of the Proletariat. Peking: Foreign Languages Press, 1961.

Orleans, Leo A. *Professional Manpower and Education in Communist China*. Washington, D.C.: Government Printing Office, 1961.

——————, ed. *Science in Contemporary China*. Stanford, Calif.: Stanford University Press, 1981.

Peck, James, and Victor Nee, eds. *China's Uninterrupted Revolution: From 1840 to the Present*. New York: Pantheon, 1975.

P'eng Shu-tse. *The Chinese Communist Party in Power*. New York: Monad Press, 1980.

Pepper, Suzanne. *China's Education Reform in the 1980s*. Berkeley: Center for Chinese Studies, University of California, 1990.

——————. *China's Universities: Post-Mao Enrollment Policies and Their Impact on the Structure of Secondary Education*. Ann Arbor: Center for Chinese Studies, University of Michigan, 1984.

——————. *Civil War in China: The Political Struggle, 1945–1949*. Berkeley: University of California Press, 1978.

Perkins, Dwight H. *Agricultural Development in China, 1368–1969*. Chicago: Aldine, 1969.

——————. *Market Control and Planning in Communist China*. Cambridge, Mass.: Harvard University Press, 1966.

——————, ed. *China's Modern Economy in Historical Perspective*. Stanford, Calif.: Stanford University Press, 1975.

——————, ed. *Rural Small-Scale Industry in the People's Republic of China*. Berkeley: University of California Press, 1977.

Perry, Elizabeth. *Rebels and Revolutionaries in North China, 1845–1945*. Stanford, Calif.: Stanford University Press, 1980.

——————, and Christine Wong, eds. *The Political Economy of Reform in Post-Mao China*. Cambridge, Mass.: Harvard University Press, 1985.

Pickowicz, Paul G. *Marxist Literary Thought in China: The Influence of Ch'u Ch'iu-pai.* Berkeley: University of California Press, 1981.

——————. *Marxist Literary Thought and China: A Conceptual Framework.* Berkeley: Center for Chinese Studies, 1980.

Polanyi, Karl. *The Great Transformation.* Boston: Beacon Press, 1957.

Price, Don C. *Russia and the Roots of the Chinese Revolution.* Cambridge, Mass.: Harvard University Press, 1974.

Price, R. F. *Education in Communist China.* London: Routledge & Kegan Paul, 1970.

Prybyla, Jan S. *The Political Economy of Communist China.* Scranton, Pa.: International Textbooks, 1970.

Rawski, Thomas G. *China's Transition to Industrialism.* Ann Arbor: University of Michigan Press, 1980.

——————. *Economic Growth and Employment in China.* New York: Oxford University Press, 1979.

Rice, Edward. *Mao's Way.* Berkeley: University of California Press, 1972.

Richman, Barry M. *Industrial Society in Communist China.* New York: Random House, 1969.

Riskin, Carl. *China's Political Economy: The Quest for Development since 1949.* New York: Oxford University Press, 1987.

Robinson, Joan. *Economic Management in China.* London: Anglo-Chinese Educational Institute, 1975.

——————. *Reports from China.* London: Anglo-Chinese Educational Institute, 1977.

Robinson, Thomas W., ed. *The Cultural Revolution in China.* Berkeley: University of California Press, 1971.

Rosen, Stanley. *Red Guard Factionalism and the Cultural Revolution in Guangzhou (Canton).* Boulder: Westview Press, 1982.

——————. *The Role of Sent-Down Youth in the Chinese Cultural Revolution: The Case of Guangzhou.* Berkeley: University of California Press, 1981.

Rosenberg, William G., and Marilyn B. Young. *Transforming Russia and China: Revolutionary Struggle in the Twentieth Century.* New York: Oxford University Press, 1982.

Rozman, Gilbert, ed. *The Modernization of China.* New York: The Free Press, 1981.

Ruan Ming. *The Empire of Deng.* Boulder: Westview Press, 1994.

Rue, John. *Mao Tse-tung in Opposition, 1927–1935.* Stanford, Calif.: Stanford University Press, 1966.

Saich, Tony, ed. *The Chinese People's Movement: Perspectives on Spring 1989.* Armonk, N.Y.: M.E. Sharpe, 1990.

Salisbury, Harrison. *The Long March: The Untold Story.* New York: Harper and Row, 1985.

Schell, Orville. *Discos and Democracy: China in the Throes of Reform.* New York: Pantheon, 1988.

——————. *To Get Rich Is Glorious.* New York: Pantheon, 1985.

Schiffrin, Harold Z. *Sun Yat-sen and the Origins of the Chinese Revolution.* Berkeley: University of California Press, 1970.

Schram, Stuart R. *Ideology and Policy in China since the Third Plenum, 1978–84.* London: Contemporary China Institute, University of London, 1984.

——————. *Mao Tse-tung.* New York: Simon & Schuster, 1967.

——————. *Mao Tse-tung Unrehearsed: Talks and Letters, 1956–71.* Middlesex: Penguin Books, 1974.

——————. *The Political Thought of Mao Tse-tung.* New York: Praeger, 1969.

——————. *La "revolution permanente" en Chine.* Paris: Mouton, 1963.

—————, ed. *Authority, Participation, and Cultural Change in China.* Cambridge: Cambridge University Press, 1973.

—————, ed. *The Scope of State Power in China.* New York: St. Martin's Press, 1985.

Schurmann, Franz. *Ideology and Organization in Communist China.* 2nd ed, rev. and enl. Berkeley: University of California Press, 1970.

Schwarcz, Vera. *Long Road Home: A China Journal.* New Haven: Yale University Press, 1984.

Schwartz, Benjamin. *Chinese Communism and the Rise of Mao.* Cambridge, Mass.: Harvard University Press, 1951.

—————. *Communism and China: Ideology in Flux.* Cambridge, Mass.: Harvard University Press, 1968.

—————. *In Search of Wealth and Power: Yen Fu and the West.* Cambridge, Mass.: Harvard University Press, 1964.

Selden, Mark. *The Political Economy of Chinese Development.* Armonk, N.Y.: M.E. Sharpe, 1993.

—————. *The Yenan Way in Revolutionary China.* Cambridge, Mass.: Harvard University Press, 1971.

—————, ed. *The People's Republic of China: A Documentary History of Revolutionary Change.* New York: Monthly Review Press, 1979.

—————, and Victor Lippit, eds. *The Transition to Socialism in China.* Armonk, N.Y.: M.E. Sharpe, 1982.

Seybolt, Peter J., ed. *The Rustification of Urban Youth in China.* White Plains, N.Y.: M.E. Sharpe, 1977.

Seymour, James D., ed. *The Fifth Modernization: China's Human Rights Movement, 1978–79.* New York: Human Rights Publishing Group, 1980.

Shaffer, Lynda. *Mao and the Workers.* Armonk, N.Y.: M.E. Sharpe, 1982.

Shanbaugh, David. *The Making of a Premier: Zhao Ziyang's Provincial Career.* Boulder: Westview Press, 1984.

Shanin, Teodor, ed. *Late Marx and the Russian Road.* New York: Monthly Review Press, 1983.

Sheel, Kamal. *Peasant Society and Marxist Intellectuals in China.* Princeton: Princeton University Press, 1989.

Sheridan, James. *China in Disintegration.* New York: The Free Press, 1975.

—————. *Chinese Warlord: The Career of Feng Yu-hsiang.* Stanford, Calif.: Stanford University Press, 1966.

Shirk, Susan L. *Competitive Comrades: Career Incentives and Student Strategies in China.* Berkeley: University of California Press, 1982.

Shue, Vivienne. *Peasant China in Transition: The Dynamics of Development toward Socialism, 1949–1956.* Berkeley: University of California Press, 1980.

—————. *The Reach of the State.* Stanford, Calif.: Stanford University Press, 1988.

Sidel, Ruth. *Women and Child Care in China.* New York: Hill & Wang, 1972.

Sidel, Victor W., and Ruth Sidel. *Serve the People: Observations on Medicine in the People's Republic of China.* New York: Josiah Macy, 1973.

Sigurdson, Jon. *Rural Industrialization in China.* Cambridge, Mass.: Harvard East Asian Monographs, 1977.

Singer, Daniel. *The Road to Gdansk.* New York: Monthly Review Press, 1982.

Siu, Bobby. *Women of China: Imperialism and Women's Resistance, 1900–1949.* London: Zed Press, 1982.

Siu, Helen F., ed. *Furrows: Peasants, Intellectuals and the State.* Stanford, Calif.: Stanford University Press, 1990.

————————, and Zelda Stern, eds. *Mao's Harvest.* New York: Oxford University Press, 1983.

Skocpol, Theda. *States and Social Revolutions: A Comparative Analysis of France, Russia, and China.* Cambridge: Cambridge University Press, 1979.

Smedley, Agnes. *The Great Road: The Life and Times of Chu Teh.* New York: Monthly Review Press, 1956.

Smil, Vaclav. *The Bad Earth: Environmental Degradation in China.* Armonk, N.Y.: M.E. Sharpe, 1984.

————————. *China's Environmental Crisis.* Armonk, N.Y.: M.E. Sharpe, 1993.

Snow, Edgar. *The Long Revolution.* New York: Random House, 1972.

————————. *The Other Side of the River.* New York: Random House, 1961.

————————. *Random Notes on Red China, 1936–1945.* Cambridge, Mass.: Harvard University Press, 1957.

————————. *Red Star Over China.* New York: Random House, 1938.

Solinger, Dorothy J. *From Lathes to Looms: China's Industrial Policy in Comparative Perspective, 1979–1982.* Stanford, Calif.: Stanford University Press, 1991.

————————. *Regional Government and Provincial Integration in Southwest China, 1949–1954: A Case Study.* Berkeley: University of California Press, 1977.

Spence, Jonathan D. *The Gate of Heavenly Peace: The Chinese and Their Revolution, 1895–1980.* New York: Viking, 1981.

————————. *To Change China: Western Advisers in China, 1620–1960.* Boston: Little Brown and Company, 1969.

————————. *The Search for Modern China.* New York: Norton, 1990.

Stacey, Judith. *Patriarchy and Socialist Revolution in China.* Berkeley: University of California Press, 1983.

Stalin, J. V. *Economic Problems of Socialism in the U.S.S.R.* Moscow: Foreign Languages Press, 1952.

Starr, John Bryan. *Continuing the Revolution: The Political Thought of Mao.* Princeton, N.J.: Princeton University Press, 1979.

State Statistical Bureau, PRC. *Main Indicators, Development of the National Economy of the People's Republic of China (1949–1978).* Beijing, 1979.

Stavis, Benedict. *The Politics of Agricultural Mechanization in China.* Ithaca: Cornell University Press, 1978.

Strong, Anna Louise. *Tomorrow's China.* New York: Committee for a Democractic Far Eastern Policy, 1948.

Su, Shaozhi. *China and the Making of the New, Socialist Spiritual Civilization.* Beijing: Institute of Marxism-Leninism-Mao Zedong Thought, Chinese Academy of Social Sciences, 1981.

————————. *Develop Marxism Under Contemporary Conditions.* Beijing: Institute of Marxism-Leninism-Mao Zedong Thought, Chinese Academy of Social Sciences, 1983.

————————. *Marxism in China.* London: Spokesman, 1983.

Su, Xiaokang and Wang Luxiang. *Deathsong of the River: A Reader's Guide to the Chinese TV Series Heshang.* Ithaca: Cornell University East Asian Program, 1991.

Sun, Yan. *The Chinese Reassessment of Socialism, 1976–1992.* Princeton, N.J.: Princeton University Press, 1992.

Sweezy, Paul M. *Post-Revolutionary Society.* New York: Monthly Review Press, 1980.

————————, and Charles Bettelheim. *On the Transition to Socialism.* New York: Monthly Review Press, 1971.

Tawney, R. H. *Land and Labour in China.* London: George Allen & Unwin, 1932.

The Tenth National Congress of the Communist Party of China (Documents). Peking: Foreign Languages Press, 1973.

Terrill, Ross. *800,000,000: The Real China.* Boston: Little, Brown & Co., 1972.

—————. *The Future of China After Mao.* New York: Dell, 1978.

—————. *Mao.* New York: Harper & Row, 1980.

Thaxton, Ralph A. *China Turned Rightside Up: Revolutionary Legitimacy in the Peasant World.* New Haven: Yale University Press, 1983.

The Thirteenth National Congress of the Communist Party of China (Documents). Beijing: Foreign Languages Press, 1987.

Thompson, E. P. *The Making of the English Working Class.* New York: Pantheon, 1964.

Thurston, Anne F. *Enemies of the People.* Cambridge, Mass.: Harvard University Press, 1988.

Tien, Hung-Mao. *Government and Politics in Kuomintang China, 1927–1937.* Stanford, Calif.: Stanford University Press, 1972.

—————. *The Great Transition: Political and Social Change in the Republic of China (Taiwan).* Stanford, Calif.: Stanford University Press, 1989.

Tiewes, Frederick C. *Politics at Mao's Court: Gao Gang and Party Factionalism in the Early 1950s.* Armonk, N.Y.: M.E. Sharpe, 1990.

—————. *Politics and Purges in China.* White Plains, N.Y.: M. E. Sharpe, 1979.

Townsend, James. *Political Participation in Communist China.* Berkeley: University of California Press, 1967.

Trotsky, Leon. *Our Revolution.* New York, 1918.

—————. *The Permanent Revolution and Results and Prospects.* New York: Pathfinder Press, 1974.

—————. *Problems of the Chinese Revolution.* New York: Pioneer Publishers, 1932.

Tsou, Tang. *America's Failure in China, 1949–1950.* 2 vols. Chicago: University of Chicago Press, 1963.

—————. *The Cultural Revolution and the Post-Mao Reforms.* Chicago: University of Chicago Press, 1986.

Tucker, Robert C. *The Marxian Revolutionary Idea.* New York: Norton, 1969.

Twitchett, Dennis and John K. Fairbank, eds. *The Cambridge History of China.* New York: Cambridge University Press, 1978–1991.

Ulam, Adam. *The Unfinished Revolution: An Essay on the Sources and Influence of Marxism and Communism.* New York: Vintage, 1964.

Unger, Jonathan. *Education under Mao: Class and Competition in Canton Schools.* New York: Columbia University Press, 1982.

—————, ed. *The Pro-Democracy Protests in China: Reports from the Provinces.* Armonk, N.Y.: M.E. Sharpe, 1991.

Union Research Institute, ed. *The Case of P'eng Teh-huai, 1959–1968.* Hong Kong: Union Research Institute, 1968.

—————, ed. *Documents of the Chinese Communist Party Central Committee.* 2 vols. Hong Kong: Union Research Institute, 1971.

—————, ed. *Who's Who in Communist China.* 2 vols. Hong Kong: Union Research Institute, 1969–70.

U.S. Central Intelligence Agency. *China: Economic Performance in 1987 and Outlook for 1988.* Washington, D.C.: Directorate of Intelligence, 1988.

—————. *The Chinese Economy in 1988 and 1989.* Washington, D.C.: Directorate of Intelligence, 1989.

——————. *People's Republic of China: Handbook of Economic Indicators.* Washington, D.C.: Directorate of Intelligence, 1976.

Vogel, Ezra. *Canton under Communism.* Cambridge, Mass.: Harvard University Press, 1969.

——————. *One Step Ahead in China: Guangdong under Reform.* Cambridge, Mass.: Harvard University Press, 1989.

Wakeman, Frederic, Jr. *The Fall of Imperial China.* New York: The Free Press, 1975.

——————. *History and Will: Philosophic Perspectives of Mao Tse-tung's Thought.* Berkeley: University of California Press, 1973.

Walder, Andrew G. *Chang Ch'un-ch'iao and Shanghai's January Revolution.* Ann Arbor: Center for Chinese Studies, University of Michigan, 1977.

——————. *Communist Neo-Traditionalism: Work and Authority in Chinese Industry.* Berkeley: University of California Press, 1986.

Wales, Nym. *Red Dust: Autobiographies of Chinese Communists.* Stanford, Calif.: Stanford University Press, 1952.

Walicki, A. *The Controversy over Capitalism.* Oxford: The Clarendon Press, 1969.

Waller, Derek J. *The Government and Politics of the People's Republic of China.* London: Hutchinson, 1981.

Wallerstein, Immanuel. *The Capitalist World-Economy.* Cambridge: Cambridge University Press, 1979.

Wang, Gungwu. *China and the World since 1949: The Impact of Independence, Modernity and Revolution.* London: Macmillan, 1977.

Wang, Ming. *Mao's Betrayal.* Moscow: Progress Publishers, 1979.

Wang, Xizhe. *Wang Xizhe Lunwen Ji.* (Collected Essays of Wang Xizhe). Hong Kong: The Seventies Magazine Press, 1981.

Wang, Y. C. *Chinese Intellectuals and the West.* Chapel Hill: University of North Carolina Press, 1966.

Wang, Yaan-iee. *The Chinese Idea.* Ph.D. Dissertation. Madison: Department of History, University of Wisconsin-Madison, 1997.

Wasserstrom, Jeffrey and Elizabeth Perry, eds. *Popular Protest and Political Culture in Modern China.* Boulder: Westview Press, 1992.

Watson, James L., ed. *Class and Social Stratification in Post-Revolutionary China.* Cambridge: Cambridge University Press, 1984.

Weber, Max. *The Religion of China.* Glencoe, Ill.: The Free Press, 1951.

——————. *The Theory of Social and Economic Organization.* New York: The Free Press, 1964.

Weil, Robert. *Red Cat, White Cat: China and the Contradictions of "Market Socialism."* New York: Monthly Review Press, 1996.

Wheelwright, E. L. and Bruce McFarlane. *The Chinese Road to Socialism: Economics of the Cultural Revolution.* New York: Monthly Review Press, 1970.

White, Gordon. *Riding the Tiger: The Politics of Economic Reform in Post-Mao China.* Stanford, Calif.: Stanford University Press, 1993.

White, Lynn T. III. *Careers in Shanghai.* Berkeley: University of California Press, 1978.

——————. *Policies of Chaos: The Organizational Causes of Violence in China's Cultural Revolution.* Princeton: Princeton University Press, 1989.

Whiting, Allen. *China Crosses the Yalu: The Decision to Enter the Korean War.* New York: Macmillan, 1960.

Whitson, William A. *A History of Chinese Communist Military Politics, 1927–1961.* New York: Praeger, 1973.

Whyte, Martin K. *Small Groups and Political Rituals in China.* Berkeley: University of California Press, 1974.

——————, and William Parrish. *Urban Life in Contemporary China.* Chicago: University of Chicago Press, 1984.

Wilson, Dick. *The Long March: The Epic of Chinese Communism's Survival.* London: Hamish Hamilton, 1971.

——————, ed. *Mao Tse-tung in the Scales of History.* New York: Cambridge University Press, 1977.

Wilson Center, ed. *The Limits of Reform in China.* Washington, D.C.: Woodrow Wilson Center for International Scholars, 1982.

Witke, Roxanne. *Comrade Chiang Ch'ing.* Boston: Little, Brown, 1977.

Wittfogel, Karl A. *Oriental Despotism.* New Haven: Yale University Press, 1957.

Wolf, Eric. *Europe and the People Without History.* Berkeley: University of California Press, 1982.

Wolf, Margery, and Roxanne Witke, eds. *Women in Chinese Society.* Stanford, Calif.: Stanford University Press, 1975.

Womack, Brantly. *The Foundations of Mao Zedong's Political Thought.* Honolulu: University Press of Hawaii, 1982.

Wong, John. *Land Reform in China: Institutional Transformation of Agriculture.* New York: Praeger, 1973.

Woo, Jung-en. *Race to the Swift: State and Finance in Korea's Industrialization.* New York: Columbia University Press, 1991.

Wood, Ellen Meiksins. *Democracy Against Capitalism.* Cambridge: Cambridge University Press, 1995.

World Bank, *Trends in Developing Economies, 1996.* Washington, D.C.: The World Bank, 1997.

Wright, Mary C. *The Last Stand of Chinese Conservatism: The T'ung Chih Restoration, 1862–1874.* rev. ed. Stanford, Calif.: Stanford University Press, 1966.

——————, ed. *China in Revolution: The First Phase, 1900–1913.* New Haven: Yale University Press, 1968.

Wu, Hongda Harry. *Laogai—The Chinese Gulag.* Boulder: Westview Press, 1992.

Wu, Yuan-Li. *The Economy of China: An Interpretation.* New York: Praeger, 1965.

Wylie, Raymond F. *The Emergence of Maoism: Mao Tse-tung, Ch'en Po-ta and the Search for Chinese Theory, 1935–1945.* Stanford, Calif.: Stanford University Press, 1980.

Xu, Dixin, et. al. *China's Search for Economic Growth.* Beijing: New World Press, 1982.

Xue, Muqiao, ed. *Almanac of China's Economy, 1981.* Hong Kong: Modern Cultural Co., 1982.

Yahuda, Michael. *Towards the End of Isolationalism: Chinese Foreign Policy After Mao.* London: Macmillan, 1983.

Yang, C. K. *The Chinese Family in the Communist Revolution.* Cambridge: MIT Press, 1959.

——————. *A Chinese Village in Early Communist Transition.* Cambridge: MIT Press, 1959.

Yao, Wen-yuan. *On the Social Basis of the Lin Piao Anti-Party Clique.* Peking: Foreign Languages Press, 1975.

Young, Marilyn B. *The Vietnam Wars 1945–1990.* New York: HarperCollins, 1991.

——————, ed. *Women in China.* Ann Arbor: Center for Chinese Studies, University of Michigan, 1973.

——————, and William Rosenberg. *Transforming Russia and China: Revolutionary Struggle in the Twentieth Century.* New York: Oxford University Press, 1982.

Yu, Guangyuan. *On the Objective Character of Laws of Development.* Beijing: Institute of Marxism-Leninism and Mao Zedong Thought, Chinese Academy of Social Sciences, 1982.

————, ed. *China's Socialist Modernization.* Beijing: Foreign Languages Press, 1984.

Yu, Mok Chiu and J. Frank Harrison, eds. *Voices from Tiananmen Square.* Montreal: Black Rose Books, 1990.

Yue, Daiyun and Carolyn Wakeman. *To the Storm: The Odyssey of a Revolutionary Chinese Woman.* Berkeley: University of California Press, 1985.

Zagoria, Donald S. *The Sino-Soviet Conflict, 1956–61.* Princeton, N.J.: Princeton University Press, 1962.

Zweig, David. *Agrarian Radicalism in China, 1968–1981.* Cambridge, Mass.: Harvard University Press, 1989.

Index